PENGUIN

THE PENGUIN SH
OF ENGLISH LITERATURE

Stephen Coote was educated at Magdalene College, Cambridge, where he was an exhibitioner, and at Birkbeck College, University of London, where he was the senior research scholar. Dr Coote is the author of critical studies of Chaucer, T.S. Eliot and English literature of the Middle Ages, as well as of biographies of Byron and William Morris. He divides his time between a Dutch barge in London and a cottage in the Oxfordshire countryside.

Stephen Coote

THE PENGUIN SHORT HISTORY
OF ENGLISH LITERATURE

PENGUIN BOOKS

PENGUIN BOOKS

Published by the Penguin Group
Penguin Books Ltd, 27 Wrights Lane, London w8 5tz, England
Penguin Books USA Inc., 375 Hudson Street, New York, New York 10014, USA
Penguin Books Australia Ltd, Ringwood, Victoria, Australia
Penguin Books Canada Ltd, 10 Alcorn Avenue, Toronto, Ontario, Canada m4v 3b2
Penguin Books (NZ) Ltd, 182–190 Wairau Road, Auckland 10, New Zealand

Penguin Books Ltd, Registered Offices: Harmondsworth, Middlesex, England

First published 1993
1 3 5 7 9 10 8 6 4 2

Set in 10/12 Monophoto Bembo
Typeset by Datix International Limited, Bungay, Suffolk
Printed in England by Clays Ltd, St Ives plc

Contents

Acknowledgements

I would like to acknowledge the following who read and commented on early drafts of the various chapters of this book: Professor Derick Brewer and Professor John Stevens, Leo Salingar, Graham Parry, David Noakes, Christopher Wordsworth, Paul Keegan and Peter Mudford. I owe a particular debt to Nicholas Everett who read the entire manuscript through for consistency. Those errors that remain I acknowledge mine.

The verse translations in the first chapter are reproduced from Michael Alexander's *The Earliest English Poems*, London, Penguin Books, 1966, with permission.

My greatest debt is to the late James Reeves who lived for poetry and introduced me to the literary life. I would like to dedicate this book to his memory.

Old English Literature

This is a chronicle of how men and women, for more than a thousand years, have expressed themselves in a literature of extraordinary fertility and a language of matchless resource.

The origins of that language reach back to the remote fifth century when conquering tribes of Jutes, Saxons and Angles first brought to the country the various dialects of a Germanic tongue now called Old English. Many of the words the invaders used survive in our vocabulary today. We have no difficulty recognizing *mann*, *wif* and *cild*. We are familiar with the *hus* in which they *libben* or live, the *mete* they *etan* and the *waeter* they *drincan*. The *bok* you are reading describes a history almost as old.

Though pronunciation has changed and modern English has freed itself of nouns that must be declined and adjectives that reflect their gender, Old English had several qualities which uniquely fitted it to survive and grow. Its users were willing to borrow words from the Latin culture of the Christian church and to absorb the Scandinavian vocabulary of later Viking raiders. Old English thus drew on European traditions, while her poets further enriched their 'wordhoard' with an imaginative range of synonyms. These last tell us a great deal about Anglo-Saxon life. In a world of war, gold and honour, the king was the heroes' treasure keeper and 'victory lord'. His warriors were his 'shield bearers' fighting in the 'iron-clad ring'. Over the heaving 'whale's road', riding the 'water's back', sailed the broad-bosomed longships with crews of 'Spear Danes' eager for fame.

Such fame was a principal preoccupation of the poet or *scop*, seated at his chieftain's hearth and regaling the company with records of their history. Wisdith, in a poem that dates perhaps from the early seventh century, offers a detailed inventory of the men who rose and fell in the great period of warrior migration a hundred years before.

While presenting this panorama of the past however, Wisdith also portrays himself in the timeless and masculine role of the Old English bard. His name implies that he is the widely travelled one, the man whose albeit imaginary journeys have disciplined him to received wisdom. Suffering, loneliness and the experience of good and evil have made Wisdith a man apart and the singer of songs who can reveal to his audience the glory and pathos of their uncertain world. This is the world created again by the stoic author of *Deor* (?seventh century), and both men look to the lord of the 'mead hall' for generous gifts in return for immortalizing his fame.

The communal and oral nature of such poetry accounts for a number of its characteristic features. All of these made it easier for the bard to improvise his work and his listeners to understand it. For example, each line, divided into halves of two stressed and a varying number of unstressed syllables, is symmetrical and alliterative. Such patterns appeal directly to the ear. Vivid poetic diction and the frequent use of parallel expressions for a single idea set the verse apart from normal speech and mark it out as a special mode of discourse, a means of imagining the world. Lastly, many set-piece passages describing such events as fights or feasts are composed from verbal formulas that were clearly part of a traditional and unwritten inheritance on which all poets could draw.

Such are some of the formal characteristics of this verse, but if Old English poetry is marked by artifice it is also characterized by deep emotion. The following lines from *The Battle of Maldon* (993) in which a band of warriors face certain defeat suggest these qualities well:

> Courage shall grow keener, clearer the will,
> the heart fiercer, as our force faileth.
> Here lies our lord levelled in the dust,
> the man all marred; he shall mourn to the end
> who thinks to wend off from this war-play now.
> Though I am white with winters I will not away,
> for I think to lodge me alongside my dear one,
> lay me down by my lord's right hand.

This passage conveys the ideal of warrior loyalty, the love of fame and honour embodied in the Germanic and originally pagan forms of the warrior life. It also suggests the reverence for conventional wisdom and the recognition of an uncertain and even malign universe which characterize the longest and most famous Old English poem, the epic *Beowulf*.

Although composed in a Christian court in seventh- or eighth-century Mercia or Northumbria, *Beowulf* is deeply sympathetic to the heroic tradition, to the culture of the hall and that view of human activity characteristic of the pagan world of southern Scandinavia two hundred years earlier. The poem thus reflects a life of fights and feasting, of ceremony, brilliant gold and sudden darkness. Here are pride in birth and physical strength, a world of sacred obligations, feud and vengeance. Beyond this, the forces of *wyrd* or fate seem to control man's destiny with mysterious omnipotence, while evil itself (personified in the poem by the monstrous Grendel, his dam and the dragon) is both primordial and powerful, something to be outwitted and destroyed by cunning and physical strength. However, while *Beowulf* contains many scenes of vivid action, it is principally conceived as a meditation on the heroic life, a philosophic vision of warrior man in his splendour and defeat.

The opening lines, for example, portray the funeral of a great king who as a young man crossed the waters to bring glory to an ailing country, just as Beowulf himself will later do. We watch the building of Hrothgar's mighty hall at Heorot, but even as this symbol of heroic society is celebrated, so we know it is waiting for the fire that will one day destroy it. Man's highest achievements are thus set against a background of inexorable change, and man himself is subject to time, weakness and age. Hrothgar has now passed his prime, and creatures of darkness prey on his fading glory.

Grendel and his dam are embodiments of primordial evil, the outcast forces of destruction who hate the order of Heorot with satanic jealousy. Hrothgar can no longer hold them at bay, and Beowulf in his shining 'war-gear' – the young hero from across the sea – is the only figure who can counter their power. When Grendel and his mother have been slain, a period of celebration ensues. There is rejoicing in victory and Beowulf's strength. Treasure is lavished on the hero and he returns home with his fame immeasurably increased. Hrothgar's words in the midst of proud success cannot however be forgotten:

> Put away arrogance,
> noble fighter! The noon of your strength
> shall last for a while now, but in a little time
> sickness of the sword will strip it from you:
> either enfolding flame or a flood's billow
> or a knife-stab or the stoop of a spear
> or the ugliness of age; or your eyes' brightness
> lessens and grows dim. Death shall soon
> have beaten you then, O brave warrior!

This speech is the pivot of the poem. It combines a love of heroism and conventional wisdom with a view of man poised between the brightness of youthful achievement and the shadow of death. If the first half of the work is a record of glory, we now move to a more sombre view.

The last section of *Beowulf* describes the ageing hero's defeat in his struggle against the dragon. The whole encounter is suffused with pessimism and the meanness of the man who has stolen the dragon's gold. With his spirit 'gloomy, death-eager, wandering', Beowulf himself seems to realize there is something fatal in this last encounter, a corrosion of confidence that eats away at the heart of the heroic ideal. In the heat of battle, all his companions save one desert him. As the dying hero offers his kingship to his last loyal retainer, so the glory of a nation withers away. Death and exile wait for all, and heroism passes into poetic legend.

2

The anonymous author of *Beowulf* drew on traditional resources to present an all-involving view of man and the supernatural, war and peace, life and death. This helps give his work its status as a heroic elegy. Great churchmen such as Alcuin of York (735–804) however had long asked what verse fundamentally sympathetic to a pagan culture could have to do with Christian salvation. This was a serious challenge to the older tradition, and a passage from *The Ecclesiastical History of the English People*, written in Latin by the Venerable Bede (probably 673–735), suggests how it was resolved.

Bede relates that when the harp was passed to the devout but unlearned Caedmon (late seventh century) he would rise from the company rather than expose his ignorance and distaste for pagan convention. One evening when this had happened and Caedmon had retreated to the cowshed, a figure appeared to him in a dream and commanded him to sing. 'What should I sing about?' the bewildered Caedmon asked. 'Sing about the creation of all things,' the figure replied. Bede says that Caedmon promptly improvised the following verses:

> Now we must praise the Keeper of Heaven's Kingdom,
> The Maker's might, and His conception,
> The deed of the Father of Glory; as He of all wonders
> – The Eternal Lord – established the beginning.
> He first created for the children of men
> Heaven as a roof, the Holy Shaper;
> Then Middle Earth did Mankind's Keeper,
> The Eternal Lord, afterward ordain,
> The earth of men, the Almighty Lord.

In these nine lines Caedmon has drawn heavily on the traditional 'wordhoard', but epithets previously reserved for pagan warriors have now been applied to the Christian God. When Caedmon was taken before St Hild, Abbess of Whitby, she and her learned advisers were so impressed by this that Caedmon was made a lay brother and offered instruction in order that he might versify the whole Christian story and so teach the people.

For Bede, concerned above all to show the operation of the divine in English history, Caedmon's discovery of his vocation was an act of God. What his account more certainly shows is how an important cultural problem was exposed and then solved by a creative intuition, an imaginative leap we may well choose to call inspired. In Caedmon's 'Creation-Hymn', two apparently contradictory cultures were reconciled and Old English poetry was joined to the great tradition of European Christianity. An enormous artistic advance had been made, and scholars sometimes refer to this as the Caedmonian revolution. What is less often recognized is the role played in this process by St Hild. A woman of commanding personality, and respected as such by Bede, the intelligence and foresight with which she used the important place offered her by her society require that she too be seen as a central figure in the making of English literature.

Though Bede goes on to describe how Caedmon versified a wide range of biblical events, modern scholars suggest that the remaining eighth-century Christian poems in Old English are the work of Caedmon's followers. One such poet is known by name. The verse of Cynewulf (late eighth or ninth century) lies firmly within contemporary patterns of Christian devotion and scholarship, motifs to which the poet in such works as *Elene* brings both his culture's natural regard for able women and an often skilful use of the formulas of Germanic heroic verse. These last were also used by the anonymous author of *Genesis* who delighted in describing God and the angels in terms of a warlord and his warriors, while heaven itself becomes an image of the earthly mead hall.

In *Exodus*, the flight of the Israelites and the crossing of the Red Sea are again imagined in terms of epic poetry, but to these effects the poet adds traditions of scriptural interpretation learned from the church fathers. Beneath the adventure there lies a serious spiritual purpose. Just as the Israelites are shown gaining the Promised Land, so Christians may enter the kingdom of God. Events in the Old Testament thus prefigure those in the New and teach all men of their salvation. This method of allegorical interpretation was to be of great importance to writers for many centuries to come, and they applied it not just to the Old and New Testaments. The whole world could be seen as an image of spiritual truth. In *The Whale*, for example, the great beast represents the Devil who lies in wait for unwary men, swallows them and drags them down to the depths of hell. Even wholly imaginary animals could be made to serve religious instruction. In *The Phoenix*, the fabulous bird, leaving its earthly paradise to die and be reborn, becomes an image of Christ's Passion and Resurrection.

Such works suggest how the church and its poets believed the true function of art was not simply to release feeling but to teach others and enhance devotion. A poem might give pleasure but it should also do something spiritually useful. It should help its hearer to pray and so assist in the most important duty of life – the pursuit of salvation. It is against such a background that we should read the masterpiece of Old English devotional verse, *The Dream of the Rood* (c. 700).

Rood is Old English for a cross, and this most famous symbol of the Christian faith appears in the narrator's dream encrusted with gold and reaching out over the whole world. At once bleeding and glorious, the cross is an image of shame and redemption – a uniquely powerful fusion of Anglo-Saxon culture with New Testament love. Christ is portrayed as the young warrior striding to embrace death and victory, while the cross itself takes on the burden of his suffering. When it speaks to the narrator of Christ's eager sacrifice and its own humiliation, the poet's skilful handling of words and emotion – his rhetoric – makes us feel we are present at the Passion itself:

> I was reared up, a rood.
>   I raised the great King
> liege lord of the heavens,
>   dared not lean from the true.
> They drove me through with dark nails:
>   on me are the deep wounds manifest,
> wide-mouthed hate-dents.
>   I durst not harm any of them.
> How they mocked at us both!
>   I was all moist with blood
> sprung from the Man's side
>   after He sent forth His soul.

As the poet of *The Dream of the Rood* obliges us to relive the agony of the Crucifixion, so his art stirs our pity and gratitude. We become ever more conscious of human sin. At the close of the work, when the poet's vision has faded, he offers a final and moving image of himself as a devout Christian alone on the worthless earth and longing to be reunited with the cross in heaven.

The heroism, sense of transitoriness and ardour for salvation that characterize *The Dream of the Rood* are also seen in some of the Elegies, that mighty handful of poems gathered in the Exeter Book, one of four manuscripts dating from about the year 1000 in which the greater part of Old English verse is preserved. The names by which these eighth-century poems have come to be known are *The Wanderer*, *The Seafarer*, *The Ruin*, *The Wife's Lament*, *The Husband's Message* and *Wulf and Eardwacer*. Each concerns loss and isolation, and coldly through the greatest of them blows a salt-edged wind and a knowledge of the heaving wastes of the sea. These build to a sense of universal desolation:

> A wise man may grasp how ghastly it shall be
> when all this world's wealth standeth waste,
> even as now, in many places, over the earth
> walls stand, wind-beaten,
> hung with hoar-frost; ruined habitations.

Such pessimism remains profoundly moving, but as we come to know more intimately the rhetorical image of themselves that these poets fashioned, so we can also begin to see how the narrators of *The Wanderer* and *The Seafarer* were deeply responsive to the Christian view of existence as this was formulated towards the much feared end of the first millennium. Aware of the anger of God towards the sinful soul, these poets present exemplary Christian images of themselves as strangers and sojourners in a corrupt and corrupting world. The author of *The Seafarer* in particular suggests that the true image of the righteous man is of a traveller or pilgrim on his way through the snares of mortal life to the eternal and heavenly Jerusalem. Such an image not only underlies some of the finest Old English poetry, but was to be developed by many of the greatest writers of the Middle Ages.

3

It is recorded that Alfred the Great (reigned 871–901) was keenly interested in Old English verse, but Alfred's literary concerns are principally associated with the revival of written prose and hence that crucial cultural achievement: the preservation of a body of advanced thought on which others could draw to describe their world. Books – rare, valuable and open to only the tiny minority of the literate – were now to take on their vital role as the repositories of what is known.

In Alfred's Wessex, the writing of such books was an urgent matter. Repeated Viking raids, cutting ever deeper into the kingdoms of England, had resulted in the sacking of churches and the burning of libraries. The centres of knowledge were being destroyed. When Alfred had finally forced the Vikings into retreat, he realized that to build his kingdom afresh he would have to develop its language and revive the learning once preserved by churchmen such as Bede. Literacy was clearly essential to this, but since Latin (for centuries the international medium of scholarship) had fallen into decay over most of England, the native tongue would have to serve. Its use in government and the law, in church matters and education, would stretch the resources of Old English to their limit and be a powerful force for national unity.

When peace was at last assured, Alfred wrote to the bishops saying that it seemed best to him, provided it did so to them, that they now 'turn into the language we all understand certain books most necessary for all men to know'. To revive the traditions of knowledge, Alfred would, with the help of scholars from England and abroad, translate the wisdom of the Latin and Christian classics into the language of his time. These translations include the *Dialogues* of St Gregory (trans. *c.* 880), one of the most influential fathers of the church. The fact that Alfred chose to translate this collection of saints' lives suggests he was determined to create for his people – such young men at least as could be spared from the army or the production of food – a literature of exemplary Christian conduct. Alfred's version of Gregory's *Pastoral Care* further shows how he wanted to place his own rule and that of his senior administrators on a firm intellectual basis, for *Pastoral Care* describes the moral and spiritual qualities required of those who have the government of others.

To provide his subjects with a sense of historical continuity, Alfred had an edited translation of Bede's *Ecclesiastical History of the English People* prepared. This work tells, with a critical concern for accuracy unique in its time, the history of England subsequent to the arrival of St Augustine of Canterbury as a missionary in 597. This event had helped establish the Roman Church as the focus of the country's European culture, and Bede's illustration of the then common belief that history is a moral pattern shaped by the hand of God would be a fundamental notion influencing writers for centuries to come. Finally, two further translations by Alfred himself reveal his more personal concerns. His version of the first fifty of the Psalms expresses the emotional side of his piety, while his work on Boethius's *Consolation of Philosophy* (the book which, more than any other, handed down the classical inheritance of reason to the Middle Ages) shows Alfred's interest in developing a language for abstract and critical thought.

Alfred's revival of literacy was sustained by many others. *The Anglo-Saxon Chronicle* (*c.* 871–1154), for example, is a laconic record of contemporary national events and thus an important source of information for Alfred's and subsequent reigns. It survived the Norman Conquest, and entries in the version from Peterborough (one of the seven centres at which the *Chronicle* was kept) continue into the harrowingly described reign of King Stephen (1135–54). While the narrative rarely rises to the level of literary interest, what is chiefly remarkable about the work is its very simplicity at a time when Latin authors in England and abroad were striving for elaborate rhetorical effect.

Conscious artifice and a concern with style and fluency were clearly of interest among later writers of Old English prose. This is particularly true of those associated with the Benedictine revival which took place during the reign of King Edgar (959–75). In this prolific period, during which many of the manuscripts in which Old English verse survives were written, the learning fostered by Alfred was placed on a firm foundation after the troubles that succeeded his reign.

The importance of Benedictine monasteries as institutions for preserving scholarship can hardly be overemphasized. The value placed on learning by St Benedict himself (the founder of Western monasticism) resulted in the making of digests or *florilegia* of the classical writers and theologians. These traditions of literacy were then passed on by an educational system based on the *trivium* or the skills of Latin grammar, rhetoric (the techniques of shaping language into persuasive and effective forms) and logic, the rational ordering of ideas. Such are the foundations of medieval and later scholarship. They were brought to bear on Old English by the ecclesiastical requirement to preach in the native tongue. For many centuries the sermon, educating people in what were held to be their spiritual, social and political duties, was an important force in preserving and developing the language. A quantity of alliterative prose sermons survives from the tenth century. Some of these, forcibly decrying the evils of the age, see further Viking raids as a divine punishment foretelling the end of the world.

It is the particular mark of Old English prose in this last great period however that it proved itself capable of dealing with almost any subject, be it history, romantic adventure such as we find in the translation *Apollonius of Tyre* (*c.* 1050), righteous indignation or the subtleties of theological argument. The lucid, powerful homilies of Aelfric (d. 1020) and Wulfstan (d. 1023) reveal a complete mastery of the medium and show how fifty years before the Norman Conquest southern England especially had, along with a remarkable body of poetic achievement, the most advanced prose literature of any region in Europe.

Medieval Literature

I

After the battle of Hastings, Old English ceased to be the main language of advanced written thought and public record. Latin and the Norman French of the conquerors became the principal tongues of church affairs and secular administration. A language without a common written standard is vulnerable however, and between the early twelfth and fourteenth centuries Old English lost many of its more complex grammatical characteristics. Nonetheless, contact with the Normans themselves greatly increased its vocabulary. By about 1350, some 900 words had been borrowed, and while much of the basic language of existence (*life, love, work* and *death*, for example) remains Old English in origin, many of the new words suggest increasingly refined aspirations. Among these words are *courteous, honour* and *noble*. Such changes mean that linguists refer to the speech of the period between about 1150 and 1350 as Early Middle English.

These subtle linguistic movements are paralleled by changes to the literature produced during the next three centuries that are equally far-ranging. Several works of devotional prose allow us to trace this development. In the central section of *The Ancrene Riwle* (*c.* 1200) for instance – a guide for anchoresses or women who had entered on a life of cloistered seclusion – the anonymous author creates a moving passage in which he suggests how Christ comes to the erring soul as a knightly lover to his lady, offering to die for her redemption. A profound change in spiritual life has clearly taken place, prompted here by the spiritual needs of women. Unlike Old English literature, the finger of an angry God no longer points to the sin-fraught exile. Love has largely superseded fear, and explorations into undiscovered regions of the heart offer fresh possibilities for introspection. An emphasis has also been placed on the humanity of Christ and the imagery of human passion.

These new ways of experiencing the world were a result of the widespread criticism and development of ideas that took place in Europe between about 1050 and 1300. This is sometimes called the twelfth-century renaissance, and books played an essential role in its progress. Though their scarcity meant that scholars had to develop elaborate memory systems to preserve their knowledge, the expansion of religious institutions and the number of teachers who went with these, along with the increasing complexity of society itself, meant that books were becoming ever more essential to clerics and laypeople alike. The number of scribes increased, a fast cursive script was developed, while copying was often organized around the *pecia* system whereby teams of scribes would reproduce a text divided into sections. By 1300, English books were sometimes being written on paper.

As part of this rebirth of learning, the skills in communication fostered by the *trivium* were greatly developed. The study of Latin flourished, and it was in Latin that the Englishman Geoffrey de Vinsauf produced his *Poetria Nova* (*c.* 1200), a treatise on rhetoric written for an international audience. This work is important, for Geoffrey's ideas point to the crucial fact that much medieval and later literature is not the result of spontaneous expression but, as Geoffrey himself says, of long-considered form and detailed preparation. When a literary concept was fully realized in the mind it could then achieve expression through practised rhetoric, the known modes of communication.

The third element of the *trivium* was logic. Contact with the Arab world had brought a greater knowledge of Aristotle to the West, and the range of Aristotle's studies provided men with a revelation of order, system, the powers of the mind. Disputation in the manner of Aristotle became a chief feature of undergraduate studies in the new universities of Oxford and Paris (the students also produced a body of witty Latin lyrics) and the rigour of such thinkers as Peter Abelard (1079–1142) pointed forward to that magisterial synthesis, the detailed and encyclopaedic reconciliation of Aristotelian thought and Christian theology, evident in the *Summa Theologiae* of St Thomas Aquinas (*c.* 1225–74).

Aquinas's work eventually became the corner-stone of Christian orthodoxy and the origin of the intellectual movement known as scholasticism. This was an attempt to demonstrate the rational basis of Christian belief by philosophic means and then illustrate the reasonableness of theology by minutely examining the inter-relationship of its parts. In addition, the scholastics also promoted a profoundly influential model of the universe which, derived from antiquity, was held to be definitive up to the late sixteenth century.

This model placed the unmoving earth at the centre of the crystal-line spheres of the planets and declared that both the universe and man himself – the macrocosm and the microcosm – were made up of the four elements: earth, air, fire and water. All created things were further ordered into a divinely ordained hierarchy or great chain of being. This ascended from inanimate stones, through plants and animals, to man whose possession of a soul placed him only a little lower than the angels. The universe was thus held to be finite, comprehensively ordered and the creation of a benevolent deity who bound it together in a supreme harmony of love.

Parallel with this emphasis on logical analysis went a new concern with subjectivity. This too was of importance for literature. The Cistercian order of monks, for example, placed great stress on medita-tion, spiritual friendship and even mysticism. St Anselm (c. 1033–1109) urged his influential audience of high-born female penitents to excite their minds and seclude themselves with God. This ardent disclosure of sin developed alongside the new tenderness for the person of Christ, and, with St Bernard of Clairvaux (1090–1153), the spiritual beauty of the Redeemer leads the soul to its mystic marriage with Christ the Bridegroom. These newly tender forms of devotion were soon popularized by the followers of St Francis of Assisi (?1181–1226) whose own radical simplicity of heart and intensity of vision make him the most attractive religious figure of the twelfth-century renaissance.

In English poetry of the period, this new intensity of religious emotion is revealed in a new form – the lyric. Nothing survives from Old English literature that quite corresponds to the lyric but, drawing on French traditions and rhymed, accented Latin verse, some of the religious poems gathered in the remarkable *Harley Lyrics* (c. 1310) show this new emphasis on the humanity of Christ and the suffering of his mother:

> 'Stond wel, moder, vnder rode,
> byholt þy sone wiþ glade mode,
> blyþe, moder, myht þou be!'

'Sone, hou shulde y bliþe stonde?
Y se þin fet, y se þin honde
    nayled to þe harde tre.'

þ is pronounced th; rode: *cross*; byholt: *behold*; blyþe: *happy*; fet: *feet*

Later writers of medieval lyric were to develop such emotions, and a large quantity of religious verse survives from the following centuries. In addition to celebrating the feasts of the church year, much of this poetry centres on the Virgin whose cult was a great humanizing force in the Middle Ages. Lyrics such as 'I syng of a mayden' (early fifteenth century) suggest the miraculous joy of the Incarnation, while in others the radiant Virgin of the Annunciation becomes the anguished mother of the *pietà* mourning the body of her son. 'Who cannot wepe, come lerne at me.' The intimacy with which the sufferings of Christ and his followers were re-experienced by believers spread out to many such devotional verses and related them directly to the lives of their audience.

A work such as 'In the vaile of restles mynd' (late fifteenth century) – an incomparable example of medieval devotional poetry – shows how the anonymous writer could borrow from the secular love poetry of the period in order to present the redeeming and mystic marriage of the soul to Christ. This suggests that the emotions of medieval faith could sometimes be expressed in the new-found language of human love. Certain of the *Harley Lyrics* thrill with this fresh refinement of sexual desire:

When þe nyhtegale singes þe wodes waxen grene;
lef ant gras ant blosme springes in Averyl, y wene,
ant loue is to myn herte gon wiþ one spere so kene
nyht ant day my blod hit drynkes; myn herte deþ me tene.

Ich have loved al þis ȝer, þat y may love namore;
ich have siked moni syk, lemmon, for þin ore.
Me nis loue never þe ner, and þat me reweþ sore.
Suete lemmon, þench on me, ich have loved þe ȝore.

Suete lemmon, y preye þe of love one speche;
whil y lyue in world so wyde oþer nulle y seche.
Wiþ þy love, my suete leof, mi blis þou mihtes eche;
a suete cos of þy mouþ mihte be my leche.

Suete lemmon, y preȝe þe of a loue-bene;

ȝef þou me lovest ase men says, lemmon, as y wene,

ant ȝef hit þi wille be, þou loke þat hit be sene.

So muchel y þenk vpon þe þat al y waxe grene.

Bituene Lyncolne ant Lyndeseye, Northaptoun and Lounde,

ne wot y non so fayr a may as y go fore-ybounde,

Suete lemmon, y preȝe þe þou louie me a stounde.

       Y wole mone my songe

       on wham þat hit ys ylong.

ȝ *is pronounced* y *or* gh; tene: *grieves*; ich: *I*; siked ... syk: *sighed ... sigh*; lemmon: *beloved*; for þin ore: *for your favour*; þench: *think*; ȝore: *for a long time*; oþer nulle y seche: *will not look for another*; leof: *beloved*; eche: *increase*; cos: *kiss*; leche: *doctor*; loue-bene: *love-boon*; wene: *think*; wot: *know*; may: *maiden*; fore-ybounde: *fettered by love*; stounde: *a while*; mone: *sing sadly*; on wham, *etc.*: *to (her) whom it is about*

The purity of this lyric has survived through nearly seven centuries to make it seem as if mankind had here fallen in love for the first time. In a sense this is true. In classical literature, sexual passion is often an intense, annoying intrusion or a comic aberration. Old English literature largely ignores it. In medieval lyric however, a newly refined love between the sexes is a proper subject for poetry. Few developments in European culture are of such significance. Writers of the Middle Ages developed a wide vocabulary of amatory gesture, and this has come to be called 'courtly love' or *fine amour*. It expressed itself in terms of the well-bred man's abasement before his lady who, like a saint, could confer grace on her unworthy supplicant, or, like a feudal lord, receive pledges of his undying service.

The ideals expressed by the love lyrics in the *Harley* manuscript reflect this aristocratic tone and touch on a further development in European society: the creation of chivalry, or the noble life of love and warfare. A new image of aristocratic man was being fashioned out of older notions of warrior companionship. The great English scholar John of Salisbury (d. 1180) declared that the perfect chivalric knight should protect the church and the poor, attack infidelity, reverence the priesthood, keep the peace and, if necessary, lay down his life for his fellow man. Others added to these requirements a refined appreciation of sexual love and courteous behaviour, qualities which mark out the 'gentil' man. In France especially, a new genre or pattern of literary conventions was developed to explore these ideas. 'Romance' originally meant to compose in the native tongue, and French became, quite literally, the lingua franca of the European secular élite.

Romance itself required a new refinement from its audience and developed the characteristic medieval motifs of the quest, the forest, the garden, the test, the meeting with the evil giant and the encounter with the beautiful beloved. Such incidents were written with great formal artistry but were rarely presented for their own sake. At its best, as in the work of the French poet Chrétien de Troyes (late twelfth century) or the Anglo-Norman *lais* of Marie de France (late twelfth century), romance could analyse the connection between a refined inner life and the demands of society. In Chrétien's depiction of knights given too exclusively to arms or love, for example, we see the importance of romance itself as a means of showing aristocratic medieval men and women in relation to their idealized view of the world. In such works of Marie's as *Guigemar*, a woman can contribute to this debate in her own voice: 'Hear, my lords, the words of Marie.' It is suggestive however that Marie herself felt obliged to speak thus against the background of those who disparaged her work, and it would be many centuries before such confident accents would be heard from a woman writer again.

Most of the surviving thirteenth- and early-fourteenth-century romances in English lack the intellectual sophistication of Marie's work. Though the octosyllabic lines of *King Horn* (c. 1225) and *Havelock the Dane* (c. 1300) have some literary qualities, and *Sir Orpheo* (c. 1300) a real appreciation of the supernatural, *Bevis of Hampton* and *Guy of Warwick* (both early fourteenth century) are largely concerned with thrills and spills and offer at best a horny-handed courtesy. They were nonetheless popular up to the time of Shakespeare.

But if these vernacular romances are of relatively small literary interest, Early Middle English poetry boasts one fine example of the opposing genre. The 'fabliau' is a comic narrative which presents the grotesque and very physical world of the bourgeois, the peasant and the clerk. This it does in an imagined sequence which shows these figures living by their wits in a world of farce. Such poetry is no more realistic or egalitarian than romance. While Chaucer is the supreme English exponent of fabliau, *Dame Sirith* (thirteenth century) – a poem which tells how a widow helped an absurdly languishing clerk to sleep with his reluctant girl-friend – is especially interesting as the first great comic narrative in the language.

Twelfth- and thirteenth-century England also had a fine school of Latin writers (historians especially) and it was the least scholarly of these who won the heart of Europe. Geoffrey of Monmouth's *History of the Kingdom of Britain* was composed in about 1135 and offers the earliest account of King Arthur whose popularity throughout the Middle Ages and beyond was enormous. Geoffrey's book was adapted and translated by the Anglo-Norman poet Wace (d. after 1171) who lavished on his version the new ideals of chivalry and made Camelot a paradigm for the courts of western Europe. Wace's poem was also a principal source for one of the most important Early Middle English verse chronicles, Layamon's *Brut* (twelfth century). This rhymed, alliterative work is chiefly heroic and military in its interests. The passage describing the death of Arthur however suggests something of the mystery which helps account for the enduring fascination of the 'matter of Britain'. In addition, one of the most interesting aspects of the poem is Layamon's brief self-portrait in the opening lines.

Layamon tells how he took a quill in his hand, applied it to the 'book-skin', set down the truer words from his sources and so digested three books into one. If his reference to three sources is somewhat fanciful, Layamon nonetheless presents himself as at once a scribe, a compiler and a commentator. He is thus the ideal medieval author, a man reverencing the authority of the past, preserving a communal and ancient wisdom and so working within a tradition. Like many medieval poets, his claim is less to originality than to the truth of his material.

Layamon's self-portrait is a revealing if deeply conservative one. Other poets were more experimental and found they could draw on the powerful, precise use of words and ordered public debate now being developed by the law. Nicholas of Guildford, for example, appears to have been a legally trained courtier looking for preferment, and he was probably the author of *The Owl and the Nightingale* (twelfth century). This is a work which, in the form of a rehearsal for a mock-trial, skilfully argues out a fundamental problem of the age: the conflict that had arisen between the Gregorian traditions of penitence represented by the Owl and the new world-delighting cult of *fine amour* enjoyed by the Nightingale. After a highly spirited confrontation in which each speaker is obliged to modify her opinion, the quick-witted Nightingale and her newly arrived allies claim the courtly bird has won the case as, technically, she has. Nonetheless, the Owl demands a retrial before Nicholas himself. We are not told what judgement was given. The issue is left for the audience to discuss.

This is the poem's most subtle ploy and points to a number of important general features of medieval poetry. First, *The Owl and the Nightingale* was not, like much Old English verse, an oral improvisation subject to the vagaries of being transcribed at a later date. Nor, like modern literature, was it a printed book circulated to thousands of anonymous and disparate readers. The longer medieval poem was a handwritten text that was first recited to an audience. Such a text could be more self-consciously wrought and more permanent than the older poetry. It could also be exactly repeated. In addition, by being the central element in a public performance, its narrator – particularly if he were the author – could develop an intricate and dramatic relationship with his aristocratic listeners. By embodying this new subtlety in a poem that requires its audience to consider serious issues in their culture, *The Owl and the Nightingale* reveals that by the close of the twelfth century literature in English could operate on the highest levels and be the vehicle of a full humanity.

2

The Early Middle English dialect of *The Owl and the Nightingale* was to be profoundly modified in the course of the next two centuries. Though the disintegration of the vast continental estates ruled by the Plantagenets might have suggested that the allegiance of the court now lay with England, French remained the chief language of the nobility. This became increasingly resented (particularly during the Hundred Years War with France) and attempts to enforce the use of French through legislation became less and less effective. However, though English was the speech of the majority, for many years it remained secondary to Latin as a medium for serious discussion and to French as a means of literary expression.

Writers wishing to instruct a lay audience nonetheless were increasingly obliged to use it. The *Ormulum* (late twelfth century), for example, is a worthy if somewhat tedious attempt to provide an English commentary on the Gospels as these were used in the mass over the church year. Such collections of saints' lives as *The Northern Passion* and *The South English Legendary* (late thirteenth century) were constantly being added to until the vast *Cursor Mundi* (early fourteenth century) became an encyclopaedia of scriptural knowledge in English. Such compilations were important to a manuscript culture. They show how verse was still considered a central means of instruction and suggest attitudes to the nature and function of books as encyclopaedias which were to influence poets of much greater achievement.

Through contact with French, the language itself continued to be enriched to the extent that from about 1350 it should be termed Middle English. It was still a remarkably regionalized tongue nonetheless. Economic development ensured that the dialect of the prosperous East Midlands (a huge and subdivisible area stretching from the Humber south to the Thames and bounded in the west by the Peak District) became the dominant form. The growth of mercantile and associated activity in London then forced the native language into new areas of expression and expertise. By 1356, the mayor and aldermen of London required that proceedings in the sheriff's courts be conducted in English, a move which reflects the decision of a powerful group of men to conduct their affairs in their own language. Six years later the king's courts followed suit.

These conscious decisions to augment the prestige of English were reinforced by a natural disaster: the Black Death which ravaged the country between 1348 and 1350. The Black Death was a force making for profound social and linguistic change. The translator John of Trevisa (1326–1412), for example, declared that before the plague schoolchildren were taught in French but afterwards those surviving 'lerneth an Englische'. This was a revolution, and Trevisa cites two Oxford-trained schoolmasters as its instigators: John of Cornwall and Richard Pencrich, men largely unknown but innovators of the greatest significance. By the last quarter of the fourteenth century, and as a result of such combined forces, Middle English was a highly developed language preparing to take its place beside the great literary vernaculars of Europe, to absorb their techniques and extend their purposes. It was to do so in the hands of a poet of genius.

3

Geoffrey Chaucer (c. 1345–1400) is 'the father of English poetry'. This popular epithet is in many ways deserved, and although nothing can explain the sudden appearance of a mind of the most acute and original sensibility, range and innovative power, it is at least possible to suggest something of Chaucer's circumstances and the traditions on which he drew, only to transfigure these with so mastering a facility that he ranks as a poet of European stature.

Chaucer's birth in an English-speaking merchant family with connections at court helps to account for his career in royal employment. This included a period of active service in France where he was briefly imprisoned, diplomatic journeys to Italy, marriage, responsible work as Comptroller of Customs for the Port of London among other posts, and burial in Westminster Abbey as a reward for his labours. Such a career suggests Chaucer's familiarity with a leisured, chivalric and French-based culture of the greatest brilliance. It also shows his experience of the specialized world of work and achievement. To such circumstances should be added Chaucer's personal interests: his active and searching piety; his knowledge of Latin, French and Italian literature; and his speculative, humane intellect which was deeply concerned with rhetoric, theology, philosophy and the several branches of medieval science. With Chaucer, a wide range of European poetry and speculation is thus brought to bear on received native traditions and thereby transforms them.

Aside from the Bible, the seminal work of Latin literature for Chaucer was Boethius's *The Consolation of Philosophy*. This he translated with the help of a French version in about 1382. In Boethius's text, the allegorical figure of Philosophy explains to the imprisoned author how the love that links the world in harmony, if pursued with excessive attachment, binds man to the great wheel of Fortune. This rules his fate unless he turns from false and fleeting happiness to God, the still centre of the revolving wheel. With Boethius, the last flowering of classical philosophy was opened to the medieval mind, offering Chaucer both a mature language of speculation and a means of exploring a fundamental issue in his work: the life of men and women in a world which draws us with its beauty and allure, but which must finally be seen as a delusion and a source of woe when compared to the power of spiritual reality.

Chaucer was early influenced by French literature, in particular the *Roman de la Rose* which is one of the central works of European culture. The product of two writers, Guillaume de Lorris (active *c.* 1230) and Jean de Meung (active *c.* 1275), the poem is an ironic and allegorical dream vision – a fantasy of male sexual attainment – which provided much of the medieval psychology of love and many of the conventions of its poetry. The work shows the complex nature of the literary dream, the folly of unreasoning lust and a wide range of influential comic and allegorical figures who beguile us even while we are supposed to recognize their errors. Such techniques are fundamental to much subsequent medieval poetry and, just as Chaucer translated Boethius, so he made a version of the opening of this work. The intellectual and technical resources on which English writers could draw were thus being greatly expanded.

Chaucer's earliest original poem was probably *The Book of the Duchess* (1368). This is an elegy, couched in the form of a dream vision, that mourns and celebrates Blanche, the wife of John of Gaunt. It also offers comfort to her widower. Chaucer, the ironically naïve narrator of the work, here reveals himself as a learned poet grafting the techniques of French literature on to the octosyllabic couplets of his native tradition and thereby fashioning for an important public occasion an English poem of unprecedented sophistication. His work is thus to be seen not as a private exploration of sensibility but as a public discussion of important matters – an intellectual courtier's contribution to a society of the highest cultural achievement.

The House of Fame suggests that Chaucer did not accept literary traditions uncritically. Although he shows himself seated in front of his book 'domb as any stoon', such silent reading was itself an advanced technique in a period when most scholars would mutter over their studies. Here, somewhat like the Dante of *The Divine Comedy* who was so impressive and liberating an influence on his work, Chaucer presents himself as the modest (sometimes comically

modest) but nonetheless self-possessed intellectual. He is a man confronting the immense resources of the past not in servile dependence
but with respect and a measure of freedom. As his dream vision
recounts the story of Dido and Aeneas (derived from the Latin of
Virgil and Ovid) and then tells of his own flight to the temple of
Fame in the grip of a delightfully loquacious eagle (a character
parodied from Dante), so Chaucer pits his personal observation
against 'auctoritee' or received ideas. His is a critical reverence for
tradition and, as his own man, he can finally tell the strident figure of
Fame: 'I wot myself best how ystonde.'

This freedom of enquiry is clearest in the third of Chaucer's early
works: *The Parliament of Fowls* (c. 1382–3), a work composed from
the seven more or less regular iambic pentameter lines of the 'rhyme
royal' stanza. Here, after studying the stern morality of the ancient
Somnium Scipionis, the troubled dreamer in the poem wanders through
an allegorical garden, past Cupid and the burning desires of Venus'
temple, and comes upon a parliament of birds presided over by the
goddess Nature. A refined but indecisive debate on love and marriage
ensues between three aristocratic eagles and the female tercel perched
on Nature's wrist. The debate gently suggests the impractical sophist-
ications of excessive *fine amour*, just as the narrator's previous encounters have hinted at the limitations of a life exclusively given either to
study or to sexual indulgence. The lesser birds however, growing
restive during the aristocrats' long debate, choose their mates and
then sing an exquisite *rondeau*. The noise of their parting wakes the
narrator. Having glimpsed something of the range of experience his
culture offers – charity, lust, *fine amour* and marriage – he returns
to his books having committed himself to no final 'auctoritee'.
Chaucer remains the intellectual searching his way among the various
alternatives offered by his time.

4

Chaucer's early dream sequences show a poet of *fine amour* exploring
his art against a range of literary and philosophical possibilities. In
Troilus and Criseyde (c. 1385) – the story of a young prince of the

Trojan royal house who suffers to win his love only to be betrayed by her and die – Chaucer applied this experience to a different mode. In one of the supreme achievements of English literature he became a master of romance. Once again, contact with Italy provided the initial stimulus, for the English poem derives from Boccaccio's *Il Filostrato*. In the accepted medieval manner, Chaucer extensively adapted and translated his original. He then added rhetorical, philosophical and theological material from Boethius, Dante and his own devising to fashion a narrative unique in its depth and technical resourcefulness. In *Troilus and Criseyde* – and with a breathtaking extension of his powers – Chaucer offers a comprehensive image of medieval courtly man in his worldly and eternal destiny.

The opening stanzas appear to tell the whole story. Chaucer it at first seems is no more than the humble transcriber of Troilus's journey 'fro wo to wele and after out of joie'. All appears predetermined. As we watch the characters struggle to achieve a worldly happiness that they cannot see is doomed, so we know – or think we know – their entire history.

Surveying the women in the temple and naïvely glad he is free from such attachments, Troilus's eyes light on the beautiful Criseyde, a young widow deserted by her treacherous father. From the start, Troilus's passion reveals itself as a seemingly hopeless devotion, a supreme expression of romantic idealism. Chaucer subtly evokes this in a manner at once impassioned and devout yet tinged with the innocence of youthful ardour. Leaving the temple, the smitten boy heads straight for the privacy of his rooms. Here he prostrates himself before the ideal of his lady and, in a hell of seemingly irremediable despair, laments his previous sins against Cupid.

Criseyde's uncle Pandarus now interrupts him in a scene of great technical audacity. The highest expressions of romance and *fine amour* are here juxtaposed to the most worldly manipulation, for the vulgar and loquacious Pandarus is one of the great comic characters of English literature. When he has extracted the truth from the young lover, Pandarus hurries to his niece and, in a superbly realistic scene of comedy and sinister emotional blackmail, tells her of Troilus's infatuation. He also arranges for Troilus to ride past Criseyde's window. All this is the subtle manipulation of a pimp – a pander. Pandarus himself is delighted by his success but, as Boethius had shown, it is Fortune who really rules worldly men, and it is Fortune who actually arranges for Criseyde to glimpse Troilus as he rides by. This scene, so richly conveying the ethos of romance, is one of the most exquisite moments in medieval English literature:

> This Troilus sat on his baye steede,
> Al armed, save his hed, ful richely;
> And wownded was his hors, and gan to blede,
> On which he rood a pas ful softely.
> But swich a knyghtly sighte, trewely,
> As was on hym, was nought, withouten faille,
> To loke on Mars, that god is of bataille.
>
> So lik a man of armes and a knyght
> He was to seen, fulfilled of heigh prowesse;
> For bothe he hadde a body and a myght
> To don that thing, as wel as hardynesse;
> And ek to seen hym in his gere hym dresse,
> So fressh, so yong, so weldy semed he,
> It was an heven upon hym for to see.
>
> His helm to-hewen was in twenty places,
> That by a tyssew heng his bak byhynde;
> His sheeld to-dasshed was with swerdes and maces,
> In which men myght many an arwe fynde
> That thirled hadde horn and nerf and rynde;
> And ay the peple cryde, 'Here cometh oure joye,
> And, next his brother, holder up of Troye!'
>
> For which he wex a litel reed for shame,
> Whan he the peple upon hym herde cryen,
> That to byholde it was a noble game,
> How sobrelich he caste down his yen.
> Criseyda gan al his chere aspien,
> And leet it so softe in hire heret synke,
> That to hireself she seyde, 'Who yaf me drynke?'

a pas: *at foot pace*; hardynesse: *boldness*; gere: *armour*; weldy: *active*; tyssew: *lace*; thirled, *etc.*: *cut through the layers of his shield*; yen: *eyes*; chere: *demeanour*

The young martial hero in his battered armour enters the city in triumph. Although he is gnawed by a secret grief, his new-found hope is nonetheless perfecting his social and military excellence. The personal demands placed on him by his love for the unseen woman who stares down at him are beginning to purge him of the seven deadly sins. These, in their interrelated order of descent, are: pride, wrath, envy, lust, gluttony, avarice and sloth. They form one of the most influential analyses of human behaviour ever made. And, just as Chaucer's much revered Dante is purged of the sins as he ascends Mount Purgatory towards the earthly paradise, so, by the close of Book Two, Troilus has moved from a hell of hopeless anguish to a refining purgatory of sexual desire.

Love it seems can indeed perfect a man and, as a result, Criseyde's passion too is kindled. She is attracted to the best a pagan world can offer. This, she knows, is much. As she tells Troilus in their last moments of intimacy, her affections were roused not by Fortune's gifts of the prince's wealth, good looks and social status, but by those noble and inward qualities that make him a gentleman and have their roots in what Criseyde herself calls 'moral vertu, grounded upon trouthe'.

At its highest, such 'trouthe' is a man's personal integrity, his being true to his word. This is the quality Troilus embodies above all and, in Book Three, it allows him to glimpse divine truth in the earthly paradise of Criseyde's arms. In the rapture of desire fulfilled, Troilus becomes aware of the beauty of a loving God who rules the world in blissful harmony. In his song at the close of Book Three, the entranced young man beholds a world pulsing with love, a love that binds earth, sea and sky in a hymning and ardent benevolence. The virtuous pagan, raised to the very height of human worth, beholds God's purposes in an ecstasy of adoration.

Herein lies Chaucer's supreme validation of human love: at its best it may so perfect a man that he can glimpse a higher order of spiritual existence. But for Troilus it is only a glimpse. Criseyde is not Dante's Beatrice to lead her lover through paradise. She is the world: beautiful and alluring, but false, fleeting and subject to Fortune. Her traitor father begs the Trojan parliament for her return in exchange for an important prisoner. The secret lovers are forced to part, and the last two books of *Troilus and Criseyde* are a picture of an ever-deepening grief.

Chaucer's presentation of the doomed lover trapped in his lonely anguish is all but unbearably insistent. Troilus loses his philosophical insight into divine truth. The advice offered by Pandarus is ever more useless and distasteful. And still Criseyde does not come. Although at their parting she protested her own 'trouthe', in her weakness and isolation she eventually succumbs to the Grecian Diomede. For the sake of a worthless protector, Criseyde abandons the height of human excellence, callously denying she ever had such a lover as Troilus. This is a moment of numbing betrayal, and to make the inevitable so surprising is a supreme creation of art. We are left hurt and resentful. Nonetheless, it is the narrator, urging on us Christian forgiveness, who eventually moves us the most:

> Ne me ne list this sely womman chyde
> Forther than the storye wol devyse.
> Hire name, allas! is punysshed so wide,
> That for hire gilt it oughte ynough suffise.
> And if I myghte excuse hire any wise,
> For she so sory was for hire untrouthe,
> Iwis, I wolde excuse hire yet for routhe.

sely: *hapless*; routhe: *pity*

In the failure of human love we learn Christian compassion. There is a more sustaining morality than *fine amour*.

Finally, with his letters ambiguously answered, Troilus's growing suspicion of Criseyde is confirmed and, in his despair, he wants only revenge and death. Fortune however has not decreed that Troilus shall kill his rival. He fights desperately but, in the end, 'dispitiously him slough the fiers Achille'. The hero's death is a matter of a single line. Troilus's soul is now freed from the sliding and deceptive world of Fortune and is led through the heavens to where 'Mercury sorted him for to dwell.' The only real freedom however is the truth of God in the permanence of eternity, and it is this perception of the power of the Creator that allows Chaucer to turn to his audience of 'yonge, fresshe folkes' at the close of his work and urge on them the precepts of Christian love. Though initiates in the fine arts of desire, these people are blessed with a revelation of the divine infinitely more powerful than that available to the pagan Troilus. They are Christians. For them, there is a higher, surer and more glorious love than *fine amour*. In the authentic medieval manner, *Troilus and Criseyde* speaks finally of God.

5

In *The Legend of the Good Women* (c. 1382–94), and perhaps as a mock-penance for writing of Criseyde's deceit, Chaucer retold in the form of the saint's life stories of classical heroines betrayed by their men. The prologues discuss the nature of dream with great sophistication, while the narratives themselves vary in tone from vivid battle scenes to lament. The work itself, written in heroic couplets, is incomplete however, and Chaucer's most famous collection of narratives is *The Canterbury Tales*.

Some fifty-eight substantial manuscripts survive to suggest the contemporary popularity of Chaucer's unfinished masterpiece, while the twenty-four completed or abandoned narratives that make up the collection themselves reveal the breadth of literary interests Chaucer could explore by having imagined pilgrims tell stories on their way to (and, it was once planned, on their way from) the national shrine of St Thomas à Becket at Canterbury. This is experimentation on the widest and most exhilarating scale.

Chaucer's pilgrims gather at the Tabard Inn at Southwark as the world undergoes its spring awakening to love and faith revived. In the *General Prologue* (c. 1387) to his work, the devout but retiring narrator depicts his various characters with a matchless appearance of observation and an eye for the skills of such professionals as the Yeoman, the Doctor and Harry Bailey, the group's landlord and leader. He shows a more formal awareness of those ideal characters who represent the three 'estates' of feudal society: the Knight, the Parson and the Ploughman. With characters such as the Monk, the Summoner and the Wife of Bath however, we are made vividly aware of sophisticated satire on both the church and secular society.

The opening narrative is *The Knight's Tale* (c. 1382), a romance once again derived from Boccaccio. Chaucer shortened and adapted his original to portray in highly rhetorical form the effects of love and war in a non-Christian society. The poem is a magnificent evocation of the power and pageantry of courtly life. It is also an exploration of *fine amour* that recognizes its highly polished ardour, points to the inherent folly of its extremism, and then explores the relation between sexual desire, violence and death. In addition, the poem is a searching philosophical work, for as the friendship of Palamon and Arcite is broken by their love for the remote Emily, so Chaucer's narrative broadens into an examination of the life of chivalric man ruled by passion and the ruthless planets. Only at the close of the work, in the noble speeches of Theseus the good ruler, are the great themes of love, violence and courtliness finally set in the context of Boethius's view of an eternal and benevolent order.

Contrast is an essential aspect of Chaucer's comprehensiveness, and the fabliaux are among the great delights of *The Canterbury Tales*. Narratives by the Friar, the Summoner and the Cannon's Yeoman offer anti-clerical themes, while there is a subtle mixture of comedy and learned allusion in the tales of the Merchant, the Reeve and the Miller. The Miller's altercation with Harry Bailey also suggests how vivid the link passages between the narratives are.

The Miller's Tale (c. 1390) itself recounts how young Nicholas convinces John, the conventionally foolish husband of the alluring Alisoun, that he will escape the coming punishment of a world flood if he hides in a barrel suspended in the rafters. Having fooled the old man into believing he is a 'type' of Noah, Nicholas then sets about getting his pleasure. However, he and Alisoun are interrupted by the ridiculous and squeamish Absolon whom Alisoun tricks into kissing her bare backside. This is a moment of uproarious comedy, and the juxtaposition of inappropriate high passion expressed in the manner of the *Harley Lyrics*, demotic dialogue and sheer physical vulgarity reveals the mature Chaucer's masterful and witty playing with levels of style:

> This Absolon doun sette hym on his knees
> And seyde, 'I am a lord at alle degrees;
> For after this I hope ther cometh moore.
> Lemman, thy grace, and sweete bryd, thyn oore!'
> The wyndow she undoth, and that in haste.
> 'Have do,' quod she, 'com of, and speed the faste,
> Lest that oure neighebores thee espie.'

> This Absolon gan wype his mouth ful drie.
> Derk was the nyght as pich, or as the cole,
> And at the wyndow out she putte hir hole,
> And Absolon, hym fil no bet ne wers,
> But with his mouth he kiste hir naked ers
> Ful savourly, er he were war of this.
>
> Abak he stirte, and thoughte it was amys,
> For wel he wiste a womman hath no berd.
> He felte a thyng al rough and long yherd,
> And seyde, 'Fy! allas! what have I do?'
>
> 'Tehee!' quod she, and clapte the wyndow to,
> And Absolon gooth forth a sory pas.

Lemman: *beloved*; oore: *compassion*

Worse is to come, however. When the vengeful Absolon returns with a red-hot coulter, Nicholas sticks his own bottom out of the window, farting horribly. The pain of his unexpected branding is such that he calls for water. John thinks the flood has come, cuts the ropes on his barrel, hurtles to the ground and breaks his arm. When the lovers convince the neighbours he is mad the result is, as promised, 'harlotrie' or timeless farce.

For Chaucer, comedy was a fruitful means of juxtaposing a divinely ordered universe against the vagaries of human interpretation. *The Wife of Bath's Prologue and Tale* are perhaps his most comprehensive experiments in this mode. They are also among his most attractive. Alisoun the Wife of Bath herself, garrulously recounting her succession of marriages, dressed with vulgar ostentation, her hearty attachment to the things of this world touched with the poignancy of advancing age, is one of the most memorable characters in the *General Prologue* and one of the most beguiling of raconteurs. The metamorphosis of the bawdy adviser from romance and the 'bad wife' of the sermons into this vivacious provincial housewife is a remarkable achievement, and one deepened and made more humane by Chaucer's shrewd exploration of the relation of human desire to divine decree.

Throughout, the Wife of Bath pits private experience against the received ecclesiastical verities. In particular, she defies the church and believes a woman should have 'maistrye' or dominance over her husband. Her accounts of her marriages vividly suggest her sexual career, while her discussion of virginity, wedlock and widowhood, along with her citation of numerous anti-feminist authorities, also reveal how *The Canterbury Tales* themselves can be seen as a uniquely entertaining *compilatio*, an encyclopaedia of received wisdom. The Wife of Bath herself is nonetheless aware of the human damage inflicted by the creation of literature when it is too exclusively the preserve of theologically minded men:

> By God! if wommen hadde writen stories,
> As clerkes han withine hire oratories,
> They woldee han writen of men moore wikkednesse
> Than al the mark of Adam may redresse.

Alisoun's indignation retains its force. Nonetheless, her own experience finally contradicts her loud assertions of feminine independence, for she tells us that when her last and most favoured husband had struck and revived her, she lived with him without contention. Married love, the subject of her tale, is eventually established on the conventional sanctities. Theology remains for Chaucer the bedrock of the deepest human experiences.

The Wife of Bath's Tale (pre-1396), Chaucer's only narrative with an Arthurian setting, develops these themes. It tells how a young rapist, condemned to death by the king's court of law, is saved by the queen's court of love. Male aggression is contrasted to female mercy as the courtly ladies charge the youth to discover what wedded women most desire. In return for a promise of marriage, a loathly lady tells the knight that this is 'maistrye'. The queen's court agree, and the horrified young man is obliged to marry his rescuer.

In their bridal chamber, the loathly lady uses arguments from Dante to convince the sometime rapist that true worth does not lie in a worldly concern for wealth, beauty and rank but in moral value. The young man is finally convinced and kisses his mentor who is at once transformed into a beauty. Conversion to virtue brings its magical reward, and the newly wedded couple spend the rest of their days in the 'parfit joy' of a mutual and sanctified relationship. By a delightful irony however, the Wife of Bath ends her tale with the hope that she herself will meet other such young squires with their transforming kisses. Life and literature are touchingly confused at the close of a work which has explored the extremes of human relationships from male and female dominance to the most delicate apprehension of a carefully maintained mutuality between the sexes.

Marriage is also the central issue in the tales told by the Merchant and the Franklin. In the first, and after another encyclopaedic debate on the advantages and woes of marriage itself, the elderly January weds the youthful May. This situation, familiar in fabliau, is ripe for exploration through comedy and farce.

The couple's nuptial feast, described with a wealth of biblical and classical allusion, is in marked contrast to the ageing husband's repulsive efforts at intimacy. This suggests the powerful juxtaposition of contrasts in a poem at once learned and comic. Such a technique is further developed at the climax. May has been courted by Damyan, a young squire languishing in the excesses of *fine amour*, a form of passion often careless about marital fidelity. All three figures then gather in January's idyllic garden where May has arranged to cuckold her now blinded husband. May, claiming she is pregnant and longing for the pears growing on the tree above them, is watched by the king and queen of the underworld as she climbs on her husband's shoulders to enjoy the favours of her lover hidden in the branches. Pluto suddenly returns January's sight, but Proserpine, true to her word, gives May the womanly quick-wittedness whereby she beguiles her husband into thinking her actions have wrought his cure. Fantasy and the grotesquely comic are thus wedded in a narrative where learning and debate combine in a rich, ironic miscellany.

The vigorous and allusive bawdy of *The Merchant's Tale* is in marked contrast to the refined analysis of 'trouthe' and 'gentilesse' in the tale told by the Franklin. Here, Chaucer's interest in the loving relation of man to wife (as well as in the development of a style of sententious aphorism) is clear when Arveragus agrees after his marriage to submit in private to his lady Dorigen provided that in public matters she obeys him. Theirs is thus a relation of friendship established on the premise 'that freendes everych oother moot obey'.

When Arveragus is then called away, Dorigen laments that the cruel rocks on the coastline appear to threaten her husband's safe return. Nonetheless, when she gently rebuffs the amorous Aurelius by saying she will only grant his wishes when the rocks have disappeared, what had appeared as a threat to wedded happiness becomes a token of its enduring foundation. Only an illusion – an untruth – can remove the rocks and threaten Dorigen's marriage. And it is just this illusion that Aurelius eventually procures through the expensive services of a magician – a dealer in lies. The rocks are indeed removed, Arveragus returns, and in a scene of high and 'gentil' pathos he insists that Dorigen honour her word to Aurelius. 'Trouthe is the hyeste thyng that man may kepe,' Arveragus declares in his anguish. So moved is Aurelius by this evidence of noble integrity that he at once releases Dorigen from her vow even as the magician, also moved by the revelation of aristocratic 'gentilesse', frees the lover from his crushing burden of indebtedness. In the words of the Gospel, the truth has set all parties free.

The anguish inflicted by Dorigen's rash promise is overcome by integrity and the 'gentil' behaviour of the freely born, those noble not just in birth but in spirit. At the end of his tale however, and with a rhetorical gesture towards the medieval delight in refined literary debate, the Franklin asks which of his characters best embodies his ideal of behaviour. While the question is unanswerable, it nonetheless obliges the audience to reflect on the deft and serious moral intricacy with which the narrative is constructed.

Where the tales of the Merchant and the Franklin reveal the extremes in Chaucer's handling of sexual passion, other works are concerned with the pathos characteristic of much fourteenth-century religious devotion. The tales of the Prioress and the Second Nun, for example, show a highly wrought concern with martyred innocence, while *The Man of Law's Tale* (*c.* 1390) is a saint's legend. This work is thus a true Christian history which recounts with pathos and fine philosophical exposition the story of Constance, the devout daughter of a believing Roman emperor. As so often in medieval religious writing however the literal surface of the narrative hints at deeper levels of interpretation. These concern the Christian duties of conversion and baptism, the right conduct of life amid the stormy waves of Fortune, and the soul's final journey to the reunion of the blessed in paradise. As a true Christian story, *The Man of Law's Tale* can thus be read as a study in faith, morality and man's eternal destiny.

Such techniques are more obliquely applied in the austerely beautiful *Clerk's Tale* (*c.* 1373). Here a wife's obedience to her tyrannical husband supposedly provides a model of the soul's obedience to God, but the narrator's sympathy is so engaged by the human melodrama of his narrative that he finds this application all but impossible to make. The Clerk's refusal to treat Griselda merely as a token woman in a priestly theological exercise obliges the audience to consider the limitations of some of their conventional ideas while also suggesting the mature Chaucer's delight in the problems posed by literary interpretation itself. This is an interest seen at its most developed in *The Nun's Priest's Tale.*

The Nun's Priest's Tale (post-1381) has been preceded by the Monk's recital of numerous incidents illustrating the destruction of men as proud and worldly as himself. This well-recognized genre was often termed the 'fall of princes', but its tedium here is such that Harry Bailey interrupts and requests a livelier tale from the Nun's Priest. The result is the finest versified animal fable in the language.

The narrative tells how a widow's proud and libidinous cockerel, ignoring a dream of his own destruction and confusing his much vaunted reason through an excessive desire for his wife, struts and sings his way to near-destruction in the maw of a fox. This is very much in the 'fall of princes' genre, and both the action and the poem's wealth of lively debate appear to raise profound issues about free will and determinism, dream lore, sexual relations, the Fall of man and his salvation. Chauntecleer the cockerel however eventually saves himself by his wit and the hullabaloo raised by the Widow, her family and neighbours. Serious questions have thus been raised only to be comically brushed aside. For all his hero's philosophical pretensions and the Nun's Priest's own ironic and mock-heroic interjections, he finally declares: 'my tale is of a cok'. The comic narrative thus undermines any attempt at wholly serious interpretation.

For all that, the Nun's Priest is an essentially virtuous man. The Pardoner however, who tells a chilling *exemplum* or moral story to illustrate how the love of money is the root of all evil, is motivated solely by the greed he appears to attack. As he recounts his story of three low-living men who go to kill Death but are diverted by a pot of gold and end up killing each other, so we can begin to see his performance as a grotesque inversion of the ideal of a preacher inspired by the Holy Ghost. The Pardoner, like the characters in his tale, is inspired simply by money and wine.

The Parson on the other hand forswears fiction completely. His tale is a sermon on the seven deadly sins. He has opted for 'moralitee', for 'virtuous matere' and prose. In so doing he offers a useful exposition of conventional medieval religious thought. Then, as we move nearer Canterbury itself, Chaucer appends to the Parson's sermon a sincere retraction of his own 'enditynges of worldly vanitees'. It is a moving moment. A great master of medieval narrative (who, in this his most ambitious work, had himself tell a romance so humorously dull that he was interrupted and obliged to substitute an improving prose fable) here dismisses his early poems, the philosophic enquiries of *Troilus and Criseyde*, his fabliaux and other romances. No longer an innovative poet or even an imagined pilgrim, Chaucer presents himself finally as a mortal man and kneels contrite before the ultimate Truth of Christian salvation. At the last, a great voice of Middle English literature is silenced as Chaucer reaches across the centuries and asks not for our critical appreciation but for our prayers.

6

The enormous influence of Chaucer's work was felt by poets in both England and Scotland. Scotland herself had already produced verse chronicles such as Barbour's *Bruce* (*c.* 1380), and her political independence ensured that 'Inglis' developed separately there. By about 1400, the language can be termed Middle Scots, and this is the tongue of the so-called Scottish Chaucerians. *The Kingis Quair* ('King's Book') of James I (1394–1437), who was long imprisoned in England, is a love vision owing something to the Boethian concerns of *The Knight's Tale*. Nonetheless, if the Scottish Chaucerians borrowed much, their genius for refashioning received genres was their own.

Robert Henryson (*c.* 1424–*c.* 1505) was an outstanding narrative poet. This is shown in his *Fabilis*, his versions of Aesop written with the tender yet shrewd observation especially apparent in his version of the town mouse and the country mouse. Henryson's masterpiece however is *The Testament of Cressid*. This recounts the anguish of Chaucer's heroine when she has been jilted by Diomede and returned to her father. Cressid curses the gods who then smite her with leprosy, and her ensuing lament to 'frivoll fortune' is one of the finest passages of medieval rhetoric. Finally, Cressid dies of remorse when she discovers Troilus has offered her charity. He, in turn, raises a tomb and inscription to her that makes no reference to her deceit. This is perfect 'gentilesse'.

In the work of William Dunbar (c. 1456–c. 1513), we see a Scottish courtly poet working in a full range of genres. One of his finest achievements is a fabliau. The characters in *The Tua Marrit Wemen and the Wedow*, unaware of the presence of the male narrator, discuss their sexual experiences with unbridled licence and occasional ironic echoes of religious imagery. In fact, Dunbar himself was a fine religious poet as the vigour of his 'Easter Hymn' makes clear. His 'Lament for the Makirs' or poets with its knell-like refrain also shows Dunbar as a master of the 'plain' style, while his poems for public occasions use 'aureate' or golden rhetoric:

> Hale, sterne superne! Hale, in eterne,
> In Godis sicht to schyne!
> Lucerne in derne for to discerne
> Be glory and grace devyne;
> Hodiern, modern, sempitern,
> Angellical regyne!
> Our tern inferne for to dispern
> Helpe, rialest rosyne.
> *Ave Maria, gracia plena!*
> Haile, fresche floure femynyne!
> Yerne us, guberne, virgin matern,
> Of reuth baith rute and ryne.

sterne: *star*; superne: *high*; Lucerne in derne: *lantern in darkness*; Hodiern, *etc.*: *of today, contemporary and for all time*; regyne: *queen*; tern inferne: *damnation*; rosyne: *rose*; Ave Maria, *etc.*: *Hail Mary, full of grace*; Yerne us, *etc.*: *desire us, govern us, virgin mother*; Of reuth, *etc.*: *the all in all of pity*

This passage from Dunbar's 'Hymn to the Virgin' shows how wrong it is to associate the skilled and influential manner of aureate diction with emotional insincerity.

In England, the monk John Lydgate (c. 1370–1450) was also an adept in 'the gold dewe-dropis of rethorik so fine', and believed this style to be among Chaucer's most important legacies. Thomas Hoc-cleve (c. 1368–c. 1450), on the other hand, produced his finest poems in the plain style. His *Regiment of Princes* is an example of conventional moral teaching which, along with Lydgate's excessively voluminous *Troy-book, Fall of Princes* and translations, reveals how verse was still a principal means of written instruction at this time.

The 33,000 lines of the *Confessio Amantis* ('The Lover's Confession') by John Gower (?1330–1408) confirm this. Gower's work is a compila-tion of 133 smooth-flowing, moral and unemphatic stories in octosyl-labic couplets skilfully retold from familiar sources. As in a penitential manual, the tales are arranged round the seven deadly sins whose various aspects they illustrate while Genius, the priest of Venus, hears the elderly lover's confession. The relation between piety and *fine amour* is thus explored, and love itself is shown as an imperative force that should lead to marriage rather than loss of self-control. The seventh book of the *Confessio Amantis* however is a vast *summa* of conventional medieval thought. Its concern with the education of a prince, along with satire on the corrupt state of the country, shows Gower reflecting on the troubled end of the reign of Richard II (1377–99). The complete work, discussing love in the widest personal and social contexts, thus fulfils Gower's wish to write 'a bok for Engelondes sake'.

Chaucer called his friend 'moral Gower', and some of his own moral and philosophical interests are examined in his *balades* 'Fortune', 'Truth' and 'Gentilesse'. 'Merciless Beauty', by contrast, is a witty parody of extreme *fine amour*. Such English courtly lyric was much influenced by the French, and Charles d'Orléans (1394–1465), cap-tured at Agincourt, was responsible for the first surviving sequence of English love poems. This includes the parodic 'Lover's Confession'. Nonetheless, some of these later secular lyrics, playing their part in the social game of love, grew stale. While comic songs and the harmless bawdy of 'I have a gentil cok' continued the tradition of 'Summer is icumen in' (early thirteenth century), it is satirical pieces like 'Swarte-smeked smethes' that offer a foretaste of the riches to be found in medieval alliterative poetry.

7

Middle English alliterative verse was mostly produced during the second half of the fourteenth century by poets from the North and West Midlands, an area that had earlier nurtured Layamon. This body of work is one of the glories of medieval literature, and the achievements of Langland and the anonymous Gawain poet (late fourteenth century) stand comparison with Chaucer.

We should first consider the form. The Middle English alliterative line most commonly consists of four stressed syllables (of which the first three usually begin with the same consonant or any vowel) and a variable number of unaccented syllables. The alliterating syllables are usually placed in pairs across a caesura. Such a measure is flexible and energetic. It is also capable of exquisite refinement.

The alliterative *Morte Arthure* (*c.* 1360) treats of the nature of the good king, the instability of Fortune and the punishment of worldly pride. The familiar 'fall of princes' genre however is handled with transforming vitality. The unknown poet delights in the full brilliance of heroic glory. Nonetheless, with an eye to the French wars and the sumptuous court of Edward III (1327–77), the work also reveals how the personal splendour of Arthur, the gleaming eyes, magnanimity and valour of 'the comlyeste of knȝtehod that undyre Cryste lyffes' merge into cruelty and God-forsaking pride when Arthur wages an unjust war. As Arthur loses the favour of God and Fortune, destruction closes round him. With the final expression of his anguish over Gawain's corpse, we are led to see the end not just of his empire, dynasty and marriage, but of his own life also. The starkness of Arthur's death is offset by no mystical promise of return. The wheel of Fortune has simply, crushingly, come full circle.

The values of Camelot are again tested in another great work of Middle English alliterative poetry, *Sir Gawain and the Green Knight* (*c.* 1385). This is an anonymous romance preserved along with *Pearl*, *Patience* and *Cleanness* in a unique manuscript now in the British Library.

Sir Gawain and the Green Knight was probably written as a Christmas entertainment. Hence its pleasure in courtly celebration and the poet's wry delight in the fictional trappings of romance – in this case a monstrous green knight who challenges the young lords of Camelot to cut off his head and then seek him out for a return of favours within a year and a day. When Gawain has accepted the challenge and the great green head has rolled to the floor, its owner snatches it up and, before riding off, reminds Gawain of his promise to meet him at the Green Chapel. The humorously grotesque merges with the morally serious. Gawain must honour his plighted word, his truth.

As Gawain rides out on his adventure, the images of the pentangle and the Blessed Virgin Mary blazoned on his shield suggest the subtle knot of physical, social and religious qualities that make him an image of all that is excellent in courtly man. Dressed in what St Paul called the whole armour of God, Gawain is to pit himself against spiritual wickedness in high places. The narrative of his journey (which is described with a cunning mixture of earnest and humour) is thus underpinned by a level of profound moral interest.

On Christmas Eve, Gawain arrives at a fabulous castle and is welcomed by Sir Bertilak, its courteous proprietor. Unbeknown to Gawain however, his host is none other than the Green Knight himself, a figure under the spell of Morgan-le-Fay whose hatred for Camelot was responsible for the beheading game challenge in the first place. It is Morgan who now organizes the unsuspecting Gawain's test in the castle. On three successive days, having agreed to exchange his winnings with Gawain, Sir Bertilak goes hunting. Gawain, meanwhile, is tempted by the blandishments of his host's wife. Sex and death are powerfully juxtaposed.

Through his social and moral qualities, Gawain manages delicately to rebuff the lady's advances, and on the first two mornings receives no more than a kiss which he then exchanges for his host's hunting trophies. On the third day however the lady offers Gawain a girdle which, she says, will make him immune to the fatal blow. Gawain takes the girdle and hides the matter from Sir Bertilak. We sympathize, but by placing self-protection before honour, and deceit before his trust in the armour of God, Gawain has fallen into moral confusion. Without being fully aware of it, he has sinned.

He then rides out to the Green Chapel. In this awesome place, trusting to the girdle rather than the goodness of God, Gawain bares his neck for the blow. The axe descends twice and is twice restrained.

The third blow draws blood to symbolize Gawain's fault. In other words, the Green Knight knows all. Though he claims to shrive Gawain, Gawain himself now realizes the depth of his guilt. Despite being the flower of chivalry, he is a 'type' or image of Adam – an ordinary man led to forget his trust in the armour of God by the wiles of a woman. Human excellence is marred by original sin and courtly values alone are no protection. Though Gawain can hope to be excused, the girdle itself remains a perpetual reminder of his weakness. He returns chastened to Camelot. Here the courtiers view the girdle as a trophy of his victory. They thus mistake a symbol of human weakness for a token of worldly success.

In its more modest range, *Patience* recounts the story of Jonah, using the Old Testament narrative to suggest how man must patiently accept God's freedom to intervene in nature and so reveal the mysterious workings of His grace. *Cleanness*, on the other hand, is a collection of exemplary stories illustrating a text from Beatitudes: 'Blessed are the pure in heart; for they shall see God.' Cleanness itself suggests physical, moral and spiritual purity (qualities which place it next to godliness) and is exemplified by such Old Testament figures as Noah. Christ is shown as the ideal type of cleanness who offers redemption to those living under the New Testament. Evil or 'fylþe' is exemplified by the vividly retold accounts of the fall of Lucifer, the Flood, the destruction of Sodom and Belshazzar's feast. In these scenes especially, the poet shows his delight in high drama, gorgeous ceremony and spectacular effects.

Pearl is a sublime *somnium* or mystical dream vision in which a father is consoled for the death of his daughter by a revelation of her happiness in the heavenly Jerusalem. The intricate form of the work is part of this spiritual significance, for the twelve lines of the 101 stanzas give a total of 1,212 lines, and twelve is the mystic number of the heavenly Jerusalem. Such rhetorical structures (properly termed numerological) continued to be used well into the seventeenth century. Here they help fashion an exquisite reliquary for vision and truth.

At the opening of the work, the distraught father laments the death of his daughter Pearl. Mourning in the bright garden of the world, his grief has a depth and sophistication unmatched elsewhere in medieval verse:

To þat spot þat I in speche expoun
I entred in þat erber grene,
In Auguste in a hyȝ seysoun,
Quen corne is coruen wyth crokez kene.
On huyle þer perle hit trendled doun
Schadowed þis worteȝ ful schyre and schene:
Gilofre, gyngure, and gromylyon,
And pyonys powdered ay betwene.
ȝif watz semly on to sene,
A fayr re flayr ȝet fro hit flot,
þer wonys þat worþly, I wot and wene,
My precious perle wythouten spot.

(That spot that I have spoken of – the arbour green – I entered in at the height of August when the corn is cut with sharp sickles. The grave where Pearl was lost from view was shaded with beautiful, shining plants: gilly-flower, ginger and gromwell, with peonies powdered in between. It was lovely to behold, yet a fairer fragrance from it flowed where lives my loveliest, I know full well, my precious Pearl without a spot.)

Forgetting that pearls are incorruptible, the father falls asleep in body but wakes in heart to receive spiritual instruction from his daughter as she stands on the borders of the earthly paradise. Wracked by immoderate grief, he longs to join her. However, he is not yet ready for beatitude. He must learn intellectual truth before he can attain to spiritual revelation. His daughter urges humility and explains how through the courtesy of God she – a mere child – is now a bride of Christ, the Lamb of God, and thus an equal of the Virgin herself.

To the suffering father this seems merely unjust. Pearl then uses the parable of the labourers in the vineyard to explain that grace is not earned through length of service but is God's gift to reformed sinners and the innocent alike. The language of human love merges with an image of salvation, but true visionary rapture is achieved when the dreamer is finally granted a sight of the adoration of the Lamb of God in the heavenly Jerusalem. This was an experience which the contemporary mystic Walter Hilton (late fourteenth century) described as 'contemplation in perfect love of God . . . which is very peace'. The jeweller's desperate desire to join his daughter is once again frustrated however and he wakes to return to the earthly city and a life of patient faith.

In addition to mystical vision, alliterative poets such as the anonymous authors of *Winner and Waster* and *The Parliament of the Three Ages* (c. 1350), *Richard the Redelesse* (c. 1360) and *Mum and Soothsegger* (c. 1400) satirized social and political abuses. The greatest of these works, far surpassing the rest in intellectual scope and passion, is William Langland's (?1330–?1400) *Piers Plowman*. This poem was the life-work of an obscure figure who may have been the illegitimate son of the Shropshire landowner who funded Langland's theological training. The poet himself lived in London for a time and earned a living singing masses for the dead. His poem exists in three versions. Of these, the B-text (1377–9) is the most appropriate for showing how Langland developed the tradition of the dream vision in order to present a personal experience of Christ's sacrifice. In this, Langland takes us to the heart of the later medieval spiritual dilemma.

Criticism of the philosophy of Thomas Aquinas – much of this led by important English thinkers such as Duns Scotus (?1265–?1308) and William of Ockham (d. ?1349) – had raised difficult theological problems about how a sinner might enter a right relationship with God. The central question, which was also Langland's question, was this: What must I do to be saved? The later Middle Ages saw the growth of a laity deeply concerned with such issues, with criticisms of ecclesiastical abuse, and engaged above all in the search for a more immediate experience of Christ than the offices of the church could always provide. Hence the concern in *Piers Plowman* for spiritual quest and Langland's satire on institutional shortcomings.

Langland's narrator, the partly allegorical and partly autobiographical Will, is first seen in a field full of fair folk 'werchynge and wandrynge as the world asketh'. In answer to his anguished question about how he may save his soul, Will is told by Holy Church (one of Langland's innumerable allegorical figures) that he must seek the truth that is God through 'kynde knowynge', or the natural knowledge of the heart. The rest of the poem will explore the meaning of this idea.

Will's first vision, which occupies the opening four *passus* or 'steps' of the poem, portrays the reformation of secular society. In his second vision (Passus V–VIII), this moral improvement is already being corrupted. Men begin turning to inner values however, and the vividly particularized figures of the seven deadly sins (a justly popular aspect of Langland's art) expose immorality through their near-heroic beastliness. Nonetheless, when newly repentant mankind has set out on his search for truth, he almost immediately gets lost. At this point, Piers Plowman himself emerges. An ordinary labouring man, Piers knows truth in the way Holy Church described, through 'kynde knowynge'. Piers immediately sets the world to work and has backsliders punished by Hunger.

In one of the great moments of the poem, a pardon arrives for society. In the stark terms of the Athanasian Creed it states simply that those who do well will be saved, while those who sin will be damned. We have already seen however that erring mankind cannot rely for long on his own resources. He needs greater spiritual help than the pardon can offer. In sheer exasperation Piers tears the document to shreds. The search for a more intimate knowledge of salvation and better ways of living now begins.

The *vita* or 'Life of Dowel, Dobet and Dobest' occupies the densely allegorical and sometimes overlong central sections of the work. Passus VIII–XII show Will searching for the virtuous life through the exercise of his intellect. Mounting satire on the spiritual ignorance of the learned however leads Will to despise such people and eventually resign his aggrieved trust to simple, unquestioning forms of faith. Old age now comes and with it a desire for repentance. Anima rebukes Will's excessive intellectualism and revives for him the ideal of Piers Plowman, the simple man with an intimate knowledge of God. As the poem progresses, so we begin to see how human history and the fate of the individual soul are dependent not on subtle theological abstractions but on simple faith in the incarnation of the God of Love in Jesus. The humanity of Christ even allows him to be identified with Piers Plowman himself. God is thus truly made man.

A deepening awareness of faith, hope and charity (the latter movingly exemplified in the story of the Good Samaritan) is then linked to scenes of the Passion. Eventually, Will's maturing spirituality allows him a personal knowledge of Christ's sacrifice. As Will views the agony on Calvary, so the power of Langland's poetry raises the emotional awareness of spiritual truth Will has been seeking all along. 'Kynde knowynge' at last allows us to see God:

'*Crucifige!*' quod a cachepol, 'I warante hym a wicche!'
'*Tolle, tolle!*' quod another, and took of kene thornes,
And began of [gr]ene thorn a garland to make,
And sette it sore on his heed and seide in envye,
'*Ave, raby!*' quod that ribaud – and threw reedes at hym,
Nailed hym with thre nailes naked on the roode,
And poison on a poole thei putte to hise lippes,
And beden hym drynken his deeth-yvel – hise dayes were ydone –
And [seiden], 'If that thow sotil be, help now thiselve;
If thow be Crist and kynges sone, com down of the roode;
Thanne shul we leve that lif thee loveth and wol noght thee deye!'
   '*Consummatum est*' quod Crist, and comsede for to swoune,
Pitousliche and pale as a prison that deieth;
The lord of lif and of light tho leide hise eighen togidres
The day for drede withdrough and derk bicam the sonne.
The wal waggede and cleef, and al the world quaved.
Dede men for that dene come out of depe graves,
And tolde why that tempeste so longe tyme durede.

('Crucify him!' said an officer, 'I warrant he's a witch.' 'Drag him away!'
said another and took sharp thorns and wove the green ones as a garland, and
placed it painfully on his head, saying maliciously, 'Hail, Rabbi!' and then
threw reeds at him. With three nails they nailed him naked to the cross.
They put poison on a pole and pressed it to his lips, and bade him drink his
death-bane – his days were done – and they said: 'If you are clever then help
yourself now. If you are Christ and the son of a king, come down off the
cross. Then we shall believe that life loves you and does not wish you to die.'
'It is finished,' said Christ and swooned, pitiable and pale as a dying prisoner.
The lord of life and light laid his eyes together. Day retreated in fear and the
sun darkened. The wall wavered and split, and all the world shook. Because
of the noise, dead men came out of their deep graves and told why the
tempest continued so long.)

Christ, descending to purgatory to rescue the souls of the righteous
pagans, is again identified with Piers Plowman, but at the close of the
poem we are made to know how sloth and greed have all but
destroyed Christ's church. Langland's anti-clerical satire is very strong
here as he shows how a friar sells forgiveness for cash and asks for no
amendment. In such ways is faith corrupted. The true spiritual life is

revealed, by contrast, as a constant search for moral reform. Nonetheless, at the end of the poem, only Conscience is left to seek once again for Piers Plowman, the perfect exemplar of the Christian life who knows truth through love alone.

8

Langland's satire and visionary insight helped reinvigorate the intellectual and spiritual forces of his day for an audience at once informed and concerned about advanced issues of the religious life. Morality plays such as the incomplete *Pride of Life*, *The Castle of Perseverance* (*c.* 1405–25), *Mankind* and *Wisdom* (*c.* 1460–70) again present, if in more popular and conventional form, the right conduct of life through dramatized allegory. For example, like the servant in Matthew's parable, the hero of *Everyman* (*c.* 1500) is obliged to account for the use he has made of his talents. As the goods of this world desert him, we feel through the powerfully spare language of the play the intense isolation of his 'pylgrymage' to God. When Everyman has finally confessed his sins, his 'Good Dedes' alone help him and he dies in the assurance of salvation.

Salvation through good deeds is also exemplified at the close of the Mystery plays. These works were again concerned to present ordinary people with a clear, orthodox and vernacular account of Christian truths in order to enhance devotion. They were performed either on scaffolds or movable 'pageants' by guilds of skilled craftsmen. Such a skilled craft was called a 'mystery', and four major English cycles of Mystery plays survive: Chester (*c.* 1375), York (pre-1378), the Townley plays from Wakefield (*c.* 1450) and the so-called 'N-Town' plays (pre-1468) once ascribed to Coventry.

The Mystery plays originated in the feast of Corpus Christi. This was designed to focus devotion on the saving majesty of Christ the King whose birth and Passion were prophesied by events in the Old Testament, events which in turn prefigured those in the New. These last centre around the Passion, Resurrection and Last Judgement, and by dramatizing them all the Mystery plays presented their audience with the whole cycle of human history from Creation to the end of time. Such effects were achieved in a language of strong and homely simplicity, a rhetoric that imitated the language of Scripture. This, the church fathers taught, is available to everyone yet absorbs the attention even of the learned.

Such a combination of directness and exegesis is clear in the Chester version of *Abraham and Isaac*. The pathos evoked by the old man obliged to sacrifice his willing son is deeply moving, but religious feeling is fully stirred, as the Expositor reminds us, not just when Abraham is viewed as an example of proper and devout behaviour, but when the sacrifice of his son is seen as a *figura* foreshadowing the Crucifixion. The Chester version replaces the biblical ram which was slain in Isaac's place with a lamb – the Lamb of God.

Christ the Lamb of God is also the central image in *The Second Shepherds' Play* from the Townley cycle. This is the work of an unnamed reviser of genius who is known as the 'Wakefield Master'. His three shepherds of the Nativity and Mak the sheep-stealer illustrate the text from St John which tells how the thief comes only to steal while Jesus the Good Shepherd comes to die that his sheep may have life more abundantly.

The play opens with Coll, Gyb and Daw lamenting in terms of medieval 'complaint' poetry the harsh life of the poor in a hard and fallen world:

> Bot we sely shepardes   that walkys on the moore,
> In fayth we ar nere handys   outt of the doore.
> No wonder, as it standys,   if we be poore,
> For the tylthe of our landys   lyys falow as the floore,
> As ye ken.
>
> We are so hamyd,
> For-taxed and ramyd,
> We are mayde hand tamyd
> With thys gentlery men.

sely: *simple*; nere handys: *near*; tylthe: *tilth*; hamyd: *hamstrung*; For-taxed: *over-taxed*; ramyd: *oppressed*; hand tamyd: *tamed*; gentlery men: *gentry*

Such bitterness is consoled to some extent by their music. When they sleep, Mak the sheep-thief enters. He is a gloriously comic and inadequate rogue. As he steals one of the sheep, religious allusions allow us to see him as a type of the Devil thieving grace from mankind. Such parodic allusion is continued when Mak and his wife bind the feet of the stolen lamb (an image of the Crucifixion) and then, parodying the Nativity, hide it in a cradle and pretend it is their own child. Eventually, the shepherds recover their lamb and punish Mak by tossing him in a blanket. After such farce, divine harmony then descends as the angels sing their Gloria and summon the shepherds to Bethlehem. Here, presenting gifts symbolic of the Incarnation, Resurrection and Christ the King, they worship the Good Shepherd, the Lamb of God. Despite their hard existence, these simple men come to know life more abundantly.

A second master of medieval drama was the 'York Realist' who revised the Passion scenes from that cycle. The York *Crucifixion* itself is an exceptional example of medieval religious drama. The unrelieved brutality of the soldiers is contrasted to the serene and forgiving Christ who silently places himself on the cross for their redemption. It is Christ triumphant however who, at the end of time – after the Resurrection and the Harrowing of Hell, Pentecost and the Assumption of the Blessed Virgin Mary – judges man according to his deeds and draws the cycles to a close on the borders of infinity.

9

The vivid emotion, comedy and colloquial language evident in Langland and the Miracle plays had their roots in sermon literature. The sermon was intended to recall the languishing soul to virtue, and great emphasis was placed on the rectitude and scholarship of the preacher himself. Sermons were also to be appropriate to their audience. Some – following the example of Christ – supplement direct instruction with parables and homely images. Those preached to university congregations however employed more complex rhetorical strategies in which a Latin phrase from the Bible was broken down into two or three topics which were then supported by citations from religious authorities.

A number of sermons, some of them written under the influence of Wycliffe (*c.* 1320–84) and the Lollards, attacked social and spiritual abuses in the church. Among their many concerns, the Lollards believed people should be able to read the Bible in their own language and then criticize society by reference to it. This was an implicit challenge to the church's authority to teach and was supported by the Wycliffite translation of Scripture. Though Lollardy itself was cruelly suppressed and remained influential only with the powerless, Wycliffe and his followers had identified important problems within contemporary theology. A return to Scripture based on reliable translations of well-edited texts was to become a key issue in the Reformation.

A number of further late-fourteenth- and early-fifteenth-century prose works suggest the climate of contemporary lay spirituality through their concern with the inner life of the individual, in particular the desire for a personal intimacy with God seen in *Piers Plowman.* In the literature associated with this fundamental cultural development, two women were to play an important role.

The Book of Margery Kempe (1433) is the first substantial surviving English autobiography and recounts the religious experiences of an extreme and sometimes hysterically pious woman. Margery Kempe herself was illiterate and dictated her work to a priest who may well have exercised some editorial control over what nonetheless remains the most vivid account of a courageous and widely travelled woman who was well able to snub overbearing ecclesiastics and withstand the rigour of examinations for heresy. If the forms taken by Margery Kempe's piety are sometimes tiresome (they angered many of her contemporaries) her sympathy with the humble and, above all, the sheer conviction with which she imagines herself playing her role among the sufferers on Calvary clearly show the affective nature of late medieval religious life. In her wide-ranging aural acquaintance with northern European patterns of intense devotion, Margery Kempe also suggests the continental basis of the new piety with its distaste for excessive theological abstraction.

Of far greater quality is the classic of English mystical prose produced by the anchoress Julian of Norwich (active 1416). In her *Revelations of Divine Love,* and in the manner of continental female mystics especially, Dame Julian offered the fruits of her meditation on a series of visions and the 'homely' courtesy of Christ, declaring that love was the Lord's meaning behind her 'shewings'. The power of Julian's work – her intellectual and imaginative clarity – makes her the first great English female writer, and her personal strength was such that she could override the church's traditional requirement of silence from women on theological matters. 'Botte for I am a woman, schulde I therfore leve [believe] that I schulde nought telle yow the goodenes of God?' The question is a landmark in the literary history of feminism.

Richard Rolle (c. 1300–49) wrote in a fervent manner for the inspiration of devout women, and his English work was known to Margery Kempe. Much of his writing is in Latin, but his elaborate style displeased the author of *The Cloud of Unknowing* whose mysticism of the Negative Way required the mind to empty itself of images of the divine and recognize the unknowable nature of God. In common with many great religious writers at the close of the Middle Ages, the anonymous author of *The Cloud of Unknowing* says of his hidden divinity that only 'by love may he be getyn and holdyn'. The intense desire for a personal knowledge of God leads once again to the exultation of mystical insight.

10

The existence of such vernacular prose works as these suggests that English prose itself was now becoming a natural medium for conveying ideas. Towards the close of the fourteenth century, the translator John of Trevisa was exercised as to whether to choose verse or prose for his writings. His patron suggested the latter, for prose 'is more dere than rhyme, more esy, and more playn to knowe and understonde'. For some, such as Bishop Peacock (?1395–?1460), the attempt to write 'the comon pepil's language' was a failure, but the great collection of Paston letters (c. 1420–1503) and handbooks devoted to a range of subjects from fishing to medicine reveal how much was now being achieved. Probably the best known of such prose works is Mandeville's *Travels* (c. 1350), a combination of fact and fantasy originally written by an Englishman in French and then translated into every major European vernacular.

The most enduring and magnificent prose work of this era however – the period of the internecine feuding of the Wars of the Roses – is the *Morte Darthur* of Sir Thomas Malory. Malory himself can perhaps be identified with a lawless 'knyght presonour' who died in 1471. His work draws heavily on earlier Arthurian material in French and English and presents the familiar cycle of birth, triumph and destruction. Malory's theme is thus the whole universe of chivalric life, and he develops this interest through his genius for interlacing stories of individuals, their nobility, follies and tragedies. These he then displays against a background of larger moral, national and historical issues.

Malory frequently cut and improved on his originals, while his variety of response can be seen in such differing episodes as the family saga of Sir Gareth, the love of Tristan and Isode at the castle of Joyous Gard and the mystical and religious themes in the quest for the Sankgreal. These last Malory humanizes even as he gives them a strange wonder. But if Malory admired Galahad and Perceval for their attainment of mystical vision at Carbonek, his deepest sympathy lay with Lancelot, 'the greatest knight of a sinful man', whose love for his master's wife Guinevere forms the subject of the concluding seventh and eighth books of the *Morte Darthur*. Here the narrative strands are woven with the skill of tragic genius. Chance and fate, love and dishonour, chivalry and betrayal, lead finally to disaster and penitence. Indeed, some of the finest narrative moments in English literature are to be found in the story of the fight in Guinevere's chamber and, above all, in the final parting of Lancelot and Guinevere themselves.

To achieve such effects, Malory created a wide-ranging literary style appropriate to a fifteenth-century gentleman, a style that is at once colloquial, polished and resonant:

for in many persones there ys no stabylite; for we may se all day, for a lytyll blaste of wyntres rasure, anone we shall deface and lay aparte trew love, for lytyll or nowght, that coste muche thynge. Thys ys no wysedome nother no stabylite, but hit ys fyeblenes of nature and grete disworshyp, whomsoever usyeth thys.

For Malory, instability is the lot of earthly man, and at the close of his cycle of romances, with the death of Arthur himself, Lancelot and Guinevere repent of their worldly values and turn to higher truths.

II

The *Morte Darthur* was one of the works printed by William Caxton (*c*. 1421–91). Caxton wrote that he learned his craft in Cologne at great expense and in order to avoid the tedium of copying by hand. He thereby became part of the technological revolution initiated by the German goldsmith Johann Gutenberg (*c*. 1400–?68). Gutenberg had discovered that casting individual letters of the alphabet as movable type made it possible to reproduce any combination of words simply, quickly and in almost unlimited numbers. This was to transform the intellectual world in ways that were both subtle and profound. Nonetheless, it would be wrong to see Caxton himself as being at the forefront of this innovation. Though he was concerned with the problems of style and vocabulary raised by his numerous translations, his *Recuyell of the Histories of Troye* (1473–4) – the first book printed in English – reveals his conservative taste for works of chivalry and instruction.

Caxton's appeal was essentially to an aristocratic audience requiring texts in the vernacular. For such people he published the poems of Chaucer, Lydgate and Gower, while his issuing of translations of such works of conventional piety as *The Golden Legend* (published version post-1483) shows a typically medieval taste for forms of devotion that were soon to rouse the scorn of the Protestant reformers. Nonetheless, it is fitting we should close the medieval period with Caxton and with printing, for it was the printing press itself which, under the pressure of radical demands, was soon to help disseminate the new ideas of the Renaissance and Reformation.

Humanism and Reform

I

During the sixteenth and early seventeenth centuries the people of England were to transform the basis of their national and spiritual life, immeasurably widen their intellectual horizons and fashion from a newly augmented language one of the great literatures of the Western world. To describe this remarkable achievement we should begin with the range of ideas that had been inherited from the immediate past, for it was these ideas, under the pressure of novel demands, that writers were soon to criticize, reject or refine in the process of creating a new poetry and a new prose.

The work of John Skelton (?1460–1529) shows many characteristics of a late medieval courtly 'maker' working with modes of rhetoric derived in part from Chaucer, his contemporaries and followers. For Skelton, such rhetorical techniques prompted the use of an 'aureate' or profuse style in poems written for courtly public occasions and a 'plain' or colloquial manner in passages of exposition and satire. The narrator of *Collyn Clout* (1521–2), for example, attacks the overweening ambition of Cardinal Wolsey through vigorous demotic speech and a rhyme-scheme known as 'Skeltonics':

> though my ryme be ragged,
> Tattered and jagged,
> Rudely raync-beaten,
> Rusty and mothe-eaten,
> Yf ye take well therwith
> It hath in it some pyth.

It was in this form that Skelton achieved some of his most assured successes, whether they be the lively vulgarity of *The Tunnyng of Elynour Rummyng* (?1517), the delicate ambivalence of *Phyllyp Sparowe* (?1509) or the lyrics in *The Garlande of Laurell* (1523) with their exquisite evocation of the high cultural refinement sustained by such great ladies of the English court as the Countess of Surrey. Indeed, the place of such women in the fostering of English literature is of great importance and too infrequently recognized.

Skelton's masterpiece however is a poem in a different kind. *Speke Parrot* (1521) is a desperate and remarkably complex attempt to show the plight of the poet in a corrupt world of absolute power. Through his image of a divinely born caged bird, Skelton again comments on the England of the all-mastering Wolsey. Wolsey's sinister international manoeuvring and, for Skelton at least, his wrong-headed interest in new methods of teaching Greek and Latin have resulted in England's moral and linguistic collapse. The poet's life becomes a tyranny of intellectual fear and confusion that can best be suggested through the farrago of multilingual quotation that Parrot screams from his cage.

Speke Parrot is one of the most extreme and important achievements of early Tudor poetry, the reaction of a complex and deeply conservative poet to new and apparently threatening forces. In particular, Skelton shows little real sympathy with the imaginative re-creation of pagan antiquity encouraged by Wolsey, with the study of Greek, the new textual criticism of the Bible or the attempts to refine the teaching of Latin through the imitation of the classics. In retrospect, it was just such issues we should see as the most interesting problems in Skelton's culture and hence the focus of intellectual development.

2

Skelton's attack on the new ways of teaching Latin and the introduction of Greek was a criticism of the English followers of the *umanisti*. These last were a group of Italian scholars originally centred around fourteenth- and fifteenth-century Florence. In their studies they had returned to the classical sources of 'humane letters' – to Latin writers such as Cicero, to the historians and later to Plato – in an attempt to find new ways of generating ideas and promoting a written and spoken eloquence greater in its purity than the crabbed Latin of the medieval schoolmen.

Many of these concerns had first been expressed by Petrarch (1304–74), Chaucer's 'lauriat poete', from whose Italian *Canzionere* – a vastly influential collection of sonnets and other pieces meditating on Petrarch's love and mourning for his lost Laura – Chaucer himself had borrowed for his hero's song in the third book of *Troilus and Criseyde*. For later Italian scholars however, Petrarch's influence lay in additional areas: in his activities as a Latin poet in the epic and pastoral manner of the ancients and as the editor of Virgil, Livy and the letters of Cicero. Petrarch's successors thus found in him a writer with a profoundly creative relation to the pagan past. They were also aware that Petrarch's acute and sometimes despairing sense of self, having found no solace in the arid disputes of the medieval schoolmen, had turned instead to an evangelical religion of grace in which God incarnate in Christ could lift the individual believer above his worldly limitations.

Such literary and religious ideas appealed deeply to the scholars of the Florentine republic where the *studia humanitatis* – grammar, rhetoric, history, poetry and moral philosophy – comprised the education of those who aspired to power. In the writings of scholars such as Andrea Poliziano (1454–94), we see how it came to be held that a study of full and properly edited texts of the classics would train a willingness to subordinate private interests to public good, to fight tyranny and corruption and so satisfy the need for personal and patriotic advance within the civic life of the community. Ironically, such scholarship was also to provide the basis for the most radical of Renaissance political theories – the amoral pursuit of power outlined in Machiavelli's *The Prince* (written 1513–14).

With their intellectual horizons so greatly expanded, such people could not rest content with a religion of dry academic dispute and mechanical 'works' or repetitious pious observances, a religion which too often urged that contempt for the world for so many centuries reiterated from Innocent III's *De Contemptu Mundi* (thirteenth century). There were aspects of human activity that were now considered admirable, and a new accommodation with the traditions of belief was required.

The religious and philosophical development of humanism is associated in Florence with Marsilio Ficino (1433–99) who, under the patronage of Cosimo di Medici, founded an academy of Platonic studies and translated into Latin the work of Plato and his followers as well as writing commentaries. Christian Platonism – given its first memorable expression in Ficino's *Theologica Platonica* ('Platonic Theory on the Immortality of Souls') – was designed to stimulate the worship of God through a new understanding of the nature of man as a rational being capable of divine insight. The influence of such ideas, developed with enthusiasm and an extraordinary breadth of scholarly reference in Pico della Mirandola's *Oration on the Dignity of Man* (1486), was to be widespread and profound, the academy itself having a reputation that stretched as far as England. In this we begin to see the revolution that was being wrought by print.

On the mainland of Europe, printers' shops had become meeting places for intellectuals, some of whom worked happily on the craft itself. This they did partly for money and partly because the new skills of proof-reading and collation went hand in hand with the new concern for critically prepared editions of the classics. The growth of printing meant that greater numbers of people had greater access to an ever-wider range of ideas. Such a formation of an enlarged reading public encouraged what is sometimes referred to as a 'knowledge explosion' and this in turn fostered a new awareness of the diversity of thought, the range of opinion. A mechanical revolution thus became a central means for evolving concepts and disseminating new ideas.

Nonetheless, Englishmen interested in these ideas still had to go abroad for instruction. William Grocyn (?1446–1519) studied with Poliziano in Florence, and by 1491 was teaching Greek in Oxford. Six years later John Colet (?1467–1519) was lecturing on the Pauline Epistles and referring to Pico and Ficino rather than scholastic commentaries. The young Henry VIII (1509–47) took an interest in humanist scholarship, while it was Lord Mountjoy, the king's companion in study, who in 1499 invited his tutor to England and so introduced to the country the undisputed leader of northern European humanism, the Dutch scholar Desiderius Erasmus (1466–1536).

In one of the several thousand of his letters that together form a monument of humanist endeavour, Erasmus declared: 'My whole purpose in life has always been twofold: to stimulate others to cultivate *bonae literae* [i.e. 'fine literature and writing'] and to bring the study of *bonae literae* into harmony with theology.' This statement is a manifesto of early northern European humanism.

Like its southern counterpart, this was a movement concerned to find solutions to the problems exposed in too much official late medieval Christian theory and practice. Under the inspiration of Erasmus's *Enchiridion Militis Christiani* ('The Manual of the Christian Knight') especially, many of the humanists of the North sought a reform of religious life by appealing to the pious laity through a return to the transforming power of the sources of faith: Scripture and the newly edited texts of the church fathers. For several periods of his career, England provided Erasmus with a base from which he could develop the manifold activities these aims required. In particular, under the influence of Colet, he perfected the humanist philological techniques he applied to his vastly influential edition of the New Testament. He also began his study of Christian Platonism.

This last interest developed out of one of the most famous of literary friendships, that between Erasmus himself and Thomas More (1478–1535), whose own early life and writings had been partly moulded by the example of Pico della Mirandola whose biography he translated. Two larger works of More's clearly reflect the influence of civic humanism and Christian Platonism. Despite its sometimes uncertain prose style, the incomplete English version of More's *History of King Richard III* (1514–18) is a vivid and important example of Christian humanist historiography. The work reflects the psychological power and dynamic narrative skill of the Roman historian Tacitus, while, in the manner prescribed by Sallust, More has selected incidents and arranged them to highlight important moral themes: in this case his political concern with tyranny and his Christian conviction of the self-destructive nature of evil. The classical models are handled with great imaginative vitality (the test of all true literary imitation) but it is the Bible and Christian ethics that provide the full moral context for More's depiction of sin.

More's *Utopia* (1516, English trans. 1551) chiefly belongs to the history of Renaissance Latin literature. It owes a considerable debt to Plato's *Republic* and was partly inspired by the Greek satirist Lucian from whom More derived the rhetorical irony by which he could jest with seriousness and deal with serious problems in an apparently light-hearted way. This is clear from More's narrator. While Raphael Hythlodaeus's first name suggests something of angelic knowledge (literally, it means 'God has healed'), his surname is a Greek compound hinting that he is 'a babbler of learned nonsense'.

In the first book we are shown his discussion with More. Their topics include a deeply felt consideration of the corruption of the rich, the suffering of the poor and the injustice of the death penalty for starving thieves. The first book also contains a debate on a central humanist issue: the problem as to whether one should serve at court in the hope of improving matters or shun a world peopled by unscrupulous rulers and their fawning courtiers. Can a thinker achieve anything in such a world through compromise, or is the true intellectual inevitably divorced from action? To Hythlodaeus, the corruption wrought by money determines the latter course, and only Utopia, where private property has been abolished, offers his ideal of a rationally planned and unchanging state. The irony lies in the fact that 'Utopia' means 'Nowhere'. Such a state does not exist.

The blueprint of an apparently ideal society that Raphael provides nonetheless reveals a high-minded, money-free collective where an Order of Literati enforce strictly rational codes. Through natural reason, these most intelligent of Utopians have also glimpsed an idea of God similar to Plato's 'world soul', and it is this that makes them sympathetic to the greatest of revelations – the Christian Platonism brought to the island by the scholarly Raphael. Perfection is for Never-Never Land however, and the basis of More's work is a witty, serious and speculative paradox. Utopia is an ideal but non-existent country of the mind, a Platonic idea to which More's art gives imagined physical reality and against which we can measure the very real defects of our own and truly existing world of error.

3

The humanist ideals of the Christian Platonists led to a widespread concern with education, and Colet himself inscribed the fundamentals of Erasmus's creed above the door of his new foundation, St Paul's School. This we may translate as: 'Academy for the instruction of boys in the faith of Christ, the best and greatest, and in good literature'. Despite the patent male bias of this – a bias that was for centuries to deprive most women of a formal education – Colet's twofold aim was widely influential, and educational writers from Erasmus to Milton emphasize a dual purpose.

The educationalists' first concern was to begin repairing the work of original sin by providing scholars with sufficient literary skills to return to the sources of faith in the Bible and the early church fathers. By so doing, pupils could begin to know God aright, love Him and so be prepared for the heavenly gift of faith. Secondly, the study of pagan and Christian authors was considered the best preparation for a man (and, very occasionally, a woman) to perform, in Milton's words, 'justly, skilful and magnanimously all the affairs, both public and private, of peace and war'. A social change of crucial importance was thus being wrought by making the printed text a central part of adolescent mental development. Such texts now served as the broad intellectual foundations of both those who composed the literature of this period and those who read it.

Their training, often in one of over 350 grammar schools founded by 1575, was all but exclusively centred around selected texts. Early studies were based on translation and paraphrase as a means of acquiring vocabulary and grammatical competence in Latin and, less often, Greek. With the advent of later humanist schoolmasters such as Spenser's teacher Richard Mulcaster (?1530–1611) however an emphasis was also placed on the worth of English. This was an important modification of Erasmus's insistence on the primacy of Latin and a huge stimulus to national pride.

The classic authors were nonetheless studied as guides to life. Poetry was seen as an inspiration to virtue because of the philosophy dressed in its irresistible eloquence, while history was the storehouse of moral example. In all cases, the ancient writers were analysed for their rhetorical effects. A rhetorical tradition stretching back through Quintillian and Cicero to Isocrates saw language as a priceless gift and its proper rhetorical structuring as the measure of a man's excellence. By the intelligent shaping of language man revealed his humanity. When transferred to Renaissance and later poetry, the result was a verse consciously addressed to a reader or listener which presented a flow of ideas through recognized formal patterns that were then embroidered with rich ornaments of style. Clearly, this is a poetry not of intuitive communion but of conscious and even ostentatious display.

4

The influence of humanist rhetoric is clear in the best poetry of Sir Thomas Wyatt (?1503–42). Though his transition to the courtly poet of humanism was not easily made and many of Wyatt's love lyrics are repetitious *vers de société*, a powerful group of works such as 'My lute awake', 'They flee from me' and 'Quondam was I in my lady's grace' achieve their excellence through a lively and concentrated organization far superior to most late medieval lyric. Their quality also lies in the persuasive voice of the narrator, in the occasional subtle employment of refrain and, above all, in the fact that these technical resources are used to protest against the humdrum of convention and what had become the deadening weight of automatic idealization and lament. In the best of these pieces, a fresh poetic mind sees old problems with a new vividness:

> They fle from me that sometyme did me seke
> With naked fote stalking in my chambre.
> I have sene theim gentill, tame and meke,
> That nowe are wyld and do not remembre
> That sometyme they put theimself in daunger
> To take bred at my hand; and nowe they raunge,
> Besely seking with a continuell chaunge.

It was such qualities that Wyatt brought to the remainder of his important work: those verses where, absorbing the techniques of Renaissance poets, he found a moral and reflective voice with which to make the past his own and redolent of true experience. Such a process was known by the rhetorical name *imitatio* and, as a source for imitation, Petrarch's sonnets in the *Canzionere* provided Wyatt with exquisitely mellifluous and small-scale examples of intricate argument. They also offered a picture of idealized longing against which he could measure his own franker emotions. At his most interesting, in poems such as 'Whoso list hunt', Wyatt could both handle the sonnet form and criticize the original argument, contrasting Petrarch's idealism to his own exhausted and bitter pursuit of futile desire.

The poetry of Wyatt's younger contemporary the Earl of Surrey

(?1517–47) again reveals the influence of the humanists, in particular their philological interest in a language that would show 'proprietie in wordys, simplicitie in sentences, plainnesse and light'. Though attracted to Petrarch's sonnets, Surrey's historical importance lies with his classical translations, his versions of the second and fourth books of the *Aeneid* being the first English attempts at blank penta-meters, or what Milton called 'heroic verse without rhyme'. Surrey culled many verbal details from the couplet version of Virgil by Gavin Douglas (?1474–1522), but his chief purpose was the subtle business of refining the appeal of English by suggesting the rhetorical and syntactical massing of Virgil's hexameters. Something of his success can be gauged by his version of Aeneas's opening of the account of his woes:

> And lo, moist night now from the welkin falls,
> And stars declining counsel us to rest,
> But since so great is thy delight to hear
> Of our mishaps, and Troia's last decay,
> Though to record the same my mind abhors
> And plaint eschews, yet thus will I begin.

welkin: *sky*

The iambic line becomes a beautifully modulated part of a larger argument, and it was for such effects as these that George Puttenham suggested in his *Art of English Poesie* (an influential text published in 1589 though written earlier and subsequently revised) that Wyatt and Surrey might justly be called 'the first reformers of our English metre and style'.

The humanists' concern with the classics and rhetoric, with teaching and the development of the native language, is also clear in the work of Sir Thomas Elyot (?1499–?1546). His most formative work – and a text well known to Shakespeare – was *The Book Named the Governor* (1531). This was influenced by the circle gathered round Thomas More, and reveals Elyot's knowledge of the thought of Erasmus, Plato and More himself. Unlike *Utopia* however, Elyot significantly modified the Platonic ideal of the state to try and bring it in line with English traditions. This he did in the humanist hope of producing 'governors' or noble administrators whose new educational training would make the country strong. Ideally, these wise, experienced and well-read men – preferably derived from good houses of long standing – would counsel the monarch, for, in Elyot's view: 'undoubtedly the best and most sure government is by one king or prince, which ruleth only for the weal of his people to him subject'.

Elyot urges that reason, nature and biblical and classical history all support this ideal of hierarchy under a single king. Take this supernaturally sanctioned order away – as, for instance, in a democracy – and the result in Elyot's view was chaos. Men's ideas, he considered, are not all of equal worth. The common people in particular are 'a monster with many heads' unfit to take part in government. Such an approach was not a novelty, but the idea of hierarchy was to be ever more volubly expressed, and Shakespeare was not alone in being influenced by Elyot's book.

This influence derived in part from the effects of printing. From the time of Caxton, English printing was predominantly vernacular and chiefly focused on London. Here, the Company of Stationers (founded 1557) dominated the trade for nearly a century, working in close, profitable association with the Crown and, by their orthodoxy and efficiency, becoming an indispensable part of the regulation of output and the suppression of undesirable books and pirate editions.

The apparent need for censorship had been felt early, and in 1559 Elizabeth I (1558–1603) issued a series of injunctions requiring new books to be approved by Privy Counsellors, the most senior churchmen or the vice-chancellors of the two universities. The right to own a press was restricted to the Master Printers who never numbered more than twenty-five up to the time of the Civil War. It was these men too who owned the lucrative monopolies on such areas as law books, Bibles, almanacs and elementary educational works. Despite restrictions and the relatively small scale of the industry (1550 saw the publication of 200 titles) availability created demand. Religious works predominated, followed by domestic and utilitarian titles and a culturally important range of translations and histories.

For example, Lord Berners (1467–1533) completed his version of the French historian Froissart by 1525, while a growing national pride can be seen in both Edward Hall's *Union of the Two Noble and Illustrate Families of York and Lancaster* (1548) and the collaboration known as Holinshed's *Chronicles* (1577). The latter again owes much to Froissart and both were to serve as sources for Shakespeare. Two years later, another of Shakespeare's sources, Plutarch's *Lives of the Noble Grecians and Romans*, was translated out of a French version by Sir Thomas North (?1535–?1601). North thus introduced into English a history based firmly on classical ideas of humanity, dramatic effect and moral grandeur in great events. Courtesy books were also popular, and Sir Thomas Hoby's translation of Castiglione's *The Courtier* (trans. 1561) provided a profoundly influential model of an important social ideal. Indeed, by the turn of the century, in the mellifluous works of such men as Philemon Holland (1552–1637) and John Florio (?1553–1625), who prepared versions of Pliny and Montaigne, we see how translation had become a developed art capable of analysis, description and revealing the full sonority of English.

5

Out of this ferment of new books, new interpretations and spiritual questioning came a further shaping force on the literature of the period, the religious movements of the Reformation. These derived originally from the mainland of Europe.

In 1515, Martin Luther (1483–1546) was a young professor at Wittenberg preparing a lecture course on St Paul's Epistle to the Romans. Dissatisfied with his own exemplary piety of 'works', mistrustful of the late medieval belief that God was contractually bound to save those who submitted to Him and did their moral best, Luther became more and more convinced of man's utter depravity and certain damnation. Out of his despair at the corrupt bondage of the will however came a crucial theological breakthrough: God would not invariably damn sinners. Rather, through His grace, God freely gave certain sinning but faithful souls the righteousness to enter into a relationship of justification with Him. Nothing man might do could earn this gift, but the result was a faith that showed itself in good works yet was not dependent on them.

It was also a deeply personal belief, an inward sense of forgiveness that had no need of a priest and the church's sacrament of penance. Every true Christian was his own priest and was entitled, so Luther at first believed, to interpret Scripture for himself. Here was a new religious formulation based on an intense emotive inwardness, on what Luther himself called 'real feeling, the true experience of a grave conflict in the heart'. In the light of this fervent conviction, the Roman Catholic beliefs in penance, indulgences, works and prayers for the dead were revealed as a seeming sham. One by one the institutions of the old church fell across much of northern Europe as the ideas of the reformers, answering so deeply to the call for an inward and personal knowledge of God, spread themselves and became involved in politics.

The writings of the Lutherans were at first smuggled into England, often with danger and at great expense. Radical circles in Oxford and Cambridge discussed their ideas, and probably from such groups as these emerged one of the great figures of Tudor literature: William Tyndale (d. 1536).

In nearly all his beliefs Tyndale was Luther's disciple, but with his prose he was his own master. In works of controversy (particularly with Thomas More who had temporarily abandoned literature for profuse and tedious polemic) Tyndale showed himself not only logical but satirical and even artfully urbane as he attacked scholasticism and the related Roman Catholic beliefs that the clergy alone could interpret Scripture, that tradition is as valid as the written word and that the authority of the church is superior on all matters. In works such as *The Parable of Wicked Mammon* and *The Obedience of the Christian Man* (both 1528) Tyndale presented the arguments for justification through faith and constantly urged the importance of Scripture's written word. Hence the supreme significance of vernacular translations of the Bible so that all might have access to the saving Word of God. As a result of this central Protestant idea, the transforming power of print was to move to the centre of consciousness. The intense and often private experience of reading became the means of the deepest spiritual discovery.

It was Tyndale's mission to further this. He was, first of all, an exceptionally gifted linguist who translated the New Testament out of the third edition of Erasmus's Greek text. This was complete by 1525 and was smuggled into England the following year. Having perfected his Hebrew, Tyndale then translated the Pentateuch, providing his text with prologues and glosses urging reformist views. Tyndale was a rigorous linguist who knew that while truth lies in accuracy, its power sometimes lies in style. His understanding of the literary qualities of Scripture was close to Augustine's belief that 'its gait was humble but the heights it reached were sublime'. Consequently, Tyndale was a master of the colloquial (we owe to him the phrase 'filthy lucre'), of spoken idiom and even of the visionary power of revelation.

The reformers' searching conflict of religious ideas is also apparent in some of the poetry of the period. Wyatt was certainly influenced by Tyndale, for probably while in the Tower he embarked on his translation of the Seven Penitential Psalms which reveal his reading of Tyndale's works. The vocabulary tells all. As Wyatt has David sing 'of faith, of frailty, of grace' and then 'of God's goodness and of Justifying', so we see a devout poet alert to contemporary nuances of the drama of salvation. For Surrey, this was Wyatt's supreme poetic achievement, and his finest elegy for him suggests a new and influential model of the English poet as the humanist gentleman of Protestant sympathies committed to the well-being of his nation.

Tyndale's language can thus be seen as the thew and sinew of much English religious and poetic thought, not least because it underlies subsequent translations of the Bible. These are intimately connected with the progress of the Reformation in England and the attempts of the reformers themselves to tie private spiritual life to the nation state through the national language. Translation proceeded fitfully nonetheless. Tyndale's assistant Miles Coverdale (1488–1568), for instance, had prepared a complete translation in 1535. Though not a sufficient linguist to work from the original Hebrew and Greek, Coverdale had the exceptional command of contemporary English most memorably revealed in his version of the Psalms. By 1537, when it was known that Henry VIII would accept an English translation of the Bible, the composite 'Matthew' version was issued. However, neither this nor Coverdale's edition was wholly satisfactory, the one being too reformist, the other too little dependent on the original languages. The result was yet a third version: the 'Great Bible' of 1539 which was essentially a revision of 'Matthew' directed by Coverdale.

The 'Great Bible', supposedly placed in every church partly at the parishioners' expense, was a work of signal importance. For the first time Englishmen had access to the truths of their religion expressed in their own language and a plain but trenchant style. Soon the English

Bible was being 'disputed, rhymed, sung and jangled in every ale-house'. By 1543, a worried government banned the lower orders from reading it. The Henrician reformation was thrown into conservative reverse, and major figures such as Coverdale left England for the advanced reforming centres of Antwerp, Strasburg and Zurich.

Further developments were to complicate and enrich both the impetus of reform and the writings produced to serve it. The figure of Archbishop Cranmer (1489–1556) is central here. In particular, during the reign of Edward VI (1547–53), Cranmer's thought was veering ever closer to the ideas of the Swiss reformers headed by Ulrich Zwingli (1484–1531). This is reflected in the two seminal works produced under Cranmer's guidance: the First and Second Edwardian Prayer Books (1549, 1552) and the collection of sermons known as the *Book of Homilies* (1547, 1563).

Both are fundamental works of English Protestantism and reflect the thinking of the Swiss reformers, some of whom were now resident in England. Under the influence of these men, the mass, the host and the altar were replaced by the sermon, the Bible and the pulpit. Such fundamental changes underlie the forms of worship outlined in Cranmer's quietly beautiful Second Edwardian Prayer Book, while his *Book of Homilies* reflects the concern of the Swiss reformers with teaching and government. In a country where church attendance was obligatory, the reading of these prayers and sermons brought the central beliefs in order, hierarchy and the basic tenets of Protestant humanism home to everyone's bosom.

The Edwardian period also produced at least one outstanding individual preacher: Hugh Latimer (?1485–1555). Latimer was inspired by the reformist belief that salvation comes from preaching the Word, from offering the congregation truly nourishing meat and 'not strawberries that come but once a year, and tarry not long but soon are gone'. Latimer's *Sermon of the Plough* (1548), in particular, is enriched with vivid colloquial language, telling anecdote and a bold and even outspoken disgust at social and clerical abuses. Latimer's strong voice was horribly silenced however in the Marian persecutions that followed Edward's premature death. He was one of 280 martyrs burned for their Protestant beliefs, and the writings of his last days are a moving testament of his faith.

Many others fled abroad, going to Strasburg and the Geneva of

John Calvin (1509–64) where they discovered purer forms of Protestantism. Part of Calvin's influence lay in the logical severity and extreme moral rigour with which he organized the church in Geneva. Those who returned from Switzerland with the advent of Elizabeth I were in turn to exercise a considerable effect on the formation of the church in England. Further, the Calvinists were also responsible for the scholarly 'Geneva Bible' which for a generation held its own against both the later 'Bishops' Bible' and even the Authorized Version of 1611. This last work – of all English translations the most stately – remains one of the literary glories of the period. It draws its strength from its devoted translation, from its numinous if slightly archaic language and, above all, from a ninety-year tradition of Protestant scholarship initiated by Tyndale, whose labours provided by far the greater part of its foundations. For generations, the Authorized Version spoke to English people as the authentic Word of God, the true voice of the church.

Other voices were soon raised in opposition to the Anglican Settlement nonetheless, and they reached a climax with the 'Martin Marprelate' tracts (1588–9). The authorities looked to Richard Hooker (?1554–1600) for their definitive reply. This he provided with *The Laws of Ecclesiastical Polity*, the first four books of which were published in 1593, the fifth in 1597, while the last long remained in manuscript. *The Laws of Ecclesiastical Polity* is a work of subtlety, grandeur and polemic designed to show that the Elizabethan Settlement outlined in the Thirty-Nine Articles was consistent with the laws of God, nature and reason, and that those who assented to these were truly part of society. Natural law and evolving tradition are here set against the supposed certainties of dogmatic revelation. These last are seen to place the rigid Calvinist outside fully humane existence.

Much has been made – and rightly – of the sonorous reasoning with which Hooker returned man to his dignity in a rational cosmos ordered after the Elizabethan conception of divine law:

Now if Nature should intermit her course, and leave altogether though it were but for a while the observation of her laws; if those principal and mother elements of the world, whereof all things in this world are made, should lose the qualities which now they have; if the frame of that heavenly arch erected over our heads should loosen and dissolve itself; if celestial spheres should forget their wonted motions, and by irregular volubility turn themselves any way as it might happen; if the prince of the lights of heaven, which now as a giant doth run his unwearied course, should as it were through a languishing faintness begin to stand and to rest himself; if the moon should wander from her beaten way, the times and seasons of the year blend themselves by disordered and confused mixture, the winds breathe out their last gasp, the clouds yield no rain, the earth be defeated of heavenly influence, the fruits of the earth pine away as children at the withered breasts of their mother no longer able to yield them relief; what would become of man himself, whom these things now all do serve? See we not plainly that obedience of creatures under the law of nature is the stay of the whole world?

It was part of the genius of Anglicanism to salvage reason from spiritual dogmatism and to enshrine it in great literature. The felicitous ostentation of Hooker's accumulated clauses and the poetic force of his imagery show how the disciplines of humanist scholarship had now given English prose exceptional resonance and resource. The true purpose of rhetoric was nonetheless always to argue a case, and Hooker's magisterial tone not only presents his theology but, by seeming in its reasonableness to be above polemic, becomes an instrument for exposing his opponents' follies of unreason. Hooker had a remarkable grip on the psychology of dogmatism (his portrait of Calvin is particularly shrewd) and the very orderliness with which he exposed his opponents highlights their crueller and more extravagant absurdities. Against these are then set the decent practices of the Anglican Church under the rule of a virtuous queen whom Hooker sees as having being saved and established by the fiat of Providence.

This last is an important theme in much Elizabethan literature – particularly in Foxe's highly influential if lurid presentation of the Marian persecutions in his *Actes and Monuments* (1563, fourth edn 1583) – and by the 1580s English writers and readers were wholly familiar with the idea of the Protestant nation state guided by the hand of God and open to the full richness of Renaissance thought.

6

They also had available a remarkably developed language in which to express these ideas. In particular, the growth of education and the expansion of printing were powerful forces for promoting both a uniform standard English and a greatly augmented vocabulary. The schoolmaster Roger Ascham (1515–68) commended the vernacular for its pith and plainness, declaring: 'I honour the Latin but I worship the English.' Before the close of the sixteenth century, writers were to claim that English was both as copious and eloquent as the ancient tongues as well as a rival to any modern one.

A number of developments helped this. By the middle of the sixteenth century many were aware that spelling required the ideal of a fixed standard, custom and usage being the guiding rules. In one respect however the timing of this change was unfortunate, for parallel with the gradual standardization of orthography went a significant change in pronunciation. Linguists refer to this as 'the great vowel shift'. In particular, the pronunciation of 'long' vowels was affected. Thus Chaucer's pronunciation of the *a* in *name* had been like that in the modern *father*, while by the sixteenth century it had taken its current form. Nonetheless, English spelling was becoming fixed before this change, with the result that written vowel sounds still do not always correspond to their accepted pronunciation.

In addition, the sixteenth and seventeenth centuries were the period of a conscious and extraordinarily vigorous attempt to enrich vocabulary. A new text might bring not only new ideas but the new words in which they were expressed. Greek, Latin, French, Italian and Spanish were all laid under contribution. Although there was hostility to excessive obscurantism – the jargon the period called 'inkhorn terms' – many of the words borrowed were soon so indispensable that it is difficult to imagine communication without them. Most of these terms were introduced in printed works where an explanation was sometimes provided in parenthesis. Elyot, for example, wrote of '*education* or the bringing up of children'. But above all it was the creation of a great literature that showed the full potential of the newly augmented language. This was recognized by Dr Johnson when, in the Preface to his *Dictionary* of 1755, he paid tribute to the

writers of the sixteenth and early seventeenth centuries as the founders
of modern English.

7

Language develops by accumulated use, literature through imaginative criticism. For Sir Philip Sidney (1554–86), the English language
of the 1580s was sufficiently mature to express 'sweetly and naturally'
the 'conceits' or notions of the mind, and Sidney's own mind
touched so many preoccupations of his time that in a brief career he
helped shape the course of literature for the next hundred years. To
his admiring contemporaries, Sidney was the English model of the
universal Renaissance man: a Protestant gentleman of humanist education committed to both the active life of *virtù* and the artistic and
patriotic ideal of creating a literature to stand beside the great
vernaculars of Europe. In particular, Sidney was responsible for
Astrophil and Stella, the first Petrarchan sonnet cycle in English; the
two versions of his pastoral prose romance *Arcadia*; and *The Apology
for Poetry* in which he laid the groundwork of his Protestant and
humanist ideal in literature.

We should begin with the criticism. *The Apology for Poetry* (written
?1581–3, published 1595) is remarkable for its clarity of argument,
range of scholarship and imaginative vision. The existence of the
work is all the more surprising when we consider that, other than
some popular ballads, the native poetic tradition seemed to offer little
between the distant example of Chaucer and Sidney's own unpublished manuscripts. Plodding translators and more or less dull didactic
writers – Thomas Drant (d. 1578), Barnaby Googe (1540–94), George
Turbeville (1540–1610), Thomas Tusser (?1524–80), the opprobrious
Thomas Churchyard (1520–1604) – are all unmentioned. So, more
regretfully, is that useful literary man of all work George Gascoigne
(?1534–77) whose medieval notions of poetry give way to fresher
ideas on invention and inspiration in the prose of his *Certain Notes of
Instruction* (1575). However, other than Spenser's *Shepherd's Calender*
(1579) and Sackville's tragedy *Gorboduc* (1561), Sidney commends
only the handful of lyrics by the Earl of Surrey (first reprinted with

works by Wyatt and others in Tottel's *Songs and Sonnets* of 1557) and
the laborious but influential *Mirror for Magistrates* (1559, fifth edn
1610), a collection of chronicles concerned with sin and Providence
and directed to fashioning a responsible governing class.

With great imaginative judgement and considerable optimism,
Sidney moved the avant-garde beyond such provincial doldrums by
constructing his case for a new poetic out of a wide range of ancient
and Renaissance authorities. These were then fashioned around the
persuasive formulas of the seven-part classical oration. Sidney's interests as a rhetorician are thus made clear.

Sidney's opening or 'exordium' skilfully renders his aristocratic
audience well disposed, attentive and receptive through the telling of
a pleasing anecdote. In his 'narration' – having revealed himself as a
poet – Sidney shows the antiquity and universal appeal of what he
calls his 'unelected vocation'. With his credentials thus established, he
then proceeds to develop his Christian-humanist view of poetry, a
view which relates the reason of man fashioned in the image and
likeness of his Creator to the fact that man's 'infected will' fell with
Adam.

The poet thus deals with both aspiration and corruption. Sidney
shows how he is superior to mere analysts of fallen nature like the
philosopher and historian since the poet's mind alone can glimpse the
eternal types 'of virtues, vices or what else' that underlie the world of
appearance. These visions of the ideal the poet then shapes in verse so
that erring men may be delighted and improved by them, even if
they cannot fully attain to such excellence themselves. In other
words, by fashioning exemplary figures such as 'a right manlike man,
as nature often erring, yet shows she would fain make', the poet
creates a 'golden' world for our profit and delight. His work is a
faithful copy or 'imitation' of the eternal verities, and this is the
process Sidney outlines in his 'proposition' – the core of his argument
– when he defines his subject thus: 'Poesy therefore is an art of
imitation, for so Aristotle termeth it in his word *mimesis*, that is to
say, a representing, counterfeiting, or figuring forth – to speak
metaphorically, a speaking picture – with this end, to teach and
delight.' Sidney here gives seminal ideas derived from Aristotle, and,
to some extent, Plato and Horace, their first effective currency in
English literary theory.

From such notions came Sidney's belief in the supreme responsibility of the poet, whether, as he shows in his 'division', he be a divinely inspired seer like David, a didactic poet like the Virgil of the *Georgics* or Sidney's favoured image: the man whose reason and faith can pierce to the centre of universal reality and whose works, with all the delight and power of words, offer a practical, rational and appealing image of the true state of human affairs.

It is this last quality that makes the poet a teacher and guide. Sidney shows in his 'proof' how the poet is indeed 'the right popular philosopher', for, as virtuous action is the end of learning, 'so Poetry, being the most familiar to teach it, and the most princely to move towards it, is the most excellent work in the most excellent workman'. Combining his Protestant and humanist sympathies, Sidney here sees the end of poetry as the moral reform of man through education. In his 'refutation', Sidney counters the 'low-creeping objections' of those who criticize poetry for being an unprofitable, lying abuse. Then, inserting a 'digression', he outlines what he sees as the defects of English drama and poetry as he knew them, pointing to their verbal affectation and lack of literary decorum. Finally, in his mildly ironic 'peroration', Sidney closes his argument by praising once again the uses of poetry and its 'virtue-breeding delightfulness'.

Sidney's own poetry is characterized both by such aims as these and by wide-ranging metrical experiment. This last includes the use of quantitative classical metres, a mode that soon proved unsuitable to the determinedly stressed nature of English. Such demanding exercises nonetheless helped build the intellectual toughness Sidney invariably demanded from verse. Such rigour further required skills of dramatic and logical organization so that the poet's work would not collapse into 'a confused mass of words, with a tinkling sound of rhyme, barely accompanied with reason'. Essential to this rigorous approach too was the appearance of genuine personal passion, that 'forcibleness or *energeia*' which the classical rhetoricians had demanded.

In order to achieve these effects in his sonnet cycle *Astrophil and Stella* (written ?1578, published 1591 and 1598), Sidney 'sought fit words to paint the blackest face of woe'. His aim was to portray the anguish of a humiliating passion he could neither fulfil nor reject in the hope of aspiring to higher things. The personal origins of this apparently lay in his infatuation for Lady Rich, the Stella or 'star' of Astrophil the 'star-lover'. The poetry of this period is never simply autobiographical however, and private passion is here explored by using and extending the public conventions of poetry – in this case the Petrarchan sonnet sequence interlaced with lyric. Tradition is thus enlivened by experience and experience shaped by poetry.

As the star-struck poet himself shows us how he was brought to love, the lover's battles of sense and reason, his inspiration, exultation and defeat, so Sidney also provides a complete image of a sometime rational man hopelessly in thrall to an absolute and ultimately destructive passion. Nonetheless, by one of the great paradoxes of art, there springs from this emotional turmoil a new poetic voice whose intellectual power marvellously controls the fire of Renaissance artifice:

> It is most true that eyes are formed to serve
> The inward light; and that the heavenly part
> Ought to be king, from whose rule who do swerve,
> Rebels to Nature, strive for their own smart.
>   It is most true, what we call Cupid's dart,
> An image is, which for ourselves we carve;
> And, fools, adore in temple of our heart,
> Till that good god make church and churchmen starve.
>   True, that true beauty virtue is indeed,
> Whereof this beauty can be but a shade,
> Which elements with mortal mixture breed;
> True, that on earth we are but pilgrims made,
>   And should in soul up to our country move;
> True; and yet true, that I must Stella love.

The triumph of love over virtue becomes the origin of art.

The destructive nature of passion is also a major theme in Sidney's *Arcadia*. This prose narrative is set in the Never-Never Land of pastoral shepherds and disguised princes. The text, which was written for Sidney's brilliant sister the Countess of Pembroke who herself achieved some distinction as a translator of the Psalms, consists of a first version (written ?1581–2) and a much lengthened, incomplete revision by Sidney himself which was further edited by others (1590, 1593, 1621). For its sources, *Arcadia* draws on the late Greek romance of Heliodorus, the chivalric *Amadis of Gaul*, while, like Sannazaro's Italian *Arcadia*, Sidney's book diversifies prose with lyric interludes. Its range and complexity however are its own.

Arcadia is a pre-Christian land whose best inhabitants live by right reason. This allows them to know Providence and the workings of God. But Arcadia is also the refuge of the fearful Basilius who, hearing a dire prophecy of his future, withdraws from his court with his wife and two daughters, Pamela and Philoclea. It is now that a pair of shipwrecked princes – Pyrocles and Musidorus – arrive and, in falling for the girls, further the passion that upsets right reason. We are shown 'a very stage-play of love' in which desire reduces every character to 'an extreme and unfortunate slavery'. This in turn brings havoc to the state. The narrative thus has remarkable intricacy but is also designed to show Sidney's most serious theme: the actions of a benevolent Providence. The events are the 'imaginative groundplot of a profitable invention' which, though the characters do not always realize this, works towards the happy ending.

The plot of *Arcadia* is inseparable from its style. The book is a remarkable display of rhetorical set-piece descriptions, debates and verbal patterning. *Prosopopoeia* creates an abundance of representative characters, great and small. Shipwrecks, battles and hunts show *descriptio* enlivened with *energeia*, while the speeches – particularly those in the trial scene – show a full command of rhetorical structure and devices. Indeed, *Arcadia* soon became a source book for these and, as such, it is right to see the work as a heroic poem. After all, 'it is not rhyming or versing that maketh a poet', Sidney wrote. Rather, 'it is that feigning of notable images of virtues, vices, or what else, with that delightful teaching, which must be the right describing note to know a poet by'. In thus combining rhetoric, instruction and pleasure, Sidney created in *Arcadia* one of the earliest and most popular works of English Protestant humanism.

8

Arcadia is diversified with pastoral verse. Because Virgil had started with this before maturing to an epic poet, Renaissance critics often regarded pastoral as an apprentice genre in which writers could try their wings 'before they make a greater flight'. As we have seen, it was as a pastoral poet that Edmund Spenser (?1552–99) early appeared with *The Shepherd's Calender* (1579).

The importance of this pseudo-anonymous publication was soon recognized. Sidney commended the 'much poetry' he found in these twelve eclogues where, through the months of the year, Spenser's rustics discuss the course of life and love from youth to age, touching also on religion, politics and poetry. The poems themselves are garnished with extensive glosses and commentaries by one 'E.K.' which point to the poet's rhetorical skills (the use of ornament in particular) and suggest that his work should be regarded as seriously as a classical text. *The Shepherd's Calender* is thus Spenser's self-conscious attempt to appear as the modern English spokesman of the humanist tradition, the inspired poet who works through 'a divine gift and heavenly instinct not to be gotten by labour and learning, but adorned with both: and poured into the wit by a certain *enthousiasmos* and celestial inspiration'.

The use of archaisms in *The Shepherd's Calender*, as in the rest of Spenser's work, suggests how he believed English must draw from its own roots in order to refashion the ancients and stand as an equal beside the great literatures of Europe. In his 'October Eclogue', Cuddie, 'the perfect pattern of a poet', is told that to achieve this aim England must have its own epic – a national image of the heroic and aristocratic life. Such ambitions were eventually to result in *The Faerie Queene* (1590–96).

Though living in Ireland, and thus at some distance from the English court, Spenser was the most comprehensive poet of Elizabethan courtly culture and its most fabulous artificer. His central concern, and the issue to which he brought the broad wealth of his learning and the political and ethical concerns of his Protestantism, was the nature of the courtier. Here was that ideal member of a very small and very powerful social group who, through his mental, moral and bodily perfections, could represent the pinnacle of human achievement.

Though satires such as *Colin Clouts Come Home Againe* (1595) and *Mother Hubberds Tale* (1590) show Spenser aware of how far real life fell short of his ideal, the educative function of *The Faerie Queene* reveals Spenser's humanist commitment to the high calling of the poet, the man of vision who must use his abilities in the service of the state. The epic poem should be patriotic and didactic, and, through literary delight, teach the relation of private morality to public strength. An immense tradition underlay so ambitious an undertaking. In his role as the learned spokesman of English Protestant humanism, Spenser embraced it with enthusiasm and created the longest great poem in the language.

Homer and Virgil had 'ensampled a good governor and a virtuous man' in their epics. Odysseus, in the view of the Renaissance, was a type of the wise hero morally resisting temptation during his journey, a strength to which the pious Aeneas added an all-mastering patriotism. Medieval chivalric romance offered the complex interlacing of narratives of moral adventure, techniques much developed in two Italian Renaissance epics: Ariosto's *Orlando Furioso* (1532) and Tasso's *Gerusalemme Liberata* (1581). From these, Spenser borrowed not only the patriotic vernacular ideal of stanzaic narrative but the belief that a richly woven plot was the true basis of the modern heroic poem. Such ideas stemmed in turn from the Italian critic Geraldo Cinthio (1504–73) who distinguished three types of epic: that which concerns the action of one man, that which shows the deeds of many and that which is essentially biographical.

In a narrative which, as Spenser shows in his 'Letter to Ralegh', he intended to present twelve questing knights riding out through the mystic realms of Faerie during the twelve days of the Faerie Queene's feast, Spenser merges all three types of epic defined by Cinthio. Though he did not live to complete his vast project, each of the heroes of his existing six books reveals a growing knowledge of a particular moral virtue. In their rich combination they can also be seen as personifying elements of the greatest of all virtues: the magnanimity embodied in Spenser's Prince Arthur. Under the delightful complexities of the plot there thus lies a thoroughgoing allegorical structure or 'darke conceit' derived from the Renaissance interpretation of the epic tradition and designed, in the words of Ariosto's sixteenth-century English translator Sir John Harington (1561–1612), to conceal and preserve 'deep mysteries of learning'.

As a great poem designed for print, the appeal of *The Faerie Queene* is further extended by the ways in which it engages the solitary reader. There is, first of all, the imaginative delight of its setting and action. This is in part Spenser's re-creation of the Elizabethan chivalry in which knights such as Sir Philip Sidney jousted before the queen during pageants of great symbolic complexity. These are a beguiling case of life imitating art in the service of political order. Their world of plaster temples, personified vices and virtues, emblazoned banners and shields – all of which were designed to suggest service of the virgin empress Elizabeth – helps us appreciate *The Faerie Queene* in which Elizabeth herself is personified politically as Gloriana and personally as the Virgin Belphoebe. Spenser's poem is thus a continuous pageant celebrating such matters and is at once decorative and deeply serious.

Let us take the opening stanza as an example of the verse Spenser created for his poem, the particular form of English he used, as well as a taste of the world we are entering and its modes of interpretation:

> A Gentle Knight was pricking on the plaine,
> Y cladd in mightie armes and siluer shielde,
> Wherein old dints of deepe wounds did remaine,
> The cruell markes of many a bloudy fielde;
> Yet armes till that time did he neuer wield:
> His angry steede did chide his foming bitt,
> As much disdayning to the curbe to yield:
> Full iolly knight he seemd, and faire did sitt,
> As one for knightly giusts and fierce encounters fitt.

pricking: *spurring his horse*; dints: *dents*; giusts: *feats of arms*

The knight pictured here represents Holiness, and his armour (like that of the hero of the medieval Gawain poet) suggests the spiritual defences of the true Christian specified by St Paul in Ephesians. His angry horse, though it is a picturesque touch, allegorizes the rider's incomplete control of his passions, and this is an image that can be found in Plato's *Phaedrus*. Right at the start, the biblical, chivalric and classical worlds combine to create a 'speaking picture', an emblem or image of a moral state. But there is more. Even today, the red cross we learn the knight has on his shield allows us to identify him with St George (it is proper that an epic should enshrine national legend), while Spenser's 'Letter to Ralegh', taking up the theme of the knight's inexperience, tells us that he started out as a 'clownishe younge man' who begged his quest from the Faerie Queene herself. Much later in Book One, we learn both that he is a British changeling who was stolen into Faerie where he was brought up as a humble ploughman, and that his name is spelled 'Georgos'.

Even this has a purpose. Spenser's use of etymology is similar to his employment of emblem. It is a form of analysis based on the Platonic belief that words partake of the nature of what they describe. Among other matters, contemporary thought derived 'Georgos' from *geos* or 'earth' and *orge* or 'tilling' (hence the ploughman story) as well as from *gera* or 'holy' and *gyon* or 'wrestler'. The knight is thus a 'holy wrestler' in the manner described by St Paul, while Guyon is the name of the knight representing Temperance in the next book. By allying his heroes through etymology in this way, Spenser suggests how succeeding knights build on the virtues established by their predecessors. Such verbal analysis also tells us that the Red Cross knight himself is associated with the flesh which, as even a casual acquaintance with Genesis will tell us, is earth. In sum, Redcrosse is a Christian Everyman, a Protestant Piers Plowman.

A brief account of Book One will help suggest how Spenser combines such moral and spiritual analysis with the events of chivalric epic.

The purpose of Redcrosse's quest is to free original mankind – the parents of Una or the undivided truth of the Anglican Church – from the power of the Devil. His fight is thus against sin. Una and her knight are first seen together in the opening canto when Redcrosse easily routs the dragon of Error in the Wandering Wood. The fallen world of man is full of delusion however and the overconfident knight (like the unwary reader) soon falls into the snares of Archimago in whose symbolically dark world of deceit Redcrosse and Una are parted as the knight falls for the illusory charms of Duessa, a representative of Roman Catholicism. The quest against outer evil becomes an experience of inner sin. Una is now in grave danger (physical hazard is at one with moral risk) while Redcrosse falls further into error.

Misled by his purely worldly chivalry, Redcrosse is taken by Duessa to the House of Pride (one of the poem's many symbolic locations which serve its structure of comparison, contrast and moral analysis) where he witnesses the pageant of the seven deadly sins. Such pageants are one of the finest aspects of Spenser's art, a powerful combination of moral concern and poetic effect. Redcrosse contrives to escape, but falls prey to Orgoglio, that spiritual pride which attacks him as soon as the flesh triumphs over the spirit. Only Providence in the form of the arrival of Arthur (the prince's appearances are a moral and narrative theme repeated in each book) can save the knight. Redcrosse then despairs at his error. This marks the beginning of his struggle back to truth, and he is comforted by Una who takes him to the House of Holiness where the process of his sanctification or moral rebirth is concluded as he repents, receives instruction and then, justified by grace, has a vision of his eternal salvation. In the words of St Paul, Redcrosse has cast off his old, corrupt self, been renewed in spirit and so put on the new man 'created in righteousness, and true holiness'. As such, Redcrosse is now ready to do battle with the dragon which has been ravishing the Eden of Una's parents.

On the literal level, we can appreciate the fight for what it certainly is: a vividly fanciful description. But the fact that it lasts three days reminds us that numbers are always important in Spenser. Here, following the manner of the medieval exegetes, we might interpret the struggle mystically as a 'type' or representation of Christ's three-day descent to harrow hell. It is easier perhaps to see it as every Christian's fight against sin or the Church Militant wrestling with the Devil, but scholars dispute how far a political interpretation – which views the struggle specifically as a history of the English Church – may be appropriate.

Doubts remain because *The Faerie Queene* is a poem and not a vast cryptogram to be eventually reduced to prose. For example, we can interpret the Wandering Wood of the first book as an allegory of worldly life and, knowing that the Latin for 'wander' is *errare*, associate it with Error who, as we have seen, is personified as a dragon at its centre. But unless we also feel something of the terror of Hansel and Gretel – those other archetypal wanderers in a witch-infested wood – then we shall fail to appreciate Spenser's particularly Renaissance interpretation of this universal state and his grasp of the human need for symbol to suggest such things. To read Spenser requires both scholarship and imagination. With these in harmony, we can begin to see Redcrosse with his eventual victory over the dragon, betrothal to Una, glimpse of heaven and return to the court of Gloriana (Elizabeth I in her public role) not as a unique character, but as a richly allusive presentation of Spenser's Protestant, sixteenth-century analysis of every true Christian's spiritual experience.

The Victorian sage Carlyle remarked somewhat tartly that few readers of *The Faerie Queene* get beyond the first book. This is a pity since such people miss another Spenser: the poet of Renaissance love. Here, from Book Two, is an example of his powers of sensuous description:

> Her snowy brest was bare to readie spoyle
>> Of hungrie eies, which n'ote therewith be fild,
>> And yet through languor of her late sweet toyle,
>> Few drops, more cleare then Nectar, forth distild,
>> That like pure Orient perles adowne it trild,
>> And her faire eyes sweet smyling in delight,
>> Moystened their firie beames, with which she thrild
>> Fraile harts, yet quenched not; like starry light
> Which sparckling on the silent waues, does seeme more bright.

n'ote therewith be fild: *could not be satisfied*; her late sweet toyle: *i.e. sexual intercourse*; trild: *trickled*; thrild: *pierced*

This sixteenth-century pin-up – her name is Acrasia which suggests impotent and incontinent pleasure – is the presiding deity of the Bower of Bliss. The Bower itself is a further example of Spenser's contriving a place – a hut, a castle or, in this instance, a garden – as an allegory of a state of mind. The Bower of Bliss indicates the lascivious and somewhat cloying eroticism that Spenser sees as the great danger threatening Guyon, his personification of Temperance or self-control.

The delights of the Bower of Bliss are both beautiful and dangerously deceitful. Spenser's verse in this passage points to a too contrived perfection – a mere hedonism in art – while, as Guyon explores the Bower itself, so we are obliged to witness a voyeuristic indulgence that coarsens while it debilitates. Acrasia's lovers are transformed to beasts. Temperance himself must not fall victim to this Circe (the analogy to Homer has been established during the journey to the

Bower which marvellously allegorizes the wanderings of Odysseus), and to escape, Guyon destroys the place with a thoroughness that some find deeply disturbing. What in fact Spenser has done is show how righteous indignation prepares the heart for the greater fullness of true love which is explored in the following books.

Spenser's knights go armed. This suggests that virtue itself is a continuous struggle, but it does not imply that virtue is a purely masculine pursuit. Virgil has his warrior maidens and, to preserve decorum, so must Spenser. He portrays the awakening of love in one such: Britomart, his personification of Chastity or true love who is a woman militantly feminine to the point of her spear. This does not mean that Chastity is frigid. Indeed, the reverse is true, and one of the most vivid sections of *The Faerie Queene* illustrates this.

Britomart has fallen in love with Artegall, Spenser's knight of Justice whose fierceness and delusion she helps him to tame and correct. The virtues of the third, fourth and fifth books of *The Faerie Queene* are respectively Chastity, Friendship and Justice. Aristotle defines their relationship – and hence the reason behind Britomart's feelings – when he says that 'love [Spenser's Chastity] is the bond that holds states together', adding that 'legislators set more store by it than justice, for concord is akin to friendship'. The eventual marriage of Britomart and Artegall will thus reconcile these elements of a well-ordered society and, reminding us that *The Faerie Queene* is a national epic, the fruit of this union of Love and Justice will be a line of rulers that culminates in Elizabeth I.

So much for the future. Before it can come about, Britomart must understand her own nature. Chastity, in other words, must be tested and explored. Britomart's love is at first reluctant and troubling, but once she has accepted it she rides out in pursuit of Artegall and performs various feats of derring-do. These include the rescue of Amoret from the House of Busirane. Amoret, a stepdaughter of Venus, represents the loving, sensuous, reproductive side of her nature that Chastity must accept. Its abuse – what we might call a perversion or aberration – Spenser presents as a pageant.

The evil Busirane holds Amoret in a paralysing enchantment. Britomart crosses the wall of fire and smoke that surrounds her prison – Chastity, in other words, is unaffected by excessive passion – and enters the castle whose dark complexities are like the corridors of a troubled brain. Here are statues and tapestries representing the fear, guilt and shame that can make physical love so problematic, while the Masque of Cupid – a fearsome pageant of figures derived from the *Romance of the Rose* – suggests how such inhibitions have become institutionalized through poetry. They evaporate in the face of a mature acceptance of sexuality. The wound in Amoret's 'bleeding breast and riven bowels' heals as she is rescued, the images crumble, and such things, Spenser tells us, are illusions which vanish to leave no scar. Britomart is now ready to move on to those stages of the unfolding of Chastity in which the virtue must be explored through more adult sensations of lust and jealousy while developing a proper understanding of the relationship of man to woman, love to justice, private to public.

The central books of *The Faerie Queene* – which are in some ways less sure and artistically satisfying than the earlier ones – present these themes through plots and subplots that show Spenser's attempt to outdo Ariosto in narrative complexity. Places like the Garden of Adonis are an education in Renaissance erotic thought, and the vision culminates – as do Spenser's more private poems – in the public celebration of marriage, in this case portrayed through a remarkable mythological pageant which shows the sheer power of poetic and moral evocation Spenser lavished on his poem.

Spenser's more private works reveal his poetic weakness as well as his unusual strengths. His *Amoretti* (1595), the sonnets prompted by the wooing of his second wife, deal with a subject unusual among sonneteers who tended to be rather careless about such proprieties. Nonetheless, while they interestingly transform many traditional themes through the sense of romance maturing towards a Christian concept of marriage, they often lack the emotional vivacity that should pulse through rhetoric if it is to be wholly convincing. The best of the sonnets – 'One day I wrote her name upon the strand' for instance – are pleasing because the conceits are well handled, but Spenser's genius lies less in this form than in such narrative and pageant as we find in two of his loveliest works: the *Epithalamion* (1595), a hymn for his own wedding, and the yet more beautiful *Prothalamion* (1596), a work commissioned by the Earl of Worcester to celebrate the double marriage of his daughters. Here, the classical and Christian worlds combine in the celebration of potency and rapturous married love, while the intricate stanza forms provide a music for these processions that is truly stately. In this stanza from the *Prothalamion*, for example, the two brides are seen as swans gliding down the Thames past a group of nymphs, one of whom sings to them a song of fulfilment with its exquisite last line refrain:

> 'Ye gentle Birdes, the world's faire ornament,
> And heavens glorie, whom this happie hower
> Doth leade unto your lovers blissful bower,
> Joy may you have, and gentle hearts content
> Of your loves couplement:
> And let faire *Venus*, that is Queene of love,
> With her heart-quelling Sonne upon you smile,
> Whose smile, they say, hath vertue to remove
> All Loves dislike, and friendships faultie guile
> For ever to assoile.
> Let endlesse Peace your steadfast hearts accord,
> And blessed Plentie wait upon your bord,
> And let your bed with pleasures chast abound,
> That fruitfull issue may to you afford,
> Which may your foes confound,
> And make your joyes redound
> Upon your Brydale day, which is not long:
> Sweete *Themmes* run softlie, till I end my Song.'

assoile: *purify*

For Spenser, marriage was a sacrament which united the rapt contemplation of female loveliness with the duty to procreate. He discussed these issues as both a lover and a philosopher and, as was natural to his time, drew on the writings of Plato as these had been interpreted by the Florentine Renaissance. Such beliefs allowed writers and painters to gaze on bodily perfection and see it as an image of the divine Forms or Platonic ideas which underlie worldly appearance. The beautiful body became a speaking picture of the beautiful soul. 'For soule is forme, and doth the bodie make,' as Spenser summarized the tradition in his *Fowre Hymnes* (1596).

No idea is more potent in Renaissance art. It is why, in the *Amoretti*, Spenser can tell his mistress that her image locked in his heart is 'the fayre Idea of your celestiall hew'. He sees her beauty as quite literally divine – a Platonic archetype. And, just as Florentine Neoplatonism finds its most graceful interpretation in the paintings of Botticelli, so Spenser's finest version of the same themes is the Primavera vision in the last book of *The Faerie Queene*. Here, amid a richly woven series of incidents designed to portray the nature of Courtesy, Spenser presents himself in his pastoral guise as Colin Clout piping on the uplands of the earthly paradise. Before him dance not just 'an hundred naked maidens lily white', but the three Graces whose interweaving movement about his rustic beloved suggests the cosmic harmony and spiritual abundance that the poet inspired to vision may view – view, that is, until the world intrudes and Colin breaks his pipe as the pageant fades.

Man must return to the common world of duty and eventual death. Calidore – the personification of Courtesy in Book Six – must end his pastoral idyll to pursue the Blatant Beast, the force of destructive gossip who nonetheless contrives to escape. The poet, meanwhile, is obliged to see everyday life as either vulgar or tragic. The first mood may inspire him to satire, while Spenser's deep sense of the transience of life led to the writing of many verses, collectively republished in 1591, that are now little read: *The Ruines of Time*, his early translation *The Ruines of Rome*, *Visions of the World's Vanitie* and such elegies as *Daphnaida* (1591) and *Astrophel* (1596), his lament for Sir Philip Sidney.

This sense of pessimism in face of the fallen world's decay is resolved in one of Spenser's finest achievements: the *Mutabilitie Cantos*, first printed in the 1609 folio of *The Faerie Queene*, and almost certainly designed as part of its projected continuation. Here was a subject that could be treated in a way wholly sympathetic to Spenser's genius. Mutability is a philosophical problem to be explored through pageant. The main action of the poem, which has all the contemporary allusiveness of Spenser's other work, consists of Mutability's attempt to extend her rights over the order of creation.

Mutability knows that all things beneath the moon are subject to her power. Now she wishes to assert what she considers her birthright and extend her influence to the seat of the planets or gods. Her struggle with Luna, which is wonderfully described, leads to an eclipse. Frightened by this, the planetary powers that rule over men call a hurried council. Mutability denies their power to decide her fate and challenges the Creator himself. A parliament of the world is called. Mutability produces a procession of the changing months and seasons and then discusses the erratic nature of the planets to prove her case before the goddess Nature.

The whole speaks most powerfully of change and decay, drawing on the widest range of learning. The great commonplaces of European thought from the church fathers to the humanists are here blended in allegory, emblem and myth. Poetic precedents from Ovid, late Latin writers, Petrarch, Chaucer and continental Renaissance predecessors show Spenser's ability to synthesize learning at its most extended. He is at once serious but delightful.

And, at the close, complete power is not ceded to death and decay. There is a greater divinity that shapes our ends. Nature gives judgement, and her laws, as Hooker wrote, are 'the stay of the whole world'. Mutability's view of universal chaos is absorbed into Nature's promise that all things die so that they may return to the timeless order of God, an order that will only be fully known at the end of the world. The poet, secure now in his desire for knowledge of the divinely beautiful, permanent and good, can temper pessimism with vision, hope and prayer.

9

The magnificent achievement of *The Faerie Queene* was in some respects old-fashioned even when the poem first appeared, but Spenser's example, both in epic and in the many other genres he explored, was to have a lasting influence on a number of writers. Michael Drayton (1563–1631), for example, was an immensely productive poet attempting nearly all the available forms. His verse chronicles, along with those of Samuel Daniel (1562–1619), are among the rarely visited flatlands of Renaissance verse. Although the better sections of Drayton's work have some feeling for dramatic situation or beauty of rhetoric, such historical narrative was still largely part of the popular, serious, but artistically inert tradition of the verse chroniclers and *The Mirror for Magistrates*. Drayton's ballad 'Fair stood the wind for France' however reminds us that the patterns of common speech are the salt of even the finest Elizabethan rhetoric, while his lifelong taste for history and topographical description found final form in his massive 'merry England' vision: *Poly-Olbion* (1622). Here, love of nature and homeland are mythologized in decorous if rather dull alexandrine couplets.

Myth was again part of the liberating and profound influence of the Latin poet Ovid on Elizabethan verse. Familiar in extract to every Elizabethan schoolboy, Ovid was to be widely translated and, more crucially, imitated. He was both the 'most learned and exquisite' rhetorician and, just as fascinatingly, the 'grand-maister of wantonesse'. As writers of prose had absorbed the sonorous cadences of Cicero and made them their own, so Ovid's mirror-bright perfection of form, his erotic analysis – sometimes flippant, sometimes tragic – and his wide response to nature allowed poets to employ the rhetorical principle of imitation in the most creative ways.

It was with *Scylla's Metamorphosis* (1589) by Thomas Lodge (?1558–1625) that the anthropomorphic, artificial Ovid was first imitated. Cocking a snook at the prudish, the Ovidian narrative made a directly sensuous appeal to the reader through its subject matter and verbal artifice. It rejoiced in a style at once 'variable, inconstant, affected, curious and most witty'. By 1593, two major works had been written in the form by figures of the generation succeeding Sidney and Spenser: Marlowe's *Hero and Leander* (issued with Chapman's conclusion in 1598) and Shakespeare's *Venus and Adonis* (1593). These were followed a year later by the publication of Shakespeare's *The Rape of Lucrece*.

Marlowe's debt to the source of his greatest narrative work is clear in his translation *All Ovid's Elegies*, which was subsequently burned as obscene, while in *Hero and Leander* itself he has so absorbed his master's lessons as to create a poem which is a triumph of artifice over nature, of ambiguity suffused with tragic awareness. This is the world of Acrasia's Bower, but Marlowe does not give a fig for temperance. His young Leander, sumptuous in body and naïve in heart, burns in his ardour. Greeting Hero in the temple of Venus (a place of polished pagan delights and aberrations that sets the tone of the whole and prefigures the partly comic attempt at homosexual rape in the second part) Leander woos his beloved with rhetoric of the greatest sophistication. Tricking out his speech with learned references in the approved manner, Leander proves virginity to be neither virtuous nor honourable:

> Men foolishly do call it virtuous,
> What virtue is it, that is born with us?
> Much less can honour be ascrib'd thereto;
> Honour is purchased by the deeds we do.

Modes of humanist rhetoric are ironically applied to seduction. Such casuistry is as delightfully audacious as Hero's eventual surrender is psychologically convincing. With an intellectual freedom that looks forward to the more cynical lyrics of Donne, nature and artifice are tellingly juxtaposed. As a result, Leander's desires are granted. The atmosphere becomes tense with febrile sex and, as love in its variously comic, cruel and potentially tragic moods is suggested, so Marlowe's verse both heightens the drama and distances us from it in a disturbing way.

This ironic humour and delight in sensuous artifice may be found again in Shakespeare's *Venus and Adonis*. It is combined here with vivid natural description and colloquial turns of speech to make a poem that is both witty and ambiguous. The initial situation is also richly comic. Venus courts Adonis with persuasions to love that are more familiar on the lips of male lovers. The goddess perceives Adonis as the essence of human beauty, but the boy himself – peevish and ludicrously virginal – is more concerned to go hunting with his mates than dally with the queen of love. Her anguish is touching but does not balk at physical force. It also finds expression in exquisite language – the 'golden' rhetoric of the 1590s – and is supported by luxurious images and a heightened sense of physical awareness. The exact natural description in the poem – the hunted hare, the horses and the boar – makes Venus' declarations of passion seem particularly contrived while also suggesting the pain, lust and danger of the natural world. At the end however, when perfect human beauty has forsaken love and lies in its own blood, we recognize the work's underlying seriousness.

The preface to *Venus and Adonis* promises 'some graver labour' in the future, and the poem itself closes with the purity of love now curdled. Love is seen as 'fickle, false and full of fraud'. *The Rape of Lucrece*, greatly developing the moral, tragic intentions of such works as Samuel Daniel's recent *Complaint of Rosalind* (1592), builds on the suggestions of Shakespeare's earlier poem to create a more ambitious if less successful work. Written at a period when the theatres were closed due to plague and at a time when drama itself was considered a 'low' form, it was Shakespeare's early attempt to write a work 'assured of acceptance'. Posterity has not endorsed this hope, though the poem itself was immediately successful and has great merits. The compulsive brutality and night-time evil of the 'lust breathed Tarquin' are evocative beyond the powers of Shakespeare's contemporaries. So too is the imagery that universalizes the sense of outrage. But what contemporaries would also have appreciated – the rhetorical laments of the too protesting Lucrece – now seems merely to hold up the action.

Although it is not strictly an epyllion (a narrative poem on erotic and mythological themes), this is a convenient place to mention the most enigmatic of Shakespeare's narrative poems. *The Phoenix and the Turtle* (1601, 1611) is the 'Kubla Khan' of Renaissance literature, a poem which has its origins in material of small worth (Chester's *Love's Martyr*) which it then transforms into intense poetry, an expression of mutual self-sacrifice for love at once incantatory and scholastic.

Three wholly contrasted works show the range of response Ovidian narrative could conjure in its most active period. John Marston's slickly cynical *The Metamorphosis of Pygmalion's Image* (1598) satirizes the romantic aspirations of the epyllion and its readers, while Henry Willoby's colloquial *Willobie his Avisa* (1594) is an early attack on the licentious artifice of the form. The poem presents a number of suitors, corrupt in their sophistication, failing to seduce the virtuous Avisa before and after her marriage. The poem was suppressed in 1599, possibly because it is a *roman-à-clef*. Some believe it to contain a portrait of Shakespeare.

George Chapman's *Ovid's Banquet of Sense* (1595) presents the Latin poet spying on his mistress in a luxurious garden, and the highly charged and sensuous atmosphere is designed to reveal a series of emblems presenting abstruse Neoplatonic thought. Such concerns are also revealed in Chapman's important translations of Homer and his continuation of Marlowe's *Hero and Leander* (1598), a work of considerable power. Chapman's themes here are guilt, misery and punishment. These mount to tragic intensity as the lovers are destroyed for having failed to conform to the ceremonious world of marriage. Such ideas are partly presented through pageant and personification, while, in a technique that Marlowe himself adapted from Ovid, the use of subsidiary myths (in this instance the story of Hymen and Eucharis who observed the rites of Ceremony) clarifies the moral purpose of the major narrative in the way that subplots do in Shakespearian tragedy.

10

In the pirated first printing of Sidney's *Astrophil and Stella* (1591) appeared some twenty-seven sonnets by 'well-languaged Daniel'. The following year a separate edition, augmented to nearly twice this size, was issued under its own title: *Delia*. The great decade of Elizabethan sonneteering was established. It was a strange mixture of dross and the purest gold. The minor sonneteers are as much translators as imitators, but the sonnet could also be a medium for improvisation of the highest order. With the sonnet, Daniel the prolix verse historian found a genre that released his talent for exquisite variation on stock ideas. Such courteous, rhetorical meditations as 'Beauty, sweet love, is like the morning dew' show how Daniel's passion derives mostly from craftsmanship and tradition. In his best works, this is inspiration enough.

Copiousness, the desired rhetorical skill of producing elegant variations on standard themes, is the explicit inspiration of *Idea*, the sonnet sequence which Drayton first published in 1594, expanding and revising it for the next twenty-five years. He declared that he was 'to variety inclined', and his sonnets show him at his poetic best, searching out fresh illustrations for old themes, a lover of wit and paradox who could skilfully contrast such tones to a more resonant beauty. If Drayton does not always avoid vulgarity, then in 'Since there's no help' he could rise to at least one moment of true greatness.

Shakespeare's *Sonnets* (written *c.* 1595–1600, published in full 1609) emerge out of the concerns of the period to speak for all time. There is no greater sequence of short poems in English literature and none more fraught with problems. Shakespeare did not authorize their publication, the proof-reading was poor, and it is possible that many of the sonnets were not originally printed in their true order, if indeed there was one. How Thomas Thorpe, the publisher of the first complete edition, obtained his copy is unknown, and the identity and precise role of Mr W.H. 'the onlie begetter' of the volume are again among the great mysteries of literary history. What does seem likely is that the 1609 quarto was not reprinted – a mere eleven copies survive – and that Shakespeare himself was content to be known for 'his sugared sonnets among his private friends'. These were first made public on a small scale in *The Passionate Pilgrim* (1598–9) and then comprehensively by Thorpe. If Shakespeare was distressed by this, he appears neither to have repudiated Thorpe's edition nor to have issued a superior one.

The *Sonnets*, developing the conventions of the genre with unparalleled force, are expressions of apparently private concerns and record the poet's relationship, real or imagined, with a beautiful young man of noble birth and the famous or infamous 'Dark Lady'. To textual problems are added biographical ones. Who were these people? Many candidates have been proposed, but while identification may be a matter of great interest, it is of no more intrinsic importance to the poetry than the actual 'story' that may or may not lie behind the sequence. Elizabethan verse is primarily concerned with the artifice of intellectual and emotional persuasion, and it is perilous to ransack it for biography.

Over 120 of the sonnets are concerned with the relationship to the Friend. At their root lies the life-enhancing potency of youthful beauty. Transforming the conventional expressions of the sonnet through imagery that identifies the young nobleman with the forces of nature and social prestige, the Poet's existence becomes wholly absorbed by this embodiment of radiant life. Here is a passion that does not look for physical consummation. It is inspired by a loveliness that is thought to be the only truth the Poet can know, but which, nonetheless, is tested through fear of death and decay, and a hell of mutual deceit and despair.

Time the destroyer – the great theme of so much Elizabethan verse – is discussed in the first nineteen sonnets, but eventually, by a profound rhetorical shift, the Poet comes to see the Friend as personifying all truth as well as all beauty, and both, he fears, will end with the Friend's death. He has urged him to marry and have children, but in

'Shall I compare thee to a summer's day', the absolute loveliness of the Friend, greater than changing nature, is recognized as the inspiration of immortal art. Poetry alone can defend its subject against time. The Poet has found his vocation, and his 'eternal lines' become the pledge of enduring fame.

The dramatic power of the sequence lies in the Poet's discovery that the Friend, so idealized in absence, is far from perfect. First, he has been encouraging rival versifiers whose work corrupts his integrity, spoils poetry with insincere and overloaded ornament and, most importantly of all, by debasing both art and the Friend, pollutes the sources of the true Poet's inspiration. Shakespeare's 'tongue-tied' muse, once a singing lark, can now only keep her silence among these wordy rivals. But if the Friend is being swayed by the flattery of insincere poets, a greater danger lurks in his innate sensual weakness. This imperfection of the ideal beloved is the paradox on which many of the greatest sonnets turn. It is a unique and painful discovery. The sensual weakness of the Friend is at times guessed at, analysed and partly excused, but in Sonnets 40–42 we are made aware of how it shows itself. The Friend had been led astray by the Poet's own mistress: the Dark Lady.

The sonnets that analyse the Poet's relation to the Dark Lady form a grotesque contrast to the idealizing works addressed to the Friend. As the sonnets to the Friend adopt and hugely extend the conventions to explore an unusual situation, so those to the Dark Lady invert the stock ideas of sonneteering to create a picture of compulsive, promiscuous sex and constant deceit. The ordered world of erotic idealism is undermined, torn to shreds and satirized. Its obverse face – the face of the mistress – is both ugly and morally objectionable.

The plainness and lust of the Dark Lady are made clear from the outset, and word-play becomes an instrument of savage analysis. The Dark Lady 'lies', and the verb expresses both untruthfulness and the act of sex itself. Intercourse and deceit are identified, the Petrarchan dream is turned to nightmare, and the way is open to the Poet's most ruthless account of compulsive lust: 'The expense of spirit in a waste of shame'. It is into such a moral slum that the Friend has been willingly inveigled. Corruption is now compounded with jealousy and despair.

The recognition of the Friend's fault introduces to the *Sonnets* a dominant theme of the plays: the divide between appearance and reality. In this case it takes the form of a cruel exposure of the Platonic dream. The beautiful body is no longer an outward, visible sign of the beautiful mind. The Friend has grown 'common', and beauty's flower becomes a cankered rose, a festering lily. The paradox is unbearable. It destroys the old order in which love and virtue were mutually inspiring. The Poet, caught between the Dark Lady, his 'worser spirit', and his 'better angel', the Friend she is seducing, has reached a crisis. All is corrupt in a meaningless world. Sonnets of resignation, of shrewd and bitter casuistry, alternate with desperate attempts to part from the Friend or remain with him at any price.

Then, remarkably and most movingly, there comes the Poet's assumption of the Friend's burden of guilt, his intuition of a redemption through love. Images such as that of the sun stained with clouds – the idea that even the most perfect things are blemished – suggest that the Poet has accepted the imperfections of the Friend, and it is such human sympathy that allows him to view his tears of contrition as a ransom for sin. Nothing in the sonnet tradition would have suggested so moving and human a love.

But if the Friend is stained, so too is the Poet. The lover of the Dark Lady is himself no constant figure from conventional sonneteering. After a long period of apostasy, of abasement both physical and intellectual, he returns to the Friend whose beauty is the Poet's 'all-the-world'. Burdened with remorse, ageing and sullied by the world, he begs a reciprocal forgiveness. Sonnet 120 is a most moving account of this. There is a feeling here of shared pain and vulnerability, an intuition that only those who love us and whom we love can redeem us. The world has no coherence, no meaning outside such love, and such love is felt to be the whole world. On this basis the Poet builds the defiant celebration of Sonnet 116:

> Let me not to the marriage of true minds
> Admit impediments, love is not love
> Which alters when it alteration finds,
> Or bends with the remover to remove.
> O no, it is an ever-fixed mark
> That looks on tempest and is never shaken;
> It is the star to every wand'ring bark,

Whose worth's unknown, although his height be taken.
Love's not Time's fool, though rosy lips and cheeks
Within his bending sickle's compass come,
Love alters not with his brief hours and weeks,
But bears it out even to the edge of doom:
    If this be error and upon me proved,
    I never writ, nor no man ever loved.

This poem is one of the greatest achievements of the Elizabethan sonnet. The ideal love that underlies the Petrarchan tradition is reasserted on a new basis. Love is seen as a universal force that redeems and makes eternal the faulted lovers. It offers a 'marriage of true minds', the holiness and ceremonious permanence of which are suggested through imitation of the words of the wedding service. In an image of the greatest beauty, love becomes the pole-star by which the erring lover – in a conceit that Wyatt among others had adapted from Petrarch – can guide his 'wand'ring bark'. Love is also stronger than Time, who appears with his familiar scythe to harvest the roses of beauty.

The precious conventions of ideal love are thus reaffirmed by being transformed. Love is now seen to offer redemption to faulted lover and faulted beloved alike in a chaste and equal union. The perfect use of form – the three quatrains and the couplet that have come to be known as the Shakespearian sonnet – the vigour of urgent speech in counterpoint over the iambic line and the exquisite delicacy of vowels and consonants do indeed make this small work the 'eternal' monument of the Poet's boast. Such is the promised immortalization of the Friend, a climax and splendid transfiguration of a long and various tradition.

The productions of minor sonneteers, hacking out plagiaristic verse at two crowns a time, encouraged an inevitable reaction. The sonnet fell into disrepute. However, by directing it towards more philosophical concerns, later poets such us Fulke Greville, Lord Brooke (1554–1628) and Ben Jonson's friend Drummond of Hawthornden (1585–1649) introduced elegiac and religious themes into the form. In the sonnets of William Alabaster (1567–1640), this latter becomes a record of an intense if temporary conversion to Roman Catholicism during the late 1590s, while the verse of another Roman Catholic, the recusant Robert Southwell (1561–95), is among the most effective religious poetry of the period.

Sir John Davies (1569–1626), a lawyer who rose to be appointed Lord Chief Justice but who died before he could take up office, parodied the sonnet's excesses in his earlier and more boisterous poetic career. Davies's principal works however, *Orchestra, or a Poem of Dancing* (1569) and *Nosce Teipsum* (1599), are those rare things: philosophical poems that succeed as poetry. *Orchestra* describes the Ptolemaic view of the universe which held that the earth was the centre of the cosmos. Round the earth dance the planets. In Davies's poem, they are as stately and entrancing as courtly masquers. *Nosce Teipsum* ('Know Thyself'), a poem in quatrains, holds within it the great commonplaces of Neoplatonic and Protestant thought seen also in Spenser. With considerable grace, Davies shows the mind, corrupt after the Fall of man, struggling out of materialism towards faith and an understanding of the soul and redemption.

II

The pastoral verse of Sidney and Spenser was widely imitated, and the popularity of the genre continued into the first third of the seventeenth century. Drayton, as we might expect, used its conventions, and his late but conservative *The Muses' Elysium* of 1630 is surprisingly fine. However, the best known of many anthologies of lyrics in the pastoral mode is *England's Helicon* (1600), a collection of slight and pretty pieces for the most part with much metrical variety and, in the best poems, a rich, *faux-naïve* or true colloquial idiom. A number of prolific minor writers appear to advantage here, while *England's Helicon* further contains two of the finest pastoral lyrics of the period: Marlowe's strong, delicately inventive 'Come live with me and be my love' and the reply attributed to Sir Walter Ralegh (?1552–1618). However, Ralegh was a greater and more various poet than this suggests. He was the author of one of the most intense verse meditations of the period, the unfinished, unpolished *Eleventh and Last Book of the Ocean to Cynthea*. Here, with turbulent imagery drawn from exact observation, Ralegh writes of his disgrace at the hands of Elizabeth I in terms of a pastoral lover – a 'Shepherd of the Ocean' as Spenser called him – begging a return to his mistress.

Much verse written for public events, including many of the more formal funeral poems, is of little intrinsic interest, but one occasional poem has outlasted the situation that gave rise to it. For the retirement of Sir Henry Lee (1590) – that influential man who organized the tournaments of Elizabethan chivalry – George Peele (?1558–?97) wrote 'His golden locks time hath to silver turned'. The lyric combines elegant and playful melancholy with judicious epithet. Its sententious and proverbial tones become the dominant manner of Ralegh's powerful conceit 'What is our life?' and his sharply satirical 'The Lie'. These tones contribute also to Sir Edward Dyer's 'My mind to me a kingdom is', and become the sole content of what remains, nonetheless, one of the most heart-rending lyrics of the period: Chidiock Tichborne's 'My prime of youth is but a frost of cares', a poem that draws on medieval traditions of complaint and was supposedly written on the eve of Tichborne's execution in 1586.

A great deal of the finest Elizabethan lyric poetry was meant to be sung – sometimes in the theatre – and the last decades of the sixteenth century and the first two of the next are the first great age of English secular music. Musicians themselves recognized the primacy of the written text, and this partnership is perfectly explored in the work of John Dowland (?1563–?1626). A well-known madrigal by another composer, 'Draw on sweet night' by John Wilbye (1574–1638), shows how a range of musical techniques such as an advanced dissonance could transfigure a pleasant lyric. But many of the lyrics are more than simply pleasant. They draw on a range of possibilities from street cries ('Fine knacks for ladies') and daily life ('Now winter nights enlarge'), through a wealth of pastoral, of witty and tormented love poems, to religious meditation such as 'Never weather-beaten sail'. Many of the finest lyrics are based on the most slender conventional conceits and, outside Shakespeare, none perhaps more perfectly shows what could be achieved than 'When thou must home to shades of underground' by Thomas Campion (1567–1620).

Shakespeare's lyrics are among the most exquisite of the period and range from the unaffected pastoral of 'It was a lover and his lass', through the delicate, intricate 'Take, oh take those lips away', to the solemn incantations of 'Fear no more the heat of the sun'. No account of the lyric poetry of this period however can omit a song in Thomas Nashe's *Summer's Last Will and Testament* (printed 1600) – a poem which is a perfect expression of Renaissance commonplace, medieval moralizing and a seemingly effortless artifice:

> Beauty is but a flower,
> Which wrinkles will devour,
> Brightness falls from the air,
> Queens have died young and fair,
> Dust hath closed Helen's eye.
> I am sick, I must die:
>> Lord have mercy on us.

Here is a verse that illustrates the inspired and often sombre beauty that the Elizabethans so frequently enshrined in their best lyric poetry.

12

A handful of the academic poor turned in the later sixteenth century to freelance writing in prose. Under the double incentive of poverty and educated intelligence they fashioned a vigorous range of new styles. Thomas Nashe (1567–?1601), who, in addition to being a poet, was the most brilliant of them, declared: 'I have written in all sorts of humours . . . more than any young man of my age in England.' This is the boast of an author who lives, however precariously, by his pen.

Patronage remained an important source of support and prestige for many such men. The stationers however were beginning to pay at least something to authors, and 'writing for the booksellers' became a recognized if somewhat despised form of work. Above all, the existence of more or less professional writers such as Nashe, Thomas Lodge (1558–1625), Robert Greene (1558–92) and the others who turned their hand to satire, fiction, controversy and criticism (as well as to less tendentious areas such as prose translation, chronicle, topography, travel writing and a wide variety of manuals) suggests both a ready market and entrepreneurs keen to supply it.

As at most times, the bulk of production was largely ephemeral, but it was out of the earlier satirical, romantic, sermonizing, allegorical and coarsely humorous work relished by the Tudor reading public that Elizabethan literary prose grew. Nashe himself first appeared in the flurry of pamphlets produced for and against episcopacy in the 'Martin Marprelate' controversy. In works such as *Have with You to Saffron-Walden* (1596), his wit is ostentatiously inventive and is joined to a dazzling energy of syntax. Loathing is made effective through laughter – so effective, indeed, that the authorities had to step in and ban the work.

Others of Nashe's pamphlets again show his energetic, allusive style. They also reveal a sometimes excessive concern for cruelty and draw heavily on medieval traditions of homily. *Pierce Penniless* (1592), for example, uses the framework of the seven deadly sins, while portraits such as that of 'Mistress Minx, the merchant's wife, that will eat no cherries, forsooth, but when they are at twenty shillings a pound', show lively and satirical observation of the 'humours' type. Nashe's major works however are *Lenten Stuff* (1593) and *The Unfortunate Traveller* (1594).

In *Lenten Stuff*, Nashe joins a delightful praise of Yarmouth to a mock-encomium of its herring in the manner of Renaissance ironic praise for things apparently mundane. Nashe makes this form his own, and nowhere is the switchback logic of a man obsessed with words more playfully effective. *The Unfortunate Traveller*, on the other hand, begins in the Tudor jest-book world of jokes and pranks but proceeds, by way of a digression on Puritanism, to a disgusting if powerful account of a Europe torn with religious violence. With its rudimentary plot and characterization, there is less a suggestion of the future novel here than an exercise in an exhilarating and subtle verbal resource. In this description of an execution, for example, the very homeliness of the similes emphasizes the cruelty of commonplace barbarity:

The executioner needed no exhortation hereunto, for of his own nature he was hackster good enough. Old excellent he was at a boneache. At the first chop with his wood-knife would he fish for a man's heart and fetch it out as easily as a plum from the bottom of a porridge pot. He would crack necks as fast as a cook cracks eggs; a fiddler cannot turn his pin so soon as he would turn a man off the ladder.

The passage ends with the victim 'splintered in shivers' and alone save for the fowls who will end his living death. Although prose was to acquire different forms of expertise, outside of Shakespeare it was sometimes to lose the profoundly imaginative resource of Nashe's subtlety and colloquial ruthlessness.

Mention should also be made of the exposures of the 'conies' or dupes of London street life by Robert Greene, a vein amusingly continued by Thomas Dekker (?1570–?1673) in his 'Bellman' pamphlets. However, if such widely popular but ephemeral works have something of the flavour of the low-living characters seen again in plays about contemporary city life, the stream of popular literature which most directly fed the drama was prose fiction.

This is a genre that should be approached by way of a literary curiosity. In 1578, John Lyly (1553/4–1606) published his *Euphues' the Anatomy of Wit*, following up its enormous success with *Euphues his England* in 1580. The books have given the language an adjective. 'Euphuism' originally highlighted Lyly's persistent use of otiose similes from natural history and the classics. It now suggests an excessive concern with fine phrases and – less obviously – an interest in alliteration. Much of this has a rhetorical basis, and elements of the euphuistic style can be found in the work of contemporary translators. Lyly's contribution was to graft on to a slight and not very pleasant moral tale a concern with style as virtually an end in itself.

The influence of Lyly's work was widespread. For example, pastoral narrative with its attendant disguises and sudden reversals is the basis of the work that supplied the plot of *As You Like It*: Thomas Lodge's *Rosalynde: Euphues' Golden Legacy* (1590). Shakespeare's play should be seen in part at least as a delicate satire on such escapism. *The Winter's Tale* is derived from Greene's *Pandosto* (1588) much as a pearl is derived from a grain of sand. Finally, Thomas Deloney's *The Gentle Craft* (?1597–8) is a true and realistic Dick Whittington story that served as the basis for Dekker's *The Shoemaker's Holiday* (published 1600).

A considerable number of manuals of instruction and works of reference also come from this period. Indeed, in 1617, Gervase Markham (1568–1637) was persuaded to sign a promise that he would produce no more books about 'the diseases or cures of any cattle, as horse, ox, cow, sheep, swine, goats etc.'. He did not keep his word. Some of the chronicle and topographical prose of the period shows the development of a sober style, while William Harrison's boast about his little garden is a delightful episode in his *Description of England* (1577). This work is more important however for its justification of Harrison's claim that 'I have had an especial eye to the truth of things.' This phrase – so simple in expression, so potent in its implications – points to areas of literary activity of the greatest importance.

The decades that saw the pamphlets of Nashe and the issuing of such works of high literary artifice as the *Arcadia* also witnessed a proliferation of books that had nothing to do with the humanist emphasis on the education of an élite. Artisans, merchants and adventurers, men busy with the practical handling of things, sought information, and the London presses published works of scientific literature and popular learning in English. These were cheap and often went through many editions. Nor were they necessarily superficial. The life-work of Richard Hakluyt (?1553–1616), *The Principal Navigations, Voyages and Discoveries of the English Nation* (1589–1600), is a monumental edition of the writings of the great seamen and includes Ralegh's thrilling account of the last fight of the *Revenge*. In addition, works of mathematics, astronomy, surgery and the trades all appeared. A wide range of people could now read in their own language not just the Bible, the challenging ideas of ancient historians and the rhetorical experiments of the humanists, but works of direct utilitarian importance in a direct, utilitarian style. Such honest prose is a hardwon, noble thing, and the strength of the writing of these practical men was eventually to play a role in the development of English that was of the greatest importance.

Shakespeare and the Drama: 1500–1642

I

To playwrights in the reigns of Elizabeth and James I all the world was a stage, but the tremendous achievement of English drama in the late sixteenth and early seventeenth centuries – the work of Marlowe, Shakespeare, Jonson and their successors – was preceded by experiments of some historical importance in which traditions from the Middle Ages can be seen reacting with the forces of Protestantism and the concerns of the early humanists. Out of such ground, genius was to flourish.

Henry VII (1485–1509) maintained a company of four professional actors who performed what were probably scripted plays, often in the banqueting halls of their master. In addition to celebratory mummings, masques and disguisings, the lavish court of Henry's son seems also to have enjoyed versions of the didactic Morality play, since it was for the edification of his royal sometime pupil that John Skelton (?1460–1529) wrote his lengthy *Magnyfycence* (?1515). Here, reworking the form of dramas such as *The Castle of Perseverance*, Skelton shows the private and political education of the kingly Magnyfycence, as courtly vices so trick him that (in a pattern widely followed in such plays) he is brought to suicidal despair and then saved through true faith.

The shorter moral plays or 'interludes' exhibit a wide range of themes and were often written with considerable dramatic inventiveness. *Mankind* (?1471), for example, vividly contrasts piety and satirical worldliness, scatological bawdy and the serious moral progress of Mankind himself from virtue through temptation by the Vice. This last was the chief comic character in such plays, a mischievous, mocking figure, nimble of speech and body, intimate with the audience and yet often given a sinister edge by his association with the Devil. In *Mankind*, he leads the hero through sloth and despair but cannot finally prevent him finding salvation. The Vice was to remain an influential memory, and Shakespeare's Feste and Richard III both consciously recall him.

Sir Thomas More keenly enjoyed such works and is a central but elusive figure in the development of the interlude. He seems to have written dramas himself, while his interest in the Greek satirist Lucian's marriage of comedy to philosophic discourse may have suggested to other members of his circle how these debates could be staged. The earliest surviving of such pieces – Henry Medwall's *Fulgens and Lucrece* (*c.* 1490-1501) – indicates how this élite drama, designed as an entertainment between the courses of a feast, could provide a disputation on true nobility as well as coarse, knockabout humour in the amorous misadventures of two servants named simply A and B. Uninhibited laughter, an interest in secular values and a reasonably open-ended debate have here replaced religious teaching.

Protestant writers, aware of the power of drama to spread ideas, used the interlude as a means of doctrinal, political and moral instruction. The strongly anti-Catholic dramas of John Bale (1495-1563), for example, popularize the basic tenets of Protestantism. His lengthy Morality play *King John* (1538) implies parallels between the medieval king's struggle with the papacy and Henry VIII's desire for a reformed church. While *Respublica* (1553) was written from a Roman Catholic viewpoint in the reign of Mary Tudor, the Scottish poet Sir David Lindsay's *Ane Satire on the Thrie Estatis* (1540, 1552, 1554) is once again directed to political and religious reform.

The humanists' emphasis on rhetoric and classical studies meant that drama was often encouraged in the schools, both to help with the boys' elocution and to bring alive the comedies of Plautus and Terence. Plays in English for schoolboys followed, and the tradition of school drama is seen at its most entertaining in a work by the sometime headmaster of Eton and Westminster. Nicholas Udall's *Ralph Roister-Doister* (1545-52) is a lively piece in doggerel couplets structured round the five acts of a Latin comedy. More importantly, the plot is carried forward by suspense and intrigue. Its hero is partly modelled on the boasting knight of classical drama, while the vigorous Matthew Merrygreek derives from the Latin parasite. Both the naturalization of such standard characters and the structural development of the plot were influential, while plays by troupes of boy actors were to have a significant place in the more professional drama of the period.

It was the boys' companies indeed that first secured the favour of the court and universities at a time when adult common players were despised and had no outstanding repertoire. Children had taken part in medieval pageants and, under William Cornish (d. 1523), the Children of the Chapel Royal acted in court disguisings. Later masters of the Chapel Royal had the boys perform in the Inns of Court, the training colleges for lawyers, which were also centres of literary activity. Under Richard Farrant (d. 1581), the boys of the Chapel Royal acquired their own theatre and acted historical dramas there. They seem to have ceased public performances around 1584. Another juvenile company – the boys of the choir school of St Paul's – presented at least two plays in most years between 1560 and 1582.

John Lyly (1553/4–1606) wrote extensively for Paul's Boys. His *Mother Bombie* (1587–90) is an excellent comedy in the classical mould, well constructed and shrewdly characterized. Nonetheless, it stands aside from Lyly's most influential work for the theatre. Fashioning the highly wrought style of his prose narrative *Euphues* into a medium for dramatic dialogue, in plays such as *Campaspe* (1584) and *Endymion* (1591), Lyly helped give the prose language of comedy its virtuoso freedom and delight in its own artifice. In addition, Lyly blended classical allusion, contemporary politics and courtly compliment with philosophic myth and intellectual debate. In *Gallathea* (1585), he played with the important comic motif of gender reversal.

Drama was also an aspect of higher education, and early plays from the universities and Inns of Court were important to the process of adapting classical and other influences to native interests. Some time between about 1552 and 1563, undergraduates at Christ's College, Cambridge, mounted a performance of *Gammer Gurton's Needle* (published 1575). The play perhaps reveals an acquaintance with the intricacies of Italian comedy and has a finely constructed and fairly complex plot in which an interest in the classics is matched by vivid social realism and knockabout farce.

It was perhaps inevitable that an interest in Plautus and Terence should have been matched by an equal fascination with tragedy, in particular the closet drama conventionally attributed to the Roman philosopher Seneca. Like the comic dramatists, Seneca had been widely read in the Middle Ages and studied for his rhetoric, but in the 1560s translators began to show an interest in his work. This eventually resulted in the publication of *Seneca, his Tenne Tragedies* (1581).

For the most part these efforts are fustian. Iambic fourteeners failed to convey the grim, majestic effects of the original, while experiments with onomatopoeia and alliteration led to the excesses Bottom was later to call his 'tyrant's vein'. Clearly, translations from Seneca could not yet provide the English stage with an effective tragic voice, nor was Seneca's rigid classical structure – his observation of the unities of time, place and action – amenable to the dominant taste for variety and spectacle. The real and very considerable importance of Seneca for Elizabethan and later dramatists lay in other areas: in the stately dignity of his style with its rich display of *sententiae* or memorable commonplaces, his philosophical concern with Fortune, and the conflict of private life and public duties. Seneca's interest in horrific events surmounted in mind at least by his stoic heroes was also profoundly influential, as was his concern to expose 'filthy lust, cloaked dissimulation, and odious treachery'. These purposes could only be fully exploited however when dramatists had developed a new mastery of English verse and an effective stage technique.

In the meantime, playwrights at the Inns of Court tried to imitate Seneca's characteristic set-piece speeches. The result was a play of largely historical interest: *Gorboduc* (1561). Despite Sidney's qualified praise and the work's contemporary success, an excessive emphasis on debate and an over-didactic concern with the effects of ill-government in a divided country make the play now seem tedious. The great developments in Elizabethan drama were to occur in the less rarefied atmosphere of the commercial theatres.

2

The first London theatres were built in 1576. Both were speculative ventures outside the City's jurisdiction, but the differences between them already hint at shifts and developments to come. The Blackfriars Theatre (the first of that name) was a roofed building hired and converted by Richard Farrant for performances by his Children of the Chapel Royal. Such 'private' theatres had a complex and sometimes antagonistic relationship with more popular auditoriums like The Theatre. This, the first of the 'public' playhouses, was managed by James Burbage (d. 1597) and was an unroofed wooden building. While it used to be thought that its plan was based on the inn yards and bear-baiting houses where paid, full-time actors usually performed when in London, there is also evidence to suggest that its builders had ideas of the Roman amphitheatre in mind.

The construction of The Theatre marks a turning-point of great significance. It suggests permanence, a more rooted professionalism among actors than had been known before. A statute of 1572 had lumped 'common players' along with jugglers, pedlars and tinkers, and declared them to be vagabonds unless they were part of the household of some great noble. If they wished to travel, they had to be licensed by two magistrates. Aristocratic protection was thus decisive, and it was just such an incorporation as 'Leicester's Men' in 1574 that encouraged Burbage to build his Theatre outside the City limits and hence away from a source of constant interference. This was eventually to triumph with the Puritans' closing of the playhouses in 1642.

In the meantime, rival companies rose and fell, but in 1594 there emerged the two adult companies which, along with the players at the Red Bull Theatre (built 1605), were to hold a virtual monopoly of the London stage for the ensuing decades. The first of these was the Admiral's Men who performed with Edward Alleyn (1566–1626), initially at his father-in-law the impresario Henslowe's theatre the Rose, and then at the Fortune. The second was Shakespeare's company, first called the Lord Chamberlain's Men, who were originally based at Burbage's Theatre. When this was pulled down by order in 1597, they performed at the Curtain. In 1599 however Burbage's son Richard moved the company across the river to Bankside and into the now famous Globe. This was partly built from the timbers of their original home.

Entry to the yard round the apron stage of the Globe cost a penny. A second penny gained access to the three tiers of galleries built out from the retaining walls, while a third offered the cushioned comfort of the higher levels of these galleries. Lords' rooms, partitioned from the galleries and close to the stage, cost sixpence. Estimates of audience capacity suggest that a full house at the public theatres consisted of some 3,000 people. The survival of the builder's contract for Henslowe's Fortune, which was modelled on the Globe, suggests how densely these audiences must have been packed.

The yard at the Fortune was a square 55 feet in each direction. The raised apron stage was 44 feet across and seems to have projected some 27½ feet into the yard. The stage at the Globe also had a trap-door big enough for two men to descend at a time. At the rear of the stage was a 'tiring house' or green room which had two or more openings on to the stage. One of these may have been hidden by a curtain which was opened to 'discover' a shop, tomb or study. The other may have been fronted by a portable raised platform or screened booth that could variously suggest a tent, scaffold or rostrum. Above these openings was the 'taras' or balcony, and from this extended the 'heavens', a cover supported by two pillars rising from the stage. This provided protection, helped define the acting area and also served as a height from which properties could be 'flown' by stagehands operating from the 'hut' above it.

A contemporary copy of a foreign visitor's sketch of the Swan Theatre – a valuable if contentious document sometimes known as the de Witt drawing – suggests that it was from a platform by the hut that a trumpeter announced the start of each performance. A flag was also flown during the action. The interior was richly painted and carved, and as early as 1576 protesting cries were heard to exclaim that 'it is an evident token of a wicked time when players wax so rich that they can build such houses'.

Entry to the so-called 'private' theatres was more expensive than to the Globe and its rivals, and such auditoriums seated only 200 to 600 people. The minimum cost of entry was sixpence. No one appears to have stood, and these candle-lit theatres in which music was an important ingredient suggest a wealthy and select audience. This is confirmed by the location of some private theatres inside the City walls, close to Westminster and the Inns of Court. It is significant that, after 1609, when the first adult company had fully established itself in an indoor theatre, playhouses built subsequently (with the exception of the Hope) all conformed to this pattern.

The existence of the companies – groups of known individuals offering their combined talents to each repertory production – led in later years at least to a certain standardization of roles. Lists have been preserved for the decade from 1623 which name actors in the King's Men who played such recognizable types as the hero, tyrant, smooth villain, lover and clown. Clearly, such a practice helped simplify the creation of new roles for actors and playwrights alike, while mannerisms – known gestures providing a form of emotional shorthand – were essential to performances in a theatre where changes of repertoire were frequent, rehearsals limited and deep familiarity with new parts all but impossible. That such gestures were indeed used is suggested by stage directions such as '*Isabella falls in love*'. It was part of the training of the apprentice boys who played the female roles to learn what such gestures entailed and convey changes of mood through them. The boys, indeed, became very experienced, and appear to have performed women's roles up to the age of nineteen or twenty.

Developments in acting styles clearly took place, and changes in nomenclature suggest that an increasing refinement of performance was being sought. What the early adult performers had offered their public was 'playing' – a suggestive term – while 'acting' at first described the orator's art of gesture. This seems to have been a speciality of the more academic boys' companies whose prose comedies sometimes satirized the 'stalking-stamping' style of the adult theatres. By the time of the first production of *Hamlet* (1600–1601) however, the further term 'personation' had been coined, perhaps by the playwright John Marston, to suggest a new emphasis on individual characterization.

To the rhetorical nature of dramatic language in the period and the stylized conventions of acting itself should be added the relative plainness of contemporary staging (though not of costuming) in the public theatres at least. All these qualities suggest how the drama of the late sixteenth and early seventeenth centuries – with the important exception of the elaborate masques performed at court – made little attempt to pretend stage illusions were reality. A crowded audience, many of them standing close to the stage and in daylight, was less likely to be beguiled by attempts at visual illusion than an audience seated in the controlled light and upholstered spaciousness of a modern theatre. The effect was thus chiefly produced by the force of language and the techniques of dramatization. It is to the great creators of these that we must now turn.

3

The sudden maturing of English drama in the decades from 1590 is an exhilarating spectacle. Possibilities barely glimpsed before were developed with an astonishing fecundity of invention. Tragedy, comedy and the history play reached heights of poetry and passionate analysis rarely if ever equalled. In the work of Shakespeare, we have a supreme witness of human genius.

Such developments sprang from humble beginnings. Robert Greene's comedy *Friar Bacon and Friar Bungay* (1589) draws an analogy between the medieval magician Roger Bacon and the dangerous, magical power of love. The relation of plots through theme in this way was to be of the greatest significance to future theatrical developments. Literary pastoralism is important to George Peele's *The Arraignment of Paris* (1581) – a work designed to flatter Elizabeth I – as well as to the charm of *The Old Wives' Tale* (1590). His *Edward I* (1591) is a strongly patriotic piece whose lavish stage requirements reflect the influence of the moral and allegorical pageants Peele designed for the City of London. His finest historical work however is *The Love of King David and Fair Bethshebe* (1594–9) with its evocative use of biblical imagery. The drama of England's history also made a strong appeal to Protestant audiences with their new sense of national identity. *The Famous Victories of Henry the Fifth* (1583–8), *Jack Straw* (1590–93), *The Troublesome Reign of King John* (1587–91), *The True Tragedy of Richard the Third* (1588–94) and *King Leir and his Three Daughters* (1588–94) reflect this concern and use material later to be transformed by Shakespeare.

Some time around 1587 came the first performance of Thomas Kyd's *The Spanish Tragedy*. This was one of the most frequently acted of Elizabethan plays, and the sheer theatricality unleashed by its technical innovations goes some way to accounting for its popularity. Kyd's language, if sometimes a little stiff, demands a virtuoso and declamatory style to make feelings, character and situation explicit. The tragic temper is varied by spectacle, dialogue and rhetorical soliloquy, much of which successfully imitates the manner of Seneca. What is only reported in classical drama however is here presented on stage. Hieronimo, maddened by the murder of his son, becomes one of the first of many heroes trapped in the vividly realized savagery of a Renaissance palace:

> I will go plain me to my lord the king,
> And cry aloud for justice through the court,
> Wearing the flints with these my withered feet,
> And either purchase justice by entreats,
> Or tire them all with my revenging threats.

The Spanish Tragedy is a drama of revenge, an issue that opened up a crucial divide between private aristocratic honour and a social order based on the Christian ethic of forgiveness. Revenge became a dominant theme among playwrights of the period, and one inherently dramatic in its presentation of the madness and blood-lust that stem from moral confusion. In addition, Kyd's central theatrical image of the drama itself – of a world made up of acting and observing roles, contriving events and manipulating characters – was a metaphor that crucially influenced subsequent dramatists' analyses of society, including Shakespeare's.

Another exceptional play from this early period makes important links between history, tragedy and Providence. This is *Arden of Faversham* (1585–92). The work is anonymous, though eighteenth-century critics once attributed the play to Shakespeare himself. Drawing on Holinshed's *Chronicles*, the drama shows how the hero 'was wretchedly murdered by means of his disloyal and wanton wife, who, for the love she bear to one Mosbie, hired two desperate ruffians, Black Will and Shakebag, to kill him'. The playwright effectively heightens the tale's sensational realism, suspense and moral concern with the punishment of sin. His dramatic blank verse is also frequently excellent.

It is with Christopher Marlowe (1564–93) however that Elizabethan drama finds its first great poetic voice and a language that shapes the desire of characters to master the world through their ideas and will, actions and speech:

> Nature, that fram'd us of four elements
> Warring within our breasts for regiment,
> Doth teach us all to have aspiring minds.
> Our souls, whose faculties can comprehend

> The wondrous architecture of the world,
> And measure every wandering planet's course,
> Still climbing after knowledge infinite,
> And always moving as the restless spheres,
> Will us to wear ourselves and never rest,
> Until we reach the ripest fruit of all,
> The sweet fruition of an earthly crown.

regiment: *rule*

The speaker here is Tamburlaine whose irrepressible energies, raising him from humble shepherd to world conqueror, are the subject of Marlowe's two plays on this exemplar of Renaissance *virtù* or the force of human personality. Tamburlaine's are indeed 'working words', and they insist on a daring re-examination of older ideas of hierarchy and of pride as the origin of the fall of princes.

In the first part of *Tamburlaine* (1587), the hero flouts the given order, literally tramples on despairing princes to gain his throne, and yet does not himself fall. Furthermore, the power of his language urges the audience into an uneasy identification with a high-aspiring mind that is at once cruel and hideously successful, self-created and carried by love and dreams beyond the limits of mortal existence. As the weak fall before this seemingly irresistible force, so we are exhilarated even as we are appalled. Only death brings sorrow and a forced close to aspiration. But it brings no repentance. In the second part of *Tamburlaine* (1588), after the hero's 'impassionate fury for the death of his lady and love, fair Zenocrate', the dying Tamburlaine stares at a map of the world declaring: 'And shall I die and this unconquered?' The aspiring Renaissance mind raises new vistas even in the face of death.

The amoral pursuit of power, the belief that 'the sweet fruition of an earthly crown' is indeed the true goal of human effort, was associated by Marlowe and his contemporaries with the much reviled and much studied figure of Machiavelli. The Italian thinker actually appears as the Prologue in Marlowe's *The Jew of Malta* (?1589). This play is a savage, cynical and grotesquely comic satire on the worldly ambitions of groups often defined by the Elizabethans as conventionally unacceptable: Turks, Catholics and Jews. The energy of the plot and the power of the language (both of which are embodied in

Barabas, the aspiring anti-hero or 'machiavel') helped create the play's ability to excite an Elizabethan audience into despising the Christians and wondering at Barabas's evil *virtù*, even while all parties remain bogymen. Set on the perilous edge of the morally acceptable, the play exploits the physical resources of the theatre with startling enthusiasm. At the end, when the smug Catholics cause the Jew to hurtle down into a caldron of boiling lead he himself has prepared, a brilliant comic spectacle raises uncomfortable laughter as the revenging machiavel is destroyed by his own endeavours.

Marlowe's *Dido, Queen of Carthage* (1587–93) is a free and poetic imitation from Virgil on the Renaissance *topos* or received idea of pleasure versus the pursuit of power and virtue. *The Massacre at Paris* (1593), despite being a successful play in its time, is for the most part a dull piece of anti-Catholic hack-work distinguished only by the speeches of the machiavellian Guise. *Edward II* (1591–3), which was Marlowe's attempt at the English chronicle or history play, is a finer work combining pace, tragic dignity and an attempt to develop plot from a range of interacting characters. Though the latter parts of the narrative tend to confusion, there is considerable force in the speeches of the hedonistic Gaveston, the machiavellian Mortimer and the tragic king himself.

Of all Marlowe's plays, *Doctor Faustus* (1592–3) remains the most compelling, his profoundly poetic reworking of one of the great European myths. The text, nonetheless, raises a number of important general points. As so often with the drama of this period, when plays belonged to the companies and were usually printed (frequently in mangled versions) only as pirated editions or to establish ownership, it is necessary to ask about the status of the two published versions of *Doctor Faustus*. The earlier is a quarto (a book on standard sheets of paper twice folded) printed in 1604 and now known as Ai. It is a somewhat scrappy version, probably made from memory, of what later appeared in a much fuller version printed in 1616. The latter was probably derived from a reprint of Ai and Marlowe's own draft, his so-called 'foul papers'. These the companies customarily gave to a scrivener or copyist to make into the prompt copy. This in turn could be altered to mark changes made in production. The fuller version of *Doctor Faustus* is called Bi, and is now considered to show what can be ascertained of Marlowe's broadest intentions for the play.

It is not clear that all the act and scene divisions in the play are Marlowe's own however. These only became standard practice after *c.* 1610 and would not have been noticeable in the continuous performances of the public theatres. Further, the lower-quality but eminently stageable comic scenes are regarded as the work of others writing under Marlowe's direction. Such collaboration was commonplace, and this early masterpiece of English Renaissance drama comes to us through a complex process that is far from untypical.

Where the political world succumbed to Tamburlaine's *virtù*, in this play the realms of knowledge have been mastered by Faustus's aspiring mind. None of them has provided him with the miracle he needs however. The height of the intellect reaches a dryness of the spirit. Faustus attempts to slake this through faith – faith in the Devil who alone seems to offer modern man power over the kingdoms of this world. Faustus eventually tries to raise the Devil with the aid of spells, but what in fact prompts his appearance is Faustus's blasphemy. The scholar's incantation – apparently the fruit of advanced study – is mere hocus-pocus. Nonetheless, by denying Christ and the old, sure order of redemption, Faustus's desires have brought hell to earth, for where Mephistopheles is, there hell is also. The conflict between the high aspirations of the worldly Renaissance imagination and the less exciting rectitude of a faith that leads to bliss is now played out between the new hero of the Elizabethan stage, his satanic companion and the trio of the Old Man and the Good and Bad Angels who derive from medieval Morality drama.

The dramatic power and intellectual force of *Doctor Faustus* lie in the conflict between the conventional morality that circumscribes Faustus's damnation and the radical exhilaration in the speeches of this sinning but often magnificent hero:

> Was this the face that launched a thousand ships,
> And burnt the topless towers of Ilium?
> Sweet Helen, make me immortal with a kiss.
> Her lips suck forth my soul: see where it flies.
> Come, Helen, come, give me my soul again.
> Here will I dwell, for heaven is in those lips,
> And all is dross that is not Helena.

The scholar's anguish expresses itself in the sublime language of

Elizabethan love poetry. Faustus embraces the spirit of Helen of Troy he has conjured up and has his soul sucked out to an immortality of damnation. The rapture is a savage irony. The Old Man despairs of Faustus's salvation. Lucifer, Beelzebub and Mephistopheles close in on their victim. Faustus's Good Angel leaves. There remains only the terrifying final soliloquy in which the hero's verse tries in vain to hold back the forces of damnation. And, at the close, we feel less a sense of just desert than of ambiguous, tragic waste and terror. In defeat, Faustus's language gives him the first full grandeur and pathos of Elizabethan tragedy, and it was such 'high-astounding' terms that provided a model for Marlowe's incomparable contemporary, William Shakespeare (1564–1616).

4

'If we wish to know the force of human genius, we should read Shakespeare. If we wish to see the insignificance of human learning, we may study his commentators.' This observation by William Hazlitt, one of the finest of Shakespeare's nineteenth-century critics, must haunt subsequent writers on England's greatest dramatist. The range, depth and imaginative richness – the sheer power and variety – of Shakespeare's work have meant that each generation discovers him anew and, in so doing, partly discovers itself.

One fact about Shakespeare's life is an item of universal knowledge: Shakespeare was born in Stratford-upon-Avon, a small town in the centre of England, probably on 23 April, and certainly in 1564. It is likely that Shakespeare attended the local grammar school where he would have followed the standard humanist curriculum, the long hours of classical grammar and translation which, for all Ben Jonson's jibes about Shakespeare's 'small Latin and less Greek', amounted to a greater familiarity with the classics and their commentators than many modern audiences can muster. The same may be said of Shakespeare and the Bible. This he would have heard from the time of his childhood, sitting in the front pew of Holy Trinity church as befitted the dignity of a member of the local mayor's family. Although Shakespeare's father seems later to have fallen into poverty (there are suggestions of a Catholic sympathy) during the period of his local prestige John Shakespeare would also have granted permission for travelling players to perform, probably in the Guildhall below his son's classroom.

On 28 November 1582, the Bishop of Worcester's office issued a special licence authorizing Shakespeare's marriage to 'Anne Hathwey of Stratford'. He was eighteen, she twenty-six and pregnant. The following May she gave birth to a daughter. On 2 February 1585, Shakespeare's twins, Hamnet and Judith, were christened. If Shakespeare's marriage has caused much speculation, other events in the so-called 'lost years' between the birth of his twins and the first of very few hostile contemporary criticisms of his drama have proliferated myths. To this period belong the stories (and they are probably no more than that) of deer-poaching, schoolmastering and sleeping off a hangover under a crab-apple tree. What is certain is that by 1592 Shakespeare had so established himself in London as both an actor and a playwright that less successful university men were jealous. Robert Greene, dying in embittered poverty, declared Shakespeare to be 'an upstart crow', an ambitious hack with a 'tiger's heart wrapped in a player's hide'. This last taunt parodies a line from *Henry VI, Part III* and is the sneer by which mediocrity pays its tribute to genius.

By 1598, having published *Venus and Adonis* and *The Rape of Lucrece* with their dedications to Henry Wriothesley, third Earl of Southampton (who, for some, is the 'lovely boy' of the *Sonnets*), Shakespeare was an established member of the Lord Chamberlain's Men. He acted with them, wrote for them and was entitled to a 10 per cent share of their profits. No other playwright of the time had so settled a professional life, while contemporaries praised Shakespeare in the highest terms. 'As Plautus and Seneca are accounted the best for comedy and tragedy among the Latins, so Shakespeare among the English is the most excellent in both kinds,' wrote Francis Meres in his *Palladis Tamia: Wit's Treasury* (1598).

With the accession of James I in 1603, Shakespeare, as one of the newly named King's Men, was a royal retainer whose work was much in demand at court. In 1609, the King's Men also purchased the lease of the 'private' Blackfriars Theatre which catered for the tastes of a wealthy and select audience. Though he lived much in London,

Shakespeare invested a large part of his money in the place of his birth, buying houses and land in Stratford and involving himself in other deals there. By 1597 he could afford New Place, the second largest house in the town. It remained in his possession until he died.

On 25 March 1616, with his health and memory failing, Shakespeare signed some revisions to his will in a shaking hand. By 23 April he was dead. Two days later, as a prosperous burgher of his native town, he was buried in the chancel of Holy Trinity. The somewhat sinister lines by his tomb cursing 'he that moves my bones' are not a last, mystical address to posterity, but a warning to generations of sextons who, as the author of *Hamlet* knew, occasionally disturbed old corpses when making new graves.

5

But Shakespeare's enduring monument is, of course, his work as a dramatist. This existed above all for the ephemeral life of the stage and the company who owned the scripts. Publication of his plays was never Shakespeare's major purpose, and during his lifetime it was intermittent and often careless. When he died, at least eighteen of his dramas remained unprinted, the potential victims of mere oblivion.

In 1623 however John Heminges and Henry Condell, two of his fellow actors in the King's Men, issued a collection of thirty-six of Shakespeare's plays in a volume now known as the First Folio. This was a labour of love, produced 'without ambition either of self-profit or fame; only to keep the memory of so worthy a friend and fellow alive, as was our Shakespeare'. Bardolatry had begun, and the First Folio, dividing the plays into comedies, histories and tragedies (labels often as contentious as they are useful), helped establish the canon of Shakespeare's work.

The First Folio is one source of those profound textual problems faced when trying to determine (or at least to reconstruct from the inevitable confusions of transmission) what Shakespeare may have written and his company performed. For example, Heminges and Condell excluded *Pericles*, which we know to be mostly Shakespeare's, and other works in which Shakespeare collaborated to a lesser degree such as *Sir Thomas More* (1595) and *The Two Noble Kinsmen* (1613–14). The 'Evil May-day' scene in the latter exists in the only surviving dramatic script in Shakespeare's hand. Heminges and Condell also included passages such as the Hecate speeches in *Macbeth*, which are possibly by Middleton, and offered that play itself in what is probably an abridged form. Again, the texts Heminges and Condell printed reflect the theatrical practices of their own time rather than Shakespeare's. The majority of the act divisions, for example, are not authorial (they should mostly be regarded as convenient reference points rather than structural features) while a law of 1606 had necessitated the removal of profanities.

Nor do the difficulties end there. As always, there were problems with compositors and proof-reading. The First Folio consists of 'quires' of six leaves or twelve pages sewn together and bound. The type was not set up in the numerical sequence of these pages however but from the centre spread of the quire outwards. The last pages to be printed were thus the first and the twelfth. Getting all the type to fit was clearly a somewhat hit-and-miss affair and, when they missed, the compositors resorted to printing verse as prose or even to leaving lines out. In addition, something in the order of seven or eight different compositors have been identified, their shifts determined, their failings analysed.

What copy were these men working from? Heminges and Condell could present their compositors with a variety of material. In addition to some of Shakespeare's own drafts or foul papers, at least five of his comedies were set from neat copies of either Shakespeare's own scripts or the company's prompt books made by the scrivener Ralph Crane. It was unlikely the company would have lent its own prompt-book version of a play to the printers since these were too valuable to lose. They were, first of all, the official version of the script approved by the Master of the Revels and licensed by him after censorship and at considerable expense. They were also proof of owning copyright. Again, the prompt books became the company's record of its performance tradition and also the source from which both individual parts and the 'plats' or cue sheets were copied.

But there were other sources on which Heminges and Condell could draw. In their Preface they write of 'stolen and surreptitious copies, maimed and deformed by the frauds and stealths of injurious impostors'. This used to be taken as implying criticism of all the small or quarto versions of individual plays printed before their own publication. Modern scholarship however takes the phrase to refer only to those 'bad quartos' which it is believed were set from the transcripts of 'memorial reconstructions'. These were sometimes made by and for bit-part actors on provincial tours. It can be shown, for example, that the principal reporter of the 'bad' 1603 quarto of *Hamlet* with its deathless howler 'To be or not to be; ay, there's the point' was the actor who played Marcellus. In other instances, the 'bad' quartos were the work of actor-reporters deliberately pirating work for publishers who then owned the copyright. By contrast, a substantial number of 'good quartos' also exist. The 1622 quarto of *Othello*, for example, probably derives from a scribal transcript of Shakespeare's own foul papers.

More substantial problems are raised when there are considerable divergences from the text printed in a reliable quarto and that reproduced in the folio. The outstanding example of this is *King Lear*. The quarto contains three hundred lines not in the folio, while the folio has one hundred lines not in the quarto. Over eight hundred smaller variants between the two also exist. What was Shakespeare's role in this? While some problems with the quarto of *King Lear* are clearly due to the inexperience of the printer, it now seems likely that the version of this supreme work presented in the First Folio represents the result of substantial changes of mind on Shakespeare's part, alterations which resulted not only in new readings but in some pruning of the play in the third and fourth acts in order to accelerate its tempo.

Interpretation of Shakespeare is thus a constant creative flux. Detailed scholarship reveals Shakespeare's own revisions and exposes the often problematic nature of his texts. Critics across the ages, developing and rejecting a multitude of theories about possible interpretation, offer a variety of sometimes conflicting insights. Directors bring to performances a further range of interpretation and the tastes of their time. Shakespearian actors, each with a unique voice, a particular personal presence, a private range of experience to offer a role, proliferate endless diversity. To be involved with a Shakespeare play is thus to be involved with a living entity, one that is complex, multifarious and capable of making the greatest demands on the subtlety of perception. It is above all a profoundly humanizing experience, and one that obliges us to recognize the provisional nature of all our theories, all our interpretations.

6

When Shakespeare began his career at the start of the 1590s, both the relative novelty of the London theatrical world and the talent it attracted were a stimulus to experiment. To enquire what contemporaries were doing was to be involved in a vigorous public arena where the potential of drama could be explored, extended, revised or revolutionized.

The new theatres themselves allowed for the constant discovery of previously unsuspected possibilities in the staging of an action, of seeing the stage as a world and the world as a stage. The talents of great actors – the clowns Will Kempe (active 1600) and Robert Armin (active 1599), Edward Alleyn (1566–1626) the 'stalking Tamburlaine' and mighty Richard Burbage (?1567–1619) the first Hamlet, Lear and Othello – all enriched these possibilities. The new language of the theatre – a poetry and prose fed from the immense resources of humanism and the vernacular and then developed with the greatest imaginative daring – encouraged the awareness of new aims and solutions to freshly discovered challenges. Lastly, in seeing how others – Kyd, Marlowe, Lyly and the rest – had used the stage as a means of transcending the merely local and, by envisaging circumstances beyond conventional experience, had tested old prejudices and habitual assumptions, Shakespeare could see the possibility of drama at its most exhilarating and profound.

The newcomer had, nonetheless, to learn his craft. The plays of Shakespeare's earliest period (the works he wrote between c. 1590 and 1594) show him experimenting with the three major genres that largely shaped his career: the history or chronicle play, tragedy and comedy. It is convenient to begin with the histories.

The chronicles of Hall and Holinshed provided Shakespeare with accounts of recent English history set against the background of Providence or the working of God's purposes in the unfolding of the nation's story. In the case of what are conventionally known as the three parts of *Henry VI* (c. 1590–91), the dramatic theme is the collapse of English power in France after the death of Henry V. Along with this goes the breakdown of authority, order, the family and Christian values at home. The country, nominally ruled by a weak king of dubious descent, is plunged into the strife of the Wars of the Roses. At the outset of his career we are thus presented with something of fundamental importance to Shakespearian drama: the analysis of how men and women behave when the ideal order of the state has collapsed. The stage becomes a mirror of the period's deepest political fears while reflecting its intense patriotism. It is recorded that over 10,000 people enjoyed the pathos of the death of the heroic Talbot, one of the cycle's best scenes.

As is appropriate to an age which saw history as exemplary – a storehouse of moral truth, a reflection of God's designs or a source of propaganda – Shakespeare's first history plays interpret their material through the great political concerns of the day: a belief in divine guidance, and the fear of anarchy, weakness and machiavellian opportunism. Only at the close of *Richard III* (1592–3) are peace and order finally restored as the triumphant Richmond is shown securing the throne at the behest of Providence to become Henry VII, the first of the Tudor dynasty.

Richard III was the most compelling character English drama had yet produced. He is above all a creature of the stage, and in developing so exhilarating a solution to the problems of dramatizing history, Shakespeare drew on a wide range of native and classical traditions. He did so as an artist testing and exploring the limits of the given. A various inheritance is thus transformed through imaginative criticism of genius. The Richard fashioned by Thomas More, the heroes of Marlowe, the comic Vice and the tyrant from the *Mirror for Magistrates* all played their part. Along with this wide interest in native sources however went Shakespeare's involvement with classical drama. In *Richard III*, Seneca and classical literary scholarship are pervasive and creative influences. For example, although the First Folio (like most drama printed after c. 1610) divides the play into five acts, the divisions Renaissance critics detected in classical tragedy may also give the work its structure.

The opening, or 'protasis', marvellously serves its formal function of introducing and establishing the background and main characters. Here we see Richard, the actor and would-be king, fashioning the drama in which he will play the leading role. He is a man self-created in the evil that will destroy him. The fascination of his wickedness works through a vividly repulsive physical presence and Richard's virtuoso delight in words. In the high theatrical excitement of his opening soliloquy a new era in English drama opens. A formal device for giving information about the speaker is transformed by the diabolic energy that is Shakespeare's subject:

> But I, that am not shaped for sportive tricks
> Nor made to court an amorous looking-glass;
> I that am rudely stamped and want love's majesty
> To strut before a wanton ambling nymph,
> I that am curtailed of this fair proportion,
> Cheated of feature by dissembling nature,
> Deformed, unfinished, sent before my time
> Into this breathing world, scarce half made up –
> And that so lamely and unfashionable
> That dogs bark at me as I halt by them –
> Why, I in this weak piping time of peace,
> Have no delight to pass away the time,
> Unless to spy my shadow in the sun
> And descant on mine own deformity.
> And therefore, since I cannot prove a lover
> To entertain these fair well-spoken days,
> I am determinèd to prove a villain
> And hate the idle pleasures of these days.

The flexibility of this verse, the handling of a rhythm that at once presses the main argument forward while eddying round on itself to find images that emphasize the fertility of Richard's bitterness, is a triumph of technique and characterization. As a poetry which both creates and criticizes character, which equally provokes sympathy, laughter, reptilian fascination and contempt, it is an exceptional creation. Language, role-playing and the manipulation of action – the very bases of drama – here combine with newly concentrated power and reveal a wholly new potential for the stage.

The audience now watches with increasing horror as, in the

'epitasis', or that part of the play where the action intensifies, Richard wades through slaughter to his throne. Clarence's nightmare creates a suitably Senecan atmosphere of omens and the macabre, while the doomed princes provide pathos. And yet, with unprecedented dramatic subtlety, we also become aware that a greater hand than Richard's is shaping the action. The ensuing 'catastasis' (the point of change in classical tragedy) rises through stunning displays of hypocrisy to the murder of the princes, but with this there also comes the sense of opposition grouping and Richard's increasing failure to control action through words. Providence is playing its role and evil is being leached of its power to destroy.

The final 'catastrophe' – the reversal which brings about the conclusion – takes place on Bosworth field. Before the battle, a Senecan climax of horror is reached as the ghosts of Richard's victims shake his soul. In the morning, the forces of Richmond, soon to be God's anointed, fight with the Devil's own. Their victory is assured. Richard, crying for his horse, is slain. At the close, the triumphant founder of the Tudor dynasty promises lasting peace, while the stage itself has now become the most powerful and various medium of political analysis in English Renaissance literature.

If the too often frigid sensationalism of *Titus Andronicus* (1592) suggests that the authority of Seneca could sometimes prove a baleful encumbrance, the Latin comedy of Plautus was a force liberating exuberance, subtlety and masterful construction. These can be seen in *The Comedy of Errors* (1594), Shakespeare's shortest play. Technically, *The Comedy of Errors* is an attempt to outdo the virtuosity of Plautus by reshaping his *Menaechmi*. The twin, parted brothers of the Latin comedy are here provided with twin, parted servants. This increases comic confusion by a geometric ratio, and the sheer exhilaration in Shakespeare's handling of the complexities of artifice is a central element in the pleasure the play affords, a revelation of a fundamental mastery of technique. Nonetheless, although the result has all the mad logic of farce, underpinning the exuberance are pain, desperation, pathos and a warm sense of the metamorphosis wrought by joy and reunion. Such an intricate perception of gaiety and seriousness mixed lies at the heart of Shakespearian comedy, giving it its exceptional human richness.

The Shakespearian comic stage was also a medium for the testing of literary convention. As a result, many of his comedies are often concerned with young men maturing from the self-conscious parade of artificial emotion under the influence of women quite as passionate, quite as brave, yet more naturally sexual than they. This is a theme broached in *The Two Gentlemen of Verona* (1590–91), an investigation into the nature of romance with its disguisings, flights, forests, robbers and Petrarchan posturings. In *The Taming of the Shrew* (1590–91) – a more sophisticated play – the tables are turned. Set within the self-referring theatrical framework of the gulling of Christopher Sly, we are shown how Petruchio, the emotionally assured man of the world, tames the shrewish Katherine by outdoing her in bravura displays of comic stridency. Husband and wife eventually find a loving relationship based on St Paul's concepts of married obedience. Lucentio's romantic wooing of Bianca however brings him a wife more shrewish than he expected.

By far the most subtle of Shakespeare's early comedies is *Love's Labour's Lost* (1594–5). This play is directed against people who exalt learning and artifice above common sense. Self-conscious language and behaviour – theatricality itself – become vehicles for exploring human nature. The courtiers of Navarre withdraw into a world of learning only to be obliged to question their vocation as the arrival of the French queen and her ladies reveals to them that the true force of desire is the real path to self-knowledge, the sparkle of a woman's eye 'the right Promethean fire'. Yet, with the entry of Marcade bringing news of the French queen's father's death – a moment which, in the theatre, can be one of shivering seriousness – artifice crumbles, and the lords are sentenced to a year of abstinence before the prospect of marriage. Such delicate theatrical complexity, Shakespeare's view of a mixed world of pain and pleasure, was to be enormously developed in the comedies of his middle years.

7

In *King John* (1596), Shakespeare presented the decline of an active monarch through foolishly self-seeking compromise or 'commodity'. Though more advanced in its examination of issues of political theory than the earlier history dramas, the work lacks the poetic and imaginative power Shakespeare brought to his second cycle of English history plays. These are the four related but independent studies of kingship and power politics: *Richard II* (1595), the two parts of *Henry IV* (1596–7, 1597–8) and *Henry V* (1598–9). In these works, Shakespeare enormously extended his vision of the stage as a medium for the analysis of political conflict, and one among innumerable approaches is to see these plays as studies in the politics of language, action and role-playing – the fundamentals of drama itself.

'We were not born to sue but to command.' Richard II's language appears to transform words into deeds as he asserts his divinely appointed role as the voice of national order. Such power, however, is largely an illusion. As the elegiac beauty of *Richard II* unfolds, we are shown how the irresponsibility of an anointed ruler is pitted against a mighty and unjustly treated subject. Bolingbroke is driven into the brutalities of power politics as he confronts the vanity of a player prince. Richard becomes the victim of his own folly, and the garden of England is ravaged.

Innately magisterial even in decline, Richard takes on ever more completely the role of the player king. He also elaborates a language of self-indulgent lament as power slips from his grasp. To this language of lament is added an imagery which structures the drama with deeply poetic resonance. Richard is throughout compared to the sun. The scene of his deposition, powerfully exploiting the physical resources of the theatre, suggests how in falling to Bolingbroke's level Richard must plummet like Phaeton, the mythical figure whose reckless driving of the chariot of the sun symbolized imperfect self-control. Now, over England, the sun itself is eclipsed. Nature is awry. Intimations of civil chaos grow louder, while words alone remain to the imprisoned and powerless king:

> I have been studying how I may compare
> This prison where I live unto the world;
> And for because the world is populous,
> And here is not a creature but myself,
> I cannot do it. Yet I'll hammer it out.
> My brain I'll prove the female to my soul,
> My soul the father, and these two beget
> A generation of still-breeding thoughts;

> And these same thoughts people this little world
> In humours like the people of this world.

Words feed on themselves to spin out fantasies. The kingly language of command is reduced to pathetic solecism. All Richard can do is play out a hollow role. Eventually, with his murder, he becomes the ultimate victim of the actions of others. Power and guilt (though not a divinely sanctioned kingship) lay their heavy burden on Bolingbroke, now Henry IV.

To move from *Richard II* to the first part of *Henry IV* is again to experience the infinite variety of Shakespeare's genius. We inhabit a different world. It is the world of a hard and efficient yet pressured and sorrowing king, of Hotspur's immoderate vitality and Falstaff's raucous humanity. Between these mutually revealing spheres however moves another figure, formed and forming himself in response to the nation: Hal, the king's son, and, for contemporary audiences, the wild boy who emerged through miraculous change to be Henry V, the nation's hero and the victor of Agincourt.

A central theme of the play is thus the education of a prince, a major topic of Renaissance thought and one to which Shakespeare brought an unequalled wealth of dramatic contrivance. The actor's art of role-playing merges with the craft of the politician as Hal explains why he associates with the lowest in the kingdom:

> I know you all, and will awhile uphold
> The unyoked humour of your idleness.
> Yet herein will I imitate the sun,
> Who doth permit the base contagious clouds
> To smother up his beauty from the world,
> That when he please again to be himself,
> Being wanted he may be more wondered at
> By breaking through the foul and ugly mists
> Of vapours that did seem to strangle him.

Such action is a political ploy. Nonetheless, by sounding 'the very bass string of humility', Hal achieves an understanding of the good lads of Eastcheap which will be part of his armoury as a mature king. From Falstaff he will learn much else besides – including the hard necessity of rejecting his teacher.

The massive figure of Falstaff bulks large in the play, literally and thematically. Falstaff is Shakespeare's great embodiment of comic humanity. He is liberating, anarchic, consistently inconsistent in his riot and melancholy, his thieving, cowardice, boasting and sheer drunken exuberance. With Falstaff, language and action are debased to glorious comedy as Hal, the future king, is associated with the lord of misrule.

Nonetheless, as the play moves to its climax on the battlefield at Shrewsbury, so Hal's experience is reflected against another figure: 'Hare-brained Hotspur, governed by a spleen'. Hotspur's impetuous language is at one with undisciplined military prowess, and both are given over to rebellion. Hal must triumph over a rival whose words and deeds run constantly to hot-headed and destructive excess. He succeeds, but Shakespeare's presentation is more subtle than this suggests. In a dramatic tableau on Shrewsbury field, we see Hal mourning like a true soldier over Hotspur whom he has slain and Falstaff who appears to be dead. Hal exits chastened but apparently free from rivals and temptation. But Falstaff is not dead. He '*riseth up*', and he does so with the comic vitality of a jack-in-the-box to play his bawdy and necessary role in *Henry IV, Part II*. Shakespeare's dramatic world permits no easy conclusions.

'I am old, I am old.' Falstaff's lament as he dandles the whore Doll Tearsheet on his knee in the second part of *Henry IV* suggests how the comic vision of this play surveys a world more sour, more soiled and often more cynical than that of the earlier work. The emblematic figure of Rumour introduces the drama's themes of deception, misinformation and rebellion. Once again, language and action are diverted from their true ends. The rebels themselves however, though dangerous, are disunited. Meanwhile, ever greater sorrow and exhaustion attend the guilty king. Eastcheap – by a superb extension of Shakespeare's art – is seen as both more squalid and yet more richly human than before. Mistress Quickly's fluttering mind, for example, marvellously conjures up a low world of broken promises, cheating and self-indulgence. The greatness of Shakespeare's comic prose becomes the perfect complement to the rhetoric of his poetry:

Thou didst swear to me upon a parcel-gilt goblet, sitting in my Dolphin chamber, at the round table, by a sea-coal fire, upon Wednesday in Wheeson week, when the Prince broke thy head for liking his father to a singing-man of Windsor – thou didst swear to me then, as I was washing thy wound, to marry me, and make me my lady thy wife. Canst thou deny it? Did not godwife Keech the butcher's wife come in and then call me 'Gossip Quickly' – coming in to borrow a mess of vinegar, telling us she had a good dish of prawns, whereby thou didst desire to eat some, whereby I told thee they were ill for a green wound? And didst thou not, when she was gone downstairs, desire me to be no more so familiarity with such poor people, saying that ere long they should call me 'madam'? And didst thou not kiss me, and bid me fetch thee thirty shillings? I put thee now to thy book-oath; deny it if thou canst.

parcel-gilt: *partly gilded*; Wheeson: *Whitsun*; Keech: *animal fat*; gossip: *neighbour*; mess: *a small quantity*; green: *unhealed*

Comedy nonetheless becomes shot through with images of disease, while the folly of old age is explored in the scenes between Falstaff, Justice Shallow and his friend Silence. Here we see an inimitable combination of hospitality, roguery and embroidered reminiscence. 'We have heard the chimes at midnight, Master Shallow.' In recalling these however, the old men conjure up a passing world of defeat and decay.

Effective action is for the young, and the young are hard. In a scene of ruthless political manoeuvring, Hal's brother tricks the rebels and condemns them to death. The king, meanwhile, is dying. Hal, who has watched the sordid life of Eastcheap at a greater and more disdainful distance than before, is brought to his father's bedside. The crown lies beside the dying man and the prince addresses it. His soliloquy, emphasizing both the temptations and the personal loneliness of power, shows him aware of his awesome responsibilities and his own ambition.

Reconciled to his son, the old king dies. Hal is now Henry V and must, as he has sworn, emerge sunlike from the base clouds of his youthful reputation. He will play his role as the rightful king of England urging heroic action through heroic speech. We are also shown how his legitimate succession is underpinned by respect for the law. Henry is obliged to reject the false paternal care of Falstaff for the strong, impartial guidance of the Lord Chief Justice. The new king's rejection of Falstaff is a hard deed but not, finally, a gratuitous one. It is the necessary if troubling action by which the youth becomes a man, and the man a virtuous ruler.

'We are no tyrant, but a Christian king.' These words are addressed by Henry to the French ambassador in *Henry V*. They suggest the play's doctrinal and exemplary concern with the strong monarch. Turning from the subtleties of *Henry IV, Part II, Henry V* exploits the conventions of epic. The excellently varied scenes of the play are linked by the high rhetoric of the Chorus speeches. These not only maintain tone and continuity but, by requiring the audience to imagine what the theatre cannot always present, emphasize the theatrical nature of what they do see. The audience are encouraged into identifying with the drama of their nation's history and to focus their attention on the king himself as an actor.

We see Henry's conscious playing of his ideal role. This might be as the good ruler listening to advice when he consults the churchmen on his legal right to the throne of France, or as the source of justice when he executes the traitors Scroop, Cambridge and Grey. We hear him quickening patriotism at Harfleur, on the eve of Agincourt and on the morning of the battle itself. The true king thereby becomes a master of an invigorating public speech:

> Once more unto the breach, dear friends, once more,
> Or close the wall up with our English dead!
> In peace there's nothing so becomes a man
> As modest stillness and humility:
> But when the blast of war blows in our ears,
> Then imitate the action of the tiger;
> Stiffen the sinews, summon up the blood,
> Disguise fair nature with hard-favoured rage;
> Then lend the eye a terrible aspect;
> Let it pry through the portage of the head
> Like the brass cannon; let the brow o'erwhelm it
> As fearfully as doth a galled rock
> O'er hang and jutty his confounded base.

The Renaissance ideal of the epic hero is here embodied on the stage. Language, action and the role of the king are made one in patriotic endeavour. Shakespeare makes Henry's soliloquy before the encounter at Agincourt the one revelation of the private burden of responsibility bravely borne in trust in God. Finally, at the close of the work, we see Henry as the bluff but sincere wooer of the French princess making a shrewd political marriage.

Against such matters are played out the scenes of low life. Often, as with the deaths of Falstaff and the Boy, these produce true pathos. The encounters with the soldier Williams reveal both humour and a manly frankness. Pistol (the braggart from the earlier plays) maintains the tone of vicarious survival. Above all however, the interplay of English, Scots, Welsh and Irish soldiers presents the nation under the sway of a great military man, one aware of the very real suffering and horror of war, of the burden of responsibility, but confident too in God and his right. *Henry V* is thus a grandiloquent assertion of national prestige modified by humour, pathos and the hard realities of political life and warfare. Yet, finally, Henry's reign is presented as a brief moment of glory only. The Chorus reminds us that this great actor of the royal part died young and that the ensuing chaos was the subject of Shakespeare's earlier cycle of history plays. Historical and theatrical reality merge.

8

Though his death is reported in *Henry V*, Falstaff had another existence outside the history plays – in Shakespeare's brilliantly inventive farce of middle-class life, *The Merry Wives of Windsor* (1597-8). In the pursuit of the bodies and purses of Mistresses Ford and Page, Falstaff becomes the trickster tricked. The lovers however, snatching married happiness out of these very incidents, round off a comedy of revenge with happy reconciliation.

The sophistication of mature Shakespearian comedy derives in part from the play between high, outgoing romance and darker forces of negativity and hate. To his absolute mastery of the intricate plot is added Shakespeare's mercurial swiftness in contrasting moods. He thereby creates tension, ambiguity, a self-conscious and self-delighting artifice that is at once intellectually exciting and emotionally engaging. In the life of the play, life itself is a form of playing, and disguise, illusion and intrigue become central.

The result is the suggestive ambiguity of response seen in *The*

Merchant of Venice (1596–7). Here the drama centres around the responses of the Christian lovers to the machinations of the Jewish money-lender Shylock, revealing him as a comic villain whose persecuted humanity nonetheless makes him almost tragic. These ambivalent attitudes are also reflected in our responses to some of the other characters. Bassanio's love for Portia, for example, is a compound of idealism and self-interest, while Portia's much vaunted mercy is, in fact, 'strained' when she turns on Shylock in the trial scene. Antonio, the merchant of Venice himself, is also a complex figure: fashionably and obscurely melancholy, generous to a fault, yet prejudiced against Shylock to a degree that prompts the Jew's understandable desire for revenge. Finally, in surrendering Bassanio to Portia, Antonio is also the one figure who does not have a place amid the happiness of the married couples. He is left on the outside.

Such a subtle testing of the delights of comedy was a fundamental Shakespearian interest. So too was his exploration of the language of love:

> How sweet the moonlight sleeps upon this bank!
> Here will we sit, and let the sounds of music
> Creep in our ears. Soft stillness and the night
> Become the touches of sweet harmony:
> Sit, Jessica. [*They sit*]
>   Look how the floor of heaven
> Is thick inlaid with pattens of bright gold,
> There's not the smallest orb which thou behold'st
> But in his motion like an angel sings,
> Still choiring to the young-eyed cherubims;
> Such harmony is in immortal souls,
> But whilst this muddy vesture of decay
> Doth grossly close it in, we cannot hear it.

>   pattens: *thin gold plates used to cover chalices*

Lorenzo's words to his betrothed convey a cosmic rapture through the richness of rhetorical language. The speech moves from a moon-kissed bank of earth, up through intimations of the divinity of heaven, to the harmony known only after death – a harmony which can nonetheless be guessed at in moments of love. Man, woman and the universe thrill to a celestial music.

This is the language of exalted passion – a supreme poetry which in his other comedies Shakespeare often tests through the artifice of wit and satire. Beatrice, the heroine of *Much Ado about Nothing* (1598), for example, comes to a measure of self-knowledge and to recognizing the power of love through being the victim of others' contrivance. This comedy is a virtuoso display of plot within plot, of the dynamic juxtaposition of farce, idealized love and unreasoning hate, vengeance and repentance, high-life crime and low-life humour.

It is partly for its wit that *Much Ado about Nothing* is so memorable. The play explores the ambiguities of its comic situations with all the subtlety of *The Merchant of Venice*, but raises to a particularly delightful pitch those exchanges of ingenious, artificial and self-delightingly intelligent dialogue by which Shakespeare's lovers convey the ebullience of their excitement and the more delicate shades of their personalities:

BEATRICE: I wonder that you will still be talking, Signior Benedick. Nobody marks you.

BENEDICK: What, my dear Lady Disdain! Are you yet living?

BEATRICE: Is it possible disdain should die while she hath such meet food to feed it as Signior Benedick? Courtesy itself must convert to disdain if you come in her presence.

BENEDICK: Then is courtesy a turncoat. But it is certain I am loved of all ladies, only you excepted. And I would I could find it in my heart that I had not a hard heart, for truly I love none.

BEATRICE: A dear happiness to women. They would else have been troubled with a pernicious suitor.

In such moments as these, *Much Ado about Nothing* exists preeminently for the stage, and as it plays daringly with illusion, reality and the variety of our emotions, so we see Shakespeare's absolute mastery of his dramatic resources and the fertility of Renaissance English.

Illusion and reality are again central themes in *A Midsummer Night's Dream* (1595). The three worlds of the play – that of the aristocratic lovers, the fairies and the 'rude mechanicals' – revolve with incomparable deftness around the drama's two locations: Athens under the rule of Theseus with its appearance of harsh law but ordered social life, and the wood outside the city, the chief realm of Oberon and the place of magic, entanglement, suffering and illusion.

All of these must be undergone before the lovers can return to society and marriage, Bottom and his troupe of actors perform their play, and the fairies take on a more modest relation to humankind than they show in the wood.

The relationship between the Fairy King and Queen themselves is expressed through a language of astonishing beauty which identifies these creatures with the forces of both the natural world and a rapturous magic:

> I know a bank where the wild thyme blows,
> Where oxlips and the nodding violet grows,
> Quite overcanopied with luscious woodbine,
> With sweet musk-roses, and with eglantine.
> There sleeps Titania sometime of the night,
> Lulled in these flowers with dances and delight;
> And there the snake throws her enamelled skin,
> Weed wide enough to wrap a fairy in;
> And with the juice of this I'll streak her eyes,
> And make her full of hateful fantasies.

Such poetry, at once vividly observed and fantastic, hints at cruelty amid its own abundance. The play's concern with nature and illusion, and sleep and the entanglements of love, is held in perfect synthesis. The language itself – fresh and of the greatest sophistication – also throws into relief the Petrarchan attitudinizing of the lovers, the warm, homely prose of the mechanicals and the glorious fustian of their play. Indeed, by a marvellous paradox, the mechanicals' wretched drama of Pyramus and Thisbe, performed in Theseus's palace for the nuptials of their master, is one of Shakespeare's supreme achievements. The comedy, illusion and grotesque high passion are genuinely hilarious, yet we are never finally sure if our tears are those of laughter or compassion for these fumbling men in whom we have invested so much love.

As You Like It (1599–1600) is Shakespeare's comedy in the pastoral mode. Deriving in part from Thomas Lodge's prose romance *Rosalynde*, it contrives to use many of the well-known themes of the genre, to develop some with delightful humour and gently to satirize others. It thereby probes the surface of this most popular form of Elizabethan fantasy literature to make it at once more delightfully artificial and more humanly shrewd.

The play offers a wealth of motifs from pastoral romance: the political upsets that drive courtiers and lovers to the forest of Arden, wicked brothers, disguised princesses, amorous shepherds, besotted noble youths, sudden reversals of fortune and, above all, a continual variety of loving encounters interspersed with song. A number of other elements test the unreality of the mode. Duke Senior's feast, for example, is interrupted by Orlando with his drawn sword. He demands food for his ancient servant. Naked steel is met with courtesy however, and while Orlando goes to fetch his retainer, Jaques offers the famous pessimism of his speech on the seven ages of man with its bitter portrayal of old age:

> With spectacles on nose and pouch on side,
> His youthful hose, well saved, a world too wide
> For his shrunk shank, and his big, manly voice,
> Turning again towards childish treble, pipes
> And whistles in his sound. Last scene of all,
> That ends this strange, eventful history,
> Is second childishness, and mere oblivion,
> Sans teeth, sans eyes, sans taste, sans everything.

But Jaques's pessimistic vision is not the play's final comment. If all the world is a stage, then the stage itself denies the fashionable attitudinizing of some of its actors. Orlando enters supporting his old and loyal servant. Human kindness counters satirical cynicism. Action contradicts speech. The couple are offered royal kindness, and the younger man can now hope to cure the excesses of passion by his pretended wooing of Ganymede who, unbeknown to him, is his mistress Rosalind in disguise. And Rosalind, despite her occasional melancholy, is Shakespeare's most ebullient heroine, his rich portrayal of a girl in the flood-tide of love. Her all-controlling, witty and passionate energy resolves each of love's dilemmas, including her own. Finally, when Rosalind reveals her true nature, she and Orlando can joyfully recognize each other as man and wife as the courtly lovers prepare for the return from Arden.

But Shakespeare has other comic worlds. 'This is Illyria, lady.' The Captain's words to Viola as she emerges from the all-transforming sea introduce the heroine of *Twelfth Night* (1600) to one of the most exquisite and satisfying provinces of the imagination ever mapped by man. Illyria is where romantic love and broad farce combine with disguise and desire, illusion and melancholy, joy, cruelty and song. In Illyria we hear biting wit and word-play, and also some of Shakespeare's most ravishing poetry. Love, around which the play centres, is felt as a powerful force, and one which can drive people to absurdity and extremes.

The play moves swiftly from rapture to slapstick, aided by a variety of characters. We are shown Orsino, a rare and exotic connoisseur of passion; and Viola, fresh, faithful and strong. The Lady Olivia has turned her back on love but, in meeting Viola disguised, discovers its desperate and convulsive power. The low-life characters add variety and comment. Sir Toby Belch, in his raucous and earthy delights, is touching as well as comic. Sir Andrew Aguecheek is absurd but pathetic. Malvolio, 'sick of self-love', the would-be courtier and wooer, the 'madman' and, finally, the one rejected character, comments bitterly on all these themes.

The overriding theme, of course, is the nature of love, and in *Twelfth Night* the final truth of love lies in the happy marriages of Olivia to Sebastian, Viola to Orsino, Sir Toby to Maria. They have grown out of illusions: Orsino's illusions of romantic passion, Olivia's unnatural withdrawal from the world. Only when these illusions have been truly overthrown however, when, with a unique combination of laughter and poetry, Viola throws off the last disguise and stands revealed as the woman she really is, can happiness and truth prevail.

Yet this is only part of Shakespeare's total effect. Orsino's relation to Viola when she is disguised as a boy provides the satire on excessive male passion revealed by the similar motif in *As You Like It*, while the final exit of the loveless and tortured Malvolio focuses the play's cruelty. The bitter-sweet tone of the entire work is constantly suggested by Feste whose shrewd sallies of wit and complex engagement with each of the play's characters make him one of the most subtle of Shakespeare's fools. The play ends with his song:

> A great while ago the world began,
>   With hey-ho, the wind and the rain;
> But that's all one, our play is done,
>   And we'll strive to please you every day.

This beautifully melancholy lyric finally leads us out of the rare existence of Illyria and so away from comedy itself.

9

Among the achievements of world literature Shakespeare's tragic sequence stands supreme. Language, action and role-playing here become vehicles for imagining the ultimates of human experience: the destructive power of love and politics, madness and the supernatural, the flawed forces of the heroes' own magnificence. Approaching such works, the historian must recognize the impossibility of his task. Shakespeare's tragedies reveal the extraordinary fertility of genius, and repeated study shows them in an ever richer light.

Romeo and Juliet (1595), Shakespeare's portrayal of 'star-crossed love' awakened, fulfilled and destroyed amid vendetta, has a universal appeal, an irreducible pathos. We watch the action move from stalking wit and murder on the city streets, through dancing and love poetry in the palace at night, and on to the moonlit ardour of the balcony scene and the parting at dawn. Romeo is a young man in the grip of dangerously impetuous desire. For Juliet, love is an imperative and marriage an act of disobedience by which – first with the help of her Nurse's conspiratorial bawdy and then through rejection of her compromises – she finds her status as a woman and tragic heroine.

The action reaches its climax in the torchlit anguish of the tomb. Here, as the speeches attain a new height of poetry, so the subtle play of images reaches its consummation. Night, which was the time of lovers' meeting, is also the darkness of the grave. The stars, flambeaux and lightning, which throughout have burned against the dark, now fully suggest the malignancy of fate and the brief flame of headlong desire, that 'lightning before death' which is tragic passion itself.

In *Romeo and Juliet*, language provides a universalizing imagery. In *Julius Caesar* (1599), it is a form of political action – of power. The most famous scene in the play (and one invented by Shakespeare rather than derived by him from his source in North's translation of Plutarch's *Lives*) shows Antony mounting the pulpit to address the citizens of Rome clustered about Caesar's corpse:

> Friends, Romans, countrymen, lend me your ears.
> I come to bury Caesar, not to praise him.
> The evil that men do lives after them;
> The good is oft interred with their bones.
> So let it be with Caesar. The noble Brutus
> Hath told you Caesar was ambitious.
> If it were so, it was a grievous fault,
> And grievously hath Caesar answered it.
> Here, under leave of Brutus and the rest –
> For Brutus is an honourable man,
> So are they all, all honourable men –
> Come I to speak in Caesar's funeral.

Ancient Rome was the seat of rhetoric, and Antony is a skilled rhetorician. Brutus has convinced the people Caesar was a tyrant and now, through the sheer power of words, Antony must persuade them to the opposite view. To achieve this, he uses two of the orator's most powerful tools: pathos and his own ethos – his presentation of himself as a worthy and responsible man. Antony thus plays the role of patriot and uses language to manipulate power. His speech, nonetheless, is ruthless demagoguery. The action it inspires is civil chaos. The republic of Rome – the Rome of the people – is revealed as a barbarous place where Cinna the poet is torn apart simply because of his name. Far from bringing order, Antony's speech has wrought the chaos which only he and the autocratic followers of Caesar can quell.

The humanist notion of language in the service of the state is here revealed as a profoundly ambiguous ideal, while the scene as a whole shows how Caesar's assassination is the focus of Shakespeare's presentation of humanity in one of its most distinctive roles. *Julius Caesar* reveals political men acting in the rivalry between idealism, expediency and the awful pursuit of the power necessary to effect change in the world. Each of the main characters is so subtly presented however that we see great historical events arising naturally out of their particular strengths and flaws.

Against the subtle and often warm humanity with which Shakespeare presents Brutus and Cassius, for example, is contrasted the short and devastating scene at the start of Act IV in which Antony and Octavius carve up the world. We hear the timeless voices of absolute power. The conspirators' minds, riven by the continuing influence of Caesar (the appearance of his ghost provides a suitably Senecan atmosphere in this Roman tragedy), dwell as much on death as on securing victory. Confusion, defeat and suicide – each presented with the greatest pathos – mean that power itself is finally possessed by Caesar's legitimate heirs.

Violence and the excitement of the political thriller are again central to the tragedy which, for many people, marks the pinnacle of Shakespeare's achievement: *Hamlet* (1600–1601). The timeless appeal of this mighty drama lies in its combination of intrigue, emotional conflict and searching philosophic melancholy. Against an obsessive background of death, Hamlet is the brooding, violent and tortured figure who, though a lover of drama himself, is yet too sophisticated easily to degrade his nature to the conventional role of a stage revenger. He thus becomes in part the eternal outsider, the genius of alienation whose moments of despairing lassitude so appealed to romantic critics.

Trapped in hideous circumstances and apparently bearing the intolerable burden of the duty to revenge his father's death, Hamlet is obliged to inhabit a shadow world, to live suspended between fact and fiction, language and action. His life is one of constant role-playing in a perilous world. Such an existence, like the book Hamlet is shown reading, becomes 'words, words, words'. For such a figure, soliloquy is a natural medium, a necessary release:

> To be, or not to be; that is the question:
> Whether 'tis nobler in the mind to suffer
> The slings and arrows of outrageous fortune,
> Or to take arms against a sea of troubles,
> And, by opposing, end them. To die, to sleep –
> No more, and by a sleep to say we end
> The heartache and the thousand natural shocks
> That flesh is heir to, 'tis a consummation
> Devoutly to be wished. To die, to sleep.
> To sleep, perchance to dream. Ay, there's the rub,
> For in that sleep of death what dreams may come
> When we have shuffled off this mortal coil

Must give us pause. There's the respect
That makes calamity of so long life.

In this most famous passage of Shakespearian drama, the language
of a tragic hero forced into the anguish of continual role-playing
examines the nature of action only to deny its possibility. The result
is infinite postponement and crippling uncertainty. By the time the
prince speaks his soliloquy, Denmark itself has become a nightmare
world of spying, testing and plotting. Almost everyone is playing a
role in the intricate deceits of language and action. Hamlet himself is
obliged to become a consummate actor. In the corrupt and conniving
court he must play the madman in order to force Claudius into
showing his hand. But the intense conflict of his emotions renders
Hamlet all but mad indeed. We barely know if he is acting or not.
His very words confuse communication. We see how the introspection of the subtle mind can so dwell on its own concerns that words
become detached from what they signify and, as an end in themselves,
'lose the name of action'. Action itself meanwhile, unmediated by
thought, is violent, effective, yet lacking the rational dignity with
which we would like to invest it and so give purpose to existence.
The result of this divorce between thought and action is a terrifying
insecurity, a vision which probes fundamental notions about the self
and its relation to others. Drama, as Hamlet the player prince wishes
it to, holds a mirror up to nature. The reflection it presents however is as profoundly disturbing to us as Hamlet's own play is to
Claudius.

The scene in the graveyard – a supreme achievement of Renaissance
pessimism – is a meditation on the futility of all language and action
in the face of death. Nonetheless, it is the climax of *Hamlet* that most
terrifyingly shows the divorce of words from deeds, actions from
intentions. Claudius's rigged fencing match, with its poisoned rapiers,
poisoned goblets and ironic interplay of error by which all the
principal characters die, concludes the plot with matchless narrative
skill. But this triumph of stagecraft provides no ready answers to the
play's deepest concerns. Action and meaning are nowhere more
completely divorced. Even the divine patterns of punishment and
Providence are confused and contradictory. Horatio attempts to
explain events to Fortinbras in terms of the conventions of revenge

tragedy, but it is right that in this image of an immensely complex world his words should be only a first and rough attempt to explain those forces of life and death and the morality of action which the play itself has so powerfully exposed.

It is part of the greatness of mature Shakespearian drama that the thrust of a whole play is often felt in each of its most significant episodes. When, after a furious storm, Othello arrives in Cyprus, the following exchange takes place:

> OTHELLO: O, my fair warrior!
>
> DESDEMONA: My dear Othello!
>
> OTHELLO:
>
> It gives me wonder great as my content
> To see you here before me. O my soul's joy,
> If after every tempest come such calms,
> May the winds blow till they have wakened death,
> And let the labouring barque climb hills of seas
> Olympus-high, and duck again as low
> As hell's from heaven. If it were now to die,
> 'Twere now to be most happy, for I fear
> My soul hath her content so absolute
> That not another comfort like to this
> Succeeds in unknown fate.
>
> DESDEMONA: The heavens forbid
> But that our loves and comforts should increase
> Even as our days do grow.
>
> OTHELLO: Amen to that, sweet Powers!
> I cannot speak enough of this content.
> It stops me here; it is too much of joy.
>
> *They kiss.*
>
> And this, and this, the greatest discords be
> That e'er our hearts shall make.
>
> IAGO (*aside*): O, you are well tuned now,
> But I'll set down the pegs that make this music,
> As honest as I am.

This small episode brings together the three chief actors in the drama. We see, in Dr Johnson's words, 'the fiery openness of Othello, magnanimous, artless, and credulous, boundless in his confidence, ardent in his affection, inflexible in his resolution and obdurate in his revenge'. Desdemona's fidelity and love are transparent. In Iago's aside we hear what Coleridge described as his 'motiveless malignity'. Iago is the consummate actor and contriver of scenes who tempts the hero to betray his greatness to 'the green-eyed monster' and so live a life of anguished jealousy in which he believes Cassio is Desdemona's lover.

Most dramatically of all, we can envisage the storm as an augury of the anguish about to fall on hero and heroine alike. The heaving seas that here quieten to happiness tragically prefigure the 'steep-down gulfs of liquid fire' which will torment Othello in eternity. The kiss that silences language in loving ecstasy – a perfect union of opposites – is in all-too-tragic contrast to those which Othello gives Desdemona before he murders her and as he himself is dying. The height of happiness is indeed the moment to begin destruction, and Iago's aside suggests the divine harmony of love he will help bring to dissonant chaos. His language of lies will create a world of false roles and hideous action.

With jealousy and the destruction of Othello's magnificence comes raging evil. Subtle variations of torture reduce him to a thing of fury and mindless language. The love that united man and woman, youth and maturity, black and white, in marriage and resplendent oratory is shattered into its warring opposites. In calling Desdemona a 'whore', Othello breaks her heart with a word. Never seriously doubting his 'honest Iago', he is unaware that the Devil's greatest trick is to convince us he doesn't exist.

This most subtly plotted of tragedies moves inexorably to the murder, to the ghastly revelations of the truth, and Othello's final anguished question to Iago as to 'Why he hath thus ensnared my soul and body'. But the purposes of evil are smothered in silence. The question remains unanswered. Nonetheless, it is out of this silence that Othello himself rises to the brief but massive dignity of tragic self-awareness and true poetry. He recaptures the nobility of language and love. Then, dying by his own hand, he falls on the lips of his murdered wife and leaves language and desire for ever. The action in Cyprus has come full circle.

Othello (1604) is a domestic tragedy wrought from the hideous entanglement of lying words. In the two related but independent versions of King Lear, language, action and role-playing are universalized into an awe-inspiring meditation on human suffering.

After an absurd competition in which Lear tries to settle the succession by dividing his kingdom, he curses his youngest and truest daughter for being unable to flatter him. While Cordelia, the pattern of integrity, refuses to distort the world through the abuse of words, her older sisters, Goneril and Regan, ruthlessly separate language from intention. Having protested a love they do not feel, they then callously abandon their ageing father. Calling down chaos, dispossessed of all that naturally raises man above the level of beasts, Lear is forced on to the storm-racked heath. Here, in the holocaust of the elements and his own mind, he is finally stripped of sanity, kingly role and the normal syntax of thought and speech. The natural bonds of the world are sundered. Chaos is a universal anguish:

EDGAR: Do, de, de, de. Sese! Come, march to wakes and fairs And market towns. Poor Tom, thy horn is dry.

LEAR: Then let them anatomize Regan; see what breeds about her heart. Is there any cause in nature that makes these hard-hearts? (*To Edgar*) You, sir, I entertain for one of my hundred, only I do not like the fashion of your garments. You will say they are Persian; but let them be changed.

KENT: Now, good my lord, lie here and rest awhile.

LEAR: Make no noise, make no noise. Draw the curtains. So, so. We'll go to supper i'the morning.

[*He sleeps*]

FOOL: And I'll go to bed at noon.

Enter the Duke of Gloucester

GLOUCESTER: Come hither, friend. Where is the King my master?

KENT: Here, sir, but trouble him not; his wits are gone.

The convergence of the main plot and subplots of *King Lear* in this meeting of the dispossessed, the insane and the feigning mad is one of the most profoundly disturbing scenes in Renaissance drama. Shakespeare uses the stage to imagine the destruction of some of the central tenets of his culture. Language, the measure of rational man, is destroyed. The role of the king as the focus of justice and authority is reduced to agonized parody. The framework of the world is wrecked, while benighted man, stripped to his essential nature, is glimpsed as nothing more than 'a poor, bare forked animal'.

The very scale of *King Lear* seems to re-enact the apparently infinite duration of true suffering, and the play's final tableau becomes a tragic inversion of the opening. A foolish king, enthroned in power and vanity before his daughters at the start, is now the sufferer before the bodies of Goneril and Regan, who have been destroyed in their mutual wickedness, and Cordelia, borne on to the stage by Lear himself. In the fullness of his grief, the king dies. Edgar, risen to heroic stature through suffering but aware that no language can give adequate public expression to the end of this tragic world, is left to take on the burdensome role of king.

Where *King Lear* shows men and women in their vanity and foolishness wrenching language from its true relation to the world and so bringing about universal chaos, *Macbeth* (1606) is Shakespeare's study in the destruction wrought from the supernatural language of diabolic prophecy. The play is his most powerful study in evil. We watch the fall of a noble mind into temptation and see worldly power won and lost at the price of damnation. If the prophecies of the Witches who appear before the hero at the start of the play appear to tell the truth, it is humankind who will translate their words into deeds and so surrender free will to sin.

In contrast to Macbeth's very real doubt and fear when confronted with the language of evil, his wife believes that through the power of words alone she can summon up the forces of hell and so personify the ruthlessness to which she aspires:

> The raven himself is hoarse
> That croaks the fatal entrance of Duncan
> Under my battlements. Come, you spirits
> That tend on mortal thoughts, unsex me here,
> And fill me from the crown to the toe top-full
> Of direst cruelty. Make thick my blood,
> Stop up th' access and passage to remorse,
> That no compunctious visitings of nature
> Shake my fell purpose, nor keep peace between
> Th' effect and it. Come to my woman's breasts,
> And take my milk for gall, you murd'ring ministers,
> Wherever in your sightless substances
> You wait on nature's mischief. Come, thick night,

And pall thee in the dunnest smoke of hell,
That my keen knife see not the wound it makes,
Nor heaven creep through the blanket of the dark
To cry, 'Hold, hold!'

Lady Macbeth's soliloquy before the arrival of King Duncan at her castle develops the play's images of night and the unnatural with the hypnotic power that characterizes them throughout. Nonetheless, by falsely casting herself in a role beyond human nature, Lady Macbeth works her own destruction. If she can taunt Macbeth, provide his alibis and excuse his wild behaviour when he is greeted by Banquo's ghost, she ends the play a pathetic wraith, broken by the insanity and guilt which eventually drive her to suicide. Evil is wholly self-destructive, and the language with which Lady Macbeth summoned up its forces creates a role whose only outcome is despair.

But the more terrible role is Macbeth's. The hero's finer moral sense tortures him with the full import of his enormity. He knows the depths he plumbs. Nowhere is this awareness more desperate than in Macbeth's second encounter with the Witches. He is the man who has murdered his sanctified king and, as the Porter scene suggests, turned his castle into hell. His stolen country is a purgatory of spying and whispering, while he himself is tortured by conscience and the ghosts of the slain who prophesy about the young who have escaped his murderous grasp. Now, in sleepless torment, Macbeth returns to the first sources of his destruction.

Again he commands the Witches to speak. Again they tell him equivocal truths. And, just as in the initial encounter the Witches' first prophecy immediately came true, so now Macbeth's suspicions of Macduff are at once confirmed. Macbeth is told of his flight to England and is obliged to realize that his actions are not all-powerful. In panic and despair, he abandons reason to mindless savagery. The firstlings of his heart become the firstlings of his hand. Language and thought no longer temper action. The role of man is abandoned for the merely bestial. Macbeth surprises Macduff's castle and orders the wholesale murder of his wife, children and servants.

Nonetheless, in the closing scenes, as Macbeth is surrounded by the triumphant forces of good, so Shakespeare manages to recapture something of our sympathy for the tyrant and mass murderer. He does so through the poetry Macbeth speaks. Macbeth's soliloquy 'Tomorrow, and tomorrow, and tomorrow' conveys a pessimism absolute in its strength and world-weary majesty. Both terror and pity are roused by the tragic hero. Yet the final images of a man so diminished by sin emphasize his degradation. Macbeth is reduced to a trapped animal as his castle is surrounded. The import of the Witches' equivocal promises of safety is revealed and, at the last, Macbeth's severed head is borne in on a pole – a grisly nothing in a world the young will have to rebuild.

Antony and Cleopatra (1606) takes an empire for its stage and the giants of history for its characters. Shakespeare created his most sumptuous tragedy out of the final struggle to establish Rome's world domination. It is a struggle fought by an Antony torn between his roles as the great lover and the great soldier; Egypt's queen, who alluringly combines both nobility and whorishness; and Octavius Caesar, the young and cold machiavellian playing for the highest political stakes. The might of Rome is thus pitted against the seductions of an Egypt at once debilitating yet glorious.

Such irreducible contradictions are present in the characters themselves and generate the dramatic conflict. For Antony, to neglect an empire or fight for its mastery is in part a gambit in the pursuit of love, in part an assertion of his military self-respect. Cleopatra is both the temptress who effeminizes his valour and the inspiration for whom alone he will make his wars. Hence the tragic paradox of glory and shame, and our ambivalent response to the confused yet heroic leader. Indeed, it is possible to see both characters as trapped in the ethos, language and gesture of a chivalry that is at once romantic yet unstably rooted in sex and blood-lust, a response to life at once richly imaginative and yet constantly brought into question by the age and worldliness of its adherents. Language, action and role-play are again tragically at variance with reality, and the ambiguities exposed are both heroic and profoundly moving.

Worldly defeat raises both Antony and Cleopatra to poetic victory. The greatness of Antony is measured by his generosity to the defecting Enobarbus, by the pathos of his own botched suicide and by the power of the poetry in which the dying hero enshrines his vision of greatness and eternal reconciliation:

> Stay for me.
> Where souls do couch on flowers we'll hand in hand,
> Dido and her Aeneas shall want troops,
> And all the haunt be ours.

The last act is Cleopatra's own and is an achievement of sublime tragic pathos. Cleopatra, rising in final fixedness of purpose to die in Roman suicide, presents a tableau of transforming majesty. We see her as a woman commanded by common passion to uncommon glory. Even Caesar is moved, and at the close, the cold voice of the *pax Romana* pays passion its lasting tribute while ushering in a time of universal peace.

Antony and Cleopatra is a tragedy of lavish spectacle, but literary convention also allowed tragedy to be combined with satire. *Timon of Athens* (1605) is Shakespeare's bitterest essay in both. Rejected by the Athenians in his hour of need, the erstwhile lavish Timon cannot compromise with a city so fundamentally immoral. He rejects her with an absoluteness that reveals itself in a language of terrible misanthropy – an exile from all mankind. Timon now has no role to play beyond being the mouthpiece of hatred. Nonetheless, in the terrible anger of wounded innocence, the self-destructive rage that can end only in death, Timon also comes close to the great, indifferent forces of the natural world. Leaving his curse engraved on his tomb by the sea, Timon finds a final, awesome silence and an eternal language of hate.

Coriolanus (1608), the last of Shakespeare's major tragedies, is again a searching meditation on man's place within the life and language of the community and the self-destructive nature of exile from these. Though not a popular play, the very real greatness of the work lies in Shakespeare's unillusioned view of man in the fitful duplicity, spite and occasional heroism of his political being.

The hero is pre-eminently a man of action, and his actions are devoted to the patriotic support of aristocratic Rome. When he turns to speak to the plebeians (people on the desperate edge of starvation) the violence of his language reveals a man whose very strengths make him a danger to the state. After his victory over the Volsces and their leader Tullus Aufidius at Corioli, the hero is led in triumph through his native city to be given high office and receive the ambiguous name of Coriolanus. That most intimate of words — a name — identifies the hero with the enemy. And it is to the enemy that Coriolanus deserts when, after refusing to show due humility to a populace manipulated by the deceitful Tribunes, he turns his back on his city. Despising the political manipulation of language, proud in his heroic isolation, Coriolanus takes on the role of Rome's greatest enemy and dedicates his actions to her destruction. In his pride, he believes he is beyond the reach of human sympathy. His language, actions and role have become hideously wrenched from their true aim.

Despite the imagery of god-like power and bestial monstrosity that envelops him — images which point to his dehumanized state — Coriolanus remains a man. Words can touch him and his emotions can be stirred. In a scene of great rhetorical power, his mother comes to him in the enemy camp and pleads for her native city. At the supreme moment of his unnaturalness, and when he is about to destroy all that gave him life, Coriolanus discovers his humanity. Tullus Aufidius however uses this moment of seeming weakness to strip his enemy of his name and then destroy him. Shakespeare's impartial, tragic gaze here achieves a final and pitiless objectivity towards political man trapped in the deceits of language, action and role.

IO

Great artists take great risks. With Shakespeare this is pre-eminently so, and several of his plays from the first years of the seventeenth century, straining at the limits of form, do not fit easily into the conventional types of tragedy, comedy and history. These works are sometimes referred to as 'problem' plays, a loose category which has the merit of focusing attention on literary experiment.

Such experiment clearly underlies the earliest of these plays: *Troilus and Cressida* (1602). In this long and highly intellectual work, the great heroes of Greek epic and Chaucerian romance are exposed through a sceptical analysis which both uses and tests the various languages of satire and social comedy, high rhetoric and Petrarchan ardour. The epic voice of the Prologue suggests one approach to the play's familiar subject, but as we see Troilus's passion juxtaposed to Pandarus's comic vulgarity and then listen to the long and brilliantly contrived debates in the Greek and Trojan camps, so we become aware of vain and decadent societies, of men acting out highly contrived roles beneath which fester the cruder forces of lust, ambition and pride.

Language and intention are thus terribly at variance as men hungry for sex and power play out their ostentatiously sophisticated roles in a corrupt and brittle world. Ulysses is a restless political manipulator, Achilles a destructive sophisticate, Hector a vain aristocrat trapped in the ruthless illusions of chivalry. Even Troilus, the most poignant of lovers, is not immune to these deceits, while Helen herself – the subject of the war – is the most empty-headed and frivolous of women. As a result, we come to appreciate the satirical Thersites's view of the Trojan war: 'All the argument is a whore and a cuckold; a good quarrel to draw emulous factions and bleed to death upon.' Beneath the intense verbalism of the characters and their constant parade of roles there thus lie actions of impulsive violence and treachery, lust and death. The result is a deeply disturbing play whose disillusioned moral intricacy, emphasizing the importance of ethical issues, refuses easy categorization.

A similar moral complexity is achieved in *Measure for Measure* (1603). Here we are moved by some of Shakespeare's most emotionally powerful and reflective poetry, drawn into some of his most painful dramatic encounters and yet beguiled by low-life comedy and a narrative artifice that does not balk at the wildest coincidence and most patent contrivance. As a result, a simple approach to *Measure for Measure* is condemned by the sheer variety of the text. Our attitude to both the characters and the narrative must be ambivalent. For instance, while the humane but lax Duke Vincentio may be criticized for allowing Vienna to fall into moral decay, that very decay has an earthy, life-enhancing bawdy which the duke is right to view more compassionately than the narrowly legalistic and hypocritical deputy he appoints in his place. Again, the coldly virtuous Angelo to whom the duke entrusts his powers, and who is betrayed into lustful cruelty by the limited experience of his heart, nonetheless touches us in his anguished moments of self-awareness. Isabella, the object of his desires, seems to suffer from spiritual pride in the very intensity of her religious vocation, yet through a narrative of elaborate comic subterfuge she develops to a sincere and moving awareness of true Christian charity.

Her brother Claudio, condemned by a judge more pernicious than himself, again moves through ambiguous areas of experience. Though he is eventually saved and allowed to marry his pregnant betrothed, Claudio first has to face in their extremity two opposed attitudes to death. On the one hand there is the measured stoicism of Vincentio's speech when he appears to Claudio disguised as a friar. On the other is the unforgettable terror of death with which Claudio himself pleads to his sister, the virgin novice, begging her to surrender her body to Angelo and so save her brother at the cost of all she holds most dear.

Such moral problems are so painful in their presentation as to border on tragedy, and yet they are resolved through comic manipulation. We are delighted and amazed at the play's final happy outcome. Throughout, we are made aware of an emphasis on compassion, the refusal readily to judge others and the belief that as we treat our fellows so we ourselves shall be treated, measure for measure. In thus combining moral profit with delight, Shakespeare's text fulfils the underlying requirements of Renaissance humanist literature, doing so with unmatched virtuosity and dazzling theatrical experiment which constantly draws attention to the play itself as a highly sophisticated work of artifice.

In *Measure for Measure*, Angelo is tricked into believing he has slept with Isabella. Only at the close of the play is it revealed to him that she was replaced in the dark by Mariana, Angelo's jilted betrothed whom he is then obliged to marry. This curious motif of the 'bed trick' – something which, like the play itself, is at once artificial yet deeply satisfying to our sense of justice – is also used in *All's Well that Ends Well*. This play greatly develops the sense of wonder, of something timeless and universal, which goes with such ancient motifs of story-telling as the 'bed trick' itself, the virgin with powers to heal an old and sickly king, loss, restoration and recognition, potent youth and wise and wintry age. Such elements are here juxtaposed to sharply observed worldly detail: the problems of class, the crudely masculine existence of the worldly Parolles, and the callous immaturity of Bertram who is loved by Helena, a maid of lower degree. Hence in part the 'problematic' nature of *All's Well that Ends Well*: its sense of specific context and, underlying this, of something more potently universal that Shakespeare was to explore in the matchless poetry of his final romances.

II

In addition to writing the lost *Cardenio* (performed 1613) and *Henry VIII*, and collaborative work on *Pericles* (*c.* 1608) and *The Two Noble Kinsmen* (1612–13), the three great plays of Shakespeare's final years are *Cymbeline* (1609–10), *The Winter's Tale* (1609–10) and *The Tempest* (1611). Each of these reveals profound and continuing experiment and an artistic intelligence of the highest order seizing on the new, pushing at the frontiers of drama and constantly delighting an audience.

The plays draw on and develop a widespread contemporary taste for romance, for narratives whose melodramatic unlikeliness can yet convey a subtle and poetic apprehension of the deep-seated desires released by the ancient motifs of fiction. For some critics, the plays' concern with loss and renewal provides an 'answer' to Shakespeare's tragic vision. For others, often with a varying Christian or anthropological emphasis, they are seen as myths and parables of reconciliation. Some critics consider their elaborate stage effects as a response to the tastes of the élite Blackfriars audience, while others again, concentrating on genre, read the plays in terms of pastoral tragicomedy.

Cymbeline reveals an extraordinary virtuosity in the handling of a rich and highly involved narrative. No great play was ever a representation of a more complex action, and part of the pleasure the work offers in the theatre lies in just the brilliance with which Shakespeare solved the formidable technical problems such a narrative presents. The unfolding of incident through the great romance themes of treachery, separation and disguise defeats adequate synopsis, and yet the audience is never aware of confusion. Rather, the intense involvement required is inherently pleasurable and at one with appreciating the facility with which Shakespeare constructed his most elaborate denouement.

The Winter's Tale again reveals a daringly experimental approach to its material and effects. The title suggests that the play is no more than an incredible trifle (much like an old wives' tale) but it also points to a concern with how the human pattern of tragically destructive anger and loving redemption is mirrored by the seasonal cycle of winter's transformation into spring. Perdita, the child and woman lost and found, symbolizes the latter in the great scene of pastoral activity in Act IV, an extraordinary combination of skilful narrative dramaturgy, sophisticated intellectual delight, comedy and quiet, radiant innocence. It is at the close however, when, in a moment of the most rare and refined illusion, the statue of Hermione comes to life before her repentant husband's gaze, that Shakespeare's concern with fairy-tale and artifice is at one with an archetypal intuition of forgiveness, reconciliation and love.

Nonetheless, it is *The Tempest* that remains the most beautiful as well as the most sophisticated of these late plays. Great poetry here creates the magic which is in part the work's medium, while the deftly imaginative artifice results in Shakespeare's most advanced essay in illusion and reality. Indeed, many of the abiding themes of his career are gathered into this work to be given final expression in a play at once delightful, profound and endlessly elusive.

The social chaos on the tempest-tossed ship of the opening scene, for example, suggests the preoccupation with anarchy evident from Shakespeare's earliest history plays, but then, when we learn that the storm has been raised by Prospero's magic in the attempt to gain power over those who have usurped his dukedom, so themes of illusion and reality, of language as a form of power and of the role of the revenger come to the fore. We see Prospero the Renaissance magus or magician as the Shakespearian hero trying to manipulate the world through words. Yet his own presence on the island itself is a usurpation over the altogether more primal world of Caliban and the spirit Ariel, temporarily and often rebelliously subdued to his employment. The magic and fantasy, the play's world of song and youthful love, are thus permeated by a powerful recognition of evil, by intricate moral ambiguity, the constant threat of violence and, above all, by a pervasive sense of enigma, illusion and metamorphosis. Mortality and stage spectacle, life and art, become inseparable:

> These our actors,
> As I foretold you, were all spirits, and
> Are melted into air, into thin air;
> And like the baseless fabric of this vision,
> The cloud-capped towers, the gorgeous palaces,
> The solemn temples, the great globe itself,
> Yea, all which it inherit, shall dissolve;
> And, like this insubstantial pageant faded,
> Leave not a rack behind. We are such stuff
> As dreams are made on, and our little life
> Is rounded with a sleep.

The world as a stage and the stage as a world evaporate in the very poetry that has created them.

At the close of the play, when Prospero forgives his enemies, abjures the role and language of the magician and hands the resolution of the action to the audience, his farewell to his art is read by many as Shakespeare's farewell to his. This is a pleasing but unlikely fantasy. Shakespeare's work is never so openly autobiographical. Indeed, on the level of personality, England's greatest poet remains her most enigmatic. In studying the works we come no nearer to the man. Rather, Shakespeare is so wholly absorbed in his art – in the imaginative exploration of mankind through the dramatist's resources of language, action, and role-play – that what we do come to appreciate is the inexhaustible richness of human invention itself. In the noble words of Ben Jonson: 'He was not of an age, but for all time.'

12

The tribute paid to Shakespeare by Jonson (1572–1637) was the more generous for the rivalry he felt towards the greater man, but if Jonson awarded Shakespeare the honours of posterity he gained for himself some of those offered by his age. He was effectively Poet Laureate (pensioned but not titled) and, though his later years were spent in poverty, the nobility of England attended his funeral in recognition of his genius.

Jonson – convivial, critical, the pundit of his age – remains a fine writer of lyric, a great satirist and a major figure in that classical and humanist tradition of literature which stretches from Sidney, through Milton and Dryden, to the other Johnson and Gray. That this tradition of humane, decorous, yet profoundly experienced poetry was also the standard by which to satirize his times is given dramatic form in Jonson's *Poetaster* (1601) where the serene values of Virgil and Horace are juxtaposed to seventeenth-century pretenders to art.

Jonson's two surviving tragedies derive from Roman history. The first is by far the greater, though neither was a popular success. *Sejanus* (1603) presents the emperor Tiberius's bestial reign of terror in a Rome where, amid parasites and fearful hypocrites – people swollen to distortion with their desire for power – liberty, language and human worth are crushed in the self-destructive intricacy of machination. In *Catiline* (1611), Jonson shows the working of conspiracy with an even darker and more self-conscious scholarship, but the play cannot be counted a dramatic success, and it is in his comedies of city life that we find Jonson's most telling portrayal of human folly. These works were profoundly influenced by classical theory. They also relate to a rich and varied native tradition which they effortlessly transcend. To this last we should briefly turn.

The rapid expansion of population and mercantile activity in London was a leading phenomenon of the age, and theatres like the Fortune produced plays designed to please the merchant classes. The immensely prolific Thomas Heywood (?1575–c. 1641), for example, wrote *The Four Prentices of London* (c. 1592–1600) in which the heroes are noble yet 'of city trades they have no scorn'. In the second part of his *If You Know Not Me You Know Nobody* (1605), praise of the great merchant Sir Thomas Gresham combines with intense patriotism. Domestic virtue and moral edification are again central to *Old Fortunatus* (1599) by Thomas Dekker (?1572–1632), while in the same year Dekker produced *The Shoemaker's Holiday* in which imaginative comic prose, romance and touching marital fidelity are allied to the eternally comfortable story of an apprentice's rise to the position of Lord Mayor.

Dekker's seemingly unlikely collaboration with the tragedian Webster in *Westward Ho!* (1604) and *Northward Ho!* (1605) led him beyond the praise of 'a fine life, a velvet life, a careful life'. Others were actively to criticize citizen tastes in drama however, and the most lasting exposure of the works produced for this market is *The Knight of the Burning Pestle* (1607) by Francis Beaumont (1584-1616). This piece is both a kind-hearted burlesque and a clever exercise on the idea of the play within the play. Contrasts between chivalry, modern aristocratic values and merchant ideals here centre around the sympathetic figure of Rafe, the apprentice and comic knight errant.

A more bitterly satirical humour is to be found in the comedies of George Chapman (c. 1560-1634) and John Marston (1576-1634). Cynicism is a marked tone in Chapman's work in the form, while Marston's comedies are the work of a verse satirist and reveal the aggressive and twisted syntax characteristic of that genre. Jonson himself came into collision with Marston and Dekker in the so-called 'war of the theatres'. He had already completed Nashe's *The Isle of Dogs* (1597) and been imprisoned for sedition as a result. Shortly after finishing the first version of *Every Man in his Humour* (1598, revised by 1616) he duelled with a fellow actor, killed him, and only escaped the gallows through a legal technicality. In *Every Man Out of his Humour* (1599) – a drama of plays within plays which discusses the problems of play writing and then satirizes the nature of satire – Jonson lightly criticized Marston in the figure of Clove. Marston himself had recently essayed an unfortunate eulogy of Jonson in his revision of the anti-theatrical diatribe *Histriomastix* (c. 1599), a portrait which is in fact nearer to parody.

Marston retaliated to the figure of Clove with an open caricature of Jonson in *Jack Drum's Entertainment* (c. 1600). He received his rebuff in *Cynthia's Revels* (1600), a boys' company play satirizing the follies of the court. The work is reminiscent of Lyly, and contains the exquisite lyric 'Queen and huntress, chaste and fair'. Jonson's *Poetaster*, written for Paul's Boys, presents caricatures of Marston and Dekker among the pretenders to art in Augustan Rome and triumphed completely over Marston's *What You Will* (c. 1601). Dekker was now recruited on Marston's side with his *Satiromastix* (1601), but Jonson himself tried to rise above the fray with *Sejanus*. Then – such is the abiding nature of the literary world – he collaborated with Marston and Chapman in *Eastward Ho!* (1605), voluntarily joining his co-authors in prison when the play was considered seditious. However, in the following year, the King's Men gave a triumphantly successful performance of Jonson's *Volpone*, one of the great comic masterpieces of the English stage.

All Jonson's immense energies are focused in *Volpone* where he deals with one of his most characteristic themes: the corruption wrought by greed on those obsessive and fantastic creatures who dupe each other on the lunatic fringes of an enterprise culture. 'This', Jonson wrote, 'is the money-get mechanic age', and Volpone's cunning scheme for getting money makes gold itself the object of a parody religion.

As a rich man without heirs, Volpone adds to his wealth through the bribes offered the apparently dying man by those hoping for an advantageous mention in his will. To secure this, people will disinherit their children, pervert the law and prostitute their wives. Volpone's bedroom becomes the centre of inverted human values where money is gained without real work, innocence is all but corrupted by glittering lust, and men are reduced to the foxes, flies, vultures, ravens and crows which give them their names.

To draw his heroic caricature of materialism, Jonson turned to a wide range of sources, his classical training especially. There was nothing frigid or pedantic about this. He confined his play largely within the unities of time (twenty-four hours), place (Venice) and action (the refusal to admit material distracting from the main narrative) not because Renaissance scholars believed Aristotle had promulgated such rules as laws. He did it because these devices help concentrate the dramatic excitement. Again, Jonson did not reduce his characters to types because Terence and Plautus had done so, but because an overmastering obsession or 'humour' caricatures itself, as the anonymous writers of medieval Morality plays had been aware. If older forms helped give a framework, the foundation of *Volpone* is passionate observation.

As a result, Volpone himself throbs with something of his creator's vitality. He relishes his own play-acting, his frequent disguises and performances which eventually lead to his undoing and that of his parasite Mosca. As a result, the effect of the play is far from simple. The energy of corruption is infectious, and if we are pleased that the villain is exposed by means of his own designs, then the worthlessness of the Venetian authorities who clap him in irons gives justice itself an ironic final twist.

Epicoene, or The Silent Woman (1609) is again concerned with man as a social (or antisocial) animal. Morose tries to shelter himself from the world's din, declaring: 'All discourses, but mine own, afflict me; they seem harsh, impertinent and irksome.' The world appears to justify his misanthropy. Morose tries to disinherit his nephew by marrying an apparently silent bride. She turns out, however, to be first a scold and then a boy in disguise. The comedy ends in separation rather than marriage, while its sexual ambiguities may be a taunt at the Puritans' objection to the portrayal of female roles in the theatre by boys.

The Alchemist (1610) again concerns itself with distorting dreams of gold. It is constructed in brilliant conformity to the unities and, in its earthy and imaginative richness of contemporary dialogue and folly, embodies Jonson's ideal of a comedy which employs

> deeds, and language, such as men do use,
> And persons, such as Comedy would choose
> When she would show an image of the times,
> And sport with human follies, not with crimes.

The particular folly here is the lure of easy money: Sir Epicure Mammon's dream that through the philosopher's stone he can 'turn the age to gold'. Interestingly, it is not alchemy itself that is satirized but the attitude which sees science (which alchemy was still widely held to be) as a fulfilment of fantasy. Face, Subtle and his consort Doll Common – rogues who have employed Lovewit's house for their purpose – are adepts in manipulating vain desires in a variety of characters: Epicure Mammon himself, Abel Drugger the tobacconist, Kastril the roistering boy and the comic Puritans Ananias and Tribulation Wholesome. The real transformations in *The Alchemist* are thus not of base metal into gold but of human folly into absurdity. When the off-stage laboratory finally blows up, fantasy explodes with it. The return of Lovewit brilliantly resolves the action but hardly restores official law and order.

A Puritan is again humiliated in Jonson's prose comedy *Bartholomew Fair* (1614). Zeal-of-the-Land Busy, a hypocritical creature of appetite, ends up in the stocks. The dramatic re-creation of a real fair allowed Jonson to celebrate the all-licensed, topsy-turvy world of *mardi gras* with great diversity of action and a matching richness of dialogue.

The simple-minded Cokes is robbed, while Justice Adam Overdo, out to spy on 'enormities', also winds up in the stocks. Nonetheless, when he ends the play by inviting all to dine with him, the foolish Cokes insists they be accompanied by the puppet show which has already offered one of the best episodes in the play. The fair itself – its vitality memorably embodied in Ursula the Pig-woman – is Jonson's image of raucous humanity, variously hypocritical, simple, vengeful and forgiving.

The plays for the commercial theatre Jonson wrote in the later stages of his career – *The Devil Is an Ass* (1616), *The Staple of News* (1626), *The New Inn* (1629) and *The Magnetic Lady* (1632) – were harshly if not wholly inaccurately described by Dryden as his 'dotages'. A fascinating and very different aspect of Jonson's dramatic art however is revealed in the series of masques he wrote as Twelfth Night entertainments for the court of James I (1603–25). Here we see an élite drama dealing explicitly with contemporary theories of political power.

Jonson had already designed the lavish and arcane symbolism of the Scottish king's triumphal entry to his new capital, and the masques extend this exploration of James's notion of the divine right of kings: the belief that James was accountable to God alone, that his position partook of divinity and that he was endowed with supernatural wisdom. In *The Golden Age Restor'd* (1615), we see how classical learning, music, poetry, dance and the lavish sets of Inigo Jones (1573–1652) present James as Jove, the benevolent guide of the nation's fate. When the Iron Age is routed in a conventional anti-masque, Astraea or Justice heralds the return of the Golden Age. Through the Neoplatonic philosophy that underpins the Jonsonian masque, the dancing courtiers come to symbolize the completeness, harmony and peace attained by the dramatic enactment of the divine king's decrees.

The Jonsonian masque was an élite celebration of a political and cultural ideal. For many, however, these sumptuous illusions disguised a more troubled reality. Though the court encouraged the highest cultural sophistication, its moral tone was low and corruption and factionalism were rife. James's assertion of divine right gave a dangerous edge to the royal prerogative, while his reckless expenditure led to increasing debt in a period of economic uncertainty and bad harvests. Further, while the king (an enthusiastic amateur theologian) failed to satisfy moderate Puritan demands for church reform, his rash creation of new titles (partly as an attempt to raise money) exacerbated a deep sense of status insecurity in a society where ancient notions of hierarchy were being eroded by the power of money and capital. This uncertainty is reflected in the work of a number of Jacobean comic writers.

The 'city' comedies of Thomas Middleton (?1580–1627), for example, combine the idiom of London life and its pace with deft plotting and realistic satire. Middleton is consistently ironic about the rabidly acquisitive London of his time. Merchants, usurers, idle aristocrats and an extravagant gentry are all exposed in a world where it is increasingly the cleverest rather than the most virtuous who succeed. In *A Trick to Catch the Old One* (1605), surface cleverness works alongside deeper moral concerns with something of the force of the *exempla* in contemporary Puritan sermons. *A Mad World, my Masters* (1605) represents the marriage of a whore to a dupe, while in *A Chaste Maid in Cheapside* (1611) sex is traded for money as the appetites and restless folly of city life control the gulls and cheats who populate it. Philip Massinger (1583–1640) borrowed the plot of *A Trick to Catch the Old One* in *A New Way to Pay Old Debts* (1621), turning it to different and Jonsonian purposes in the humiliation of the great comic figure of Sir Giles Overreach, the loan shark. Overreach is the focus of Massinger's violent and deeply conservative satire on a corrupt Jacobean world, a world where titles are sold to the *nouveaux riches* and, as traditional social ties collapse, so madness looms.

13

'Horror waits on princes.' This phrase by the Jacobean playwright John Webster (?1580–?1625) suggests the claustrophobic world of moral confusion, lust, revenge and bloodshed characteristic of many of Shakespeare's contemporaries and successors in tragedy. While these motifs had been fundamental to the genre from the time of Kyd, they were frequently given an added force in the work of later writers by their relation to what was widely seen as the profligate and corrupting power of the Jacobean court.

Such disquiet can be felt in *The Revenger's Tragedy* (1606). Some attribute this piece to Thomas Middleton, others consider it to be the work of Cyril Tourneur (?1575–1626) whose only other known play is *The Atheist's Tragedy* (1609). This last may be a somewhat confused attempt to rework the themes of the earlier drama on a philosophic basis.

The title of *The Revenger's Tragedy* suggests familiar Jacobean motifs but not the extraordinary energy of the work's intense, image-laden language of horror and satire in which the deceits of human vengeance are contrasted (not always with the greatest dramatic facility) to the divine punishment of lust and greed. The play alludes strongly to the contemporary social situation, relating the luxury and self-indulgence of the court to the breakdown of traditional stability. The world of the play seems set on an irreversible course to damnation. 'It is our blood to err, though hell gape wide.' This almost Calvinist sense of predestined suffering is heightened by strong visual effects: torchlit processions of the corrupt, murder amid revelry, and a revenger carrying the skull of his poisoned mistress. This last is the symbol of the vanity of all worldly effort, and the hero addresses it in a justly famous soliloquy:

> Does the silk-worm expend her yellow labours
> For thee? for thee does she undo herself?
> Are lordships sold to maintain ladyships
> For the poor benefit of a bewitching minute?

With the accession of James I, dramatic criticism of society had to be written against a background of tightening censorship. In the first year of the new reign, Jonson had been summoned before the Privy Council because of the parallels drawn between *Sejanus* and the life and policies of the new king. Within three to four years, the theatrical companies all came under royal control, while censorship of critical comments on the court, foreign powers and religious controversy was a major force in narrowing the serious treatment of political, social and spiritual issues. The relative freedom of the 1590s had gone. By 1605, Jonson, along with Chapman and Marston, was under sentence of mutilation for the criticisms contained in *Eastward Ho!*.

Chapman's own tragedies are the recondite works of a deeply learned poet, and plays such as *Bussy d'Ambois* (1604, revised ?1610) concern the relation of the great man to cosmic harmony. To describe this, Chapman drew on Marlowe, the Morality play, Seneca and Giordano Bruno's *Spaccio della Bestia Trionfante* ('The Expulsion of the Triumphant Beast'), an influential and arcane work much read in the court circles to which Chapman was attached. Bussy is both the idealist and the malcontent whose mission is to cleanse the Augean stables of the world, a world which traps him in its corrupt workings. Chapman views Bussy as a hero whose great and illicit passions, if they work his own destruction, nonetheless make him superior to the other characters by virtue of their relation to spiritual truth.

Webster praised Chapman for his 'full and heightn'd style', placing him alongside his other masters: Jonson, Shakespeare, Dekker, Heywood and the partnership of Beaumont and Fletcher. Webster thus offers his work as a drama rooted in the theatrical practice of his time and drawing on the widest range of example. His work can also be seen as part of the protest against corruption and tyranny at court. Nonetheless, for all the surface allure of Webster's drama – its rich and vivid language of moral exhaustion, its flashes of realistic characterization and its appearance of advanced ethical disillusion – his work is too often merely factitious, the product of Bernard Shaw's 'Tussaud laureate'.

Webster's two major tragedies – *The White Devil* (c. 1612) and *The Duchess of Malfi* (c. 1613) – employ the sensational, machiavellian intrigues of corrupt Italian courts and exploit the opportunities these afforded for satire and the analysis of the morality of revenge. Flamineo, Webster's scholar-villain in *The White Devil*, carries much of the burden of his author's scepticism, and if he has moments when he powerfully suggests a man adrift in a world without moral bearings, he is often too obviously manipulated by the plot. When the heroine – an adultress implicated in two murders – reveals herself at her trial as a pleasure-loving girl more innocent than her accusers, the sensation of dramatic irony is perhaps more important than any real moral questioning the situation may prompt.

The Duchess of Malfi dwells on torture and suffering as the heroine's brothers try to bring this woman who has married beneath her 'by degrees to mortification'. Such moral sensationalism is found again in the famous dialogue between the duchess and her tormentor when Bosola tells her that, despite her rank, the duchess is merely 'a box of worm-seed, at best, but a salvatory of green mummy!' As she rises to her moment of heroic defiance however – 'I am Duchess of Malfi still' – so we see how for Webster rank asserts itself against a vicious world. Nonetheless, Webster's final comment on the futility of action in a meaningless universe comes when, dying at the hands of a lunatic, Bosola tells how he killed the wrong man in the dark and by accident. The tragic and ironic are equally balanced. As Webster wrote in his tragicomedy *The Devil's Law-Case* (*c.* 1617): 'rareness and difficulty give estimation'. This self-conscious striving for extreme effect finally vitiates the seriousness of his tragic vision.

Such contrivance links Webster with those technical preoccupations which led to the decline of Jacobean tragedy in the work of Francis Beaumont (1584–1616) and John Fletcher (1579–1625). Either singly or in partnership these men produced some fifty-four plays for the private theatres. They show a distinct narrowing of horizons, and in tragicomedies like *Philaster* (*c.* 1609) the comprehensive and profound questioning of the older dramatists has been replaced by elegant facility and a polite if shallow concern with hypothetical issues of honour and love. In *The Maid's Tragedy* (*c.* 1610), lust and erotic pathos are substitutes for passion, while dramatic issues in many other works are often resolved merely through a neat turn of the plot.

Thomas Middleton (?1570–1627) was an altogether greater playwright who, in addition to writing comedies of city life and designing pageants for the City fathers, composed the most successful and controversial political satire of the Jacobean stage: *A Game of Chess* (1624). This work bitterly exposes King James's attempt to cement a Catholic alliance through a royal marriage with Spain and suggests the critical edge of Middleton's parliamentarian, City and Puritan sympathies. To assume that every Puritan was a narrow killjoy is to miss an important element in some of the best plays of the 1630s and 1640s.

Middleton embodies this critical trend at its most successful in his two major tragedies, *Women Beware Women* (*c.* 1621) and *The Changeling* (1622). Here, a Puritan and city emphasis on personal responsibility and economic pressures, along with a subtle and probing social realism, places Middleton's heroines against a consistent and psychologically convincing background.

In *Women Beware Women*, there is careful attention to probability in the greater part of the play's sensational action. This allows Middleton to portray the tragic conflict between aristocratic ideas of love and sex on the one hand and merchant concerns on the other. Through his shrewd characterization of the nobly born Bianca, a woman who has eloped with the bourgeois Leantio whom she then abandons for her seducer the Duke of Florence, Middleton brilliantly conveys the alleged moral depravity of the Italian states, an aristocratic world whose social code is rotten to the core. To the deft portrayal of character and moral analysis is added Middleton's technical expertise. For example, Bianca is seduced while we watch a game of chess. The 'game' of lust is paralleled in the movement of the chess-pieces in a society where manipulation and skill are all-important. Bianca's subsequent descent into a remorseless vanity of corruption and murder reveals both Middleton's ability to portray women trapped in moral confusion and the effect of evil in a world where

> Lust and forgetfulness have been amongst us,
> And we are brought to nothing.

These themes also characterize *The Changeling*. This play is a collaborative work, some of the main passages and the much criticized madhouse scenes of the subplot being the work of William Rowley (*c.* 1585–1626). However, in his presentation of the relationship between Beatrice-Joanna and de Flores, Middleton suggests tragic entanglement with an absolute assurance of insight and technique.

Beatrice-Joanna, engaged to Piraquo and in love with Alsemero, is worshipped by the hideous de Flores whom she hires to murder her betrothed. To the morally shallow and spoiled girl, the murder seems at first a matter merely of giving orders, paying money and using people. Death is just a commodity. The greatness of Middleton's presentation however lies in his showing Beatrice-Joanna's at first unconscious attraction to de Flores's all-mastering sexual drive. She is stirred by the instrument of her own wickedness and then trapped by the ambiguities of language. De Flores's price for the 'deed' of murder will be Beatrice-Joanna's body. The vocabulary of death becomes the language of desire as de Flores obliges Beatrice-Joanna to realize her own depravity, even as he forces his attentions on her:

BEATRICE-JOANNA:
> Why, 'tis impossible thou canst be so wicked,
> Or shelter such a cunning cruelty,
> To make his death the murderer of my honour!
> Thy language is so bold and vicious,
> I cannot see which way I can forgive it
> With any modesty.

DE FLORES:
>   Push, you forget yourself!
> A woman dipp'd in blood and talk of modesty?

Middleton is unsurpassed in the portrayal of a morally trivial woman trapped by desire into finally recognizing the depth of her own sin as the workings of Providence drive both her and de Flores to death.

With domestic tragedies such as *The Fatal Dowry* (c. 1619) by Fletcher's collaborator Philip Massinger (1583–1640), the form becomes merely cold and parasitic, a confused combination of romance and elementary stoicism. It has lost touch with the passion first seen in *Arden of Faversham* and continued in such popular dramas as Heywood's *A Woman Killed with Kindness* (1603) and that masterly analysis of self-destruction, the anonymous *Yorkshire Tragedy* (c. 1606).

In *The Broken Heart* (1629) by John Ford (1586–?1639), stoicism and pathos are shown as the decorous way to face madness, death and 'the silent griefs which cut the heart-strings'. In *Perkin Warbeck* (1633), Ford revived the history play for an interesting study in delusion, but his most famous work is *'Tis Pity She's a Whore* (1632). Here an incestuous affair is treated as a pathetic instance of star-crossed love. While the heroine is tearfully remorseful after her pregnancy and marriage, Giovanni the free-thinking hero becomes almost a Marlovian rebel as he enters with Annabella's heart impaled on his dagger's end.

Ford is by far the best of the Caroline dramatists. With the tragedies of James Shirley (1596–1666), plot becomes virtually an end in itself, while in Sir John Suckling's *Aglaura* (1637), the refined cult of platonic love becomes the centre of an all-too-precious dramatic concern. Indeed, the great experiment in drama itself was now coming rapidly to an end. While the court beguiled its brief hours of peace with masques of increasing elaboration, voices deeply mistrustful of the theatre were becoming louder. Finally, on 2 September 1642, the traditional objections to the drama were given legal form in the *First Ordinance of the Long Parliament against Stage-Plays and Interludes*. The theatres were to remain closed for twenty years of civil war and interregnum. When they reopened, it was to new plays and wholly different values.

From Donne to Dryden

_____

I

While playwrights of the early seventeenth century were fashioning language into a supreme theatrical medium, other poets were submitting lyric, satire and elegy to a searching re-examination. The most brilliant of these figures was John Donne (1572–1631).

Donne's was a life of passionate intellectual and personal drama. Reared as a Roman Catholic in a Protestant nation state, aware of being part of a group often summoned to suffering and martyrdom, Donne called the basis of his creed in doubt and read and questioned his way towards a hard-won, restless Anglicanism. Yet the man who annotated nearly fifteen hundred works of theology and argument was no mere bookish recluse. Donne was a soldier of fortune, the author of perhaps the finest collection of love lyrics in the language and a man whose naked ambition and sheer recklessness trapped him in servile hopes of court patronage. From these he was finally called to the deanery of St Paul's and emerged as one of the most popular preachers and mighty poets of Christian salvation.

Donne's early prose *Paradoxes* (published 1633) give an indication of the manner of his thought. When he argues that 'a wise man is known by much laughing' or proves 'the gifts of the body are better than those of the mind', Donne was writing in a long-established rhetorical tradition. The plenitude of his inventiveness however suggests a sceptical fascination with the workings of reason as these are revealed through the display of wit.

Wit as ingenuity – the creation of far-fetched arguments or conceits – was a prized rhetorical achievement, and Donne's skill earned him the highest praise from his contemporaries. For later critics such as Dryden and Dr Johnson however, men working in different modes of literary decorum, such effects supposedly revealed a lack of taste which earned Donne and his followers the misleading name of 'metaphysical'. They were accused of linking together grotesque, recondite ideas, and so failing to achieve the central and classical voice of broad human experience. It took later generations of critics, first Coleridge and then T.S. Eliot, to rediscover in Donne's poetry the thought of a complex and very masculine brain, one which dwelt on the nature of its own perceptions and, by bringing a passionately critical intellect to bear on the traditions of rhetoric, revealed its force through the quality of its wit.

Such wit is often allied to worldly cynicism in Donne's Elegies and Satires, works which pay tribute to the classics by revolutionizing them. The Elegies, for example, frequently surpass their Ovidian model in the sceptical analysis of base human motive, in the sheer versatility of 'The Autumnal' and, above all, in the sensual, colloquial force, the vividly re-enacted drama of 'His Picture' and 'To his Mistress Going to Bed'. In this last work, a new style of love poetry comes to maturity as Donne re-creates the appearance of passionately articulate self-awareness:

> License my roving hands, and let them go
> Before, behind, between, above, below.
> O my America, my new found land,
> My kingdom, safeliest when with one man manned,
> My mine of precious stones, my empery,
> How blest am I in this discovering thee!
> To enter in these bonds, is to be free;
> Then where my hand is set, my seal shall be.

empery: *empire*

This passage is one of the great achievements of seventeenth-century erotic wit, a combination of passion and artifice that seems to re-create the wonder and excitement of sexual arousal itself. The woman is a virgin continent to be explored for her hidden wealth and 'manned'. Such puns, as in Shakespeare's *Sonnets*, lead to profound emotional insights. In the last line, for example, the poet in bed, naked and erect, envisages his body as a seal which, in the act of love, will validate the union of the lovers themselves. This appearance of a dramatized self – a central feature in all Donne's work – is conveyed here through a language at once knotty, colloquial and capable of supreme sensuousness. Donne's 'strong lines', as contemporaries called them, can thus be seen as a liberating force of criticism which swept away nymphs and goddesses, pining Petrarchan lovers and a mellifluousness of tone that all too easily sank to servile imitation.

In the Satires, Donne was concerned to develop what some contemporaries thought they had discovered in Latin satire: the harsh tones of classical moral outrage. In Joseph Hall's *Virgidemiarum* (1597) and his rival John Marston's *Scourge of Villanie* (1598), for example, we hear the 'savage indignation' of Juvenal and what was believed to be the dense syntax of Persius. These are re-created through the 'persona' or assumed personality of the intellectually superior malcontent. Though Donne could also clothe a moral type in the foolish fashions of the day, he had an alert sense of the relative foolishness of all human activity, whether this be the teeming life of the streets and court or his own scholarship. With 'Satire III', such scepticism becomes a matter of intense personal seriousness, for this is the work in which Donne criticized the aberrations of all Christian sects in his search for 'true religion'. The tough syntax of the poem is not a literary affectation but the voice of a great intellect in turmoil:

> To adore, or scorn an image, or protest,
> May all be bad; doubt wisely, in strange way
> To stand inquiring right, is not to stray;
> To sleep, or run wrong is. On a huge hill,
> Cragged, and steep, Truth stands, and he that will
> Reach her, about must, and about must go;
> And what the hill's suddenness resists, win so;
> Yet strive so, that before age, death's twilight,
> Thy soul rest, for none can work in that night,
> To will, implies delay, therefore do now.

Donne's wit is here the medium of his radical play of mind. It is the discourse of a restlessly argumentative intellect which dramatizes aspects of a complex and obsessive intelligence. Clearly, this is not the verse of Sidney's 'right popular philosopher' proceeding through formal logic and ornament to settled verities. An acutely questioning self-awareness has intervened to make Donne's the poetry of a highly civilized small group such as that gathered round the great literary patron Lucy, Countess of Bedford (d. 1627), a coterie that was sufficiently daring to question convention in pursuit of the fresh and tougher truths of experience. It was also a group sufficiently small to subsist on the passing of manuscripts. The greater part of Donne's poems were published posthumously by his son. They are thus the records of a poetic revolution wrought among the few.

Such qualities can be seen again in the love lyrics that make up Donne's *Songs and Sonnets*. These were probably written over some twenty years. None can be readily dated, and few if any should be given a precise biographical significance. Each however concentrates with a unique rhetoric the colloquial force and erotic passion of the other early works, while the testing, inclusive reference of their wit invariably dramatizes aspects of relationship. These may be cynical, sensuous, mystically celebratory, or give voice to a mournful sense of loss.

Donne's cynical lyrics vary between the flippancy of 'Go, and catch a falling star' and the more intricate worldly satire of 'Love's Alchemy' and the 'Farewell to love' with its ironic and closely observed analysis of the demystification of desire in post-coital enervation. Persuasions to love itself sometimes attain the outrageous casuistry of 'The Flea'. Here, a girl's loss of honour in surrendering her virginity is compared to the loss of blood suffered in a flea bite which, since the flea has bitten the poet too, mixes the blood of both man and woman in its shell, even as the lovers' bed will join their bodies.

In 'The Ecstasy', by contrast, Donne discussed with witty yet passionate rigour the deepest relation between shared spiritual love and the natural needs of the body. United, these offer that rapture which is the subject of 'The Dream' and 'The Good Morrow'. These poems are among the great celebrations of intimacy in English literature. It is perhaps in 'The Sun Rising' however that Donne's combination of stanza form and speech rhythm, observation of the world and celebration of the idea that the lovers in their bed are the world, is most wittily yet profoundly expressed. The tradition of the *aubade*, or the lover's lament for the coming of dawn, is here transformed as the poet seeks to persuade the sun to irradiate a triumphant and mutual passion:

> Thy beams, so reverend, and strong
> Why shouldst thou think?

I could eclipse and cloud them with a wink,
But that I would not lose her sight so long:
   If her eyes have not blinded thine,
    Look, and tomorrow late, tell me,
  Whether both th'Indias of spice and mine
  Be where thou left'st them, or lie here with me.
Ask for those kings whom thou saw'st yesterday,
And thou shalt hear, All here in one bed lay.

both th'Indias: *the East and West Indies*

Such deep erotic satisfaction is also the subject of 'The Anniversary', 'Love's Growth' and 'The Canonization'. In these works we again see Donne as one of the supreme analysts of passion fulfilled, a man drawing on the notions of scholasticism for conceits that convey a sense of wonder all the more miraculous for the sceptical intellect that apprehends it.

Such learned references in Donne's poetry were drawn from a memory stocked with the arcana and commonplaces of science and theology, and were then juxtaposed to sharply immediate perception. By a transforming paradox, this meeting of opposites frequently 'interinanimates' both, and from this flows a new awareness of the complexity of experience. In poems such as 'The Canonization', for example, the doctrine of the intercession of saints suggests how rare yet spiritually powerful is a mutual human relationship. In 'Air and Angels', adapting Aquinas's belief that God permits the heavenly hosts to assume a body of condensed air in order to appear to men, Donne shows a lover's progress between a too acute sensuousness and a too ethereal idealism:

    Every thy hair for love to work upon
  Is much too much, some fitter must be sought;
    For, nor in nothing, nor in things
  Extreme, and scatt'ring bright, can love inhere;
    Then as an angel, face, and wings
  Of air, not pure as it, yet pure doth wear,
    So thy love may be my love's sphere;
      Just such disparity
  As is 'twixt air and angels' purity,
'Twixt women's love, and men's will ever be.

Love itself is here irradiated with a sense of the divine. But if Donne's is a voice of celebration, he is occasionally a great poet of love's defeat. We see this particularly in 'Twicknam Garden' and, above all, in one of his finest works, 'A Nocturnal upon S. Lucy's Day, Being the Shortest Day'. Here the desolation of a love occluded by death offers a sense of universal loss, the nothingness of the bereaved and learned self as it seeks a greater darkness in which to prepare for spiritual truth:

> Since she enjoys her long night's festival,
> Let me prepare towards her, and let me call
> This hour her vigil, and her eve, since this
> Both the year's, and the day's deep midnight is.

With the death of the beloved, the poet becomes an eremite devoted to the holy service of his departed saint.

Although such poems seem to touch an unworldly ardour, Donne was in fact very much concerned with the world at this stage of his career. Hence his writing of verse letters, obsequies and occasional pieces to aristocratic figures. These can sometimes seem mannered and over-ingeniously flattering when compared to his major and more popular work. Nonetheless, while it is right to see some of these verses as the poet's labour as he drudged for patronage – a necessary task in a society where advancement lay in the gift of the great – it is also important not to miss their discussion of attitudes crucial to Donne's maturing thought.

Amid the compliment and professions of friendship, for example, we are offered glimpses of a corrupt and perilous world of relative values, disillusion and vulnerability, the futility and spite of fallen man. In 'The Storm' and 'The Calm' – perhaps the most stimulating of Donne's Epistles – he also debunked the heroic pretensions of the military adventures in which he followed Essex and Ralegh. What in Hakluyt might be a chronicle of national endeavour, here becomes a re-creation of diminishingly painful experience raised to an almost surreal intensity by prodigious wit.

Such techniques are further developed in those most bizarre works *The Progress of the Soul* and the two *Anniversaries* (1611–12). These last were written to commemorate the death of Elizabeth Drury, a girl Donne had never seen, and were then printed by her influential father. Donne was later to regret this publicity both as a stain on his gentleman's amateur status and because these essays in extreme hyperbole were persistently misunderstood. What Donne was here concerned to achieve however was a contrast between the powers of Christian innocence imagined in his ideal of Elizabeth Drury and the decay of a corrupt, fallen world. The issue was thus between faith and virtue on the one hand and the toils of worldliness on the other. It is an old theme, but one examined here in the glare of new problems, in particular that scepticism which was to transform the intellectual life of the century.

At its most fundamental, the scepticism with which Donne had already approached literary convention challenged the ordered world inherited from Aquinas and the scholastics. It declared that ultimate truth cannot be approached by reason alone since, in a notion given classic formulation by Montaigne in *The Apology for Raymond Sebond* (*c.* 1576), reason works only on sense data and cannot be definitively checked. The central questions that sprang from this dilemma were whether and how one may know God – in other words, is belief a matter of faith or reason? – and whether and how one may gain a knowledge of the physical world – in other words, is fact only opinion or can some enquiries be verified?

In the *Anniversaries*, Donne set his face against the empirical investigation of nature that was soon to prove if not the final answer to these questions then at least their most powerful reply. He suggests that to let oneself be 'taught by sense, and Fantasy' is only to pile up useless and pedantic confusion. If the new astronomy of Galileo and Copernicus shows that the universe is not the regular, serene construct of the scholastics, then that is not a stimulus to inventing new theories but proof that the physical world is irremediably corrupt. If the links in the great chain of being are broken, then matters are worse than ever we thought:

> new philosophy calls all in doubt,
> The element of fire is quite put out;
> The sun is lost, and th'earth, and no mans wit
> Can well direct him where to look for it.
> And freely men confess that this world's spent,
> When in the planets, and the firmament

> They seek so many new; they see that this
> Is crumbled out again to his atomies.
> 'Tis all in pieces, all coherence gone.

Donne's answer to this predicament was 'fideism': not sharper telescopes but intenser prayer, not knowledge but virtue, not science but faith. When the soul, shot like a bullet from a rusted gun, courses through the celestial spheres, Donne shows it does not stop to question their movement but hurtles to the seat of all knowledge – the bosom of God. Meanwhile, with the removal of such inspiring virtue as Elizabeth Drury's, the rest of mankind is left to stagger on in a dark, decaying world lit only by the ghostly memory of the heroine's worth. The intellect at its most extended can only expose its own fallacies, and we must finally admit that the mysteries of Christ 'are not to be chawed by reason, but to be swallowed by faith'.

This last quotation comes from Donne the preacher. The sermons are the greatest of his prose works, but were preceded by a number of pieces which show Donne involved in both the personal quest for religious experience and the worldly pursuit of profitable employment. His *Pseudo-Martyr* (1610) and *Biathanatos* – a work unpublished in his lifetime – suggest the problems this entailed. *Pseudo-Martyr*, for example, was designed to appeal to James I by suggesting that Roman Catholics went against the rule of nature when they refused to swear to the king's supremacy in church matters and so laid themselves open to the death penalty. As with *Ignatius his Conclave* (1611), the work relishes a convert's scabrous anti-Catholic satire. In the labyrinthine and sceptical paradoxes of *Biathanatos*, on the other hand, Donne argued for the morality of suicide with an involvement rooted in acute personal experience.

And it is the obsession with death and the last things that characterizes Donne's mature religious works. The *Devotions on Emergent Occasions* (published 1624) were written when Donne's doctors had declared him too ill to read, let alone compose. The afflicted body houses a soaring mind however. Donne's emotions range over the fear of solitude and physical disintegration, the relation between sickness and sin, sin and death. The entire universe is raided for images because man himself – John Donne – is an image of the universe, an epitome, a microcosm. It is this belief that underlies the most famous passage in Donne's prose:

No man is an island, entire of itself; every man is a piece of the continent, a part of the main; if a clod be washed away by the sea, Europe is the less, as well as if a promontory were, as well as if a manor of thy friends, or of thine own were; any man's death diminishes me, because I am involved in mankind; and therefore never send to know for whom the bell tolls; it tolls for thee.

The moment of union is perceived but, as is appropriate for a sick-bed meditation, is perceived in the instant of its dissolution.

It is for his sermons that Donne is best known as a writer of religious prose. In the Jacobean period especially, occupied by preachers of great distinction, the pulpit gained extraordinary influence as a focus of spiritual thought and the dissemination of ideas. Led by the king, the court itself relished the finesse of religious analysis, and connoisseurs of style and content memorized sermons and took notes on a form of literature that was both popular and learned. Donne's contribution should not be seen in isolation.

Many preachers, particularly those of a Puritan persuasion, argued for an unornamented clarity of style. Others dressed spiritual matters in the garment of learning. While Thomas Adams (c. 1583–ante-1660) combined both in a manner that is often theatrical and powerfully directed to the abuses of the time, Lancelot Andrewes (1555–1626) brought his immense erudition in fifteen languages to passages of Scripture, each word and syllable of which he believed to be divinely inspired. As a result, each word and syllable is examined with the pious ardour of a philologist revealing the depths of the Word of God.

With Andrewes, human drama is often conveyed through a tiny yet telling comment in parenthesis. With Donne it moves to the centre of the stage. The immediate impact of the man, of course, is irrecoverably lost, but his devout biographer Izaac Walton (1593–1683) described Donne 'preaching to himself like an angel from a cloud' and appealing to the consciences of others 'with a most particular grace and an unexpressable addition of comeliness'.

The literary style of Donne's sermons is partly a distinctive reworking of its many sources. For example, Donne could exploit rhetorical patterning with the startling virtuosity of the sermon preached to the Earl of Carlisle in *c.* 1622 where he describes the agony of being 'secluded eternally, eternally, eternally from the sight of God'. From Seneca, Tacitus and their Renaissance editor Justus Lipsius however Donne and many others derived an anti-Ciceronian style. This was carefully contrived with a dramatic, irregular immediacy to express a concern with personal experience rather than settled certainties. Sermons such as *Death's Duel* (published 1632) however suggest that of all the influences on Donne's sermon style the Geneva and Authorized versions of the Bible – the parallelism of the Psalms, the visionary urgency of the Prophets and the evangelical fervour of St Paul especially – were the most telling. Nonetheless, when all the influences have been traced, what finally impresses is the compelling sense of Donne's unique spiritual sensibility, the range and drama of a religious intellect for which every aspect of the world could be a metaphor of the soul's experience.

As part of this technique, the sermons frequently juxtapose macabre effects with the tremblingly numinous, decay with resurrection. On the one hand is the conviction that 'Between that excremental jelly that thy body is made of at first, and that jelly which thy body dissolves to at last; there is not so noisome, so putrid a thing in nature.' In contrast is the image of the redeemed soul springing up in heaven like a lily from the red soil of its first creation. Between these experiences come the life of prayer and temptation, the imagining of the last things and, finally, an awareness of mercy.

This was not lightly won, and Donne's religious poetry dramatizes his spiritual conflicts with great power and formal mastery. However, since distinctions in the psychology of faith are not always as easy to discern as those in Donne's love lyrics, it is important to emphasize the variety in his religious poetry. The sonnets in 'La Corona', for example, draw on the church's traditions of oral prayer to fashion a devout and accomplished celebration of the mysteries of faith that was to some extent influenced by Roman Catholic practices. 'The Litany', by contrast, while not perhaps a wholly successful poem, is an attempt to express the modest, sober delight in daily piety which is a great achievement of seventeenth-century Anglicanism, and one which finds its truest expression in the work of George Herbert and Thomas Ken (1637–1711).

It is in the *Holy Sonnets*, however, that we hear Donne's most dramatic voice. Once again, it is the voice of a spiritual tradition – that of intense and affective private meditation. This merges here with Donne's Calvinist concern with a God who has arbitrarily predestined the eternal damnation of some souls and the belief that it is only through His grace that the chosen sinner may repent, be imputed righteous and so enter a state of justification. The personal realization of such ideas was terrifying – 'those are my best days, when I shake with fear' – and it forms the true spiritual centre of Donne's alternately defiant and submissive drama of sin and judgement. Around this centres the fear of physical decay. Sonnets such as 'Oh my black Soul!', 'At the round earth's imagin'd corners' and 'Death be not proud' contain doomsday in their small compass.

In 'Good Friday, riding westwards' Donne investigated the paradoxes of Christian faith with intensely dramatic wit, but it is in the 'Hymn to God my God, in my Sickness' and a 'Hymn to God the Father' that his relish of paradox and the strong speech rhythms of personal drama merge most tellingly with theology and faith. In these poems we watch Donne's advance towards the unity of the human and divine. In the first hymn, Donne's body is again a microcosm, a little world hurrying to decay. Yet, in its pain, it also imitates Christ's Passion and so may eventually rise like him to paradise. Finally, at the close of the second hymn, Donne hovers on the edge of death in a state at once confessional, wittily serious and almost ready to accept the extinction of his turbulent personality:

> I have a sin of fear, that when I have spun
> My last thread, I shall perish on the shore;
> But swear by thy self, that at my death thy son
> Shall shine as he shines now, and heretofore;
> And, having done that, thou hast done,
> I fear no more.

In the end, Donne's own name – that very personal token of self – becomes something to offer in wit to God and so a means of surrendering the human to the divine.

2

The courtiers addressed by Donne in many of his sermons were also the recipients of verses by Ben Jonson (1572–1637), and it is a measure of Jonson's stature that, in addition to being one of the leading playwrights of the age, he was also its most influential court poet.

Drawing extensively on the classics and Renaissance theorists, Jonson's non-dramatic poetry elaborates the ideals and criticizes the shortcomings of those involved in his vision of a cultured, socially responsible life of 'manners, arms and arts'. In these works, Jonson thus aspired to a seventeenth-century version of the urbane and moral gentleman of Latin literature: sociable yet self-contained, grave but unpedantic, a man in whom the virtues of the golden mean have been refined in the fires of art and personal integrity. Jonson thereby presents himself as an arbiter of civil virtue, an English Horace.

In the prose of his *Timber, or Discoveries* (1640–41), and often through extensive and unacknowledged paraphrase of Vives and other scholars, Jonson showed how the classical basis of his poetry was rooted in nature, exercise, imitation, study and art. The classical rhetoricians were the masters of his particular practice. Their works were to be used only as guides however, not as commanders. What Jonson was seeking was to relate an awareness of his own time to the timeless values of the past, and to do so in a distinctive idiom. To achieve this, he perfected the rhetoric of the middle voice in which he declared: 'the language is plain, and pleasing: even without stopping, round without swelling; all well-tuned, composed, elegant, and accurate'.

These qualities can be seen in Jonson's Epigrams: 'the ripest of my studies'. In pieces such as 'Inviting a Friend to Supper', the courteous social tone, tinged with fantasy, is modulated through reminiscences of Martial to create the ideal of a shared and civilized enjoyment of good food, good talk and good books. A sense of self-knowledge and self-respect, of constancy tempered by experience, is the subject of 'An Epistle Answering to One that Asked to be Sealed of the Tribe of Ben', an informal group that numbered some of the finest intellects of the age.

A shared sense of high values is also clear in Jonson's praise of other literary and artistic men, though this was something that did not always come naturally to him. The torrential release of pent-up irritation in 'An Expostulation with Inigo Jones' vividly suggests Jonson's envy of a rival's success at court and his refusal to believe that this great architect and scene designer's skills ranked with his own poetic arts. Jonson's tribute to William Camden, his master at Westminster, achieves a moving reverence. When Jonson writes of Shakespeare however, in a poem printed in the First Folio, his lines are among the most generous of the age.

Jonson's epitaphs to his children temper contradictory feelings of grief and Christian acceptance through an art that seems to belie the emotions that sustain it. In Jonson's two odes to himself, his deep feeling for the integrity of that art is asserted against the allegedly gimcrack tastes of his age. In his few religious pieces, such art also expresses a sinner's measured awareness of his own iniquity.

A contemporary is supposed to have declared that Jonson 'never writes of love, or, if he does, does it not naturally'. This is hard but not wholly unfair. 'My Picture Left in Scotland' has a delicate, honest pathos, and Jonson was capable of both the shrewd cynicism of 'That Women Are but Men's Shadows' as well as the artifice and high compliment of 'Drink to me only with thine eyes'. In 'See the chariot at hand here of Love', such artifice creates its own exotic sense of wonder:

> Have you seen but a bright lily grow,
>   Before rude hand hath touch'd it?
> Ha' you mark'd but the fall o'the snow
>   Before the soil hath smutch'd it?
> Ha' you felt the wool o'the beaver?
>   Or swan's down ever?
> Or have smelt o'the bud of the brier?
>   Or the nard in the fire?
> Or have tasted the bag of the bee?
> O so white! O so soft! O so sweet is she!

nard: *ambergris*

It is as the poet of the civilized aristocratic community however that Jonson is at his best, the mutual and by no means automatic respect of patron and poet serving to create a Roman ideal of behaviour, an aristocracy of mind as much as birth. Consequently, Jonson was a fine writer of eulogies. These, as in the excellent 'To Sir Robert Wroth', are often tempered by a moral concern for the corruptions of the city and court, a feeling for the virtues of country existence and a piety in which the classical ideal of the good life blends easily with a restrained Christian faith. Bravery, patriotism and friendship – the aristocratic life of action – are celebrated in the Pindaric ode to Cary and Morrison, but it is a tribute to the breadth of Jonson's classicism that he could also celebrate the scatological and mock-heroic exuberance of 'On the Famous Voyage'.

Such poems to the aristocracy suggest the great importance of patronage to the creative life of the age. When Jonson wrote in praise of his patroness the Countess of Bedford, for example, a new image of woman emerged, one that was aristocratic, liberal and educated, and allowed her to move on an equal and graceful footing with men. In 'A Farewell for a Gentlewoman', this is tempered by a stoic, Christian rejection of worldliness. In one of Jonson's finest achievements, the 'Elegy on Lady Jane Paulet', such faith creates a genuine sense of exultation.

It is in 'To Penshurst' however that such concerns combined to form Jonson's supreme evocation of Christian humanism as well as a work which inaugurated the important tradition of the country-house poem. The ancestral seat of the Sidneys here becomes the focus of all aspects of the good life. Modest yet dignified, blessed by the heritage of a great poet and rich in the bounty of nature, Penshurst is the centre of a humane community where all – peasant and poet – join in Sir Robert's courteous hospitality. Rural England is remade through the classics into an image of harmony, decency and integrity, fit and able to welcome the king and so be part of a patriotic ideal. And at the basis of this public excellence lies private virtue. The lady of the house is 'noble, fruitful, chaste withal', while the children, encouraged in rectitude by the example of their parents, are pious and keen to learn the ways of aristocratic merit. Jonson's vision is thus comprehensive and humane, Christian and classical, private and public. However we may question its political implications, it remains a noble image of a civilizing ideal.

3

Jonson's royalist vision is, along with his distinctive reworking of classical sources, an element in the work of Robert Herrick (1591–1674). Yet Herrick's voice is his own, as is his belatedly Elizabethan Arcadia 'of Maypoles, hock-carts, wassails, wakes' to which, in *Hesperides* (1648), he brought the refining contrivance of wit and sensuality. Viewed in the light of Horace, rural Devon becomes, for all its occasional rustic monotony, a world of modest and dignified content, of ceremonious versifying and the rituals of country life – a place to realize the influential ideal of unambitious retirement and the happy man. In *Noble Numbers* (1648), Herrick's collection of religious verse, such peace is praised as a gift from God.

But Herrick's is also the world of 'cleanly wantonness', of erotic dream, the 'liquefaction' of a woman's clothes and the white, hairless flesh of his Julia's leg. This sensuousness is the more telling for its sophisticated simplicity and, at its best, is returned to nature. This might be through the incandescent magic of 'The Night-Piece, To Julia' or the ardent yet earthy refinement of ceremony in 'Corinna's Going A-Maying' with its undertow of delight hastening to death. This classic theme is given its purest expression in Herrick's 'To Daffodils' and 'Gather ye rosebuds'.

In 'Ask me no more' by Thomas Carew (1594/5–1640), beauty's fading roses are enshrined in his mistress's cheek, yet compared to Herrick there is a coldly fastidious and urbane contrivance in many of Carew's lyrics. His 'Elegy on the Death of Dr Donne, Dean of St Paul's' nonetheless remains the most judicious critique of the master the age produced. Other courtly poets influenced by Jonson achieved fame for a slender handful of lyrics or even a single poem. In 'Ye meaner beauties of the night', for example, Sir Henry Wotton (1568–1639) wove an exquisite tribute to the tragic queen of Bohemia, doing so in terms of both pastoral and a fashionable Neoplatonism. Such Platonic themes were explored again in the lyrics of Lord Herbert of Cherbury (1582–1648), a considerable philosopher whose three poems entitled 'Platonic Love' analyse desire as a means of spiritual intuition.

It is in the Caroline court masque however that this cult of

Neoplatonism is seen at its most lavish. These works were all mounted after the beginning of the eleven-year period of the personal rule of Charles I (reigned 1625–49). They were thus a serious attempt to justify royal autocracy against parliamentary concern at the arbitrary raising of taxes and a supposed Roman Catholic bias in the king's support for the ritualistic doctrines urged by William Laud, the most influential man in the Caroline church. Neoplatonism thus served a political purpose. In Carew's sumptuous *Coelum Britannicum* (1634), for example, the perfection of the Stuarts is shown reforming the heavens themselves. On the eve of civil war, in the *Salmacida Spolia* (1640) of Sir William Davenant (1606–88), it is the king's secret and Platonic wisdom that makes him Philogenes, the 'Lover of his People', who can allegedly dispel dissension and restore harmony.

Such themes are seen again in the early poems of Edmund Waller (1606–87). Here the queen of England is cast as the queen of love to whose perfections only 'Sacred Charles' may aspire. Waller's formal importance lies, along with that of his friend Sir John Denham (1615–69), in the refining of the heroic couplet, a development that was profoundly to affect the poets of the Restoration after 1660. It is as a Caroline royalist we might view Waller here however, a man writing with a fervent and cultured belief in the divine right of kings and producing in such works as 'Go lovely rose' a perfect example of Cavalier lyric grace.

Cavalier lyric itself was the work of gentlemen amateurs, and Sir William Davenant in 'The Lark now leaves his Watry Nest' suggests the facility that characterizes this poetry at its best. The Cavalier spirit is most fully associated however with two further poets: Sir John Suckling (1609–42) and the 'extraordinary handsome' Richard Lovelace (1618–56/7).

A light and libertine grace characterizes the best of Suckling's love lyrics, the carefree raffishness of a versifier who, in his roll-call of Cavalier wits called 'A Sessions of the Poets', does not even bother to appear, being more happily engaged with bowls and girls. A lighter version of the cynical Donne informs such lyrics as 'Of thee, kind boy', 'Oh! for some honest lover's ghost' and the neat metrics of 'Why so pale and wan, fond lover'. In 'A Song to a Lute', Suckling's acute ear helped him towards a vivid parody of Ben Jonson, the godfather of all the Cavalier poets. In 'A Ballad upon a Wedding',

Suckling's tone of the libertine *faux-naïf* conveys charm, shrewdness and delicacy.

Of all the Cavalier poets however, it is Richard Lovelace who best reveals the grace and occasional shortcomings of these men: their wit and fastidious lyric artifice, their love of beauty, loyalty and love itself. 'Gratiana Dancing and Singing' focuses a world of chivalric desire, while 'Amarantha sweet and fair' promises more physical delights. But just as Herrick could alternate sensual contrivance with a Horatian ideal of steadfast retirement, so in 'The Grasshopper' Lovelace juxtaposes the sunshine world of Cavalier hedonism with those retired pleasures of friendship and wine that serve as an antidote to defeat when 'dropping December shall come weeping in'.

There is thus a subtle seriousness in Lovelace's work that deepens to pathos his Cavalier insouciance. This is most perfectly captured in two lyrics whose closing lines have become proverbial. In 'To Lucasta. Going to the Wars' the passion of the Cavalier soldier is shown to be rooted in a greater love of honour, while in 'To Althea. From Prison' the constrained poet claims that real liberty lies in the tangle of his lady's hair, in the abiding love of his king and the pleasures of an albeit enforced retirement. The concluding stanza of the poem reads like a manifesto of the Cavalier ideal:

> Stone walls do not a prison make,
>   Nor iron bars a cage:
> Minds innocent and quiet take
>   That for a hermitage.
> If I have freedom in my love,
>   And in my soul am free,
> Angels alone, that soar above,
>   Enjoy such liberty.

Grace, wit and integrity here contrive paradoxes with which to deny the humiliations of a crueller and cruder existence. But *Lucasta*, the volume from which this poem comes, was published in 1649, the year of the execution of Lovelace's king and so of the rude conclusion of the Cavalier dream itself.

4

The religious lyrics of George Herbert (1593–1633), first published posthumously in *The Temple* (1633) and frequently reprinted, are 'a picture of the many spiritual Conflicts that have past betwixt God and my Soul, before I could subject mine to the will of Jesus my Master: in whose service I have now found perfect freedom'. Herbert's lyrics are thus the fruit of a profound engagement with the rites, beliefs and personal demands of the national church as the believer, deeply influenced by the High Anglican community established by Nicholas Ferrar at Little Gidding, discovers the unworldly depths of his vocation.

A great many of Herbert's poems, especially those of spiritual doubt, were written in the period that led up to his time of crisis between 1628 and 1629. What he had to forgo in the pursuit of faith – pride in intellect and birth, and worldly pleasure – is shown in 'The Pearl', the poem of a man who has surrendered all in response to God. The following year Herbert was ordained, and his public career and private pilgrimage came to their conclusion in the three years he spent as an Anglican minister in rural Bemerton, near Salisbury. Here he embodied the ideal set out in his prose work *A Priest to the Temple, or The Country Parson* (published 1652), his chaste yet ceremonious piety marking a high point in Anglican spirituality before the decades of open religious conflict.

The poems in *The Temple* are divided into three sections: 'The Church-Porch' or the place of moral instruction, the concluding 'Church Militant' and the long, central group of lyrics named simply 'The Church'. The architectural and spiritual image underlying *The Temple* thus allowed Herbert to offer a picture of the full Anglican life, its public institutions and private struggles.

The public and institutional side of Herbert's Anglicanism shows how he wished to steer a middle way between popery and extreme Puritanism. This is the theme of 'The British Church' whose priest preaches the redemption and offers the communion vouchsafed by the Easter Passion. The meeting of sin and love on Calvary lies at the theological heart of the volume, and the drama of Easter itself makes up the first sequence of poems in Herbert's collection. These works include the emblematic 'Easter Wings', a lyric whose shape and argument celebrate the soaring spiritual freedom won both for the world and for the individual by Christ's Resurrection.

In addition to such meditative sequences, *The Temple* contains a vivid discussion of the true nature of Christian prosody. In his youth, Herbert was clearly drawn to an elaborate poetry 'curling with metaphor a plain intention', but in 'The Forerunners' and his two 'Jordan' poems he put forward the self-imposed ideal of a plain style, one that forswore pride in artifice and the intricate rhetoric of a pastoral Helicon, replacing these with the purer waters of Christian baptism and the rivers of the Promised Land. The result, in poems like 'Denial', 'Virtue' and 'Life', is a Christian verse at once homely, shapely and based on a faith whose truths simply uttered are poetry enough. In the end, a truly devout art need express no more than every Christian's joy in singing '*My God and King*'.

In Herbert's lyrics of spiritual conflict these technical qualities are often merged with a colloquial, dramatic immediacy and the use of a single extended conceit. In works such as 'The Collar', these techniques allowed Herbert to portray his crisis in all its energy while preserving a detached and even ironic commentary. But it is as the poet of chaste and joyous thanksgiving, of the rebellious soul remade in love and submission, that Herbert is at his characteristic best. In his earthly life, the recovery of faith was also the recovery of humanity and the true poet:

> And now in age I bud again,
> After so many deaths I live and write;
> I once more smell the dew and rain,
> And relish versing: O my only light,
> It cannot be
> That I am he
> On whom thy tempests fell all night.

The stylistic ideals outlined in the 'Jordan' poems here express a beatitude that is simple and wholesome, a sense of wonder after pain. Safe in the fold of the Anglican Church, the poet's delights are a foretaste of that divine banquet of the blessed in paradise which in 'Love', the final poem in his volume, Herbert is bidden to join. At the last, his 'many spiritual Conflicts' are indeed quietened in the service of God.

It was widely recognized by contemporaries that in so wholly dedicating his muse to Christ, Herbert had fashioned a body of poetry which, in its power and scope, deserved an honourable place beside the Scriptures themselves. *The Temple* was hugely influential and widely imitated. None took its substance more to heart than Henry Vaughan (1621/2–95). In 1650, Vaughan issued one of the most intense accounts of spiritual awakening in seventeenth-century poetry: his *Silex Scintillans* ('The Flashing Flintstone'), republished in a revised form in 1655. Sustaining all these lyrics is a tremulous intimation of supernatural joy, the rapture of a man who, having glimpsed the radiance of eternity amid spiritual darkness, is inspired to speak in tongues.

External circumstances prompted the suffering that was a prelude to this revelation. The first of these circumstances was the death of Vaughan's younger brother which inspired many poems. Darkness and a glimmering hope characterize such works as 'Silence, and stealth of days' and 'My Soul, there is a Country'. At their most powerful, Vaughan's intimations of Christian immortality are qualified by an awareness of human sin and suffering. Light and dark are set in dramatic contrast.

The second force working on Vaughan was the example of that 'blessed man, Mr George Herbert, whose holy life and verse gained many pious Converts, (of whom I am the least)'. The influence of *The Temple* is felt everywhere in *Silex Scintillans*, yet there was a crucial difference in the situations of the two men. For the Herbert of 'The British Church', Anglicanism was the moated castle of true faith. Vaughan's similarly titled poem is a lament for an institution disestablished by the parliamentarians.

Deprived of communal doctrine and celebration, Vaughan was obliged to turn to other modes of spiritual explanation. He found them in the Hermetic texts which were erroneously believed to contain the ancient Egyptian wisdom of Hermes Trismegistus which had in turn been passed to Orpheus, Pythagoras and Plato. The Hermetic texts were widely interpreted as apparently genuine and primary sources of a spiritual revelation that saw man as the image of God and the world as a shadow of His splendour. Both 'The Shower' and 'The Waterfall' elaborate objects from nature into closely argued images of spiritual restoration. The 'Cock Crowing' wakes from 'dreams of Paradise and light' to carol its celebration of the divine in expectation of the Second Coming. In 'The Retreat', employing the Platonic elements in this philosophy, Vaughan could think of the happy days of his 'Angell-infancy' when, in relative innocence, the beauty of a cloud prompted memories of his soul's origins in paradise. But paradise closed against Vaughan the poet. The lyrics added to his edition of 1655 are often, though by no means always, of a lower quality, while his *Thalia Rediviva* (1678) is a dull volume.

To another poet Eden remained open, a shining field of 'Orient and Immortal Wheat'. The poems of Thomas Traherne (1637–74), along with his finer prose work *Centuries of Meditation*, were rediscovered at the start of this century and present an image of the mystic's recovery of childhood innocence and light, the felicity of a man who has shunned the baits of the world and recaptured 'the Highest Reason' in a blissful union with God in nature. If Traherne's verse is sometimes undisciplined in its enthusiasm, it remains extraordinarily potent in its joy. Nonetheless, in 'Solitude' he wrote a moving study of mystic vision occluded.

The spiritual career of Richard Crashaw (1612/13–49) was not a return to childhood but a pilgrimage that took him from High Anglican circles in Cambridge through to a conversion to Roman Catholicism and eventual death at Loretto. His *Steps to the Temple* (1646, 1648) reveals the influence of both Spanish mysticism and the intensely artificial rhetoric of the continental baroque style. Paradox, wit and a sensuousness allied to spirituality characterize poems like 'The Weeper', but if the artifice of such works occasionally seems taken to excess, Crashaw's 'Hymn' to Saint Theresa and 'The Flaming Heart' reveal the power of a poet

> Drest in the glorious madness of a Muse,
> Whose feet can walk the milky way.

The contrast in style and spirituality between Herbert and Crashaw suggests the extraordinary diversity of seventeenth-century religious lyric, and it might be expected that so rich an age would produce a number of lesser yet highly talented poets. Bishop Henry King (1592–1669), for example, wrote a quantity of amatory verse in the style of Jonson and Donne, but in 'The Exequy', an elegy on the death of his young wife, he rose to an imaginative pitch of tenderness and Christian hope that is wholly exceptional:

> 'Tis true, with shame and grief I yield,
> Thou like the Van first took'st the field,
> And gotten hast the victory
> In thus adventuring to die
> Before me, whose more years might crave
> A just precedence in the grave.
> But heark! My pulse like a soft drum
> Beats my approach, tells thee I come;
> And slow howe'er my marches be,
> I shall at last sit down by thee.

> Van: *front-line troops*

In these lines, King combines the early-seventeenth-century lyric poet's concern with love, death and spiritual consolation in a conceit at once evocative and exquisitely tender.

5

The decadence of the 'metaphysical' style can be seen in the highly influential work of John Cleveland (1613–58). Here, contorted wit often becomes an end in itself, something at once bizarre and ostentatious. Cleveland's elegy on the death of Edward King (the subject also of Milton's 'Lycidas') shows this affectation at its worst. The acutely self-conscious poet here denies his vocation and claims a genuine simplicity of grief in lines that are among the most mannered the age produced:

> I like not tears in tune, nor will I prize
> His artificial grief, that scans his eyes;
> Mine weep down pious beads, but why should I
> Confine them to the muses' rosary.

This sort of writing was very popular among superficially clever young men, and Cleveland's love lyrics and elegies were widely imitated. It was when such a style was adapted to satire however that Cleveland's savage and mauling wit is seen at its most effective.

A similar concern with witty artifice again characterizes much of the early work of Abraham Cowley (1618–67) whose *Poetical Blossoms* (1633) is a volume full of recollections of the Elizabethans and was once again widely imitated. In *The Mistress* (1647), Cowley showed himself a follower of Donne. A more genuinely quickened sensibility may be found in his classical imitations such as Horace's 'The Country Mouse', but while Cowley's Pindaric odes were factitious if influential experiments, occasional poems such as 'On the Death of Mr William Hervey' offer a true, personal sense of loss as Cowley recalls the pastoral scenes of his youth and bids them become 'dark as the grave wherein my Friend is laid'.

An altogether greater poet – the finest late flowering indeed of 'metaphysical' wit – is Andrew Marvell (1621–78). His erotic poems show particular aspects of his excellence. 'The Definition of Love', for example, derives its power from the dramatic contrast between the poet's frustrated ardour and the geometrical imagery, rational to the point of ruthlessness, with which he proves the impossibility of sexual fulfilment. A second love poem, the exquisite 'To his Coy Mistress', again shows Marvell juxtaposing passion and logic while bringing to its apogee one of the great themes of Renaissance classicism: the seizing of erotic pleasure before the onset of inevitable death. In what is perhaps the best-known seventeenth-century image of the triumph of time, the delicacy of Marvell's octosyllabic couplets juxtaposes immensity and the specific, life and love, the macabre certainty of death and a power at once visionary and quietly ironic:

> But at my back I always hear
> Times winged Charriot hurrying near:
> And yonder all before us lye
> Desarts of vast Eternity.
> Thy Beauty shall no more be found;
> Nor, in thy marble Vault, shall sound
> My echoing Song: then worms shall try
> That long preserv'd Virginity:
> And your quaint Honour turn to dust;
> And into ashes all my Lust.
> The Grave's a fine and private place,
> But none I think do there embrace.

Marvell also brought the sophisticated artifice of his love poetry to his religious lyrics and, in 'The Coronet', investigated the problems posed by the pride of the artist when in conflict with the humility of the believer. Seeking to redress the sins or thorns with which he has persecuted his Saviour, Marvell shows himself bringing the skills of his love poetry (the garlands he wove for his mistresses) to his religious verse only to find vanity lurking in the lines. Christ alone can punish such pride by trampling on his work. By a final paradox however, Marvell's poetry honours his Redeemer by crowning Christ's feet even in the moment of art's destruction.

Marvell's dialogues between the soul and pleasure and the soul and the body again discuss the conflict of spirituality and worldliness, an issue which in 'On a Drop of Dew' receives its most subtle exploration through delicately realized conceit. Finally, in 'Bermudas', Marvell offered a picture of the English 'elect' guided by the hand of God towards a new Eden in the New World.

Another major Renaissance theme brought to its summation in Marvell's poetry is the relative merit of the active and contemplative lives. 'The Garden' is Marvell's great lyric in praise of the contemplative life. The nine stanzas of this poem move inwards from the discordant world of men towards harmony, Hermetic unity in nature and pre-lapsarian innocence. As the mind withdraws ever further into itself, so the soul achieves a moment of release and a vision of heaven as it is imagined perching on the fruit trees in the garden:

> Here at the Fountains sliding foot,
> Or at some Fruit-trees mossy root,
> Casting the Bodies Vest aside,
> My Soul into the boughs does glide:
> There like a Bird it sits, and sings,
> Then whets, and combs its silver Wings;
> And, till prepar'd for longer flight,
> Waves in its Plumes the various Light.

whets: *preens*

The theme of action and withdrawal is again central to two of Marvell's other major poems: 'An Horatian Ode upon Cromwell's Return from Ireland' and his summation of the country-house poem: 'Upon Appleton House'.

Appleton House itself was the family home of Thomas, Lord Fairfax, general of the parliamentarian armies until 1650 when he retired because of his disapproval of the execution of Charles I and the involvement of English forces in Scotland. Marvell was appointed tutor to his daughter who appears in the poem as an image of perfection at the close of a long and intricately patterned account of God's providential plan for England and the universe. As Marvell surveys his patron's estate, so its gardens and fields, peasants and landed gentry re-enact the recent course of English history. Reformation and revolution are given emblematic form in the landscapes of Nun Appleton.

The formal planting of the borders round the house, for example, wittily suggests the military order over which Fairfax – for a while the man of destiny – had command until conscience obliged him to withdraw from the active life. The grand design of Providence continues to unfold nonetheless. The moving scenes that Marvell creates, which in others of his lyrics suggested the violent conflicts of sexual desire, now shadow forth the most violent conflict of all – the Civil War. Then, as night falls, so suggestions of the Apocalypse accompany it. Throughout, and with a most subtle power of allusion, Marvell uses the country-house poem to suggest the drama of a nation involved in the mighty course of the workings of Providence.

Such a providential interpretation of history is central to others of Marvell's political poems and to his exploration of the complexities of the active life in a time of national conflict, a time when it was widely believed England and her people had been selected by God for His special purposes. The best known of these political poems is the 'Horatian Ode', written between May and July 1650, and so in the period after the execution of the king when Cromwell, like the young Augustus praised by Horace, was in a position to seize power after civil war. Marvell's poem is an exceptionally delicate balance between opposing forces and feelings. In the well-known passage on the execution of the king, for example, Marvell's humanity raises our sympathy for Charles, but equally important is his appreciation of the problems posed by the new forces unleashed with Cromwell. That Cromwell is fierce and destructive is as clear as that he is noble. More importantly, Cromwell is seen as a providential agent – the instrument of God in the destiny of the nation. Charles is the sacrificial victim, while Cromwell is seen as a divine force who will be able to extend the power of England and the true Protestant cause.

Five years later, in 'The First Anniversary of the Government under his Highness the Lord Protector', this religious interpretation of Cromwell's political role is yet more triumphantly celebrated. Cromwell is now seen as the divinely appointed leader ruling an elect nation in conformity with God's will. He is thus preparing England for the Second Coming. Paradise is imminent, and 'if these the Times, then this must be the Man'. Marvell, whose lyric poems had brought to their glorious fulfilment so many traditions of seventeenth-century humanist thought, here sees his nation poised on the borders of eternity itself.

But paradise was not regained. Instead of being led into the Promised Land, with the Restoration of Charles II (1660–85), the people of England chose 'a captain back for Egypt'. Marvell, now a Member of Parliament, began his period as a Restoration satirist. The political and religious vision of an earthly paradise had faded, but in his lines to another poet Marvell paid generous tribute to the man who, blind and old, had created the supreme work of seventeenth-century Protestant humanism and paradise lost – John Milton (1608–74).

6

At the centre of Milton's life and art lay an ineradicable sense of vocation, the commitment of a mighty Protestant and humanist scholar to his God, his nation and the national voice through which that God might speak. Perhaps no great poet ever prepared himself more arduously for his task. An autobiographical passage from his Latin *Second Defence of the English People* (1654) tells how at home and later at St Paul's School Milton began that study of the classical and Christian inheritance by which, as he wrote in his pamphlet *Of Education* (1644), he hoped the scholar might take his place in the civic community and 'repair the ruins of our first parents by regaining to know God aright'. These social and religious principles shaped his entire career.

That career was to take Milton to Cambridge where 'the Lady of Christ's', chafing at the outmoded teaching, appears to have been rusticated for a while in his second year. Milton's skill at public disputation however – the chief means then used for developing logical and verbal ability – was widely recognized, and Milton also played his role in the light-hearted Vacation Exercise of 1628, producing both a burlesque Latin speech of exceptional coarseness (a talent that was to serve him well in his pamphleteering) and the English poem 'Hail native language'. Here, Milton's reverence for the power of English, his sense of wonder at the potential of his own tongue, is already united with the ambition to tackle 'some graver subject' than the present occasion afforded.

An extensive period of private study, of what, in *The Reason of Church Government* (1641), Milton was to call 'industrious and select reading', now ensued. Though Milton was later to blame this for the origins of his blindness, he was placing before himself all the then known fields of human knowledge. In a Latin poem he thanked his indulgent father for supporting him through this period of omnivorous study, but the dispiriting impression that his talents were slow to ripen was expressed in his sonnet 'How soon hath time'.

In fact, and in addition to studies in music and mathematics undertaken for relaxation, by 1634 Milton had composed the masque now called *Comus*, while in 1637 – the year in which he wrote 'Lycidas' – he set out on his tour of Europe. In Naples however Milton heard of the death of his school friend Charles Diodati and of the outbreak of the Bishops' War against Scotland, the prelude to the Civil War itself. In his early thirties, ashamed to be travelling while his compatriots were fighting for liberty and resolved that, for the honour of his native land and tongue, he would 'leave something so written to aftertimes, as they would not willingly let it die', Milton turned for home, to political pamphleteering and the eventual publication of his poems.

7

Milton's *Poems* of 1645 are one of the ripest fruits of seventeenth-century Protestant humanism, a collection which draws on a full range of classical and contemporary European culture to fashion the image of a poet who is at once the graceful inhabitant of a Caroline Arcadia (the publisher, probably in an attempt to boost sales, compared him to Waller) as well as an inspired prophet, the *vates* of Virgil and the mouthpiece of God.

Milton had no doubt that his poetic inspiration, though secured by wide study and experience, was a divine gift, a speaking in tongues that united the believer, the artist and the citizen to the figure of the seer. In the opening work of his 1645 volume – the ode 'On the Morning of Christ's Nativity' (written 1639) – Milton writes of the poet's lips touched by a hallowed fire, the very image of the inspired Isaiah. Such an image, along with the work's formal construction, suggests that these are verses not of private faith and conflict but examples of glorious and lofty hymns sung in public celebration.

Milton's subject in the ode is nothing less than the significance of the birth of Christ in terms of universal history: the belief that, with the Nativity, a new order of true spiritual redemption replaced the old world of nature, death and the false gods of paganism. To achieve so mighty a purpose, Milton wove together allusions to the fourth eclogue of Virgil (where the image of a return to the Golden Age was long believed to be a pagan prophecy of the birth of Christ), the intricacy of Italian *canzone* forms and the Elizabethan pastoralism of Sidney, 'sage and serious Spenser' and the Shakespeare of *A Midsummer Night's Dream*. The result is a new, distinctive language of a muscular, flexible and exquisite formality. It conveys both the burden of Milton's thought and the rapture of his subject. In particular, we hear the music of the spheres which (as Milton also showed in 'At a Solemn Musick') would sound to man when the earthly paradise was restored:

> Such music (as 'tis said)
> Before was never made,
>   But when of old the sons of morning sung,
> While the creator great
> His constellations set,
>   And the well-balanced world on hinges hung,
> And cast the dark foundations deep,
> And bid the welt'ring waves their oozy channel keep.

>   sons of morning: *the angels*; welt'ring: *tumbling*

188

With the birth of Christ, an era of universal peace seems to unite heaven and earth in Virgil's hope that 'Time will run back, and fetch the age of gold.' But at the numerical centre of the poem – as at the heart of Christian belief – lies a deeper understanding of history than that available to the pagan Virgil. This is the Christian knowledge that only after the Passion and Last Judgement, at the end of mortal time, will Christ the King finally bring about the golden era of paradise regained. The Nativity and the defeat of the pagan gods (the subject of the second half of the poem) are but a prelude to that mighty vision.

By associating himself with Isaiah in the Nativity ode and with Ezekiel in his less perfect poem on 'The Passion', Milton revealed his belief in the divine inspiration of his Christian poetry. In other works from the volume of 1645 that biblical source is supplemented by more specifically Renaissance concerns: in particular a Protestant Neoplatonism which viewed the moral life of man against a pastoral backdrop. 'L'Allegro' and 'Il Penseroso' (?1631) – that most lovely pairing of poems – suggest what this entailed.

Both verses can be appreciated as gracefully evocative studies in mirth and melancholy, action and contemplation. The light octosyllabic couplets contain, among other things, the most delicate evocations of a pastoral landscape at once flower scented and fairy trod. Beneath the sensuous description however lies a firm and controlling sense of intellectual purpose. This derived from Milton's studies and the wish, expressed in his Latin Seventh Prolusion (?1632), to rise through natural knowledge to the mystic insight treasured by the Hermetic magus, the follower of Orpheus. In the two English poems, Milton suggests this process partly through his mythological references. What at first appear as ornaments are clues to a deeper intention.

In 'L'Allegro', for example, shunning illusory melancholy, Milton evokes Euphrosyne or Mirth, one of the three Graces and a figure whose divine origins and powers sharpen the poet's perception through joy, poetry and music. This leads to the possibility of that supreme art by which Orpheus, the first disciple of Hermes Trismegistus, could, with an almost Christ-like influence, restore the lost soul to life and power. Re-animating joy thus leads through nature, love and art to that supreme expression of human potential mythologized in the figure of the legendary poet.

As Milton had shown in his Latin elegy to Charles Diodati, the mystic insight melancholy brings can only be won through a chaste and priest-like devotion to art. Hence the image in 'Il Penseroso' of the poet in retired evening contemplation reading Hermes, Plato and the tragedians in the pursuit of Orphic wisdom. At this stage in his career however it was in the music and ceremony of the Anglican Church that Milton claimed to find the surest path to ecstasy, and in 'Il Penseroso' it is as a devout hermit that he finally pictures himself, living in chaste contemplation and hoping to reach 'something like prophetic strain'.

For Milton, the life of contemplative withdrawal was not, however, the highest good. In a famous passage in *Areopagitica* (1644) he wrote: 'I cannot praise a fugitive and cloistered virtue, unexercised and unbreathed.' Indeed, it was essential to Milton's entire concept of 'the true wayfaring Christian' – one living in a fallen world where good and evil can be known only through their mutually defining contrasts – that the mind be exposed to the baits and seeming pleasures of vice. Knowing these for what they are, the virtuous soul should then resist them through mental strength. At the heart of such a belief lies a wholesale commitment to moral choice and individual responsibility. These are the subjects of *Comus*.

Milton had briefly essayed the masque's combination of music and poetry in *Arcades* (?1633). In 1634 however he collaborated with the composer Henry Lawes to produce a full-scale work to celebrate the installation of the Earl of Bridgwater as Lord President of Wales. Fletcher, Tasso and Guarini helped provide the element of pastoral dramaturgy while, in the tradition of the Jonsonian masque, *Comus* is a learned and Neoplatonic entertainment which reveals the spiritual worth of its participants.

Many of Milton's most cherished notions enriched the work. The masque's combination of music and poetry, for example, exercises the twin skills of Orpheus, and the Attendant Spirit (originally played by Lawes) is shown as a figure of Orphic power who can guide and protect the characters as they wander in the wood of error. It is here that Comus has his home. In contrast to the ideal of the inspired and philosophic mind sought by virtue, Comus is the suave and alluringly sensuous son of Bacchus and Circe who tempts the soul to betray its powers to a bestial life of self-indulgence.

The music has already associated Comus with all that stands against the Orphic harmonies of true virtue, and the Lady at the centre of the action is able to resist his blandishments. While her tempter speaks 'false rules pranked in reason's garb', her natural chastity of mind is expressed through a rhetoric which knows that temperance is the law of God and that it can, if needs be, speak with the awful voice of divine authority. Comus realizes the Lady's power even as he offers her a glass of tempting liquid. The Brothers now enter and dash the glass from Comus's hands. This suggests that virtue requires active protection, but it is only when the Attendant Spirit summons the river goddess Sabrina – the full image of true and loving chastity – that the Lady is freed from Comus's paralysing enchantment and can be presented in all her integrity to her father. As the masque closes, so the exquisite tetrameter couplets sung by the Attendant Spirit urge the minds of the audience upwards to the divine abodes of rapturous virtue which his Orphic art alone may reveal.

Milton first published *Comus* reluctantly and anonymously in 1637, being aware of what he considered its relative immaturity. This sense of unripeness and the premature also haunts the most considerable work in Milton's volume of 1645: the pastoral elegy 'Lycidas'.

In 1638 there had appeared a volume of poems mourning the death by drowning of Edward King, a Fellow of Christ's College, Cambridge, a clergyman and minor poet. Milton's is the longest of the thirteen elegies in the book, but while the majority of these pieces are unmemorable exercises in the manner of Cleveland (who, as we have seen, contributed to the volume) 'Lycidas' is one of the supreme achievements of English poetry. It attains this status through the power of a learned imagination which transforms the conventional artifice of Arcadia into a thrilling and passionate metaphor, a metaphor in which Milton could discuss his responses as a Christian poet to the gratuitous death of a good man.

In the opening paragraph, grief and a feeling of immaturity are deepened by the sense of irrecoverable loss in the silencing of a young poet. Such emotions swell to a passionate call for the consolations of art as Milton, bitterly critical of corruption in the church, juxtaposes the horrific image of Lycidas's corpse to the remembered beauties of a pastoral landscape, a landscape once enjoyed in youthful friendship, mirth and song. The extremes of nature – its loveliness and cruelty –

characterize the first two-thirds of the poem, but beneath these lies an oppressive and questioning sense of outrage. What is the place of a poet in such a perilous world? Even the inspired Orpheus, Milton reminds us, was torn to pieces by the insanity of the Thracian women. There is no guarantee that a virtuous life spent in the strict service of the thankless muse will not be cut short or that art will be saved from the ravages of barbarity. The death of King (a shepherd so much more virtuous than the corrupt pastors satirized in St Peter's bitter speech) makes Milton shockingly aware of nature's destructiveness and, in his grief, his friend becomes a metaphor of his own sense of the perilousness of his vocation.

In his confusion, the poet turns again to the beauties of the natural world. Yet, in the end, such comforts are an illusion. While the speaker lets his 'frail thoughts dally with false surmise' other images of Lycidas's corpse blight his fantasy. Only the classical vision of dolphins wafting the body of the hapless youth offers, perhaps, some sense of consolation in the natural world. But the natural world, its cruelties and partial compensations are not the poet's only resource. A higher order of mercy has been won by Christ. 'The natural man', St Paul declared, 'knows not the things of God, for they are spiritually discerned.' And it is with such spiritual quickening that the poet finally sees Lycidas living in eternity, in a resurrection to paradise where the groves and rivers of Arcady have their heavenly counterpart and the lyrics of the pastoral poet are transformed into the alleluias sung round the throne of God:

> Weep no more, woeful shepherds weep no more
> For Lycidas your sorrow is not dead,
> Sunk though he be beneath the watery floor,
> So sinks the day-star in the ocean bed,
> And yet anon repairs his drooping head,
> And tricks his beams, and with new spangled ore,
> Flames in the forehead of the morning sky:
> So Lycidas sank low, but mounted high,
> Through the dear might of him that walked the waves;
> Where other groves, and other streams along,
> With nectar pure his oozy locks he laves,
> And hears the unexpressive nuptial song,

In the blest kingdoms of meek joy and love.
There entertain him all the saints above,
In solemn troops, and sweet societies
That sing, and singing in their glory move,
And wipe the tears for ever from his eyes.

The natural world gives way to the divine, and in this new understanding the poet completes the passage of his mourning. His grief assuaged, he is ready for a new day, 'fresh woods and pastures new'.

8

With the moving exception of 'When I consider how my light is spent' (?1652) and 'Methought I saw my late espoused saint', Milton's sonnets from the years of the Civil War and the Protectorate concern either political figures such as Cromwell and Fairfax or political events such as the massacre of the Protestant Vaudois ('Avenge O Lord thy slaughtered saints') and an imminent royalist attack on London ('Captain or colonel, or knight in arms'). These years were chiefly spent, however, in pamphleteering.

The pamphlets Milton wrote between 1641 and 1660 chart the development of his social, religious and political thought. At the centre of them all lies his commitment to an increasingly radical Puritanism. The theological basis of this was developed in his Latin *De Doctrina Christiana* ('Concerning Christian Doctrine') which he worked on between his return from Italy and the Restoration. Here he outlined the extreme Protestant view that Scripture alone is the guide to truth and that its simplicity, when aided by divine illumination, makes clear all we need to know of salvation. Every believer, Milton continues, has the right to interpret Scripture for himself, and he came to acknowledge that no one – least of all Laud and the High Anglican bishops – should stand in the way of this free enquiry.

In *Of Reformation in England* (1641), the first of five anti-prelatical tracts, Milton took on what he saw as his public duty 'to vindicate the spotless truth from an ignominious bondage'. Just as the poet of the 1645 volume sees himself as a prophet inspired like Isaiah, so in these pamphlets, as he makes clear amid the wearisome self-justification and iron sarcasm of *An Apology for Smectymnus* (1642), Milton now speaks with a righteous indignation that is a gift of God's imparting.

Such a belief in prophetic denunciation was accompanied by both theoretical and visionary aims. At this stage in his career, Milton believed that his ideals could be achieved by replacing the corrupt sway of the bishops with a Presbyterian church, one in which Bible-reading Protestants would be able to elect the truly virtuous as their leaders. The fire of passionate idealism – perhaps Milton's most important contribution to political literature – burns in his prose as he throws aside merely legal objections in his concern to replace the laws of man with the law of God and a hope of the millennium, or the thousand-year rule of Christ over the elect.

Having written on religious freedom, Milton then surveyed the domestic world and, in particular, *The Doctrine and Discipline of Divorce* (1643). Painfully personal concerns may have underlain this interest, for in 1642 he had married Mary Powell, the eighteen-year-old daughter of a royalist family who had left him at the outbreak of war and after a month of marriage. Political circumstances may also have kept the couple apart, but they were only to live together again in 1645. In the meantime, Milton had published pamphlets on divorce that were to make him notorious.

Searching the Bible for precedents, Milton became convinced that wedlock should not be preferred 'before the good of man and the plain exigence of charity'. Once again, the spirit was the true guide to Scripture and suggested a Puritan ideal of marriage based on the God-given superiority of the man and his holy, loving bond with a woman, the companion of his mind as well as of his bed. Together they might find a love, happiness and peace that were glorious to God. Without such mutual support, the man condemned to 'grind in the mill of an undelighted and servile copulation', neither party could enjoy the liberty and clear conscience in which to work for salvation and the public good.

Milton's concern with the upbringing of children is discussed in *Of Education*, a work which is the last great fanfare for the educational ideals of northern European Protestant humanism: the belief that learning should train the whole man to virtue, public life and godliness. Milton's ambitious and frankly élitist programme was designed to produce ideal citizens for the Puritan Commonwealth, that millenarian foretaste of the Second Coming imagined in the finest of his prose works: *Areopagitica* (1644).

The Areopagus was the democratically elected supremê court in ancient Athens and was much acclaimed in seventeenth-century England. The title of Milton's pamphlet compares it explicitly to the Long Parliament which, having in 1641 abolished the Star Chamber that had controlled censorship since the time of Elizabeth I, was now under pressure from the Presbyterians to reintroduce a licensed press. Milton himself was moving away from his earlier Presbyterian enthusiasm however – '*New Presbyter* is but old *Priest* writ large', he wrote in a sonnet of *c.* 1646 – and was now adopting a position of increasingly radical Independence.

'Give me the liberty to know, to utter and to argue freely according to conscience, above all liberties.' Beneath this ringing acclamation lies a belief in the duty of the adult Puritan not to live under 'a perpetual childhood of prescription'. Rather, he must search for truth and test his own moral strength in a world where good and evil are inextricably intertwined. Good books contain reason – the image of God in man – while the search for truth itself must of necessity result in much arguing, much writing, many opinions.

Areopagitica presents Milton's image of an open society of all honest Puritans united 'in one general and brotherly search after Truth'. There is nothing vague about such people or the language they use. Give them a censored text and 'every alert reader', Milton declares, will be ready 'to ding the book a quoit's distance from him'. Forcibly to constrain such readers under censorship is to deny them genuine moral choice, the right to test their self-discipline and so work towards a greater knowledge of God and the building of a godly nation, an England fit for the millennium:

Methinks I see in my mind a noble and puissant nation rousing herself like a strong man after sleep, and shaking her invincible locks. Methinks I see her as an eagle mewing her mighty youth, and kindling her undazzled eyes at the full midday beam; purging and unscaling her long-abused sight at the fountain itself of heavenly radiance; while the whole noise of timorous and flocking birds, with those also that love the twilight, flutter about, amazed at what she means, and in their envious gabble would prognosticate a year of sects and schisms.

mewing: *preening*

Among other extreme radical views being published at this time were the ideas being formulated by Leveller groups within the army. Freedom of the press was essential to the dissemination of these, and in *England's Birth-Right Justified* – a pamphlet almost certainly by the Leveller leader John Lilburne (1615–57) – a free press is again seen as a bulwark against tyranny. Pamphlets such as *England's Misery and Remedy* (1645) and the historic *Agreement of the People* (1647) set out the most audacious political concepts, often in a plain yet telling English, to stir up radical ideas in a new audience of ordinary working people. Men who had begun the century with the extreme theory of the divine right of kings set out in James I's *True Law of Free Monarchies* (1598) were now replacing belief in absolute monarchy with notions of popular sovereignty, of the multitude as a body of individuals who could sweep away king and Parliament in order to reconstruct society on the basis of equality. In the pamphlets of Gerrard Winstanley (1609–post-1660), the leader of the pacifist Diggers, the inspired language of Christian communism describes the dream of a second Eden.

With the execution of the king, these radical parliamentarians seemed to have secured the first step towards paradise regained. 'The old world is running up like parchment in the fire,' Winstanley wrote. Yet executing the king as a tyrant was a fearsome step. Forced through by a purged Parliament claiming to act as a court of law, it raised the greatest legal and ethical difficulties. These Milton set out to answer in *The Tenure of Kings and Magistrates* (1649). Here, bitterly attacking Presbyterian attempts to compromise the new Jerusalem, Milton urged the courage and moral rigour needed to seize the freedom offered by God and build the Puritan Commonwealth. Drawing on the Bible, Aristotle, classical history and the political and legal theory of thinkers such as Suarez and Buchanan, Milton advanced the argument that all men were originally born free but, after the Fall, banded together in mutual defence and voluntarily gave rule to one king. Promoting a radical view of popular sovereignty, Milton believed the people had the right to take such power back if the king abused his trust.

This idea Milton repeated in *Eikonoklastes* (1649), his attack on an influential collection of the late king's writings entitled *Eikon Basilike* (1649) or 'The Image of the King'. Milton wrote this pamphlet at the behest of the Commonwealth to which he was now Secretary for the Foreign Tongues, and it was in Latin – the international language of debate – that Milton also routed the attacks of the French scholar Salmacius (Claude Saumaise) and so justified the ways of the regicides to a horrified Europe. The effort of the controversy cost him the remains of his sight.

Nonetheless, to place such an advanced ideal of Puritan freedom at the centre of his theory was to find that most men could not live up to the ideal. While more sophisticated political thinkers of the 1650s such as James Harrington (1611–77), the author of *The Commonwealth of Oceana* (1656), were insisting that the foundation of a moral commonwealth was not good men but good laws, Milton's belief that only the virtuous could appreciate freedom led inexorably to a disillusioned élitism that condemned 'the rest' for loving not freedom but licence.

It was from such a position, and faced with the imminent popular return of the Stuart monarchy, that Milton published the most tortuously desperate of his pamphlets: *The Ready and Easy Way to Establish a Free Commonwealth* (1660). Here, urging that 'the general defection of a misguided and abused multitude' had so betrayed the workings of Providence as to forfeit 'the right of their election what the government shall be', Milton argued that only a perpetual council of the virtuous could save the republic from ridicule. The euphoria of an elect nation preparing for paradise has slumped to that most unholy of tyrannies – the permanent rule of the godly. But events were to overtake him. While Milton hid in fear of condign punishment, the people of England welcomed the return of their king.

9

Debarred from founding a heaven on earth, Milton sought the paradise within. In defeat, the poet was reborn. Between 1658 and 1663 he dictated his epic *Paradise Lost*, publishing it first as ten books in 1667 and then in a revised edition of twelve books in 1674. It is insufficient however to read *Paradise Lost* simply as a personal response to private circumstances. Though Milton could present himself as blind and persecuted in a contumelious world – and do so with all the heart-rending power of the lines that open his seventh book – it is proper to view the poem itself as a magnificently comprehensive answer to the range of demands which created the possibility of writing a vernacular epic in the first place.

Chief among these was a poet aware of his power, believing this to be divinely inspired and working within an intellectual tradition which held that an epic in the poet's mother tongue was the highest ideal for poetry. This was an ideal further enriched by the conviction that such a poem should be Christian in its subject and 'doctrinal and exemplary' in its purpose. The subject matter or 'argument' of an epic should thus be centred on man's deepest and most interesting problems, while its exposition should contain the modes of previous and similar works.

In Milton's case, these last were the epics of Homer and Virgil, the Ovid of the *Metamorphoses*, narratives from medieval and Renaissance romance traditions and, to some extent, the great body of hexameral literature or writings on the six days of creation. Of these, *La Semaine, ou Creation du Monde* (1578) which Joshua Sylvester (1563–1618) had translated from Du Bartas's French was perhaps the most influential. The poet should use and refashion the conventions of such works – invocations to the muses, heroic similes, wars, games, debates, passages of exposition, and so on – and might then criticize their shortcomings in the light of his own zealous Protestantism.

Part of Milton's purpose is achieved through such an examination of the traditions within which he worked, while his subject itself was the mightiest and most urgent available to him: the reasons how and why sin came into the world, the origins of death and, by extension, the place of salvation within the universal history of fallen man. A poem about revolt from God, about sin and the Fall, the intention behind *Paradise Lost* is to bring some souls – Milton's 'fit audience though few' – to an awareness of God's merciful Providence not just on the level of reason but through the spiritual quickening great poetry can achieve. *Paradise Lost* thus works through the tradition of an encyclopaedic Christian humanism, extending it so as to investigate the moral and spiritual awareness of its audience. These are learned men and women, fallen but of good will, who live in a world where virtue and vice are inextricably tangled – a world where paradise has indeed been lost. To achieve this, the poet conducted them in a language of massive yet subtle resonance through heaven, earth and the hell where the work begins.

The first two books of *Paradise Lost* have been universally admired for the imaginative power with which Milton presented the rebel angels, the 'huge affliction and dismay' of those who have defied God and so embody the range of vices fallen man is prone to. This effect is achieved partly through carefully contrived rhetoric. Writing in '*English* Heroic Verse without Rime', the magisterial artifice creates 'true musical delight' through the skilful handling of 'apt Numbers, fit quantity of Syllables, and the sense variously drawn out of one verse into another'. Such a technique allowed Milton to juxtapose the high voice of inspired description, with which, like an Old Testament prophet, he believed he created his divine fiction, to the malicious calculation with which Satan deceives his followers. Holy truth gives way to the manipulation of words. Rhetoric becomes deceit.

We are shown this in the debate in Pandemonium where degrees of evil – Moloch's self-destructive ambition, Belial's 'ignoble ease and peaceful sloth' and Mammon's corrupt acceptance of defeat – are contrasted to Satan's demagoguery. At the conclusion of the council, Satan springs his carefully contrived surprise. This is the heroic effort to destroy the newly made world which Satan alone can undertake. To wonder at the defiant magnificence of the sin that has corrupted us (despite all that is said to expose and demean it) is to recognize what a grip such sin now has. Milton's epic points constantly to the troubled ambiguities of our fallen nature.

But Milton's purpose was logical and intellectual persuasion as well as emotional proof. His poem attempts to convince us that the unquestionable truth of biblical revelation means that an all-knowing God was just in allowing Adam and Eve to be tempted and, of their free will, to choose sin and its inevitable punishment, thereby opening the way for that voluntary sacrifice of Christ which showed the mercy of God in bringing good out of evil.

The philosophic issues this raised (and which it is widely considered Milton did not satisfactorily resolve) are discussed between God and

Christ in the poem's third book. Few find these debates the most satisfying element in the poem. In the *De Doctrina Christiana*, Milton stated his belief that God revealed Himself in the Bible 'not as He really is, but in such a manner as may be within the scope of our comprehension'. Since reason is the image of God in man, it was appropriate to present Him largely through a poetry of logical exposition (a poetry skilfully contrasted to the debate in hell), but there is an intellectually unpleasing arbitrariness to the theology and an obsessive logic-chopping in these sections which is at variance with Milton's true genius for presenting Christian truth through the subtle exploration of myth. This he achieved magnificently in Book Four.

Milton believed that in the world of fallen man, after Adam had tasted the apple, good and evil were 'as two twins cleaving together' and that the one could only be known by the other. This post-lapsarian consciousness is what helps to make his description of Eden so effective. Certain knowledge of the Fall pervades the narrative, while much of the description of paradise itself is what the diminished Satan, carrying 'hell within him', views. Eden is thus glimpsed in terms of its imminent destruction, and such emotive subtlety is worked deep into the classical allusions and heroic similes that offer some of Milton's finest effects:

> The birds their choir apply; airs, vernal airs,
> Breathing the smell of field and grove, attune
> The trembling leaves, while universal Pan
> Knit with the Graces and the Hours in dance
> Led on the eternal spring. Not that fair field
> Of Enna, where Proserpine gathering flowers
> Herself a fairer flower by gloomy Dis
> Was gathered, which cost Ceres all that pain
> To seek her through the world; nor that sweet grove
> Of Daphne by Orontes, and the inspired
> Castalian spring, might with this Paradise
> Of Eden strive.

The verse throbs with a spiritual homesickness for paradise truly lost.

Such pathos also shrouds Adam and Eve as they are presented naked but 'with native Honour clad'. Their language has the sweet dignity of pre-lapsarian rhetoric, yet the subject of their talk is the forbidden fruit hanging on the Tree of Knowledge, the object of God's arbitrary and absolute prohibition. As we hear more about this so Satan, looking on 'with jealous leer malign', discovers the means of their corruption. The innocence we can understand is innocence threatened, and this is raised to its most poignant as we are told of the satiated bliss of the lovers, lulled by nightingales, yet with Satan 'squat like a Toad, close at the ear of Eve'. There are bad dreams even in paradise.

There is also legitimate intellectual enquiry. Books Five to Eight are largely occupied by the dialogues between Adam and the angel Raphael who has been sent to warn 'our primitive great sire' of Satan's plotting. Raphael's history of the war in heaven warns of the perils of disobedience to God, while the account of the Creation that is so soon to fall leads to Adam's description of God's fashioning Eve. Once again, his joy in his spouse and the ideal of marriage are brought into doubt. In the rapture of his love for Eve, Adam declares: 'All higher wisdom in her presence falls.' We are given a presentiment of the perilous rift between human love and spiritual duty – the conflict which, in Book Nine, will lead to the Fall of man.

Book Nine of *Paradise Lost* is one of the supreme achievements of English Protestant humanism. The passion of the narrator rises to the height of his argument, while the events, recounted with the greatest drama and sympathy, lead us to see that in the Fall of man Adam discovered his full humanity – the sinning, foolish, demeaned yet heroically loving self that all the guiltless pastoralism of Eden could never show.

At the centre of this conflict lies Milton's fundamental concern with freedom and choice: the freedom to submit to God's prohibition on eating the apple and the choice of disobedience made for love. Eve, seduced by the serpent's rhetoric and her own confused ambition – as well as the mere prompting of hunger – falls into sin through innocent credulity. Adam falls by consciously choosing human love rather than obeying God. This is the error wherein his greatness lies. If the price is death, it is also human life as we can know it, something infinitely more tender than coldly obedient abstinence. If Adam's is now the world of fault, fury and long suffering, of the weary history of human degradation narrated by the archangel in the penultimate book, it is also the world of work and struggle, the world of achievement won through effort and of love known in a fallen universe:

> They looking back, all the eastern side beheld
> Of Paradise, so late their happy seat,
> Waved over by that flaming brand, the gate
> With dreadful faces thronged and fiery arms:
> Some natural tears they dropped, but wiped them soon;
> The world was all before them, where to choose
> Their place of rest, and providence their guide:
> They hand in hand with wandering steps and slow,
> Through Eden took their solitary way.

It is a profoundly moving conclusion, and one centred deep within the purposes of the poem itself with its burdensome certainty of paradise lost and full humanity won.

10

In 1671 there appeared *Paradise Regain'd. A Poem. In IV Books. To which is added Samson Agonistes. Paradise Regained* is a brief biblical epic, much influenced by commentaries on the Book of Job. It is a slighter and more didactic work than *Paradise Lost* and more austere in style. It portrays Satan's tempting Christ in the wilderness in order to test the paradoxical nature of the second Adam, the God made man. Christ is portrayed as a figure who should conquer such temptations even as the first Adam succumbed to them. In this Christ succeeds, but the conflict has little of the emotional power of the ninth book of *Paradise Lost*.

Though never intended for the stage, *Samson Agonistes* is written in conformity with Aristotle's rules for the structure of classical tragedy. The poetry and the various episodes also combine reminiscences of Sophocles and Euripides with biblical allusions drawn especially from the Psalms, works in which Milton the translator found great consolation with the onset of full blindness. The result is a self-consciously literary attempt to examine a problematic episode from Old Testament history in terms of classical precedent, seventeenth-century theology and the experience of the defeated 'elect'.

Samson, led on to the stage like the blind hero of *Oedipus at Colonus*, speaks a language that recalls the prophecy of Jewish redemption expressed at the opening of Luke's Gospel. Personal and national defeat however is the present overwhelming concern: the Israelites in bondage and their captive saviour 'eyeless in Gaza at the mill with slaves'. The appalling deprivation of blindness leads to the most passionate outbursts in the play:

> O dark, dark, dark, amid the blaze of noon,
> Irrecoverably dark, total eclipse
> Without all hope of day!
> O first-created beam, and thou great word,
> Let there be light and light was over all;
> Why am I thus bereaved thy prime decree?
> The sun to me is dark
> And silent as the moon,
> When she deserts the night
> Hid in her vacant interlunar cave.

The hero, certain of his divine election, has now to reveal his understanding that, in the manner of Adam, he has betrayed his spiritual responsibilities through the wiles of a woman and so merited the punishment of a God in whom he retains an absolute trust. The tinkling mediocrity of the Chorus speeches (the speeches of a chosen people who have, like the Civil War Puritans of Milton's last pamphlets, weakly betrayed their cause) implicitly contrasts their own uncertainty to the heroic resolve of the protagonist.

That resolve has to be tested and known weakness overcome. Hence the ambivalent (and for many unpleasant) episode of the encounter between Samson and Dalila in which the hero resists her temptations with a newly invigorated savagery of purpose. The confrontation with Harapha of Gath further quickens the hero's resolve and, sure in his commitment to God's as yet unrevealed purposes, Samson is led out to the play's catastrophe. This is a deeply ambivalent combination of vengeance, divine guidance and sheer destructive natural force through which the sinning yet elect hero moves to his victory in death. As classical decorum required, this episode is narrated by a messenger.

While a majority of readers are likely to feel moral disgust at the catastrophe (and certainly not the glib platitudes of catharsis mouthed by the hero's father and the unreliable Chorus) Milton perhaps intended here a sense of the elect man brought into conflict with God, a conflict which only the most rigorous Puritan faith could find tragically satisfying. *Samson Agonistes* remains a profoundly disturbing work, and the problematic forces working within it are diminished by too easy a reverence for its status as a classic of our literature. Milton's vision remains to trouble us still.

II

The Civil War helped establish the propaganda power of the press, but from the beginning of the century printers had exploited its potential for popular entertainment and instruction. Writers also hoped to profit by this, and among the most interesting experiments in prose fiction from the early decades of the century is Lady Mary Wroth's *Urania* (1621), a work which adopts both the euphuistic prose and the exotic contrivance of pastoral romance. Where the work itself is most interesting is in those scenes which appear to draw on real life for their matter, manner and dialogue. To many of Lady Wroth's audience, this appeared scandalous, and the opprobrium heaped on her went along with her book itself being willed into obscurity. Writing from a desperate need for money, Lady Wroth initiated the pattern for many subsequent women writers and their struggle with the deeply engrained prejudice against women publishing their work.

The early decades of the century saw the publication of a large number of courtesy books, most of them aimed at fashioning the socially dominant image of the gentleman. A vast quantity of religious matter also appeared. Translations were sold along with diatribes on subjects as diverse as women, witches and tobacco, as well as accounts of real and imaginary voyages. Sir Thomas Overbury exposed 'An Affectate Traveller' in his co-operative anthology of *Characters* (1614) which developed the taste for the witty use of rhetoric and ethical analysis found again in Joseph Hall's *Characters of Virtues and Vices*

(1608), a work which combines sermon *exempla* with imitation of the ancient Greek character-writer Theophrastus. The early English essay also drew on the classics as well as on Montaigne, on the literature of advice and reflection and, in particular, on the philosophical interests of Francis Bacon (1561–1626).

Bacon's *Essays or Counsels, Civil and Moral* (1625), first issued as ten sequences of aphorisms in 1597, were finally enlarged to fifty-eight pieces. In the later editions, the style is more digressive, but an anti-Ciceronian brevity, a cold ruthlessness and even cynicism characterize these attempts at what, in *The Advancement of Learning* (1605), Bacon had seen as the necessity for an empirical enquiry into the 'culture of the mind'. If Bacon's essays on abstract topics sometimes glow with rich conceits, it is the chill pith of disillusion that perhaps makes the greatest impression. 'There is little friendship in the world,' he wrote, 'and least of all between equals, which was wont to be so magnified.'

Biographical writing in the first half of the century is most closely associated with Izaac Walton. His life of Donne (1640) has already been mentioned, though as with the others he completed – Wotton (1651), Hooker (1665), Herbert (1670) and Sanderson (1678) – beneath the avowed use of documents and sometimes grating modesty there lies a tendency to hagiography which too readily slides into High Church propaganda. In Walton's *The Compleat Angler*, first published in 1653 and, like his other works, frequently revised, those 'that hate contentions, and love quietness, and virtue, and Angling' are treated to one of the most purely delightful of books. Passages of Arcadian idyll such as Auceps on the nightingale or the paragraphs on the milkmaid's song are joined with instruction in the manner of Virgil's *Georgics* to praise a skill which disciplines the whole man.

Biography and didactic character writing combine with satire and good counsel in the works of Thomas Fuller (1608–61) who, in addition to being a biographer, was a preacher, essayist, wit and antiquary. John Aubrey (1626–97), whose biographical anecdotes are a source of information and gossiping delight, was also an antiquarian who attempted an archaeological account of the society he thought built Stonehenge.

Sir Walter Ralegh (?1552–1618), whose incomplete *History of the World* (1614) was composed while he was in the Tower, reveals a keen intellect in the process of assessing older humanist notions of history. Ralegh brought a daringly critical approach to his subject which allowed historical evidence to be studied for what it could tell about divine purpose and moral responsibility. Recorded history – the theatre of God's judgements – was thus a storehouse both of moral example and of experience to analyse, and Ralegh's own analyses of the shortcomings of tyrannical kings especially were to be profoundly influential on the Civil War parliamentarians. The poetry of Ralegh's richly developed thematic images also reveals him sharing with many contemporaries a profound sense of pessimism in the face of death. In a famous passage, he wrote: 'Thou hast drawn together all the far-fetched greatness, all the pride, cruelty, and ambition of man, and covered it over with those two narrow words, *Hic jacet*.' The encyclopaedic range, force and organization of the *History*, along with its often beautiful prose, make it one of the great if neglected works of the period.

Bacon's *History of Henry VII* (published 1622) is a portrait of a close, careful ruler shrewdly exploiting the realities of political experience to maintain his power. In Bacon's epistemological works however, this concern with experience and experiment is fired by a new and radical vision of science in the service of man. Bacon declared he had taken all knowledge as his province and, in the fragment called 'The Great Instauration' (published 1620) or 'restoration' of true learning, revealed himself as a powerful pioneer in the taxonomy of the sciences. In *The Advancement of Learning* (1605), and in opposition to conservative clerics, Bacon put forward the idea that the natural world – the book of God's material works – is a rich storehouse to be investigated for the glory of the Creator and the relief of man.

Having shown that science was not inimical to religion (and so made it sympathetic to Puritans) Bacon set about giving it the dignity of philosophic method. His technique was induction, or the drawing of general laws from a number of particular instances. To effect his daring attempt to free men from dependence on received authority and so advance the revolutionary idea that inductive knowledge implied progress, Bacon had to isolate and criticize habitual mental weaknesses. These he called the 'Idols'.

The idols of the tribe are universal human errors such as too uncritical a belief in regularities. The idols of the cave are individual quirks and special pleading. The idols of the theatre are such false systems or 'vanities of learning' as the contentious and sophistic manner of the Aristotelian schoolmen whose thought still formed the staple of English university education. In addition, 'fantastic' learning such as Hermeticism (among whose activities Bacon missed the elements of 'genuine' science) were similarly dismissed. Bacon then countered the sceptics by declaring the errors of sense perception could be corrected by repeated piecemeal observation.

In opposing the 'delicate' learning of rhetorical humanism, Bacon defined his fourth pantheon: the idols of the market-place. These exert their tyranny by subjecting men to a concern with words rather than things. This might be through a belletrist concern with style or the belief that words such as 'Fortune' describe substantive entities. 'Here therefore is the first distemper of learning, when men study words and not matter.' Bacon's objections to mere rhetorical copiousness gave a philosophic rationale to calls for a plain style already practised by some Puritan divines and the writers of utilitarian prose. Indeed, his ideas were to provide a basis for the 'mathematical plainness' later advocated by the Royal Society when, after the Restoration, scientific progress carefully presented itself in terms of institutionalized, gentlemanly respectability and patriotic endeavour.

Wholly different is the significantly titled life-work of Robert Burton (1577–1640), *The Anatomy of Melancholy* (first edn 1621). Alone in the libraries of Christ Church, Oxford, Burton turned over more than twelve hundred volumes in creating what initially appears as an orderly medical treatise. In fact, this semblance of method soon collapses under the fantastication of the melancholic excess it purports to anatomize. Burton's text, made up from a tissue of other texts, drives on with the apparent force of argument until we realize that that argument has become the opposite of itself. What remains is not stable fact but a shrewd and often cynical awareness of unending contrariety and the vivid languages through which this is expressed. To relish Burton is to love the diversity of Babel.

For another great prose stylist of the age, the Norwich doctor Sir Thomas Browne (1605–82), truth lay partly in the ideas of Bacon. Browne's *Pseudodoxia Epidemica* ('Vulgar Errors') of 1646 is in some degree a response to Bacon's call for a 'calendar' of common misunderstandings. Browne paid formal tribute to the Baconian ideal when he wrote he wished the book might have been the work of 'some co-operating advancers'. Fortunately, it is entirely his own – a collocation of massive erudition and curiosity which works through a critical use of authority, reason and experience. As Browne discusses if there are griffins in nature or whether 'Lampries have nine eies', so he reveals, as Coleridge wrote, 'the Humorist constantly mingling and flashing across the Philosopher'.

Such enquiries of Browne's were not purely materialistic since science, he believed, could work to the glory of God. 'Those highly magnify him, whose judicious enquiry into his Acts, and deliberate research into his Creation, return the duty of a devout and learned admiration.' This is 'The Religion of a Doctor' embodied in Browne's *Religio Medici* (first authorized edn 1643). The book is one of the supreme achievements of seventeenth-century English prose, and what animates the carefully contrived biblical parallelism and wide-ranging vocabulary is a soaring yet quizzical fideism that is in some respects comparable to Donne's. The resulting statement of faith is a portrait of a mind enamoured of paradox:

As for those wingy mysteries in Divinity, and airy subtelties of Religion, which have unhing'd the brains of better heads, they never stretch the *Pia Mater* of mine; me thinks there be not impossibilities enough in Religion for an active faith; the deepest mysteries ours contains have not only been illustrated, but maintained, by syllogism, and the rule of reason: I love to lose my self in a mystery, to pursue my Reason to an *oh altitudo*. 'Tis my solitary recreation to pose my apprehension with those involved enigmas and riddles of the Trinity, with Incarnation, and Resurrection. I can answer all the objections of Satan, and my rebellious reason with that odd resolution I learned of Tertullian, *Certum est, quia impossibile est*. I desire to exercise my faith in the difficultest points, for to credit ordinary and visible objects is not faith but persuasion.

Pia mater: *the skin round the brain*; Certum est, *etc.*: *It is certain because it is impossible*

The microcosm contains the macrocosm, and man is a spiritual being. 'There is surely a piece of Divinity in us,' Browne wrote, 'something that was before the Elements, and owes no homage unto the Sun.' The order of the universe, the secret hieroglyphs of nature and the mysteries of the Resurrection will finally make this clear when the elect soul, redeemed from time, glories in the eternal present of its Maker.

Such thoughts underlie both the *Hydriotaphia* or *Urn-Burial* (1658) and its companion piece *The Garden of Cyrus*. In the latter work, by curiously pursuing the number five through 'the orderly book of nature', Browne glimpses the handiwork of 'the ordainer of order and mystical Mathematics of the City of Heaven'. In *Hydriotaphia* on the other hand – a work inspired by the discovery of some Saxon funerary urns which Browne believed to be Roman – an antiquarian's account of burial rites advances through the rich cadences of the great fifth chapter meditation on death the leveller to an account of the futility of pride and of death transfigured by resurrection.

In Browne's *Christian Morals* (published 1716), the imaginative reach of the earlier works has been subdued by the influence of Christian stoicism and the maxims of the copybook. Yet here too a concern for religious tolerance is keenly felt as when Browne writes of 'this strict enquiring Age, wherein, for the most part, Probably, and Perhaps, will hardly serve to mollify the Spirit of captious Contradictors'. Other writers also sought the grounds of tolerance. For Jeremy Taylor (1613–67), the author of *Holy Living* (1650) and *Holy Dying* (1651), 'Contentedness in all estates is a duty of religion', and he believed 'a holy life is the best determination of all questions, and the surest way to knowledge'. The influential group gathered about Lord Falkland (?1610–43) at Great Tew again sought tolerance and freedom of enquiry, as did the Cambridge Platonists: Henry More (1614–87), John Smith (?1612–52), Ralph Cudworth (1617–88) and Nathaniel Culverwel (1618/19–?51). For their leader, Benjamin Whichcote (1609–83), Proverbs provided the motto: 'The spirit of man is the candle of the Lord.' Though its light was the reason of a well-tempered conscience fortified through revelation, much of the writing of this group is diffuse, mystic, obscure.

One of the most searching answers to contemporary problems of science and belief, language and truth, the state of nature and the nature of the state had been propounded as early as the 1640s. The *Leviathan* (published 1651) of Thomas Hobbes (1588–1679) is one of the great yet dangerous achievements of seventeenth-century English prose.

Hobbes's philosophical revolution lay in bringing the deductive methods of Euclid and Galileo to the political problem of ensuring the stability of the state. Human beings are to be studied like the physical universe and irrefutable conclusions are to be drawn from basic premises. The first of these premises is what contemporaries felt to be Hobbes's contentious and subversive materialism. Man is seen as mere matter in motion, a machine whose movements are governed by passions derived from the senses which are then interpreted through reason. Man the automaton discovers himself in the fear, appetite and conflict aroused by contact with other such machines. Life becomes a desperate struggle for superiority, a race which 'we must suppose to have no other *goal*, nor other *garland*, but being foremost, and in it'. The final phrase cuts through illusion to the nightmare of natural man and the savagery of an existence with 'no arts, no letters; no society; and which is worst of all, continual fear, and danger of violent death; and the life of man, solitary, poor, nasty, brutish, and short'.

The ordinary words, scrubbed by logic and marshalled into the syntax of a shrewd observer, give English a new force. We all sometimes believe that life is 'nasty, brutish, and short'. And for Hobbes, this state of nature is a permanent threat. Peace cannot be secured by searching for 'natural rights' but only by rearing the huge structure of an artificial commonwealth: the supreme Leviathan which a process of rigorous deductive reasoning eventually tells us we must absolutely obey. In a world of matter in conflict there are no immaterial essences like goodness, justice or kindness. These are mere words – 'insignificant speech'. The might which keeps peace alone gives the right to rule. In the end, man must submit to Leviathan, his own discovery, and so surrender to absolutism if he is to be free from anarchy.

I2

Some contemporary poets attempted the epic. Cowley's biblical *Davideis* (1656) however, lacking in narrative tension, is unfinished. Sir William Davenant's *Gondibert* (1651) tried to found epic on the drama, but any real interest the work might have is in his *Discourse upon Gondibert* and Hobbes's *Answer* of 1650. The poet urges the didactic utility of courtly and martial epic, while the philosopher condemns the 'ambitious obscurity' of the strong lines favoured by the metaphysicals, dismissing them as no more than riddles. A public, rational prosody is again in the making.

It is this pursuit that helps account for the importance of John Denham (1615–69) and Edmund Waller (1606–87) to the poetry of the Restoration. Denham's *Cooper's Hill* (first printed 1642 and subsequently revised) combines the topographical and moral interests of earlier work with two important Restoration concerns: a public voice in which to discuss social and political matters, and the creation of a refined and rational style which mirrors social order. For Denham, the restrained landscape around Windsor allowed him to present an account of disciplined royal rule and harmonious social relationships in couplets that are, like the Thames itself,

> Though deep, yet clear, though gentle yet not dull,
> Strong without rage, without o'er-flowing full.

The poems of Charles Cotton (1630–87) enjoy this sense of locale without explicitly politicizing it, but other poets were seeking a more heroic means of presenting Restoration public life. Chief among these figures was John Dryden (1631–1700).

Early in his career Dryden had written his *Heroique Stanzas* (1659) on the death of Cromwell but, changing with the nation, in 1660 he composed his *Astraea Redux*. The central notion here is the return with Charles II of a golden age of peace, plenty and the arts, along with the establishment of a strong and divinely sanctioned monarchy. Such themes are central to all Dryden's political writing and here find expression in a metrical regularity which matches his concern with social order.

The most considerable early statement of Dryden's beliefs however is *Annus Mirabilis* of 1666. This poem uses the stanza form of Davenant's *Gondibert*, and celebrates the English victory in the First Dutch War, seeing this as the work of a strong and newly united nation guided by Providence. What is particularly noticeable however is the rich experimentation of Dryden's technique, his exuberant and somewhat excessive display of invention, fancy and elocution. For Dryden, such rhetorical copiousness revealed the proper wit of a heroic poem and was the product of genuine inspiration, the fire of passionate and learned insight. This, at its best, makes Dryden a great philosophical poet and not the spokesman of the tame and occasionally satiric neo-classicism for which he has too often been slighted.

Dryden was not alone in attempting eulogy in the early years of the Restoration. Waller's *Instructions to a Painter* (1665) is another panegyric celebrating the Duke of York's naval victory over the Dutch. But such enthusiasm was not to last. Corruption at court and incompetence in the government under Clarendon began to suggest that heroic ideals were groundless. Heroic verse became a basis for satire. In 1667, when the Dutch inflicted a crushing defeat on the ill-prepared English navy, Andrew Marvell wrote his *Last Instructions to a Painter*, one of the great political poems of the Restoration period.

Savage patriotic indignation here finds a vividly indecorous language for a corrupt and indecorous court manipulated by Clarendon. Heroic portrait becomes cartoon – the only art such a government can inspire. Reminiscences of Juvenal create lively images of courtly degradation, while balance and panegyric are reserved only for the Country party of honest parliamentarians. The humanist tradition has here been vividly extended. New and influential dimensions for satire have been found, and the genre was to acquire increasing importance.

Marvell offered his praise to another Restoration satirist: Samuel Butler (1612–80), the author of *Hudibras* (1662, 1663, 1680). Butler's is an immensely long and intermittently brilliant three-part burlesque of heroic romance in which he satirizes those Puritan dogmatists whose abuse of language is a cover for minds working furiously to their own squalid advantage. The particular objects of Butler's attack are his Presbyterian anti-hero, his Independent squire Ralph, Hudibras's beloved Widow and Sidrophel the Hermetic magician. These figures are blown to nightmare proportions, and what made them so popular to Restoration audiences was the poet's vigorously demotic attempt to laugh off the still prevalent menace of sectarianism:

> When *Tinkers* bawl'd aloud, to settle
> *Church Discipline*, for patching *Kettle*,
> No *Sow-gelder* did blow his horn
> To geld a Cat, but cry'd *Reform*.
> The *Oyster-women* lock'd their Fish up,

And trudg'd away to cry *No Bishop*.
The *Mouse-trap* men laid Save-alls by,
And 'gainst *Ev'l Counsellors* did cry.

Butler's swift octosyllabic couplets create a variety of the bleakly absurd, an epic of 'insignificant speech' in which there is no palliative save remorseless scorn to make men aware of their faults.

Verse satire, along with sharply pointed and often libertine lyrics that develop the Cavalier mode, circulated among the Restoration courtiers, what Pope was later to call that 'mob of gentlemen who wrote with ease'. This group included the Earl of Roscommon (?1633–85), the enlightened author of an *Essay on Translated Verse* (1684), the playwright Sir George Etherege (?1634–91), Charles Sackville, Earl of Dorset (1638–1706), Sir Charles Sedley (1639–1701) and the unattractive John Sheffield, Earl of Mulgrave (1648–1721), author of an *Essay on Satyr* (?1680). The greatest of these figures however was John Wilmot, Earl of Rochester (1647–80), whose libertine extravagance and verbal mastery epitomize the values of these men.

Something of the subtle excellence of Rochester's craft may be seen in his lyric 'Love and Life'. Here Hobbesian man, the materialist joying in the present moment, is juxtaposed to the sentimental cant of his loving Phyllis. Such delicate contrasts of register, allied to a libertine lack of restraint and an incisive and even tragic sense of hypocrisy and nihilistic hedonism, also characterize Rochester's satire at its best. For example, beneath the comedy of 'Signor Dildo' chased up the Mall by voracious royal ladies lies a distressing sense of human waste. This rarely rises to sustained political comment, though the notorious 'Sodom', if it is Rochester's, compares unnatural tyranny to 'unnatural vice'. But Rochester's finest satire is social: the exultation and disillusioned insight of the claret-drinking satyr who, in 'A Ramble in St James's Park', shows he could tolerate the joys of mutual deception if his Corinna chased pleasure with virile men rather than 'whiffling fools'. In 'Tunbridge Wells', vivid social realism and an excellent control of the couplet provide portraits of contemporary imbeciles in the manner of Dorset's 'A Faithful Catalogue of our Most Eminent Ninnies' (1678).

Rochester's literary satires such as *Timon* show the influence of Boileau's refinement of the satiric couplet as well as a new interest in the smoothness of Horace. This latter is especially clear in *An Allusion to Horace, the Tenth Satyr of the First Book* (1675/6), an important early example of sustained classical imitation in satire which related the contemporary world to the values of Augustan Rome. In this work, Rochester deftly criticized his literary contemporaries and set out his version of the widely influential ideal of a subtly proportioned and varied prosody to inveigle rather than bludgeon or puzzle the elegant reader.

In 'Artemisia to Chloë', this technical refinement is enriched by an ear for dialogue and a subtle satiric indirectness, a range of moral viewpoints varying between the strained idealism of the literary Artemisia, the ebullient 'fine lady' – one of the great comic creations of Restoration satire – and Corinna, the ruthless survivor in a corrupt world of sexual politics. Only in *A Satyr against Reason and Mankind* did Rochester (soon to die a penitent rake) create a more powerful if less subtle poem, a coruscating vision of bestial, Hobbesian man tortured by reason and trapped in his own tragically wilful energies until

> old age and experience, hand in hand,
> Lead him to death, and make him understand,
> After a search so painful and so long,
> That all his life he has been in the wrong.
> Huddled in dirt the reasoning engine lies,
> Who was so proud, so witty, and so wise.

The range of experiment in Restoration satire can be seen again in the work of John Oldham (1655–83). His best-known work, the *Satyrs on the Jesuits* (1679), is historically important as a miscellany combining Elizabethan and Clevelandesque styles with classical imitation and mock-encomium. Diverse traditions are here brought to bear on a contemporary national issue: the fear of royal absolutism and Roman Catholicism rife during the Popish Plot. Dryden was indebted to this formal breakthrough in political satire – his admiration is expressed in his moving epitaph on the young poet – but there is a monotonous and gloomy hyperbole about these works that masks Oldham's real talents.

As an imitator of Horace, Juvenal and Boileau, Oldham (along with Rochester to whom he was much indebted) helped establish the sustained modernized imitation as a major poetic technique. However,

Oldham's surest success lay in the authoritative indignation he brought to another topic of contemporary concern: the precarious life of the professional writer. *A Satyr Addressed to a Friend* shows the desperate shifts such people are forced to, while in *Spenser's Ghost* Oldham wrote a bitterly impassioned section on the death of the hapless Butler. The perils and conflicts of the literary life were becoming a major topic of literature itself.

13

This is particularly clear with that very small number of intrepid women who chose to write. As the 'matchless Orinda', Katherine Philips (1631–64) and her circle created an ideal of pastoral retirement in which Philips herself was the poet of romantic and platonic ideas of friendship. Such notions continued the ideals of Caroline court poetry, developing them in a manner which concentrated particularly on the world of civilized and refined feeling that women can create in their own society. Lyrics such as 'To my Excellent Lucasia on our Friendship', for example, suggest a feminine world free both from male prejudice and from the political turmoil of the Civil War and Interregnum:

> No bridegroom's nor crown-conquerer's mirth
>   To mine compared can be:
> They have but pieces of this Earth
>   I've all the world in thee.

This was a world of retirement and scholarship in which Philips could write on philosophic and religious matters as well as producing a quantity of translations from French literature. These included St Amant's influential *La Solitude* and Corneille's *Pompey* which was performed in Dublin in 1662 and then published anonymously. This last was a stipulation of the greatest importance to Philips who, like all contemporary women authors, realized that her reputation would be irreversibly compromised if her name appeared in print. 'Should I once own it publicly,' she wrote of her work, 'I think I should never be able to show my face again.' The painful divide between her roles as a lady and as a writer is here made graphic, and that Philips felt it deeply is made clear in a letter to her friend Dorothy Osborne when, much to her intense distress, a pirated volume of her poems was issued by a London printer six months before her death.

In writing to Dorothy Osborne (1627–95), Philips suggests how important letters were to women as a means of self-expression, and Osborne's own letters provide a most sensitive account of a woman's frustrated passions. They are also full of the most finely observed domestic detail, and it was partly these areas of concern that resulted in two interesting biographies written by women, both of which which were long to remain in manuscript.

The first of these, Anne Fanshaw's account of the adventures faced by her husband and herself during the Civil War and its aftermath, is a remarkable combination of dangers endured with courage, affection and intelligence. Lucy Hutchinson's biography of her husband, the *Life of Colonel Hutchinson*, is vigorous if less delicately observed than Fanshaw's work, and suggests a mind whose natural bent was towards historical analysis, objectivity and, eventually, theological speculation. Her fragment of autobiography is more intimately revealing. Here, as she describes her work on translating Lucretius (hers was the first English version of the poem), she suggests both what a literary woman could aspire to and the conditions in which she was obliged to work. Hutchinson was later to disparage the Latin poet's atheism

which even at the first I did not employ any serious study in, for I turned it into English in a room where my children practised the several qualities they were taught with their tutors, and I numbered the syllables of my translation by the threads of the canvass I wrought in, and set them down with a pen and ink that stood by me.

All the time they did not aim at publication under their own names, women were encouraged to write as a graceful accomplishment, to submit their work to the correction of formally educated men and even to circulate it in manuscript. A number of poetic genres were particularly theirs. These included epitaphs and panegyrics on their families and friends, death-bed exhortation, poems on the deaths of children and spiritual meditations. These last were a major and influential form of Nonconformist literature, and the Quakers especially were to encourage their production by women.

The problems faced by literary women in the later seventeenth century are most clearly seen in the work of Margaret Cavendish, Duchess of Newcastle (1624–74). *The True Relation of my Birth, Breeding and Life* (1656), along with her biography of her husband, suggests the courage and resourcefulness many royalist women showed during the Civil War and Interregnum. These works are also an important addition to a literary genre in which women made a distinctive contribution. Nonetheless, the desire to publish her works under her own name brought Cavendish the cruel notoriety of the freak, and not only men were appalled by her defiance of convention. 'Mad Madge' however looked on her detractors with scorn. Her ambitions obliged her to think deeply about the position of women in society and to decry both the assumption of male superiority and the general inadequacy of female education. As she wrote in *The World's Olio* (1655), matters would be greatly improved for women 'if we were bred in schools to mature our brains and to manure our understandings, that we might bring forth the fruits of knowledge'. Cavendish herself was widely self-educated, and women who did not follow her – women who cultivated the increasingly influential image of leisure and passive virtue – she held in contempt. In a number of her tales, she explored these feminist ideas further, and her works in this field are important and interesting examples of the development of prose fiction.

This is a genre chiefly associated in the Restoration period with Aphra Behn (?1640–89), the first professional woman of letters in England. The importance of this role in the history of women's writing is clear but was long denied Behn by obloquy and then indifference to her work. Such responses – the effective suppression of the writing of a woman widely known in her day – are painfully characteristic of the difficulties encountered in establishing a tradition of feminine writing. In addition, to lose Behn was also to lose an innovator in prose fiction of great importance.

In *Love Letters between a Nobleman and his Sister* (attributed to Behn in the edition of 1683), she developed that form of writing in which women had always been allowed to excel, and portrayed (if in a somewhat ponderous baroque prose) a set of developing situations and characters. The use of letters – the genre of the epistolary novel – was soon to be widely influential, but of all her narratives it is

Oroonoko (1688) that forms the basis of Behn's reputation. Here, revitalizing the conventions of romance through imaginative criticism of considerable originality, Behn wrote a work where political convictions and vivid factual description play against a narrative whose exotic nature becomes a means of pointed and immediate moral analysis.

Much of this approach derives from Behn's own experiences of a voyage to Surinam, and her insistence on the factual aspects of her fiction marks an important technical advance. So too does her ability to address important contemporary issues. Her hero derives from the disguised aristocrats who in the artifice of conventional romance find love among the shepherdesses, but Oroonoko himself – the first black hero in English prose – is a prince lured into the most degrading slavery for love. Innately noble, prizing freedom and honour above life, his moral stature throws into terrible relief the barbarous conduct of the white masters who in the end murder him. In terms of contemporary English history, the novel and its values can be seen as a reflection of Behn's own romantically High Tory loyalties in a period of growing Whig opposition, while as a portrayal of power relationships and racism, *Oroonoko* is also an early analysis of colonialism. It is thus a work of prose fiction in which old conventions have been put to radical new uses and so enable the writer to explore the real world.

As a woman living by her pen in a licentious age, Behn provided the market with what it would buy. A narrative such as *The Nun, or The Fair Vow-Breaker* (undated), for example, is a neatly contrived sensational tale embracing the hypocrisy of convent life, passion, bigamy and murder. It is also a study of the effects on women of a permissive male society. As Behn announces at the start: 'the women are taught, by the lives of the men, to live up to all their vices'. Isabella does indeed become a criminal, breaks her vows to man and God, and is eventually punished. She nonetheless redeems herself in the eyes of the crowd if not of God, and Behn's melodrama is tempered by her vigorous pleasure in the irreligious and sensual, by her awareness of the desperation of a trapped woman and by the pitiless realism with which she describes Isabella's contriving the double murder of the women who have pursued her. Such a denial of the genteel and submissive woman however, along with Behn's increasingly unfashionable Tory politics, led to her rapid fall into ignominy. Women's ready way into literature was thus barred by the image of a 'lewd harlot' whose work caused her reputation to be wholly destroyed.

<h1 style="text-align:center">14</h1>

Behn had begun her literary career in the theatre where she wrote seventeen plays and enjoyed the esteem of her male peers until forced by political rivals from the stage. An insatiable hunger for drama had not been wholly starved during the Commonwealth. Farces and fragments were occasionally performed, plays were still printed, while music drama survived in the two parts of Davenant's *The Siege of Rhodes* (1656, 1657). This dull but epoch-making work used actresses and movable scenery while, as what Dryden called the 'first light' of the heroic play in England, Davenant's work suggested the seminal theme of love and honour played out at length in an exotic setting and with elaborate symmetries of plot. Neither part of the work however used the heroic couplets later considered essential.

With the Restoration of the theatre-loving Charles II, Thomas Killigrew (1612–83) and Davenant were allowed to form the King's Men and the Duke's Men at the Theatre Royal, Drury Lane, and Covent Garden. Both worked a repertory system for an audience swayed by aristocratic tastes. Both also employed actresses and used lavish sets and costumes on an illusionistic stage. However, while Killigrew inherited the rights to earlier dramas, Davenant sought out new work at a time when, as John Evelyn wrote of a 1667 production of *Hamlet*, 'the old plays began to disgust this refined age'.

One dubious innovation was the heroic play. Roger Boyle, Earl of Orrery (1621–79), had written at royal command *The General* (1662), an awkward and precious work in the French tragic manner, following this with the extravagant *Mustapha* (1665). Much to his later regret however it was Dryden who was the chief exponent of the form, and it was Dryden who declared that 'an heroic play ought to be an imitation, in little, of an heroic poem'. The ideal was to draw all things 'as far above the ordinary proportions of the stage as that is beyond the common words and actions of human life'. The result, in works such as *The Indian Queen* (1664) and *The Indian Emperor* (1665), is artifice, rhymed aristocratic rant and an often excessive ingenuity of argument and imagery. The heroic dramas of Elkanah Settle (1648–1724), along with those of Nathaniel Lee (1645/52–92) and the early Thomas Otway (1652–85), continue this mode but are merely wearisome in their extravagance.

Blank-verse tragedy was attempted in 1677 with Lee's *The Rival Queens*. Dryden's *All for Love, or The World Well Lost* (1677) – a version of *Antony and Cleopatra* – suggests the importance of a Shakespeare 'refined' for the age and is an attempt to compress Jacobean vastness into the classical constraints of one location, one day and ten characters. One of the strengths of *All for Love* is pathos, a mood further developed in Thomas Otway's *The Orphan* (1680). Like Lee and Dryden, Otway also tried to discuss political issues, but in *Venice Preserv'd, or A Plot Discovered* (1682), he went beyond contemporary circumstances to combine revenge tragedy, pathos and bawdy comic satire with the well-worn themes of love and honour. In the characters of Pierre and Jaffeir especially, he created figures who rise above mere convention and move away from aristocratic heroes towards pathos. Such a development is again clear in the 'she-tragedies' of John Banks (active 1677–96), and suggests traits soon to be developed by Nicholas Rowe (1674–1718) and others.

One feature of lasting importance was to spring from this mostly forgettable dramatic work: the publication of criticism, or what Dryden called 'a standard of judging well'. Since much of this criticism concerns the drama, we might begin with the play that is the shrewdest and most amusing attack on heroic drama: *The Rehearsal* (1671) of Buckingham, Samuel Butler and the apologist of the Royal Society, Thomas Sprat. Dryden, the new Poet Laureate, appears in the play as the conceited Bayes whose self-incriminating comments ridicule him as he rehearses his latest effort in the absurd rant of love and honour. The parody is perceptive and was widely popular.

Dryden's own criticism however has at its best a breadth and humanity, a judicious and sceptical mistrust of dogmatic theory, which shows the practical writer and widely appreciative reader searching for methods to evaluate, compare and contrast. Dryden was looking for reasoned grounds in literary practice, and in the dramatic criticism contained in his prefaces, prologues and epilogues to individual plays, as well as in that considerable achievement *Of Dramatic Poesy* (1668), he raises (even if he does not always answer) many of the great central issues of criticism.

Dryden was acutely aware of the fecund literary endeavour of the previous hundred years. In common with his contemporaries, he was also interested in the disciplined theories which French neo-classical critics such as Rapin, Boileau and Le Bossu had derived from Aristotle and Horace. Hence Dryden's interest (sometimes vitiated by too great a concern merely to defend his own practice) in the dramatic unities, as well as convention and realism, art and nature, the status of tragicomedy (an area of some weakness) and the defence of rhyme.

At its most creative, Dryden's was a constantly negotiated position in the fundamental debate between the rule of ancient authority and the greater experimental licence of the 'moderns'. Dryden's aim was always to see how a work could be judged as effective in its kind rather than determine how it fitted a particular theory. Unlike Thomas Rymer (1641–1713), for example, author of *The Tragedies of the Last Age Consider'd* (1678), Dryden refused to play both judge and prosecuting counsel in the court of neo-classicism. As a result, if he could not always achieve the sophistication of Rymer's attempt to unite tragic notions of pity and fear with the concept of poetic justice, he at least avoided the pitfalls of describing *Othello* as 'a bloody farce, without salt or savour'.

Rightly and inevitably, the example of Shakespeare was central to Dryden's thinking and if, in the pursuit of a refined prosody, he found Shakespeare 'pestered' with figurative images, in his version of *Troilus and Cressida* (1679), he abstained from refining when he found the language more 'significant' than 'pure'. And it is in his analysis of the Jacobean dramatists – Shakespeare, Beaumont and Fletcher and, above all, Ben Jonson – that Dryden reveals the innovative subtlety and power of his critical approach. He defines what he sees as the general characteristics of these writers admirably. Indeed, Johnson praised Dryden's depiction of Shakespeare as 'a perpetual model of encomiastick criticism; exact without minuteness, and lofty without exaggeration'. Dryden also reveals a sense of historical development, while his analysis of *Epicoene* is the first example of extended practical criticism in English, a piece that moves easily between the analysis of technique, the abstraction of theory and a knowledge of evolving technical terms.

Above all, Dryden created in these critical writings an English of flexible ease capable of abstract discussion. If the refined tone of gentlemanly conversation sometimes reveals the shortcomings of such an approach – playing hide-and-seek with the precise definition of such key terms as 'nature', or preferring the witty riposte to the well-reasoned response – the breadth and fairness of his approach richly deserve Johnson's comment that 'Dryden may properly be considered as the father of English criticism.'

Dryden's critical comments on comedy were more distinguished than his theatrical practice. Earlier comic writers such as Richard Brome (*c.* 1590–*c.* 1652) and James Shirley (1596–1666) in works such as *Love in a Maze* (1631) and *Hyde Park* (1632) had pointed forward to the fashionable wit and social élitism of the Restoration comic stage. It is with the work of Sir George Etherege (?1634–91) however that Restoration 'genteel comedy' achieved its first success. *The Comical Revenge, or Love in a Tub* (1664) unites a high plot and a low one through Sir Frederick Frollick, an early rake hero. Etherege followed this in 1668 with *She Wou'd if She Cou'd*, an upper-middle-class comedy of wit and sexual cynicism where dialogue becomes a centre of dramatic interest. Such work is altogether more sophisticated than the comedy of humours maintained by Thomas Shadwell or the low farces of Tom Durfey (1653–1723) and Edward Ravenscroft (1644–1704). It is in *The Man of Mode* (1676) however that Etherege achieved his most important and most ambiguous work. Dorimant, who is probably a portrait of Rochester, is the 'exquisite fiend' – attractive, cruel, manipulative, a Hobbesian rake delighting in the glory and power of sexual conquest – who in the end finds his match in the shrewd and shrewish Harriet. Etherege's is a world of duelling wit and passion here thrown into relief by the absurd Sir Fopling Flutter.

The moral complexity of Etherege is further developed in the work of William Wycherley (?1640–1716), author of *The Country Wife* (1675). The various strands of the plot are handled with a self-delighting expertise that enhances both the artificiality and the range of satirical analysis, while the scenes of *double entendre* in which wit becomes a form of sexuality support Wycherley's unsettling and obsessive word-play. For example, Wycherly's Horner is the spuriously impotent giver of cuckold's horns whose name sounds like 'Honour' and who, knowing himself to be no better than anyone else, exposes folly and hypocrisy in marriage with as much relish as he enjoys the seductions from which he emerges scot-free. The moral relativism of *The Country Wife* is the sophisticated achievement of a satiric age, and although *The Plain Dealer* (1676) attempts to show the follies of misplaced idealism in the figure of Manly (a character who became the author's sobriquet) the play's too strident contrast of dark emotion and sentimental romance lacks the subtlety of Wycherley's masterpiece.

The third major comic dramatist of the late seventeenth century is William Congreve (1670–1729). Indeed, *The Way of the World* (1700) is one of the greatest English comedies. The very considerable complexity of the plot reflects the ways of a complex, mercenary existence, while the variety and brilliance of the language are also a means of characterization. The plot turns on the inheritance of money, and while Fainall and Mrs Marwood are shown as characters motivated by selfish individualism, Mirabell, the reformed rake, acts in response to finer feelings of generosity and so helps to restore social order. His brilliant dialogues with Fainall and Millamant discuss legal, financial and marital issues with remarkable wit and openness, while the genuine concern for morality and a tone more decorous than that in earlier work suggest a movement away from the Restoration libertine ethos.

This had been forcibly urged in Jeremy Collier's *Short View of the Immorality and Profaneness of the English Stage* (1698), while the values of a more bourgeois audience were also beginning to show their influence. Although *The Relapse* (acted 1696) and *The Provoked Wife* (1697) of Sir John Vanbrugh (1664–1726) assert the moral force of presenting vice directly, and comedies such as *The Recruiting Officer* (1706) and *The Beaux' Stratagem* (1707) of George Farquhar (1678–1707) made interesting diversions into the ordinary social world of the early eighteenth century, the dramatic work of Richard Steele (1672–1729) shows an attempt to deal sentimentally with middle-class life – a fundamental shift in taste most usefully discussed in the context of the succeeding age.

15

The Restoration was also an important period of experimentation in the styles of continuous prose. The decades that saw the polished ease of Dryden, the noble intensity of Clarendon and the spiritual genius of Bunyan should not be reduced merely to the cliché of the search for a plain style advocated by members of the Royal Society. Indeed, on closer inspection, even the writing of these men proves more diverse than their pronouncements, taken in isolation, might suggest.

The scientific endeavours of the later Commonwealth period had been co-ordinated in Oxford by William Wilkins (1614–72) whose *Essay towards a Real Character and a Philosophical Language* (1668) shows the contemporary interest in curing the dissensions caused by words, in allying words to things in the Baconian manner, and so healing the wounds of controversy. In 1660, Wilkins was appointed first Secretary to the Royal Society and, under his influence, his pupil Thomas Sprat (1635–1713) issued his *History of the Royal Society* (1667).

The millenarian expectations that had fired the Puritan experimenters are here transformed by the belief that the Restoration of Charles II had indeed ushered in a new age of enquiry and 'passion allayed'. Sprat urged the Fellows of the Royal Society to avoid verbal wrangling by the use of 'a close, naked, natural way of speaking; positive expressions; clear senses; a native easiness: bringing all things as near the mathematical plainness as they can; and preferring the language of artisans, countrymen, and merchants before that of wits or scholars'. Such a utilitarian prose style was to be employed in the Society's *Transactions* especially and so became the means of providing scientific endeavour with an appropriate manner of discourse.

Others were also involved in experiment. The revisions made by Joseph Glanville (1636–80) to a work originally and significantly titled *The Vanity of Dogmatizing* (1661, 1676) chart a movement away from a laboured attempt to write in the manner of Browne towards Sprat's ideal of a scientific plain style, a style most nearly achieved by Robert Hooke (1635–1703) in his beautifully illustrated *Micrographia* (1665). John Evelyn (1620–1706), a pious man of universal interests, was also an early advocate of the Royal Society and praised its Fellows' search for a plain style. In his own *Sylva, or A Discourse of*

Forest Trees (1664) however, Evelyn's patriotic and scientific interests are blended with a poetic awareness of his subject (Browne was a friend) and a prolix and allusive learning that has something of the cumbrous amateur.

Evelyn's immense *Diary* is a dignified reflection of his multifarious interests and was written partly for his descendants, but it is Samuel Pepys (1633–1703), writing in shorthand and for his own purposes, who is the supreme English diarist. Begun at the opening of 1660 and concluding nine years later with the touching passage on his deepening blindness (a sorrow increased by the fact that he would no longer be able easily to write the records of his most intimate life) Pepys's *Diary* has the freshness of frank and unselfconscious confession. It is at once an account of the nation in a period of tumultuous change and the warm record of the personal life and progress of an energetic state official, a man with a mastery of organization and observation. The myriad details of everyday life are juxtaposed to the great set pieces of the Restoration and the Fire, but it is in the account of the major infidelity of Pepys's life – his wife's discovery of his affair with her companion – that the diarist's genius for self-revelation is most fully and movingly revealed.

Pepys's *Diary* is the record of a man involved in national events. *The History of the Rebellion* (1704) by Edward Hyde, Earl of Clarendon (1609–74), is the work of one who shaped them. Completed during his exile, the *History* is magisterial in its conspectus and often penetrating in its analysis. Nowhere is this clearer than in the many portraits Clarendon worked into the narrative. Figures as different as Strafford, Hampden and Cromwell that 'brave bad man' are all assessed, but it is in the character of Lord Falkland of Great Tew (a determining influence on Clarendon) that the statesman marshals the full weight of his experience to create the most convincing, tragic picture of idealism crushed by conflict. For many generations, this great work was to provide the definitive interpretation of the Civil War, and it remains a great work of English historiography. Gilbert Burnet (1645–1715) also firmly believed 'those who have themselves been engaged in affairs are the fittest to write history'. Hence his *History of my Own Times* (published 1724, 1734), a rambling, anecdotal work, much biased by political principle yet valuable as the only first-hand account of political events in the reigns of the later Stuarts.

A number of spiritual autobiographies also date from this period.

The Puritan concern with self-examination and the workings of grace were a major force in this. The immense *Reliquiae Baxterianae* (1696) of Richard Baxter (1615–91) is a record of the efforts of a remarkably broad and critical mind to find a true, modest Puritanism with which to inspire others. Nonconformist spiritual autobiographies include the plain yet often vivid *Journal* (1694) of George Fox (1624–91), the founder of the Quakers, but of all these dissenting works the most powerful and perennially fascinating remains *Grace Abounding to the Chief of Sinners* (1666), the spiritual history of one of the supreme masters of English prose, John Bunyan (1628–88).

Bunyan's use of a plain style is a measure of his spiritual integrity. 'God did not play in convincing of me,' he wrote in the Preface to *Grace Abounding*; 'the Devil did not play in tempting of me; neither did I play when I sunk into the bottomless pit, when *the pangs of hell caught hold upon me*: wherefore I may not play in my relating of them, but be plain and simple, and lay down the thing as it was.' The passionate simplicity of such prose is the vehicle of a man unshakeable in his conviction that he has been called from sin to grace and that God has summoned him to a spiritual mission. As *Grace Abounding* unfolds, so Bunyan's absolute and comprehensive understanding of the spiritual fever played along his pulses makes us aware that his is the voice of the central Puritan experience, of religious crisis set in an ordinary world of exact and truthful images:

Now was the battle won, and down fell I, as a bird that is shot from the top of a tree, into great guilt and fearful despair. Thus getting out of my bed, I went moping into the field; but God knows, with as heavy a heart as mortal man, I think, could bear; where, for the space of two hours, I was like a man bereft of life, and as now past all recovery, and bound over to eternal punishment.

Bunyan's directness, vivid colloquial exposition and idiomatic dialogue suggest his familiarity with the life of the literate poor and lower middle classes, even as his biblical cadences suggest the all-pervading force of Scripture. The small and sinning tradesman whose story is *The Life and Death of Mr Badman* (1680) exists in a known world of pettiness leading to damnation. Some of the events in that millenarian vision *The Holy War* (1682) are modelled on occurrences in Bunyan's native Bedford, but it is in the first part of *The Pilgrim's Progress*, written in 1676 when Bunyan was ending a third term of imprisonment for his beliefs, that the tremendous forces of the Word within fused into his most enduring achievement.

The absolute demand of the call to redemption, the spiritual uncertainty and tribulation of Puritan man – all the suffering Bunyan himself so intensely knew – speak through the allegory of Christian's flight from the City of Destruction. Allegories of place – the Slough of Despond and Vanity Fair – are realized through an exact knowledge of what they stand for. The hypocrites and tempters – Mr Worldly-Wiseman, for example – speak with the insidious colloquial ordinariness of the spiritually inert and so suggest the perilous nature of everyday experience. Events such as the fight with Apollyon and, most especially, the moment when the burden of original sin falls from Christian's back are episodes of high spiritual drama. But it is perhaps in his vision of the Celestial City that the colloquial and the biblical merge into Bunyan's final expression of the eternal poor man's inextinguishable certainty of spiritual joy.

To turn to contemporary political and religious controversy is to anticipate the genius of Locke, but we should first consider the book that Locke himself eventually reduced to the detritus of history: the *Patriarcha* (published 1680) of Sir Robert Filmer (*c.* 1588–1653). Writing during the years of the personal rule of Charles I, Filmer turned back to paradise to find in Adam his model of natural and hereditary kingship. The first patriarch is the only true exemplar, and 'as the father over one family, so the king, as father over many families, extends his care to preserve, feed, clothe, instruct, and defend the whole commonwealth'. The monarchical authority of the Stuarts is thus seen as the will of God, a benevolent expression of true order. And it is these ideas, absurd in themselves but potent in their mythologies, that underlie one of the most considerable political poems of the age, Dryden's *Absalom and Achitophel* (1681).

16

Absalom and Achitophel is in part a response to a political event, in part a solution to a literary problem. By the early 1680s the Whig party under the leadership of Shaftesbury had brought the Exclusion Crisis to its head by their attempt to settle the succession on Charles II's illegitimate but Protestant son the Duke of Monmouth rather than the king's Roman Catholic brother. Divine right, it seemed, might be subdued to the will of Parliament. Dryden's poem was one element in the pro-royalist Tory campaign to influence a London jury who were currently trying Shaftesbury on a bill of indictment. The work is thus avowedly propagandist.

In the attempt to achieve its eventually frustrated purpose, Dryden's poem had to assert a heroic vision of Tory philosophy (a particular problem given the notoriously lax morals of the king) while satirizing the Whigs in a manner that would be trenchant yet avoid the uncouth. Dryden's solution was to combine allegorical biblical narrative with epic modes and sprightly raillery. By so doing, he effected an important development in English satiric and political poetry.

To give a sense of both objective distance and royal spiritual force, Dryden presented Charles as King David whose natural son Absalom (the Duke of Monmouth) is the fruit of well-known royal promiscuity – the joys of the king's natural body. The people of England, in a parallel much favoured by the Puritans, are presented as the Jews, 'a headstrong, moody, murmuring race' whose latest aberration is the Whig cause, what Dryden calls 'the dregs of a democracy'. Turbulence and a fretting and destructive energy characterize the allegedly impious Whigs, and these forces are in large part conveyed through one of the poem's most influential devices – the satiric portrait.

'How easy it is to call rogue and villain, and that wittily! But how hard to make a man appear a fool, a blockhead, or a knave, without using any of those opprobrious terms,' Dryden wrote. In his portrait of Zimri (the Whig Duke of Buckingham) Dryden reveals the raillery which allowed him to create a suavely destructive portrait of an inconstant man, a portrait that has its classical origins in Juvenal:

> Some of their Chiefs were Princes of the Land:
> In the first Rank of these did *Zimri* stand:
> A man so various, that he seem'd to be
> Not one, but all Mankinds Epitome.
> Stiff in Opinions, always in the wrong;
> Was every thing by starts, and nothing long:
> But, in the course of one revolving Moon,

> Was Chymist, Fidler, States-man, and Buffoon:
> Then all for Women, Painting, Rhiming, Drinking;
> Besides ten thousand freaks that dy'd in thinking.
> Blest Madman, who coud every hour employ,
> With something New to wish, or to enjoy!

This is refined, modern, sophisticated. It is also skilfully contrasted to the more ruthless, self-destructive energies of Achitophel (Shaftesbury) whose diabolic intentions towards Absalom are conveyed by parodic allusions to Milton's Satan.

Dryden attempted to give those courtiers loyal to the Crown the dignity of Virgilian heroes. This was necessary to his purpose because such men had to be shown as faithful to an institution that was not simply royal but divine. The king's natural body might have fathered Absalom, but it is with the sanctified voice of true paternalistic kingship that he must finally crush rebellion. When 'the God-like David' speaks at the close, raillery gives way to the authority of sanctified monarchy. For Dryden, there was still a divinity that hedged a king, and his closing lines are an attempt to express this. A doctrine of power that was soon to be decisively routed on a philosophical level here receives its last major poetic presentation.

Dryden renewed his attack on the Whigs in *The Medall* (1682) and in the portraits of Doeg (the egregious Elkanah Settle) and Og (Thomas Shadwell) which he added to the second part of *Absalom and Achitophel*, a work mostly by Nahum Tate. Dryden's most effective satire of Shadwell however is contained in *MacFlecknoe* (written ?1676, published 1682 and 1684).

MacFlecknoe shows the same excellent raillery as *Absalom and Achitophel* but is perhaps more truly in the mock-heroic vein since epic here serves constantly to point the contrast between Virgilian majesty and the absurd reality of Shadwell himself. Shadwell is presented as the would-be heir to the classical tradition of Jonson and is to be crowned by the notoriously bad poet Richard Flecknoe as heir to 'all the realms of Non-sense'. The poem is fundamentally derisory – Shadwell is laughed into immortality – and although Pope was to take many hints from the work, *MacFlecknoe* lacks the searing analysis of cultural decay offered in the *Dunciad*. Dryden's poem is hilarious lampoon while Pope's is tragic satire.

The later 1680s showed England's greatest public poet exercising his skill in political eulogy, while over a hundred prologues and epilogues for plays (an interest from Dryden's earliest years) developed a variety of themes with relaxed, topical excellence. It is a measure of the flexibility of Dryden's mature genius however that amid so much activity he was also developing the religious and philosophic interests characteristic of his later work. Indeed, now in his fifties, Dryden's mind was discovering its fullest reach. The public poet was undergoing a period of private spiritual questioning.

In 1682, Dryden issued his *Religio Laici* ('A Layman's Religion'), a poem on a matter of crucial importance to him: the nature of religious authority. A new gravity is at once apparent with the mixture of scientific and religious imagery seen in the opening. As the thrust of the argument develops, so Dryden enhances the intellectual energy that flows through the varied rhythm of his couplets with philosophical history, confession and satire. He thereby exposes what he viewed as the shortcomings of deism, Roman Catholicism and extreme Puritanism. Intellectual modesty, a recognition of the unknowableness of God and the belief that 'Common Quiet is Mankind's concern' lead Dryden eventually to the Anglican Church. He solves admirably the stylistic problems of being 'plain and natural, and yet majestick', and his solution deserves more praise than it sometimes receives. Nonetheless, Anglicanism was not the final answer to Dryden's theological problems, and in 1685 he was received into the Roman Church.

This development was far more than the poet's cynical attempt to ally himself with James II (1685–8). He was still searching for what is implicit in so much of his poetry – a surrender to authority, an escape from the potential anarchy of individualism which Dryden often associated with sin and which he clearly recognized in himself. Hence the force of the confessional passages in what is otherwise the rather unsatisfactory combination of theology, contemporary comment and beast fable in the poem of his conversion, *The Hind and the Panther* (1687):

> My thoughtless youth was wing'd with vain desires,
> My manhood, long misled by wand'ring fires,
> Follow'd false lights; and when their glimpse was gone,

> My pride struck out new sparkles of her own.
> Such was I, such by nature still I am,
> Be thine the glory, and be mine the shame.
> Good life be now my task: my doubts are done.

The poetic force lies less in the spiritual drama than in the quiet undertow of modest self-acceptance.

With such awareness there went a refreshed concern with the spiritual force of art that many poets in 'this lubrique and adult'rate age' had often smirched. Of all the classically sanctioned forms that conveyed this sense of inspiration, the Pindaric ode was both the most powerful and the most difficult to use. With the possible exception of Cowley, only Dryden among contemporary poets could achieve the force of many passages in the ode to Anne Killigrew (1686) and 'A Song for St Cecilia's Day' (1687).

'What Passions cannot Musick raise and quell!' In that sublime example of the English baroque called *Alexander's Feast* (1697), Dryden considered this issue at a more profound level. The passions that music raises can indeed be awesome, as Purcell's setting tries to suggest. The conquering hero is made wantonly and absurdly destructive by the very power of the pagan bard who celebrates his victories. Music is a Dionysiac terror, a real and threatening force that is complemented yet not destroyed by the heavenly harmonies of St Cecilia. Worldly desires and heavenly rapture are both part of man's spiritual experience, and in *Alexander's Feast* Dryden sets them side by side as an emblem of man's divided experience.

With the Glorious Revolution of 1688 and the accession of the Protestant William and Mary (1689–1702, 1689–94), Dryden was deprived of the posts of Historiographer Royal and Poet Laureate. (Ironically, the latter went to Shadwell.) Dryden now returned to writing plays and to an activity he had pursued since the start of the decade – translation. In this last endeavour, and with his sumptuous and carefully planned translation of Virgil, Dryden capitalized on the device of publishing by subscription. Though on this occasion there were only 350 subscribers, and less than a third of these paid the full five guineas to be commemorated with special engravings in the text, Dryden himself netted a considerable sum for his labour. Publishing by subscription was to become an important source of income for publishers and writers alike. It helped free both from the dominance of a single patron and so became a major stage in the developing career of the professional author.

Aside from their role in the history of publishing, the importance of Dryden's translations – especially the *Sylvae* (1685) and the *Fables Ancient and Modern* (1700) – lies not in their literalness but in the range of their assured, increasingly free identification with the masters of the past. In addition to translating Virgil, Dryden turned to Boccaccio, Chaucer and, above all, Ovid. In this attempt to refashion the past for modern needs, we see the humanist endeavour in action. It was an endeavour that also bore fruit in some of Dryden's finest late work: in the passionate gravity of 'To the Memory of Mr Oldham' (1684) and the patriotic, Horatian ideal espoused in 'To my Honour'd Kinsman, John Driden' (published 1700). This last work is strong in the classical poise of the man who, in the last year of the century and of his own life, could calmly review a period of the greatest turbulence and declare:

> 'Tis well an Old Age is out
> And time to begin a New.

But that new age, in truth, had already begun.

Science, Satire and Sentiment

I

A chief spokesman of the new age was John Locke (1632–1704) whose thought – measured in expression, magisterial in its range – touched on the central problems of science and perception, religion, politics, education and language, to propose solutions that influenced the conduct of life and the writing of literature for over a century.

In the *Essay Concerning Human Understanding* (1690), Locke cast himself as one clearing the detritus of illusory thought, the 'curious and inexplicable web of perplexed words' which had been spun by 'the writers and wranglers in religion'. In this, as in so much else, Locke revealed himself as a man working in the traditions of the Royal Society. And it was the scientists, 'the incomparable Mr Newton' in particular, who were so crucial an influence on his thought.

For Locke, all human knowledge proceeded from sensations falling on the brain. He believed that at birth the mind was a blank innocent, free from innate notions. It was a *tabula rasa* on which experience wrote its endless variety of 'ideas'. These ideas might be of an object's primary qualities – of what, following Newton, Locke saw as the fundamental mathematical properties of 'solidity, extension, figure, motion or rest, and number' – or those secondary qualities which strike us for instance as an object's taste or smell. The mind is passive when it receives such simple ideas from sensation but active when, whether reasonably or not, it goes about associating them into complex notions or abstractions. If the mind chooses to associate simple ideas on the basis of rigorous discrimination then it is using judgement; if however it is merely enjoying random similarities in order 'to make up pleasant pictures and agreeable visions in the fancy' then it is being deluded by wit down the dangerous path to poetry and rhetoric.

Beyond sensation and the snares of fancy there lay for Locke the mind's ability to construct rational arguments – what he called 'demonstration'. In particular, he believed the mind could construct arguments to prove the existence of God. Just as Newton's physics required God to be the Prime Mover of matter into motion and suggested that the Creator was uniformly present in the infinity of space, so for Locke 'the works of nature, in every part of them, sufficiently evidence a deity'.

This was an idea as old as Cicero. Man, the thinking second cause, could demonstrate the necessity of an infinite First Cause with a logic 'equal to mathematical certainty'. Further, the design of the universe revealed, in the title of John Ray's book, *The Wisdom of God Manifested in the Works of the Creation* (1691). Such an intricate balance made nature appear as a divinely animated machine, a celestial clock, and such a mechanism of necessity required a celestial clock-maker. In the words of Archbishop Tillotson (1630–94): 'As any curious work, or rare engine doth argue the wit of the artificer; so the variety, and order, and regularity, and fitness of the works of God, argue the infinite wisdom of him who made them.'

Others such as Joseph Addison (1672–1719) could temper too facile an optimism in celestial mechanics with a 'secret horror' at the smallness of man as he contemplated the silence of interstellar space. Nonetheless, it was Addison himself – the supreme popularizer of the age – who, confident that the infinity of space was also the infinity of God, could fuse Locke, Newton and Cicero with the words of the Psalmist to write the most enraptured vision of scientific man beholding the heavens as they turned in newly discovered glory:

> The spacious firmament on high,
> With all the blue ethereal sky,
> And spangled heavens, a shining frame,
> Their great original proclaim:
> The unwearied sun from day to day,
> Does his creator's power display,
> And publishes to every land
> The work of an almighty hand.

But how far was this divine and rational universe a Christian universe? Locke was himself a sincere believer (he died listening to the Psalms) and in his significantly titled *The Reasonableness of Christ-*

ianity (1695) he showed that Christian teaching, 'self-love and social' are all of a piece. Miracles, mysteries and other revelations – especially the tenets of papist dogma ridiculed in John Toland's *Christianity Not Mysterious* (1696) – can only serve what Locke himself called 'a religion suited to vulgar appetites; and the state of mankind in this world, destined to labour'. Nonetheless, with the Roman Catholic James II (1685–8) succeeding to the throne, religious extremism once again seemed to threaten the basis of political stability. Locke's solutions to these problems were perhaps his most influential writings.

In his *Letters Concerning Toleration* (1690), originally written in Latin, Locke proposed that religious dogmas cannot be imposed or forbidden by the state since such notions exist on the level of speculation rather than as certain knowledge. Consequently, rulers and magistrates should tolerate all save atheists (whose disbelief forbids them recognizing divine punishment as the ultimate sanction of social bonds) as well as such groups as Roman Catholics whose deepest allegiance was to a foreign prince. The Crown however, secretly in the pay of the French and open in its avowal of Catholic sympathies, pursued the policies that had fomented the Exclusion Crisis of the early 1680s. These were brought to a head by the abdication of James II in the Glorious Revolution of 1688.

Parliamentary resistance to the Catholic heir was originally led by Shaftesbury and had resulted in the formation of the first political parties: the royalist Tories and the opposition Whigs. Though some men such as the politically experienced and moderate George Savile, Marquess of Halifax (1633–95), had tried to set patriotism above party – in the elegant wit of *The Character of a Trimmer* (1684) Halifax compared parliamentary wrangling to a boys' snowball fight – Shaftesbury himself was also motivated by a challenging vision of trade and national prosperity.

Dutch merchants had thrived with democratic religious toleration, and Shaftesbury nourished similar hopes of English commercial expansion. Hence in part his interest in religious freedom and his concern to remove the threat posed by a Roman Catholic heir. And it was Locke who, as Shaftesbury's adviser and confidant, formulated not only the philosophic grounds of religious toleration, but the principles of a new constitution which would eventually justify the Glorious

Revolution and so help determine the nature of English politics for over a century.

The first of Locke's *Two Treatises of Government* (written 1679–89, revised 1689, published 1690) demolished with devastating exactitude the patriarchal basis of kingship we have seen developed in the work of Sir Robert Filmer. In place of kings established by biblical precedent, Locke urged a notion of kingship based on the consent of the people, a consent they could withdraw if a monarch proved tyrannical. Nonetheless, although Locke held a democratic view of popular sovereignty and urged the choosing of a representative legislative assembly to balance the executive power of the king and his servants, he did not believe in modern forms of democratic government: the idea of one person, one vote. Because 'government has no other end but the preservation of property', the legislative assembly must reflect the importance of the propertied interest. Throughout the eighteenth century, the British Parliament was an oligarchy of the landed gentry.

It was these men who nonetheless created the England wryly admired by Voltaire (1694–1778) in his *Lettres philosophiques*, first published in an English translation as *Letters Concerning the English Nation* (1733) and so, perhaps, an honorary volume of English literature. Voltaire saw that partly under the guidance of Locke, belief in absolute and divine kingship had been quietly replaced by a mixed constitution of Commons, Lords and a monarch invited to rule by Parliament. Politics was henceforth to be fought out in the ever shifting allegiances of party. In addition, a Toleration Act of 1689 allowed freedom of worship to Roman Catholics and Dissenters, even if it laid them under heavy penalties and forbade them representative office.

Such advances in political and religious liberty were matched by developments in trade. A revolution in commerce – the founding of the Bank of England, the Stock Exchange and the National Debt – led to extraordinary new wealth and the haphazard accumulation of what was eventually to become an empire. Shaftesbury's dream was being realized. By 1760, Britain had annexed most of India, much of North America and the wealth of the West Indies. Her merchants held the purse-strings of world trade.

Such new wealth created its own problems of ethics and analysis.

While conventional moralists, drawing on classical sources, were quick to point out that excessive riches corrupted empires, the radical Bernard Mandeville (1670–1733), taking a materialist approach in *The Fable of the Bees* (published 1705 as *The Grumbling Hive* and finally revised in 1724), argued that for ineradicably wilful mankind it was not pure enterprise but 'fraud, luxury and pride' that were the spurs to prosperity. Private vices apparently stimulated the public benefits of wealth, and for urging such a view Mandeville was to see his book banned and his name thrown into disrepute.

Others suggested that where trade went the civilizing arts would follow, and, with wealth and the arts, there allegedly went peace and a love of country, as well as the belief that political freedom accompanies trade. Such ideas were expressed by poets as various as the deftly colloquial lyricist Matthew Prior (1664–1721), Pope in *Windsor Forest* (1713), John Dyer (*c.* 1700–58) in *The Fleece* (1757) and most famously in the verses Thomson inserted into his drama on a great English patriot, *Alfred* (1740):

> When Britain first, at heaven's command,
>   Arose from out the azure main,
> This was the charter of the land,
>   And guardian angels sung this strain –
>   'Rule, Britannia, rule the waves;
>   Britons never will be slaves.'

To some in what was now one of the most powerful nations on earth, such sentiments seemed nothing less than a self-evident truth.

2

It was out of such a newly invigorated life of politics, business and religious dissent that there emerged one of the great writers of the early part of the eighteenth century: Daniel Defoe (?1660–1731).

The country created after the Glorious Revolution was a marketplace of intense competition, and Defoe was an early victim. In 1692, the dissenting Whig merchant who had greeted William III in verse was bankrupt to the tune of £17,000. Defoe turned his extraordinary energies to political pamphleteering. By 1703, he was in government secret service and pouring out propaganda works in prose and verse. In response to fears over William's Dutch sympathies, for example, Defoe wrote *The True Born Englishman* (1701), arguing that the history of the country made a nonsense of ideas of racial purity.

In religious polemic, Defoe assumed a number of satirical masks, but his *Shortest Way with Dissenters* (1702), affecting to expose High Church attitudes through mimicry of their more bigoted notions, grievously backfired. Defoe was proceeded against for seditious libel, arrested, imprisoned and sentenced to public humiliation. In response, he wrote his *Hymn to the Pillory* (1703), a courageous exposure of political injustice. Though the mob that might have taunted him wreathed him with flowers, this was the turning-point in Defoe's life. Destitute and despised by many, he accepted an offer from the moderate Tory leader Robert Harley, Earl of Oxford, to write and edit his thrice-weekly *Review* (1704–12).

In addition to journalism and works on psychology and the occult such as *The Apparition of Mrs Veal* (1705), Defoe wrote essays in historical journalism, re-creating great natural disasters through the imaginative use of historical records. These culminated in an undoubted masterpiece of historical reconstruction: *A Journal of the Plague Year* (1722). This picture of London in agony is told by a Puritan manufacturer aware of the hand of Providence in all things, yet fascinated too by the details of collective urban life. These he relates through Defoe's masterly use of an informal, apparently artless style. Horror, pathos and macabre humour jostle with statistics, scientific reflection and a concern with the financial and moral effects of the plague. Suggesting the breadth and literary novelty Defoe brought to Elizabethan plague pamphlets, *A Journal of the Plague Year* is a Dissenter's ledger of man's courage and fickle iniquity, a work of fact transformed by imagination.

In his own business and his work for Harley, Defoe himself had travelled extensively in his native country. The result was *A Tour through the Whole Island of Great Britain* (1724, 1725, 1727). Defoe's travelogue develops a newly revived interest in topographical description to present a detailed, various and occasionally elegiac account of the nation's life, towns and commerce.

It was as an author of commercial and moral works however that

Defoe revealed himself as a skilled writer for craftsmen and small shopkeepers, providing works in a 'free and familiar' style which continued the tradition of the vernacular as a living medium of printed instruction. Again, near the end of his career, and amid the detailed practical advice of *The Complete English Tradesman* (1725), Defoe advocated an influential ethical ideal of commerce. Trade, he declared, is 'a plain visible scene of honest life, shewn best in its native appearance, without disguise; supported by prudence and frugality'. Such a concern with moral values is also clear in Defoe's *The Family Instructor* (1715, 1718). Here, in dialogues that vividly capture the tone of middle-class family life, he urged the ideal of a companionable relationship between man and wife.

The many reprintings of Defoe's works in these genres suggest how popular books of instruction and morality were. This fact leads naturally to a discussion of titles written for a large market and to a recognition of that important figure in eighteenth-century literature – the Grub Street 'hack'. In 1725, Defoe himself declared: 'Writing is become a very considerable branch of the English commerce. The booksellers are the master manufacturers or employers. The several writers, authors, copyers, sub-writers, and all other operators with pen and ink are the workmen employed by the said manufacturers.' Defoe's *Essay upon Literature* (1726) shows that literature itself can be seen as an industry, and such commercial matters were a vital influence on the material now being published.

Expansion had been helped by a change in the law. Though pre-publication licensing, now under a Secretary of State, had been reintroduced by a Printing Act of 1662, this finally lapsed in 1695. While other methods of partial control were soon devised, pre-publication censorship itself was at last abandoned. This was a major advance, and it was in such an atmosphere of greater freedom that the new commercial developments flourished.

The once influential Stationers' Company still held the lucrative market in almanacs, but real initiative now lay with individual entrepreneurs who owned the rights in what they produced and were tending to specialize in particular fields. By the end of the seventeenth century, the influential Jacob Tonson (1656–1736) was publishing scholarly editions and a range of more popular works, supplying these through wholesalers to retail booksellers and a growing provincial trade. This last required both a system for distribution and a measure of advertising through newspapers and lists of publications such as the *Term Catalogues* (first issued 1668). The publisher as the financing and organizing entrepreneur of the book trade was coming into existence.

Crucial to the emerging publisher's activity was the ownership of copyright, his purchase of and control over the intellectual property created by an author and recorded in the particular words of his manuscript. With an increasingly competitive market, it became important for publishers both to define the status of this copyright ownership and to protect it against piracy. In 1710, an Act for the Encouragement of Learning (usually known as the 'Copyright Act') confirmed owners' rights in existing copies for a further twenty-one years and stipulated a renewable fourteen-year ownership on any new copies they might acquire. With their back-lists thus legally secured, the publishers developed a flourishing reprint trade around the works of such figures as Shakespeare, Milton, Bunyan, Addison and Steele.

While levels of literacy are exceptionally difficult to determine for this period, it is possible that half the male population in England and a rather smaller percentage of women were at least functionally literate. Though many might enjoy reprints of older texts (and clearly had an insatiable appetite for theological and moralizing works) new books in an immense variety of fields were now being called for. Authors were needed to supply these, and writing both to order and for money became ever more widely practised. Schoolmasters and clergymen supplemented their stipends by working for the publishers. A few, such as Defoe and a small number of courageous and financially pressed women, turned to writing full-time. Such people – usually given a one-off payment calculated by the printed sheet – helped lay the foundations of the profession of letters in England. As a new group in a rapidly changing world, they also became the centre of an often savage and searching debate about the value of literature produced for cash.

It was out of such a commercial world, and with a sudden and wholly unpredictable fusion of his interests, that there emerged Defoe's great myth of economic man: *Robinson Crusoe* (1719). Defoe himself was now almost sixty, and with this work his genius ripened to produce the first of those books on which his status as a great imaginative writer depends.

As an adventure story, *Robinson Crusoe* has every element of allure: a rebellious son, storms, pirates, slavery and shipwreck on a cannibal island. The style – rapid and accumulative – is capable of suspense, exposition and even pathos. Crusoe's struggle to reach land after the shipwreck itself, for example, is a masterly passage of action, while the detailed observation exactly conveys the blunt horror of loss and loneliness. When Crusoe scans the beach after he has swum ashore, so he glimpses the relics of his companions: 'three of their hats, one cap, and two shoes that were not fellows'.

Crusoe's isolation is at the core of the book and underlies every event on the island with primal insecurity. Such solitude also takes on a religious dimension. The hero becomes a Protestant Everyman reduced to the most barren existence by his adventurous but rebellious urge against the God-given authority of his father and his place in 'the upper station of low life'. In his isolation, the born entrepreneur must at once assert his native resilience to subdue a hostile environment (and so, by his labour, acquire dominion over its natural resources) and come to recognize what in the unsuccessful third part of the book is called 'the great superintendency of Divine Providence in the minutest affairs of this world'. Crusoe is thus a Puritan business man keeping his accounts, acquiring property rights over his island, and, as he rises from subsistence to comparative comfort, a man asking questions about manufacture, technological resources and the economic basis of labour. His ideas in these respects are thoroughly colonialist, the early impulses of a mercantile civilization. Man Friday, for instance, exists for him largely as an economic factor.

But the Puritan entrepreneur at his ledger is also the Nonconformist writing a memoir in the tradition that tabulated instances of God's providence. We have seen that Crusoe is at first in rebellion against these, and the reader's identification with a hero caught between the conflicting forces of human initiative and divine decree partly accounts for the dramatic interest. Sickness however eventually makes Crusoe aware that the universe is ruled by a benevolent God. Through grace and Bible reading the sinner is reborn. God's punishments give way to a mercy displayed in both Crusoe's eventual rescue and his final discovery of his immense wealth. In what is often regarded as the prototype of the English novel, Puritan man, initially rebellious towards God, has discovered the ways of grace and capitalism.

Defoe also wrote two fictions centred on women: *Moll Flanders* (1722) and *Roxana* (1724). Just as *Robinson Crusoe* developed the Puritan tradition of spiritual autobiography in order to present a heroic view of capitalist man and the workings of Providence, so these two narratives are offered in the form of women's lives edited by Defoe with a view to their moral and spiritual content. Both works are thus fictions presented as edifying fact. Furthermore, both works are also the product of a profoundly innovative imagination in the process of exploring the society for which such books were produced. Old formulas are here recast to deal with new problems.

Defoe's concern in each of these works was to develop his view of the relationship between money, class and sexual partnerships, setting these fundamental issues in the context of a male-centred world of ferocious daily competition and the eternal pattern of the sinner in the hands of God. On the one side there is thus the terror of powerlessness and poverty, the chilling perception of this Hobbes of the market-place that 'distress removes from the soul all relation, affection, sense of justice, all the obligations, either moral or religious, that secure one man against another'. On the other side is the Dissenter's recognition that this desperate trial of morality is played out before the gaze of God.

For the writer of fiction, there was also the requirement to entertain. The full title suggests what can be expected from the earlier of Defoe's works: *The Fortunes and Misfortunes of the Famous Moll Flanders, who was born in Newgate, and during a life of continu'd variety for threescore years, besides her childhood, was twelve year a whore, five times a wife (whereof once to her own brother), twelve year a thief, eight year a transported felon in Virginia, at last grew rich, liv'd honest, and died a penitent.* The influence of the picaresque rogue's tale is evident.

The younger Moll, abandoned by a mother who has been transported to America for theft, longs for the gentility she identifies with independence. Her model for this is ironically a local seamstress, a woman free to earn her own living but who is also a whore. Such economic initiative and the use of sex as a bargaining counter characterize the young Moll's own progress as she exploits the vast resources of her cunning to survive in a hostile male world. This is the Moll that most interests us and whose worldly shrewdness and resilience win our ambiguous admiration. Her story, nonetheless, is told by the older Moll – Moll the respectable bourgeois penitent. It is this woman who sees (or affects to see) the hand of Providence in the bizarre coincidences that have led her towards worldly security. At the close of the work, happy with the man she loves, with her affectionate son (a product of her incestuous relationship) and her genteel status obtained through money inherited from her mother and augmented by the profits of crime, Moll can believe that it is the mercy of God which has brought her to the state where she can finally afford to be a Christian gentlewoman.

In Defoe's last novel, *Roxana* (1724), the ambiguous moral focus of *Moll Flanders* is sharpened to tragic clarity. Roxana lives in a world where she is obliged to exploit her sexuality to avoid destitution. Joying in her independence, she rises to a ringing assertion of personal liberty. The novel shows the terrible social, psychological and spiritual price that must be paid for such freedom, a freedom which Defoe exposes as illusory. In so doing, he also achieved developments in the art of prose fiction that were of exceptional formal importance. External events are now matched with internal development, an exposure of corruption in society with a portrait of its effects on an ambitious individual trapped and destroyed by 'the opposite circumstances of a *Wife* and a *Whore*'. As the work reaches its searing conclusion, so we realize that this considerable formal achievement is the spiritual biography of a woman in hell.

3

Women themselves were also writing and even, on occasions, publishing. This was despite the difficulties placed in the way of those who wished to preserve their reputations by avoiding men's disparagement of female learning. Such women had to face the increasing emphasis placed on the domesticated and submissive woman, and to brave the reputations of Aphra Behn and those who had followed her into Grub Street. Only a very small number dared openly protest. In 1694, for example, Mary Astell (1666–1731) wrote her *Reflections on Marriage*, following these three years later with *A Serious Proposal to the Ladies*. Recent scholarship has also allowed us to hear again the well-argued, bitterly experienced works of such poets as Lady Mary Chudleigh (1656–1710) and the finer Sarah Fyge Egerton (?1669–1722) in which they inveigh against 'these finite males' who would 'our thoughts control'.

A small number of women, often under the pressure of personal circumstances, defied this control and began to cater for the varied tastes of the growing reading public – a public which nonetheless remained fairly small, leisured and able to afford publications whose average cost was between one and two shillings. Such an audience drew its numbers increasingly from the middle classes, and in ways both powerful and various these people were to help determine the literature writers produced. This in turn required authors who lived by their pens to be proficient in a variety of genres, and just as Defoe published political pamphlets, historical re-creations, educational works and prose fiction, so Mary de la Riviere Manley (1663–1724) wrote plays, political satire, fiction and journalism. In her day, she was both widely popular and notorious as the skilful self-publicist of a number of scandalous satirical works such as *The Secret History of Queen Zarah and the Zaraians* (1705). Ironically claiming to be a translation from the Italian, this work, like Manley's *The New Atalantis* (1709), is a racy exposé of high-society scandal written with a keen awareness of its political implications.

The work of Eliza Haywood (1693–1756) is more various and altogether more influential. Escaping an unhappy marriage and determined to support herself by writing, Haywood too produced works of satirical scandal such as *The Secret History of the Present Intrigues of the Court of Caramania*, issued anonymously in 1727. Her experiments in prose fiction however are of more considerable interest for they show a prolific author freely experimenting and developing narrative forms, moulding and being moulded by the requirements of her readers and establishing a number of factors central to the evolving novel. None of these is of more importance than her belief that the aristocratic figures from romance are not the only characters of interest in narrative fiction. As Haywood wrote in the opening pages of *The Disguised Prince, or The Beautiful Parisian* (1728): 'Nature confines her blessings not to the *Great* alone.' She continued:

As the following sheets, therefore, contain only real matters of fact, and have, indeed, something so very surprising in themselves, that they stand not in need of any embellishments from fiction: I shall take my heroine such as I find her, and believe the reader will easily pass by the meanness of her birth, in favour of a thousand other good qualities she was possessed of.

Once again, the emphasis is on blurring the distinction between fact and fiction, but by claiming that an ordinary woman and the trial of her virtue by aristocratic men are proper subjects for her work, Haywood was asserting that the experience of her middle-class readers was an appropriate subject for serious reflection. The novel could acquire the respectability of the audience for whom it was being created.

In Haywood's numerous epistolary novels, the letter itself (always tolerated as a medium for women's expression) is developed as a means of analysis, while in *The History of Betsy Thoughtless* (1751) Haywood created a character who was to be developed into one of the great archetypes of fiction: the innocent and naïve woman enmeshed in well-described social predicaments through which she is obliged to progress towards a greater maturity.

4

In *The History of Betsy Thoughtless*, the heroine is at one stage lured into a painful marriage. Haywood's concern with the position of women and their attempts to discover their lives in a society where female propriety was being increasingly emphasized is clear from her journalism, in particular her editorship of the *Female Spectator*, a periodical she ran between 1744 and 1746 and which was often reprinted in volume form. Indeed, the opening decades of the eighteenth century witness to the rise of the journal as an important means of providing the reading public with information, entertainment and guidance on important new images of men and women in society.

The *Athenian Gazette* (1691–97), for example, had covered a wide range of concerns in question-and-answer form, while the *Gentleman's Journal* (1692) aimed to include 'news, history, philosophy, musick, translations &c.'. There were many others, but by far the most influential journals of the period were *The Tatler* (1709–11) and *The Spectator* (1711–12). Each was the joint work of Joseph Addison and Sir Richard Steele (1672–1729), sometimes with the assistance of others. In these hugely successful papers, the widest range of interests was covered in an English at once informal but polished, and addressed by equals to an audience of intelligent middle-class men and women. Here were new and articulate voices of the greatest importance.

Both journals, *The Spectator* in particular, developed the essay in the direction of the lay sermon, quietly insisting on a morality that was utilitarian and at times even smug. It avoided nonetheless both the libidinous extremes of Restoration cynicism and the harsh world of the unsociable Puritan, the man who 'thinks himself obliged in duty to be sad and disconsolate'. Instead, the virtues of home and the woman's place within it, of trade, cheerfulness and polite learning were all insisted upon. New areas of literary appreciation joined with an interest in the powers of the imagination and the basis of virtue in sentiment or moral feeling. An image of men as benevolent and compassionate, practical, virtuous and refined was developed alongside a highly restrictive image of women as prudent, beautiful and virtuous beings on whom the wealth of the world may be lavished but who were formed chiefly 'to temper mankind, and soothe them into tenderness and compassion'.

Steele was the originator of *The Tatler*, and his earlier work gives an indication of the interests he brought to his journalism. His first book had been *The Christian Hero, or An Argument Proving that No Principles but Those of Religion Are Sufficient to Make a Great Man* (1701). This title suggests the didactic, moralizing side of Steele's character which in his essays prompted him to argue that it was personal meanness which forbade men from seeing how the word 'Christian' carries with it 'all that is great, worthy, friendly, generous, and heroic'. In such a universe, 'self-love and social' are the same, while, under the influence of Christian teaching, that central eighteenth-century figure, the man of feeling, is beginning to be defined.

Morality and sentiment were again important to Steele's comedies. In such works as *The Conscious Lovers* (1722), Steele was developing a new approach to comedy, one designed both to portray his ideal of the sentimental hero or heroine and to appeal to a predominantly middle-class audience among whom women were now an important group. These were the people who had also begun to reject the licentiousness of Restoration comedy roundly criticized in Jeremy Collier's *A Short View of the Immorality and Profaneness of the English Stage* (1698). Instead of a predominance of wit, there was now to be an abundance of sentiment – the hugely influential idea that virtue in distress is appealing and a suitable vehicle for moralizing.

Others had also been giving theatrical expression to this ideal of a 'joy too exquisite for laughter'. Steele himself praised the works of Susanna Centlivre (*c.* 1670–1723) and admired the lachrymose and occasionally absurd sentiments in *The Careless Husband* (1704) of Colley Cibber (1671–1757), singling them out for their familial piety, 'agreeableness of behaviour', virtue and innocence. These he then contrasted to the worldly cynicism of such earlier comedies as Etherege's *The Man of Mode* (1676) which Steele reluctantly admired for its truth to nature but saw as 'Nature in its utmost corruption and degeneracy'.

Sentimental tragedies such as *The Distress'd Mother* (1712) of Ambrose Philips (*c.* 1675–1749) were also praised in *The Spectator*. This genre included such works as Thomas Otway's *The Orphan* (1680) and Nicholas Rowe's *The Fair Penitent* (1703) in which the heroines eventually submit to the punishments inflicted on them for asserting their sexuality against the ideal of the domestic, familial woman. In George Lillo's hugely popular *The London Merchant* (1731), it is the bourgeois hero who falls through the agency of a worldly female to discover tearful morality and forgiveness in his ruin.

An interest in moralizing sentiment and narrative is seen again in a number of pieces Steele wrote for *The Spectator*. These include the pathetic story of the callous Inkle and the loving Yarico, a narrative told by a virtuous woman in response to taunts on the fickleness of her sex. This tale so touches the writer that he finally leaves the room with fashionable and decorous tears in his eyes. Rather more successful is the balance of sentiment and benevolent satire in Steele's portrayal of the misprized love of Sir Roger de Coverly.

Sir Roger is the most memorable of the characters who constitute the club of which the quietly observing Mr Spectator is himself a member. Sir Roger represents the Whig authors' moderate view of the old Tory landed gentry – paternalistic, benevolent, a shade obtuse. Sir Roger's friend Will Wimble delightfully suggests the life of the dependent younger son, but it is in the character of Sir Andrew Freeport that Steele depicts his ideal of the great Whig merchant, the cultured man of business, master in the London of trading activity so well described in *Spectators* 69 and 454. And it is Sir Andrew, confident that free trade and good accounting are the sure paths to success, who eventually raises himself to the status of the great Whig magnate, the new model of the landed gentry favoured by the Hanoverian monarchs as men whose property was the basis of their parliamentary power.

Such themes are supplemented in *The Spectator* by an interest in literature and aesthetics. In these fields, Addison as a philosopher of the imagination was the more considerable figure. His contributions, however, should not be seen in isolation. Morals and aesthetics had been united, for example, in the various works of Anthony Ashley Cooper, third Earl of Shaftesbury (1671–1713), which were collectively reprinted as *Characteristicks of Men, Manners, Opinions, Times* (1711). For Shaftesbury, to philosophize was 'to learn what is just in society, and beautiful in nature, and the order of the world'. Man can do this on the basis of his moral sense and independently of God's command. Man is now seen as naturally virtuous through taste and inclination. Virtue itself lies in the affections and these, as well as being their own reward, contribute to the general good.

Such an intuitive moral sense was dependent as much on feeling as on thought, and Shaftesbury encouraged his readers to make 'a formal descent on the territories of the heart'. Here they would learn to identify the beautiful with the good and glimpse in the grandeur of the universe how 'every thing is govern'd, order'd, or regulat'd *for the best*, by a designing principle, or mind, necessarily good and permanent'. Shaftesbury saw nature as the handiwork of God the supreme artist, while man was the 'mortal artist, who can thus imitate the Creator'. This he does not by copying outward appearances nor, as Locke believed, by tacking on to his work the deceitful embellishments of rhetoric, but by being at one with the organizing and creative principle of nature itself. 'Like that Sovereign Artist or Universal Plastic Nature, he forms a whole, coherent and proportion'd in itself, with due subjection and subordinancy of constituent parts.' Such ideas, greatly developed by German thinkers, were to return to English poetry a century later in the work of Coleridge.

Others were also pursuing the sublime. In the works of the irascible John Dennis (1657–1734), for example, the writer records how the Alps produced in him 'a delightful horror, a terrible joy'. Nonetheless, as there was nothing in nature without rule and order, the same was true of poetry which should be an exact imitation of nature. Hence the importance both of received critical rules (a concern Dennis argued should not be taken to excess) and of the Christian religion as the basis of 'all that is sublime and majestick in reason'. Poetry kindles passion to inform thought and faith. Milton becomes the great English exemplar of this, and Dennis's praise of his work was to be influential on later eighteenth-century poets.

Addison too wrote a series of influential papers on Milton, analysing *Paradise Lost* partly in terms of classical theory and so providing for his audience a popularization of his own wide reading and a sense of the worth of their shared literary heritage. As opposed to Dennis, Addison also urged the value of the ballad tradition, finding in 'Chevy Chase' a fundamental and noble humanity comparable to Horace and Virgil, and in 'The Two Children in the Wood' a natural simplicity which he declared truly affecting. Once again, the psychological basis of aesthetics is stressed, a matter of great importance to future developments.

Addison derived his theoretical approach partly from Locke, arguing that ideas derive from sense impressions (the sight particularly) and can be combined and altered in the mind by a power he called the primary imagination. Stimulated by the sublime, the uncommon and the beautiful, the primary imagination is a legitimate means by which we may perceive the Divine Artificer operating in His works. The poet, recording his experience of this, uses his secondary imagination, while, in creating new worlds of magical delight – what Dryden called 'the fairy kind of writing' – Addison claims 'we are led, as it were, into a new Creation'. The artist makes additions to nature and extends the variety of God's works. Shakespeare, with 'nothing to support him but the strength of his own genius', was a chief exemplar of the faculty, but Spenser, whose works were edited in 1715 by John Hughes (1677–1720), was also held to have peopled the fairyland of poetry through allegorical fancy.

5

Other writers, particularly those of a conservative bent, maintained the traditions of humanist learning against these newer forces. However, when Sir William Temple (1628–99) published his *Essay upon the Ancient and Modern Learning* (1690) and cited the *Epistles* of Phalaris and the *Fables* of Aesop in support of his pessimistic contention that 'the oldest books we have are still in their kind the best', he roused the criticism of Richard Bentley (1662–1742), the finest classical scholar of his day. In an appendix to William Wotton's *Reflections upon Ancient and Modern Learning* (1694), Bentley employed his own modern scholarship to prove the first of the works mentioned by Temple was a forgery, while much of the second was later than Temple supposed. At its broadest, this originally French-inspired battle between the ancients and the moderns was the engagement of received wisdom with critical enquiry, tradition with innovation. Crucially, it was also a debate entered by Temple's secretary and one of the supreme figures of eighteenth-century English literature: Jonathan Swift (1667–1745).

In Temple's library at Moor Park, Swift the young Anglo-Irishman gave himself the education the old-fashioned curriculum of Trinity College, Dublin, could not supply. Working on Temple's fastidious prose, Swift laid both the basis of his own appreciation of style and the foundation of many of his general opinions. It was at Moor Park too that he met the much younger Esther Johnson, the 'Stella' of his poetry and letters, with whom for twenty-five years he was to conduct a relationship of scrupulous and self-defensive propriety. After his master's death, Swift published Temple's fragmentary reply to Bentley, but his chief contribution to the debate between the ancients and the moderns was *The Battle of the Books* (1704).

Couched in a mock-heroic form that owes much to Virgil, Swift's satire is concerned to denigrate what, like Temple, he saw as the jejune and spiteful arrogance of the moderns. These writers, comparable to the Spider in the fable Swift inserted into his plot, spin out their works merely from their own insane and vulgar pride 'which feeding and engendering on itself, turns all into excrement and venom'. In the end, such writers produce nothing but cobwebs. By contrast, the ideal of decorum, of the wide-ranging and scholarly study of nature through tradition, is represented by the Bee whose foraging among the flowers of the ancients furnishes mankind with nutritious honey or what, in a telling phrase, Swift called 'sweetness and light'. The enemies of civilization are thus defined by their vulgarity. They are the hacks and dunces who figure so largely in the satire of the period. And it is just such a character who is the supposed author of the greatest of Swift's early works, *A Tale of a Tub* (1704).

This prodigiously versatile satire is written in one of Swift's most effective modes: the subversive imitation of a well-known genre. In *A Tale of a Tub*, Swift took the form of the Grub Street treatise and, by pushing its conventions into parody, created an ironically self-damning exercise in intellectual aberration – the madness of the unfettered imagination which produces both hack literature and heretical religion. The supposed narrator of the work is a recently discharged lunatic earning a meagre living in the garrets of Grub Street. He proudly calls himself 'a true modern', and his conduct of his entire book ironically displays the faults of the modern dunce. In his enthusiastic pursuit of originality at all costs, the Hack reveals a mind cut adrift from tradition and reasonable restraint. With a last self-damning statement he declares: 'In my disposure of employments of the brain, I have thought fit to make *invention* the *master*, and to give *method* and *reason* the office of its *lackeys*.' This is the Spider triumphant.

It is also the method of religious bigots and political tyrants, the origin of the corrosive evil of those fanatics who bring barbarism and destruction to a commonwealth. The Hack's purpose in the core of his work is to illustrate these tendencies in popery and Nonconformism. This he does through the allegorical tale of three brothers: Peter the Roman Catholic, Jack the Calvinist and Martin the moderate Anglican. Each inherits a coat from their father symbolic of true Christian doctrine and which it is charged they should not alter in any detail. As his tale progresses, so the Hack exposes the ingenious mendacity, intellectual aberration and sheer arrogance with which Peter and Jack trim their coats to the worldly fashions of their time.

What sharpens the edge of the satire, its threatening and pessimistic anxiety, is Swift's ability so to identify with the thought of his Hack as to enlarge his knowledge of lunacy into a vision of universal delusion. In 'A Digression concerning the Original, the Use, and Improvement of Madness in a Commonwealth', we see how the philosopher constructing his new system is merely yet terribly a victim of paranoia: 'For what man in the natural state or course of thinking, did ever conceive it in his power to reduce the notions of all mankind exactly to the same length, and breadth, and height of his own?' Again, world conquerors and street-corner thugs are one, since 'The very same principle that influences a *bully* to break the windows of a whore who has jilted him, naturally stirs up a great prince to raise mighty armies and dream of nothing but sieges, battles, and victories.' The whole world is a lunatic asylum where horrors are magnified by reason and enquiry, and where our only hope is ironically 'the sublime and refined point of felicity, called *the possession of being well deceived*; the serene peaceful state, of being a fool among knaves'.

'But to return to madness': whatever the baying enthusiasts of the *Tale* may assert, their fanaticism has nothing to do with divine revelation. Swift was part of a tradition which saw such disorders as psychosomatic – an effect of the body. In *A Tale of a Tub*, for example, the sublime afflatus of the deluded Aeolists is a rushing, mighty wind that rises from their own guts. Inspiration is eructation, and on this they base a whole divisive faith. For Swift, man is never more physical than when he aspires above the senses.

In *A Discourse Concerning the Mechanical Operation of the Spirit* (1704, 1710) – a piece satirically couched in the form of a 'Letter to a Friend' and published anonymously along with *The Battle of the Books* and *A Tale of a Tub* – sublimated sexual desire is seen as the basis of religious enthusiasm. 'I have been informed by certain sanguine brethren of the first class that in the height and *orgasmus* of their spiritual exercise, it has been frequent with them *****; immediately after which they found the *spirit* to relax and flag of a sudden with nerves, and they were forced to hasten to a conclusion.' Enthusiasm is shown as an upward displacement of the physical. The brain sits atop the bowel. Swift's scatological vision is at one with his refusal to forget that man is physical, animal, bestial. It was a vision that, after prolonged exposure to the deceits of political life, was to help shape the ironies of *Gulliver's Travels*.

In 'A Meditation upon a Broomstick' (1701), Swift parodied the theological device of arguing by analogy, finally coming up with the absurd statement: 'Surely mortal man is a broomstick!' The bathos of the supposed divine is brilliantly deflating, yet such was the versatility of Swift's imagination that on this basis he could rear a horrifying vision of aged man as a decaying entity whose 'last days are spent in slavery to women, and generally the least deserving, till, worn out to the stumps, like his brother besom, he is either kicked out of doors, or made use of to kindle flames for others to warm themselves by'. Bathos and something close to tragedy are held together in this brief, ironic masterpiece.

The 'Meditation' was a practical joke played on a pious lady who apparently took it in good part. More hilarious and more topical were Swift's April Fool's tricks perpetrated against the astrologer John Partridge. As the head dunce of the almanac trade, Partridge was an obvious target. What made him particularly abhorrent to Swift was the fact that Partridge's *Merlinus Liberatus*, selling upwards of 20,000 copies a year, was a vehicle for Low Church propaganda and, in particular, opposition to the Sacramental Test. This tendentious piece of legislation (and one central to Swift's career) denied real influence to Roman Catholics and Nonconformists by admitting only communicating Anglicans to public office.

Swift attacked Partridge in the imagined character of Isaac Bickerstaff, an astrologer who, in his 'Predictions for the Year 1708', gleefully prophesied Partridge's death. On the evening of 29 March 1708, Swift's 'Elegy on Mr Partridge, the Almanac-Maker' was hawked in the streets, while for All Fool's Day there appeared 'The Accomplishment of the First of Mr Bickerstaff's Predictions'. Partridge was placed in the absurd position of having to declare himself alive. The following year, in the deliciously funny 'Vindication of Isaac Bickerstaff', his efforts were turned against him. With crowning absurdity, Partridge's very defence of his continuing existence is used to prove him effectively dead.

The years to 1714 were immensely productive for Swift. He now had a position in the Anglican Church in Ireland but was in London on ecclesiastical business and mixing in the most lively literary and political circles. The Whigs Addison and Steele were particular friends, and the figure of Isaac Bickerstaff became the *nom de plume* of writers for *The Tatler*.

Swift himself contributed a number of papers. These include two of his most successful early poems: 'A Description of the Morning' (1709) and 'A Description of a City Shower' (1710), works in which the conventions of epic simile are parodied through a vivid observation of London street scenes, a comic perception of low life at once exact and humane. Now that Swift had set aside his early and unsuccessful attempts at the Pindaric ode, his sharp, ironic relish for the actual allowed him to reveal the variety of ways in which language is used and abused. These might be the barely literate trivialities recorded in 'Verses Wrote in a Lady's Ivory Table-Book' (?1698), the warm demotic of 'The Humble Petition of Frances Harris' (1701) or the combination of the homely, the surreal and the pathetic in his imitation of Ovid's *Baucis and Philemon* (1706). Near the close of his career, Swift was still recording the brain-numbing clichés gathered in *A Complete Collection of Genteel and Ingenious Conversation* (1738), while in a *Tatler* paper of 1710 he offered 'an admirable pattern of the present polite way of writing' in a letter replete with shoddy punctuation, crass elisions, neologisms and clichés.

Under the wit lay the serious if wrong-headed purpose outlined in Swift's *Proposal for Correcting, Improving and Ascertaining the English Tongue* (1712), his hope that if English were 'once refined to a certain standard, perhaps there might be ways found out to fix it for ever'. This call for 'ascertainment', for setting established standards by rules, was repeated by many. At various times, and often with an envious glance towards the standardization attempted in Italy and by the Académie Française, writers as different as Dryden, Addison and Defoe had called for a body to fix usage in a permanent form. Reason, regulation and authority seemed essential if language were not to descend into chaos. But if Latin and Greek appeared to provide models of permanence, they were languages almost exclusively of the pen. To fix the language for ever was to atrophy it. Happily, Swift's academy never materialized. His influential proposal died with Queen Anne (1702–14), and by the middle of the century the greater wisdom of the true lexicographer prevailed when Dr Johnson declared that 'sounds are too volatile and subtile for legal restraints'.

Far more important to Swift than these activities was the political and ecclesiastical purpose behind his visits to England. He had been sent by his superiors to argue for the remission of First Fruits, the dues paid by the Anglican Church in Ireland to the Crown. It was becoming clear however that Swift's favoured Whig party would consent to this only if the Sacramental Test were repealed, thereby giving greater influence to Irish Dissenters. Such a threat led Swift to formulate High Church opposition views in his *Sentiments of a Church of England Man* (1711) and other related works. However, in his *Argument to Prove that the Abolishing of Christianity in England May, as Things Now Stand, Be Attended with Some Inconvenience* (1711), the ironist triumphed over the avowed authoritarian.

In what is one of his finest prose satires, Swift again adopted the voice of the naïve narrator whose expression of his opinions damns him unaware. The supposed writer is a mere nominal Christian, one of those contemporary figures who advocated an occasional conformity to the Church of England since this was both socially respectable and commercially useful. There is not a hint of spirituality about such a belief. The church is merely a useful place for meeting business associates and for 'rendezvouzes of gallantry'. Swift's work is a chilling indictment of the worldliness of the spiritually enfeebled whose belief is a matter of convenience.

But faith was also a matter of politics, and hence of party. As early as 1701 Swift had composed his *Discourse of the Contests and Dissensions between the Nobles and the Commons in Athens and Rome* which defended Whig ideas and personalities through an implied parallel between ancient and contemporary history. It was becoming increasingly clear however that the Whigs were antipathetic to Swift's High Church views. Furthermore, power was slipping from their hands. When the forty-year-old Swift, fired with political zeal and personal ambition, changed his allegiance to Harley and the Tory party, there began that intense period of activity when, as he wrote in his *Memoirs, Relating to That Change in the Queen's Ministry* (published 1765), his was the 'good pen' employed to 'keep up the spirit raised in the people, to assert the principles, and justify the proceedings of the new ministers'.

A chief place for the employment of his pen was the weekly Tory *Examiner*. Both here and in his related pamphlets such as *The Conduct of the Allies* (1711), disingenuously claiming to rise above party faction, Swift discovered the reach of his powers for propaganda and abuse. The Whig merchant oligarchy, he now alleges, is a conspiracy of 'moneyed men', Dissenters and foreigners who, under the corrupt sway of the great general Marlborough, are determined to continue the vastly expensive wars against Louis XIV purely for the interest received on their loans to government.

But the Tory leaders, Harley and Bolingbroke, were divided even in success, and Swift confided to Stella that mediating between them was 'a plaguy ticklish piece of work'. His very personal letters from this period were posthumously published as the *Journal to Stella* (1766) and they provide an insight into the couple's long and curious relationship. Ostensibly written to both Stella and her female companion, the Stella whom Swift had fashioned for himself is the real recipient of these confidences about their author's contacts with the great. The language, veering from political analysis to the shared privacies of baby-talk, is both intimate and distancing, the closest Swift could come to, and a barrier against, complete commitment. The compelling need to write expresses the depth of Swift's attachment, but the distance, the separation such letters imply, is suggestive of a deeper emotional truth.

And there was another young woman who was powerfully drawn to him in these London years: Esther Vanhomrigh, who would wreck her life as the lover of a genius too self-defensive fully to respond, too deeply involved easily to let her go. She became the Vanessa of his imagination and of *Cadenus and Vanessa* (written 1713, published 1735), the poem in which Swift explored the passions roused by contact with a woman half his age. Here, partly through his use of mythology, Swift brings out the pain and absurdity, his own 'shame, disappointment, grief, surprise', as a beautiful and virtuous gentlewoman, sanitized through his teaching to his ideal of a near-masculine perfection, falls for him and kindles his ageing passion. The greatest virtue turns to the greatest folly:

> But what success Vanessa met,
> Is to the world a secret yet,
> Whether the nymph, to please her swain,
> Talks in a high romantic strain;
> Or whether he at last descends

To love with less seraphic ends;
Or to compound the business, whether
They temper love and books together;
Shall never to mankind be told,
Nor dares the conscious muse unfold.

There is mystery and privacy at the heart of the poem, but these were defences that offered Vanessa no protection. As early as 1699, in his resolutions written for 'When I Come to Be Old', Swift's first vow had been 'not to marry a young woman'. It was a vow he kept.

Surprised by a love he could neither accept nor abandon, frustrated in his hopes of preferment and torn by anxiety as the rift in the ministry widened, Swift still had the energy to develop his literary friendships with the Tory Scriblerus Club: Harley, Arbuthnot, Pope, Parnell and Gay. These influential men were united to ridicule the dullness of false learning and pedantry in the invented figure of Martinus Scriblerus, a modern dunce whose unfinished *Memoirs* were finally published in 1741. But with the death of Queen Anne and the fall of the Tories, Swift's years of apparent influence in London suddenly ended. Merely an Irish dean when he had hoped to be an English bishop, bitterly at odds with Addison and Steele and separated from newer literary friends by his return to his home, the collapse of his hopes seemed total. Exile and misanthropy appeared his only lot.

He was also increasingly troubled by bouts of the deafness and giddiness that had afflicted him since early manhood. Sensing a coolness towards him from both Stella and Vanessa, Swift now threw himself into his deanery chores with the stoic and sometimes grim sense of duty that characterizes his sermons and his ideal of the conduct of his vocation outlined in a *Letter to a Young Gentleman Lately Entered into Holy Orders* (1720). Sermons, he declares here, are to be sober, restrained. 'Proper words in proper places, makes the true definition of a style.' Such a style, he adds, can only be found in intellectual modesty.

Three years later the relationship with Vanessa ended, possibly after acrimony, with her death. From this period too dates the insoluble conundrum of whether there was a secret marriage with Stella. Whatever the facts of this, the truest account of their relationship remains the poems Swift wrote to her, often on the occasion of her birthday. Here, a combination of irony, tenderness and occasional admonishment portrays an affection free from spurious idealism. Slowly too Swift now acquired new friends, and by 1720 he felt impelled into the political arena once more. A new figure emerges: Swift the Irish patriot. It was a title given by others, and one which he always denied.

By 1720, Ireland had been effectively reduced to the status of a colony run from London by the Whigs. A blatant example of this exploitation was the licence sold to William Wood for the manufacture of Irish small change. There was widespread fear that this coinage would be debased and lead to inflation, as well as resentment at the fact that the privilege had been granted without reference to the Irish themselves. While others such as William Molyneux in his *Case of Ireland* (1698) had advanced the theories propounded by Locke to suggest that the Irish (or, at least, the very small body of Anglo-Irish settlers) enjoyed the same rights and liberties as the English, Swift knew that in Ireland power grew out of the barrel of a gun. Political philosophy was one thing, practice another. He needed to shock the Irish into action: 'in reason, all government without consent of the governed, is the very definition of slavery: but in fact, eleven men well armed, will certainly subdue one single man in his shirt'. Such is the vivid, pungent insight of M.B., the patriotic draper of Dublin, who is the alleged author of Swift's five *Drapier's Letters* (1724).

Swift's is a nightmare vision of inflation, of farmers paying their rents with three cartloads of Wood's coins and of squires requiring 250 horses to collect them. In these letters, Swift orchestrated the most daring political campaign of his life, writing to 'the whole people of Ireland' in terms of the most fervent liberty. In the end he was successful and Wood's patent was withdrawn. The people of Ireland fêted Swift as their liberator, though his concern, in truth, was not to free them but merely to ease the worst abuses of their slavery. It was a partial if passionate vision of human rights.

If Ireland was a victim of speculators, she was also considered a fit subject for the more heartless extremes of economic theory. Such autocratic economic schemes roused Swift's indignation, and the result was the finest of his short prose satires: *A Modest Proposal for Preventing the Children of Poor People from Being a Burthen to their*

Parents or the Country, and for Making them Beneficial to the Public (1729). Once again, we are offered the subversive imitation of a well-known form (in this case the economic tract) and a narrator who unwittingly condemns himself. In terms of contemporary economic theory, the alleged author is made ridiculous by proposing to increase wealth by lessening the population, but it is for the gruesome simplicity of his methods that he stands utterly condemned: 'I have been assured by a very knowing American of my acquaintance in London, that a young healthy child, well nursed, is at a year old a most delicious, nourishing, and wholesome food, whether *stewed*, *roasted*, *baked*, or *boiled*, and I make no doubt that it will equally serve in a *fricassee* or *ragout*.' Infanticide and cannibalism, argued with a logic of repellent self-satisfaction, make *A Modest Proposal* a horrific parody of inhuman schemes for economic reform and a bitter satire on the heartless ingenuity of the mercantilist imagination.

It was in these Irish years that Swift also wrote one of the supreme works of European satire: *Gulliver's Travels* (1726). His irony, misanthropy and indignation, his experience both of the world and of the literary means by which its follies might be exposed, are here fused in images that have become proverbial. But it is important not to diminish *Gulliver's Travels* by seeing it simply as a work of unrelenting pessimism. If Swift wrote the book to 'vex the world', he could also write to Pope: 'I tell you after all that I do not hate mankind; it is *vous autres* who hate them because you would have them reasonable animals, and are angry for being disappointed.' *Gulliver's Travels* is a similarly unillusioned view of man's pride and folly, a work of the bleakest irony but not finally of tragic despair.

Books of voyages serve as the genre which the ironist subverts, but the new lands discovered are the old, eternal ones of human folly. Nor is the narrator himself immune to this. His restless voyages outwards are also a journeying inwards towards confusion. Swift's favoured device of the self-deluded narrator grandly offering his work for the improvement of mankind is never more subtly employed. Gulliver's deepening disillusion ends in fantastic and self-condemnatory bitterness.

The process begins in Lilliput where the image of Gulliver tied down by the little people is a powerful exposition of the triumph of pettiness. Despite the stringent social and legal institutions of Lilliput, smallness of physical bearing goes with smallness of moral stature. No schemes for virtue guarantee rectitude. The spectacle of the ministers 'leaping and creeping' for political preferment is a timeless comment on what even quite intelligent people will undergo for public office. The origins of the war with Blefuscu show what they do when they get it.

Though Gulliver himself – a far more useful figure than the ministers – saves the burning royal palace by urinating on it, he wins for this the hatred of the empress. When he preserves the state by destroying the enemy fleet, he rouses the resentment of the emperor since he refuses to annihilate the inhabitants of Blefuscu itself. Few rulers easily forgo the means of mass destruction. Similarly, few ministers like to see others promoted over their heads. The emperor, Flimnap and Skyresh Bolgolam connive at Gulliver's execution. The sentence is commuted to blinding and starvation, but when Gulliver escapes he does not seek revenge. Nonetheless, if he appears virtuous, the emphasis on his physical functions reminds us that Gulliver is a man and therefore inherently physical and gross.

Such a paradox is the subject of the voyage to Brobdingnag. The giants of this country are physically repellent. Nipples are the size of human heads. Enormous lice root at the beggars' flesh. The female odours of the maids of honour tighten the gorge. Gulliver himself is in physical danger from dogs, snails, monkeys and the mound of cow dung he boastingly tries to jump. It is he who is now the little man leaping and creeping to the great.

Patriotism is his boast. English government, religion and history, he suggests, are the best in the world. Nonetheless, after probing questions, the enlightened monarch of Brobdingnag can only conclude that English history is a catalogue of faction and murder, while the men themselves are 'the most pernicious race of little odious vermin that nature ever suffered to crawl upon the surface of the earth'. Gulliver, deeply hurt, tries to court the giant king's favour by describing the secrets of gunpowder. The king is appalled, and Gulliver dismisses him as a mere foreign moralist ignorant of abstract philosophy and wholly inferior to the mighty achievements of European culture. The bigoted, vicious little Gulliver betrays himself to an audience who cannot easily feel superior. In the maze of Swift's irony, we constantly encounter ourselves.

The third book of *Gulliver's Travels*, though written last, is artistically the least satisfactory. The miscellaneous structure contains, nonetheless, some of Swift's finest satirical insights, particularly on the nature of abstract thought. In particular, he shows how extreme abstraction denies the body. On the flying island of Laputa, the sweating, excreting carcass of the earlier books is ignored. As the professors of mathematics and music wander with one eye pointing up and the other directed inwards, they are unaware of their wives' infidelities and worry instead that the earth will fall into the sun. They are quite capable of punishing the inhabitants of Balnibarbi however, a subject state like Ireland whose economy has been wrecked by modern science.

Swift reserves his sharpest satire here for the Academy of Lagado. This is his vision of the Royal Society and of a mechanistic science which allegedly perverts the intellect through warping curiosity. Instead of the humanists' belief that the proper study of mankind is man – however corrupt he may be – Swift's scientists seek to extract sunlight from cucumbers, and nutrition from human excrement, and to revive a dead dog by blowing air up its anus. This trivializing of the intellect also perverts the language. In pursuit of things rather than words, the scientists of Lagado reduce language merely to nouns as part of a project for abandoning it altogether. They then jejunely propose the easy solution to all problems, including political ones. The ordure of politicians will supposedly reveal state conspiracies, for example, while brain surgery will cure party faction.

Gulliver's voyage to the kingdom of the Houyhnhnms is one of the great challenging achievements of eighteenth-century satire, a horrific insight into the paradoxes of moral extremism and of man trapped between the polar opposites of his nature. We here move away from satire on particular follies to Swift the unillusioned ironist's satire on man himself: his pride, his vaunted reason and his repellent moral superiority. With great psychological insight, Swift reveals these last as a combination of the self-hatred and self-glorification that stem from man's refusal to accept his inherent baseness and limitations. To realize this discovery, Swift fashioned three of his most potent satirical images: the repulsive, shit-slinging Yahoos; the rational Houyhnhnms, horse-like creatures whose name ironically means 'the perfection of nature'; and Gulliver himself, the deluded narrator caught between them.

The horrified Gulliver is eventually forced to recognize his kinship with the Yahoos and, in his bitterness, he assumes that the Yahoos personify all that man is. Pride and revulsion then lead the deluded Gulliver to think that his own humanity lies in something superior. He clings to his absurd and self-condemning belief that he can aspire to be a rational horse. Proud, illusioned man warps his already crippled nature by thinking that he is above all reasonable. This belief in his own rationality however merely topples him into the ridiculous extremes of misanthropy revealed by Gulliver at the close of the work. He cannot bear the decent sea captain who offers him the means of his return to England. He cannot bear the sight and smell of his wife and children, preferring instead the company of his horses. In his deluded bitterness, Gulliver joins Swift's other maddened authors – the hack of *A Tale of a Tub*, the projector in *A Modest Proposal* – and offers his views for the universal improvement of mankind. His failure to reform them only deepens his misanthropy. By a final paradox, *Gulliver's Travels* itself becomes a record of the insights of a deluded man into the follies of the world, a work of reform that has effected no improvement.

Swift published *Gulliver's Travels* while Stella was dying, and his love for her is given noble and poignant expression in 'On the Death of Mrs Johnson' (1727), one of the most moving of his prose pieces. With the exception of the ironically subversive *Directions to Servants* (posthumously published in 1745) and his work on *Genteel Conversation* however, Swift's major late work is mostly in verse. Four notorious scatological poems, similar in tone to 'The Progress of Beauty' (1719), date from this period: 'The Lady's Dressing Room' (1730), 'A Beautiful Young Nymph Going to Bed', *Strephon and Chloe* and 'Cassinus and Peter' (all 1731). Each unmasks gross female physicality beneath the paint and petticoats to expose the self-deluded idealism of the men who have made women their goddesses. As Cassinus declares:

> No wonder how I lost my wits;
> Oh! Celia, Celia, Celia shits!

Scriblerian wit characterizes *On Poetry, a Rhapsody* (1733), a self-help manual on being a poetic dunce which, by a typically Swiftian irony, exhibits the poet's immense control of the variety of expression afforded by his preferred medium of the octosyllabic couplet. While 'The Legion Club' (1736) is a searing attack on corruption in the Irish Parliament, the finest of these late poems is *Verses on the Death of Dr Swift* (1731). Here, following La Rochefoucauld's maxim that 'in the adversity of our best friends we find something that does not displease us', Swift imagines the hard-faced reactions of his colleagues to news of his death. Then he imagines an anonymous character speaking disinterestedly in his praise. Swift writes his own epitaph as, near the end of his literary career and eleven years before a commission of lunacy found him to be 'of unsound mind and memory', he has his speaker declare: 'Fair LIBERTY was all his cry.' The boast is repeated in the Latin of Swift's memorial slab with the further reflection that, in death, savage indignation could no longer tear his heart.

6

Swift's genius was to have a great influence on his Scriblerian friends. For instance, when he wrote to Pope 'what think you of a Newgate pastoral, among the whores and thieves there?' he gave John Gay (1685–1732) the idea for *The Beggar's Opera* (1728). Gay further borrowed from *The Rehearsal* the device of a critical discussion of the play within the play, and his targets are contemporary music, contemporary political and social life and the literary modes of pastoral and romance. For the high artifice of the Italianate, Handelian aria, Gay and his musician John Pepusch (1667–1752) substituted the ballad form popularized by Addison.

It is suggestive of the work's subtlety however that the lyrical beauty of duets such as 'Over the hills and far away' draws its imagery from the grim realities of criminal transportation, just as references to the lovers' knot offer elegantly macabre parallels with the hangman's noose. Again, the ironies of pastoral innocence among thieves transfigure the passion of Polly Peachum into something truly ideal, while prison life itself – the duplicities of Peachum and Lockit especially – is a comment on the rabid self-interest characteristic of Walpole's government and the mercantile society that had just endured the first stock-market crash with the bursting of the South Sea Bubble. Speculators, politicians and thieves are one, but Polly and Macheath, united in love, suggest how complex and various the strands of *The Beggar's Opera* are.

Pastoral itself was a widely practised and much debated genre, Addison's protégé Ambrose Philips (*c.* 1675–1749) delighting the 'little senate' at Button's coffee-house with his *Pastorals* (collectively published 1710). These mixed sentimental pathos and the sometimes coyly *faux-naïve* in what the critic Thomas Tickell (1686–1740) called a 'pleasing delusion'. The most liberating use of the classical eclogue and georgic however lay in parody. In Gay's *The Shepherd's Week* (1714), his Grubbinols and Blouzelindas succeed because the literary artifice is both heightened and tested by the characters being the sons and daughters of toil, comic figures whose touching emotions are expressed through parody of a highly sophisticated form.

Lady Mary Wortley Montagu (1689–1762) developed such parody in a different direction with her *Town Eclogues* (1711). 'Saturday' is a lament for beauty's ruin by smallpox, a disfigurement the author herself suffered and which made her an early advocate of inoculation. There is no trace of emotional self-indulgence here but rather a brave, ironic lament for lost worldly delights. Despite her assertions to the contrary, Lady Mary was a woman of wide self-education. Much of her work, in deference to restraining conventions against which she complained, was issued anonymously. Her shrewd and humane *Letters*, especially those describing her experiences in Turkey, are among the most attractive of the age.

Gay's *Fables* (1722, 1736) were his most admired works, and pieces such as 'The Elephant and the Bookseller' and 'The Wild Boar and the Ram' still have their point, sometimes a sharply satirical one. The most pleasing of Gay's non-dramatic works however remains *Trivia, or The Art of Walking the Streets of London* (1716). Here, developing the manner of Swift's city poems, Gay found the evocative in the ordinary and allied his precise observation to both an excellent control of the heroic couplet and a satiric inversion of the forms of georgic. The result is fresh, vividly urban and, in the famous passage describing an apple-seller decapitated in the thawing ice of the Thames, rich with that comic sympathy reached through literary satire that characterizes Gay's work at its best.

At the opposite extreme, the early eighteenth century was also one of the great ages of hymn writing. Much of this was the work of Nonconformists whose verses often preserved the emotional drama of sin and redemption which the labours of Anglican divines tended to skirt, rationalizing them away in the interests of fashionable optimism and a bland, lucrative support of the status quo. Chief among these dissenting hymn writers was Isaac Watts (1674–1748), whose *Divine Songs for Children* (1716) contained such verses as '' Tis the voice of the sluggard' and 'How doth the little busy bee', both to be brilliantly parodied by Lewis Carroll. The existence of parody itself however points to the influence of Watts's achievement, and his desire 'to promote the pious entertainment of souls truly serious, even of the meanest capacity'.

Poetic diction was here eschewed so Watts could write in the language of ordinary people. This was an honest and ancient purpose that was made fashionable in the middle third of the century but which came to be considered as a radical statement of the rights of man at its close. Here however, at the beginning of the age, Watts the Nonconformist speaks for every Christian and achieves purposes most others could only preach. In his *Hymns and Spiritual Songs* (1707), for example, Watts attained the sublime in 'When I survey the wondrous cross', while in *The Psalms of David Imitated* (1719) his absolute faith is combined with a massive, precise simplicity and a truly Horatian dignity of common thought memorably expressed:

> Time like an ever-rolling stream
>   Bears all its sons away;
> They fly forgotten as a dream
>   Dies at the opening day.

Other poets nurtured Horatian dreams of rural retirement. Perhaps under the civilizing influence of Sir William Temple, John Pomfret (1667–1702) described his ideal of a modest and book-lined country retreat, of health, charity, friendship and bachelor freedom. An innocent delight in the pleasures of life is also the subject of *The Spleen* (1737) by Matthew Green (1696–1737), but the most evocative of these poems is 'A Nocturnal Reverie' (1713) by Anne Finch, Countess of Winchilsea (1661–1720). The exact, sensitive description, the wish to wander in nature 'till morning breaks, and all's confused again', preserves the undertow of truly grateful release, something deeper than the catalogue of delight in her 'Petition for Absolute Retreat' and closer to the alert, hypochondriacal sensitivity of her poem on the spleen.

Enjoyment of the natural world led to such descriptive poems as Dyer's *Grongar Hill* (third edn 1726) and the wish to 'draw the landskip bright and strong'. There is nothing of the political analogy of *Cooper's Hill* here. The beauty of nature teaches a passive acceptance of conventional morality, a philosophic quietness heightened by the pleasing macabre of the ruined castle with its moss, toads and ivy. These romantic effects (the word had first been used in respect of landscape by Addison in *A Letter from Italy* as early as 1705) were to become increasingly important. 'A Night-Piece on Death' (1721) by Thomas Parnell (1679–1718), for instance, despite the final vision of heavenly light, is an early example of a long line of eighteenth-century verses on levelling death and the melancholy fascination of 'angels, epitaphs and bones'.

But nature had other lessons than teaching the rustic moralist to die. A large number of didactic and utilitarian poems such as John Philips's *Cyder* (1708) date from this period, enlarging their themes with patriotic statements and historical set pieces in conscious if often deadening imitation of Milton's prosody and the Virgilian georgic. Mere imitation was not enough however. Scientists, philosophers and aestheticians had proclaimed a divine world of orderly and benevolent nature in which man's best feelings were at one with the common good. It was against such a background that in 1726 the young Scots poet James Thomson (1700–48) issued the first version of his *Winter*. As Thomson revised and amplified his work, so there emerged one of the most important nature poems of the century, *The Seasons* (1730, 1744, 1746).

As the seasons of his poem unfold, so Thomson shows the workings of 'the various God' in the natural world. The poet, anxious to peruse divine Nature's 'all-instructing page', records the findings of what Addison called the primary imagination. Minute observation of particulars (partly Thomson's own, partly derived from the growing body of scientific literature) rise to scenes of sentiment and pathos such as the death of the shepherd amid the snows of *Winter*, or to warmly benevolent visions of labouring men in harmony with animals and the land. In such passages as the sheep-shearing episode from *Summer*, we see ordinary people working with a harmonious enthusiasm that at once assures the wealth of Britain as a great trading nation and allows Britain herself to be compared to the mighty Roman empire. Extensive paragraphs of patriotic panegyric then lead to the section in *Autumn* where the blessings of industry and commerce are praised as the origins of civilization itself, of comfort, pleasure, elegance, grace and democracy.

This is the Whig tradition of progress apostrophized, and it was to be the subject of Thomson's *Liberty* (1735-6) as well as the great injunction to 'Toil, and be glad!' in his Spenserian allegory of the triumph of effort over apathy in *The Castle of Indolence* (1748). Such a rapturous praise of Britain's 'infinite progression' was also to have its more dubious expression in the jingoistic warmongering of Thomson's 'Britannia' (1729).

An important aspect of Thomson's delight in progress was the advance of science, and many passages in *The Seasons* and 'To the Memory of Sir Isaac Newton' (1727) either describe the beauties of nature in scientific terms or praise the scientific mind itself. It was also this interest in scientific exactitude that was responsible for the most widely criticized aspect of Thomson's verse – his use of periphrases such as 'the busy nations' for bees or 'the feathered eddy' for homing swallows. Originally employed in the interests of precise or evocative labelling, such phrases now have the deadening weight of merely artificial poetic diction.

As well as praising scientific advances, Thomson also drew on Locke and Shaftesbury and on the delight in the divine order of nature popularized in such works as William Derham's *Physico-Theology* (1713) and *Astro-Theology* (1715). The closing paragraph of *Summer*, for example, shows a Lockeian concern with how ideas 'compound, divide and into order shift' as the mind progresses upwards to what, in *Spring*, becomes a Shaftesburian ecstasy:

> By swift degrees the love of Nature works,
> And warms the bosom; till at last, sublimed
> To rapture and enthusiastic heat,
> We feel the present Deity, and taste
> The joy of God to see a happy world!

Man approaches the borders of the infinite in rapt contemplation.

However, as Thomson reveals in the concluding passage of *Winter* (the section which most powerfully shows the destructive powers of nature) no mortal can fully know the divine purpose until, after death and resurrection, 'the storms of wintery time' are over and the round of the mortal seasons is subsumed into the benevolent cycle of eternity.

So popular a poem as *The Seasons* was a valuable literary property, and nearly a quarter of a century after Thomson's death the work was the subject of an important ruling on publishers' control of copyright. Even in his lifetime however, Thomson – who was obliged to live precariously on patronage and sinecures – was irked by his treatment at the hand of his booksellers, declaring that 'ruthless wasps oft rob the painful bee'. Writing was still the most uncertain of livings. In the words of Alexander Pope (1688–1744), himself a highly successful player of the game: 'the life of a wit is a warfare upon earth'.

7

An important part of the arsenal deployed in that warfare was a mastery of technique. For Pope, this meant the ideal of 'correctness'. Correctness implied an exquisite sensitivity to rhythm, to matching form with content, and an appreciation of those broader issues of critical and humane decorum which in Pope's later works are the focus of his moral values.

As early as the Preface to his *Pastorals* (written 1704–7, published 1709) Pope had declared that the 'numbers' or metre of pastoral poetry 'should be the smoothest, the most easy and flowing imaginable'. These lines from 'Summer' suggest the graceful artifice he could already achieve:

> Where'er you walk, cool gales shall fan the glade,
> Trees, where you sit, shall crowd into a shade:
> Where'er you tread, the blushing flowers shall rise,
> And all things flourish where you turn your eyes.

But Pope recognized the limitations of those 'who haunt Parnassus but to please their ear', and in his daringly precocious *Essay on Criticism* (written 1709, published 1711) he set out to define his broad ideal of the literary life and to satirize those who fell short of it.

Drawing on the wide and sometimes contradictory range of the critical tradition from Aristotle, Horace and Longinus to Renaissance theorists and such modern writers as Dryden and Roscommon, Pope's *Essay* is an attempt to establish standards for writing and judging well. To achieve this, he took account both of received rules and of imaginative freedom, advancing an urbane and unpedantic acceptance of the ancients as the basis for a just appreciation of good literature. Pope realized that both the inspired easiness of manner he praised in Horace and the 'great Sublime' of Longinus were aspects of poetic integrity and that these were fused most aptly in the works of Homer. All other poets from Virgil onwards could learn from Homer since his practice was at one with the truest rules of all – those of nature. It is nature as an inner, life-giving principle of sincere and unaffected excellence that is the ground of Pope's critical ideal:

> First follow *Nature*, and your judgement frame
> By her just standard, which is still the same:
> Unerring NATURE, still divinely bright,
> One clear, unchang'd and universal light,
> Life, force, and beauty must to all impart,
> At once the source, and end, and test of Art.

Great art gives final form to the great, general truths of human nature, to 'what oft was thought, but ne'er so well express'd'.

Against these values stood all that Pope objected to: the pride of false critics with their self-seeking, partial rule-mongering, and their over-zealous concern with style and technical matters at the expense of the whole. True criticism is now seen as the muse's handmaid, and the qualities of the true critic himself are defined as essentially moral ones – 'truth and candour', the very values, indeed, we expect from a good friend. The grounds of excellence in life and art thus lie in shared and decorous humanity. This was a vision Pope was to elaborate in numerous ways and eventually give a tragic power in the face of certain defeat.

In this early period, Pope also attempted to give patriotic and political expression to his enthusiasms in *Windsor Forest* (final version

1713). His praise of a Stuart monarch here and his attack on foreign tyrants give a particular slant to his patriotism and prepare the way for his later role as Poet Laureate to the Tory opposition and a Roman Catholic writer living a life of high integrity under considerable social and political disadvantages. Despite some fine descriptive passages in the poem however, the most considerable work of Pope's early period is also one of the most subtle of eighteenth-century poems: *The Rape of the Lock*.

This poem appears to have been based on a real incident between Lord Petre and Miss Arabella Fermor which had then developed into a serious rift between the two Roman Catholic families. Pope reworked the original events into a mock-epic narrative in which a baron snips the lock from the beautiful Belinda's head only to lose it as it is transported to heaven. Socially, the poem was designed as an attempt to laugh the original families back together again and so recommend the virtues of 'good Humour'. As the work grew from the two-canto version of 1712 into the five-canto version of 1714 however, so it also became Pope's medium for the engagement of the values of his art with those of the world of eighteenth-century high society.

The poem preserves a constantly delighted but critical engagement with the surfaces and underlying tensions of that world. We are shown its vanities, trivialities and shortcomings, often in terms of a comparison with the ancient and heroic values of Homeric and Virgilian epic. Such resonances at once satirize and give evocative splendour to a modern life of fashion, coffee-drinking and courtship over card games. Belinda herself is at the centre of these, and the famous description of her toilet, rich with the bounty of world trade, suggests the nuances by which Pope's poem works:

> And now, unveil'd, the Toilet stands display'd,
> Each silver vase in mystic order laid.
> First, rob'd in white, the Nymph intent adores,
> With head uncover'd, the cosmetic powers.
> A heav'nly image in the glass appears,
> To that she bends, to that her eyes she rears;
> Th'inferior priestess, at her altar's side,
> Trembling, begins the sacred rites of Pride.

Unnumber'd treasures ope at once, and here
The various off'rings of the world appear;
From each she nicely culls with curious toil,
And decks the goddess with the glitt'ring spoil.
This casket India's glowing gems unlocks,
And all Arabia breathes from yonder box.
The tortoise here and elephant unite,
Transform'd to combs, the speckled, and the white.
Here files of pins extend their shining rows,
Puffs, powders, patches, bibles, billet-doux.
Now awful beauty puts on all its arms;
The fair each moment rises in her charms,
Repairs her smiles, awakens every grace,
And calls forth all the wonders of her face;
Sees by degrees a purer blush arise,
And keener lightnings quicken in her eyes.

Th'inferior priestess: *Belinda's maid*

The 'rites of Pride' are at once sacred and profane, a vanity and a
praise of mysterious feminine allure. In terms of heroic allusion, the
preparations of a beautiful woman are also the arming of a female
warrior for her contests in the war of the sexes, but the exactly
observed physical world suggests the confusions of the moral one.
Cosmetics, love letters and Scripture are all of equal value in this life
of vanity.

Pope also shows how this world of youth, society and desire – of
elegant, flirtatious women and male ardour at once refined to romantic longing yet eager for the main chance – is one in which personal
and social pressures confuse the workings of nature and a woman's
perception of her true self. For example, the Sylphs that attend and
apparently protect Belinda (and who are surely the most imaginatively delicate of all the literary inventions of this period) are rendered
powerless by the real force of human passion.

In a life of mere flirtatious gallantry, the Sylphs can prompt the
behaviour of the coquette, the termagant and the prude, but the
illusory, superficial aspect of this is suggested by their lack of true
moral perception. Theirs is a view of existence where it is all one
for a woman to 'stain her honour, or her new brocade', or 'lose her

heart, or necklace, at a ball'. The Sylphs may protect women in the superficial deceits of the sex war but, as the Baron leans forward to sever the lock at the conclusion of the remarkably described card game, Ariel discovers 'an earthly lover' lurking in Belinda's heart. He is powerless in the face of Belinda's tacit but apparently deep consent to the 'rape' itself.

In view of this, the heroine's subsequent protests are merely expressions of temperament and spleen rather than true outrage. They are an affectation of morality. Particularly when it is claiming to be virtuous, Belinda's world contains self-deceptions far more dangerous than the Baron's ploy. For example, Clarissa's plea for good humour based on a realistic and even elegiac awareness of how transitory life is rings out nobly even if it goes unheard, but it was Clarissa who provided the Baron with the scissors to snip the lock in the first place. The skirmishes of the sex war continue. The poet however has shown the moral and emotional perils that accompany them and, finally, it is his art that can provide the concluding image of glory and eternal fame as the ravished lock is transported to the stars.

Between the years 1715 and 1726, Pope devoted his considerable energies largely to translation and editorial work. His love for Homer was deep, and his earlier translations of episodes from the Greek poet encouraged him to believe he could produce an equivalent of Dryden's Virgil. Money was also a spur to a far from wealthy Roman Catholic living under financial penalties for his faith. However, publishing his work by subscription, Pope was eventually to free himself from pecuniary worries. Indeed, the publication of the *Iliad* and the *Odyssey* marks a high-water point in the history of subscription publishing. Pope worked his publisher Joseph Lintot hard to obtain those aristocratic subscribers who would then be seen as collaborating to fund a work of national cultural importance. However, fiercely independent as always, Pope chose to dedicate the work not to a member of the aristocracy but to Congreve, a man from his own profession. With earnings of over £5,000 gained without direct, single patronage, Pope's Homer gave a new status to the career of the writer.

Pope appears to have translated an average of fifty lines a day. While his use of collaborators in the *Odyssey* was to arouse some antagonism, the sheer labour of the translation itself was supplemented by footnotes and essays on Homeric topics that called for exhaustive supplementary reading. But an academic purpose was not Pope's principal aim. For him, Homer was above all the poet of imagination or 'invention' – the recorder of a lost world who had also fashioned an enduring poetic one. When the work finally appeared, the professional scholars were naturally suspicious of an outsider of quality, but, despite the translation's occasionally strained elevation and politeness, Johnson, Coleridge and generations of the reading public were to acknowledge the success of Pope's achievement.

Pope's labours on Shakespeare are problematic. His Preface promised more that his textual scholarship could deliver. Just as the *Essay on Criticism* had prompted the furious if sometimes telling comments of John Dennis, so now Pope had to face the acute strictures of Bentley's disciple Lewis Theobald in his *Shakespeare Restored, or A Specimen of the Many Errors as Well Committed as Unamended by Mr Pope in his Late Edition of This Poet* (1726). The battle of the books was being prolonged, and some of Theobald's points were to be silently included in later printings of the Shakespeare edition, while the critic himself was to be pilloried in the first version of the *Dunciad* (1728, 1729), Pope's mock-epic on what he viewed as the blighted cultural existence of his country. At the end of his life, Pope was to expand this poem into a vision of the collapse of the entire humanist tradition, and the *Dunciad* is best considered as the crowning achievement of his career.

Meanwhile, between the publication of the *Iliad* and the Shakespeare, Pope issued his own *Works* (1717), a volume that contained two important new pieces: the *Elegy to the Memory of an Unfortunate Lady* and *Eloisa to Abelard*. The latter is an intense and psychologically shrewd reworking of the Ovidian heroic epistle. Pope took the well-known story of the twelfth-century lovers and, in the figure of Eloisa, powerfully re-created the emotions of a woman torn between love of God and love of man, a confusion of the mind in which Abelard and the Creator are alternately fused and wrenched apart in the raptures of painful contemplation.

The diversity of Pope's writing at this time reveals the breadth of his virtuosity. He had already attempted pastoral, moralized description and mock-heroic. He had recently tried translation, editorial work, satire and the Ovidian epistle. Now he was to concentrate these energies, to secure his philosophical position and become the critical spokesman of his society. In his own words, he 'stoop'd to truth, and moraliz'd his song'.

According to Joseph Spence (1699–1768), whose *Observations, Anecdotes, and Characters of Books and Men* provides the most useful and intimate account of Pope's conversation, the poet was thinking at this time of a large-scale work on morality to be illustrated by passages of satire and eulogy. This grand project never fully materialized but what remains are some of the central works of Pope's maturity: his *Essay on Man* (published anonymously 1733, 1734), his *Epistles to Several Persons* (1731–5) and his imitations of Horace.

Though widely popular in its day, the *Essay on Man* is perhaps the least satisfactory of these pieces, a work of eclectic moralizing attractively arranged after a conventional rhetorical pattern but often fitful and awkward in its shifts of tone and perspective. Pope's fundamental argument however is derived from the age-old conception of the great chain of being and the paradox of man's nature suspended between the beasts and the angels.

While the great chain of being, as the creation of a perfect God, must of itself be perfect – the embodiment of a universe where 'whatever IS, is RIGHT' – man's own limited and divided nature means he cannot always understand God's purposes. 'The glory, jest, and riddle of the world', man is both impelled by self-love and ideally restrained by reason. Self-love is shown as powered by the 'ruling Passion' which we must 'rectify' when we can but which, in any case, always has an equivalent virtue attached to it, and one which reason can turn to the general advantage. As Pope shows in Book Three, man in the state of nature enjoyed the benefit of knowing that 'self-love and social' were the same. It was part of Pope's optimism to suggest that modern society educates contemporary man towards a similar awareness of loving community. Such personal and social happiness is 'our being's end and aim', and, in the *Essay*'s last book, Pope reveals its origins in self-knowledge: in accepting our place in the great chain of being and working in charitable benevolence.

Many of these ideas underlie Pope's *Epistles* or *Moral Essays*, but increasingly the literary power of these works is shown less in their benevolent, optimistic message than in the imaginative power with which Pope re-created the forces of the chaotic and the perverse for purposes of satire.

The earliest of the *Moral Essays* was the *Epistle to Burlington* (1731). Addressed to the most cultivated amateur of the arts in England, the leader of the Palladian revival in architecture and a man whose taste was of profound influence, Pope's poem is an attempt both to establish the basis of artistic discrimination in nature and good sense, and to describe the errors of vulgarity. Burlington himself emerges as the ideal type of the connoisseur whose humane balance of the rules and nature develops to a patriotic sense of what true taste can effect in public works. By contrast, the spendthrift Timon indulges a mere ephemeral vulgarity that is at once comic and grossly unnatural.

The *Epistle to Bathurst, of the Use of Riches* (1733) develops this sense of the unnatural as a perversion of good sense and decency. Bathurst himself is seen as the ideal of the man who can balance generosity with prudence, just as in the broader sphere it is Providence which ensures that the extremes in men's use of wealth are balanced out for the public good. John Kyrle, the Man of Ross, is seen (in a passage of somewhat strained eulogy) as the pattern of charity, an individual raised to symbolic status through Christian and Horatian imagery. The concluding tale of Sir Balaam illustrates how riches corrupt. But the satirist's most powerful lines occur in such passages as those on the deaths of the self-destructive Hopkins and Villiers. Here, imaginative invective creates memorable cartoons out of the very filth of poverty itself. This tendency to locate the finest literary effects in alert satiric intelligence rather than generalized statement is seen again in the *Epistle to Lord Cobham, of the Knowledge and Characters of Men* (1734). Here, despite much analysis of the 'ruling Passion', it is the satirical insight that is the most telling, as in the image of the 'frugal Crone' dying as she blows out her death-bed candle in order to save money.

In the *Epistle to a Lady* (1735), Pope took the image of painting to create a gallery of satiric portraits of women, balancing their inconstancy – their lack of true 'character' – against the restraint and personal integrity of his much admired dedicatee Martha Blount. Pope's attempt made throughout the *Moral Essays* to juxtapose the follies of the world to the decorum of his friends is most satisfactorily resolved in this poem.

The alleged moral and emotional instability of women – a theme touched on in the earlier portraits of Belinda and Clarissa in *The Rape of the Lock* – is here developed into a kaleidoscopic impression of social, sexual and intellectual inconstancy, of frustrated and trivial purposes dictated by a mere couple of ruling passions that supposedly suffice for the whole sex: 'Love of Pleasure, and the Love of Sway'. These find their ironic fulfilment in the memorable portrait of Atossa (the Duchess of Marlborough) and finally dwindle to the tragic fatuousness of old age:

> See how the world its veterans rewards!
> A youth of frolics, an old age of cards;
> Fair to no purpose, artful to no end,
> Young without lovers, old without a friend,
> A fop their passion, but their prize a sot,
> Alive, ridiculous, and dead, forgot!

In couplets of chilling if energetic virtuosity, Pope expresses the futility of wasted energy. These he then compares to the superior merits of Martha Blount whose virtues make her almost at one with her poet.

The naming of names in the *Moral Essays* led to the sort of outcry familiar in Pope's career. His response was to turn to one of the supreme poets of the Augustan era and imitate his works with a view to the ironic parallels that could be drawn between ancient Rome and contemporary London. As Pope expressed the matter in the 1735 edition of his works: 'The occasion of my publishing these *Imitations* was the clamour raised by some of my *Epistles*. An answer from Horace was both more full, and of more dignity, than I could have made in my own person.'

In his *Imitations of Horace* (1733–8), Pope could at once relate himself to timeless values of decorum and be at his most personally and suggestively intimate. He also deliberately emphasizes the sense of active virtue under siege. In *Satire II, i*, Pope the Roman Catholic living with the inconvenience of fines and property penalties is the embodiment of Horatian virtue in the corrupt world of the Walpole administration. The virtuous Bolingbroke, ousted by the Whigs, is portrayed as the ideal of the friend in *Epistle I, i*. That Bolingbroke out of office is implicitly compared to the great Roman patron

Maecenas in office makes the corruption of contemporary cultural and political life look all the more scandalous. In the survey of English literary history in *Epistle II, i*, this gulf between civilization in the Rome of Augustus and the England of George Augustus (George II) becomes glaring.

The *Imitations* are prefaced by one of Pope's finest achievements: the *Epistle to Dr Arbuthnot* (1735), his literary self-portrait and apologia. The work, addressed to a fellow Scriblerian, thus combines the themes of friendship and decorum familiar from the *Imitations*. These are then allied to the Scriblerians' contempt for hack writers and pedantry which Pope had already given voice to in the first version of the *Dunciad* and his prose satire *Peri-Bathous, or The Art of Sinking in Poetry* (1728). What makes the *Epistle* specially powerful however is its skilful balance of outrage and deferential intimacy, its portrayal of besieged integrity through marvellously varied and energetic language.

The colloquial and the forms of restrained eulogy and of masculine, assertive moral force are admirably contrasted to the sly deflation of literary smugness in the portrait of Addison (Atticus) and the fury of imaginative invective with which Pope created his image of Sporus or Lord Hervey (1696–1743). In collaboration with Lady Mary Wortley Montagu – a woman whom Pope had satirized with all the spite of a rejected lover – Hervey had written the *Verses Addressed to the Imitator of Horace* (1733), perhaps the only one of innumerable satires on the poet that achieves real literary merit. The portrait in the *Epistle* was Pope's revenge. Where Lady Mary had been transformed into Sappho, a filthy bluestocking, Hervey now becomes Sporus, Nero's eunuch, and a nightmare image of impotent, ambiguous, diabolically shape-shifting worldliness that is contrasted to the decorous integrity of Twickenham and Pope himself. Increasingly, the poet becomes the hero of his own vitriolic pessimism.

In the two Dialogues that form the *Epilogue to the Satires* (1738), this moral isolation takes on the heroic and even tragic force of self-assertion. The benevolent universe of the *Essay on Man* (what Swift saw as mere illusioned optimism) is here inverted with all the anger of intense disappointment. Walpole's England is seen as irremediably corrupt, and Pope himself is the lone voice of bitter integrity. 'The condition of morality', he wrote to a friend, 'is so desperate, as to be above all human hands.'

Such moral decay, Pope believed, was reflected in declining literary standards, and in both versions of the *Dunciad* (1728–9, 1742–3) he set out to show how the collapse of learning, and of the humane values of intellectual dignity and decorum, was wrought in his age by the hacks and fools who were shown besieging the poet in the *Epistle to Dr Arbuthnot*. The minions of the goddess Dulness, these people are cast as the forces of cultural night and of a final silencing and absolute despair.

The first version of the *Dunciad* (1728–9), we have seen, took Pope's critic Lewis Theobald for its hero. Though rooted in personal animosity, the satirist's image of his enemy broadens to an attack on the poisons eroding every aspect of what Pope regarded as the sole domain of contemporary high literary culture – the aristocratic male preserve of poetry and its classical basis. Theobald is the quintessence of the forces attacking this. He is presented as a penniless hack toiling over his wretched works in a room very similar to the lurid world presented in his own *Cave of Poverty* (1714). Such physical squalor is at one with Theobald's mental and moral confusion. His Shakespearian scholarship is lampooned as mere pedantry that fogs the broad and cultured humanist appreciation of great literature. Theobald's own works – vulgarly indecorous pantomimes and confusing, soporific poems – reveal the futile energies of a poet who has sold out to the corrupting taste of Whig merchants in the City – the stock-jobbers and market men who need little in the way of culture beyond pulp, pageantry and pornography.

As such, Theobald is the ideal follower of the goddess Dulness, the mythical incarnation of the anti-intellectual and a figure far more insidious than mere boneheadedness. Dulness is the fog-bound, restless force of uncritical mental life who thrives in such a world as Theobald's and who, in answer to her hierophant's prayer, emerges to choose him as her earthly king.

Like an ancient epic hero, Theobald is first entertained with heroic games – here the antics of money-grubbing publishers and their followers – and is then granted a prophetic vision in which Elkanah Settle, a founding father of English dullness, prophesies the return of cultural chaos. However, when in the revised *New Dunciad* (1742–3) Pope replaced Theobald with Colley Cibber, the Poet Laureate, his mock-epic became, in its greater range and passion, a vision of tragic despair, of the final overwhelming of culture by the powers of Dulness embodied in Cibber and his wretched associates.

The official voice of national literary culture, author of the zestful, boasting *Apology for the Life of Mr Colley Cibber* (1740) – the first English work to contain considerable critical accounts of particular actors' stage techniques – Cibber was himself a playwright as well as a comic actor and theatrical manager in a period of decline in drama. In the *New Dunciad*, Cibber stands for the complete abasement of cultural life. He is the focus of national, political and intellectual defeat.

In the opening book, Cibber's Grub Street study, close to the brothels and the lunatic hospital at Bedlam, is a sort of Lockeian hell – at once an actual room, a brain, a bowel and a stage where dull and incongruous literary ideas collide and copulate under the chaotic sway of self-applauding Dulness. Cibber himself emerges as the archetypal hack whose works extend the powers of a corrupt City and government. Eventually, Dulness transports him to her 'sacred Dome' where she anoints him as the emblem of her folly.

In the ensuing three books of the *New Dunciad*, Pope presents a crowded, harrowing scene of intellectual decay. The heroic games over which Cibber presides with all the panoply of Milton's Satan show us a world of vulgar publishers racing in pursuit of an illusory poet, slipping on the shit-stained track and being fortified by the very excrement that is their true medium. Pissing competitions – that most juvenile of male activities – suggest the antics such men will perform in order to obtain the *romans-à-clef* of figures like Mary de la Riviere Manley and Eliza Haywood. The latter's reputation both in her life and posthumously was badly damaged by this. Meanwhile, hacks desperately seeking patronage tickle a rich lord (the imagery suggests the mutual masturbation that is the physical equivalent of fawning dedications) while, amid the turds floating in the common sewer of an abased tradition, others dive and wallow in cultural filth. Heroic journeys to the underworld are parodied in Cibber's visit to the nether regions where, on a clouded hill, Settle reveals the progress of barbarism: the Goths and Vandals, the 'Peel'd, patch'd and pyebald, linsey-wolsey brothers' of the Dark and Middle Ages and their modern successors.

The fourth book illustrates the fulfilment of Settle's prophecies. The dunces, summoned by an apocalyptic fart, attend their queen. Allegedly pedantic editors such as Richard Bentley jostle with those who further narrow cultural horizons: pedantic schoolmasters clamping a 'jingling padlock on the mind', and lax tutors who, on the Grand Tour of Europe, give their libidinous charges free rein and so ensure that all classic learning is lost on classic ground. Then follow obsessive virtuosi whose interests have narrowed to collecting coins, flowers and butterflies. To such spavined wits – intellectually, culturally and politically quiescent – Dulness awards her degrees.

As Dulness's empire spreads, so Nature begins to sleep. The power that in the *Essay on Criticism* and the *Epistles* was the source of all truth collapses under the sheer force of corruption. Even the poet himself is finally overwhelmed:

> Lo! thy dread Empire, CHAOS! is restor'd;
> Light dies before thy uncreating word:
> Thy hand, great Anarch! lets the curtain fall;
> And Universal Darkness buries All.

Pope's poem rises to a tragic force, as epic – the supreme mode of national pride – is here inverted to expose utter national despair: 'a total oblivion of all Obligations, divine, civil, moral, or rational'. The great humanist tradition has perished in meaningless cacophony.

8

Despite the profound pessimism of the *Dunciad* and the abiding force of its attack on the values that wither culture, the 1740s were a decade of the most various and fertile literary experiment. Nowhere is this clearer than in prose fiction. Usually in unacknowledged ways, the experiments of such women writers as Eliza Haywood and Elizabeth Singer Rowe, author of *Letters Moral and Entertaining* (1729–33), were developed by male writers. In 1740, for example, the middle-aged printer Samuel Richardson (1689–1761) was asked to produce a guide to correspondence. Realizing like women novelists before him how a work of instruction could also be a work of the imagination – a revelation of character and morality – Richardson put his original project aside and, in two months of hectic activity, produced one of the seminal works of eighteenth-century fiction, the enormously popular *Pamela, or Virtue Rewarded* (1740).

In her letters to her father, Pamela tries to show herself as a model serving girl defending her honour against the advances of her master, Mr B. Sex, status and the sentimentalists' love of virtue in distress at first seem allied to the theme of 'faithless men, and ruin'd maids' familiar from the sensational novels of Mrs Manley. Richardson's purposes however were more overtly moral than this, just as his middle-class awareness was more decorous than that which had permitted Defoe's rogues-and-whores' lives of sixteen years before. Yet, as with Richardson's later works, it was not for its action that *Pamela* was principally admired, but for its sentiment and for the subtle, minute-by-minute revelation of moral awareness. This was enhanced by a strong didactic purpose – Richardson's hope that his book would 'cultivate the principles of virtue and religion in the minds of the youth of both sexes'. Faith, self-analysis and the ethics of the conduct-books are one.

In Richardson's masterpiece *Clarissa* (1747–8), these elements are raised to tragic intensity. His heroine is of a higher class and educational level than her predecessor, older and more mature. Her agony derives from social and psychological issues of greater interest, while Richardson's use of several correspondents allows for constantly shifting analyses of action and feeling. These, while they extend over enormous and often repetitious length (the novel is about a million words long), also help create the imprisoning sense of remorseless conflict that lies at the heart of this epic of sentiment.

The conflict itself springs from the money-driven ambition of the Harlowe family, in particular the aspirations of the heroine's brother James to a peerage. Clarissa, the passively innocent female, having both an inheritance and an unwelcome aristocratic suitor in the rakish Lovelace, appears to thwart her family's aims. Clarissa and Lovelace are at the centre of the novel. The heroine, made increasingly desperate as her family world closes vengefully round her, finds in her letters to the lively Anna Howe a means of expression that is at once an escape, a therapy and an analysis of her emotional claustrophobia. That the writing of such letters is forbidden by Clarissa's family makes her assertion of self a crime against some of her deepest values.

Lovelace (pronounced 'loveless') troubles the heroine's naïvety, and Clarissa at first believes she can reform a rake whose sinister fascination fills her dreams and waking thoughts with the ambiguous allure of sexuality. It is a sexuality born of male obsession – an obsession with its own energies, with revenge for being jilted as a younger man – and an overpowering phallic pride. This last is swollen by the very challenge posed to it: 'to carry off such a girl as this, in spite of all her watchful and implacable friends; and in spite of a prudence and reserve that I never met with in any of the sex: what a triumph! What a triumph over the whole sex!' Lovelace's letters, when not toiling in convention, have a radical and challenging force that survives all attempts to label him a mere villain.

Lovelace takes Clarissa to London and imprisons her in a brothel where, after protracted skirmishing and delay – a period which raises to its height Richardson's presentation of the persecuted maiden and of characters in intricate and deadly combat – he drugs her and rapes her. The violation of the purity that has obsessed him but which remains morally intact (thereby disproving the libertine ethic that every woman is at heart a rake) reduces Lovelace to a victim of his own lust. He is diminished even as Clarissa, straining on the borders of sanity, rises to her final role of injured saint.

For modern readers, this is the least satisfactory section of the novel. At great length and with an often unctuously cloying sentimentality, Clarissa prepares for death, and for the coffin on which she writes her last letters to her penitent family and which will be both her body's final prison and the means to her spirit's eventual freedom. Exemplary even in death, Clarissa passes beyond the material world with the spirituality that the conduct-books had shown as belonging to the virtuous Christian.

In *The History of Sir Charles Grandison* (1753–4), Richardson's last novel, the protagonist is the personification of exemplary Christian virtue in a man, but the didactic and moralizing side of Richardson's art here takes precedence over the drama of moral conflict.

Among women novelists of the 1740s, Sarah Fielding (1710–68) is the most interesting. *The Adventures of David Simple* (1744) is the work by which this widely educated woman is best remembered, and in it she creates a considerable sense of the innocent and guileless trapped in a duplicitous and often cruel world. David 'in search of a real friend' is constantly the victim, as (with more assured narrative success) is his beloved Cynthia. The presentation of the latter is a convincing account of a powerless woman constantly the victim of both men and the more domineering of her own sex. In the last volume, this pessimistic apprehension of a malign universe is powerfully conveyed through a narrative centring around the financial suffering Sarah Fielding herself was familiar with.

Sarah's brother Henry Fielding (1707–54) began his literary career in the theatre where he worked in numerous critical and satiric modes. It was in *The Historical Register for 1736* (1737) and its afterpiece *Euridice Hissed* that Fielding revealed the full strength of his anti-Walpole feelings. The government grew alarmed and passed the Licensing Act of 1737 which brought drama under the direct censorship of the Lord Chamberlain – a control that was not relinquished until 1968. With the theatre closed to his satirical talents however, Fielding turned to non-dramatic writing. In *Jonathan Wild*, published in 1743 but probably written earlier, he developed an idea also noted in his 'Modern Glossary' in the *Covent Garden Journal*, no. 4 (1752). Here, Fielding defined the word 'Great' thus: 'Applied to Things, signifies Bigness; when applied to a Man, often Littleness or Meanness.' Applied to Walpole, 'Great' meant low, criminal cunning and a comic parallel between the Prime Minister and the country's most notorious villain.

But Fielding's neo-Scriblerian irony, the generous, open disposition of the gentleman author who believed that literature should preserve the poise of good conversation, was most effectively levelled at what he saw as the self-serving nastiness of Richardson's *Pamela*. Believing the work to be by Colley Cibber – always an acceptable butt – Fielding published in 1741 his parodic *Shamela*. Here, the calculating heroine defends her 'vartue' only to inflame. Virtue rewarded is merely cynicism triumphant, and such satire of Richardson helped shape Fielding's engagement with prose fiction. His particular development of the novel – that most popular, prolific and lawless of forms – was enriched however by the other modes he called on in the attempt to shape narratives which explore the problems of virtue. This critical borrowing, the shaping of the new through a dialogue with the old, is clear in Fielding's next work: *The History of the Adventures of Joseph Andrews, and his Friend Mr Abraham Adams* (1742).

Joseph is the virtuous brother of Richardson's virtuous Pamela. Deeply in love with Fanny Goodwill, he refuses the advances of his employer, the ageing Lady Booby (the aunt of Richardson's squire) and is sacked for his chastity. The prospect of an ardent, lily-white youth preserving his virginity for his true love while pursued by a monstrous harridan is delightfully comic, but as the novel develops, so the anti-Richardsonian elements merge with others.

Joseph's narrative, for example, draws on romance and folk-tale motifs of mistaken identity, gypsy kidnappings, occasional melodrama and the final discovery of true paternity and true love. Elements from the picaresque novel of the road allow for seemingly chance encounters in what is in fact a most carefully constructed plot, as well as the telling of exemplary but apparently superimposed narratives. In his Preface, Fielding defined the novel itself as a 'comic epic poem in prose'. It is comic in so far as its characters are drawn from low life, yet it is different to burlesque in that these characters are representatives of human nature rather than caricatures of individuals. Epic is parodied in the fights with mops and chamber pots that provide some of the broader comedy, but in the figure of Parson Adams (the most developed of the major characters) slapstick is wedded to a moral purpose through the influence of Cervantes's *Don Quixote* (1605, 1615).

Just as the good, unworldly Spanish don appears ridiculous by imagining a universe where all is governed by the modes of romance, so the absent-minded and unworldly Adams appears as a type of the Christian fool described by St Paul. The human warmth of Adams's dogged integrity shines through however as he is surrounded by the hypocrisy and vanity of others. These, for Fielding, were the twin forces of 'affectation' from which arose the truly ridiculous. Snobs, braggarts, uncharitable clergymen like Parson Trulliber, canting lawyers and avaricious doctors populate Adams's bruising progress through the novel as he himself embodies the benevolent, natural man disciplined by Christian charity.

Indeed, Adams is introduced as a type of the Good Samaritan. In a famous episode, Joseph has been stripped and robbed. The passengers on a passing stage-coach find various reasons for not helping the naked youth, who

> must have perished, unless the postillion (a lad who hath since been transported for robbing a hen-roost) had voluntarily stripped off a great coat, his only garment, at the same time swearing a great oath (for which he was rebuked by the passengers) that he would rather ride in his shirt all his life, than suffer a fellow-creature to lie in so miserable a condition.

Here, in miniature, is that natural goodness which pettifogging hypocrisy so often causes to suffer. It is the same goodness Adams shows at the inn when the snobbish landlady and the greedy surgeon and parson leave the suffering Joseph until Adams himself, recognizing the youth's livery, rushes upstairs to succour him.

The only other character willing to help was Betty the chambermaid whose good nature and compassion, Fielding shows, were closely allied to a physical desire for the young man. Sexual openness is seen to go with true benevolence and, in *Tom Jones* (1749), Fielding explored this perception more fully. The novel also shows him developing his impressive technical skills to produce one of the great comic masterpieces of English literature.

Tom Jones is plotted with a dextrous fecundity of invention that is in itself deeply satisfying. Many of the narrative elements that appeared in *Joseph Andrews* – the discovery of true identity, adventures on the road, inserted narratives – are re-used in the later work, but where Joseph had about him a suggestion of the ridiculous, Tom emerges as a richer character capable both of some development and of exemplifying serious aspects of his creator's moral awareness. In particular, Tom is the focus of a typically eighteenth-century concern with benevolence. For Fielding, there was nothing overly theoretical or mawkishly sentimental about this. Benevolence is the spontaneous expression of a full and radiant personality which both attracts affection and responds in kind. It is a quality that the infant foundling hero shows from the start.

Tom matures as a natural, healthy boy, intensely loyal to his gamekeeper friends and warm in his feelings for their daughter Molly. His attractive personality exactly conveys Fielding's conception of benevolence, but it is from the very impulsiveness of his good nature that Tom's troubles spring. These accidents cause him to be compared unfavourably to the odious Blifil, his opposite and, it eventually transpires, his half-brother. The contrast is thus drawn between inhibited, self-seeking hypocrisy on the one hand and a heedless, open benevolence on the other.

Fielding's portrayal of innocent virtue as spontaneous and physically aware (the very opposite, indeed, of the prudential chastity of Richardson's characters) was regarded by many with disapproval. Fielding himself was conscious of the danger he ran but, as he argued in his dedicatory Preface to Lord Lyttelton, he believed his novel contained nothing prejudicial to religion and decency, adding: 'I have endeavoured strongly to inculcate that virtue and innocence can scarce ever be injured but by indiscretion; and that it is this alone which often betrays them into the snares that deceit and villainy spread for them.'

In the early part of the novel, these snares and deceits are chiefly the work of Blifil. Blifil cunningly exploits Tom's escapades so that he is banished by the exemplary if somewhat wooden Squire Allworthy from the security of Paradise Hall. He is thereby denied the chance of wedding the radiant Sophia, the heroine whose intuitive dislike of Blifil is so strong that she too eventually leaves home rather than compromise her feelings by marriage. Such events could easily become melodramatic, but Fielding controls the reader's response through the urbane, smiling wisdom of his narratorial voice. In the introductions to each of his books and the somewhat too frequent essays interpolated into his narrative, Fielding discusses a range of literary and moral issues that suggest the ideals of the polished and rational gentleman, a character who emerges as the most trustworthy moral focus in the novel.

This wry yet decorous *hauteur* is present even in the details of the action, at once describing and interpreting it. For example, when Tom has been driven from Paradise Hall, he throws himself down by a river in his grief. We are told: 'Here he presently fell into the most violent agonies, tearing his hair from his head, and using other actions which generally accompany fits of madness, rage and despair.' Tom's outburst is a matter of a single polished sentence which describes yet smilingly refuses to linger over excess.

Such detachment helps account for the various comic effects Fielding achieves in the remarkable central section of his novel. We are aware of his balance and control amid the seeming chaos as a gallimaufry of comic characters, pursuing their various ends, compel the hero into escapades that at once worsen his plight and yet are central to its resolution. The wealth of expertise here justifies Fielding's neo-classical contention, described in the introduction to Book Nine, that the good writer has 'invention', judgement, learning and a rich acquaintance with high and low life. Comedy and melodrama, virtuous maids and loose wives, squires, serving girls and soldiers, angry fathers and irate husbands, professional pessimists and blabbing friends, career about the good yet indulgent hero to create the most compelling picture of innocence and hypocrisy in a bustling world. And over-arching all is the pure bravery of Sophia's love for Tom and the hero's own aspirations after her – a chastity of the spirit maintained despite the lapses of a virile young body.

It is in London that Tom reaches the nadir of his existence when he becomes the kept man of the ageing Lady Bellaston and is also accused of murder. Even during this period however he retains his affection for Sophia whose father – the comic ogre Squire Western – is forcing her into marriage with Blifil. It also emerges that it was Blifil himself who helped orchestrate Tom's arrest. Here at the conclusion, and with the greatest dexterity, Fielding manages to suggest the developing seriousness of Tom's position and the benevolent concurrence of circumstances that will at once render Blifil's machinations harmless, free Tom and allow him to discover that by birth he is the illegitimate nephew of Squire Allworthy, and finally to marry Sophia. At the close of the novel, and to reinforce the theme of happiness in a benevolent world, we are told that the hero has 'acquired a discretion and prudence very uncommon in one of his lively parts'. Benevolence and experience have created a rounded human being.

Tom Jones concludes with the virtuous made happy and wise. In Fielding's last novel *Amelia* (1751), the tone has changed to a more cloying sentimentality. The ironic zest has gone, and in its place is an analysis of weakness and patient suffering in a harsh world of social abuses – a world of crime and punishment that the ailing author knew from his work as a magistrate. Illness and exhaustion were eventually to crush him however, and Fielding's last work, his *Journal of a Voyage to Lisbon*, was published in 1755 after his death there.

Fielding and many other leading literary figures of the period paid tribute to Charlotte Lennox (?1727–1804) whose novel *The Female Quixote* (1752) is an amusing if not always well-constructed account of the effect on the female mind of reading too many romances. Lennox's heroine Arabella – beautiful and well educated – lives in a world in which the ordinary and the good are constantly distorted in the light of the conventions of fiction. Characters are invariably seen as ravishers or princes in disguise, and the tension between this and the increasingly exasperated efforts of Arabella's suitor Mr Glanville is well handled, throwing into relief the perils attending the heroine's entry into the real world of love and marriage.

One minor erotic masterpiece dates from this period. In 1748–9, John Cleland (1710–89) published his *Memoirs of a Woman of Pleasure*. This work, better known by the name of its heroine Fanny Hill, presents a picture of a young girl's sexual awakening, education and final arrival in 'the bosom of virtue'. Largely avoiding the prurient and the merely technical (though, as the scene of male homosexual seduction shows, not invariably flouting the received social bigotries) *Fanny Hill* rises to present a rapturous evocation of physical and emotional union.

Novelists with more conventional aims worked in other modes. Cervantes and picaresque fiction were particularly influential, and the most important picaresque novelist of this period was Tobias Smollett (1721–71). Smollett translated Le Sage's French picaresque *Gil Blas* and, in *The Adventures of Roderick Random* (1748), paid tribute to the work's influence on him. Smollett's partly autobiographical first novel reveals many of his characteristic strengths and weaknesses. Grotesque, splenetic portraits and coarse, violent episodes are set within scenes of often excellent reportage. These are frequently barbed with an anger that is energetic but rarely the product of a deeply considered moral position. Indeed, the very randomness of the picaresque form itself was at one with Smollett's own view of chaos and chance in human affairs. 'I am old enough', he wrote to the actor David Garrick (1717–79), 'to have seen and observed that we are all playthings of fortune, and that it depends on something as insignificant and precarious as the tossing up of a halfpenny whether a man rise to affluence and honours, or continues to his dying day struggling with the difficulties and disgraces of life.' In Smollett's novels, displaced persons are usually represented in just such a chaotic world where tyranny, cruelty and immorality are for the most part triumphant and happy endings are often a merely factitious literary contrivance – a form of sentimentality which is the obverse of Smollett's cynicism.

Smollett also wrote an acerbic volume of *Travels through France and Italy* (1766), but in 1771 he returned to fiction with his most popular novel: *The Expedition of Humphry Clinker*. This work is altogether happier and more subtle than Smollett's earlier fictions. It presents a search for moral and physical well-being, and the author's use of the epistolary form allows for a richer interplay of character and its development than before. Of the two chief correspondents, the young Jery Melford soon realizes that his uncle Matthew Bramble 'affects misanthropy, in order to conceal the sensibility of a heart which is tender, even to a degree of weakness'. Bramble himself matures from this misanthropy partly through the discovery of Humphry Clinker himself, the illegitimate child of his youth.

The wealth of experiment in the prose fiction of this period is nowhere more evident than in the work of Laurence Sterne (1713–68). In *The Life and Opinions of Tristram Shandy, Gentleman* (1760–67), he created a unique medium for investigating some of the fundamental interests of the era: Locke's psychology of the association of ideas, the nature of sentimentalism, the conventions of prose fiction. This suggests a seriousness however which the exuberant comic intelligence of the narrator effortlessly subverts. *Tristram Shandy* is vivid with the careering and often crack-brained mental life that is its subject. To summarize a novel built from endless digressions is an impossibility, but to read it is to be cornered by a raconteur of genius, a man whose very existence depends on our attention being held by his association of ideas, his act of creation, his words.

These themes are clear from the start, especially in Sterne's description of the act of creation which gives life to his narrator. Every month, the ageing Walter Shandy has wound the family clock and then had intercourse with his wife. In Mrs Shandy's mind these two actions have become so associated that, at the moment of rapture, she confuses them: '*Pray, my dear*, quoth my mother, *have you not forgot to wind up the clock?* —— *Good G—!* cried my father, making an exclamation, but taking care to moderate his voice at the same time, —— *Did ever woman, since the creation of the world, interrupt a man with such a silly question?'* Here we see the novel's themes of frustrated sexual pleasure, interruption and digression, the obsessive and quirky association of ideas, centred on creation and the abiding eighteenth-century metaphor of the world as a timepiece. These ideas combine with the novel's preoccupation with measured time, psychological time and time the agent of mortality. Meanwhile, the sperm which is to mature into Tristram Shandy follows its difficult, debilitating path to life.

Its birth some scores of pages later is accompanied by two accidents. First, Tristram's nose – a feature invariably associated with the penis and which Walter Shandy believes to be an emblem of a man's fate – is crushed by the nurse's forceps. Later, his male organ itself is cruelly cut short by an accident with a dormer window. Tristram (that name most hated by his father who believes, contrary to Locke, that some names have a talismanic quality) is for ever associated with *tristia* or 'sadness'. The boy himself becomes the subject of his father's learned tome the *Tristia-paedia* or 'The Education of Tristram' which, like the novel, cannot keep pace with the growth of its subject.

Sterne's work is thus a mirror maze forever reflecting its own varieties of mental confusion. For example, just as the narrator's Uncle Toby (that gentle character obsessed with battles) is led by a wound in his groin to an obsessive study of the siege warfare in which he was emasculated, so Tristram displaces his own frustrated sexual energy into his writing. Literature becomes a metaphor, a sublimation of desire. In its obsessional quality it also becomes a hobby-horse – Sterne's subtle image (partly sexual, partly infantile) for those interests that develop to a ruling passion and so lock characters in a world of words which deny real communication. Other means have therefore to be sought, as when the down-to-earth Corporal Trim describes bachelor liberty to Uncle Toby as he pursues the amorous Widow Wadman:

Whilst a man is free, – cried the corporal, giving a flourish with his stick thus –

A thousand of my father's most subtle syllogisms could not have said more for celibacy.

To break with formal control was to establish other modes of communication in a world where words themselves are deceptive.

Chief among these modes for Sterne was sentimentalism. Uncle Toby, preserving the life of a fly and saying, 'This world surely is wide enough to hold both thee and me', suggests an intuitive delicacy which, especially in those scenes involving the tubercular narrator's journeys through France and his thoughts of Toby's death, are worked up to a tearful pitch. Sterne's somewhat mawkish *Journal to Eliza* (1768), the dying author's account of an extra-marital affair, is again a mixture of fact and fantasy, comedy and wish-fulfilment, all artfully contrived. In his *Sentimental Journey through France and Italy* (1768) however, Sterne's self-portrait as Parson Yorick (a descendant, we are to believe, of Hamlet's jester) is his most sophisticated account of the motions of a heart surrendering to the flow of feeling, to wit, sensuality and sensibility.

In Sterne's work, sentimental notes are precariously balanced by irony. For other novelists they became something to be explored for their own sake. Two of the more noticeable novels of sensibility – *The Fool of Quality* (1766–72) by Henry Brooke (c. 1703–72) and *The Man of Feeling* (1771) by Henry Mackenzie (1745–1831) – develop these emotional extremes especially far. The first is a loosely structured combination of morality, social optimism, tears and jingoism, while the second is in many ways the apotheosis of sentimentality, an epicurean retreat to weeping and ethereal love confessed on a dying breath. A new type of hero is here coming into existence. The sensibility which for Addison and Steele had wedded man to society is now seen to isolate him by the very intensity of its perception. Passion – however stilted in expression – is claiming its mastery.

9

Passion was also overthrowing reason in the realms of philosophy. Here the British school of empirical philosophers made a major contribution. For example, the ideas elaborated by Locke around the framework of Newtonian physics had been questioned as early as 1710 when George Berkeley (1685–1753) published his *Treatise Concerning the Principles of Human Knowledge*. Examining the problem of how ideas which are in the mind could be suggested by physical objects which are outside of it, Berkeley suggested that we can only know the former. The external world exists as it is perceived and not in any objective, physical sense at all. Our ideas about it, Berkeley then argued, are prompted in us by God whose own infinite mind, surveying His Creation, gives the universe a continuity which mere human perception could never provide.

In the work of David Hume (1711–76), even this crutch is removed. Hume agreed with Berkeley that all we can know is our own impressions and the faint traces these leave in the memory and the imagination. However, in his *Treatise of Human Nature: An Attempt to Introduce the Experimental Method of Reasoning into Moral Subjects* (1739–40), Hume argued that as a result of this limitation, concepts such as 'God', 'mind', 'self' and the 'laws of nature' are merely fictions created by the imagination. Even cause and effect – the idea that fire burns or magnets attract – is not a law but merely a result of customary associations. These, unverifiable though they may be, are nonetheless the basis of human nature. The proper study of mankind remains, in the strictest sense of the phrase, man himself. He wanders beyond his own limits at his peril:

Let us fix our attention out of ourselves as much as possible: let us chase our imagination to the heavens, or to the utmost limits of the universe; we never really advance a step beyond ourselves, nor can we conceive any kind of existence, but those perceptions, which have appear'd in that narrow compass. This is the universe of the imagination, nor have we any idea but what is there produc'd.

God is thus a figment of human thought, and theology, as Hume revealed in his *Natural History of Religion* (1757) and *Dialogues Concerning Natural Religion* (published posthumously 1779), is necessarily a branch of anthropology and psychology. This was an insight which Hume himself applied to the Christian faith with an irony that made *le bon David* especially welcome among the *philosophes* of the French Enlightenment, even as it ensured his notoriety at home. The irony and poise of a great age of satire are honed to exquisite sharpness as Hume declares:

The *Christian Religion* not only was at first attended with miracles, but even at this day cannot be believed by any reasonable person without one. Mere reason is insufficient to convince us of its veracity: And whoever is moved by *Faith* to assent to it, is conscious of a continued miracle in his own person, which subverts all the principles of his understanding, and gives him a determination to believe what is most contrary to custom and experience.

Since there is no such thing as a rational belief, neither religion nor reason itself can be an adequate ground for morality. Moral judgement has to lie in the special emotional constitution of man himself – in particular the association of virtue with pleasure and vice with pain – and the fortunate notion that the attractions of virtue appear to be good for society. Hume elaborated these ideas in his *Enquiry Concerning the Principles of Morals* (1751) where he developed a notion of personal merit anchored in the patrician values of his own social circle. These values of benevolence, courtesy, humour, and so on, are, he claimed, shared and appreciated on an intuitive basis:

The minds of all men are similar in their feelings and operations, nor can any one be actuated by any affection, of which all the others are not, in some degree, susceptible. As in strings equally wound up, the motion of one communicates itself to the rest; so all the affections readily pass from one person to another, and beget correspondent movements in every human creature.

For the smiling philosopher of the eighteenth century, the moral life has something of the excellence of a string quartet. It cannot however muffle its own more ominous chords. In Hume's philosophy, the rational mind has displaced its long-held dominion and left us in a world where 'reason is, and ought only to be, the slave of the passions'. Hume's conclusion is a landmark in Western thought.

10

One of the best-known aesthetic treatises of the century is *A Philosophical Enquiry into the Origin of our Ideas of the Sublime and the Beautiful* (1757) by Edmund Burke (1729–97). This work, admitting less genuinely imaginative developments than the theories of either Shaftesbury or Young, is Burke's allegedly scientific attempt to prove that 'the standard both of reason and of taste is the same in all human creatures'.

Taking from Locke the notion that ideas derive from the senses, the belief that the senses are common to all leads to the conclusion that ideas of the sublime and the beautiful must be universal too. Works of art, Burke suggests, communicate through 'sympathy', or the power to 'transfer their passions from one breast to another'. When these passions derive from sensations of love and pleasure then they are the source of the beautiful and are essentially social. When, however, they involve the fundamentally selfish pleasure of safely contemplating the dangerous and the painful, then they are the founts of the sublime.

This last inevitably carries with it a sense of veiled menace, as in Milton's description of death where 'all is dark, uncertain, confused, terrible, and sublime to the last degree'. When the poet introduces into such passages 'those modes of speech that mark a strong and lively feeling in himself' – when his own excitement, that is, transcends what Burke disparaged as the littleness of mere rational description – then the sublime becomes the individual poet's and reader's universal experience of the highest aesthetic attainment.

The pursuit of such emotive effects took a wide range of forms, especially among those poets of the second half of the eighteenth century who developed the ideas of Addison and Shaftesbury. For many, Thomson also proved a fertile influence. Some figures such as Erasmus Darwin (1731–1802), with his explication of Linnaeus in *The Botanic Garden* (1791), developed Thomson's georgic mode by attempting to 'enlist imagination under the banner of science'. Didactic verse in heavily Miltonic diction proved, however, to be a literary cul-de-sac.

Mark Akenside (1721–70) attempted a blank-verse rendering of Addison's ideas in *The Pleasures of Imagination* (1744, revised edn 1772), hoping thereby to turn away from the manner of Pope towards a poetry that would graft Greek 'simplicity' on to Virgilian refinement. Akenside's response to 'the simple and solitary genius of antiquity' was an important change of emphasis. In addition, Akenside's invocation to the Evening Star in his *Odes on Several Subjects* (1745) is a combination typical in its period of learning and nature viewed in the melancholy softness of dusk.

Melancholy, indeed, was to become a cult, and one of its chief spokesmen was Edward Young (1683–1765). Young had begun his career as a tragic playwright and didactic poet. In *The Universal Passion* (1725–8) he showed his skills as a satirist, while in 1759 he published his *Conjectures on Original Composition*. This work is of importance for its emphasis on the poetic imagination as a mysterious, organic process different to the genius acquired by learning. The essay was to become well known in Germany where it was to influence the thinkers from whom Coleridge later borrowed many of his ideas. It was as the poet of *The Complaint, or Night-Thoughts on Life, Death and Immortality* (1742–5, 1750) however that Young was best known. Here, in cumbersomely dogmatic and repetitive blank verse, he developed the graveyard meditations – the mixed suggestions of Christian morality and personal tragedy – that were to make his international reputation. This initiative was followed by such poets as Robert Blair (1700–46) in the sensationalistic lines of *The Grave* (1743) and by the prose effusions of James Hervey's (1714–58) *Meditations among the Tombs* (1745–7).

After the opening three decades of the century, women poets, reacting against the reputations of Behn, Manley and Haywood, cultivated a tone adjusted to the demands of propriety. This gave them a measure of acceptance. Lady Winchilsea, for example, was welcomed into literary circles, despite her initial misapprehensions. A number of other women poets had their work published in such widely circulating journals as the *Gentleman's Magazine*, while collections of women's verse funded by subscription became increasingly common. Difficulties had been far from swept away, however.

While the wholesale condemnation of women's efforts had largely ceased (even the misanthropic Swift solicited subscriptions for a woman friend in Dublin), the problems posed by pressing at the limits of convention and the difficulties of obtaining a sufficient education still daunted many women. Nor should be forgotten either the weight of women's domestic responsibilities or the considerable opposition a fine poet like Mary Leapor (1722–46) realized she would face from women themselves. Leapor's *Epistle to Artemisia* is a painfully accurate account of this last.

Nonetheless, by the middle of the century, Thomas Seward felt able to publish 'The Female Right to Literature' (1748). By the later 1750s, anthologies of women's poetry were appearing, and Dr Johnson declared: 'the revolution of the years has now produced a generation of Amazons of the pen, who with the spirit of their predecessors have set masculine tyranny at defiance, asserted their claim to the regions of science, and seem resolved to contest the usurpations of virility'. A life wholly given over to literature remained precarious however. Through truly heroic effort Elizabeth Carter (1717–1806) gained for herself a unique scholarly and literary eminence, others such as Charlotte Lennox (?1729–1804), principally known as a novelist, could complain of her 'present slavery to the Booksellers, whom I have the mortification to see adding to their heaps by my labours, which scarce produce me a scanty and precarious subsistence'. Lennox herself was eventually obliged to live on the charity of the Royal Literary Fund.

Improving education, changing attitudes and above all the individual efforts of women themselves resulted by the 1770s in the circles of 'Bluestockings' where intellectual women could meet and talk. Catherine Macaulay's *History of England* (1763), Elizabeth Montagu's *Essay on the Writings and Genius of Shakespeare* (1769) and Hester Chapone's *Letters on the Improvement of the Mind* (1773) indicate what women were now achieving. In poetry, this is clear from the *Poems* of Anna Barbauld (1743–1825) whose 'Corsica' is a powerful blank-verse discussion of political freedom. In the 1780s, the appearance of such poets as Helen Williams (1761–1827), the sonneteer Charlotte Smith

(1749–1806) and Anna Seward (1742–1809) confirms this advance.

Literary horizons were changing, and attitudes to Spenser were now becoming an important touchstone of contemporary taste. Hume reviled him, and the young Pope wrote a parody of his manner in 'The Alley'. Thomson himself, while fully aware of what could be seen as the 'ludicrous' qualities of Spenser's apparent quaintness, nonetheless managed a range of tones in *The Castle of Indolence*. These vary from dreamy sensuousness to satire. A tender, humorous pathos characterizes the Spenserian stanzas of *The Schoolmistress* (1737, 1748) by William Shenstone (1714–63), an attitude which the poet himself unfortunately described as 'simpering'. An artificial sense of contrivance is also apparent in *The Minstrel, or The Progress of Genius* (1771–4) by James Beattie (1735–1803). In this popular if rather disappointing poem, the Spenserian stanza is used to trace the growth of the poet's mind amid scenes which suggest a fashionable delight in romantically picturesque landscape.

Beattie derived much of his approach from the account of the minstrel in *The Reliques of Ancient English Poetry* (1765) compiled by Thomas Percy (1729–1811). The historical importance of this work lies in its publication of material from the rich oral tradition of the ballads. These are works of uncertain date and origin. Some are clearly medieval, others may be contemporary with Shakespeare, while a few are obviously later. Many are English and derive from the Midlands and the North, while among the very finest ballads are those from the border counties and Scotland.

Composed in four-line rhyming stanzas, the ballads hold within their seemingly simple construction worlds of extreme drama – worlds of love, murder and revenge, political and personal tragedy, and the realms of the supernatural. 'Clerk Saunders', with its portrayal of sexual ecstasy; 'The Unquiet Grave', where the mourning lover begs a kiss from the 'clay-cold lips' of the dead; 'The Wife of Usher's Well', whose heroine is visited by the ghosts of her sons until dawn comes and 'the channerin worm doth chide': these are works truly sublime. 'Thomas the Rhymer' is a supreme depiction of the poet's imaginative world of sexuality and ruthless enslavement. 'Sir Patrick Spens' captures a moment of ineluctable tragedy as the poem's doomed hero walks on the beach. The mother in 'Edward, Edward', taunting her son with the murder she has made him commit, reveals a shocking ruthlessness as the young man realizes that his crime has sundered him from all humanity. Such works might woo poets in any age from too precious a muse, and Percy's book was to be a major influence for the next fifty years.

Indeed, as early as 1724 David Mallet had tried a serious imitation of the form in his 'William and Margaret'. Though Mallet's poem is not of the highest quality, the combination of simple expression and high drama that he had tried to imitate moved that rather pompous literary figure Aaron Hill (1685–1750). In a review, Hill described the allure that such a work as Mallet's held for contemporaries, significantly calling his ballad 'a plain and noble masterpiece of the *natural* way of writing, without turns, points, conceits, flights, raptures, or affectation of what kind so ever'. Simplicity, naturalness of expression and a primitive emotion untouched by society were coming to be seen as desirable.

Such poetic and scholarly activity in the field of the ballad (evident in English literature long before the climactic publication of the *Lyrical Ballads* in 1798) was in part a reaction to neo-classical canons of 'correctness' and the main English tradition of verse from Waller to Pope. Joseph Warton (1722–1800), for instance, in his *Essay on the Genius and Writings of Pope* (two vols, 1756, 1782) argued that 'the sublime and the pathetic are the two chief nerves of genuine poesy. What is there transcendently sublime or pathetic in Pope?' Bishop Hurd (1720–1808) in his *Letters on Chivalry and Romance* (1763) similarly lamented that while the neo-classical poets had brought a great deal of good sense to their work, 'what we have lost is a world of fine fabling'.

Spenser in particular, no longer read as a mirror for courtiers but as a reflection of a newer critical interest in the powers of the imagination, was now seen as a chief exponent of this 'fairy way' of writing. Thomas Warton (1728–90), Joseph's brother, praised 'magic Spenser's wildly warbled song' which he analysed in his *Observations on the Faerie Queene* (1754). Warton's antiquarian and critical interests eventually led him to consult over seven hundred medieval manuscripts for his pioneering if diffuse and uncompleted *History of English Poetry from the Twelfth to the Close of the Sixteenth Century* (1774–81).

Another English poet enlisted with Spenser in the attack on 'wit and rhyme, sentiment and satire, polished numbers, sparkling couplets, and pointed periods' was Milton, especially the Milton of the 1645 volume. As with *The Faerie Queene*, this work was now read principally for its expressive effects. The Wartons' own poems reveal the influence of the isolated and melancholy night-time musings of 'Il Penseroso', and Thomas Warton in particular declared 'Lycidas' to be a sure test of a 'true taste for poetry'. For their friend William Collins (1721–59) in his 'Ode on the Poetical Character' (1746), Milton was also the last poet to hear the strains of divine inspiration.

Collins's career had begun with the mannered exoticism of his *Persian Eclogues* (1742), but in his 'Ode on the Poetical Character' he used a partly Spenserian allegory to develop his idea of the poet as the vehicle of holy and imaginative truth. Collins's 'Ode' presents a mythical tableau of the creative imagination and, as so often in his work, literature itself becomes the subject of poetry. Milton, as we have seen, is the exemplar of his ideal, and in the best known of Collins's descriptive odes – that to Evening – the unrhymed lines of a Milton translation of Horace were Collins's inspiration for fastidiously self-conscious literary effects:

> Then lead, calm vot'ress, where some sheety lake
> Cheers the lone heath, or some time-hallowed pile,
>   Or upland fallows grey
>   Reflect its last cool gleam.
> But when chill blust'ring winds, or driving rain,
> Forbid my willing feet, be mine the hut,
>   That from the mountain's side
>   Views wilds, and swelling floods,
> And hamlets brown, and dim-discovered spires,
> And hears their simple bell, and marks o'er all
>   Thy dewy fingers draw
>   The gradual dusky veil.

Collins's landscape is the typically picturesque one of the later eighteenth century, a combination of fairy romance, lone and melancholy meditation, ruins and the sublime. Collins was particularly drawn to subjects that could be treated as moral allegory: 'Liberty', 'Pity', 'Fear', 'Simplicity', 'Mercy' and 'Peace'. These are often effectively combined with patriotic sentiments, as in his moving 'Ode Written in the Beginning of the Year 1746'. Social and moral virtues are thus advanced in these works, often by an appeal to the sublime.

One of the chief models for this approach was the 'greater odes' of

Pindar. These Collins read in Greek while preserving in his own work the usual English practice of writing irregular stanzas or strophes. However, just as Thomas Blackwell (1701–57) in his *Enquiry into the Life and Writings of Homer* (1735) had viewed his subject in terms of primitive and passionate bardic energy, so Pindar is seen here as a means of going beyond polite, social verse to more demanding experiment. Collins's 'Ode to Fear' shows this particularly well. His subject is the terror roused by tragedy, and this allows him to compare the Greek tragedians with Shakespeare.

The association of the primitive with great art and a world where 'lives are yet sincere and plain' is made clear in Collins's unfinished 'Ode on the Popular Superstitions of the Highlands of Scotland, Considered as the Subject of Poetry'. Addressed to John Home (1722–1808), whose tragedy *Douglas* (1756) is one of the more interesting works in a period of generally benighted tragic endeavour, Collins shows in this ode a world of 'old Runic bards' inspiring choral dirges and 'some sounding tale of war's alarms'. Such scenes, while daring to depart from sober truth, 'are still to nature true' and are held to be the source for great contemporary poetry, even as they supposedly gave rise to *Macbeth*.

Among the Scots themselves, there was a new interest in the revival of their literary culture. If contemporary Scots dialects seemed suitable only for sentimental, humorous and mock-antique purposes, the three volumes of James Watson's *A Collection of Comic and Serious Scots Poems Both Ancient and Modern* (1706, 1709, 1711) suggested something of the glories of the past, while the first volume of Allan Ramsay's *Tea-Table Miscellany* (1724–37) offered an anthology in which the native vernacular tradition was presented in a way 'improved' for contemporary taste.

While Ramsay's own poems are often a hybrid of Scots and English, the works of Robert Fergusson (1750–74) offer vivid pictures of Edinburgh life in Scots dialect. And it was Fergusson whom Robert Burns (1759–96), the greatest of eighteenth-century Scots poets, recognized as 'my elder brother in the muse'. Burns, who was to delight connoisseurs as a 'Heaven-taught ploughman', was not in fact the uneducated rustic that contemporary critical opinion would have liked, an image which Burns himself indulged in his Preface to his *Poems Chiefly in the Scottish Dialect* (1786). He had a comparatively wide if informal education and he was familiar with the English writers from Shakespeare, through Milton and Dryden, to Thomson and Mackenzie whose *Man of Feeling* made a considerable impression on him. It was however a modernization of Blind Harry's *Wallace* and the poems of Fergusson that helped suggest to Burns the possibilities of combining older Scots literature with the dialect of his native Ayrshire.

But technical considerations, whatever their interest, were insufficient. 'I never had the least thought or inclination of turning poet', Burns wrote, 'till I got once healthily in love.' Burns is one of the greatest singers of love songs, and works such as 'A Red, Red Rose' and that tender reworking of a traditional air 'Oh wert thou in the cauld blast' show how creatively he could fuse feeling with his knowledge of the older Scots literary tradition. This last was deepened by Burns's work on James Johnson's *Scots Musical Museum* (1787–1803), and music, indeed, was central to much of Burns's writing, as all the world knows from 'Auld Lang Syne'.

Burns made only one attempt at folk legend in the magnificently eerie yet comic 'Tam o' Shanter', but a number of his finest works such as 'The Twa Dogs' and 'To a Louse' reveal a subtle satirical skill based on real indignation and a shrewd awareness of social nuance. This tone is less acerbic in the charming and popular 'To a Mouse', but the roistering poet of 'The Jolly Beggars' was also the man who could detect religious hypocrisy with unerring skill. In 'The Holy Fair', for example, unconstrained human nature is in fresh and life-enhancing contrast to the bigotries of Calvinism, and it is this feisty naturalness that finally triumphs over a dour, theological obsession with sin:

> How monie hearts this day converts
>> O' Sinners and o' Lasses!
> Their hearts o' stane gin night are gane,
>> As saft as ony flesh is.
> There's some are fou o' love divine;
>> There's some are fou o' brandy;
> An' monie jobs that day begin
>> May end in Houghmagandie.

Their hearts, *etc.*: *by night their stony hearts have become*; fou: *drunk*; Houghmagandie: *fornication*

It is in 'Holy Willie's Prayer' however that the self-satisfaction of the rigid Calvinist is most ruthlessly exposed through the expression of its own blind complacency. As a portrait of self-delusion, the satire ranks with the best of Swift. Only James Hogg (1770–1835), the so-called 'Ettrick Shepherd' and author of sentimental Scots songs, would produce a more terrible if melodramatic picture of Calvinism in *The Private Memoirs and Confessions of a Justified Sinner* (1824).

Scots literary critics such as Hugh Blair (1718–1800) were now concerned with the working of the creative imagination, while Blair himself had also been impressed with the *Fragments of Ancient Poetry Collected in the Highlands of Scotland and Translated from the Gaelic or Erse Language* (1760) by James Macpherson (1736–96). Blair had just been appointed Regius Professor of Rhetoric at the University of Edinburgh – essentially the first professor of English literature – and he was a scholar of formidable range. Though he was living in a great age of contemporary Gaelic poetry, Blair seems to have been interested less in this than in the lure held by Macpherson's volume which appeared to suggest that some of his fragments of Gaelic poetry belonged to an epic describing the ancient wars of Fingal. In 1762, Macpherson, who clearly had some knowledge of the Gaelic ballads, obligingly produced his *Fingal, an Ancient Epic Poem, in Six Books: together with several other poems, composed by Ossian the son of Fingal, Translated from the Gaelic Language.*

Macpherson's poem was a learned forgery or pastiche that took Europe by storm. Here, it was widely believed, was a new Homer, a bard who had emerged from a primitive society with an epic that was both tender and sublime. Genuine publications such as Percy's *Five Pieces of Runic Poetry* (1763) and Evan Evans's *Specimens of the Poetry of the Ancient Welsh Bards* (1764) went largely unread while the public surrendered to more heady pleasures: 'Weep on the rocks of roaring winds, O maid of Inistore! Bend thy fair head over the waves, thou lovelier than the ghost of the hills, – when it moves, in a sun beam, at noon, over the silence of Morven! He is fallen! thy youth is low! pale beneath the sword of Cuthullin!'

Another literary forgery also created an imagined past. Between 1768 and 1770, Thomas Chatterton (1752–70) imagined a medieval version of his native Bristol centred on the monk Thomas Rowley and his circle. Seven years after Chatterton's suicide, the great

Chaucerian scholar Thomas Tyrwhitt edited the poems, and controversy raged about their authenticity. Though there are clear traces of eighteenth-century sentiment in poems such as 'An Excelente Balade of Charitie' (and many of the discerning immediately saw through them) the pathos of Chatterton's early death was, for later generations, to provide an image of the dreaming artist crushed by a heedless society. Further, Chatterton's metrical experiments were to influence Coleridge and Scott, just as the novel play of vowels and consonants in the 'Mynstrelles Songe' from *Aella: A Tragycal Enterlude* was to beguile Keats.

Many traits in the verse of this period are brought together in the work of one of the finest poets of the late eighteenth century: Thomas Gray (1716–71). While on the Grand Tour with Horace Walpole (1717–97) – that central figure in contemporary taste – Gray had crossed the mighty valley of the Grande Chartreuse and been suitably impressed by the sublime. When Gray and Walpole had parted, Gray returned to the scene alone and was moved to write his Latin 'Alcaic Ode'. Here an intense response to the sublime is joined to the private sensibility of the learned poet in retreat. This is a central feature in some of Gray's finest work, and was to be deepened by a pressing awareness of human anguish. This last is particularly clear in three poems Gray wrote in 1742 after his friend West's early death: the 'Ode on a Distant Prospect of Eton College', the 'Ode to Adversity' and the 'Sonnet on the Death of Mr Richard West'.

The Eton College ode is prefaced by a Greek epigraph that may be translated: 'I am a man, a sufficient cause for being unhappy.' It is this learned, suffering voice of experience which describes the innocent paradise of a boyhood like Gray's own, setting it amid Gothic beauty and balancing its heedless joy against personifications of anguish suggestive of the tragic sublime and a conventional moral wisdom as old as Sophocles. In the 'Ode to Adversity', the Greek tragedians are again an inspiration, while the language, as in the 'Ode to Spring', is consciously learned and artificial.

The 'Ode to Spring' especially reveals a tissue of borrowings from Milton and others, and suggests that Gray's poetry requires not only an alert sensibility but what, amid the many concerns discussed in his correspondence (and, with Horace Walpole, Gray was one of the masters of the eighteenth-century letter), the poet called 'a long acquaintance with the good writers ancient and modern'. In Gray's poetry, the learned and literary imagination, spurred by allusion, rises to revelations of the sublime. This required a heightened diction. 'The language of the age is never the language of poetry', Gray declared, but at its best – as in the 'Sonnet on the Death of Mr Richard West' – such artifice is not pursued to the point of frigid mannerism. Here, the terse expression of 'lonely anguish' is so intense that it sunders the poet from the familiar comforts of his art. The desolation is thereby all the more acute.

Gray was capable of burlesquing his learned manner as he shows in his 'Ode on the Death of a Favourite Cat, Drowned in a Tub of Gold Fishes'. In the 'Elegy Written in a Country Churchyard' (1751) however he created a work which, in Dr Johnson's words, 'abounds with images which find a mirror in every mind, and with sentiments to which every bosom returns an echo'. The 'Elegy' remains one of the best loved of English poems. The melancholy meditation in the Gothic churchyard is uttered by an intense sensibility that rounds the subtle play of vowel sounds into seemingly timeless description. The felicitous melancholy (so superior to Young's strained labourings) is then contrasted to luminous images of life and love which make existence itself – however evanescent and hard done by – all the more precious. From this contrast arise those lines especially praised by Dr Johnson for their originality and universal pathos:

> For who to dumb Forgetfulness a prey
> This pleasing anxious being e'er resigned,
> Left the warm precincts of the cheerful day,
> Nor cast one longing lingering look behind?

Such awareness is the right even of the virtuous poor, but its throbbing intensity is the particular province of the poet. The concluding section of the 'Elegy' presents Gray's first full image of his conception of the poet as the familiar of nature and the frenzy of inspiration, the victim of inevitable death and the representative of unworldly integrity.

In 'The Progress of Poesy' (written 1751–4, published 1757), Gray revealed his conventional belief (expressed by Thomson among others) that truly inspired poetry is a life-enhancing source of peace and joy intimately connected with political liberty – with 'the unconquerable Mind and Freedom's holy flame'. As the ode develops, so Gray shows how Poesy, retreating to Rome after the collapse of ancient Greek democracy, eventually alighted in England to inspire Shakespeare, Milton and Dryden. Gray consciously places himself in this tradition, cruelly aware of a dwindling order of merit yet satirically contrasting his own integrity to the enfeebled and corrupting power of 'the Great' of his day.

In 'The Bard: A Pindaric Ode' (1757), this equation of inspired poetry with a free nation becomes Gray's principal subject. His central figure of the Druid was not a fortuitous choice, for the Druids were seen as patriot poet-priests and spokesmen of a 'Gothic liberty'. These were themes readily joined to the contemporary interest in the ancient resources of the northern European tradition. Gray himself – as part of a never completed history of English poetry – translated a number of Scandinavian fragments, suggesting their association with the sublime by calling such pieces as 'The Descent of Odin' and 'The Fatal Sisters' (1757) odes. A visit to Scotland had rekindled his awareness of the natural sublime, while he was inspired to complete 'The Bard' by the visit of a blind Welsh harper to Cambridge where Gray had spent the greater part of his life in scholarly retreat.

'The Bard' fuses these interests in one magnificent set piece based on the now disproved idea that, although Edward I supposedly slaughtered the Welsh bards in 1283, their works, as Gray wrote in his notebooks, 'still remain, the Language (tho' decaying) still lives, and the art of their versification is known and practised to this day among them'. It was an art also practised by Gray himself in the internal rhymes of the Bard's speech as, having prophesied the ruin of Edward's house and the revival of poetry with the coming of the Welsh Tudors, the last of the priestly line hurls himself from his precipice to the freedom of death:

> '. . . Enough for me: with joy I see
> The different doom our fates assign.
> Be thine despair and sceptered care;
> To triumph, and to die are mine.'
> He spoke, and headlong from the mountain's height
> Deep in the roaring tide he plunged to endless night.

Prophecy and the sublime, poetry, freedom and the imaginative resources of history are here joined in one powerful image. 'I felt myself the Bard,' Gray declared, and through his widely influential metaphor he could say things he could never utter in his own person.

A number of Gray's poems such as 'The Candidate' (1764), written against the corrupt Earl of Sandwich's election to the High Stewardship of Cambridge University, show the force of his satirical venom. This incident was also the subject of a similarly entitled poem by the prolific Charles Churchill (1732–64), a political radical who is perhaps best known for his *Rosciad* (1761), a satire on the acting profession. Other satirists such as Christopher Anstey (1724–1805) in his *New Bath Guide* (1766), a collection of verse letters which uses the anacreontic metre of Gray's 'The Candidate', took satire in the direction of light verse.

An altogether more profound vein of moral commentary is to be found in the work of George Crabbe (1754–1832), a poet who, in his long career, was admired by figures as diverse as Jane Austen and Byron. *The Village* (1783), with its depiction of poverty on the bleak Suffolk coast, marks Crabbe's out as an original poetic sensibility, the work of a man who used the conventions of the heroic couplet to show his local world 'As Truth will have it, but as Bards will not'. Crabbe's gift of observation led him to describe the lives neither of the rich nor of pastoral poverty but of the 'middling classes'. This was a new realm for poetry where, Crabbe believed,

more originality, more variety of fortune, will be met with; because, on the one hand, they do not live in the eye of the world, and, therefore, are not kept in awe by the dread of observation and indecorum; neither, on the other, are they debarred by their want of means from the cultivation of mind and the pursuits of wealth and ambition, which are necessary to the development of character displayed in the variety of situations to which this class is liable.

The Parish Register (1803) is a series of sketches of village manners, but it is 'Peter Grimes' from *The Borough* (1810) that shows Crabbe's ability to unite psychological drama with description and unobtrusive moral suggestion. Drunken sadism, the exploitation of children and their deaths while in Grimes's hideous employ lead to his psychological exile and spiritual collapse. Crabbe's presentation of this state through landscape description is powerful, profound and precise:

> There anchoring, Peter chose from man to hide,
> There hang his head, and view the lazy tide
> In its hot slimy channel slowly glide;
> Where the small eels that left the deeper way
> From the warm shore, within the shallows play;
> Where gaping mussels, left upon the mud,
> Slope their slow passage to the fallen flood; —
> Here dull and hopeless he'd lie down and trace
> How sidelong crabs had scrawled their crooked race;
> Or sadly listen to the tuneless cry
> Of fishing gull or clanging golden-eye . . .

Another considerable poet began his career with satire before being obliged by periods of spiritual despair into some of the most profound areas of eighteenth-century religious poetry. In 1782, William Cowper (1731–1800) published his *Table-Talk*. Cowper's satirist figure is specifically Christian in the values by which he measures a corrupt society. Rather more successful however is *The Task* (1785). This is a poem covering a miscellany of subjects and modes from Miltonic parody and mock-georgic, through fresh natural description (often moralized, as it is again in 'Yardley Oak' and 'The Poplar-Field'), to social comment on the local poor and the abuses of the slave trade. We are throughout aware of Cowper's Christian humanitarianism, an awareness sometimes heightened by the spiritual reflections of Cowper the 'stricken deer', a man living in precious domestic cheerfulness and peeping out at the world 'through loopholes of retreat'.

Cowper himself wrote that *The Task* was not composed 'to serve occasions of poetic pomp', and its combination of detailed domesticity and nervous personal revelation (characteristics found again in his sometimes sprightly letters) is also seen in a more moving form in the couplets of 'On the Receipt of my Mother's Picture Out of Norfolk' (1790, published 1798). This combination of detailed local description and personal reflection was to influence a later generation of poets – Coleridge especially – but it is neither here nor in his comic mock-ballad 'The Diverting History of John Gilpin' that Cowper's finest powers lay. His spiritual melancholia made him an excellent poet of religious experience. He collaborated with John Newton (1725–1807) on the *Olney Hymns* (1779), for example, Cowper himself writing two of the best known: 'God moves in a mysterious way' and the more personal 'Oh for a closer walk with God'.

Both these works reveal a faith longed for and finally won through a surrender to divine mercy, but it is as the poet of religious despair – of the anguished voice convinced of the soul's damnation – that Cowper is seen at his most powerful and experimental. The Sapphic stanzas of 'Hatred and vengeance' – often known as 'Lines Written during a Period of Insanity' – grate on the ear with the terror of a man 'fed with judgement, in a fleshly tomb'. The most fearful of these works however is 'The Castaway'. Based on an incident in Richard Walter's *Voyage round the World . . . by George Anson* (1748), Cowper's nightmare picture of death by drowning is given a terrible personal application in the final stanzas:

> No voice divine the storm allayed,
>   No light propitious shone,
> When, snatched from all effective aid,
>   We perished, each alone:
> But I beneath a rougher sea,
> And whelmed in deeper gulphs than he.

The scholarly investigation of past literature which inspired so many poets in this period was also to affect one of the greatest and most original of eighteenth-century hymn writers: Christopher Smart (1722–71). Smart knew the lectures delivered by Robert Lowth (1710–87) at Oxford on the sacred poetry of the Hebrews and was familiar with Lowth's investigation of the parallelism in the Psalms especially. In the last decade of his life, after writing much conventional work and while restrained in a lunatic asylum for religious mania, Smart wrote *A Song to David* (1763) and *Jubilate Agno* or 'Rejoice in the Lamb' (1759–63, published 1939). Both poems rhapsodically praise the wisdom of God in the creation.

Cowper's despair and Smart's exaltation are far removed from the blandness of much eighteenth-century Anglicanism. Dissent, too, had become moribund, and the spiritual vacuum was filled by a new voice: 'I felt my heart strangely warmed. I felt that I did trust in Christ, Christ alone for salvation; and an assurance was given me that he had taken *my* sins, even *mine*, and saved me from the law of sin and death.' These are the words of John Wesley (1703–91) whose *Journal* (1739) records his spiritual trials, his fervent open-air preaching and his highly influential brand of emotive Puritanism stripped of radical politics. Methodism, originally designed as a spiritual exercise within the Anglican Church, was intensely moral, socially conservative and thrift-conscious, yet emotional to the point of hysteria, anti-intellectual and even philistine in its attitudes. It was to become, nonetheless, a force of profound social cohesion, especially among those of the middle and working classes to whom other institutions remained closed.

Wesley himself combined the theological force of a Luther with the administrative genius of a Calvin, and along with his innumerable sermons, he and his brother Charles (1707–88) were the authors of some 3,000 hymns. These include 'Love divine, all loves excelling' and 'Hail the day that sees him rise'. Along with a wealth of other Nonconformist work, the hymns of the later eighteenth century reveal the exceptional influence of popular verse in creating social and religious attitudes.

II

The decades between the 1740s and the 1780s saw a wide variety of experiment in verse and prose, but the dominating presence of the era – indeed, one of the supreme figures of English literary history – was Samuel Johnson (1707–84). In what he himself described as an 'age of authors', no man gave himself more completely to authorship. To the heroic energies Johnson brought to establishing his place as a man of letters, however, he united a moral imagination at once social and Christian yet tempered by a pessimism that rises on occasions to tragic dignity. This never-wavering integrity of purpose illuminates all Johnson's work, his life and that prodigious gift for friendship revealed in his letters and conversation.

When, at the age of twenty-seven, Johnson arrived in London, he had already published his translation of a *Voyage to Abyssinia* (trans. 1733) by the Portugese Jesuit Father Lobo, taking a French version as his source. This occasionally controversial work is memorable for its level-headed Preface, written with the magisterial yet subtle rhetoric that characterizes Johnson's style, and for the fact that it contains material Johnson himself was later to draw on for his prose master-piece *Rasselas*. Once in London, Johnson gravitated naturally to the centre of the literary world and began work for Edward Cave (1691–1754) on his influential *Gentleman's Magazine*. Johnson supplied Cave with a prodigious quantity of material, much of which is of high quality and suggests the breadth of his concerns.

Lives of the famous always attracted him. 'Biography is,' he declared, 'of the various kinds of narrative writing, that which is most eagerly read, and most easily applied to the purposes of life.' Such a combination of the commercial with the moral is suggestive, and Johnson offered Cave eight essays in the form. These pieces are characterized less by original research (Johnson was content to rely on readily available sources or even translation) than by a careful selection of characteristic incidents shaped around moral commentary. This technique is seen to particular advantage in *The Life of Dr Herman Boerhaave* (1739), a man whose energy of intellect and moral probity appealed to Johnson as 'an admirable example of temperance, fortitude, humility and devotion'. The biographical and political work Johnson wrote at this period is seen at its best however in two of his most important early works: his verse satire *London* (1738) and his *Account of the Life of Mr Richard Savage* (1744).

The earlier work is an imitation of Juvenal whose satiric fury, sharp contrasts of vice with moral tirade, and near-tragic pessimism in the face of human folly were all congenial to Johnson's temperament. In the imitation, the contrast of the corrupt town to the innocence of the country becomes a means of opposing virtue to the rabid political and social corruption caused by the obsessive worship of money. The latter is given a variety of specific illustration but rises above its immediate occasion through the force of deeply felt general reflection:

> This mournful truth is everywhere confessed,
> SLOW RISES WORTH BY POVERTY DEPRESSED:
> But here more slow, where all are slaves to gold,
> Where looks are merchandise, and smiles are sold;
> Where won by bribes, by flatteries implored,
> The groom retails the favours of his lord.

The *Life of Richard Savage* is Johnson's major attempt at a long biography. To his inherently melodramatic subject – the cruel treat-ment by a mother of her talented but illegitimate child and that child's growth to self-destructive bohemianism – Johnson brought his own vigorous humanity and capacity for moral reflection. Savage remains for Johnson a poet whose work 'uniformly tended to the exaltation of the mind, and the propagation of morality and piety', while his life exemplified a particularly Johnsonian theme: the tyranny of fantasy over reason and the consequent unhappy loss of self-knowledge and self-control.

In 1747, a meeting with Robert Dodsley led to Johnson's publishing his *Plan for a Dictionary of the English Language*. This took the form of a letter to the fourth Lord Chesterfield (1694–1773). Chesterfield himself, an amateur of literature and author of the *Letters to his Son* (1774) – an informal course on courtesy which insists that 'manners must adorn knowledge, and smooth its way through the world' – appeared ready to play the patron in return for a dedication. That he then proceeded to do virtually nothing to earn this honour was later to rouse the forces of Johnson's magnificent sarcasm.

Summing up his original aims for the project, Johnson wrote: 'This . . . is my idea of an English Dictionary; a dictionary by which the pronunciation of our language may be fixed, and its attainment facilitated; by which its purity may be preserved, its use ascertained, and its duration lengthened.' Some of these purposes – long held as desirable – were to be modified as, over the course of the next seven years, the *Dictionary* absorbed a large part of Johnson's titanic energies. In the end, the two folio volumes made his name but not his fortune.

Johnson followed earlier European scholars in appending illustrative quotations to his definitions, and this procedure represents his most distinctive contribution to English dictionary making. The major English writers from Sidney onwards were consulted, and the passages gleaned were not originally intended to be merely illustrative. The moralist, the encyclopaedist and the man of letters were combined in the wish to cite improving and elegant extracts and so 'intersperse with verdure and flowers the dusty deserts of barren philology'.

Johnson recognized that it was on his definitions that he could expect 'malignity most frequently to fasten'. In some rare instances he courted this with his wit, as when he defined *oats* as 'A grain, which in England is generally given to horses, but in Scotland supports the people.' In other cases, as with the notorious *cough*, Johnson was betrayed by verbosity: 'A convulsion of the lungs, vellicated by some sharp serosity.' The general standard however is high and often elegant, as in the satisfying definition of *needle*: 'A small instrument pointed at one end to pierce cloth, and perforated at the other to receive the thread, used in sewing.'

A chief means of defining standard usage in the *Dictionary* was proscription. Johnson's proscriptive aims were as clear as Swift's. 'I have endeavoured to refine our language to grammatical purity,' he wrote, 'and to clear it from colloquial barbarisms, licentious idioms, and irregular combinations.' Obsolete and technical terms from menial trades were usually omitted, while vulgar terms and neologisms such as *bamboozle* were sometimes included only to be criticized. Gallicisms were always condemned.

But to Johnson, every activity – even what he referred to as the harmless drudgery of making a dictionary – had its moral dimension, and in some of the most moving parts of his Preface philological arguments are joined to moral, patriotic and personal reflections. Johnson came, for example, to accept the impossibility of fixing the language in a final form, and such a recognition led to a stoic meditation on mutability and the hope that 'the spirit of English liberty' would resist the false and authoritarian pronouncements of an academy. Johnson was also aware that a man who had completed so mighty an undertaking must face his own limitations: his failure to understand some words and his inability adequately to resolve all the technical problems his project raised. Above all, the Preface is characterized by the peculiarly Johnsonian recognition that the over-ambitious imagination, conjuring up possibilities beyond its competence, must finally accept that such fantasies 'were the dreams of a poet doomed at last to wake a lexicographer'. For Johnson, chastened pride was an essential of self-knowledge.

Johnson's Preface is the moving declaration of a man who has so established his independence of mind as to look with contempt on those lesser figures who would batten on his fame. Chesterfield in particular, who had offered nothing beyond an initial £10, now angled for a dedication by writing favourable reviews of the *Dictionary* in *The World*. The brief letter Johnson sent to Chesterfield on the completion of his enormous project is a masterpiece of barely restrained contempt, a document at once historically important as a symbol of the end of the age of patronage and humanely valuable as the expression of an individual who was resoundingly his own man.

To support this independence, Johnson revived the periodical essay and, in so doing, established himself as the foremost moralist of the day. *The Rambler*, which appeared twice weekly for the two years from 20 March 1750, was founded explicitly 'to consider the moral discipline of the mind'. Nearly all the papers were Johnson's own and most avoid 'the topicks of the day', concentrating instead on self-knowledge and 'a life usefully and virtuously employed'. If, as some contemporaries complained, the tone is somewhat too solemnly uniform and masculine, variety is achieved through the occasional use of Eastern tales and allegorical narratives, characters and letters. Literary topics such as the new, realistic novel, Spenserian imitation and Miltonic epic are all discussed. The scholar's ills of solitude and the feverish imagination are analysed and, though Johnson himself was to dismiss the essays as 'too wordy', there are amid much general reflection and abstract, Latinate English moments of great imagistic power and linguistic accuracy such as when Johnson wrote: 'Sorrow is a kind of rust of the soul, which every new idea contributes in its passage to scour away.'

The twenty-nine papers Johnson contributed to *The Adventurer* are usually less ponderous and include such amusing pieces as no. 84 which describes the varieties of snobbery revealed by the passengers in a stage-coach. A similar breadth of interests is seen again in the *Idler* papers which Johnson published in the *Universal Chronicle* between 13 April 1758 and 6 April 1760. Here the character of Dick Minim, retailer of the lethal literary platitude, is a particularly happy invention, though the series closes with Johnson's powerful Eastertide reflections. Such Christian hope and resignation (evident too in Johnson's prayers and private meditations) also conclude the greatest of his poems: *The Vanity of Human Wishes* (1749).

The Vanity of Human Wishes is one of the supreme achievements of eighteenth-century poetry and a work which focuses Johnson's moral views with a passion that touches the sublime. His concern is with general truths: his belief that human life is everywhere and at all times the same, and his conviction that it is the duty of the poet to express fundamentals rather than 'number the streaks of the tulip, or describe the different shades in the verdure of the forest'. These are views broadened by Johnson's Christian humanism. Juvenal, as the source for imitation, provides the classical model to be assimilated to the native tradition, while Johnson's faith — too deeply inured to suffering to trifle with a facile optimism — provides the sombre ground of true hope. Against this are then placed his representative portraits of vain aspiration. We are shown Wolsey in his scarlet pride and the Swedish monarch Charles XII condemned to pitiful exile. Yet it is not the great alone who fall victim to the fallacies of hope. The scholar too is a dupe of 'th'eternal jest':

> When first the college roll receives his name,
> The young enthusiast quits his ease for fame;
> Through all his veins the fever of renown
> Burns from the strong contagion of the gown;
> O'er Bodley's dome his future labours spread,
> And Bacon's mansion trembles o'er his head.
> Are these thy views? proceed, illustrious youth,
> And Virtue guard thee to the throne of Truth!
> Yet should thy soul indulge the generous heat,
> Till captive Science yields her last retreat;
> Should Reason guide thee with her brightest ray,
> And pour on misty Doubt resistless day;
> Should no false Kindness lure to loose delight,
> Nor Praise relax, nor Difficulty fright;
> Should tempting Novelty thy cell refrain,
> And Sloth effuse her opiate fumes in vain;
> Should Beauty blunt on fops her fatal dart,
> Nor claim the triumph of a lettered heart;
> Should no disease thy torpid veins invade,
> Nor Melancholy's phantoms haunt thy shade;
> Yet hope not life from grief or danger free,
> Nor think the doom of man reversed for thee:
> Deign on the passing world to turn thine eyes,
> And pause awhile from letters to be wise;
> There mark what ills the scholar's life assail,
> Toil, envy, want, the patron and the gaol.
> See nations slowly wise, and meanly just,

> To buried merit raise the tardy bust.
> If dreams yet flatter, once again attend,
> Hear Lydiat's life, and Galileo's end.

Bodley's dome: *the Bodleian library in Oxford*; Bacon's mansion: *the study of the medieval scholar Roger Bacon, destined to fall when a greater philosopher passed under it*; Lydiat: *Oxford scholar who died in poverty*

The great Johnsonian themes of intellectual effort and moral discipline are here described against a profound acceptance that all is vanity: vanity as pride, vanity as disappointed endeavour. Nothing can be securely built on worldly foundations, and the last paragraph of the poem provides a terrifying view of man imagined in a godless, destructive world and left to 'roll darkling down the torrent of his fate'. The Johnson of intense religious melancholia and 'inspissated gloom', the Johnson who was to face and survive nervous collapse, knew the terrors of despair as perhaps only the greatly spiritual can. Nor was there exaltation readily to counter this. Instead, humility and hope, dignity and faith, provide a powerfully traditional and deeply moving sense of purpose from which vanity in all its forms has been finally expunged.

The greatest of Johnson's prose reflections remains his prose tale *Rasselas* (1759). In its relatively brief compass, *Rasselas* contrives to present a broad survey of the fallacies of hope and the growing awareness of its youthful hero and heroine that quixotic idealism must be tempered with experience. They must learn how 'Human life is everywhere a state in which much is to be endured, and little to be enjoyed.' Even in the Happy Valley of Abyssinia the hero is afflicted by a nameless ennui, yet all the experience of the philosopher Imlac fails to convince him that existence in the real world can be made happy by making the right choice of life. Rasselas, Imlac, the prince's sister Nekayah and her companion Pekuah eventually escape to this real world, but revellers and stoics, wealthy men and shepherds variously illustrate the fleeting nature of happiness, the fallacies of escapism and the limitations of philosophy.

More insidious still is the 'hunger of the imagination that preys incessantly on life'. This very Johnsonian theme reaches its climax in Imlac's meditation on the Pyramids:

I consider this mighty structure as a monument of the insufficiency of human enjoyments. A king. whose power is unlimited, and whose treasures surmount all real and imaginary wants, is compelled to solace, by the erection of a pyramid, the satiety of dominion and tastelessness of pleasures, and to amuse the tediousness of declining life by seeing thousands labouring without end, and one stone, for no purpose, laid upon another. Whatever thou art, that, not content with a moderate condition, imaginest happiness in royal magnificence, and dreamest that command and riches can feed the appetite of novelty with perpetual gratifications, survey the pyramids, and confess thy folly!

Johnson shows how religious retreat provides no permanent answer, while scholarship, yielding again to the 'dangerous prevalence of the imagination', is exposed in the figure of the elderly and insane astronomer who is gradually cured of his delusions by the presence of human companionship. This is one of the most moving sections of the tale, and it would be wrong to characterize *Rasselas* as wholly negative or entirely pessimistic. For the princess, at least, an awareness of the importance of faith begins to dawn, while in the conclusion 'in which nothing is concluded' we see how the characters have attained some acceptance of the fact that if hope invariably aspires to fantasy the mind can at least recognize this fact and accept it.

Johnson wrote *Rasselas* in a week to defray the expenses of his mother's funeral and clear some personal debts. A number of his lesser pieces from this period also helped to support him while he worked on another large project – his edition of Shakespeare (1765).

It was during this period that there arose what Edward Gibbon referred to as that 'idolatry for the gigantic genius of Shakespeare, which is inculcated from our infancy as the first duty of an Englishman'. From the 1740s, the romantic comedies grew in popularity, and Garrick in particular contributed to broadening the awareness of Shakespeare on the stage. Editorial and critical interest in Shakespeare is also seen in a growing number of editions and critical essays, but Johnson remains the most interesting eighteenth-century student of Shakespeare. In his *Proposals for Printing the Dramatic Works of William Shakespeare* (1756) he wrote: 'the business of him who republishes an ancient book is, to correct what is corrupt, and explain what is obscure'. In the Preface to his edition, Johnson illustrates his awareness of the many and considerable difficulties this involved, problems enhanced by the fact that 'careful collation of the oldest copies' was not always possible, many of the quartos being unavailable to him. His annotations of particular words and phrases, however, show the expertise of the lexicographer.

It is less as an editor than as a Shakespearian critic that Johnson stands above his contemporaries. To read these sections of his Preface is to be aware of a powerful insight focused on the text as a vehicle for performance, appreciating its qualities and attempting to analyse these through received principles which are themselves subject to modification in the light of Shakespeare's unique excellence. Johnson's position was far from being one of abject veneration however, and he shows an interesting awareness of the 'gradual and comparative' ways in which works 'of which the excellence is not absolute and definitive' come to be appreciated. Johnson finds the underlying reason for Shakespeare's continuing attraction in his lively representation of general human nature, his instructiveness, and his powers of construction and dialogue. 'Shakespeare', he declared, 'always makes nature predominate over accident.' This central tenet of his theory Johnson elaborated thus:

His characters are not modified by the customs of particular places, unpractised by the rest of the world; by the peculiarities of studies or professions, which can operate but upon small numbers; or by the accidents of transient fashions or temporary opinions: they are always the genuine progeny of common humanity, such as the world will always supply, and observation will always find.

It is one with this approach that, for Johnson, Shakespeare is not disturbed by false notions of decorum or troubled by mixing tragedy with what Johnson saw as his superior gift for comedy. This was a matter particularly disturbing to the strict neo-classical critic, but is shown by Johnson to be an essential part of Shakespeare's imitation of nature. 'The interchanges of mingled scenes seldom fail to produce the intended vicissitudes of passion,' he declared, and he went on to argue powerfully against a coldly correct veneration for the rules. He urged instead 'the nobler beauties of variety and instruction' and declared 'the greatest graces of a play are to copy nature and instruct life'.

Here Johnson's moral and didactic bias emerges. Believing 'it is always a writer's duty to make the world better', he censures Shakespeare for appearing 'so much more careful to please than to instruct that he seems to write without any moral purpose'. He found fault too with 'a disproportionate pomp of diction and a wearisome train of circumlocution', with Shakespeare's set speeches and his puns. Such alleged faults Johnson tried to explain by adopting a historical estimate of Shakespeare, seeing him as a writer as naturally impelling as Homer but hampered by an age that 'was yet struggling to emerge from barbarity'. The Preface is thus a broadly argued work of neo-classical criticism that asks interesting questions of that tradition itself while revealing a deep engagement with Shakespeare and the prob-lems of literary analysis.

A portion of Johnson's work centres around his friends and often witnesses to the extraordinary breadth of his knowledge, his generos-ity and the fertilizing influence of his genius. For example, Johnson assisted Robert Chambers with a series of lectures on the law when Chambers himself had been appointed to the Vinerian Lectureship at Oxford in succession to Sir William Blackstone (1723–80), author of the four-volume *Commentaries on the Laws of England* (1765–9). For his old school friend Dr John Taylor he wrote a number of sermons, including the one Taylor delivered at the funeral of Johnson's wife. For David Garrick, the actor-manager who had helped mount a production of *Irene* (1749) – Johnson's somewhat ponderous tragedy of Christian and pagan love and betrayal – Johnson wrote a Prologue to celebrate the reopening of the Drury Lane Theatre in 1747. In these verses he charted 'the wild vicissitudes of taste' in English drama since Shakespeare, relating these to the expectations of the audience rather than the caprice or weakness of individual authors. The Pro-logue concludes with the hope that the present audience will have the stature to appreciate new work of high moral and artistic quality.

It is to James Boswell (1740–95) that we owe the popular portrait of Johnson as the 'Great Cham' of English letters, the heroic conversa-tionalist talking for victory, omniscient, moral and vigorously at the centre of life – 'a huge uncouth figure, with a little dark wig which scarcely covered his head, and his clothes hanging loose about him'.

Boswell first met Johnson in 1763. A prickly exchange led to a warm friendship, and the older man soon responded to Boswell's impetuous curiosity, his vivid and often anguished concern with the present moment. Johnson's letters to Boswell, in their combination of personal with general reflection, are among the most warming of his works. For his part, Boswell, who had recently quarrelled with his father, found in Johnson that greatness of stature to which he was irresistibly compelled. Within the next few years Boswell was to seek the acquaintance of Voltaire and Rousseau, the Corsican hero Pasquale Paoli, Frederick the Great and Hume, whose atheist's death he felt compelled to observe with ruthlessly intrusive curiosity. For Boswell, the life around him was of an irresistibly fascinating variety to be observed and, above all, recorded. His 'Journal' – that training ground of the great biographer – shows how he found himself one of the most interesting of phenomena to watch.

With Johnson however, Boswell was no mere passive recorder. Blessed with a powerful memory and trained as a lawyer in the techniques of examination, Boswell encouraged his subject to develop in front of him. And it was on the basis of such a friendship that Boswell persuaded Johnson to make the remarkable expedition recorded in Johnson's *Journey to the Western Islands of Scotland* (1775) and Boswell's *Tour of the Hebrides* (1785). The difference between the books is the measure of the men. Johnson's account is philosophical, an attempt to view life and manners among an ancient pastoral people still suffering from the degradations of 1745. Boswell's account is altogether more specific and vivacious, and it is Johnson the London clubman in this most different of environments who always compels: Johnson wading ashore to Iona, Johnson crossing to Raasay while the boatmen sung in Gaelic and Johnson himself sat 'high on the stern, like a magnificent Triton'. Above all, we are presented with Johnson talking, the individual man giving vent to his philosophic opinions.

When Boswell came to write his *Life of Johnson* (1791), it was just such a figure, magnificent in his response whether surprised into dining with Wilkes or talking to his king, who emerged from Boswell's memory, his skilled reworking of his notes and his scrupulous researches among Johnson's letters and his friends. The *Life* remains one of the most compelling biographies in the English language.

In 1776, Johnson wrote to Boswell that he was himself 'engaged to write little Lives, and little Prefaces, to a little edition of the English Poets'. This project was to develop into a history of English poetry from Cowley to Gray, though its origins were more mundane.

Alexander Donaldson, an enterprising Scottish publisher forbidden like all such men from exporting his titles to England, had recently opened a bookshop in London. Here he proceeded to sell his own edition of Thomson's *Seasons* after the expiry of its 28-year period of copyright. Andrew Millar, the holder of the original copy, challenged Donaldson's right to do this on the grounds that the Act of 1710 only imposed certain specific conditions on what remained, under common law, his perpetual property. The Scots courts ruled for the defendant and when, in 1774, Millar appealed this verdict to the House of Lords, he was, much to his surprise, again defeated. The English judges now held that an exclusive and permanent monopoly on a title was against the public interest. It kept prices artificially high and was not in the spirit of an Act designed to encourage learning. This verdict in *Millar* v. *Donaldson* (1744) was of historic importance to the British publishing trade. The period of protectionism and permanent monopoly was over, and the publisher now emerged as a highly competitive figure in a free market.

A healthy back-list was desirable for his profit, and reprint series (soon to be released in 'edition' bindings) were to become the popular products of the relatively small family firms whose titles were now supplied through wholesalers to bookshops in the provinces and London's fashionable West End. Between 1777 and 1782, for example, John Bell issued the 109 volumes of his *Poets of Great Britain*. These accompanied his *Shakespeare* (1774) and the twenty-one volumes of *The British Theatre* (1776–8). In belated competition, Edward Dilly, a publisher of the older school, decided to issue ten volumes of the work of poets active after 1660. It was for these that Johnson wrote his *Prefaces, Biographical and Critical* (1779, 1781), now generally known as *The Lives of the Poets*.

For Johnson, 'Poetry is the art of uniting pleasure with truth, by calling imagination to the help of reason.' His view of literary pleasure was an essentially pragmatic one, the experience of a writer who knows his craft and a reader who relishes his study. Johnson makes this particularly clear in a passage from his 'Life of Dryden':

Works of the imagination excel by their allurement and delight; by their power of attracting and detaining the attention. That book is good in vain, which the reader throws away. He only is the master, who keeps the mind in pleasing captivity; whose pages are perused with eagerness, and in the hope of pleasure are perused again; and whose conclusion is perceived with an eye of sorrow, such as the traveller casts upon departing day.

As he had already established in his Preface to Shakespeare, this power to hold many minds in pleasurable allurement depended on a writer bringing technical skills to bear on fundamental human truths. 'Great thoughts', Johnson wrote in his 'Life of Cowley', 'are always general.' This did not mean however that they were simply a matter of received commonplaces. Johnson was scornful of Pope's notion of 'what oft was thought but ne'er so well express'd'. What he sought was new truths about human nature, imaginatively expressed but agreeable to common reason. It was on just such a basis that he praised Gray's 'Elegy'. It was also on these criteria that Johnson established some of his more controversial judgements, his criticism of 'Lycidas' and the 'metaphysical' poets especially. But Johnson was too responsive a reader to dismiss what he could not wholly admire and, like Dryden, he wanted to write criticism that was 'not a dull collection of theorems, nor a rude detection of faults'. In what he saw as the misdirected energies of the metaphysicals Johnson discovered some truth and much worth. Above all, these poets were free from the vices of servile imitation.

Johnson believed that such mixed results could be partly explained by a historical estimate of the time and circumstances in which an author lived. He also thought that one of the most effective forms of criticism was extended comparison between authors. This was a technique at which he excelled, and it is seen at its best in his comparison of Dryden and Pope in his 'Life of Pope'. Here, biographical and historical information, the general and the particular, are united in what Johnson himself praised in Dryden's own criticism as 'a gay and vigorous dissertation, where delight is mingled with instruction, and where the author proves his right of judgement, by the power of his performance'.

Other than the *Lives*, Johnson wrote little at the end of his career beyond the satirical 'Short Song of Congratulation' (1780) and 'On the Death of Dr Robert Levet' (1782). The latter is one of the masterpieces of eighteenth-century verse and a poem in which Johnson may be seen at his most magnificently characteristic. Redolent with Christian charity, with a knowledge of the vanity of worldly hope and the worth of simple goodness, the poem raises a particular and otherwise largely unknown man to an abiding image of life worthily lived. Grave, general and deeply felt, the poem is truly Johnsonian in its massive and humane integrity.

12

In 1764, Johnson established his club, later known as the Literary Club, as a forum for his powers as a conversationalist and a focus for some of the most brilliant men of his day. The circle that eventually gathered on Monday nights at the Turk's Head in Soho included Burke, Gibbon, Boswell, Garrick, Sir Joshua Reynolds and Adam Smith, as well as one of the most various and delightful minor masters of the eighteenth century: Oliver Goldsmith (?1730–74).

As feckless in his life as he was graceful in his prose, Goldsmith showed in his *Enquiry into the Present State of Polite Learning* (1759) a keen awareness of how poverty drove authors to hack writing, over-production, 'tedious compilations, and periodical magazines'. Goldsmith himself produced a great quantity of such work, though often at a more than adequate level of competence. Between 1760 and 1761, for instance, Goldsmith wrote his 'Chinese Letters' for the *Public Ledger*. Modelled on Montesquieu's *Lettres persanes* (1721) and their English imitators, these pieces were later reprinted as *The Citizen of the World* (1762). They purport to offer the views of the Chinese sage Lien Chi Altangi on the comedy of English daily life, and its manners and virtues as well as such characters as the enigmatic, benevolent Man in Black.

Interest in national characteristics is also evident in Goldsmith's poem *The Traveller* (1764) where, in passages of considerable descriptive and reflective assurance, the narrator conducts a search for happiness through Europe, narrating the various virtues and frailties of its peoples until he is forced to conclude, in a couplet supplied by Johnson:

> Vain, very vain, my weary search to find
> That bliss which only centres in the mind.

Others poets such as Richard Jago (1715–81) in his *Edge-Hill* (1767) continued the verse of landscape description, enlarging this with strong feelings of local patriotism and paeans to progress, but one of the most attractive works in this descriptive and moralizing mode is Goldsmith's *The Deserted Village* (1770). Though at times too abstract in its language and slackly repetitive in its versification, there is amid the sentimental reminiscence much heartfelt observation and harsh criticism of the spread of luxury and the enclosure of common lands to make pleasure parks for the gentry.

The Vicar of Wakefield (1766), Goldsmith's only sustained work of prose fiction, is centred around religious faith maintained in adversity and the familial virtues of hearth and home. The novel presents the exemplary Dr Primrose's loss and providential recovery of his happiness, interspersing scenes of wryly observed pastoral comedy with those of sentiment. There is much here of the fairy-tale, and something too of the Book of Job, but although the work contains Goldsmith's finest lyric – 'When lovely woman stoops to folly' – the balance of sentiment with comedy is not as finely achieved as it was in his stage work.

In his *Essay on the Theatre* (1773), Goldsmith clearly distinguished two types of comedy: the sentimental work of Steele and his followers and what Goldsmith himself termed laughing comedy. In *The Good Natur'd Man* (1768), he turned an affectionately critical eye on the excesses of benevolence embodied in Mr Honeywood whose charity and over-scrupulous concern not to hurt others' feelings lead to comic confusion. In *She Stoops to Conquer* (1773) however, Goldsmith's attack on sentimentalism was more overtly critical. His character of Marlow is a shrewd portrayal of that type of English gentleman who is confident with women of the lower orders but is reduced to stammering embarrassment in the presence of a Miss Hardcastle. It is the great comic character of Tony Lumpkin however – part boor, part trickster, but above all a natural man – who exposes the inherent hypocrisy in Marlow's attitude and helps Kate to 'stoop' from her true social position to play the barmaid and so win her lover's heart. Excellently contrived and far from merely polemical, *She Stoops to Conquer* is the finest achievement of Goldsmith's versatile talent.

The Rivals (1775) by Richard Brinsley Sheridan (1751–1816) is a brilliantly light-hearted rebuff to 'the sentimental muse'. Although the subplot of Faulkland and Julia perhaps slightly unbalances the work and the deft speed of its plotting, the major characters – the comic literary heroine Lydia Languish, Sir Lucius O'Trigger the stage Irishman and Mrs Malaprop above all – are brilliantly and timelessly effective. In *The School for Scandal* (1777), this dexterity is applied with greater comic invention and sharper social comment to reveal the true nature of the hypocritical Joseph Surface and his good-natured if reckless brother Charles. The congeries of scandal-mongers is excellently observed as they 'strike a character dead at every word', but it is the revelations afforded by the famous 'screen scene' that show Sheridan's true theatrical genius and provide the high point of eighteenth-century laughing comedy.

Among other members of the Literary Club was Sir Joshua Reynolds (1723–92) who painted Johnson's portrait on several occasions, contributed a paper to *The Idler* and acknowledged Johnson's debt in helping to formulate the aesthetic theory embodied in Reynolds's *Discourses* (1797). These were delivered during his long presidency of the Royal Academy and present a neo-classical theory of the visual arts.

Another member of the Literary Club was Edward Gibbon (1737–94), author of the century's supreme work of philosophical scholarship, *The History of the Decline and Fall of the Roman Empire* (1776–88), and of the brief, elegant masterpiece entitled *Memoirs of my Life and Writings* (1796). The *Memoirs* depict the making of 'the historian of the Roman empire'. The work tells of Gibbon's voracious youthful reading, his brief undergraduate residence amid the scholarly torpor of Oxford, parental disapproval at his conversion to Roman Catholicism and his enforced stay in Switzerland. Here, in the process of being weaned from his new-found faith and an unsuitable love affair, Gibbon immersed himself in the ancient and modern scholarship that was to make him a true member of the European Enlightenment.

The *Memoirs* also offer a much quoted passage in which Gibbon tells of the discovery of his vocation. Extensive reading had prepared him for the Grand Tour, while Rome itself kindled him to sleepless excitement. He was on the ground trod by the senators of his admired republic, and 'It was at Rome on the fifteenth of October 1764, as I sat musing amid the ruins of the Capitol while the barefooted friars were singing Vespers in the temple of Jupiter, that the idea of writing the decline and fall of the City first started to my mind.'

This was a vision to be realized through years of labour. Gibbon's

History begins with the panoptic vision of the first three chapters and their subtle portrayal of a tolerant and civilized empire founded by Augustus on the thinly disguised ruins of the republic. Gibbon then showed the corruption of civic virtue by the enervating wealth of empire which preferred 'effeminacy' and the hiring of mercenary soldiers to the maintenance of a patriotic citizen army. Like Montesquieu, Gibbon went on to suggest how 'the luxury of Asia' – partly the product of a soporific climate – in time led to the oriental despotism he richly if not altogether fairly symbolized in Byzantium. Here, Gibbon believed, absolute power and political abnegation were rivalled in their corrosive effects by the disputed tenets of a dogmatic and monkish Christianity. These, he suggested, scorned both the state and human dignity in preference for the brutalizing disciplines of the soul. This aspect of the *History* – the unfavourable contrast drawn between the tolerant polytheism of classical Rome and the narrow bigotry of Christian Byzantium – was one of the most controversial aspects of the book. It is the concluding passage of the work however – Gibbon's description of the fall of Constantinople – that is his greatest achievement. Scholarship, narrative power and the moral imagination are here united in what may fairly claim to be the supreme passage of English historical prose.

Gibbon's learning is worked into a magisterial feat of historical enquiry, and as a scholar he was always quick to acknowledge his debts. In particular, he paid generous tribute to another member of the Literary Club and the greatest political economist of his age, Adam Smith (1723–90). It is for *An Enquiry into the Nature and Causes of the Wealth of Nations* (1776) that Smith is now chiefly remembered. The work is a lucid and powerfully influential model of the workings of the commercial society that was now being hugely augmented by the powers of the Industrial Revolution. It is thus a response to forces of the utmost importance.

At the basis of the work is a description of economic activity seen in terms of the benefits allegedly brought to all by unfettered growth based on the division of labour. Looking with an admiring glance on 'the new works at Sheffield, Manchester, or Birmingham', Smith illustrated the benefits of the division of labour with his famous example of pin manufacture. Where one man, he shows, undertaking all the operations required in making a pin, might produce only one a day, ten men, dividing the labour between them, might make 50,000 pins in a day.

Smith alleges that an increasing division of labour of this type produces a developing material society which in turn binds people together in ever more complex mutual dependence. Such dependence, however, is neither planned nor altruistic. 'It is not from the benevolence of the butcher, the brewer, or the baker, that we expect our dinner, but from their regard to their own interest.' The pursuit of self-interest does not necessarily lead to an antagonistic society, however. Rather, it promotes the accumulation of capital which can in turn be re-employed to produce yet more goods and opportunities for work in an ever-expanding market.

Self-interest thus promotes general welfare, and Smith thought that such beneficial sequences of events, independent of our particular purposes, are like scientific laws of nature. It is by letting them operate as freely as we may that economic benefits will come. We thrive, he thought, by encouraging free trade rather than enforcing government intervention. He realized, however, the deleterious effects of the division of labour on the poor who were thereby often condemned to mindless drudgery, and he recommended compulsory education to help offset these. He also suggested a minimum wage which must be 'consistent with common humanity'. For the great economist, market forces were not the only morality.

After Smith had been elected to the Literary Club, he is reported to have said of another member, Edmund Burke (1729–97), that Burke was the only man who, without communication, thought on these topics exactly as he did. Burke indeed prided himself on his economic studies, and a belief in the forces of free trade, which through the century had so subtly insinuated themselves into the older social order, underlay his reverence for the continuing life of the traditional establishment. Such beliefs were also the basis of his attacks on contemporary political abuses. In the earlier and longer part of his career, Burke focused his attacks on three principal areas: the attempts made by the royal court to limit parliamentary sovereignty, the government's policy towards the American colonies and the arbitrary rule and corrupting wealth of the East India Company.

In speeches, books and pamphlets, Burke developed the position that characterized his mature political thought, enlarging his approach through the broad sweep of his rhetoric, his use of a language which sees the specific in terms of strongly felt yet loosely defined moral principles. In particular, there is his reiterated belief, expressed in his *Letter to the Sheriffs of Bristol on the Affairs of America* (1777), that political science is not, like mathematics, a matter of clear-cut rules. Rather, it is a question of restraint and of piecemeal adjustments to a highly complicated organism already hallowed by long existence. In his *Thoughts on the Causes of the Present Discontents* (1770), Burke also urged the notion of the organized political party as a group of independently minded men free from an absolute obligation to the views of their particular electors and publicly committed to a joint national policy by which they would stand or fall.

The third of Burke's great early campaigns, and the one on which he most prided himself, was his attack on the abuses of the East India Company. In particular, there was his attempt to move the impeachment of the chief architect of these abuses, Warren Hastings. Burke's speeches in this cause are a brilliantly sustained and devastating criticism of the men whose new wealth was appearing to usurp the power of the traditional landed gentry at home and who had also ruthlessly abused the rights and dignities of the native Indian princes. Burke's *Speech on Fox's East India Bill* (1783) is a masterpiece of political oratory in which the regular fall of opprobrious adjectives is a body-blow to the very tyranny they ridicule.

The speech asserts that political power is based on trust, accountability and the freedoms granted by ancient charter. It also culminates in a fervid rhetoric in which Burke's case is finally seen as resting not, as Locke had argued, on the natural rights of freely associated individuals, but on man's duty of submission to an emotive but ill-defined concept of divine law. To this Burke was to cling with ever greater desperation. Indeed, it was to be the heart of his response to an event which now seemed to question the very existence of the established order itself. That event, which was soon to force all thinking people into radicalism or reaction, was one of the climactic moments of European history – the French Revolution.

Revolutions, Reaction and Reform

I

Some of the greatest imaginative writing in English literature springs from the confrontation of radicals and conservatives at the close of the eighteenth century. No event focused this debate more sharply than the French Revolution. While for many the violent replacement of an old and corrupt order appeared to offer a world of new hope and freedom, for others the loss of traditional institutions seemed to foreshadow the end of civilized existence itself. Among the latter figures was the parliamentary orator Edmund Burke (1729–97).

'I thought ten thousand swords must have leaped from their scabbards to avenge even a look that threatened her with insult. – But the age of chivalry is gone. – That of sophisters, economists, and calculators has succeeded; and the glory of Europe is extinguished for ever.' Thus Burke on the imprisonment of Marie Antoinette and the early days of the French Revolution whose traumatic progress towards the Terror Burke predicted and which caused him to write his most influential work of conservative propaganda, the *Reflections on the Revolution in France and on the Proceedings in Certain Societies in London Relative to that Event* (1790).

The full title of Burke's treatise suggests the core of his concern. Early in 1790 the dissenting minister Richard Price had preached a sermon in support of the ideals underlying the turmoil in France. Burke's essay was designed as a crusade against the spread of such radical innovation and the overthrow of the traditional liberties he saw enshrined in the church, the hereditary power of the monarchy and the greater landed families. These values formed the centrepiece of his attack on the new philosophy of the rights of man. Round them Burke then marshalled the forces of his occasionally soaring rhetoric, his shrewdly pointed epigrams and the grave and even solemn manner of his theoretical exposition.

For Burke, the ancient principle of inheritance guaranteed the rights of the people as these were embodied in the traditional political order, an order handed down through the generations from Magna Carta to the Glorious Revolution. Such a principle – 'a partnership not only between those who are living, but between those who are living, those who are dead and those who are to be born' – placed stability beyond the reach of innovating individuals and appeared to give the British constitution itself the solidity of an institution divinely ordained.

To this permanent body men must completely and willingly subdue their natural rights in order to enjoy what Burke saw as 'the *real* rights of man' – protection under the law and the security of private profit and inherited wealth. It was not for anyone to change such a system at his will, nor was this an institution in which every person could have his say. The state, in Burke's opinion, was only to be governed by 'a true natural aristocracy' of the landed gentry, the conservative intellectual élite and those few greater merchants and manufacturers who, growing rich on the forces of the Industrial Revolution, had been assimilated into the traditional order. Such men, controlling a wholly unrepresentative Parliament, formed a public of less than half a million in a nation several times that size.

While many were to welcome Burke's statement of traditional views, for others such ideas were anathema. In particular, Burke's *Reflections* were answered in one of the most lively of English political treatises, *The Rights of Man* (1791) by the revolutionary Thomas Paine (1737–1809). Paine had already played an important propagandist role in the American War of Independence where his *Common Sense* (1776), the self-educated radical's vigorous and down-to-earth exposition of liberal ideals, had galvanized the energies of a continent. For Paine, the newly free Americans had wrought 'a revolution in the principles and practice of governments'. They had abolished monarchy and hereditary power, committed themselves to a representative assembly, yet sufficiently restricted that 'necessary evil' so individual initiative could flourish in the unfettered hands of the naturally talented.

It was from such a basis, and in the radical heyday of the early 1790s, that Paine attacked the 'quixotic age of chivalric nonsense' he saw embodied in the writings of Burke. He had himself been in France during the events of 1789 – Lafayette gave him the keys of the

Bastille to present to Washington – and Paine's hatred of hereditary monarchy, institutional privilege and the 'political superstition' he found in Burke's writings won him sympathizers among both the newly wealthy manufacturers and the literate poor in England.

For the former group, Paine's vision of levelling the old and unrepresentative hierarchy of rank to a world of competitive individualism voiced the feelings of 'enterprise and industry', especially the aspirations of Dissenters from the nation's industrial world whom the Test and Corporation Acts proscribed from public office. For the poor, Paine's exposure of exploitation, of what, in *The Rights of Man*, he saw as the weak 'governed like animals, for the pleasure of their riders', was an irresistible call to freedom, and one supported by demands for state-subsidized education and social security. Paine's sixpenny pamphlet was a best-seller, and for writing it he was tried in his absence for seditious libel and outlawed from his homeland.

Paine's later works show little diminution of these radical energies, despite the counter-revolutionary feelings that were becoming ever stronger in the country and which were to delay necessary changes in the constitution until the Great Reform Bill of 1832. *Agrarian Justice* (1795), for example, is a bitter denunciation of inequality, but it was *The Age of Reason* (1792–5) that was comprehensively to establish Paine's notoriety. Here, developing the Enlightenment's attack on the socially repressive and theologically obscurantist aspects of the priesthood, Paine joined the call to recognize the benevolence of the Supreme Being and the moral teachings of Christ in a world rationally understood. For popularizing these issues and the familiar biblical difficulties with chronology, Paine came to be regarded in England and America alike as the spokesman of Antichrist.

Similar ideas had been propounded however by both Voltaire and the other French philosopher who was so crucial an influence on the English literature of this period: Jean-Jacques Rousseau (1712–78). 'Man', as Rousseau declared in *The Social Contract* (1762), 'is born free, but is everywhere in chains.' Natural man – Rousseau's influential ideal of the 'noble savage' – is compassionate and instinctive. The repressive forces of society with their concern for property and domination however have corrupted him. Education, as Rousseau observed in the *Nouvelle Héloïse* (1761) and *Emile* (1762), has also warped the pace of his natural growth. Only a society based on the 'general will' – the collective opinion of the sovereign people – can begin to bring about a better state of affairs. Such ideas on nature influenced a number of English novelists of sentiment. Rousseau's political opinions were also of profound consequence to the philosopher who was to shape the minds of two generations of English radicals, William Godwin (1756–1836).

For such poets as the younger Wordsworth, Coleridge and Shelley, Godwin was 'a sun in the firmament of reputation'. His social philosophy, developed in his *Enquiry Concerning Political Justice* (1793), was read enthusiastically for its attack on the 'brute engine' of government and its dismissal of a politics of rights in favour of the idea that 'to a rational being there can be but one rule of conduct, justice, and one mode of ascertaining that rule, the exercise of his understanding'. Eschewing bloody revolution, Godwin the rationalist set the individual, independent in his own understanding and motivated by right reason, truth and justice, against the coercion of the state. Such a man ideally pledged his wisdom 'to make others free, virtuous and wise'.

Godwin wrote passionately against the injustices of the economic system and the oppression of the poor by taxation and the new industrial world, contrasting these realities to a Utopian ideal of the small rural community. In the most successful of his novels, *Caleb Williams* (1794), a number of these issues are further discussed as Godwin, repelled by the mounting conservatism about him, determined 'to expose the evils which arise out of the present system of artificial society', especially as these were revealed in the workings of its legal system. In addition, *Caleb Williams* is a psychologically compelling novel of revenge, pursuit and the pursuer pursued. These qualities make the work superior to *Hermsprong, or Man as He Is Not* (1796) by the radical Robert Bage (1728–1801)

If law and government appeared to some contemporaries as one system of injustice, conventional gender roles were another, and in her *Vindication of the Rights of Woman* (1792) Mary Wollstonecraft (1759-97), the companion of Godwin's middle years and the mother of his daughter, set out the earliest exposition of feminism based on a comprehensive system of ethics. The aristocracy, described in Wollstonecraft's *Vindication of the Rights of Men* (1790) as 'profligates of rank, emasculated by hereditary effeminacy', were to be replaced by a society in which inalienable civil liberties would bring out the natural goodness of all.

In particular, married women (who, it was generally held, had no separate civil existence during the term of their marriage) were to be educated as useful members of society. They were to be independent, able to earn their living, advance the progress of society and assume their role as virtuous mothers to a new generation of libertarians. The anger at restrictions expressed by many literary women for nearly a century are here gathered to a climax and then focused by Wollstonecraft's powerful insight into the fact that the personal is also the political. 'Strengthen the female mind by enlarging it, and there will be an end to blind obedience; but as blind obedience is ever sought for by power, tyrants and sensualists are in the right when they endeavour to keep woman in the dark, because the former only want slaves, and the latter a plaything.' Here was an argument as profound – and as shocking – as anything in Paine.

2

In the work of William Blake (1757-1827), such revolutionary ideals were joined with profound spiritual vision. To achieve this meant a fundamental criticism of the nature of poetry itself, and a lyric in Blake's early *Poetical Sketches* (1783) complains of the uninspired quality of much contemporary verse, lamenting 'the sounds are forc'd, the notes are few'. In Blake's *Songs of Innocence* (1789), the radical broke completely with the traditions of the eighteenth century. The classical satirist, steeped in the past, is replaced by the infant thrilling with the forces of the eternal and divine. The rapture of a free imagination becomes the touchstone of a blighted world.

In the 'Introduction' to Blake's book, it is the child himself who calls the adult piper's tune, summoning the forces of untrammelled joy and so inspiring art:

> Piping down the valleys wild
> Piping songs of pleasant glee
> On a cloud I saw a child.

And he laughing said to me:

'Pipe a song about a Lamb';
So I piped with merry chear,
'Piper pipe that song again' –
So I piped, he wept to hear.

In poems such as 'Infant Joy' and 'The Echoing Green', this exuberance is further explored, while in verses like 'The Lamb' Blake's vision is broadened to suggest an entire world of innocence where animals and children, settled in a peaceable kingdom, live in natural harmony under God.

The Christian idea of sacrifice inherent in the Lamb nonetheless points to the more troubling use of innocence in these works – innocence as naïvety in a corrupt adult world. Poems such as 'The Little Black Boy', with its simple, loving resolution of racial tension, suggest what we know to be the crueller complexities of a more problematic existence. 'Holy Thursday' with its vision of charity children lit 'with a radiance all their own' reminds us terribly of a world of loss and institutional cruelty. The wretched child described in 'The Chimney Sweeper', orphaned, exploited, yet touched by visionary rapture, evokes unbearable poignancy when he finally puts his trust in the order of the universe as he knows it. The voices of these children who can imagine heaven in their abused simplicity expose the knowledge of corruption we too complacently harbour in our adult selves.

Such innocence remained for Blake a visionary means of spiritual integrity. And it was a power that could transform the world. Not for him the lifeless, mathematical print of ideas on the blank sheet of the mind favoured by eighteenth-century philosophers. The man who lived in the blaze of revelation felt bound to declare: 'I know that This World Is a World of IMAGINATION & Vision.' The universe is no longer an accumulation of statistics but a symbol of a spiritual state. Glimpsed through the eyes of the imagination, the world reveals not boundaries but the limitless. Blake declared this ideal in his *Auguries of Innocence* (c. 1803) when he besought his readers

To see a world in a grain of sand
And a heaven in a wild flower,

> Hold infinity in the palm of your hand
> And eternity in an hour.

The poet becomes a prophet of the imagination and his words remake the world as a symbol of our deepest intuitions.

What obscured this benign vision was man's fall from spiritual wholeness into blinkered materialism, what Blake called seeing with a single eye. Man, born for rapture, murders his soul as he squints down a microscope. Blake knew very well the men who were the false prophets of such a view:

> I turn my eyes to the Schools and Universities of Eürope
> And there behold the Loom of Locke, whose Woof rages dire,
> Wash'd by the Water-wheels of Newton: black the cloth
> In heavy wreathes folds over every Nation: cruel Works
> Of many Wheels I view, wheel without wheel, with cogs
>   tyrannic
> Moving by compulsion each other.

The logical mind weaves shrouds for the soul. From such a denial of spiritual integrity, from the will to order, dominate and exploit, emerged all that Blake stood against: an institutionalized and repressive government, heedless of poverty, harnessing the Industrial Revolution for the benefit of the few and served by a hypocritical church which preached a life-denying morality of restraint.

In the *Songs of Experience* (1794), this benighted England becomes the world of the dark wood, of the weeping prophet and of God conceived as ancient, repressive, vindictive. The earth pines in her bondage. The orphans of 'Holy Thursday' are now 'fed with cold and usurous hand'. The little chimney-sweep sings notes of woe while his parents go to church and praise 'God & his Priest & King' – the very instruments of their repression. In 'London', the city becomes the seat of despair, of man alienated from his true self and forcing on his kind 'the mind-forg'd manacles' of soulless dominion. In this chain-gang of the spirit, exploited children weep while the powers that hire the soldier murder his soul while forcing him to protect their palaces.

Most insidious of all is the corruption of the sexual life. The nurse in the *Songs of Innocence* now detects innuendo as she hears the children whispering in the dale. Jealousy and a pining, enforced virginity are seen as the work of priests as they turn 'The Garden of Love' into a cemetery. Prostitutes spread a syphilis of the spirit as well as of the body. Passion is irreparably blighted:

> O Rose thou art sick.
> The invisible worm,
> That flies in the night
> In the howling storm:
>
> Has found out thy bed
> Of crimson joy:
> And his dark secret love
> Does thy life destroy.

And it is in the jungle of experience that we glimpse one of Blake's most potent symbols – 'The Tyger', a force beyond reason and a portion of eternity 'too great for the eye of man'. The flaming tiger however is the counterpart of the gentle lamb. Both are of the spirit and both witness to the incomprehensible immensity of the spiritual life.

Nonetheless, there are those who retreat from the fullness and embattled complexity of existence. One of Blake's first long poetic works, *The Book of Thel* (1789), portrays this problem in a symbolic narrative, the form in which Blake was now to explore some of his most advanced ideas. These ideas were developed partly from Protestant, Bible-reading groups of radical artisans, and partly from the revolutionary circle gathered around Godwin's publisher Joseph Johnson and which included Paine, Joseph Priestley and the artist Fuseli. Complex though these beautifully illustrated works are, they contain one of the most comprehensive indictments of the political and commercial exploitation that was forming around Blake. As such, they are among the first poems of the modern world.

The virgin Thel cannot accept the fact of her own death, an acceptance which perhaps marks the first step to adult spiritual understanding. When Thel learns of the love of God that is lavished on even the humblest clay she can at last believe she will be absorbed into the earth after death and so continue in oneness with all things under God. What she cannot accept is the clay's revelation that, in the full world of experience, death and life are inextricably mixed. The pining virgin of the vales of Har is terrified of conflict. Eventually, she flees back to her home where she ends the poem as she began it, in a purposeless half-existence unable fully to rise to either innocence or experience, those contrary states of the soul which are life itself.

Those who accept life however know that 'without contraries there is no progression. Attraction and repulsion, reason and energy, love and hate, are necessary to human existence.' Such is Blake's discovery in one of his most remarkable works, *The Marriage of Heaven and Hell* (1790–93). The poem opens in anger at repression, and the fact that this section is the first sustained example of free verse in English suggests how the tyranny of rhyme and metre is only one of the many constraints now to be thrown off. In *The Marriage of Heaven and Hell*, the tiger of the *Songs of Experience* leaps out to glorify the uninhibited human being whose body is united with the soul as both flood with the energy which alone is eternal delight.

In this blaze of inspiration, the poet is at one with the prophets Isaiah and Ezekiel with whom he dines at the feast of the imagination and from whom he learns to trust his inmost powers. The hell of the priests becomes the heaven of the spiritually abundant, and its 'proverbs' form the most radical declaration of independence issued during the eighteenth century. As Blake's vision unfolds, anger and euphoria go hand in hand. The sons of joy wake to chant their 'Song of Liberty' and, with the recognition that 'every thing that lives is Holy', the tyranny of empire trembles.

Or does it? In 1791, the House of Commons rejected a bill to abolish the slave trade, and in the same year Blake probably began one of the finest of his prophetic books, his *Visions of the Daughters of Albion*. This work is a profound and subtle study of those imperialist male attitudes which subdue sexual, spiritual and political freedom to a brutal servitude in which even the oppressor himself is enchained.

In the rapturous acceptance of her sexuality, American Oothoon speeds over the waters (often, for Blake, a symbol of materialism) to her lover Theotormon. In her exultant course however she is seized by Bromion ('the roaring one') and raped. The lascivious murmurings of Bromion's foreplay are those of the imperialist as he rapes

Oothoon's 'soft American plains', stamps her 'swarthy children of the sun' with the brand of slavery and suppresses women under terror and violence. Though Oothoon herself eventually rises to a triumphant praise of unpossessive eroticism, the link between sexual and political perversion made in the poem is both explicit and shrewd.

Blake's concern with the central political event of this period was first expressed in *The French Revolution* (1791), a work based on the imagined re-creation of history. Fully to develop his analysis of the corruption and redemption of contemporary society however Blake had to explore other means. In *The Book of Urizen* (1794), he offered his key to that system of symbolic characters which makes him one of the greatest mythographers of the human condition between Hesiod and Freud.

Urizen ('Your Reason') will later be portrayed as the most important of Blake's four principles of life or 'Zoas' which, in the divine state of perfection, live in unity. Urizen's book is Blake's Genesis. It portrays its central figure asserting his desolate and abstract powers, separating from the forces of passion, sensation and instinct, and so falling from spiritual unity into bleak materialism. Los the 'eternal prophet' rages in the madness of this separation of the intuitive from the rational. With titanic effort, he creates a body for Urizen to save him from total annihilation, but the effort reduces Los himself to exhaustion and further self-division. Enitharmon, his female half, separates from him, and their subsequent attempts to reunite through sex are shown as repellent to the denizens of eternity. The eventual fruit of this union however is Orc whom Los and Enitharmon bind to a rock out of jealousy and fear. Blake thereby suggests the dark, vindictive world of repression and guilt inflicted on man from his childhood.

Urizen meanwhile refines the horrors of scientific materialism:

> He formed scales to weigh;
> He formed massy weights;
> He formed a brazen quadrant;
> He formed golden compasses
> And began to explore the Abyss
> And he planted a garden of fruits.

Urizen's wanderings in the abyss of the material world increase the pain of its inhabitants as a deadly 'Net of Religion' is secreted from his body. Aeons of suffering create the world with which we are all familiar. Nonetheless, at the close of Blake's poem, a small band of people is seen escaping from this Egyptian bondage. With them lies the future.

Blake's mythological interpretation of subsequent human existence is most readily discussed in its historical sequence rather than the chronological order of the books in which it was expressed. 'Africa' from *The Song of Los* (1795), for example, briefly portrays the spiritual corruption of man from Adam to the rationalist Voltaire. We have now reached the ultimate period of materialistic tyranny, and this is embodied in England by the chief of Urizen's evil followers, the guardian prince of Albion. He is a figure who emerges in his true power in one of the finest of Blake's prophetic books, *America* (1793).

In this poem, Blake's ability to mythologize his political enthusiasms in a manner that relates them to man's other deepest impulses is seen at its most dramatic. Orc, the son of Los and Enitharmon, has now reached puberty. The energy that is eternal delight, and which for Blake springs always from the body, causes Orc to free himself from parental bondage and have intercourse with fallen nature. Adolescent rebellion and desire are raised to cosmic forces as Orc, 'a Human fire fierce glowing', rises over the sea of materialism that stretches between England and her enslaved American colonies.

George Washington and his companions thrill with the new ideals of life, liberty and the pursuit of happiness while the vengeful Angel of Albion, rebuked by Orc, summons his armed forces. These refuse to rise and support him. Rebellion rages through America as Albion's Angel, flaming in lurid vengeance, attacks the States with plague. But Albion reaps the whirlwind he has sown. America is freed, while in England 'the millions sent up a howl of anguish and threw off their hammerd mail'. The energies of Orc thrill through their bodies, and only the repressive power of Urizen, deluging the country with counter-revolutionary propaganda, freezes forces that cannot be permanently crushed.

Europe, written in 1794, the year of the Treason Trials and just before the 'Gagging Acts' savagely restrained what could be said at public meetings, portrays how this repression was once thrown off by the French Revolution. We are shown how, after the binding of Orc, the female principle of Enitharmon is unnaturally dominant, inflicting on the world that sleep of the spirit in which the nightmare cruelties of established religion enforce the veneration of virginity and an obsession with death. Blinded to the infinite, self-repressing humankind creates a druidical faith with 'God a tyrant crown'd'.

This is Blake's image of the repressive world of Pitt and Burke who are shown defending the old Newtonian rationalism against the rising forces of Orc. Both men, however, are spiritually dead. As the end of night approaches, the sex traps of Enitharmon prove powerless. Orc flames out, and 'in the vineyards of red France appear'd the light of his fury'. Los the prophet exults in majesty, and in 'Asia' from *The Song of Los* we see how all the brass-bound laws of Urizen cannot save the tyrant from the apocalypse and the energies which ensure that empire will eventually be overthrown.

Such works reveal Blake as the prophet of universal political and spiritual freedom and show the poet himself as the spokesman of revolt. As the forces of counter-revolution became ever more dominant in the late 1790s however, Blake was obliged more closely to examine the role of the poet as prophet. In *Milton* (completed 1804), he elaborated one of the most radical conceptions of his task ever voiced by an English writer. The poet is now nothing less than the vehicle of divine inspiration, and his works bring the world ever nearer to the intimation of cosmic unity embodied in Christ, the saviour whose Second Coming will redeem benighted Albion body and soul.

Milton is an exceptional account of the mystic's heroic duty to wrestle for the salvation of his country and for all mankind. At its greatest, the work pulses with the radical innocence and challenge so memorably expressed in its most famous lines:

> And did those feet in ancient time
> Walk upon England's mountains green?
> And was the holy Lamb of God,
> On England's pleasant pastures seen?

> And did the Countenance Divine,
> Shine forth upon our clouded hills?
> And was Jerusalem builded here,
> Among these dark Satanic Mills?

> Bring me my Bow of burning gold:
> Bring me my Arrows of desire:
> Bring me my Spear: O clouds unfold!
> Bring me my Chariot of fire!
>
> I will not cease from Mental Fight,
> Nor shall my Sword sleep in my hand:
> Till we have built Jerusalem,
> In England's green & pleasant Land.

It is now the duty of the armed prophet to sweep away political repression, industrial exploitation and sexual fear so that the world may ascend from spiritual division into the fullness and blessedness of the risen Christ.

Blake had given his first epic interpretation of man's lapse into division and of the eventual coming of the heavenly city in *Vala, or The Four Zoas* (completed 1803), a work which for all its occasional power is often marred by the poet's failure to give full imaginative reality to his mythological figures. This limitation – the result, perhaps, of the isolated prophet being his own chief audience after the decline of the radical 1790s – is not wholly avoided in the last of Blake's major works. *Jerusalem* (completed 1820) remains nonetheless an exceptional *tour de force*.

This immense vision operates on several levels, somewhat in the manner of Dante's *Divine Comedy*, a work which was profoundly to involve the ageing Blake. Alienated Albion, for example, has fallen from Christ-like unity and now toils in materialism and strife. He is at once the embodiment of all nations and of England herself sundered from the biblical lands of spiritual truth. Albion is also each individual Englishman plunged ever deeper into the life-denying forces of conventional righteousness. Albion's eventual redemption is thus the salvation of both the one and the many.

In addition, Los the eternal prophet, labouring to build his City of Art, is in part every true poet and in part Blake himself striving to reunite his vision of a shining London with eternity. This is a herculean confrontation, and in its epic scope *Jerusalem* is Blake's triumphant assertion of man over materialism and of Christianity uniquely interpreted as the freedom of the body and mind to exercise the divine arts of the imagination. Above all, *Jerusalem* is the testament of a prophet whose visionary courage retains its power to challenge and inspire man's deepest resources against those torments with which he threatens to blind himself:

> I rest not from my great task!
> To open the Eternal Worlds, to open the immortal Eyes
> Of Man inwards into the Worlds of Thought: into Eternity
> Ever expanding in the Bosom of God, the Human Imagination.

In this profound purpose, Blake remains one of the first and greatest poets of the maladies of the modern world.

3

It is William Wordsworth (1770–1850) who nonetheless remains the focal poetic voice of the period. In the greatest of his poetry – that written between about 1793 and 1807 – Wordsworth's was a voice of searchingly comprehensive humanity, and one fully and often painfully engaged in the visionary's struggle with the forces of radicalism and reaction. It was also a voice that transformed the received modes of utterance. At the core of Wordsworth's poetry there thus lies a mastering concern with the nature of man, and to explore this fully meant testing poetic conventions to their limit.

Wordsworth's earliest published work shows him bringing new vigour to eighteenth-century notions of the picturesque and the sublime. The couplets of *An Evening Walk* (1793) reveal a powerful, direct observation of Wordsworth's native Lake District and conclude with a technically sophisticated description of man and nature viewed in kindly twilight. The portrait of a beggar woman however, while essentially an essay in sentiment, points forward to Wordsworth's social concerns.

These were sharpened by visits to the mainland of Europe. A walking tour of the Swiss Alps made in the Cambridge long vacation of 1790 heightened Wordsworth's exhilarated response to the grandeur of nature, but when he came to express this in his *Descriptive Sketches* (1793) other concerns had deepened his response. He now cast himself as the melancholy lover and ardent republican wandering amid a natural grandeur which at times threatens to overwhelm. The literary and the biographical here merge, for the lover is the young Wordsworth who was now the father of an illegitimate child, while the republican is the youth who had entered Paris on the anniversary of the fall of the Bastille, breathed the air of freedom and given his commitment to revolution as the only answer to the suffering of the poor. *Descriptive Sketches* is thus the work of a young radical, 'a patriot of the world'.

The course of events was to force this exploration to a crisis. In France, Robespierre was proving with conclusive horror that violent revolution begets more bloodshed, while in 1793 England herself declared war on the infant republic and so made Wordsworth's return to France an impossibility. In 'the ravage of this most unnatural strife', cruelly separated from personal responsibilities and obliged to watch his own country repressing the erstwhile forces of freedom, Wordsworth gave vent to his feelings in his unpublished 'Letter to the Bishop of Llandaff'. This is a coruscating attack on the smugness of institutional injustice.

It was also the product of a despair that was to develop to hallucinatory anguish. Alone on Salisbury Plain, a houseless vagrant stripped to the essential man, Wordsworth began to experience flame-enfolded visions of human sacrifice, a feeling for the poor as the most authentic embodiments of experience and an intuition of the timeless, calamitous nature of human suffering. In *Incidents upon Salisbury Plain*, the destitute and the outcast speak for mankind, and the only palliative seems to be 'human Reason's naked self' – Godwin's philosophy of progress, idealism and education.

But if the Terror had shown the moral failure of revolution, the citizens of the French Republic, marching into other lands and becoming 'oppressors in their turn', were revealing that a supposed love of liberty could be a mask for cynical ambition. Such deceit is explored in the character of Oswald, the villain of Wordsworth's five-act drama *The Borderers* (1796–7, published 1842). Oswald is 'a young man of great intellectual powers, yet without any solid principles of genuine benevolence'. Reason is here revealed as the tool of base emotion, while

> Suffering is permanent, obscure and dark,
> And shows the nature of infinity.

Fully to come to terms with this intuition meant a profound reorientation of Wordsworth's thought, and his next important poems are an attempt to move beyond impassioned intellectual protest towards a presentation of the poor that awakens the reader's sense of kinship with the common lot of man.

The old man in 'The Old Cumberland Beggar', living 'in the eye of Nature', is seen as precious for his unique self and the benevolence he evokes in the small rural community. The hapless wife of 'The Ruined Cottage', dying amid the disintegration of her entire way of life, rouses in the Pedlar who tells her story not the ardour of the social reformer but the tender, quiet compassion of those who are at one with the timeless truths of existence. In the power of this insight, the Pedlar becomes the poet of the human heart and the embodiment of Wordsworth's ideal as he defined this in the 1800 Preface to the *Lyrical Ballads*. Here the poet is

a man speaking to men: a man, it is true, endowed with more lively sensibility, more enthusiasm and tenderness, who has a greater knowledge of human nature, and a more comprehensive soul, than are supposed to be common among mankind; a man pleased with his own passions and volitions, and who rejoices more than other men in the spirit of life that is in him; delighting to contemplate similar volitions and passions as manifested in the goings-on of the Universe, and habitually compelled to create them where he does not find them.

The volume of *Lyrical Ballads*, first issued anonymously by Wordsworth and Coleridge in 1798, is probably the best-known collaborative exercise in English literature. Wordsworth and Coleridge had met in the autumn of 1795, and their almost daily contact was sustained by mutual recognition of genius and the fertilizing excitement of a common purpose. At this stage, both poets believed that verse stripped of high literary contrivance and written in the language of the lower and middle classes could best express the fundamentals of human nature. In particular, it would allow the poet to be at one with men who 'have never known false refinements, wayward and artificial desires, false criticisms, effeminate habits of thinking and feeling, or who, having known these things, have outgrown them'.

This was a call to primitivism which for the past thirty years had found its most popular expression in the ballad. What was so revolutionary about Wordsworth and Coleridge's volume was thus not its methods but the rigour with which it pursued its aims and the poets' daring to express the universal experience of ordinary people at a time of political reaction. In the England of 1798, this last came dangerously close to an assertion of the rights of man. Hence the long campaign waged against the *Lyrical Ballads* after 1803 by Francis Jeffrey (1773–1850), editor of the influential *Edinburgh Review*. This was a campaign which gave Wordsworth's apparently Jacobin sentiments a prominence out of all proportion to the true direction of his work.

Wordsworth's contributions to the *Lyrical Ballads* were based on subjects from ordinary life and were designed to raise that quickened response to daily existence which it was thought had been besmirched by 'the lethargy of custom'. Just as the old Cumberland beggar stirred the charitable impulses of those around him, so Wordsworth's poems would inspire their audience to see the world freshly, sympathetically and naturally. By so doing, it was hoped the poet would also be able to reveal 'the great and simple affections of our nature' and so awaken in his public that sense of community which is the special power of the poet speaking as a man to men.

Wordsworth's aim was thus morally serious and intellectually controlled. It is grievously to misinterpret his purpose to assume that his definition of poetry as 'the spontaneous overflow of powerful feelings' was a call to uncontrolled emotion. 'Spontaneous' in its eighteenth-century sense means to achieve something by an act of free will. As we have seen, what distinguishes the true poet from the mere versifier is the poet's greater responsiveness to experience and his capacity to think 'long and deeply'. When combined, these intellectual powers allow him to discover 'what is really important to man'. The skill of his art then permits him to re-create such discoveries and so offer them to his audience as an experience rather than merely as moral truisms.

This emphasis on the re-creation of experience gave rise to Wordsworth's statement that in his poetry 'the feeling therein developed gives importance to the action and situation and not the action and situation to the feeling'. We are to be moved not by the ruin of princes but by 'Simon Lee, the Old Huntsman' reduced to helpless age and tearfully grateful for true kindness, or by the plight of a shepherd forced to sell 'The Last of the Flock' and so keep his children from starving.

The element of near-bathos in such poems is often used to challenge the reader. The little girl in 'We Are Seven', unable to accept an adult awareness of death, probes with exquisite pathos the continuing reality of the dead in our imaginations. When Wordsworth combines such effects with the supernatural (a wholly appropriate element in ballad literature) the effect is as subtly ruthless as folk-tale. Goody Blake, cursing her oppressor, raises the poem in which she appears through the sentimental and the macabre to profound issues of natural justice. 'Peter Bell', in the most daring of Wordsworth's ballads – and one not issued until 1819 – attains the redemptive discovery 'that man's heart is a holy thing' through the most advanced use of the comic, the melodramatic and the supernatural.

These elements find their surest combination in 'The Idiot Boy' and 'The Thorn'. In the first of these works, the irrational mind sees more deeply into the nature of life than the commonsensical. The Idiot Boy's vision of the world has unique imaginative validity, while what Wordsworth calls his mother's 'strength, disinterestedness and grandeur of love' are shown as a miracle-working affection which brings health and community to the world. When this feeling of community has been lost, as in the betrayal of Martha Ray the infanticide, Wordsworth rises through gossip and the macabre to a sense of primal desolation:

> I did not speak – I saw her face;
> Her face! it was enough for me;
> I turned about and heard her cry,
> 'Oh misery! oh misery!'

The poems Wordsworth added to the 1800 edition of the *Lyrical Ballads* (several of which were written during a remarkable snow-bound winter in Germany) are among the finest of his achievements. The 'Lucy' poems in particular are verses of love and loss which hold within their delicate simplicity a meditation on time and death which

REVOLUTIONS, REACTION AND REFORM

rises to universal stature. The lover and his idealized beloved –
sequestered, unregarded souls – are subject to the universal experiences
of humanity. In 'A slumber did my spirit seal', love's hope of
deathless perfection is exposed as an illusion. Lucy, moulded by
nature and her own imagination, is seen to live in sympathy with a
world whose inevitable end is death. She passes from love's fantasy of
a universe without time into true eternity:

> A slumber did my spirit seal
>   I had no human fears:
> She seemed a thing that could not feel
>   The touch of earthly years.
>
> No motion has she now, no force;
>   She neither hears nor sees;
> Rolled round in earth's diurnal course,
>   With rocks, and stones, and trees.

Love passes but grief abides, hallowing its object until in the last
poem of the cycle Lucy becomes the virgin spirit of England and all
that binds the poet to his home. In life and death, Lucy and her lover
are thus individual portions of general truth, just as in the 'Matthew'
poems the old man is a symbol of an existence fully and benevolently
led: useful, kindly, sorrow-ridden, but abiding in the memory as an
archetype of all that man might be.

This deeply conservative valuation of hearth and home achieves its
most moving expression in two narrative poems Wordsworth wrote
after he and his sister Dorothy (1771–1855) had returned from
Germany and settled at Dove Cottage, Grasmere. Both 'The Brothers'
and 'Michael' are pastorals, and each transforms what had previously
been enjoyed as a medium for high artifice into a vehicle for tragedy.
This is verse 'written with a view to shew that men who do not wear
fine cloathes can feel deeply'. The honest poor remain Wordsworth's
embodiments of essential humanity, but the colloquialism of the
ballads has now been replaced by blank verse of an easy yet refined
conversational tone.

In 'The Brothers', a tragic accident reveals the depth of sensitivity
natural to unaffected man. It is 'Michael' however that most assuredly
suggests the grave and tender dignity of Wordsworth's meditations

on 'man, the heart of man, and human life'. To read 'Michael' is to perceive a vision of mankind toiling in the vastness of the natural world, moral in his doggedness, tender amid a sustaining family, independent and yet the victim of blind chance. It is such chance which obliges the young Luke to leave his parents, seek work in the city and there find the means of his corruption. Old Matthew's world of elemental values is rent apart. The ageing shepherd himself dies, his cottage crumbles, and his patrimony passes to a stranger. There remain only the few piled stones of the sheepfold he began to build with Luke. These stand to this day as the token of a sundered family and, more movingly, as a symbol of Michael's enduring affection for his son and 'the strength of love'.

If 'Michael' reveals the threat caused to the individual by material pressures and the corruption of the town, the work also suggests a complementary intuition of nature as a moral force. In others of Wordsworth's verses, this belief in the sustaining and redemptive power of the natural world – the visionary awareness of cosmic unity and rapture – becomes the source of the poet's authority as a prophet and moralist. To express so profound a knowledge meant revising eighteenth-century traditions of the picturesque and the sublime, and several pieces among the *Lyrical Ballads* develop Wordsworth's intense awareness of the transfiguring power of his joy in nature.

'To my Sister' invites Dorothy to 'the hour of feeling' in the natural world and a rapture more potent than that known by 'toiling reason'. A similarly Rousseauesque emphasis is seen again in 'Expostulation and Reply' and 'The Tables Turned'. Here, a direct perception of the world, a 'wise passiveness' unencumbered by learned preoccupations, is shown as the source of moral and spiritual growth. These simple but subtle expressions of faith in nature have the freedom of a young man speaking to others with impetuous enthusiasm. An altogether more profound and searching work – a sublime afterthought added to the first edition of the *Lyrical Ballads* when the work was in proof – was 'Lines Composed a Few Miles above Tintern Abbey, on Revisiting the Banks of the Wye during a Tour, July 13, 1798'.

If the title and some of the detailed opening description suggest earlier examples of picturesque writing, Wordsworth's poem remains a profoundly original imaginative achievement, a major advance beyond eighteenth-century convention. The valley of the Wye itself, the quiet centre of the returning wanderer's thoughts, is described with a detail that conveys a sense of natural order at once vivid and eternal. Beyond the pleasures of the picturesque with their emphasis on the eye and the external aspects of nature however lies a deeper moral awareness, a sense of completeness in multiplicity. This is what Wordsworth, with Virgilian pathos, calls 'the still, sad music of humanity'.

But the poem now progresses beyond such moral reflection. Wordsworth recalls how he has at times seen nature with the inner eye of the visionary. As he becomes aware of his own sublime communion with all things, so he suggests a mystic's sense of the unity of Creation. Inspiring nature is a force of rapture, a power that reveals the workings of the soul:

> For I have learned
> To look on nature, not as in the hour
> Of thoughtless youth; but hearing oftentimes
> The still, sad music of humanity,
> Nor harsh nor grating, though of ample power
> To chasten and subdue. And I have felt
> A presence that disturbs me with the joy
> Of elevated thoughts; a sense sublime
> Of something far more deeply interfused,
> Whose dwelling is the light of setting suns,
> And the round ocean and the living air,
> And the blue sky, and in the mind of man:
> A motion and a spirit, that impels
> All thinking things, all objects of all thought,
> And rolls through all things.

At the close of the poem, these enraptured perceptions are made more affecting by the tender intensity of the lines in which Wordsworth turns to share his discoveries with his sister. Quite as much as Coleridge, Dorothy in her pure and direct response to nature had weaned her brother from Godwinian rationalism.

It was during this period that Coleridge urged Wordsworth to undertake a major philosophic poem to be called *The Recluse*. Some passages of a work 'having for its principal subject the sensations and opinions of a poet living in retirement' were completed, but, daunted by the scale of the undertaking, Wordsworth felt it necessary to review his powers and the origins of those forces that had made him a poet.

During the winter in Germany, Wordsworth wrote extensively about those incidents in his childhood that had shaped his imagination, eventually working these into the first of several versions of the poem, all unpublished in his lifetime, which we now know as *The Prelude*. After the move to Grasmere, inspiration seems to have failed Wordsworth, but between 1804 and 1805 he worked on a five-book version of the poem which was then expanded to thirteen books and eventually published posthumously in 1850. Though largely unknown in the first half of the nineteenth century, the various drafts of the work are the most sustained example of Wordsworth's genius. Here, the intuitions of the divine glimpsed in 'Tintern Abbey' are given a full autobiographical explanation and shown as the basis of the moral, spiritual and poetic life. The poet himself becomes the subject of his epic. Allusions to Milton suggest the scale of Wordworth's 'heroic argument' – the growth of the poet's mind.

The Prelude charts this growth from infancy to manhood. We are shown the development of human consciousness under the sway of an imagination united to the grandeur of nature. Even the baby as 'an inmate of this active universe' receives impulses from the world of nature and, through the growing power of his imagination, feels himself at one with the spirit of all things. This quick association of ideas, impelled by the moulding and transforming imagination, creates a moral being in harmony with a purposeful and benevolent universe:

> Dust as we are, the immortal spirit grows
> Like harmony in music; there is a dark
> Inscrutable workmanship which reconciles
> Discordant elements, makes them cling together
> In one society.

The heady joys and fears of boyhood – Wordsworth's remarkable descriptions of skating, boating and bird-nesting in the Lake District – developed these sensations with what is seen as a sanctifying and stengthening power. In those 'spots of time' when he was at one with all things, the boy learned to recognize 'a grandeur in the beatings of the heart'. Such moments of cosmic rapture provided both Words-worth's deepest apprehensions of spiritual truth and his origins as a poet. 'I saw one world and felt that it was joy.'

This power survived into Wordsworth's undergraduate days when it was consciously developed, but if he was now aware of a certain 'inner falling off', his concern for the lot of the common man was growing, along with an awareness of the power of poetry. His crossing of the Alps described in Book VI still offered intuitions of spiritual truth, one of those 'spots of time' which later allowed him to preserve a sense of spiritual wholeness amid 'the strife of singularity' so painfully inflicted on man in the hell of London.

Later books of *The Prelude* describe Wordsworth's experiences in France: his republicanism, his affair with Annette Vallon (fictionalized as the tragic story of Vaudracour and Julia), his 'substantial dread' during the Terror and his continuing support of the ideals underlying the Revolution. Wordsworth also provides an account of the spiritual confusion inflicted on him during his period of Godwinian rationalism and – most movingly – the recuperative power of Dorothy's 'exquisite regard for common things' and Coleridge's philosophical ministrations.

Re-emerging as 'a sensitive and a creative soul', and finding 'once more in Man an object of delight', the mature forces of Wordsworth's imagination attain 'intellectual love' and that height of human consciousness embodied in the role of the poet. The concluding description of the ascent of Snowdon – one of Wordsworth's finest achievements – becomes a symbol of the poet's climb to the height of his inspired powers and to that state of vision in which, dedicating himself to humanity, he becomes one of the 'Prophets of Nature', men who offer

> A lasting inspiration, sanctified
> By reason, blest by faith.

The world is transformed through the power of the imagination and the poet takes on his heroic role as the seer speaking as a man to men.

During intervals in the composition of what we now call *The Prelude*, Wordsworth composed some of the shorter pieces later published in his *Poems in Two Volumes* (1807). Among the finest of these is 'Resolution and Independence'. In its daring use of subject matter and sense of the authenticity of the experience of the poorest, this work is the triumphant conclusion of ideas first developed in the *Lyrical Ballads*.

Rejoicing in a day of exceptional beauty, the poet is suddenly plunged into the depths of a despair. This is made all the bleaker by his awareness of the spiritual peril endured by poets who, like himself, live in a blaze of the spirit that so easily turns to 'despondency and madness' The sudden appearance of the leech-gatherer however – primeval, poor and fraught with a stoic acceptance of the extremes of human suffering – suggests a response to life altogether more heroic in its resolute shouldering of a demanding fate. Eventually, the leech-gatherer is seen as a symbol of man's life upon the earth. In his primal dignity, he becomes a talisman to ward off too self-indulgent a despair.

Two further poems – 'The Solitary Reaper' and 'To a Highland Girl' – again use rural figures to suggest the timeless mystery of sorrowful humanity and its radiant beauty. Several poems to birds and flowers reflect a similar intensity of response, the most famous of these being 'I wandered lonely as a cloud'. This is perhaps the most anthologized poem in English literature, and one that takes us to the core of Wordsworth's poetic beliefs. In her remarkable *Journal* (1800–1803), Dorothy had described the scene pictured by Wordsworth with magical directness. In her brother's lyric however, the vision of the daffodils is reflected by the poet's 'greater organic sensibility'. He has that power of imagination whereby he can relive such 'spots of time'. For the true poet, the re-created memory of such deeply perceived scenes becomes an assurance of spiritual grace:

> For oft, when on my couch I lie
> In vacant or in pensive mood,
> They flash upon that inward eye
> Which is the bliss of solitude;
> And then my heart with pleasure fills
> And dances with the daffodils.

Nonetheless, partly because of Coleridge's apparently declining powers, Wordsworth was troubled by the thought that such inner resources might fail him too. In March 1802, and as a challenge to despondency, he wrote 'To the Cuckoo', 'My heart leaps up' and the first section of his complex but splendid 'Ode: Intimations of Immortality from Recollections of Early Childhood'.

The opening stanzas of this work are an example of Wordsworth's sensuous response to language, and dramatize sensations of joy in the natural world. These alternate between a present and a remembered rapture. Such moods are darkened nonetheless by a pessimistic acceptance that 'the visionary gleam' of childhood has largely faded. Wordsworth explains this decline through an analogy with Plato's myth of man's exile from the realms of truth. Just as the dwellers in Plato's cave only dimly recall the archetypes of divine beauty, so 'shades of the prison house' close round man as he matures and realizes that visionary rapture fades into 'the light of common day'.

There is a special poignancy here, for the particular little boy Wordsworth took as his subject was his friend's son Hartley Coleridge (1796–1849) who was to become a sweetly sad minor poet writing sonnets on his own emotional shortcomings. The final stanzas of Wordsworth's poem however are a more heroic attempt to find value in a world of joy occluded. Wordsworth suggests that to the adult mind, memories of childhood rapture still prompt thoughts of 'the fountain-light of all our day'. Glimmerings of truth remain, while 'the years that bring the philosophic mind' temper early rapture to a mature acceptance that the human condition is sustained by spiritual truth. In the end, celebration is still possible.

The greatness of the Immortality ode lies in its densely articulated acceptance of joy, loss and evanescent insight. It has a grandeur built on a spiritual variety. Tragically, this proved insupportable:

> Me this unchartered freedom tires;
> I feel the weight of chance-desires:
> My hopes no more must change their name.
> I long for a repose that ever is the same.

These lines from the 'Ode to Duty' are an admission of spiritual exhaustion. This was a feeling deepened by the loss of Wordsworth's brother in 1805, who is mourned in the 'Elegiac Stanzas Suggested by a Picture of Peele Castle'. In stoic fortitude, the seer now gives way to the man. The overtly moral and the abstract increasingly replace the visionary in Wordsworth's writing.

This decline was accompanied by a hardening of the poet's political views. A number of sonnets in *Poems in Two Volumes*, inspired by Milton's works in the form, show Wordsworth taking on the role of patriot and critic. The rise of Napoleon and the fact that Britain stood virtually alone against his power produced some virulently anti-French and nationalistic works, as well as those finer meditations on political liberty: the sonnets 'On the Extinction of the Venetian Republic' and 'To Toussaint L'Ouverture'. The treaty of Amiens in 1802 allowed Wordsworth to visit Annette and their child in France, and to record his emotions in the tender lines of 'It is a beauteous evening calm and free'. But if love of country had inspired 'Fair Star of evening' and the admirable 'On Westminster Bridge', the continuing danger of Napoleon and Wordsworth's frank criticism of his own countrymen caused him to write a number of strikingly nationalistic pieces and to urge that liberty was built on 'ceaseless effort, vigilance, and virtue'.

During the later years of the Napoleonic Wars, Wordsworth was engaged with a long poem on these subjects that was eventually published in 1814 to celebrate the apparent end of the struggle with Bonaparte. *The Excursion* was the major work by which Wordsworth's contemporaries evaluated him. Though now little read, the poem marks an important development in the poet's career. In the figures of the Solitary, the Wanderer and the Pastor, Wordsworth was able to suggest his maturing view of what, in the prefatory 'Home at Grasmere', he called 'true Community'.

The Excursion draws on earlier traditions of the didactic poetry of retirement and suggests a Burkeian sense of received values and local traditions, that attachment to what Burke himself called 'the little platoon'. Both writers saw this, in Burke's words, as 'the first link in the series by which we proceed towards a love of our country and to mankind'. In Wordsworth's poem, these impulses are perceived by figures who derive from the fundamentals of his art. Indeed, the three central characters are essentially autobiographical.

The Solitary, for example, deeply responsive to the sublime in nature, nonetheless retains after his tragic experiences of personal grief and political disillusion that cynical intellectualism from which Wordsworth himself had been rescued by Coleridge and Dorothy. The Wanderer, a character identical to the earlier figure of the Pedlar, is Wordsworth's ideal of the rural and charismatic personality who has been reared amid nature but whose enthusiasms have been tempered by family tradition and piety. The Wanderer's meditation in the revised version of 'The Ruined Cottage' shows an unstrained human sympathy along with a faith that allows him to see tragic incidents redeemed by hope. Duty and trust in Providence, each underpinned by a response to the beauties of nature, finally permit the Wanderer to achieve a philosophic stability far more deeply rooted than the Solitary's wild vacillation.

Such traditional wisdom is reinforced in the tales told by the Pastor. These broaden out to touch on political events, and in the concluding books, the Wanderer provides a view of England at once victorious and prosperous yet overshadowed by the evils of the Industrial Revolution. Natural piety, tinged in later revisions with Christian doctrine and supported by Wordsworth's passionate plea for universal education, are seen as the basis on which a nation in the hour of trial preserved itself. England is thus shown to have found in traditional resources the power to thwart the perils of innovation. Such a conclusion was widely popular and, despite criticism, the seven editions of *The Excursion* slowly established Wordsworth's reputation as a voice of national sentiment.

The opinions expressed in the work nonetheless led to an ever narrowing conservatism. The visionary gleam had largely faded, and Wordsworth's poetry over the next thirty-five years contains an excessive quantity of the merely humdrum. Some sonnets such as 'Surprised by joy' (1815) or a few of those addressed to the River Duddon (1820) recapture the old power, as does that on King's College Chapel in the *Ecclesiastical Sonnets* of 1822. 'Laodamia' (1815) shows Wordsworth's powerful, puritanical response to the pagan world, while 'Yarrow Revisited' (1835) and the lines 'Composed upon an Evening of Extraordinary Splendour and Beauty' (1820) recapture something of the earlier power. Finally, the 'Extempore Effusion on the Death of James Hogg' (1835) is a poet's moving tribute to his departed peers.

Four years after writing this poem, Wordsworth was given an honorary doctorate by Oxford University and in 1843 he was made Poet Laureate. He was the most revered of living poets, but if a younger generation realized his true powers had long been spent, the publication of *The Prelude* in 1850 revealed (despite many considering it inferior to *The Excursion*) the full scope of his achievement and Wordsworth's lifelong attempt to relate the individual to the visionary powers of nature and the responsibilities of society.

4

'I am not *fit* for *public* life; yet the light shall stream to a far distance from the taper in my cottage window.' So wrote Samuel Taylor Coleridge (1772–1834) early in his career. The sentence is suggestive both of Coleridge's role as a writer and of his methods. To borrow a phrase from his commentary on Shakespeare's *Venus and Adonis*: 'how many images and feelings are here brought together without effort and without discord'.

There is, first of all, a subtle appeal to truth through the imagination. The image of the candle burning in the night-time cottage is a symbol of the writer's task, a symbol which draws on the rural and the mystical (the sense of divine illumination shining amid the circumambient darkness) to suggest the man of poetic insight set apart yet dedicating his mind to the service of others. He has taken on the precarious role of the professional intellectual, the man of letters, and Coleridge's luminous if fitful mind did indeed provide the light in which many of his contemporaries were to see themselves more clearly. Virtually no major writer of the early nineteenth century was unaffected by him. For the early Wordsworth, Coleridge was the greatest of living men. Byron and Shelley both felt the force of his mind. His conversation stirred Keats's creativity, while the great prose writers Hazlitt and De Quincey might discuss him, criticize him or, like Charles Lamb, dedicate their finest essays to him.

To appeal to such people required a richly developed concept of the writer's place in society and of the nature and function of the audience he was addressing. In the great prose works of his later career, Coleridge was to refine these notions with magisterial comprehensiveness and to do so on the basis of insights central to his own experience – insights that were explored in his poetry, enriched through his contacts with philosophical developments in Germany, and then made public through his journalism, his lectures on literary topics and his political publications.

At the core of all these activities lay a concern with human perception which, in the words of Coleridge's admirer John Stuart Mill (1806–73), 'expresses the revolt of the human mind against the philosophy of the eighteenth century'. In place of the strictly rational, the radical and the secular comes a concern with the divine power of the imagination which 'dissolves, diffuses, dissipates, in order to recreate'. The imagination is a God-like and life-bringing force in which nature and the mind of man work on each other with joyous interchange, refashioning the world and inspiring the rapturous awareness that we are in infinitely subtle ways an organic part of the '*one Life*' of the universe.

It is pre-eminently the role of the poet to show that man's true state is not to pine in devastating homesickness (a spiritual death of which the author of *The Rime of the Ancient Mariner* was the heroic analyst) but rather to thrive amid abundance, wholeness and the living harmony of the spirit. As Coleridge wrote in the great fourteenth chapter of the *Biographia Literaria* (1817):

The poet, described in ideal perfection, brings the whole soul of man into activity, with the subordination of its faculties to each other, according to their relative worth and dignity. He diffuses a spirit and tone of unity that blends and (as it were) fuses, each into each, by that synthetic and magical power to which we have exclusively appropriated the name of imagination. This power . . . reveals itself in the balance and reconciliation of opposite or discordant qualities: of sameness, with difference; of the general, with the concrete; the idea, with the image; the individual, with the representative; the sense of novelty and freshness, with old and familiar objects; a more than usual state of emotion, with more than usual order; judgement ever awake and steady in self-possession, with enthusiasm and feeling profound or vehement.

This is the light of the burning candle. It is an assertion of the primacy of man's soul and imagination which, however threatened by the surrounding darkness, illuminates Coleridge's entire career.

It was a career in which moments of the highest achievement nonetheless alternated with incidents of sheer farce and periods of despairing dependence on alcohol and drugs. Coleridge lived constantly with his 'idea-pot' bubbling, his mind fed with omnivorous reading, vision-wearied and harried by a crying need for community.

The brilliant charity boy at Christ's Hospital became the radical undergraduate reading Paine, Godwin, Voltaire and David Hartley, whose *Observations on Man, his Frame, his Duty and his Expectations* (1749) was early to convince Coleridge that the mind was a material entity working through a deterministic 'association of ideas'. Then, abandoning intellectual effort, Coleridge suddenly enlisted in the Dragoons as Silas Tomkyn Comberbache only to be bailed out two months later on a plea of 'insanity'. Meeting in Oxford with the poet Robert Southey (1774–1843), a figure whose own career is a distressing parody of greater men's drift from radicalism to reaction, Coleridge gave himself with catastrophic enthusiasm to the scheme he named 'Pantisocracy'. This aimed to found a commune in America that would comprise 'all that is good in Godwin'. Southey, wooed from such madcap idealism by the chance of an inheritance, nonetheless urged Coleridge to marry his fellow pantisocrat Sara Fricker. This was a relationship that was later to cause the greatest pain.

In his *Conciones ad Populum, or Addresses to the People* (1795), Coleridge criticized the war against France while attacking the extremism of the Revolution. He also decried atheism, urging instead an early form of Christian Socialism and education for the poor. Above all, he was now writing and revising his early poetry. In the finest of these pieces, 'The Eolian Harp' (1796), he wrote a subtly beautiful portrayal of young married love. Drawing on the reflective, conversational style of eighteenth-century writers – in particular the now largely forgotten 'picturesque' sonnets of William Bowles (1762–1850) and the 'divine Chit chat' of Cowper – Coleridge created a philosophic poem at once advanced and tender.

The work develops from the 'Innocence and Love' of the young married couple in their rural cottage through to the vision of a fantasy paradise roused by the music of the wind blowing on the lute. As the work progresses however, so the outer landscape becomes an increasingly complex reflection of inner intuitions. It takes on the qualities of what Coleridge later called 'a symbolic language for something within me that already and forever exists', an awareness (greatly enhanced in the revisions made to the poem in 1828) of cosmic harmony and the '*one Life*'. Man and wife, man and nature, are felt to be in sympathy, even as the music of the lute prompts the notion that the breath of God moves over them all to inspire the universal harmony that is in part made and in part glimpsed by the poet's imagination. His awakened mind re-creates the world in unity just as God Himself originally created and continues to sustain it. In the well-known words of the *Biographia Literaria*: 'The primary imagination I hold to be the living power and prime agent of all human perception, and as a repetition in the finite mind of the eternal act of creation in the infinite I AM.'

This awareness of divine unity is expressed in poetry through the power of what Coleridge called the artist's 'secondary imagination' and is experienced again in the central paragraph of 'Reflections on Having Left a Place of Retirement' (1796). In both poems however the visionary moment is seen as essentially a self-indulgence – albeit a refreshing and sanctifying one – compared to a fully Christian recognition of original sin, the need for faith and redemption and man's involvement in the struggle of 'science, freedom, and the truth in Christ'. There is thus a tension here between the philosophical exploration of the joys of what Coleridge calls 'the unregenerate mind' and the pull of traditional religion.

This was a deepening crisis Coleridge was eventually to feel with the force of a natural disaster. As he wrote in the *Biographia Literaria*: 'the fontal truths of natural religion and the books of Revelation alike contributed to the flood; and it was long ere my ark touched on Ararat, and rested'. Coleridge's study of German literature, in particular the philosophy of Immanuel Kant (1724–1804) and his followers, was eventually to suggest a solution to these problems. In the meantime, the need for 'Bread & Cheese' obliged Coleridge to launch *The Watchman*, a weekly newspaper expounding advanced religious and political views. In September 1795, he also met Wordsworth.

Coleridge described Wordsworth as 'a very great man – the only man, to whom *at all times* & in *all modes of excellence* I feel myself inferior'. His reading of Wordsworth's early poems had convinced Coleridge of the elder man's power to transform perception through poetry, and during the second half of 1797 and into early the following year their conversations at Nether Stowey 'turned frequently on the two cardinal points of poetry, the power of exciting the sympathy of the reader by a faithful adherence to the truth of nature, and the power of giving the interest of novelty by the modifying colours of the imagination'. For Coleridge, this was to be an intensely fruitful period in which he wrote some of his finest conversational verses and three matchless poems: *The Rime of the Ancient Mariner*, 'Kubla Khan' and *Christabel*.

The greatest of the conversational poems – 'This Lime-Tree Bower my Prison' and 'Frost at Midnight' – are at once grand and intimate discussions of man's place in the natural world. Each is also a triumph of the imagination in action. In the first, unable to accompany the Wordsworths and Charles and Mary Lamb on their walk, Coleridge pictures their progress with a power of evocation derived from the most exact natural description (a faculty partially kindled perhaps by Dorothy Wordsworth) and then imagines from his own retirement the deep joy worked by the scene on Lamb, temporarily released from the horrors of London. Nature provides a benediction which joins with the poet's love and rises to an intuition of the 'Almighty Spirit'.

In 'Frost at Midnight', this tenderness, grandeur and exquisite observation are focused on Coleridge's infant son Hartley, named after the philosopher whose theory of the association of ideas subtly structures the poem. Coleridge's mind here moves backwards and forwards in time and space from the interior of the cottage to nature and from his own city boyhood to that imagined for Hartley amid a world of sublime physical and spiritual freedom in which God will mould his spirit to virtue:

> Therefore all seasons shall be sweet to thee,
> Whether the summer clothe the general earth
> With greenness, or the redbreast sit and sing
> Betwixt the tufts of snow on the bare branch
> Or mossy apple-tree, while the nigh thatch
> Smokes in the sun-thaw; whether the eve-drops fall
> Heard only in the trances of the blast,
> Or if the secret ministry of frost
> Shall hang them up in silent icicles,
> Quietly shining to the quiet Moon.

This exquisite paragraph, deftly linking back to the opening lines, is at once a climax and a return in a poem of circling thoughts. In particular, it suggests an identification with nature imagined through a love for others and the poet's special power to direct the mind to 'the loveliness and the works of the world around us'.

This world was nonetheless under threat. Coleridge's 'Fears in Solitude: Written in April 1798, during the Alarm of Invasion' was composed at a time when Napoleon was poised to cross the Channel and in a year that marked the high point of the conservative backlash in England. Coleridge himself was to show his intellectual disillusion with the French Revolution in 'France: An Ode' (1798), but in the former poem he achieved an altogether richer combination of the public and the private as he moved from delighted sympathy with nature to an awareness of political peril.

In seeing the threat of invasion as a divine punishment, Coleridge also offers a powerful indictment of contemporary England – its imperialism, political corruption and immoral pursuit of wealth, its betrayal of Christian values and its repellent warmongering. He urges those still pure and manly, those whose integrity has been preserved by the Burkeian values of hearth and home, to repel an enemy yet more corrupt than the worst in their homeland. He upbraids both the radical and the complacent and then evokes England through a swelling patriotism in which the beauty of the land is seen as the true nurse of virtue. The poem concludes with a moving return to the vistas of its opening and to the quiet, secret values of Nether Stowey with its church, cottages and family, its private peace and public virtue. We come finally to see that it is Burke's little platoon, safe in its visionary landscape, that stands firm against French rationalism, atheism and innovation.

In addition to working on his verse drama *Osorio* (revised and successfully produced in 1813 as *Remorse*), book reviewing, and writing leading articles for the *Morning Post*, Coleridge had also embarked on *The Rime of the Ancient Mariner*, one of the most remarkable poems in English literature and a work that was subsequently published in the *Lyrical Ballads*.

Coleridge and Wordsworth had agreed that work on the *Lyrical Ballads* should be so divided that Coleridge's efforts would be 'directed to persons and characters supernatural, or at least romantic; yet so as to transfer from our inward nature a human interest and a semblance of truth sufficient to procure for these shadows of imagination that willing suspension of disbelief for the moment, which constitutes poetic faith'. *The Rime of the Ancient Mariner* is Coleridge's supreme expression of these ideas, a poem of fearful spiritual insight wedded to an archetypal plot:

Argument: How a Ship, having first sailed to the Equator, was driven by Storms to the cold Country towards the South Pole; how the Ancient Mariner cruelly and in contempt of the laws of hospitality killed a Sea-bird and how he was followed by many and strange Judgements: and in what manner he came back to his own Country.

This elemental simplicity, curiously satisfying even in précis, is matched by the Mariner's own 'strange power of speech', the language in which he recites the torments of his season in hell. This language is far more than a rejection of earlier poetic tradition, a young man's eager iconoclasm. Language is no longer seen as the clothing of thought and as subject to the rules of rhetoric. It is shaped instead by the poet's passion, the unity of 'heart and intellect' in the imagination which in turn fuses him with his subject, 'elevating, as it were, Words into Things, & living Things too'. Such language is not a report on experience but the experience itself. And that experience is of spiritual death, of the soul stifled and of nature glimpsed as an image of utter despair. The rapt contemplation of the conversational poems – Coleridge's awareness of the '*one Life*' – has been metamorphosed into its terrible opposite:

> Alone, alone, all, all alone,
> Alone on a wide wide sea!
> And never a saint took pity on
> My soul in agony.

In its anguished polarities of isolation and community, of warm social existence invaded by the experience of living death – above all, perhaps, in its intuition of spiritual menace abiding despite redemption – *The Rime of the Ancient Mariner* brings 'the whole soul of man into activity'. It does so by appealing through the imagination to the 'reason', for Coleridge, developing Kantian ideas, a faculty altogether more comprehensive than mechanical 'understanding' since it subsumes the exercise of logic into a unity with intuition and our subjective selves. In a very real sense, we grasp the poem at a level which makes explanation invariably seem partial and inadequate. *The Rime of the Ancient Mariner* is not, to use terms central to Coleridge's own criticism, an allegorical narrative but a symbolic one. Its meaning does not lie in prose explanation but in its power to seize the imagination. As a result, its structure – the sequence of events and experiences – is not 'mechanical' but 'organic', growing in meaning as these incidents become 'the living *educts* of the Imagination'. What the imagination sees however is an existential crisis, the nightmare life-in-death that was to haunt Coleridge himself until his harassed days became an appalling repetition of his earlier insights.

Christabel uses a freer version of the ballad form to create an atmosphere of Gothic horror at once delicate and sinister. The very incompleteness of the poem enhances these feelings, for we are made aware of evil without fully understanding its purpose. The standard trappings of Gothic horror – the remote castle and the wood, the virgin Christabel in peril and the subtly wicked Geraldine – dramatize a confrontation with evil through disturbing suggestions of the sexual, the supernatural and the power of dream. Throughout his career, Coleridge was fascinated by the ability of dreams to suggest truths beyond the range of rational analysis, and in the *Lay Sermons* (1816–17) he offered speculations on their nature which correspond closely to his notions on the power of poetry to enter into and transform what it describes.

Visions encouraged by the opium Coleridge was now beginning to take heavily both nourished and dissipated these imaginative powers, and his addiction had already led to the writing of that most incandescent of dream poems: 'Kubla Khan'. Even more than *The Rime of the Ancient Mariner* and *Christabel*, this drug-inspired reverie (supposedly interrupted by the unexpected visit of a person from Porlock) defies rational analysis. We perceive in the work what we can bring to it only to find our knowledge transformed into something more terrible and strange. If the work springs from Coleridge's voluminous reading, it also surges from the measureless caverns of the mind, mixing the sacred with oriental splendour, sexual fear, rapture and exultant music. In the end, the poem becomes the work of the *vates*, of the poet glimpsed not as a benevolent seer but as a shaman, primordial and awe-inspiring:

> Beware! Beware!
> His flashing eyes, his floating hair!
> Weave a circle round him thrice,
> And close your eyes with holy dread,
> For he on honey-dew hath fed,
> And drunk the milk of Paradise.

But the exultant shaman was also the troubled philosopher, and it is suggestive of the immense energies of Coleridge's mind that while he was writing these poems he was also undergoing an intellectual crisis. He had come to question both how we may have knowledge of the outward existence of objects – the manner in which they can be understood as existing independently of our perception – and how morality can be soundly based on the impulses of conscience rather than on abstract reasoning.

The philosophic system of Kant was to direct Coleridge towards an understanding of how subject and object react on each other (a perception already explored in his poetry) and to a recognition of the superiority of the Kantian concept of 'reason' over a narrow and rationalist 'understanding'. Kant was also to reveal how reason itself directs the will to the discovery of those moral ends, and how, as Coleridge wrote in *The Friend* (1809–10), 'conscience . . . unconditionally commands us to attribute reality, and actual existence, to those ideas and those only, without which the conscience itself would be baseless and contradictory, to the ideas of soul, of free-will, of immortality, and of God!' Such a philosophic undertaking was an attempt to overthrow the tyranny of mechanistic reasoning and to assert from a secured intellectual base that 'deep thinking is attainable only by a man of deep feeling, and that all truth is a species of revelation'. In this, Kant's thought goes to the heart of Coleridge's needs, and to the deep-seated urge among many of the finest minds of the age to argue for the primacy of man's spiritual life.

For Coleridge – and hence for those influenced by him – this was an area further opened up by the aesthetic ideas of Kant's followers: Friedrich Schelling (1775–1854), the poetic drama of Johann Christoph Friedrich von Schiller (1759–1805) and the writings of August Wilhelm Schlegel (1767–1845) with their notions of the unconscious and of organic form in art. These were ideas which, if their use often exposes Coleridge to the vexed issue of his frequent and blatant plagiarism, nonetheless introduced into English literary discussion concepts which broke away from classical notions of form, revealing a critical vocabulary which allowed contemporaries to discuss the literature of the past and present in terms of more pressing current needs.

Such ideas were deepened and clarified in the growing body of Coleridge's critical thought, but if he eventually returned from Germany full of ambitious literary plans – his translation of Schiller's *Wallenstein* (Part I) was the chief of these to be completed – he was also to face a crisis in his personal life. His oldest son had died in his absence, and relations with an increasingly unsympathetic wife were strained. He also met and fell deeply in love with Sara Hutchinson, the sister of Wordsworth's future wife Mary.

The poems nurtured by this guilt-ridden affair – the Gothic ballad 'Love', 'The Keepsake', 'To Asra' and 'A Day-Dream' among others – are more constricted than the earlier work and reflect the stifling of Coleridge's creative forces that is so poignantly recorded in his Notebooks. Entries here show with an almost unbearable immediacy how the transforming perception of joy had collapsed to debilitating lassitude – the spiritual death of the Ancient Mariner. Amid vivid but tortured natural descriptions beats a constant refrain: 'I have done nothing!' The overwhelming feeling is of spiritual fracture, of the mind gazing at its reflection in the jagged fragments of a shattered wholeness.

This sense of despair amid a natural world that no longer answers to the poet's craving for joy finds its most complete expression in two versions of a single work: 'Dejection: A Letter' (1802), a poem which Coleridge six months later refashioned into the intellectually more disciplined 'Dejection: An Ode'. The last is a supreme work in a form that the poets of the nineteenth century were often to make a vehicle for some of their most profound perceptions.

As a love poem, the 'Letter' is the rawer and more personal of the two poems, a work whose effort to record a welter of experience conveys the mind's struggle to cope with its desolating sense of failure, self-pity, recrimination – the inner sterility that knows the natural joy it has lost and which it then poignantly offers to the distant beloved as a sustaining truth. Nature, imagination and human love thus remain at the heart of Coleridge's concern. In one of the greatest of his letters – that written to William Sotheby in 1802 – Coleridge declared that 'a Poet's *Heart & Intellect* should be *Combined, intimately* combined & *unified*, with the great appearances in Nature'. In the 'Letter' and the 'Ode' however there is no answering joy between the poet and his world. Dejection smothers the spiritual force of the imagination until nature is an empty pageant and the stars glitter in purposeless beauty. The poet himself becomes the victim of

> A grief without a pang, void, dark, and drear,
>   A stifled, drowsy, unimpassioned grief,
>   Which finds no natural outlet, no relief,
>   In word, or sigh, or tear . . .

The Aeolian lute no longer rings with universal harmony but grates with cosmic dissonance, with storm, fear, war-music and the cry of a lost and homesick child. Yet it is amid this primal statement of the anguish and isolation of the nineteenth-century artist – that alienation and world-sorrow which signal a profound shift in artistic awareness – that there beats the insistent knowledge that joy is our truth and birthright:

> With light heart may she rise,
>   Gay fancy, cheerful eyes,
>   Joy lift her spirit, joy attune her voice;
> To her may all things live, from pole to pole,
>   Their life the eddying of her living soul!

So profound a crisis was followed by a period of dreary self-exile and wandering across Europe: Malta, Sicily, Rome. Eventually returning to London, Coleridge planned a career in journalism and lecturing, but the Wordsworths and Sara Hutchinson lured him to rural Coleorton. Here, a recital of the completed *Prelude* once again revealed the force of Wordsworth's achievement and the power of his personality. Coleridge recorded the effect of the reading in a poem in which Wordsworth is revered as the undoubted master.

By 1808, Coleridge was back in London. He began lecturing 'On Poetry and the Principles of Taste' and also launched his second periodical, *The Friend* (1809). A letter of the time outlines Coleridge's purposes here: 'I do not write this work for the multitude of men; but for those, who either by Rank, or Fortune, or Official situation, or by Talents & Habits of Reflection, are to influence the multitude – I write to found true PRINCIPLES, to oppose false PRINCIPLES in Legislation, Philosophy, Morals, International Law.'

This passage suggests Coleridge's concern with public affairs and the moral education of an important group in society he was later to call the 'clerisy'. These people – 'the learned of all denominations' – have a responsibility towards the mass of the nation in terms both of teaching them and of acting as a regulatory force in a time of rapid and often ugly social change. The duties of the clerisy consisted above all in securing those values of civilization by which men develop their full humanity within an organic community, one that was cohesive but dynamic rather than merely individualistic, mercenary and competitive.

Underlying the political thought in *The Friend* is a concern with how the state must promote this concept of social justice, a benevolence founded on family values. Coleridge proposed that government itself – which he saw as a means of regulating a society of growing individuals rather than a uniquely powerful means of bringing that growth about – should help secure work for every man and thus the grounds for 'the development of those faculties which are essential to his human nature by the knowledge of his moral and religious duties, and the increase of his intellectual powers in as great a degree as is compatible with the other ends of social union'. This is a humane requirement in which we see Coleridge endeavouring to preserve his regard for the spiritual life and for the imagination especially as 'the distinguishing characteristic of man as a progressive being'.

It was such beliefs that caused Coleridge to inveigh against the crueller aspects of the commercial spirit and of what, in conversation with Henry Crabb Robinson (1775–1867), the diarist of the contemporary literary world, he was to call 'Soul-murder'. In his awareness of the spiritual and social perils of the Industrial Revolution, Coleridge thus looks forward to the great Victorian social commentators. He also looked – and often with worried memories of the French Revolution – on immediate contemporary conditions. If the England of 1815–18, the period after the defeat of Napoleon, was marked by national triumph and conservatism, it was also a period of intense working-class unrest, of bad harvests, of the Luddite riots and of violent protest violently repressed.

In the 'Statesman's Manual' (1816) – the first of his *Lay Sermons* – Coleridge asked his aristocratic audience to 'plead *for* the poor and ignorant, and not *to* them'. In his fear of mass democratic movements, the idea of a responsible and traditional social hierarchy founded on an imagination enriched by the Scriptures as the true '*educts* of the imagination' is opposed to those followers of eighteenth-century radical enlightenment whose thoughts 'partake in the general contagion of . . . mechanic philosophy, and are the *product* of an unenlivened generalizing Understanding'. In the second Sermon, addressed to 'the Higher and Middle Classes on the Existing Distresses and Discontents', Coleridge again inveighed against the effects of unbalanced commercial greed as well as the writings of radical journalists such as William Cobbett (?1763–1835), William Hazlitt (1778–1830) and Leigh Hunt (1784–1859), analysing what he saw as their deleterious effect on the working classes. In their place, Coleridge urged a Burkeian traditionalism: 'the ancient feeling of rank and ancestry', and the virtues of a gentry class exercising their duties 'in the sight of God and their country'.

Coleridge also assigned a central role in the clerisy to the poet. In this he drew on his own experience, his relationship with Wordsworth and his reading of Shakespeare. Many of Coleridge's lectures on Shakespeare were given in the despairing years immediately after 1810 when, having broken with both Wordsworth (who, he was told, had dismissed him as 'a rotten drunkard') and also Sara Hutchinson, Coleridge plunged into the slough of London and opium. Tortured with self-disgust and even contemplating suicide, his mental strength was nonetheless such that he now wrought a revolution in English literary criticism.

At the centre of Coleridge's Shakespeare studies lies his concern with the functioning of Shakespeare's imagination – the supreme human faculty working in the supreme English poet. To develop this interest, Coleridge founded his discussion on a European basis, bringing to his subject the critical insights of Schelling on organic form and then contrasting an analysis of Shakespeare in this mode to the 'mechanical' structure of Greek and French classicism. The result was an advance from older notions of Shakespeare's lack of dramatic propriety to a view, argued with a poet's consummate subtlety of response, 'that in all points from the most important to the most minute the judgement of Shakespeare is commensurate with his genius'.

The greatest of the lectures – those on *Romeo and Juliet*, *Hamlet* and *The Tempest* – reveal Shakespeare working and Coleridge analysing in a way that shows images, characters and scenes developing out of each other and being shaped by an internal logic of feeling. Writing in a manner that truly imitates nature, Shakespeare finally reveals 'a power and an implicit wisdom deeper than consciousness'. These lectures invariably send us back to the plays with an enhanced sense of excitement, and it is Coleridge's Shakespeare which lies at the basis of much of the finest modern Shakespearian criticism. His influence was profound indeed.

In Coleridge's opinion, it was Wordsworth who stood 'nearest of all modern writers to Shakespeare'. In the sixth chapter of the *Biographia Literaria*, he paid tribute to Wordsworth's powers in a paragraph which, while defining the effect on him of hearing Wordsworth recite his early verse, actually suggests Coleridge's own ideal of poetry itself:

the union of deep feeling with profound thought; the fine balance of truth in observing, with the imaginative faculty of modifying, the objects observed; and above all the original gift of spreading the tone, the atmosphere, and with it the depth and height of the ideal world around forms, incidents, and situations, of which, for the common view, custom had bedimmed all the lustre, had dried up the sparkle and the dew drops.

Coleridge nonetheless now took issue with Wordsworth over the discussion of poetic diction in the Preface to the *Lyrical Ballads*, suggesting that a form of purified rusticity 'will not differ from the language of any other man of common-sense, however learned or refined he may be, except as far as the notions, which the rustic has to convey, are fewer and more indiscriminate'. He was to attack the central figure in *The Excursion* in similar terms, terms which point to Coleridge's aristocratic, anti-revolutionary, Burkeian concept of the poet's role amid the clerisy. The ideas underlying the *Lyrical Ballads* are now seen as a political aberration, and much of the discussion of Wordsworth is a polemical attempt to define his '*real* characteristics' in terms of the Tory culture which a younger generation were to spurn as reactionary.

A further subject broached in the *Biographia Literaria* is 'the poet, described in ideal perfection'. It is in these passages that Coleridge defines the relation of the primary and secondary imaginations. He sees this as a relation between the mind's ability to distinguish and combine experiences of the world and the self, and the poet's 'esemplastic power' whereby language, imagery and metre, rising naturally out of the poet's sensations rather than being merely copied from received forms, allow him to unite head, heart and the natural world and so create a truly organic art. This is an art in which form and content, purpose and effect, show us that we are all in our individuality part of the '*one Life*'.

Coleridge also believed that the great poet must be a philosopher, and the *Biographia Literaria* provides an account of his own development towards the ideas of Kant and his conviction that Christianity, 'though not discoverable by human reason, is yet in accordance with it'. This belief, bringing subjective and objective, man and the natural world, into imaginative harmony with God, underlies the book's magnificent closing paragraph:

It is night, sacred night! the upraised eye views only the starry heaven which manifests itself alone: and the outward beholding is fixed on the sparks twinkling in the awful depth, though suns of other worlds, only to preserve the soul steady and collected in its pure act of inward adoration to the great I AM, and to the filial Word that re-affirmeth from eternity to eternity, whose choral echo is the universe.

Coleridge's later religious thought was developed in his *Aids to Reflection* (1825) and *On the Constitution of the Church and State* (1829). The former, reacting equally against rationalism, 'shapeless feelings' and rigid conventional orthodoxy, puts in their place the felt need for divine law, for the spiritual and redemptive, bringing to bear on these the Kantian idea of a free and responsible will which accepts the authority of conscience. This was a conclusion that was deeply to affect the development of Christianity in England and the nineteenth-century search for an inner proof of faith.

In a similar way, *On the Constitution of the Church and State*, despite its opposition to Catholic emancipation and what was eventually to be the 1832 Reform Bill, was to influence Victorian thinkers such as Thomas Carlyle (1795–1881) in their search for a society more cultured and cohesive than that created by the Industrial Revolution. Indeed, Carlyle's image of the ageing Coleridge looking down on smoky London 'like a sage escaped from the inanities of life's battles' suggests how the light of Coleridge's mind – that candle burning in darkness – eventually spread out across time as well as space.

5

Much of the finest prose fiction in this period was the creation of women writers. Although at the time their pre-eminence was widely recognized, their reputations were in many cases subsequently eclipsed with the result that a distinctive tradition was obscured. One of the great achievements of modern feminist criticism has been to re-establish the role of novelists as diverse as Fanny Burney, Mary Wollstonecraft and Maria Edgeworth, and so provide a context for the greatest of them – Jane Austen.

The novel of manners and social comedy, of character placed in a specific and closely defined environment, was in large part the creation of Fanny Burney (1752–1840). The title of her first work, *Evelina, or The History of a Young Lady's Entrance into the World* (1778), suggests the confrontation of the sensitive innocent with the oppressive terrors of society. Burney herself acknowledged the influence of Eliza Haywood's *History of Betsy Thoughtless* in this, but her own *Early Diary* (published posthumously 1889) and her subsequent records of her life at court suggest how deeply rooted in personal experience was her presentation of a young woman required to survive in a dangerous, confining society, and to do so with becoming modesty.

This sense of entrapment – of the social peril surrounding the young eighteenth-century woman – is conveyed by Burney in a style in which assured surface polish covers a sense of fear amounting at times to claustrophobia. Powerlessness and betrayal are among her frequently recurring motifs, and the description of a coach journey in her second novel *Cecilia* (1782) focuses these with particular power.

Enclosed in the coach, hurrying to her husband whom she believes to be involved in a duel, her journey harassed by a stupid companion, a drunken driver and the mob, Burney wrote:

This moment, for the unhappy Cecilia, teemed with calamity; she was wholly overpowered; terror for Delville, horror for herself, hurry, confusion, heat, and fatigue, all assailing her at once, while all means of repelling them were denied her, the attack was too strong for her fears, feelings, and faculties, and her reason suddenly, yet totally failing her, she madly called out.

In *Cecilia*, Burney's theme of woman's peril is revealed through the sheer inadequacy of the men on whom she is obliged to rely, while in *Camilla* (1796) it is debt involuntarily incurred which becomes the source of shameful anxiety. Burney's novels present an acutely observed and frequently painful sense of entrapment, helplessness and the requirement that characters nonetheless preserve their moral autonomy. As such, they are important analyses of women's role in society.

Such awareness is taken up again in what are, nonetheless, the far less assured novels of Elizabeth Inchbald (1753–1821) and Charlotte Smith (1749–1806). The work of the first derives in part from Inchbald's long experience in the theatre and, in the case of *A Simple Story* (1791), from her Roman Catholicism. The latter theme is clumsily handled however, and the greater interest of the work lies in the sparring relation between the heroine and Lord Elmwood (a priest absolved from his vows) over issues of freedom in marriage. This last is also a theme in some of Charlotte Smith's novels, while such works of hers as *The Old Manor House* (1793) extend into political criticism and show in particular the author's enthusiasm for republican principles.

It is in the fiction of Mary Wollstonecraft that the position of women is explored with the most radical and passionate intelligence. Her early and largely autobiographical novel *Mary* (1788) at once analyses and condemns the conditions that have made women weak-willed and dependent through lack of education. Much of the work is also concerned with the woman of sensibility trapped into a repellently loveless marriage and seeking escape in friendship. The anguish inflicted by the prospect of enforced and loveless sex is powerfully expressed, but the only ending that can be imagined is the release of death.

In Wollstonecraft's unfinished *The Wrongs of Woman* (1798), this analysis is taken much further in a seering portrait of women's enforced ignorance and sexual exploitation, and the degrading imprisonment of a loveless marriage. 'I had been caught in a trap and caught for life,' declares the heroine in a novel where feminine sensibility is often so powerfully pitted against patriarchal norms that the work's radical force was felt to be deeply threatening. Wollstonecraft's fictions are central works of feminist consciousness, and their focus on the psychological and spiritual damage worked by the conditions of eighteenth-century marriage reinforces, as in no other novels of the age, why the right choice in marriage itself was a central subject in contemporary women's writing. Wollstonecraft's own experiences, and those of her circle, are again the subject of Mary Hay's *Memoirs of Emma Courtney* (1796), and Amelia Opie's *Adeline Mowbray* (1804).

Melodramatic fear is the particular province of the Gothic horror novel. In *The Castle of Otranto* (1765) by Horace Walpole (1711–97), heavy-handed pastiche elements derived from the supernatural in *Hamlet* and *Macbeth* suggest an attempt to assert the superiority of seventeenth-century dramatic licence over classical canons. They also offer what were to become the stock trappings of the form. Here are the gloomy castle with its dark vaults and murderous, lustful lord, an innocent heroine and 'the fleshless jaws and empty sockets of a skeleton, wrapt in a hermit's cowl'. Such sensationalism, while somewhat tempered in *The Champion of Virtue, a Gothic Story* (1771, reprinted as *The Old English Baron*) by Clara Reeve (1729–1807), reaches its height in *The Monk* (1795) by M.G. Lewis (1775–1818).

In such novels by Ann Radcliffe (1764–1823) as *The Sicilian Romance* (1790) and *The Romance of the Forest* (1791), a heightened sense of that powerless, sensitive intelligence explored by Fanny Burney is developed through Gothic effects. In Radcliffe's best-known work, *The Mysteries of Udolpho* (1794), what are presented as supernatural events are finally shown to have natural causes. Nonetheless, the power of terror they raise in the highly charged sensibilities of the heroine allows the writer to develop genuine suspense, a powerful sense of subjectivity and a degree of internal narration which become a vehicle for intelligent but essentially passive female consciousness.

While shocking effects were immensely popular, it is in its ability to provide a forum for the workings of the subconscious and the socially deviant that the Gothic novel achieved its full literary status. In *Vathek* (1784) by the extravagant William Beckford (1759–1844), for example, excitement is intimately connected with damnation and an experience of the living dead, of 'persons in search of repose and consolation, but who sought them in vain; for everyone carried within him a heart tormented in flames'. In *Melmoth the Wanderer* (1820) by Charles Robert Maturin (1782–1824), the anti-hero suggests a psychological sense of evil and exile, themes also explored, much to Coleridge's disgust, in Maturin's stage work *Bertram* (1816).

Indeed, it says much of the low state of the drama at this period that Maturin, along with R.L. Shiel (1791–1851) and Sheridan Knowles (1784–1862), was one of the most popular dramatists of his day. In an age of vast theatres and a vulgar profusion of stage effects – an age when the censor was employed as much to suppress political allusions as immorality – these authors' works appealed to an undemanding audience. While lesser writers might plunder such dramas for sensational effects, the most interesting plays of the period are usually closet dramas. Among these is *Death's Jest Book* (begun *c.* 1825, published 1850) by Thomas Lovell Beddoes (1803–49). This piece was intended, Beddoes declared, as an example 'of what might be called the florid in Gothic poetry'. The lyrics in the work show great metrical dexterity, while the violent imagery of the Jacobean dramatists helps create a meditation on death that is obsessive if not always coherent, and shot through with passages of lurid genius.

The ideals of the Enlightenment play an important role in the novels of Maria Edgeworth (1767–1849). The eponymous heroine of *Belinda* (1801), for example, progresses through the novel reconciling characters and restoring domestic harmony through her virtue and intelligence. These are qualities which point to the follies of the social world about her, a world which derives from Fanny Burney's novel of manners.

Two of Maria Edgeworth's works break new ground. In 1800 she published *Castle Rackrent, an Hibernian Tale Taken from Fact, and from the Manners of the Irish Squires before the Year 1782.* The full title suggests the novelist's interest in communities other than the English middle classes. In pitting the folly and extravagance of the old Irish squirearchy against the harder and more efficient world of the professional classes, Edgeworth at once painted a vivid series of portraits of unfamiliar people from all ranks while addressing a broad social problem. In her narrator Thaddy Quirk, she also began to suggest the possibilities of demotic story-telling as a means of giving authentic colour to her material. In 'The Absentee' from her second set of *Tales of Fashionable Life* (1812), a wide social canvas is again offered, along with a criticism of the society that was causing Ireland's decline. These last works were profoundly to influence Walter Scott, just as *Belinda* was deeply admired by Jane Austen.

6

The novels of Jane Austen (1775–1817), at once delightful and profound, are among the supreme achievements of English literature. They show a mind of the shrewdest intelligence adapting the available traditions and deepening the resources of art with consummate craftsmanship.

Northanger Abbey, written between 1797 and 1798 but published posthumously in 1818, was among the first of Austen's novels to be written. Appropriately, the reading and writing of fiction are among its central concerns. By creating in Catherine Morland a young lady from the minor gentry who feels herself to be obsessed with the Gothic horrors of Mrs Radcliffe and her school, Jane Austen broaches one of her central themes: the perils of letting imagination and feeling have sway over reason and discretion. In showing Catherine's marriage to the wealthy Henry Tilney however, Austen also reveals her abiding interest in a young woman's progress towards the self-knowledge and social position suggested by her loving dependence on a mature, courteous and prosperous man. The novel's contrast between the supposed terrors of the imagination and the altogether more interesting real world with its cruelties and natural joys reveals the shrewdness of Jane Austen's irony and her profound sense of how the drama of daily life is rooted in the conservative realities of social existence.

Such are the foundations of Austen's art, and in a period when the novel itself was often disparaged as a vulgarly subversive form, *Northanger Abbey* contains an important defence of the genre. Condemning the detractors of Fanny Burney and Maria Edgeworth, Jane Austen declares that theirs are works 'in which the greatest powers of the mind are displayed, in which the most thorough knowledge of human nature, the happiest delineation of its varieties, the liveliest effusions of wit and humour are conveyed to the world in the best chosen language'. This is a powerful statement of the novel's role as the medium through which the world can be intimately re-imagined, investigated and criticized. It is also suggests the supremely important role played by women in its creation.

At the close of *Sense and Sensibility*, a work begun in 1797 but not published until 1811, the volatile Marianne Dashwood finds herself 'submitting to new attachments, entering on new duties, placed in a new home, a wife, the mistress of a family, and the patroness of a village'. This is the conventional benevolence, Jane Austen's view of a woman's true and responsible place in the world. The novel however shows the high price that must sometimes be paid for this, especially by those whose 'sensibility' drives them beyond the hardheaded but ultimately sustaining confinements of convention.

In a motif common among Tory novelists of the period, a hedonistic young man named Willoughby, a character ultimately exposed as repellently selfish, comes into the neighbourhood and wreaks havoc by allowing Marianne to indulge her emotionalism. This deliberate cult of the self – the assertion of will over restraint – is exposed, with great psychological verisimilitude, as a force at once warmly impulsive but absurd, blind, vulnerable and potentially tragic. Marianne is brought to nervous collapse and the edge of death. In this decline she achieves self-knowledge and is finally rewarded with social prestige. Nonetheless, there hovers over the conclusion of the novel (especially when Marianne's marriage is compared to her sister Elinor's) a suggestion of the loss involved in the chastening of the self and the cost of the happiness which to others comes naturally.

Pride and Prejudice, published in 1813 but originally drafted as 'First Impressions' in 1796, is the most delightful of Jane Austen's works, and arguably the most delightful novel in English literature. The structure is exquisitely deft, the characterization in the highest degree memorable, while the irony has a radiant shrewdness unmatched elsewhere:

It is a truth universally acknowledged, that a single man in possession of a good fortune, must be in want of a wife.

However little known the feelings or views of such a man may be on his entering a neighbourhood, this truth is so well fixed in the minds of the surrounding families, that he is considered as the rightful property of some one or other of their daughters.

'My dear Mr Bennet,' said his lady to him one day, 'have you heard that Netherfield Park is let at last?'

Here are marriage, property and intrigue. At the heart of the novelist's exploration of them lies the exhilarating suspense of the relationship between Elizabeth Bennet and Darcy, and Jane Austen's delicate probing of the values of the gentry.

The moments of high comedy in the novel are always related to deeper issues. Elizabeth's rejection of the odious Mr Collins suggests her independence and self-esteem, but when Collins is accepted by her friend Charlotte Lucas we see the reality of marriage as a necessary step if a woman was to avoid the wretchedness of ageing spinsterhood. Conversely, in the elopement of Lydia and Wickham, we are shown the dangers of feckless relationships unsupported by money. It is the gradual realization by Elizabeth and Darcy of their love and their consequent growth to self-knowledge that lie at the core of the book however. Two powerful characters learn the wider values on which their marriage will be based. In Darcy's case, this entails a less haughty sense of rank which in turn allows him to blend benevolence with a full awareness of his duties. For Elizabeth, knowledge of Darcy's true moral stature causes her to check her headstrong reliance on her own judgement (a fault common among Austen's heroines) and so take her rightful place as the wife of a great hereditary gentleman and the mistress of Pemberly.

Jane Austen herself considered Pride and Prejudice to be 'rather too light, and bright, and sparkling; it wants shade'. This is a hard judgement, but it does suggest the greater seriousness to be found in her remaining works. The comic characters in Pride and Prejudice –

Mr and Mrs Bennet, Mr Collins and that monstrous snob Lady Catherine de Burgh – make us laugh even as they parody erroneous views of marriage and class. In the world of *Mansfield Park* (1814) however, such errors become the sign of a deep-seated and profoundly threatening moral vulgarity.

Mansfield Park takes Jane Austen's favourite situation – '3 or 4 Families in a Country Village' – and works this into a commentary on the values of the ruling classes in a period of unsettling social change. The novel is her most considerable achievement, ranking indeed as one of the major works of nineteenth-century fiction. At the centre of *Mansfield Park* stands the house itself: dignified to the point of sombreness, ordered, ceremonious and enclosed. It suggests the power of the gentry and the solidity of their traditions, as well as being – with all the emotive connotations of that word – a home. Into this suggestive environment comes Fanny Price, the poor relation who will best embody the house's ideal values of self-contained moral strength and fortitude, and who will eventually inherit many of its responsibilities.

Into the village also come Henry and Mary Crawford, the bright London socialites whose considerable but superficial attractiveness masks a worldly restlessness. This pair's tempting brilliance eventually serves to test the values of the indigenous 'small platoon'. The enemies without expose the dangers within, the personal flaws of the hereditary and patriarchal gentry. Sir Thomas Bertram, whose house stands for this traditional order and who is felt throughout as an awesome source of moral responsibility, has nonetheless partly failed his children. His patrician concern with form is a denial of deeper and more nourishing values. 'He had meant them to be good, but his care had been directed to the understanding and manners, not the disposition; and of the necessity of self-denial and humility, he feared they had never heard from any lips that could profit them.'

Lady Bertram, one of the most convincingly stupid women in English literature and a portrait as sharply critical as anything in Wollstonecraft, parodies the ideal stillness of the house in her debilitating lassitude. Her role as mother has passed to the odious Mrs Norris whose destructive and vulgar meanness of spirit – officious, ingratiating and restless – is a principal cause for the commonplace pettiness of the Bertram daughters and has contributed perhaps to the fecklessness of the older son. Only Edmund stands (for the greater part of the novel at least) as the true type of the young Christian gentleman, courteous and charitable.

The mounting of the melodramatic *Lovers' Vows* during the absence of Sir Thomas is a supreme example of the subtlety of Jane Austen's moral art. The country seat becomes a theatre of illusions. Love is made, hearts are broken, and lives and peace destroyed. Edmund is tempted by the siren charms of Mary Crawford, and it is only the providential return of Sir Thomas himself that prevents Fanny from being forced into this social chaos. She thereby preserves her role as the modest Christian heroine. The return of Sir Thomas is a moment of high drama, of conflict between role-playing, hedonistic individualism and the old order.

It is also a moment of developing self-knowledge. Edmund comes to realize that during this period of trial only Fanny has retained her moral integrity. She too must be further tested however. If she can withstand Henry Crawford, as the poor relation at Mansfield Park she must also make a choice about her roots. The remarkable passage describing her return to the sluttish chaos of her parents' house and her dawning realization that the Park is her true home – the place where her heart is – is excellently achieved. Such moments help prepare Fanny for her final roles as Edmund the clergyman's wife and as Sir Thomas the aristocrat's favourite relation, as well as for her replacing Mrs Norris and so becoming the quiet moral centre of the gentry values of Mansfield Park itself.

Emma (1815) recaptures something of the brilliance of *Pride and Prejudice*, elevating this into a work of the most assured mastery. If the range of social comment is narrower than in *Mansfield Park*, the psychological verisimilitude is of exceptional liveliness. Emma herself dominates the novel, even as she tries to manipulate its other characters through matchmaking schemes that betray her lack of insight and self-knowledge. Where a Maria Edgeworth heroine such as Belinda dispenses wisdom and reconciliation from a position of enlightened virtue, Emma tries to act in the same way while wholly unaware of her unsuitability for this role. As a result, we are offered a beautifully wrought minuet of error in which only Mr Knightly – that very finished portrait of the English gentleman – asserts the values of true gentility.

The arrival of Frank Churchill and Jane Fairfax, preceded by the wonderful scene in which Mr Elton proposes to Emma while under the influence of Mr Weston's good wine, provides the intrigue of the secret engagement. The dilemmas reach a narrative and moral climax in the scene at Box Hill where Knightly again shows his essential strength, Emma her lack of true decorum. Embarrassment however eventually leads to self-knowledge. Emma discovers that far from being a heroine in the Maria Edgeworth mode she has been merely interfering and deluded:

How to understand it all! How to understand the deceptions, she had been thus practising on herself, and living under! – The blunders, the blindness of her own head and heart! ... she perceived she had acted most weakly; that she had been imposed on by others in a most mortifying degree; that she had been imposing on herself in a degree yet more mortifying; that she was wretched, and should probably find this day but the beginning of wretchedness.

The deft suggestion of comic melodrama at the close of this passage is beautifully achieved, but far from leading to tragedy, Emma's deepening self-knowledge results in the recognition that she truly loves Knightly and so to the novel's happy conclusion.

Persuasion (1818), Jane Austen's last completed novel, is her most subtly wrought work and the one in which her concern with manners is revealed at its most profound. Manners are here far more than the pleasantries of social polish. They are the fundamental means of communication in gentry society, an index not merely of class, intelligence and sensitivity, but of forbearance and submission to authority, of personal integrity and moral rectitude. At their best, they express a full and balanced humanity, while at their worst they are a carapace for narrowness and cold calculation. It is in such a world that the most mature of Jane Austen's heroines has to discover the truth about her feelings and the nature of the world about her. In a situation of the utmost delicacy, Anne Eliot, with a shallow snob for a father and a limited though well-meaning adviser in Lady Russell, has been persuaded to reject the man she loves.

Captain Wentworth, in Lady Russell's words, possesses nothing to recommend him but himself. His real qualities, partly expressed through his being an officer in the navy that had saved the country from the threat of Napoleon, include the healthy ambition by which Wentworth makes himself rich, along with an underlying steadfastness of heart and the subtle, courteous delicacy of perception through which he comes to appreciate the real qualities of the woman he loves.

Anne too – natural, warm and dignified in her unfulfilled spinster life – has also to accept the rightness of her feelings as Wentworth's true qualities are revealed. More subtly, and in a way that shows Jane Austen's belief that submission to the established hierarchies is always preferable to ardent individualism, she has to come to terms with the fact that while Lady Russell's initial advice to reject Wentworth was misconceived, she herself was right to accept it. In the end, Anne finds a proven happiness in society through the acceptance of error and suffering rather than in defiance and self-assertion. Jane Austen here shows that it is manners as the expression of a full and benevolent awareness of self and others that bring content, binding together the fully human amid a sharply exposed world of shallow snobs, villains and mere fools.

7

One of Jane Austen's greatest admirers was Sir Walter Scott (1771–1832). His admiration however was the tribute paid by a great talent to a wholly different order of genius. Where Jane Austen, in one of her masterly incisive letters, had compared herself to a miniature painter bent over 'the little bit (two inches wide) of ivory on which I work with so fine a brush', Scott recognized himself as the master of 'the Big Bow-Wow strain'.

Scott's novels, begun after he had ceded dominance in the field of verse narrative to Byron, achieved spectacular popularity. Scott was both an early example of that alluring figure the best-selling author and, at a more important level, as the father of the historical novel, an innovator of great importance. In his *Lives of the Novelists* prefixed to Ballantyne's Novelists' Library (1821–4), Scott suggested that the two chief requirements of the writer of historical fiction were 'poetical imagination' and a sound knowledge of the characters and manners of the age depicted. *Waverley* (1814), the first of Scott's novels and the one whose title gave its name to his whole output of prose fiction, shows the writer combining these elements in a way developed in much of his later work. Scotland in 1745 – the year of the Jacobite rising – provides the subject, while Waverley himself, attracted to all things Scottish by dreams of romance, is an example of a frequently used device.

Waverley is the first of many young and often rather colourless visitors to Scotland who are suddenly precipitated into complex intrigues and mild love affairs, and whose adventures allow Scott to portray through vividly picturesque evocations of local character, dialect and landscape a sense of primitive society undergoing change. Revolution and social disturbance thus lie at the heart of such works, and against these Scott juxtaposes newer, bourgeois values of order, community and commercial prosperity. A contrast is thus drawn between an old heroic way of life – glamorous, dangerous and anachronistic – and a newer, British world of pragmatic conservatism. By focusing on climactic moments in Scotland's past, Scott's fiction allows us to see history being made. We watch – in a manner deeply influenced by the writers of the eighteenth-century Scottish Enlightenment – characters developing under the force of given circumstances and received values. In achieving such a perspective, Scott greatly widened the possibilities for prose fiction, and his influence was to be immense.

In *Guy Mannering* (1815), his second and more densely plotted novel, the theme of the lost heir and of ancestral estates restored allowed Scott to show his true genius for portraying old-world characters: Dandie Dinmont the courageous, honest farmer and, above all, the wonderfully exotic Meg Merrilies – gipsy, thief and choric prophetess – whose evocative, ballad-like language, cursing the brutal ways of the modern world, provides nostalgic sentiment for 'the gude auld rules'. Poetry and social commentary are one. In the modern world however reverence for the past can lead to comedy as Scott showed in Sir Arthur Wardour, the vain and vulnerable aristocrat of *The Antiquary* (1816) who actually knows less about the traditions he boasts of than the historian Oldbuck. The past truly belongs only to scholars, while the present is inhabited by those who, like Edie Ochiltree the wandering beggar and Caxon the barber, might regret its passing into the hands of villainous Jacobins, or be part of the timeless world of work and tragedy like the fishing family of the Mucklebackits. It is in such portraits as these – palpable, poetic and, in their earthy Scottishness, moving easily between realism and the supernatural – that we see one of the finest aspects of Scott's art.

In *Old Mortality* (1816), Scott relied far more on written sources to create a study of political and religious extremism among the seventeenth-century Scots Covenanters led by the fanatical Balfour of Burley and the royalists under 'Bonnie Dundee'. Here moderation fails, and the defeat of the Covenanters at Prestonpans and the subsequent revenge of the government forces create a tragic situation in which only the prudent and unglamorous survive. *Rob Roy* (1817) portrays attitudes at once critical of and nostalgic for the old heroic way of life. For all their romance however – and the imperious Diana Vernon is one of Scott's finest creations – the old ways are nonetheless shown as lawless, corrupt or merely shabby when compared to the more sustaining world of public order.

Such a theme was treated again in *Redgauntlet* (1824) where an attempt to revive the Jacobite cause is the focus for an examination of the two worlds of Scottish history – the heroic but anachronistic Jacobites embodied in the do-or-die ardour of Redgauntlet himself and the adroit good humour of the Hanoverian General Campbell who quietly sends the would-be rebels home. The fire of Redgauntlet raises the glamour of passionate conviction only to show its irrelevance in the modern world. In addition, the insertion of the brilliantly narrated 'Wandering Willie's Tale' allows Scott further reflections on the complex relationship between the present and life under 'the feudal yoke', between the old Scotland of warring clans and the new order symbolized by Alan Fairford, friend of the conventional plot figure Darsie Latimer.

The vitality of *Redgauntlet* and of 'Wandering Willie's Tale' in particular lies to a large extent in the vigorous use of Scots dialect. This was a daring innovation since such speech patterns had for long been associated with low comedy and the sentimental debasement of the Burns tradition. Scott himself however considered characterization through such language to be his most significant contribution to prose fiction, and while in his love scenes his technique is often wooden, he believed like 'my friend Wordsworth' that the speech of intelligent ordinary people was uniquely powerful. He declared that 'the antique force and simplicity of their language, often tinctured with the Oriental eloquence of Scripture, in the mouths of those of an elevated understanding, gives pathos to their grief, and dignity to their resentment'. This was a principle that received its finest treatment in what is probably the greatest of Scott's novels – *The Heart of Midlothian* (1818).

The first part of this novel has a powerful unity lacking in much of Scott's work. This it achieves through its concentration on the remarkable character of Jeannie Deans, a figure created partly to show 'the possibility of rendering a fictitious personage interesting by mere dignity of mind and rectitude of principle, assisted by unpretending good sense and temper, without any of the beauty, grace, talent, accomplishment, and wit, to which a heroine of romance is supposed to have a prescriptive right'. This is a most interesting formal problem and Scott solved it triumphantly, for Jeannie Deans is indeed the embodiment of unadorned moral rectitude, while her exciting quest for justice – her determination to save her sister from being wrongly hanged as an infanticide – shows the possibility of true heroic action in the world.

Jeannie's is also a quest around which Scott manages to weave his concern with historical and social pressures – the disruptive Presbyterian ardour of the Covenanters embodied in Davie Deans, the vividly described Porteous Riots of 1736 which are one of the great achievements of early historical fiction, and the parallel implied with threats to social stability in contemporary Britain. Jeannie Deans herself, the personification of integrity, courage and feminine, domestic virtues, also portrays Scott's belief in the power of spoken language. Of her quest itself, she says: 'writing winna do it – a letter canna look, and pray, and beg, and beseech, as the human voice can do to the human heart'. Her climactic interview with the English queen does indeed secure a royal pardon in what is perhaps the most profoundly dramatic scene Scott ever wrote.

Scott's prolific output of full-length novels was to a considerable degree the result of his attempt to discharge the crippling bankruptcy caused by the crash of the publishing firm Constable in 1826. While this led to the writing of works of variable quality which survey English and Scottish history from the Middle Ages to Scott's own day, two of his finest works are the short stories contained in

Chronicles of the Canongate (1827). Both 'The Highland Widow' and 'The Two Drovers' are tragedies of national character plotted with the stark inexorability of the ballad.

Other writers were also to explore aspects of Scottish life. These include Susan Ferrier (1782–1854) in *Marriage* (1818) and *The Inheritance* (1824), and John Galt (1779–1839) in his *Annals of the Parish* (1821) and his portrait of a self-regarding small-town Machiavelli in *The Provost* (1822). *The Entail* (1823) shows Galt's ability to create scenes of pathos, melodrama and obsession, while John Lockhart's (1794–1854) accounts of Lowland life in *Adam Blair* (1822) and *Matthew Wald* (1824) also contain powerful moments of guilt and obsession. The greatest Scots study of religious mania remains however James Hogg's (1770–1835) *Private Memoirs and Confessions of a Justified Sinner* (1824), a powerful if sometimes crude melodrama of the diabolic effects wrought by Calvinism and the supernatural on an unstable character.

8

The astonishing popular success of Scott's novels – 1,000 copies of *Waverley* were sold within weeks, 2,000 within three months and 40,000 by 1829 – suggests the energy and entrepreneurial skill that were now going into the book trade. Such figures also indicate the ever-widening spread of literacy and a huge growth in the reading public.

This last was often commented on. The literary editor Henry Southern (1799–1853), for example, marvelled at the prospect 'of a whole nation, employing nearly all its leisure hours from the highest to the lowest rank in *reading*'. In an article for the *Edinburgh Review* in 1812, Jeffrey estimated that 200,000 of the 'middling classes' were regular readers, while the aristocracy contributed 20,000 more. Nor was literacy confined to these groups alone. The Presbyterian emphasis on Bible study had resulted in a Scottish educational system second to none, while the 1780s saw the growth of the Sunday School movement in England.

These evangelical initiatives were to be of the utmost social importance and found their leader in Hannah More (1745–1833) whose Religious Tract Society sold improving works in tens of thousands. These were distributed by the middle classes to the poor. A huge potential readership had been discovered, and where the saints went the scientists and publishers followed. Henry Brougham (1778–1868), the reforming Lord Chancellor, founded the Society for the Diffusion of Useful Knowledge in 1827 and, under the editorship of Charles Knight (1791–1873), 30,000 fortnightly parts of the *Library of Useful Knowledge* were sold at sixpence each.

Literacy created a market that mechanization was to feed. In particular, supplies of paper had to be greatly augmented. The result was a decline in quality as chemical additives supplemented the rags traditionally used in paper manufacture. By 1807, a French paper-making machine had been introduced to London, and the use of these Fourdrinier mills opened the way to mass production. Taxes on paper – introduced like those on newsprint to restrict the circulation of radical opinion during the Napoleonic Wars – nonetheless kept costs high. Although the levies were halved in 1836, the taxes themselves were not finally abolished until 1861. Again, while typesetting continued in its traditional form – highly regulated wages making this the most expensive element in production – iron presses were introduced as early as 1800. By the middle of the following decade, these were being driven by steam at the offices of *The Times* (founded 1785, so named 1788) which was now selling 8,000 copies a day. Finally, the introduction of lithography allowed for the mass reproduction of illustrations.

The publishers who capitalized on these developments were often men of high calibre, aware that their initiatives were replacing aristocratic patronage and concerned that theirs should be 'a liberal profession, and not a mere business of the pence'. They had taken over wholly from the printers as the dominant economic force in the trade and were prepared to take considerable risks, sometimes spectacularly paying the price for this. A publisher's borrowings could amount to £40,000 on the eve of his trade sale when the booksellers of London and Edinburgh were invited to a dinner and an auction of wares. It was hoped that such expenses would be quickly recouped, but where sales of a large cheap edition might bring the publisher substantial returns, the bookseller had to operate on the tightest margins.

He had to compete in a highly expensive market and against the popularity of the circulating libraries – institutions much used by Jane Austen and her family. He had also to be aware of the prices charged by his fellow traders who, after 1790, and following the initiative of James Lackington, no longer maintained fixed retail prices. Frequent attempts were made throughout the nineteenth century to secure booksellers' profits, but the Bookselling Regulations of 1829 proved impossible to enforce and, in an atmosphere favourable to free trade, unregulated market forces were to ruin many retailers.

The early decades of the nineteenth century saw the rise of two great figures in the publishing world: Archibald Constable (1774–1827) in Edinburgh and John Murray (1778–1843), a Scot who emigrated to found a dynasty in London. Each was to profit from a writer of genius – Constable from Scott and Murray from Byron.

In his full and readable if not always accurate *Life of Walter Scott* (1837–8), John Lockhart described Constable as 'the grand Napoleon of the realms of print'. Constable's rise and fall were indeed spectacular, the latter causing as much pain to the London book trade as it did to Scott himself. In the golden years before the crash however, Scott and Constable made each other's fortunes. Scott himself rightly regarded his novels as 'a mine of wealth' and Lockhart calculated his annual profit in the years around 1818 to have been in the region of £10,000. Constable also shared with Scott an interest in the indigenous literature of Scotland and, true to the Enlightenment traditions of Edinburgh, was for a time the proprietor of the *Encyclopaedia Britannica* (first edn 1768–71). Finally, *Constable's Miscellany* was to be an important leader in developments in cheap mass marketing.

John Murray acted for a while as Constable's London agent, but his move to Albemarle Street in 1812 signalled the foundation of one of the most distinguished literary meeting places in Regency London. Here Scott and Coleridge might rub shoulders with scientists like Sir Humphry Davy, while it was to the inner circle of this illustrious group that Byron was to write some of his most vivid letters.

The most impressive evidence of the desire for widespread and high-quality literary debate was the enormous success of the period's reviews.

Though the clerical wit Sidney Smith (1771–1845) quipped that he never read a book before reviewing it since 'it prejudices a man so', he and Francis Jeffrey were soon to discover that in the *Edinburgh Review* (founded 1802) they had an instrument of the greatest influence. Smith's own writings such as *Peter Plymley to [his] Brother Abraham Who Lives in the Country* (1808) reveal a humane satirist nourished by Enlightenment wit and love of liberty, and the *Edinburgh* itself (for all its mauling of the *Lyrical Ballads*) was to preserve an essentially liberal line.

Writing for the *Edinburgh* also laid the foundations of the careers of such men as Carlyle and the historian Thomas Babington Macaulay (1800–59) whose 22,000-word article on Milton suggests the range and scale that readers were prepared to tackle. When Jeffrey stated that he expected four people to read each copy of the 13,000 print run of the *Edinburgh*, it is possible to see the scale of its influence.

The doggedly productive Southey declared that 'the most profitable line of composition is reviewing', adding that an article in Murray's Tory *Quarterly Review* brought him more than his three-volume *History of Brazil* (1810–29). The Reviews did indeed pay exceptionally well and were an important source of writers' income. Jeffrey, for example, offered between ten and twenty guineas a sheet for an article. Flat fee arrangements with authors of books nonetheless remained common, publishers no doubt feeling them justified by their heavy investment in advertising, marketing and origination costs. Scott however helped open the way for the very considerable sums earned by later generations of novelists, selling rights to only one edition at a time and renegotiating fees for reprints. The Copyright Act of 1814 helped considerably here by extending the old fourteen-year term of renewal to twenty-eight years or the life of the author, whichever was the longer. When rights in a successful edition reverted to the author they could be resold at a considerable profit.

Such profits were partly assured by the very high price of books themselves. The three volumes of *Waverley* – a format which established the long reign of the 'three-decker' novel – retailed at a guinea each, while the volumes of *Kenilworth* (1821) were half as much again. Reprints were less dear, but it was only in the 1830s that cheap editions started to appear. Despite these prices, the early decades of the nineteenth century saw somewhere between 1,000 and 1,500 titles issued annually to a reading public that clamoured for new work. For example, 7,000 copies of Scott's *The Fortunes of Nigel* (1822) were sold by half-past ten on the morning of the book's publication.

Poetry too could be phenomenally successful. Here Scott again led the market, though others had earlier shown an interest in narrative verse. Southey, with an instinct he lacked the genius to exploit, set out to 'try the different mythologies that are almost new to poetry'. The sad result was several largely unreadable epics. Southey's earlier poetry suggests his radical enthusiasms, but his development towards banality and reaction is shown in the work Byron was to laugh into immortality: *A Vision of Judgement* (1821).

Byron described Samuel Rogers (1763–1855) as 'the last of the *best* school'. By this he meant Rogers was a poet in the eighteenth-century descriptive mode. *The Pleasures of Memory* (1792) gives the philosophy of Hartley a mildly pleasing, melancholy cast, while *Italy* (1822, 1828) is a blandly anecdotal work by a man happy enough with being a wealthy connoisseur and dreaming in his best-known lyric of happiness in 'a cot beside the hill'. Rogers's discursive mode was to be followed by Thomas Campbell (1777–1844) in his early work, but Campbell's battle pieces such as 'Hohenlinden' are far superior and may be interestingly compared with what remains the finest military elegy of the period, 'The Burial of Sir John Moore at Corunna' by Charles Wolfe (1791–1823). It was Scott however who was now to capture public taste spectacularly with his romances of Scottish history.

The best of Scott's narrative poems – *The Lay of the Last Minstrel* (1805), *Marmion* (1808) and *The Lady of the Lake* (1810) – draw on many resources to provide the escapist pleasures of romantic archaeology. Scott had known Percy's *Reliques* since his boyhood and had himself collected and edited the works in *Minstrelsy of the Scottish Border* (1802). He felt that medieval metrical romance provided freedom of form and the opportunity for introducing popular superstitions amid highly coloured descriptions of life led under 'the influence of a rude spirit of chivalry'.

A love of the Scottish landscape also underlies these densely plotted dramas. The result is history seen as a nostalgic yet thrilling arena for pageantry and lawless passion. Hero villains such as Marmion, guilt-ridden yet almost superhuman, become the focus of a 'harmless art' and an escape from the rigours of 'the iron time'. To the infinitely more serious Wordsworth, such poetry was culpably frivolous, and in his own narrative poem *The White Doe of Rylstone* (1815) he censured poets whose aim was 'pleasure light and fugitive'. Public taste – no necessary barometer of poetic worth – responded eagerly nonetheless. Twenty-eight thousand copies of *Marmion* were sold in four years, so preparing the way for that contemporary cult figure – the Byronic hero.

9

The poetry and brief, tumultuous career of George Gordon, sixth Baron Byron (1788–1824), offered writers across Europe a contradictory image of the artist as the dark-souled outsider, the misunderstood genius and the raffish aristocrat 'managing his pen', as Scott declared, 'with the careless and negligent ease of a man of quality'. Most influentially of all, Byron was seen as the heroic freedom-fighter, the poet who gave up his life to the cause of Greek liberty. Such potent variety made Byron a figure of almost mythic force throughout his career, while the 'Byronic' itself became a guarantee of all that was new, radical and dangerous.

The beginnings were inauspicious nonetheless. Byron's early collection *Fugitive Pieces* (1806) was voluntarily suppressed when accused of immorality, but was reissued in revised form as *Poems on Various Occasions* (1807). This was followed by his third volume, *Hours of Idleness* (1807), a collection of attitudinizing and often heavy-handed lyrics, much influenced by the popular sentimentalism seen in the *Irish Melodies* (1808–34) of Thomas Moore (1779–1852). The volume was savagely attacked by the *Edinburgh Review* and Byron responded with *English Bards and Scots Reviewers* (1809), a literary satire modelled on the imitations of Pope he found in such works as the *Baviad* (1794) and the *Maeviad* (1795) by William Gifford (1756–1826), editor of the *Quarterly*.

While much of Byron's early satire is clumsy to the point of gaucheness, it nonetheless declares his lasting contempt for what he considered the commonplace and conservative vulgarity of the 'Lake

Poets' – Southey, Coleridge and Wordsworth. Later, Byron would focus his magnificently comprehensive disdain for this generation in what remains his most successful poem: *The Vision of Judgement* (1822). Meanwhile, he published the work with which, as he later wrote, he woke to find himself famous.

The first two cantos of *Childe Harold's Pilgrimage* (1812) derive from Byron's Grand Tour through Portugal, Spain, Turkey and Greece. At their best they have the vividness of good travel writing and the exoticism captured in Byron's lyric to Theresa Macri, the 'Maid of Athens'. The loose 'Spenserian' style and lack of formal development however allow the work to descend into little more than an anthology of fashionable attitudes.

We hear the narrator's expression of libertarian ideals, his hatred of warfare, his contempt for the exploitative forces of the great European powers and his ardent wish that the suppressed Greek people should win their freedom. Such concerns were later to find more complex and mature expression, but for contemporaries, Byron's highly coloured radicalism was made particularly alluring by the figure of Childe Harold himself, 'the cheerless thing, the man without a friend'. Childe Harold – the bored, blasé aristocrat and cynical, melancholy outsider – was the first Byronic hero, and a figure often alluringly identified with Byron himself. In this he became his creator's passport to the glittering circles of the Regency Whig aristocracy. This was the world of one of Byron's finest lyrics, 'She walks in beauty like the night', of Lady Caroline Lamb and, eventually, of Byron's disastrous marriage.

It was in such a society, and 'amidst balls and fooleries', that Byron wrote the narrative poems which established his enormous contemporary popularity: *The Giaour* (1813), *The Bride of Abydos* (1813), *The Corsair* (1814), *Lara* (1814), *Parisina* (1816) and *The Siege of Corinth* (1816). In these frankly sensationalist and often clumsy works, a series of heroes 'warped by the world in Disappointment's school', give vent to their anarchically individualistic passions. They do so in highly melodramatic plots and amid escapist and usually Eastern worlds, worlds already explored in what Byron called 'Southey's unsaleables' and which were later sentimentalized in Moore's *Lalla Rookh* (1817).

The misanthropy, vengeance and sexual passion here owe something to Milton's Satan, to Scott, Mrs Radcliffe and Schiller. The heroes' guilt and haughty isolation also draw on Byron's own bizarre ancestry, his experiences of homosexuality (an illicit love for the choirboy Eddlestone was metamorphosed into the 'Thyrza' lyrics) and the likelihood of an incestuous relationship with his half-sister – a motif developed in *Parisina*. Nonetheless, despite appearing as a challenge to conservative, Burkeian precepts, these poems are remarkably free of any coherent ideological interest.

With the inevitable collapse of his marriage (bitterly evoked in the lines 'Fare Thee Well!') Byron came to identify himself ever more closely with his most famous creation. The third canto of *Childe Harold's Pilgrimage* (1816) nonetheless marks a considerable advance in technique. The Childe now becomes a focus for Byron's own misanthropic sense of intolerable wrong and his portrayal of suffering genius stirred to anger by contemporary politics. Napoleon – the faulted and humiliated hero – is seen as an *alter ego*, while Wellington and Waterloo (the ball before the battle is vividly evoked) suggest the ghastly glamour of war and the despotism being forced on Europe by the victors. In addition, mountain peaks and storm are apostrophized as the true haunt of genius – much to the irritation of Wordsworth who considered these passages to be merely laboured plagiarism – while the artist becomes the supreme embodiment of the Byronic ideal.

Byron's *Journal* and letters to his half-sister show how deeply the landscapes of Switzerland fed these troubled moods, just as they also offered the settings for two further works: *The Prisoner of Chillon* (1816) and *Manfred* (1817). At Chillon, Byron and Shelley had been told of the castle's most famous political prisoner, François Bonivard. Byron almost immediately worked this anecdote into his most successful non-satiric narrative poem. *The Prisoner of Chillon*, free of the irksome contempt for ordinary humanity so evident in the third canto of *Childe Harold*, portrays liberty and imprisonment, imaginative life and death, with an economy that gives true pathos to its final irony:

> At last men came to set me free;
> I asked not why, and recked not where;
> It was at length the same to me,

> Fettered or fetterless to be,
> I learned to love despair.

This power and coherence are largely absent from *Manfred*, the poet's attempt to give dramatic form to the Byronic hero's remorse for inexpiable crime. Byron himself described the work as being 'of a very wild, metaphysical, and inexplicable kind', but the piece is essentially a confused melodrama. Manfred himself, fallen from greatness to satanic evil, is presented as a superman divorced from nature's healing powers and Christian salvation. He is proud, independent, yet ultimately unconvincing.

While such hysterical tones are not wholly absent from the fourth canto of *Childe Harold's Pilgrimage* (1818), the best stanzas develop ideas already seen in *The Lament of Tasso* (1817). We are shown the triumph of true nobility over despotism and time, while, as a description of the sights of Italy, there is much here in the tradition of meditations among the ruins. Finally, the note of personal anguish often gains dignity from its philosophical context:

> But I have lived, and have not lived in vain:
> My mind may lose its force, my blood its fire,
> And my frame perish even in conquering pain,
> But there is that within me which shall tire
> Torture and Time, and breathe when I expire;
> Something unearthly, which they deem not of,
> Like the remembered tone of a mute lyre,
> Shall on their softened spirits sink, and move
> In hearts all rocky now the late remorse of love.

The possibilities of the *Childe Harold* mode had been fully exploited however. A re-reading of Pope helped convince Byron that he had long been on a false poetic path, while he also continued to disparage both the manner of Wordsworth and the luxurious effects now being sought by the 'Cockney school' of Keats and the radical Leigh Hunt.

Byron's true genius was being poured into his letters at this time. He had early achieved a mastery of expression in the form. His letters from Greece and Turkey are superior to anything in the first two cantos of *Childe Harold's Pilgrimage*, just as those from the period of his separation surpass the third section of that work. A letter to Moore describing carnival in Venice (a missive which included the excellent lyric 'We'll go no more a-roving') and others to Murray and his circle are among the finest works of early-nineteenth-century prose. In these remarkably vibrant pieces, Byron's mercurial intelligence, his subtlety and relish of life are caught with all the seemingly negligent brio of a great Regency gentleman. The style is the man. The problem was how to transfer it to poetry.

Worldly wit, melancholy and levity could be found in the work of Winthrop Mackworth Praed (1802–39), but it was *Whistlecraft* (1817–18) by Praed's Etonian friend John Hookham Frere (1796–1846) that provided the most fruitful solution. Here was a work written in imitation of Italian *ottava rima* burlesque. In *Beppo* (1818), this manner became Byron's own:

> Oh! that I had the art of easy writing
>   What should be easy reading! could I scale
> Parnassus, where the Muses sit indicting
>   Those pretty poems never known to fail,
> How quickly would I print (the world delighting)
>   A Grecian, Syrian, or *Ass*yrian tale;
> And sell you, mixed with western sentimentalism,
> Some samples of the finest Orientalism.
>
> But I am but a nameless sort of person,
>   (A broken Dandy lately on my travels)
> And take for rhyme, to hook my rambling verse on,
>   The first that Walker's Lexicon unravels,
> And when I can't find that, I put a worse on,
>   Not caring as I ought for critics' cavils;
> I've half a mind to tumble down to prose,
> But verse is more in fashion – so here goes!

The mocking ease and the satire of Byron's oriental mode, his tilt at commercialism and ironic self-deprecation are a wholly unexpected triumph. The dandy and the poet are finally one. Carefree but never careless, Byron is about to enjoy a preposterous tale of marital infidelity with a full awareness of how its freedoms would shock English readers into an awareness of their own corseted smugness.

This satiric technique was to find its fullest expression in the sixteen completed cantos of *Don Juan* (1819–24), the great comic epic of the early nineteenth century. Originally intended to be 'a little quietly facetious upon everything', *Don Juan* is a fluent and subtly observed exposure of what Byron saw as England's besetting vice: 'cant political, cant poetical, cant religious, cant moral'. Beyond this, the work is a celebration of natural impulse wittily tempered both by Byron the 'broken Dandy' as he narrates the poem and by his hero's own progress from adolescent innocence to the point where he becomes 'gradually *gâté* and *blasé*'.

The opening canto of *Don Juan* is a brilliant, vivid analysis of romantic passion – of the prudery that denies it, of the youthful ardour that over-idealizes it and, above all, of those little temptations and self-deceits which lead to the glorious comic climax in Donna Julia's bedroom and the pathos of her letter to Juan. In these last stanzas the narrator at once smiles and shows the tragedy in the situation. *Don Juan* as a whole is built on such subtle juxtapositions of the real and the ideal, a simultaneity of response in which the narrator's breadth of experience is the final stabilizing voice.

This technique is seen in the shipwreck scene with its combination of tragic heroism, selfishness and sheer practical comedy. It is in the love between Juan and Haidee however that Byron's approach is most fully justified. Here is a pagan, Mediterranean freedom, a feeling of joy which also inspired the passionate plea for political liberty in Byron's lyric 'The Isles of Greece'. We are shown a sexuality at once innocent and incandescent, treasured for the rapture with which it binds the ardent to nature, yet lamented and just a little laughed at by an ageing poet who knows such bliss is true but unrepeatable – a stage in life, something regretfully outgrown:

> A long long kiss, a kiss of youth, and love,
>   And beauty, all concentrating like rays
> Into one focus, kindled from above;
>   Such kisses as belong to early days,
> Where heart, and soul, and sense, in concert move,
>   And the blood's lava, and the pulse a blaze,
> Each kiss a heart-quake, – for a kiss's strength,
> I think, it must be reckon'd by its length.

What replaces such rapture is the experience of war. The central cantos of *Don Juan* describing the siege of Ismail are a remarkable and too neglected achievement. Here, with an impartiality which compares with Stendhal and Tolstoy, Byron suggests the barbarity, thrill and blood-lust of war, the incompetence of the generals who conduct it and the rapaciousness of the rulers who urge it. These passages are among the few and are by far the finest meditations on warfare in a period of almost continuous military engagement.

Byron's concern to 'sketch your world exactly as it goes' produces excellent satire, a telling variety of effect which, as Juan's saving of a little girl amid appalling scenes of genocide suggests, is far more than merely cynical. It is this depth and range of response – validated by the narrator's worldly wisdom – which also allow him to begin to portray a complex and sophisticated ideal of womanhood in Aurora Raby. Here, in the last cantos of the work, Byron's indignation at the self-serving cant of the English aristocracy is supported by a subtle social awareness and a narrative skill which verges on the verse novel.

The writing of so long and challenging a poem was attended by periods of doubt and delay, and such intervals were filled with experiments in different modes. Byron had shown in *Mazeppa* (1819) how an older man's recital of his youthful passions could at once highlight the folly and delight of these. A number of neo-classical tragedies on the man of virtue also date from this period, as does the provocative melodrama *Cain* (1821). However, standing out among these works is one undoubted masterpiece: *The Vision of Judgement*.

When, to commemorate the death of George III, Southey published *A Vision of Judgement* (1821), he used his position as Laureate to attack what he called the 'Satanic school' of poetry. This was a clear if oblique reference to Byron, but the response it elicited was far more than a retort to a personal snub. Taking Southey as its object, *The Vision of Judgement* is a comprehensive satire on early-nineteenth-century England – its poetic, political, moral and religious cant. Southey's fantasy of the dead king's ascent to heaven, his shaming of his radical enemies and their damnation are here turned on their head. A poem in which a smug renegade to conservatism took on the powers of celestial judgement and identified the deity with the status quo is laughed into absurdity. Byron's liberal scorn travesties Southey's ponderous epic machinery and technical experiments while also satirizing his politics and professional vulgarity.

Satan, metamorphosed into a great Regency aristocrat and largely indifferent to the fate of so little a thing as a king's soul, provides an unanswerable indictment of George III's pawky virtues and his complacent acceptance of all that ran counter to the great Whig principles of national and personal freedom. When Southey himself – the author of works both revolutionary and reactionary – shuffles on to the scene, we are shown how all the political and religious cant of a corrupt order is maintained by a renegade hack:

> He said – (I only give the heads) – he said,
>   He meant no harm in scribbling; 'twas his way
> Upon all topics; 'twas, besides, his bread,
>   Of which he butter'd both sides; 'twould delay
> Too long the assembly (he was pleased to dread)
>   And take up rather more time than a day,
> To name his works – he would but cite a few –
> Wat Tyler – Rhymes on Blenheim – Waterloo.

Byron's loathing of a corrupt system is focused in amused, magnificent scorn for poetic ineptitude and hypocrisy. A reading of Southey's *Vision* eventually puts the company to flight. Southey himself is thrown down to the Lakes, while George III finally slips into heaven more by luck than divine judgement. Personal revenge is here united with satire on political and religious humbug as a great poem effortlessly supplants a bad one – so effortlessly, indeed, that Leigh Hunt's brother was imprisoned for publishing it. *The Vision of Judgement* is a masterpiece of opposition and Byron's finest single achievement. But for Byron himself it could be no final answer. 'Who would write,' he once declared, 'who had anything better to do?' Throughout his life, Byron had yearned for action. Now there lay before him Greece, its war of independence and death at Missolonghi.

This was the tragic conclusion that was to transfigure Byron's life and verse into one of the supreme romantic myths. Across Europe, patriots such as Mazzini and painters and musicians as diverse as Turner, Delacroix, Schumann and Berlioz were all inspired by him. Poets and novelists from the Spanish Espronceda to the Russian Lermontov were profoundly influenced by his work, while Byron and the Byronic are central to two supreme European masterpieces:

Pushkin's *Eugene Onegin* and the second part of Goethe's *Faust*, where the death of Euphorion suggests a self-destructive idealism which is mourned but ultimately rejected. Only in his own country was Byron less honoured. Though he stands with Shakespeare and Scott among the British writers with the greatest influence on the mainland of Europe, Byron's place in Poets' Corner was not finally granted until 1969.

10

For Percy Bysshe Shelley (1792–1822), poets were 'the unacknowledged legislators of the world'. Behind this famous phrase lies Shelley's belief that poetry springs from the sublime faculty of the imagination which rouses sympathy and love. These last he thought of as the basis of the moral life and hence as the foundations of a just and worthy society. Such ideas inevitably led Shelley to conceive his own poetry as a radical inspiration to reform, a means of changing the world.

In his youthful Gothic romance *St Irvyne* (1810), one of the characters speaks for Shelley himself when he declares: 'I was now about seventeen: I had dived into the depths of metaphysical calculations.' Pliny, Lucretius, works of modern science and Enlightenment philosophy, all left an early mark on Shelley's mind, and *The Necessity of Atheism* (1811), the brief tract that caused him to be sent down from Oxford, shows a sceptical mind clearly influenced by Hume.

It was *Queen Mab* (1813) however, written after Shelley's elopement with Harriet Westbrook and his discovery of Godwin's work, that first revealed the true radical. Supplemented by explanatory notes on the reading that also underlay his *Declaration of Rights* (1812) and *Refutation of Deism* (1814), *Queen Mab* is a long visionary poem which emphasizes how the 'Spirit of Nature' pulses in all people and makes an absurdity of selfishness and pride. The soul should impart joy rather than seek to dominate. War, religion, capitalist exploitation and even a carnivorous diet are all shown as corrosive forces, while in lines that underscore Shelley's entire thinking, he declared:

> Power, like a desolating pestilence,
> Pollutes whate'er it touches; and obedience,
> Bane of all genius, virtue, freedom, truth,
> Makes slaves of men, and, of the human frame
> A mechanized automaton.

By contrast, the free and innocent mind, no longer fearing death and hell, and untroubled by sexual and political coercion, will virtuously pursue 'the gradual paths of an aspiring change'. Here was a message that, despite its moments of adolescent posturing, was profoundly to influence radicals from Robert Owen (1771–1858) onwards. *Queen Mab* is thus a challenge to public reform.

Shelley's commitment to community was deeply felt, but in *Alastor, or The Spirit of Solitude* (1816) he explored its reverse in a powerful symbolic narrative which shows the lethal effects of 'self-centred seclusion' on a young poet of genius. In pursuit of knowledge and his image of the ideal, the nameless hero of the work ignores his social existence. He also rejects the realities of sexual desire as proffered love is shunned for a more ethereal passion. Enmeshed in such destructive fantasies, the youth runs despairing across the world and, in his exhilarating but solipsistic anguish, eventually dies, the tragic victim of the perils of idealism.

A similar awareness of the dangers of isolated intensity is clear in *Frankenstein* (1818) by Mary Wollstonecraft Shelley (1797–1851). The poet had met her at the home of her father William Godwin, the philosopher whom Shelley so prized but who was to cause him much irksome financial embarrassment. By June 1814, the couple had declared their love and travelled to Switzerland, a journey recorded in their joint *History of a Six Weeks' Tour* (1817). In 1816 however, accompanied by Mary's half-sister Claire Clairmont – a mistress of Byron's and the mother of his child – Shelley and Mary visited Geneva where they met Byron himself. It was during this visit that Mary had the nightmare which led to her writing her first novel.

Though she was to write futuristic works such as *The Last Man* (1826) and several historical fictions, *Frankenstein* is the work on which Mary Shelley's fame rests. Mannered and fustian though her style often is, her father's themes of social justice and the pursuer pursued, as well as her husband's scientific and philosophical interests, are here welded into one of the great myths of spiritual isolation. Frankenstein creates the monster in an obsessive mood, and its ugliness causes it to be ostracized. In his lonely agony, the monster yearns for love and insists Frankenstein create a mate for him. 'Everywhere I see bliss, from which I alone am irrevocably excluded. I was benevolent and good; misery made me a fiend. Make me happy, and I shall again be virtuous.' Though Frankenstein responds, he eventually destroys his new creation and the monster kills Frankenstein's bride in revenge. Creator and created, both now murderers, become pursuer and pursued. Amid the Arctic wastes, the monster claims Frankenstein as his last victim and slopes off to die. Isolation, ostracism and egotism have paid their terrible price.

A number of poems in Shelley's 'Esdaile Notebook' reveal how his early work was deeply influenced by Wordsworth. *Alastor* is in part a criticism of the Wordsworthian 'egotistical sublime', and Shelley's second journey through Switzerland reveals his continued questioning of the nature mysticism of both Coleridge and Wordsworth himself. For example, where Coleridge in his 'Hymn before Sunrise in the Vale of Chamouni' (adapted from a German original, 1802) had stood 'entranced in prayer' to worship the benevolent power of God, Shelley's meditation 'Mont Blanc' (1816) is altogether less reassuring. Through the very intensity of Shelley's observation, the mountain becomes a complex, shifting symbol of the amoral world of nature, and it chastens the poet into a realization of the unbridgeable gap between the mind of man and the might of God.

Shelley's 'Hymn to Intellectual Beauty' (1816) shows the supreme importance of imaginative inspiration to his work. In its description of heightened but evanescent awareness, the 'Hymn' describes 'the interpenetration of a divine nature' through our own. For Shelley, such revelations were 'the best and happiest moments of the happiest and best minds', and in *The Defence of Poetry* he was later to show how their record constituted the very basis of his art.

On his return to England, and in the agonizing period after the suicide of his first wife Harriet and his loss of custody of their children, Shelley wrote *A Proposal for Putting Reform to the Vote throughout the Kingdom* (1817), publishing it under the pseudonym 'the Hermit of Marlow'. Written in a period of acute social stress when many were urging the reform of a Parliament that was about to repeal the

Habeas Corpus Act, Shelley's pamphlet was a request for an open discussion of the constitution and a Godwinian appeal 'to proceed gradually and with caution'.

It was during this period at Marlow that Shelley also developed his acquaintance with Leigh Hunt, Keats, Hazlitt and, above all, Thomas Love Peacock. Discussions with Peacock especially drew on a range of issues to create a rich and diverse approach to literature. In general, a stand was taken against the influence of the German thought popularized by Mme de Staël in *De l'Allemagne* (1810–13) and which now found its chief spokesman in Coleridge. The work of the 'Lake School' itself was seen as reactionary, solipsistic and narrowly Christian. In its place came a critical, often comic, classically Greek and pagan ethos, a view resolutely opposed to institutional repression.

In Shelley's fragmentary 'Essay on Christianity' (?1817), the 'otherness' and unknowability of God are again asserted, since 'where indefiniteness ends idolatry and anthropomorphism begin'. These last are shown to lead to a repressive priesthood who 'have not failed to attribute to the universal cause a character analogous to their own'. Included in such repressive attitudes was a negative view of sex. In Peacock's mediocre poem *Rhododaphne* (1818), society and self-repression destroy sexual happiness, but in Shelley's *The Revolt of Islam* (1818) erotic freedom is united with political liberty.

The twelve cantos of Shelley's poem are clearly directed to the central political issue of the age: the ugly collapse of the French Revolution and the reactionary beliefs consequent on this. Shelley's Preface obliquely but significantly points to Wordsworth and Coleridge as the prime literary embodiments of this view in England. By contrast, his own poem is a densely wrought fable designed to rekindle enthusiasm for bloodless revolution, for free and fulfilling sexual passion (in the original version the artificiality of restraint was emphasized by the hero and heroine being brother and sister), for ardent feminism and for idealistic social commitment.

In *The Revolt of Islam*, the French Revolution is optimistically rewritten as the newly liberated inhabitants of the Golden City hymn wisdom, beauty and equality at a vegetarian feast. Although such happiness is brutally wrecked by the forces of reaction when Laon and Cythna themselves are sacrificed, they finally ascend to the realm of the ideal and take their place among the 'mighty senate' who will forever inspire freedom and the belief that love is 'the sole law which should govern the moral world'. The victory of the tyrants is a hollow one, and the collapse of such shameful grandeur was again memorably expressed in Shelley's most famous sonnet, 'Ozymandias' (written 1818). Here, battered fragments of the ancient Egyptian art Shelley had seen in the British Museum become an image for tyranny and its vain boast of power.

Early in 1818, Shelley and his immediate circle left England for ever, and it was in Italy – the 'Paradise of exiles' – that Shelley's greatest works were written. This was, nonetheless, a time of profound personal crisis. There were delicate and difficult negotiations with Byron over Claire's child, the death of Shelley's own children and friction between himself and Mary. The 'Lines Written among the Euganean Hills' (written 1818), with their cycles of personal and social death and rebirth, their contrasts of despair with thrilling if transitory illuminations of nature and political hope, suggest the divisions in Shelley's own mind and his longing for a repose 'far from passion, pain and guilt'.

In *Julian and Maddalo* (written 1818), Shelley created a highly sophisticated poem from his contact with Byron. The work has great psychological, intellectual and technical originality, and shuns both the explicit and the openly didactic. While Julian is a representation of the idealistic Shelley and Maddalo of the cynical Byron, the poem suggests the greater complexity that underlies both figures. We are made to feel the interaction of two very different men whose clash of temperaments suggests irreconcilable views of the world.

The Gothic figure of the restrained lunatic in the poem – a character powerfully suggestive of the fears and idealisms that lie below the surface of every man – becomes a focus of interest for both Julian and Maddalo. He does not validate the views of either however. When Julian returns to the scene many years later he finds Maddalo's daughter grown to beautiful womanhood, but the secrecy that surrounds her account of the lunatic's faith and Julian's own silence on the point deepen the poem's concern with the essential unknowableness of other minds, the continuities and chasms in our social lives. *Julian and Maddalo* is an extraordinary and very complex achievement which points forward to the verse soliloquies of Browning. Only the sprightly and idealistic 'Letter to Maria Gisborne' (written 1820) surpasses the work in the technical dexterity of its couplets.

Shelley's greatest achievement from this period was his Aeschylean drama *Prometheus Unbound* (1820). No work more comprehensively focuses Shelley's rapturous lyric impulse and epic voice, his esoteric learning and mythopoeic imagination, his classicism and political idealism. *Prometheus Unbound* is an exultant work in praise of humankind's potential, and Shelley himself recognized it as 'the most perfect of my products'. However, he advised Leigh Hunt that it was written 'only for the elect', and Mary Shelley added that 'it requires a mind as subtle and penetrating as his own to understand the mystic meanings scattered throughout'.

This is a wise warning. The airy complexities of *Prometheus Unbound* make it resistant to brief analysis. Nonetheless, the refusal of the suffering Titan to give way to external force or inner despair, his acceptance of the punishment inflicted by Jupiter and the heroic idealism by which he renounces revenge and declares, 'I wish no living thing to suffer pain', are all profoundly stirring. The giant who represents the creative power of the human mind – this Jesus-like figure who suffers for the world he would redeem – finally breaks the cycle of 'the despot's rage, the slave's revenge'. His moral victory marks an epoch in the history of the world and, with the fall of Jupiter, Prometheus himself becomes the ideal representative of a new order of forgiveness and of man:

> Equal, unclassed, tribeless, and nationless,
> Exempt from awe, worship, degree, the king
> Over himself; just, gentle, wise.

The ideals of the French Revolution have here been established not through bloodshed but by the exercise of a full humanity.

The heroism by which Prometheus becomes 'the type of the highest perfection of moral and intellectual nature' also prepares him for love, for what, in the Platonic wording of *The Defence of Poetry*, Shelley was to call 'a going out of our nature, and an identification of ourselves with the beautiful'. This ideal is symbolized in the magnificent figure of Asia, the incarnation of Celestial Venus, veiled, dazzling and resplendent in the glorious pageant of her descent to earth. The rapturous celebrations of the fourth act of *Prometheus Unbound*, held after the union of Asia and Prometheus, are among the supreme creations of English lyric poetry. We are present at a cosmic dance where 'Love ... folds over the world its healing wings.' As Demogorgon, the voice of destiny, surveys the triumph of freedom, so words at once celebratory and admonitory give expression to Shelley's most deeply held convictions:

> To suffer woes which Hope thinks infinite;
> To forgive wrongs darker than death or night;
>   To defy Power, which seems omnipotent;
> To love, and bear; to hope till Hope creates
> From its own wreck the thing it contemplates;
>   Neither to change, nor falter, nor repent;
> This, like thy glory, Titan, is to be
> Good, great and joyous, beautiful and free;
> This is alone Life, Joy, Empire, and Victory.

Where *Prometheus Unbound* is an esoteric work in praise of the ideal, *The Cenci* (1820) is a powerful tragedy in the Jacobean mode which focuses on the corruption of society as this was mirrored in sixteenth-century Rome. *The Cenci* is the only tragedy of the period to rise to a measure of real greatness, and in the heroine Beatrice, Shelley created a compelling figure whose native idealism is corrupted by the world of her incestuous father. Just as Cenci's manic obsession with sin drives him to the most repulsive refinements of sexual depravity, so Beatrice's moral rectitude hardens to the 'pernicious mistake' of mass murder and revenge. She loses her humanity in a brutal world and, in the final tragic heightening of the drama, comes to realize that by vowing vengeance she has been at one with the depraved. The idealism of *Prometheus Unbound* is here horribly inverted.

The Cenci was the only work of Shelley's to have an authorized reprinting in his lifetime, but two further pieces were deliberately composed for a popular audience at a period of national crisis: *The Masque of Anarchy* (1819) and *Oedipus Tyrannus, or Swellfoot the Tyrant* (1820). The latter is the lesser of the two works, though as a satire on the scandalous divorce of George IV (1820–30) it was immediately withdrawn on threats of prosecution from the Society for the Suppression of Vice. *The Masque of Anarchy* is an altogether more interesting work. It was written in horrified reaction to the 'Peterloo massacre' when armed troops rode down a large but peaceful demonstration for reform. Shelley saw such despotism as anarchy itself, the reactionary hysteria that shouts, 'I am God, and King, and Law!' The soil of England calls on the people to rise up and, by peacefully demanding their rights, to shame the murderers by their moral and numerical superiority.

Shelley's populist enthusiasms were again expressed in 'Men of England' which was later to become a rallying song of the British Communist Party. In *A Philosophic View of Reform* (1819) however Shelley developed his views on a broader basis. He gave a prose account of the historical analysis offered in his 'Ode to Liberty' (written 1820) and an expression of his belief that the great upsurge of creative writing in early-nineteenth-century England was a presentiment of national reform, an idea that he was again to develop in *The Defence of Poetry*. Shelley also advanced his radical views on the redistribution of wealth and his faith in that gradual process of emancipation whereby 'the people may become habituated [to] exercising the functions of sovereignty, in proportion as they acquire the possession of it'.

Shelley's political enthusiasms spilled over into a number of his shorter poems, works which reveal him as one of the most varied and expert artificers of lyric poetry. He had a technical mastery even Wordsworth could admire, and slight but exquisite pieces such as 'To Constantia, Singing', 'To Night' and 'With a Guitar, to Jane' long helped to foster a view of Shelley as merely 'the beautiful and ineffectual angel' of Matthew Arnold's phrase. 'Stanzas Written in Dejection near Naples' have a desolation that just avoids self-pity, while Shelley's 'Ode' to that city is a Pindaric hymn to her short-lived republican constitution. Outside *Prometheus Unbound* however, Shelley's supreme lyric is his 'Ode to the West Wind' (written 1819).

The poem is written in the *terza rima* form Shelley derived from his reading of Dante, a form which the relative paucity of rhymes in English makes exceptionally difficult to use. The nervous thrill of Shelley's response to nature however is here transformed through the power of art and imagination into a longing to be united with a force at once physical and prophetic. Perhaps no nature poem of the period more surely expresses the primal amorality of nature itself, its maenad fury and pagan ruthlessness. Here is no conservative reassurance, no comfortable mysticism. Shelley's ode is a damaged spirit's invocation to a primitive deity, a plea to exalt him in its fury and trumpet the radical prophecy of hope and rebirth.

Shelley declared that 'I always seek in what I see the manifestation of something beyond the present and tangible object.' In 'The Cloud' (1820), advanced meteorology and esoteric imagery create a Platonic symbol of the spirit of man born of the world yet a 'nursling of the Sky', a force of beauty and regeneration. In the less explicit symbolism of 'To a Skylark' (1820), Shelley achieved a more subtle work. The bird, suspended between reality and poetic image, pours forth an exultant song which suggests to the poet both celestial rapture and human limitation – the plight of the poet himself who must learn what he can of inspired truth from the natural world.

The Platonic element in Shelley's thought is seen in a number of somewhat abstruse poems from this period. In *The Sensitive Plant* (written 1820, published posthumously), mankind is compared to the mimosa, a delicate and rather plain flower which 'desires what it has not, the Beautiful'. In its garden world of mutability, a place where even the lovely woman who tends it is subject to death, a belief in the timeless forms of Beauty and Truth – in Platonic archetypes beyond the world of appearance – is seen as a modest yet sustaining creed. *The Witch of Atlas* (written 1820, published posthumously), in a poem full of Shelley's mythological learning, is an embodiment of the Ideal and of the forces that can lift man above spiritual slavery. Shelley is here concerned to show the playful operation of these powers, and his poem itself is capricious to the point of being irksome – a view expressed by many readers from Mary Shelley onwards.

Mary's silence about *Epipsychidion* (1821) is also revealing, since what she was later to call Shelley's 'Pisan Platonics' is an account of the poet's search for the human embodiment of his ideal (here Emilia Viviani or the 'Emily' of the poem) and of his own sexual career. The result is a revealing but fervid and sometimes over-compensatory mix of Dantesque erotic idealism and free love, Platonism and penetration. For all its attack on the restrictions of convention, its soaring idealism and Shelley's closing assertion that art is the final achievement of erotic pursuit, he was soon to ask for the work to be suppressed.

The months after the publication of *Epipsychidion* saw the production of two supreme works in which Shelley's views of the nature of poetry and the role of the poet were given their most profound treatment. In *Peter Bell the Third* (written 1819, published posthumously), Shelley had already given comic expression to the corrupt society of bigots, money-makers, right-wing critics and dull, turncoat versifiers who destroy poetry. As a satire on Wordsworth especially, this is a trenchant piece. However, in 1820, Peacock published his *Four Ages of Poetry* where – half seriously and half in jest – he developed the Enlightenment view that the efficacy of poetry declines as society becomes more advanced. Peacock urged that the sciences should take poetry's place since literature's appeal to the emotions (especially in the hands of the 'Lake School') was too often a mask for political reaction and intellectual obscurity. 'Poetry', in short, 'is the mental rattle that awakened the attention of the intellect in the infancy of society.' Shelley's answer to this utilitarian critique – an answer not fully available until its publication in 1840 – was the triumphant praise of the imagination contained in *The Defence of Poetry* (written 1821).

Shelley here accepts that, in common with government, law and scientific advance, poetry has its origins in the synthesizing powers of the imagination rather than mere analytical reasoning. He asserts however that of these activities only poetry does not clog and shackle the spirit. 'We have more moral, political, and historical wisdom than we know how to reduce into practice,' he wrote, adding: 'Man having enslaved the elements remains himself a slave.' Poetry alone can free man and offer the mind a wider view of its powers.

Shelley suggests that, of all the arts, poetry is the least hampered by its own material, for unlike paint and stone, metrical language especially 'is a more direct representation of the actions and passions of our internal being'. It is through language that the imagination most readily apprehends the ideal order of truth. The moment of poetic inspiration is 'the interpenetration of a divine nature through our own'. Evanescent as this experience may be, poetry preserves and communicates these 'visitations of divinity', kindling the imagination of its readers and stirring a loving overflow of our nature, a heightening of moral awareness.

Great poetry in thus going out to the world is a social force, 'the most unfailing herald, companion, and follower of the awakening of a great people to work a beneficial change'. The great poet himself 'not only beholds intensely the present as it is, and discovers those laws according to which present things ought to be ordered, but he beholds the future in the present, and his thoughts are the germs of the flower and the fruit of the latest time'. By rousing others to an intimation of the ideal, poets are at once prophets and legislators, the supreme fulfilments of the human mind glimpsing its divine potential and laying down for others the means of attaining to this. What for Peacock was the baby's rattle Shelley heard as the trumpet blast of a golden future, the triumph of the spirit over a material world. Such is also the theme of his most nearly perfect work: *Adonais* (1821).

This poem is an elegy for John Keats whose early death from tuberculosis Shelley believed had been hastened by hostile reviews. A cancelled passage from the Preface rightly suggests that the reviewers themselves had been motivated by political bias masquerading as snobbery. In *Adonais*, these men become the embodiments of philistin- ism and reaction, the enemies of truth. Shelley's work, by contrast, illustrates his belief that great poetry rouses others to a state of divine inspiration. This the poem achieves by bringing together the founda- tions of Shelley's art into a work at once subtle and sublime. The Spenserian stanza, used from the time of the 'Esdaile Notebook' and *The Revolt of Islam*, is here given a weight and speed that are purely Shelley's own. Again, just as in 'Lycidas' Greek and Judaeo-Christian elements are combined, so *Adonais* absorbs these into what Shelley had learned of the sublime from Dante and Milton himself.

In the first part of the poem, personifications realized with the utmost physical acuteness lament the hero and the annihilation of a young genius by the philistines. Keats's thoughts and the objects of his thoughts swell to a universal lament, a wailing like that of the worshippers in the ancient world for whom the death of Venus' beloved Adonis (the mythical basis of Shelley's poem) was a prelude to the desolation of winter. Nonetheless, the world revives with the returning year. Shelley's celebration of vernal life has a pagan force unmatched outside the Greek and Latin classics and his own 'Ode to the West Wind'. The body of Adonais however rots and blossoms in this mutable world of nature and spring:

> The leprous corpse, touched by the spirit tender,
> Exhales itself in flowers of gentle breath.

The corpse is mourned by Urania (Venus in her embodiment as heavenly love, astronomy and divine inspiration) and by the shepherds, or Keats's poetic peers. Shelley himself, 'a pardlike Spirit beautiful and swift', also comes to the tomb and, in the tragedy of young idealism destroyed, recognizes his own fate as one condemned by the world.

And it is Shelley the poet, inspired by the thought of Keats and his art, who now rises above mourning to affirm that Keats's spirit, safe from 'the contagion of the world's slow stain', has been returned to the divine power that throbs through the mutable world but is itself beyond change. Shelley here conveys an unsurpassed sense of cosmic rapture and spiritual power as he suggests how the imagination wins humankind's birthright – a place in the divine world of truth. Poetry becomes a dying into a greater life, and in the sublime concluding stanza it is poetry's kindling of imaginative sympathy and love which raises Shelley himself to that celestial sphere whither the soul of Keats beckons him:

> The breath whose might I have invoked in song
> Descends on me; my spirit's bark is driven,
> Far from the shore, far from the trembling throng
> Whose sails were never to the tempest given;
> The massy earth and sphered skies are riven!
> I am borne darkly, fearfully, afar;
> Whilst, burning through the inmost veil of Heaven,
> The soul of Adonais, like a star,
> Beacons from the abode where the Eternal are.

This stanza is Shelley's supreme assertion of the individual's intimation of immortality. In *Hellas*, a lyric drama modelled on *The Persians* of Aeschylus and published in 1822 to encourage British support for the Greek War of Independence, the Athenian ideal of political liberty tempered by charity is seen as the one value to be treasured in the fluctuating world of power politics. The unfinished *Charles the First* however appears to be more sceptical about political motives.

This was indeed a period of the greatest stress and disillusion for Shelley. He was becoming increasingly jealous and contemptuous of

Byron, while 'When passion's trance is overpast' suggests difficulties with Mary that were to cause the ever suggestible poet to turn to Jane Williams, for whom he was to write some of his most pleasing lyrics. Nonetheless, 'I feel too little certainty of the future, and too little satisfaction with regard to the past, to undertake any subject seriously and deeply,' Shelley wrote. Yet it is this very disillusion which is combated by Rousseau in Shelley's last but unfinished poem *The Triumph of Life* (written 1822). Rousseau here reveals himself as a man in whom views of the ideal have been eclipsed. As a result, he has been largely subdued by the turbid cruelty and lust of the world, forces which Shelley powerfully suggests in his Dantesque description of life's degrading but triumphant procession. Nonetheless, some meaning and purpose must be sought here:

> 'Then, what is life?' I cried.

The poem breaks off at this point, its great, unanswerable question for ever poised above silence.

Shelley himself was now planning to cross the Bay of Spezia and welcome Leigh Hunt to Italy, but his boat was caught in a sudden squall and went down. There was little to identify Shelley's body when it was eventually found save for his nankeen trousers and a volume of Keats's poems folded back in his jacket pocket.

II

In 'Sleep and Poetry', one of his earliest published verses, John Keats (1795–1821) declared:

> O for ten years, that I may overwhelm
> Myself in poesy; so I may do the deed
> That my own soul has to itself decreed.

Tragically, far less than the hoped-for time was allotted him, but in the brief half-decade of his creativity Keats not only composed the mighty handful of poems that eventually secured his posthumous fame but wrote a volume of letters which provide the most compelling self-portrait.

Keats's sonnet 'On First Looking into Chapman's Homer' exactly conveys the intense literary excitement – the feeling of new worlds opening – that underlies his *Poems* of 1817. It also suggests two of Keats's most important imaginative resources: the mythic world of ancient Greece and the English poetry of the sixteenth and seventeenth centuries. Keats's interest in these fields was shared with the friends to whom he wrote his early verse epistles. These included the minor versifier G.F. Mathew (b. 1795) and the more substantial figure of John Hamilton Reynolds (1794–1852), author of *The Garden of Florence* (1821) as well as of a shrewd parody of what he guessed to be the manner of Wordsworth's 'Peter Bell'. In addition, there was Charles Brown (1787–1842) with whom Keats was later to collaborate on the tragedy *Otho the Great* (1819) and Charles Cowden Clarke (1787–1877) who was to introduce Keats to Leigh Hunt (1784–1859) and his circle in Hampstead.

Hunt the radical journalist and minor poet was a vital influence on the early Keats, developing his taste not only for liberal politics but for the fine arts, for the narratives of the Italian Middle Ages – Hunt's own *Tale of Rimini* (1816) is his best-known work in this form – and for a view of poetry in which prettified natural description and a light and somewhat commonplace sensuality create an essentially escapist aesthetic. It was what the reviewers saw as the political and social threat in this combination – its liberal politics and sexuality allied to a use of classical mythology by men who had never been to a university – which inspired *Blackwood's Magazine*'s notorious attack on Keats, Hunt and 'the Cockney School of poetry'.

Hunt himself described Keats's genius as characterized by 'energy and voluptuousness, each able at will to take leave of each other, and possessing, in their union, a high feeling of humanity'. In the *Poems* of 1817, this union was only fitfully achieved. Neither 'I stood tiptoe' nor 'Sleep and Poetry' – the two most substantial works in the volume – avoids a cloying vulgarity. Nonetheless, Keats's awareness of his own potential and his intuition that in myth especially the poetic imagination could lift the world of experience to the realms of the ideal prefigure later achievements.

Keats's realization of the empathic power of the imagination was to be of the greatest consequence to his work and was a faculty which, as his thought and technique matured, led him to his most profound insights. Already it was his credo. 'I am certain of nothing', he wrote to his friend Benjamin Bailey in 1817, 'but of the holiness of the Heart's affections and the truth of the Imagination – What the Imagination seizes as Beauty must be truth.'

With *Endymion* (1818), Keats tried to create the great literary work of truth and beauty, the 'joy for ever' which he held to be mankind's defence against spiritual death. An early sonnet 'Written in Disgust of Vulgar Superstition' claimed that Sunday church bells rang the knell of Christianity, and *Endymion* attempts to replace supposedly worn-out forms of worship with an innocent and sensuous paganism. In the poem, human love and ideal beauty (the shepherd hero and the moon goddess) are eventually one. Despite stylistic absurdities – kisses are 'slippery blisses' while breasts are 'milky sovereignties' – Keats has here contrasted an exquisitely realized Arcadian landscape against a reactionary present, and art and imagination have been set against conventional morality. This was a partial achievement for which he was to be violently attacked. Wordsworth drily dismissed the lines from the work Keats recited to him as 'a very pretty piece of paganism'. For the reviewers of *Blackwood's*, the *Quarterly Review* and the *British Critic*, Keats's poem was a vulgar affront to morality, a threat to the beleaguered status quo. Aesthetic limitations were made to serve political polemic.

But Keats's own ideas were developing rapidly beyond what he called the 'Chamber of Maiden Thought'. At the close of 1817, while he was finishing *Endymion*, he was becoming aware of the artist's need for more complex experience. He now set out in a letter his concept of 'Negative Capability', that necessary creative state 'where man is capable of being in uncertainties, mysteries, doubts, without any irritable reaching after fact & reason'. Sensation and empathy lead 'the chameleon poet' to that state of intensity in which he 'has as much delight in conceiving an Iago as an Imogen'.

The purely aesthetic elements in this stance, the belief that beauty alone is a sufficient end for art, was soon to prove unsatisfactory. The artist's very ability to see deeply into the nature of things brings him face to face with the reality of suffering. By March 1818, in his epistle 'To John Hamilton Reynolds', Keats described how he had seen all too distinctly into the heart of 'an eternal fierce destruction'. This was a truth his poetry would now have to accommodate. Beside love and beauty stood suffering and death.

These are the themes of Keats's Italian tale *Isabella, or The Pot of Basil* (1820). The form had been made popular by Leigh Hunt among others, and in the same year as Keats's poem 'Barry Cornwall' or Bryan Waller Proctor (1787–1874) issued his *Sicilian Story*, a slight work which uses the same melodramatic narrative from Boccaccio as *Isabella*.

For Keats, Boccaccio's tale, in which the sister and an employee of two proud and heartless capitalists fall in love and so rouse the fury of the brothers that they murder the young man and bury him secretly in the forest, was a means of opposing ideal tenderness to a mercenary world. The first half of the poem contains a powerful indictment of commercial exploitation. In the second half, Isabella's discovery of Lorenzo's body, and her severing of its head and hiding it in a pot of basil, which the brothers then steal, lead to her madness. Such scenes offered considerable scope for Grand Guignol and pathos. Though Keats exploited these with an effect he was soon to dismiss as 'mawkish', *Isabella* is an important attempt to suggest the coexistence of beauty and suffering.

In the first version of *Hyperion* (written 1818–19), these themes are raised to a cosmic level. Light *ottava rima* is replaced by an individual and magnificent reworking of Miltonic grandeur. Keats's poem is an attempt to give epic dignity to inwardness and subjectivity. What he called 'the grand march of intellect' had brought contemporary poetry to a fresh awareness of the workings of the imagination, but it had done so at what seemed to be the cost of epic grandeur and objectivity. *Hyperion* was Keats's attempt to give just such an epic and objective account of the rise of the new forces of perception. To achieve this, he turned once again to myth.

In the ancient tale of the overthrow of the Titans by the Olympian gods, Keats found a vehicle for his optimistic view of evolutionary improvement. 'All civilized countries', he wrote, 'become gradually more enlighten'd and there should be a continual change for the better.' Progress leads to the replacement of an old order by a younger and superior one. For Keats, this inevitably meant the triumph of his own ideals, and Oceanus's long speech to the fallen Titans in the second book asserts

> the eternal law
> That first in beauty should be first in might.

It is on this basis that Apollo eventually rises to power.

Keats's depiction of the fallen Titans in the opening books has a hushed and monumental magnificence, just as the portrayal of the anguished Hyperion suggests the paranoia of a threatened dictator. The fear of this upholder of a threatened order is a remarkable achievement, but it is in his depiction of the young Apollo as he aspires to divinity that Keats's art is seen straining at its limits. Here, as the god of poetry and healing dies into his new life of rapt and intuitive empathy with the world of suffering and beauty, so Keats provides a heroic image of the birth of a new sensibility. We see the poet as a deity whose imaginative strength will be the foundation of a new order.

The fragmentary third book of *Hyperion* ends on the boundaries of the imaginative divine. In *The Eve of Saint Agnes* (1820), the triumph of the visionary and loving over the spiritually inert is finally assured.

The poem opens and closes with death: the Gothic beadsman spectral in his life-denying piety and the sin and ashes of an unwanted, conventional faith. Contrasted to him in this precisely observed yet headily sensuous poem – a work in which highly realized physical detail effortlessly partakes of symbolism – are the vulgar rout of party-goers and the chaste and lovely Madeline. We see the heroine of the work lost to the world in the erotic fantasies promised to those young virgins who correctly perform the rituals of St Agnes's Eve. At the heart of the poem lies Keats's concern with how these dreams, innocent but solipsistic, can merge with the physical reality of Madeline's adored and ardent Porphyro. The ideal will thereby be joined with the real, the imagined with the actual, man with woman.

Porphyro's heedless entry into his enemies' house and his persuading of the ancient Angela to bring him to Madeline's bedroom are the active principle in this union. Through masculine assertion, the young lover wins his way into an erotic paradise of supreme sensual richness and refinement, a place of moonlit stained glass, rustling silk and music. But the union of the lovers has also been unwittingly prepared for by Madeline herself. After she rises from her bed 'like a missioned spirit, unaware' and helps old Angela's steps, she hovers on the borders of dream and reality. When Porphyro's music wakens her, so she moves from virgin fantasy to sudden and painful disillusion. The real world is less attractive than dream. Finally however the physical reality of Porphyro blends with Madeline's imaginings. Sexuality and imaginative vision join in a moment of sublime ardour. Thus united, they affirm the world with an abundance beyond anything known to the party guests, to Angela or to the beadsman – the forces of worldliness and restraint who are left to nightmare and death as the lovers flee.

Where *The Eve of Saint Agnes* shows the triumph of love and imagination, 'La Belle Dame sans Merci' – Keats's second great poem in the Gothic mode – chillingly suggests the destructive power of the erotic and of dream itself. At the heart of passion the knight finds death, and he is left to wander in a waste land of the spirit. The vivid but desolate natural description and the refusal to give a logical explanation of events suggest the immense power of Keats's 'negative capability'. By the poem's refusal to reach out after fact and reason, we are made to feel the full force and mystery of an archetypal experience.

Keats's own tortured love poems to Fanny Brawne suggest how, as he was dying, he found love to be a compound of torturing jealousy and fear that such passion would stifle his poetic impulse. In the most achieved of these works – the sonnet 'Bright Star' – he also suggested the transitory nature of erotic happiness itself by yearning after the fixity of the star whose steadfastness and impartiality ultimately deny the transitory nature of human passion. In the great series of odes Keats issued in his volume of 1820 – that masterpiece of youthful genius – these themes are treated with the greatest subtlety.

Technically, the odes are a development of Keats's earlier experiments with the form and with the interwoven richness of sonnet patterns. Their subject matter however is the poet's abiding preoccupation with the imagination as it reaches out to union with the beautiful. In the greatest of these works, he also suggests the undertow of disillusion that accompanies such ecstasy, the human suffering which forever questions the visionary transcendence achieved by art.

In the 'Ode to Psyche', it is the imagination exultant that is Keats's principal concern. The poem is a reworking of a tale from late classical mythology through which he suggests the power of the imagination to create the soul by its own power and then, through art, to build the temple in which the soul is worshipped. The climax of this effort comes when 'the warm love' is finally let in. The sexual passion of Cupid and Psyche – the union of the soul with physical rapture – is thus the imagination's ultimate fulfilment.

Fully human passion is something which the carved figures in Keats's 'Ode on a Grecian Urn' at once suggest and deny. Art – or more precisely the plastic arts – exists in a timeless dimension. Though the spectator must see the details in a sequence, in reality all these elements are frozen in an eternal present. The lovers, musicians and worshippers on the urn exist simultaneously and for ever in their intensity and joy. They are immune to time, stilled in expectation. This is at once the glory and the limitation of the world conjured up by an *objet d'art*. The urn exults but simplifies intuitions of ecstasy by seeming to deny our painful knowledge of transience and suffering. Seen in this way, the carved scenes can be viewed as ultimately frigid. The urn becomes a 'Cold Pastoral', the final words dangerously close to an aesthete's substitute for bodily love and the experience of disillusion and age.

Such issues also lie at the heart of Keats's 'Ode to a Nightingale'. Here the aching ecstasy roused by the bird's song is felt like a form of spiritual homesickness, a longing to be at one with beauty. Opiates and wine at first seem the way to this union and to the attainment of a rapture which transcends the human misery so powerfully described in the ode's third stanza. Eventually however poetry itself is seen as the most effective means of exaltation. In a miraculous passage, Keats's imagination conjures up a landscape of palpitating loveliness:

> I cannot see what flowers are at my feet,
>   Nor what soft incense hangs upon the boughs,
> But, in embalmed darkness, guess each sweet
>   Wherewith the seasonable month endows
> The grass, the thicket, and the fruit-tree wild –
>   White hawthorn, and the pastoral eglantine;
>   Fast fading violets covered up in leaves;
>   And mid-May's eldest child,
>   The coming musk-rose, full of dewy wine,
>   The murmurous haunt of flies on summer eves.

A world of beauty is here imagined through the power of language.

This is achieved in so richly orchestrated a way that we are hardly aware that we are the onlookers of a purely illusory landscape created by the poet himself as he imagines it blossoming in the hushed spring darkness.

Inspired by the nightingale's song, his thoughts now ascend from the transfigured physical world, through the imagined ecstasy of death, to the timeless present of the nightingale's song. But the exhilaration created through words is also subtly destroyed by them. The ultimate imaginative view of 'faery lands forlorn' evaporates in its extremity as the full associations of the last word 'toll' the poet back from his near-loss of selfhood to the real and human world of sorrow and death. Exultant fancy is finally a 'deceiving elf' and art is an anodyne – sublime but evanescent.

Keats suggests in the 'Ode on Melancholy' that this perception of the interrelatedness of joy and pain, beauty and corruption, love and death, is a glorious burden known by the finest spirits only:

> Ay, in the very temple of Delight
>   Veiled Melancholy has her sovereign shrine,
>   Though guessed of none save him whose strenuous tongue
>   Can burst Joy's grape against his palate fine;
> His soul shall taste the sadness of her might,
>   And be among her cloudy trophies hung.

In the 'Ode to Indolence', this is a weight of knowledge to be shrugged away, but it is 'To Autumn', written some months after the other odes, that is Keats's most subtly beautiful acceptance of mutability. The three stanzas of the poem move from early autumnal fullness, through the voluptuous abundance of harvesting, to the magnificent conclusion where, in the subtle associations roused by the imagery, Keats suggests the coming of winter as 'gathering swallows twitter in the skies'. Man's dependence on the cycle of nature points to the fullness of life, its decline and the acceptance of change.

Between the completion of the 'Ode to Indolence' and 'To Autumn' Keats began his narrative poem *Lamia* (1820). The confident, Drydenesque polish of this piece is in marked contrast to Keats's more usual modes. The technique appears particularly well however in the passage describing the heroine's metamorphosis from snake to woman in which the reptilian and the sexual are merged with the demonic. These are the forces with which Lamia will woo the young Lycius. Lamia's destructive yet alluring beauty thus belongs to the worlds of faerie and the imagination, worlds that are ultimately destroyed by everyday experience and satiety. And it is these that lead to the most destructive force of all: the scientific rationalism represented in the poem by the philosopher Apollonius whose cold stare annihilates the bliss of Lamia and the young Lycius in their 'purple-lined palace of sweet sin'.

The year 1819 also saw the co-writing of the tragedy *Otho the Great* – a work intended for Covent Garden but to which Keats gave little of his genius and which was subsequently rejected – as well as the composition of *The Cap and the Bells*, an unsuccessful serio–comic poem. This last work can be connected to a number of Keats's other attempts to bring the colloquial and ironic to poetry, but such verse never equals the quality of his letters. There remains however his last great but uncompleted poem: *The Fall of Hyperion* (published 1857).

This is the work which marks Keats's move towards an altogether deeper and more tragic vision of his art. The Arcadian delights of his earliest poetry are here wished away as the dreaming poet is confronted by a series of challenges. In meeting these he passes through an agonizing process of rebirth in which he finally encounters Moneta, the goddess of memory and the mother of the muses. That he can meet this awesome presence at all is an indication that, as a poet, Keats has passed beyond the dreaming stage of luxurious self-indulgence and has taken on the true poet's burden of pain and agonized consciousness. This is a form of awareness Keats suggests through the face of Moneta herself:

> Then saw I a wan face,
> Not pined by human sorrows, but bright-blanched
> By an immortal sickness which kills not;
> It works a constant change, which happy death
> Can put no end to; deathwards progressing
> To no death was that visage; it had passed
> The lily and the snow; and beyond these
> I must not think now, though I saw that face –
> But for her eyes I should have fled away.

These lines are at once a moment of vision and of commitment.

What the true poet sees – what intuition and imagination reveal to him – is a deep and humanist awareness that truth lies in suffering, in the mysterious weight of anguish with which the world is burdened. This he sees is the only true and sufficient subject for poetry. It was a discovery the dying poet himself however was given no time to explore.

I 2

While the French Revolution had sharply divided writers, many of whom were also becoming aware of the insidious effects of the Industrial Revolution, others were to face the brutal impact of yet a third upheaval: the profound changes that were taking place across the world of agriculture. In the countryside of the early nineteenth century, the quickening pace of enclosure and the pursuit of ever-greater profits led to the loss of common rights and old stabilities, a curtailment of those marginal freedoms enjoyed by the rural poor. This is the background to the work of John Clare (1793–1864).

A fashion for 'peasant poetry' partly accounted for the success of Clare's two early volumes: *Poems Descriptive of Rural Life* (1820) and *The Village Minstrel* (1821). Clare had discovered Thomson's *Seasons* at about the age of thirteen, and if eighteenth-century poetic diction – the bane of another 'peasant poet' Robert Bloomfield (1766–1823) – can be heard in these works, Clare's true countryman's sense of constantly varied activity and accurate observation are also evident.

Such strengths appear again in one of the loveliest of volumes dedicated to the English countryside: *The Shepherd's Calendar* (1827). Here Clare's pictorial gifts and the love of detail that made him an expert naturalist create scenes of the most moving and unpretentious humanity. The natural world combines with elements of the picturesque to create a finely realized sense of the local and the specific. We are shown the weary thresher emptying cornseed out of his boots at the end of a hard day, and the shepherd dancing his children on his knee while the dog under his chair, 'starting and whispering in his sleep', dreams of chasing stray lambs.

Clare's gentle observation extended to all created things. Poems such as 'Summer Images' and 'The Lark's Nest' reveal him as one of the finest writers of animal poetry, while his occasional use of rural idiom – the pigeon 'suthers by on rapid wing', the wild duck 'wherries to the distant flood' – give these works an authenticity and accuracy that have an almost mystical intensity. But if on the one hand there is a deep sense of love and communion in this work, there is on the other the troubling state in which Clare himself 'notic'd every thing as anxious'. In a poem such as 'The Dream', this last rises to a terrible picture of the end of the world, a nightmare of nature awry. For all its return to normality in the last line, here is an ominous precursor of the intensities of Clare's madness.

In his Preface to *The Shepherd's Calendar*, Clare wrote: 'I hope my low station in life will not be set off as a foil against my verses.' This appalling sentence is riddled with a profound knowledge of the social divisions of early-nineteenth-century England. In fact, like *The Rural Muse* (1835), the volume was not a commercial success, and Clare was forced to remain in poverty, a world that roused the indignation found in 'The Parish'. Clare stated that this work was written 'under the pressure of heavy distress, with embittered feelings, under a state of anxiety and oppression almost amounting to slavery, when the prosperity of one class was founded on the adversity and distress of the other'. The resulting satire presents a world of the most sordid catchpenny exploitation, of 'fresh rates wanted from the needy poor', of Farmer Bigg, young Headlong Racket, Cheetum, Saveall and Miss Peevish Scornful. Here is a world where the weak end up in the workhouse – that 'makeshift shed for misery' – while the sensitive are driven insane.

Uprooted from his native village, Clare now began to feel the horror of landscapes shadowed by 'vague unpersonifying things'. In a poem such as 'Autumn' this reaches visionary intensity. The flat acres of Northamptonshire, cracked and burning in the breathless air, are seen with the religious awe of the Psalmist:

> Hill-tops like hot iron glitter bright in the sun,
> And the rivers we're eying burn to gold as they run;
> Burning hot is the ground, liquid gold is the air;
> Whoever looks round sees Eternity there.

Such knowledge inflicts a loneliness in which even love takes on the threat of a loss of identity, the evaporation of the familiar world into the land of shadows suggested in Clare's 'An Invite to Eternity'. There is the subtlety of a profound isolation here, and with it goes an emotional bravery so complete that rancour and self-pity have been burned away. At last the fractured ego draws itself together and, in a final moment of longing, imagines the cool and silent benediction of sleep and death:

> I AM – yet what I am, none cares nor knows;
>   My friends forsake me like a memory lost:
> I am the self-consumer of my woes –
>   They rise and vanish in oblivion's host,
> Like shadows in love's frenzied stifled throes
>   And yet I am, and live – like vapours tost
> Into the nothingness of scorn and noise,
>   Into the living sea of waking dreams,
> Where there is neither sense of life or joys,
>   But the vast shipwreck of my life's esteems;
> Even the dearest that I love the best
>   Are strange – nay, rather, stranger than the rest.
> I long for scenes where man has never trod,
>   A place where woman never smiled or wept,
> There to abide with my Creator God
>   And sleep as I in childhood sweetly slept,
> Untroubling and untroubled where I lie
>   The grass below, above, the vaulted sky.

In the voice of the ordinary working man the great themes of the age find some of their most profoundly moving accents.

13

A great age of poetry was also a great age of critical writing. In the novels of Thomas Love Peacock (1785–1866), this takes the form of satire conveyed through sparkling dialogue. *Headlong Hall* (1816), Peacock's first venture in the mode, gathers his 'humours' characters at a Christmas house party where, over long dinners, the true meaning of progress and other matters is discussed. In *Melincourt* (1817), an altogether more powerful work, Peacock inveighs against the reactionary ideas that had set in after Waterloo. Southey appears as Mr Feathernest, Coleridge as Mr Mystic, Wordsworth – in an allusion to his government sinecure – as Mr Paperstamp, while the *Quarterly* becomes the *Legitimate Review*. There is a sense of deepening bigotry in this book, but it is *Nightmare Abbey* (1818) that remains Peacock's most assured literary satire.

'Sir, I have quarrelled with my wife; and a man who has quarrelled with his wife is absolved from duty to his country.' Mr Cypress's haughty and defiant gloom laughingly catches the manner of Byron at the time of his exile, just as the excellent lyric 'There is a fever of the spirit' parodies his verse with a deftness that surpasses its original. *Nightmare Abbey* is a satire on Gothic gloom and anti-liberalism, and its positive values are suggested by Mr Hilary. 'To represent vice and misery as the necessary accompaniments of genius, is as mischievous as it is false, and the feeling is as unclassical as the language in which it is usually expressed.'

This is very much in the spirit of the Marlow group, and Shelley himself – portrayed in the figure of young Scythrop – is amusingly satirized for his love affairs and for writing so obscurely that he has found only seven readers. Scythrop is also ridiculed for his 'passion for reforming the world'. In this he represents the risks of excessive liberalism, just as Coleridge in the character of Mr Flosky reveals the dangers of an intellectually obscure Kantianism and a reactionary response to the French Revolution. This last produces particularly barbed satire. Flosky believes 'that the overthrow of the feudal fortress of tyranny and superstition was the greatest calamity that had ever befallen humankind; and their only hope now was to rake the rubbish together, and rebuild it without any of those loopholes by which the light had originally crept in'. This is a merciless attack on the Coleridge of *The Friend*.

With *Maid Marian* (1822) and *The Misfortunes of Elfin* (1829), Peacock turned to historical romance as a not altogether satisfactory medium for satirizing the present. In *Crotchet Castle* (1831) and *Gryll Grange* (1861) however he returned to his original mode. The earlier of these two books is a powerful satire on the state of the country on the eve of the Reform Bill. Like the Byron of *Don Juan*, Peacock was well aware of the besetting sin of the nation: 'Where the Greeks had modesty, we have cant; where they had patriotism, we have cant; where they had anything that exalts, delights, or adorns humanity, we have nothing but cant, cant, cant.' Those who constantly tout the 'march of mind' – that favoured commonplace of the Victorians – form the objects of one such attack, but the clash between the mob and the more settled values of traditional England, the caricatures of dishonest tradesmen aspiring to gentility and the figure of Sir Simon Steeltrap MP, Lord of the United Manors of Spring-gun and Tread-mill, suggest the dawning values of a new age. In *Gryll Grange*, Peacock's most finely achieved novel, cant and the horrors of rabid progress are set against a warm, wise and sceptical view of the world, an epicurean tranquillity.

This is a spirit altogether different to that found in the work of William Hazlitt (1778–1830) who wrote of himself:

I am not in the ordinary acceptance of the term, *a good-natured man*, that is, many things annoy me besides what interferes with my own ease and interest. I hate a lie; a piece of injustice wounds me to the quick, though nothing but the report of it reaches me. Therefore I have made many enemies and few friends; for the public know nothing of well-wishers and keep a wary eye on those that would reform them.

Here is a man incapable of compromise, a writer whose lucid honesty is at one with his style.

Such individualism had its roots with the radical Dissenters among whom Hazlitt was reared. He was one of the few major writers of his generation not to turn his back on the ideals of the French Revolution which, in his youth, he believed to be the dawn of a new era. 'Little did I dream', he later wrote, 'that long before my eyes should close, that dawn would be overcast, and set once more in the night of despotism.' This is the authentic voice of Hazlitt: introspective, pessimistic, continuously analytical.

After the failure of his *Essay on the Principles of Human Action* (1805), Hazlitt turned from philosophic and political writing to literary criticism. Between 1817 and 1825 he produced those volumes which not only drew one of the first and most influential maps of English literary history between the sixteenth century and his own, but assure Hazlitt's place among the greatest of critical writers.

Hazlitt's enthusiasms were widely based. He could see in both the *Characters of Shakespeare's Plays* (1817) and the eighteenth-century novelists discussed in *The English Comic Writers* (1819) those qualities of energy or 'gusto' which communicate the imaginative life. It is this personal response, the presence of a mind that has thought deeply, read widely and above all experienced life in many varieties – a mind which relishes literature as a magnifying mirror of its own experience – that gives Hazlitt's criticism its inspiring force.

His Shakespeare criticism also marks a decisive break from the erroneous tradition of reading the plays in terms of inappropriate classical norms. Such a response was supported by the background knowledge shown in *The Dramatic Literature of the Age of Elizabeth* (1820). Hazlitt's *Lectures on the English Poets* (1818) construct a canon that reflects his high regard for Pope, Swift and Samuel Butler (the poets of the sixteenth and earlier seventeenth centuries receive rather scant attention) while his discussion of Wordsworth shows Hazlitt engaged with the currents of his own time in a manner that achieves its fullest expression in *The Spirit of the Age* (1825).

In this book, the youth who is shown in 'My First Acquaintance with Poets' to have responded to the *Lyrical Ballads* with idealistic ardour is here replaced by the older, less illusioned but equally passionate critic. Wordsworth in particular is a subject for troubled admiration.

The current of his feelings is deep, but narrow; the range of his understanding is lofty and aspiring rather than discursive. The force, the originality, the absolute truth and identity with which he feels some things, makes him indifferent to so many others. The simplicity and enthusiasm of his feelings, with respect to nature, renders him bigoted and intolerant in his judgements of men and things.

In *The Spirit of the Age*, a great critic engages with his great contemporaries. The result is the exciting combativeness of analysis underpinned by intellectual biography.

Biography of a different kind is offered in Hazlitt's *Liber Amoris* (1823), his cloying account of the humiliations of infatuation. It is the essays collected in *The Round Table* (1817), *Table Talk* (1821–2), *The Plain Speaker* (1826) and his *Literary Remains* (1836) however that give the most considered portrait of the whole man. The style of the essays varies from the idiomatic and conversational manner of 'The Fight' – that exceptional account of intelligence surveying brutality – through to philosophic exposition. These works have the 'gusto' Hazlitt himself so admired in other writers. Here it takes the form of a direct and virile mind communicating with absolute assurance. It is that most difficult of achievements, the ease of the familiar style: 'To write a genuine familiar or truly English style, is to write as any one would speak in common conversation, who had a thorough command and choice of words, or who could discourse with ease, force, and perspicuity, setting aside all pedantic and oratorical flourishes.'

In the greatest of the essays – 'On a Sundial', for example, or 'On Going a Journey' and 'The Indian Jugglers' – Hazlitt's is a style in which the keenest observation and sense of life are allied to a sharp and exceptionally well-informed mind. We are offered a view of the world that is melancholy and sometimes bitter, a little haughty yet alive with the troubled honesty seen so clearly in 'On the Disadvantages of Intellectual Superiority'.

'No man will ever unfold the capacities of his own intellect who does not at least checker his life with solitude.' For Thomas De Quincey (1785–1859), this retreat from the pressures of daily experience took the form of intense study and the hallucinations of opium addiction. By his early thirties, De Quincey had run through his small inheritance and was obliged to turn to journalism. In 1822 he published the first and superior version of his *Confessions of an English Opium Eater* in the *London Magazine* (revised in 1856 for a collected edition 1853–60). This book is a classic of drug literature, and in an age of widespread and entirely legal addiction it guaranteed De Quincey's contemporary fame.

The great literary merit of the work lies in the success with which De Quincey achieved his purpose of revealing 'something of the grandeur which belongs *potentially* to human dreams'. In prose powerfully influenced by what he called the 'impassioned' quality of the writers of the seventeenth century, De Quincey not only described the paradises and nightmare worlds of the dreaming mind but showed their subtle psychological interconnectedness. In his 'Suspira de Profundis', he called these patterns 'involutes' and, through his spiralling analyses, began to lay bare the patterns of his unconscious. Half a century before Freud and Jung, De Quincey came to the conclusion that dreams 'throw dark reflections from eternities below all life upon the mirrors of that *camera obscura* – the sleeping mind'.

Such analyses chart the far recesses of literary introspection, while 'dream fuges' like 'The English Mail Coach' suggest both the lapidary brilliance with which his style captures moments of psychological insight as well as the diffuseness which perhaps inevitably accompanied his subject and technique. The concluding paragraph of the essay nonetheless is the most glorious word-picture of the effects of music since Hooker's passage on the organ in his *Ecclesiastical Polity*.

Poetry too was considered by De Quincey as a means of intuitive communion, and in 'The Literature of Knowledge and the Literature of Power' he describes reading Milton as an 'exercise and expansion to your own latent capacity of sympathy with the infinite'. This concern with the psychological effects of literature achieves its most acute literary insight in De Quincey's essay 'On the Knocking at the Gate in *Macbeth*'. A more ironic concern with horror can be seen in 'Murder Considered as One of the Fine Arts', but De Quincey's most sustained pieces of literary criticism and biography are contained in the essays published in *Tait's Magazine* between 1835 and 1840 and collected as *Reminiscences of the English Lake Poets*.

De Quincey had a prolonged if strained relationship with the figures involved and recognized that the term 'Lake Poets' itself is something of a misnomer. Though sometimes inaccurate on points of detail (and much resented by their subjects and their heirs for the personal criticism that accompanies praise of their work) essays such as 'Recollections of Grasmere' are vivid prose renditions of the world of Wordsworth's poetry. The portraits of Wordsworth and Coleridge themselves – especially the latter which is an exceptional account of being in the presence of genius – employ telling anecdote shrewdly to create contrasted images of two complex men with whom De Quincey himself was at once impressed and disillusioned.

Friendship with Wordsworth and Coleridge – indeed, with the greater part of the contemporary literary world – was a stimulating comfort in the life of Charles Lamb (1775–1834). His early sentimental romance *Rosamund Gray* (1798) was followed by *John Woodvil* (1802), a pastiche of the seventeenth-century drama which was one of Lamb's abiding enthusiasms. This interest also resulted in his *Specimens of English Dramatic Poets Who Lived about the Time of Shakespeare* (1808).

Such criticisms as this well-made selection contains show Lamb to be concerned with character and the poetry to be found in individual moments of these works rather than with broader issues of theme and construction. His longest critical essay – 'On the Tragedies of Shakespeare' – deprecates the elaborate and illusionistic stage performances of his day in favour of private reading and meditation on the text. Such an approach often joins with the enthusiasms of the bibliophile in Lamb's vivid and playfully random letters to his friends.

Lamb's adoption of the role of the Shakespearian fool helped him occasionally to hide the sadness of his own life: his enforced drudgery in the East India Office and his care for his periodically deranged sister who had murdered their mother. It also allowed him fully to evolve the persona adopted in the essays published by the *London Magazine* in the 1820s and republished as *Essays of Elia* (1823) and *Last Essays* (1833).

Though Lamb had early achieved some moderate poetic success with 'The Old Familiar Faces' and 'On an Infant Dying as Soon as It Was Born', it is as the master of an artfully literary prose that Lamb found his truest manner. Hooker, Browne, Walton, Fuller and Burton attracted him, while, just as Sterne had rifled the last of these, so Sterne's own manner can be seen in such pieces as 'The Character of the Late Elia' with its reminiscences of Yorick. Such 'fine Shandeian lights and shades' again give substance to 'All Fools Day' and 'Barbara S—'.

With Lamb, the essay is no longer chiefly a mode of intellectual enquiry and moral address, though 'Modern Gallantry' and 'Old China' make serious points. Rather, the essay becomes a medium for a delightful literary treatment of life's small pleasures and reassurances. These are found in such pieces as the 'Dissertation upon Roast Pig' and 'Mrs Battle's Opinions on Whist'. 'Dream Children' is a bachelor's somewhat cloying reverie, but it suggests the interest in childhood that led Lamb and his sister Mary to compose their somewhat overrated *Tales from Shakespeare* (1807) and *Adventures of Ulysses* (1808). The fullest and most subtle portrait of the writer nonetheless remains 'The Superannuated Man' from Lamb's *Last Essays*.

Where Lamb was quintessentially the Londoner, Mary Russell Mitford (1787–1855) was the prose-painter of the countryside. *Our Village* (1824–32) is a warm and delightful minor masterpiece of rural description, of weather, work and characters. Like Jane Austen, whom she much admired, the author hoped to make readers of her small country scene intimate with every person it contained, though her social range is wider if considerably shallower than her mentor's. Mary Russell Mitford knew the fields, woods and animals of her area with the familiarity of another writer whom she also greatly admired: Gilbert White (1720–93). Exquisitely observed detail, subtle picturesque description and, above all, a sense that the scientific eye is at one with a love of specific places and the animals and humans who inhabit them make *The Natural History of Selborne* (1789) an inspiring work of continuing importance.

Biography as a form of political comment is suggested in the long series of *Imaginary Conversations* (1824–9) by the minor poet Walter Savage Landor (1775–1864). Dialogues between historical figures ranging from Cicero to Wordsworth suggest something of Landor's ardently liberal views (the republicanism of a haughty and impractical classicist) but the dramatic impact is too often blunted by the bland yet curiously stilted style.

The *Autobiography* (1850) of Leigh Hunt, another man whose life was to stretch well into the Victorian era, is touched by sentimentality. While admiring the fruits of progress, the work also looks back to the time when the author saw the good of mankind stemming 'from a Whig, a Radical, or prospective' stance. This was the attitude taken in much of the journalism Hunt undertook with his brother. It was naturally a dangerous position. *The Examiner* was successfully prosecuted, while the short-lived *Liberal* was fined for printing Byron's *The Vision of Judgement*. Nonetheless, though Hunt was a brave man (and his brother perhaps more so) the voluminous quantities of journalism he produced rarely rise above the pleasantly informal.

The same cannot be said of William Cobbett (?1763–1835) in whose writings the social problems of the age come into sharp and angry focus. 'It is to blaspheme God', Cobbett wrote in his *Cottage Economy* (1822), 'to suppose that he created men to be miserable, to hunger, thirst, and perish with cold, in the midst of that abundance which is the fruit of their own labour.' In the detailed account of the state of the nation given in his *Rural Rides* (1830) and vigorously reinforced in his *Political Register* (1802–35), delight in a vision of the security and comparative comfort of 'Old England' is juxtaposed to a blistering hatred of the proprietors and manufacturers who were now inflicting what Cobbett saw as the unparalleled exploitation of labour.

In Cobbett's writing we see how a new social order was being created through the ever increasing power of capital. What Cobbett loathingly called 'the *Thing*' was emanating from the 'monstrous Wen' of London. Cobbett was to take increasingly radical steps in his attempt to return the country to older and more humane ways. Parliamentary reform was vital to this. Burke's élite – the ancient, pragmatic aristocracy which in theory stood against revolutionary assault – now appeared rotten to the core. As his thought progressed, so Cobbett came to urge that popular mass pressure must win not simply a few mild constitutional changes from such people but a democracy in which parliaments were elected annually by every male over the age of eighteen. Only in this way could poverty and exploitation be removed.

Contempt for institutional corruption also underlay the long career of Jeremy Bentham (1748–1832). Like many others in the revolutionary 1790s, Bentham had seen the rottenness of the political system in France and England, urged democratic representation and then retreated as apparent liberty turned to terror, and terror to invasion, conquest and empire. By the close of the first decade of the nineteenth century however, Bentham had come to recognize that his utilitarian principle of seeking 'the greatest happiness of the greatest number' could never be effected by a Parliament based on patronage, the influence of the Crown and what, in a publication of 1818, he called '*Church of Englandism*'.

In 1823, Bentham inaugurated the magazine that was to broadcast his attack on these establishment values. The *Westminster Review* became the great focus of liberal thought in the country. After the partial liberties granted by the Reform Act of 1832, it was to remain a beacon of modern ideas in an industrial nation, a nation that was now poised to take on world leadership and, from the raucous power of steam and the expansion of commerce, to forge the immensely diverse world of Victorian values.

Victorian Values

I

'The time for levity, insincerity, and idle babble and play-acting, in all kinds, is gone by; it is a serious, grave time.' So wrote Thomas Carlyle (1795–1881) of the Britain of the 1840s, and his tone suggests the moral earnestness with which the Victorians faced the new and manifold problems of becoming the world's first industrial power. Much Victorian poetry, fiction, philosophy and social criticism explores the painful awareness that while enterprise was bringing the country unprecedented material wealth, in the bleak cities of the workshop of the world, philistinism, poverty, exploitation and economic upheaval were leading to a divided nation. No writer more forcefully brought this 'condition-of-England question' to the public's attention than Carlyle himself. He was that most Victorian of figures, the prophet and sage.

Carlyle initially appeared in these roles as the author of *Signs of the Times* (1828) where he inveighed against an industrial culture which seemed to have mechanized the mind while crushing the spirit between the cog-wheels of profit. Carlyle asserted that instead of drawing on his 'dynamic' nature, on the well-springs of 'Love, and Fear, and Wonder, of Enthusiasm, Poetry, Religion', modern man exalted the mechanical and relied on mere systems for inculcating belief, education and morality. He further declared that the psychological had ceded to the physical in science, in metaphysics and above all in politics where groups such as the Utilitarians assumed that albeit radical adjustments to the machinery of government were sufficient to ensure a fully human existence.

In defiant rebuff, Carlyle argued that 'man is not the creature and product of Mechanism; but, in a far truer sense, its creator and producer'. This is a belief that would ring down the age, and Carlyle's particular development of the idea was to suggest that the man of true wisdom is the 'hero', the individual who has been disciplined by struggle and self-denial in the pursuit of spiritual enlightenment.

Beneath this assertion lay the profound crisis in Carlyle's own spiritual life. He had been reared in a family of poor, devoutly Calvinist Scots, but had early lost his faith. This void was eventually filled by his study of the great German thinkers of the late eighteenth and early nineteenth centuries: Kant, Fichte, Schelling, Schlegel and, above all, Goethe who became Carlyle's mentor and his early model for the hero as man of letters. In the distinctions such men drew between logic and intuitive understanding, in their assertion of a transcendent spiritual reality, Carlyle found a potent counter-charm to a world that seemed to be 'one huge, dead, immeasurable Steam-engine, rolling on, in its dead indifference, to grind me limb from limb'.

This was a process of illumination Carlyle portrayed in one of the most remarkable books of the nineteenth century: *Sartor Resartus* (1833–4). The title may be translated as 'The Tailor Refashioned' and points to the underlying metaphor of the work, a metaphor derived from Swift's *A Tale of a Tub*. Just as clothes at once cover and reveal the body and are themselves subject to change through time, so the physical and intellectual worlds of man are a 'bodying forth' of the spiritual reality that underlies them. In Carlyle's reading of German transcendentalism, clothes and ideas are the shifting carapace of the Ideal and must be refashioned through the hero's constant work so as to keep mankind aware of his true spiritual nature. Once such efforts were the special responsibility of the priest. Now, in a time of apparent religious inertia, this role of the hero falls to the writer.

To an audience in the 1830s such ideas were sufficiently advanced, but *Sartor Resartus* was made both more difficult and more comprehensive by two further factors: the densely rhythmic and metaphorical qualities of Carlyle's style and the elaborate construction of this intensely literary work, a construction which constantly draws attention to the book's status as a work of art. Both qualities derive in part from German sources, but Carlyle also drew on such masters of the comic profound as Rabelais, Swift and Sterne.

The 'philosophy of clothes' itself is presented through the disjointed jottings and imaginative leaps of one Professor Teufelsdrockh or 'Devil's dung'. These in turn are expounded by his laborious English editor. In Book II, the editor essays a biographical approach to explanation. The result is a picture of Carlyle's own development from an idyllic childhood of joy and simple religious faith, through 'the nightmare, Unbelief' and the Byronic pangs of misprized love, to the 'Everlasting Yea' – the refusal to be cowed by the griefs of the world – and so to the subjective, religious experience of true vocation, the renunciation of pleasure and the deliberate choice of doing *the Duty which lies nearest thee*'. Rational thought has here been superseded by intuitive certainty, the mechanical by the spiritual, self by service.

The particular form of *Sartor Resartus* also allowed Carlyle to develop his social criticism. Agitation for the Reform Bill during 1831–2 had moved him to profound sympathy with the lot of the poor whom he saw perishing 'like neglected, foundered Draught-Cattle, of Hunger and Overwork'. Such a division in society between the 'Dandies' and the 'Drudges', between the heedless and the desperate, Carlyle believed was a profoundly immoral danger and one for which the English aristocracy might eventually have to answer, just as the Bourbons had in 1789. In *The French Revolution* (1837), the work by which he was to make his name, Carlyle explored the implications of this, taking on himself what he considered the prime duties of the historian: to warn of present ills through a vivid reinterpretation of the past and to show in the patterns of history the workings of a just Providence.

The constant use of the present tense in *The French Revolution* is at one with the vivid power with which Carlyle suggested the multiplicity of life existing simultaneously in the great moments of history, his sense of individuals swept up in momentous events they only partly understand. This failure of understanding – in particular the blindness of the French ruling classes to the misery around them and their own selfish attachment to a society whose symbols of power had been emptied of moral force – was a disturbing issue to the English aristocracy in a period of economic tension and social distress.

Carlyle's suggestion that, far from being a monstrous aberration, the events of 1789 had an awful moral force was particularly disquieting, especially as the terror he depicted has an elemental inevitability, a sense of divine justice working through human wrong. Nowhere is this range of approach more powerfully focused than in Carlyle's account of the moments after the fall of the Bastille:

O evening sun of July, how, at this hour, thy beams fall slant on reapers amid peaceful woody fields; on old women spinning in cottages; on ships far out in the silent main; on Balls at the Orangerie of Versailles, where the high-rouged Dames of the palace even now are dancing with the double-jacketed Hussar-Officers; – and also on this roaring Hell-porch of a Hotel-de-la-Ville! Babel Tower, with the confusion of tongues, were not Bedlam added with the conflagration of thoughts, was no type of it. One forest of distracted steel bristles, endless, in front of an Electoral Committee; points itself, in horrid radii, against this and the other accused breast. It was the Titans warring with Olympus; and they, scarcely crediting it, have *conquered*: prodigy of prodigies; delirious, – as it could not but be. Denunciation, vengeance; blaze of triumph on the dark ground of terror; all outward, all inward things fallen into one general wreck of madness!

In the hungry England of the early 1840s, dangerous discontent was also rife. Despite wide-ranging alterations in administration, the problems of poverty in a rapidly rising industrial population still loomed large, while the moderate electoral changes forced by agitation for the 1832 Reform Bill appeared increasingly inadequate. The immensely painful process of adapting the institutions of a rural economy governed by parsons, squires and landed magnates to the new and often frightening world of urban and industrial democracy had only just begun. The cry for greater reform grew louder and, in 1838, William Lovett and Francis Place drew up the 'People's Charter'.

This called for universal male suffrage, equally sized electoral districts, the payment of MPs as a substitute for a property qualification, secret ballots and annual elections. 'The Charter' became a battle-cry, while riots and strikes were commonplace. It was into such a troubled world that Carlyle launched his long essay on *Chartism* (1839), calling the attention of all to the 'condition-of-England question' and suggesting, in words that would be borrowed for the *Communist Manifesto* (1848), the horrors of a world where 'Cash Payment has become the sole nexus of man to man!'

Unequal as a performance though *Chartism* is, it marks an important consolidation of some of Carlyle's principal views, in particular his outright rejection of the chief demands of the Chartists themselves. He did not see an extension of the vote as an answer to the human misery the movement expressed, a wretchedness to which Carlyle the man responded with quickened sympathy. He considered that what was wanted was a reform not of the franchise but of the leaders of society, the replacement of *laissez-faire* theorists by the 'strong man'. In the end, the democratic demands of the Chartists are heard as an inarticulate cry for authoritarian rule: 'Guide me, govern me! I am mad and miserable and cannot guide myself!'

Such ideas led directly to the volume of lectures Carlyle published as *Heroes, Hero-Worship and the Heroic in History* (1841) with its often tedious elaboration of the idea that 'Universal History, the history of what man has accomplished in this world, is at bottom the History of the Great Men who have worked here.' Carlyle chose six types as representative of his ideal: gods, prophets, poets, priests, men of letters and – a subject of increasing interest to him – the king. In his analysis, such figures as Luther, Knox, Cromwell and Napoleon are bearers of the ideal to the rest of mankind. They are men who, often starting 'in a minority of one', become leaders of thousands. In the present time, such figures would cut through the 'bewildering, inextricable jungle of delusion, confusion, falsehoods and absurdities' sown by such creeds as utilitarianism. Like the great men of times past, the modern hero would inspire belief in noble moral authority and, avoiding the perils of democracy, lead the people where the hereditary aristocracy had failed them.

Carlyle saw such leadership as pre-eminently fitted to the hero as man of letters. 'He that can write a true Book, to persuade England, is he not the Bishop and Archbishop, the Primate of England and of all England?' This vague but heady combination of faith, literature and guidance answered to a need felt deeply among intellectuals of the 1840s, people concerned about evident social distress and yet as wary of full democracy as they were of scepticism, unbelief, religious novelty and spiritual conservatism. Carlyle as prophet, speaking in terms of 'stern old-Hebrew denunciation', and purveying feelings and duties recognizably religious in tone yet unconnected with any church, was listened to by figures as diverse as Mill, Thackeray, Dickens, Mrs Gaskell, George Eliot, Tennyson and Browning. One work above all claimed their attention: *Past and Present* (1843).

In this book, Carlyle's historical interests were powerfully integrated with his concern over the 'condition-of-England question'. He painted with vivid indignation the seemingly insoluble crisis of mass unemployment amid abundance, the miseries and desperate shifts of the poor, as well as the Midas rich, paralysed and wretched amid their wealth. Caricature figures such as Plugson of Undershot, the utilitarian manufacturer, and the Hon. Alcides Dolittle MP add satire to tragedy. Industrialism, the greatest of modern phenomena, is shown to have led to absurdity and inhuman misery. The dilettante aristocracy are merely feckless, while the commercial 'Mammonists' bring a new spiritual degradation into man's relationships. 'We have profoundly forgotten everywhere that *Cash-payment* is not the sole relation of human beings.' Amid contemporary moral amnesia however work is degraded, leadership lost, and scepticism, atheism and sheer greed create an irresponsible society.

So much for the 'Present'. For the 'Past' there existed a more healthy ideal. In the recently edited *Chronicle* of Jocelin de Brakelond, Carlyle found a description of daily life in the monastery of Bury St Edmunds and, in Abbot Samson, an exemplar of the strong man who could revive the world about him. Samson's corner of twelfth-century England, regulated by a figure at once strong, active and hard-headed – above all a man of deep but simple and instinctive faith – becomes the centre of a life lived without competitive economic individualism, free from the cash nexus and supplying a focus for men's allegedly natural desire to subordinate themselves to superiors. Here, for Carlyle, was a model of the new aristocracy he hoped would lead England, an aristocracy that was at once moral and hard-working.

Past and Present was the last of Carlyle's writings positively to influence the greater part of his contemporaries, and his later works reveal, by and large, a grotesque narrowing of human sympathy. The hero of *Oliver Cromwell's Letters and Speeches, with Elucidations* (1845), for example, is praised for his harsh treatment of the Levellers and 'a whole submarine world of Calvinistic Sansculottism, Five-point Charter and the Rights of Man'. This again seems to imply that in the Puritan leader the author thought he had found the type of hero required by Victorian England.

Such attitudes were to alienate many of Carlyle's more intelligent readers, a process furthered by his monstrous *Occasional Discourse on the Nigger Question* (1849). This was an attack on the imagined effects of banning the slave trade, a campaign which is surely one of the Victorians' most enduring achievements. *Latter-Day Pamphlets* (1850), with their onslaught on the 'universal syllabub of philanthropic twaddle', completed this process of alienation, despite Carlyle's telling criticisms of official maladministration and the great influence wielded by the vigour of his prose style.

While the *Life of John Sterling* (1851) is an altogether more generous piece and reveals a humanity seen again in Carlyle's posthumous *Reminiscences* (1881), the great work of his last years was *The History of Frederick the Great* (1858–65). This is a laborious if heroically sustained whitewashing of one of the more unpleasant characters from European history, a warmonger whose closely described campaigns made him, for Carlyle, a last representative of the true king. But the triumph of the hero was the defeat of the artist, and this was a failure lamented by many of Carlyle's contemporaries. The man who had so earnestly drawn their attention to the 'condition-of-England question' in the end had failed them. 'Carlyle has led us out into the desert', wrote Arthur Hugh Clough, 'and has left us there.'

Where Carlyle looked to the redemption of Victorian society in a revised ideal of aristocratic leadership, others sought spiritual authority in the practices of the Christian church. Piety is fundamental to an understanding of the Victorian world, and in an age of widespread regular worship, a broadly evangelical approach characterized by a belief in the saving gift of faith, literalistic Bible reading and virtuous behaviour as the true test of belief was common to Anglicans and Dissenters alike.

While such an approach often led to energetic philanthropy it could also harden to complacency, and when the popular religious poet John Keble (1792–1866) preached his sermon 'National Apostasy' in 1833 there came into existence an approach to the religious life that was profoundly to influence contemporary spirituality. Named the 'Oxford Movement' after the academic home of its leaders, its tenets were developed by Edward Pusey (1800–82), R.H. Froude (1803–36) and the man who was to emerge as the greatest spiritual psychologist of the nineteenth century, John Henry Newman (1801–90)

Against the fundamental assumptions of the evangelicals, the followers of the Oxford Movement urged an apostolic faith, a veneration for the corporate traditions of the church. In *Tracts for the Times*

(1833–41), Newman and his colleagues defended the church against secular encroachment and the congregation's exclusive reliance on private judgement. In his sermons, Newman also sought to raise the spirituality of current religious practice by a direct, chastely delivered appeal to joyful self-discipline, the sacraments and the inward growth of the spiritual life within the apostolic tradition.

It was with this last concern that Newman made his most distinctive contribution. In a society where scientific advance gave ever-increasing prestige to 'Explicit Reason', Newman urged the claims of 'Implicit Reason', portraying with the greatest subtlety how the spiritual life develops through the force of something more than the rigour of logic. This was a position Newman was to maintain throughout his life, declaring in his last work, *An Essay in Aid of a Grammar of Assent* (1870): 'while I can prove Christianity divine to my own satisfaction, I shall not be able to force it on anyone else'.

For Newman, belief was a matter not of argument but of a growing, complex web of probabilities and associations, memories, instincts and received convention. These forces evolve in the mind of the seeker after truth until, like the mountaineer, he gains a particular position 'by personal endowments and by practice, rather than by rule, leaving no track behind him, and unable to teach another'. This process of logical reluctance giving way to Implicit Reason, the almost unconscious motions of the mind towards submission to its Maker, again underlies Newman's most famous hymn 'Lead Kindly Light'.

This work was published in *Lyra Apostolica* (1836), a volume of verses by anonymous Tractarians. However, by 1841, when he issued *Tract 90*, Newman's own spiritual growth and reverence for the traditional authority of the church had led him to the point where he could accept that the Thirty-Nine Articles of Anglican orthodoxy were a stepping-stone to Roman dogma. Despite Catholic emancipation having been granted in 1829, in the furore that followed the apostasy of the Anglican Church's most subtle theologian, Newman retired to his religious community at Littlemore. Here, in 1845, he was received into the Roman Church. He felt, he wrote, 'like one who, in the middle of his days, is beginning life again'.

In his *Essay on the Development of Christian Doctrine* (1845), Newman drew an important if not always convincing analogy between the growth of the individual's spiritual career and the gradual elaboration of theology. This was an attempt to show that Roman Catholic dogma had refined and developed ideas implicit in the earliest days of the church rather than inventing what Protestants saw as superstitious accretions. Newman was here positing a seminal concept of spiritual and intellectual evolution, a 'warfare of ideas, striving for the mastery, each of them enterprising, engrossing, imperious, more or less incompatible with the rest, and rallying followers or rousing foes according as it acts upon the faith, the prejudices, or the interests of individuals'.

This highly influential approach was a first defence of Roman Catholicism, but just as in his days with the Oxford Movement Newman had helped to change the life of the Anglican Church so, after his conversion, he was to alter the image of Roman Catholics among English Protestants. The hero of his novel *Loss and Gain* (1848), for example, offers a thinly veiled self-portrait of a young man who 'could not ultimately escape his destiny of being a Catholic'. Newman's most influential approach to this task of religious propaganda however was to encourage Roman Catholics to present themselves in terms of an educated urbanity that denied the caricatures of their opponents while suggesting the lack of civilized qualities in many Protestants themselves. Roman Catholics were to appear, in other words, not as devils but as gentlemen.

As early as 1841, in the satirical passages of *The Tamworth Reading Room*, Newman had attacked the idea that the pursuit of knowledge was identical with the pursuit of virtue. By the middle of the century, and responding against hostility to the founding of a papal hierarchy in England under his opponent Cardinal Manning, Newman was to develop his ideas on education in one of his greatest books: *The Idea of a University Defined and Illustrated* (1873).

Underpinning this last work is a conviction that faith within the church is the crowning glory of man. The sublimities of Implicit Reason are not necessarily inimical to the workings of Explicit Reason however. Indeed, they are their support and a matter of such importance as to be controlled by ecclesiastical rather than academic authorities. However this last point may be viewed, there is no doubting the subtle refinement and joy in Newman's advocating a university concerned with developing the enlarged and cultured mind. The freely ranging intellect is Newman's answer to the philistinism of fact-cramming. The true university, he declared, is 'an Alma Mater, knowing her children one by one, not a foundry, or a mint, or a treadmill'. The university is not a machine annually turning out the 'qualified' for the job market, but a place of true human fulfilment:

If the intellect is so excellent a portion of us, and its cultivation so excellent, it is not only beautiful, perfect, admirable and noble in itself, but in a true and high sense it must be useful to the possessor and to all around him; not useful in any low, mechanical, mercantile sense, but as a diffusing good, or as a blessing, or a gift, or a power, or a treasure, first to the owner, then through him to the world.

The passage conveys eloquent and heartfelt praise of those qualities which stand against the narrowed intellect in a mechanized and philistine world.

Newman's attempts to win a sympathetic hearing for Roman Catholics in England were greatly helped by the popularity of *The Dream of Gerontius* (1865), a poem on the terror of death and the intercession of prayers, faith and heavenly vision. It was his confrontation with Charles Kingsley (1819–75) however that was to produce one of Newman's best-known works, the autobiographical *Apologia pro Vita sua* (1864).

Kingsley himself was, along with F.D. Maurice (1805–72), the leader of the movement known as 'Christian Socialism' and a writer whose novels and journalism were another means of drawing attention to the 'condition-of-England question'. The approach of these men was profoundly inimical to the leaders of the Oxford Movement. Maurice had a major controversy with Pusey over eternal damnation, while Kingsley's novel *Hypatia* (1853), a work that draws analogies between the ancient world and modern Christianity, was conceived as an attack on Roman Catholics. Newman responded with the inferior *Callista* (1856) and then, after a pamphlet war, with the *Apologia*.

This was a work written under enormous pressures of time and emotion, and Newman was constantly in tears as he completed it. If the anecdotal sense of individuality is often missing, the autobiography remains an eloquent intellectual history made vivid by Newman's realization of his mental growth towards submission to authority and above all by the power of deep but disciplined spirituality. 'If I looked into a mirror and did not see my face, I should have the sort of feeling which actually comes upon me, when I look into this living busy world, and see no reflexion of its Creator,' he wrote. Such a sentence articulated a widespread Victorian fear and, as a result, the *Apologia* was a work that was to make the Cardinal himself one of the most respected and best loved of Victorian sages.

The search for moral and spiritual authority in the work of Carlyle and Newman forms the most powerful contrast to the ideas of the philosopher praised by Lord Asquith as the 'Purveyor-general of Thought for the early Victorians', and a man whose life and writings remain one of the most potent critiques of mass industrial society, John Stuart Mill (1806–73).

Mill was reared at the heart of philosophic radicalism. His father, James Mill (1773–1836), was the author of a critical *History of British India* (1818), a work whose intellectual debts show him as an exponent of utilitarianism and a polymath of formidable range. The extraordinary education he gave his son is recounted in the latter's *Autobiography* (1873). The boy began Greek at three, Latin at eight, logic at twelve and political economy at thirteen. Science became a hobby and history an enthusiasm, while throughout James Mill encouraged his son to argue and order rather than merely assemble facts. The well-meant purpose behind so arduous a training was to make Mill what he eventually became – a professional reformer. By his teenage years, and armed with the academic resources of a man of middle age, Mill was editing the dense and complex works of Bentham, writing for the *Westminster Review* and pursuing his own voracious reading while holding down a job in the East India Office.

Mill was also the leader of a group of young, radical debaters who met to set the world to rights by ardent and informed discussion of the principles of Bentham, the economics of Ricardo and the metaphysics of Hartley. Against the ideas of Thomas Malthus (1766–1834) presented in his *Essay on the Principle of Population* (1798) – the notion that the conditions of the poor will never be improved since in times of plenty population increases geometrically while food supplies increase only arithmetically – the young men urged birth control, and Mill himself was actually arrested for distributing literature on this tendentious subject.

In the period before the 1832 Reform Bill, the young men also argued for representative government, for complete freedom of discussion (ideas which led to their advocating votes for women) and for the reform of a society administered by aristocrats and the church under a legal system whose faults Bentham had spent a lifetime analysing. Above all, the group held to a belief in the 'unlimited possibility of improving the moral and intellectual condition of mankind by education'. Here was a Utopian vision in which sentiment was discounted, and if, under the pressure of extreme rationalism, Mill himself temporarily became what he called 'a mere reasoning machine', he was as yet unaware of the psychological dangers of this. 'I had', he wrote, 'what might truly be called an object in life; to be a reformer of the world. My conception of my own happiness was entirely identified with this object.'

But would Mill be happy if the desired reforms were ever to come about? His answer to this cruelly honest question was given in the chapter of his *Autobiography* entitled 'A Crisis in my Mental Life':

an irrepressible self-consciousness distinctly answered, 'No!' At this my heart sank within me: the whole foundation on which my life was constructed fell down. All my happiness was to have been found in the continual pursuit of this end. The end had ceased to charm, and how could there ever again be any interest in the means? I seemed to have nothing left to live for.

The greatest happiness of the greatest number had led to the misery of the youth who promoted it.

In the drought of this intellectual and spiritual crisis, Mill was obliged to recognize how his education had failed to nourish 'the internal culture of the individual'. His consequent unhappiness was acute, and it was in large part the chance discovery of Wordsworth that brought relief. In Wordsworth's poems, he found 'not mere outward beauty, but states of feeling, and of thought coloured by feeling, under the excitement of beauty'. The subjective and the inward were asserting their claim. Where Bentham had urged the philistine view that 'quantity of pleasure being equal, push-pin is as good as poetry', his disciple was now to elaborate an altogether more humane appreciation of the culture of the mind.

The Christian Socialist followers of Coleridge and the early work of Carlyle also began to make Mill aware of the complexity of human existence. His horizons had been hugely expanded, and the results of his adoption of an altogether broader vision than that in which he had been reared were first seen in three long and beautifully argued essays: 'Bentham' and 'Coleridge', published by the *Westminster Review* in 1838 and 1840, and the wholesale reinterpretation of his first master argued in *Utilitarianism* (1861).

In the first of these works, Bentham's genius for reducing abstract terms to their component parts and then revealing how 'error lurks in generalities' is praised for its genuine contribution to moral and political reform. Bentham remains 'the great questioner of things established'. However, his failure to elaborate feeling or recognize that man is 'a being capable of pursuing spiritual perfection as an end' is shown to have had a deleterious effect on his logic.

In 'Coleridge', an essay which is a fascinating account of the near-universal Victorian distaste for the eighteenth century as 'an age without earnestness', the poet is praised for seeking the human needs originally served by those lax parts of the church and state which many radicals wished to reform. In particular, Mill praised Coleridge's notion of the 'clerisy' for the benevolent effects it had had on revitalizing ecclesiastical circles, and for his analysis of the national basis of 'the two antagonistic interests of Permanence and Progression' in the English constitution. An awareness of historical and local forces has here replaced a belief in model institutions. Bentham and Coleridge – for Mill the seminal thinkers of the time – have been brought into a constructive relationship, and 'whoever could master the premises and combine the methods of both, would possess the entire English philosophy of this age'. On such a basis Mill himself would now advance.

Initially in conjunction with Auguste Comte, a French philosopher who had urged that the rationalist thought of the eighteenth century should be superseded by a 'positivist' epoch in which science supported a spiritual religion of humanity, Mill became convinced the state should be considered a 'mutual insurance company' for the large part of its members who cannot help themselves. Such liberal socialism held a potent promise for the future, and Mill was to develop his ideas in the conclusion to his *System of Logic* (1843) and *Principles of Political Economy* (1848). The notion of 'the greatest happiness of the greatest number' has here been broadened by an awareness of the needs of the individual, Mill's early training by a suppler analysis. Above all, a mechanical concept of man has given place to an organic one, a view that is at once Mill's own and yet in the tradition of the great Victorian sages: 'Human nature is not a machine to be built after a model, and set to do exactly the work prescribed for it, but a tree, which requires to grow and develop itself on all sides, according to the tendency of the inward forces which make it a living thing.'

Contemporaneous with Mill's intellectual and spiritual transformation came a change in his emotional life. He now met and fell in love with Harriet Taylor, a woman whom he was to praise in his *Autobiography* as the 'chief blessing of my existence, as well as the source of a great part of all that I have attempted to do, or hope to effect hereafter, for human improvement'. For Mill, Harriet Taylor combined the rational and instinctive in a manner that was a constant wonder and delight. She contributed decisively to his arguments for the greater self-government of the working classes and, though Mill was a feminist from his youth, her enthusiasm also influenced his *On the Subjection of Women*, an essay published in 1869 but written much earlier.

This lucid and imaginative work sympathetically portrays the lot of the 'subjected' while satirizing male chauvinism by reference to ideas of evolutionary progress. Seeking an image for ancient notions of patriarchy, Mill declared that it was 'as if a gigantic dolmen . . . occupied the site of St Paul's and received daily worship, while the surrounding Christian churches were only resorted to on feasts and festivals'. Comte's view that woman as 'the spontaneous priestess of Humanity' occupied a complementary but lower position to man led to a rift between the thinkers however, while as the MP for Westminster, Mill unsuccessfully proposed that the word 'man' in the 1867 Reform Bill be replaced by 'person'. His agitation for women's right to vote was the leading initiative in this area before the rise of the suffragettes.

More immediately relevant to our purposes, Mill also raised the question of a specifically feminine literature. He understood very clearly the limitations imposed on women by masculine traditions of education and culture, but declared pessimistically: 'If women's literature is destined to have a different collective character to that of men, much longer time is necessary than has yet elapsed before it can emancipate itself from the influence of accepted models, and guide itself by its own impulses.' In works of fiction especially, this attempt to create a distinctive feminine voice is a central issue in the Victorian literary world.

It was with the onset of tuberculosis (which in Harriet's case proved fatal) that the couple gave final shape to what has become perhaps Mill's best-known work, the essay *On Liberty* (1859). This marks a high point of Victorian liberal thought and is a vigorously argued defence of the individual's right to develop his or her 'internal culture' and rebuff the stifling effects of convention and authority.

Compulsion and punishment, Mill argues, can only justly interfere with an individual's liberty of action when the protection of others is at stake. While argument and entreaty are entirely valid – diversity of opinion was, after all, what Mill was seeking – coercion itself is immoral. 'The only part of the conduct of anyone, for which he is amenable to society, is that which concerns others. In the part which merely concerns himself, his independence is, of right, absolute. Over himself, over his own body and mind, the individual is sovereign.' To this end, Mill argued that what society must promote is not a rigid idea of truth but the virtue of liberty, something that Mill himself nonetheless feared that the 'social tyranny' of Victorian values was eroding. For the greatest philosopher of Victorian liberalism, Mrs Grundy was too evidently at work.

Others disagreed. 'What is meant by the complaint that there is no individuality now?' wrote Thomas Babington Macaulay (1800–59). 'Genius takes its own course, as it always did. Bolder invention was never known in science than in our time.' And he went on to instance steamships, the electric telegraph and gaslights as triumphs of Victorian inventiveness.

In so doing, Macaulay was advocating the view that was to help make him the most popular of nineteenth-century historians: the Whig belief that an aristocratic tradition of practical and empirical politics was the true British pathway to freedom, a freedom which manifested itself in ever greater material prosperity. Untrammelled by both mysticism and intricate paper theory, vigorous and optimistic, such a doctrine spoke reassuringly to the creators of wealth and empire. Against the grim warnings of Carlyle's *French Revolution*, Macaulay juxtaposed the solid achievements of the Glorious

Revolution and the reforms of 1832. Tradition, it seemed, gave the impetus to change, and change could be happily identified with progress. This was the exhilarated face of the Victorian vision and was to be powerfully influential.

Publications in the *Edinburgh Review* – later collected as *Critical and Historical Essays* (1843) – and the rhetorical triumph of Macaulay's speech in support of the Reform Bill itself had early popularized his ideas. With the *Lays of Ancient Rome* (1842), he combined the literary and historical in a manner reminiscent of Scott and showed himself a master of vivid action in a great age of narrative verse. It was Macaulay's unfinished *History of England from the Accession of James II* (1849–61) however that was his most assured popular success.

In this work, Macaulay made available the fruits of his immense reading and voluminous memory through a disciplined practice of 'the all-important art of making meaning pellucid'. To such rhetorical and philosophical confidence he brought those further gifts which, in his essay on *History* (1828), he described as 'the art of narration, the art of interesting the affections, and presenting pictures to the imagination'. Macaulay's handling of broad historical structures is indeed compelling. He could also be both pathetic and scathing, while the past is vividly brought to life by his use of telling anecdote. Above all, Macaulay had a politician's grasp of political reality and a propagandist's skill for isolating popular emotive issues. By advocating change within a broad tradition of continuity, by insisting that a glorious present derived from a stable past, Macaulay offered his age a reassuring vision. 'The history of our country during the last one hundred and sixty years', he wrote, 'is eminently the history of physical, of moral, and of intellectual improvement.'

Such optimistic faith in progress and reform was a powerful force in Victorian England, yet even these were not without their problematic aspects. A few months before the passing of the Reform Act itself an unknown young man, destined for the church, had set out on a five-year circumnavigation of the globe. The scientific researches of Charles Darwin (1809–82), first offered to the public in *The Origin of Species* (1859), were to give the Victorians one of their most challenging accounts of progress and man's place in a universe that now seemed to be ruled neither by God nor by man himself and to be set on a purposeless course where mere chance ensured the survival of the fittest.

Until Darwin published *The Origin of Species*, the views expounded by William Paley (1743–1805) in his *Natural Theology, or Evidences of the Existence and Attributes of the Deity* (1802) had provided the best-known account of a universe believed to be a mere six thousand years old and populated by separate and divinely created species. Of these, man himself was held to be the most glorious evidence of 'the Power, Wisdom and Goodness of God'. To observe nature was, in this comfortable view, to observe in detail how a benevolent Maker adapted His creatures to their environments and so revealed His goodness.

The evidence of fossils and geology had nonetheless begun to suggest to scientists such as Sir Charles Lyell (1797–1875), author of *The Principles of Geology* (1830–33), that such changes in the structure of the earth as had evidently occurred were the result not of cataclysmic natural eruptions alone, but of slow changes over millions of years. The earth seemed very much older than had once been thought and nature appeared to exist in a state of flux over aeons of time. Above all, the Book of Genesis no longer offered an adequate account of creation. Popular lecturers tried to interpret the fossil evidence as suggesting 'a progress Godwards', and the works of Philip Gosse (1810–88) – recalled in Edmund Gosse's beautiful biography *Father and Son* (1907) – show the degree of imaginative interpretation, piety and poetic delight with which a devout scholar could still approach his task. It was such a mode of thought that Darwin was finally to shatter.

Observing slight but telling differences between the giant tortoises of the Galapagos Islands, it seemed to Darwin that evolution from a common ancestor appeared the most likely explanation for diversities within a species. Darwin's reading of Lyell suggested the great age of the earth and so the possible time in which such varieties could develop. In addition, Malthus's *Essay on Population* prompted the idea that when a community expands at a greater rate than its supply of food then only the best adapted will survive. By 1838, Darwin had come to believe that over aeons of time a process of natural selection favoured those species whose particular characteristics best helped them find mates and food. There was no God necessarily overseeing the welfare of each separately created species but rather a constant warfare upon earth: 'Owing to this struggle for life, any variation, however slight and from whatever cause proceeding, if it be in any degree profitable to an individual of any species, in its infinitely complex relations to other organic beings and to external nature, will tend to the preservation of that individual, and will generally be inherited by its offspring.'

In this view – though *The Origin of Species* is too carefully argued to state the matter so boldly – a benevolent Creator becomes a redundant hypothesis and man himself an animal struggling for survival in a purposeless world. The clear implication that far from being the supreme work of God men are first cousins to the primates would not be made public by Darwin himself however until 1871 when he issued *The Descent of Man*.

It would be a gross simplification to assume that Darwin's work was the sole and immediate cause of the religious doubt that underlies so much of the finest Victorian literature. In Germany, for example, exponents of the Higher Criticism of Scripture such as David Friedrich Strauss in *Das Leben Jesu* (translated by George Eliot in 1846) had built on the rationalist analysis of the eighteenth century to question not only the supernatural context of the Gospels but the degree to which their account of historical events was conditioned by the traditional myths of the society in which their authors wrote. Far from being the product of direct, divine inspiration as the evangelicals hoped, Scripture was coming to be seen as a received text which should be examined as rigorously as a tragedy by Sophocles or an ode by Horace. In addition, writers like Ludwig Feuerbach, whose *Essence of Christianity* George Eliot translated in 1841, were to develop an anthropological approach to religion and argue that God is a projection of mankind's inner nature created through 'the irresistible power of the imagination'. To see a separation between man and God was thus cruelly to alienate man himself from his own highest good, a good which Feuerbach believed was truly revealed in loving human relationships.

The sources of the widespread and often agonizing religious doubt of the Victorians were thus many and complex, while the variety of responses to them was yet more so. An age in which Newman could salute Darwin for advocating an evolutionary argument similar to his own admits no easy formulas. It suggests rather that Victorian values were argued with the greatest intellectual subtlety and resource, while Victorian England itself witnessed a period of the most challenging debate on the fundamental issues of existence.

2

The gigantic figure of Dickens towers over the fiction of the early Victorian period, but before the full emergence of his genius other novelists turned their attention to the 'condition-of-England question'. Many of these authors were women, for as the versatile Harriet Martineau (1802–76) declared in her *Autobiography* (1877), women could express themselves in fiction 'with more freedom and earnestness than under any other form'. On to the eighteenth-century novelists' concern with courtship and marriage was now grafted a well-informed and often profound awareness of the social problems caused by industrialization, poverty and the position of women themselves. In Martineau's *Illustrations of Political Economy* (1832), pieces such as 'A Manchester Strike' offer a telling picture of the moral pressures on a strike leader and are arguably the origin of the 'social problem' novels of the 1840s.

Other women were to follow Martineau's lead. Charlotte Elizabeth, the devoutly evangelical Mrs Tonna (1790–1846), campaigned against abuses in the employment of women and children in *Helen Fleetwood* (1841). In *Michael Armstrong, the Factory Boy* (1839–40) – a horrific picture of child exploitation researched under the auspices of the reformer Lord Shaftesbury – Frances Trollope (1780–1863) again revealed the miseries of the industrial world to a largely middle-class audience. The writings of both women were to have some influence on the passing of such legislation as the Ten Hours Act of 1847. In addition, Mrs Trollope's melodramatic *Jessie Phillips* (1842–3) portrays the seduction of a seamstress and the murder of her illegitimate baby, a theme which Mrs Tonna and Elizabeth Stone (active 1840–73) were also to use as a focus for their discussion of the sexual exploitation of women, as were Mrs Gaskell and George Eliot.

One of the greatest politicians of the Victorian era also turned his literary attention to the 'condition-of-England question', though *Vivian Grey* (1826–7), the first novel of Benjamin Disraeli (1804–81), is essentially a political *roman-à-clef* strongly marked by Byronic posturing and the gossip about high society which characterized the so-called 'silver fork' novels popular from the mid-1820s to the mid-1840s.

Coningsby (1844) however was written 'to vindicate the just claims of the Tory party to be the popular political confederation of the country' and to outline Disraeli's hopes for what he termed the 'Young England' alliance. In *Coningsby* itself, Sidonia, the mysterious and powerful Jew, inspires the aristocratic hero with a heavily charged mix of the romantic feudalism found in Kenelm Digby's *Broad Stone of Honour, or The True Sense and Practice of Chivalry* (1822), the High Church beliefs of the Oxford Movement and a contempt for what were seen as the mercenary policies of the Whigs and the soulless materialism of the followers of Bentham. Social and industrial reform, along with a belief in 'the irresistible power of the individual', is here combined with a Carlylean hope in a revived and moral aristocracy. The principal aim of the Young England party was thus to create a new and strongly united nation – an alliance of workers and peers in a world of revived faith and responsibility.

In *Sybil, or The Two Nations* (1845), Disraeli offered his most powerful picture of 'the condition of the people' and his ideas for reform. These are presented against a background of fervent Chartist unrest, and part of the strength of the novel lies in the contrast Disraeli drew between a wealthy, self-seeking aristocracy and the appalling conditions of the industrial poor, between gilded clubs and a world where 'an English girl, for twelve, sometimes sixteen hours a day, hauls and hurries tubs of coal up subterranean roads, dark, precipitous and plashy'. Caught between these two extremes, Charles Egremont discovers that in England there are

'Two Nations; between whom there is no intercourse and no sympathy; who are as ignorant of each other's habits, thoughts and feelings, as if they were dwellers in different zones, or inhabitants of different planets; who are formed by a different breeding, are fed by a different food, are ordered by different manners, and are not governed by the same laws.'

'You speak of—' said Egremont, hesitatingly.

'THE RICH AND THE POOR.'

Disraeli's novel offers exceptionally powerful descriptions of the

lot of the poor, of unemployment, squalor and the appalling exploitation of the 'tommy shop' where factory owners forced their workers
into debt by charging high prices for staple foods or paying them in
kind. By contrast, Egremont's love affair with the beautiful Sybil –
an apparently working-class 'religious' or nun who preserves a sense
of faith and charity in this heartless world and who finally emerges as
being of aristocratic descent – is both melodramatic and faintly
ridiculous. The interplay of angry observation and the ardent urging
of reform is compelling nonetheless.

Other novelists drawn to the 'condition-of-England question' were
critical of Disraeli's romantic feudalism, and Charles Kingsley's *Yeast*
(1848) presents the Christian Socialists' belief that the answer to
current problems lay not in the conspicuous charity of peer to serf
but in making the poor better able to shift for themselves. The
Christian Socialists also asserted that a reform of society could only
spring from inner religious change, from brotherly co-operation,
self-help and self-improvement. The movement was in large part a
response to the Chartist agitation of the 1840s. That it was also
essentially anti-democratic is revealed by Kingsley's powerful novel:
Alton Locke, Tailor and Poet: An Autobiography (1850).

Alton Locke portrays the hero's struggle to educate himself amid
squalor and class conflict. Locke himself becomes a famous working-
class poet and is provoked into taking part in physical-force Chartism.
He is gaoled, and only after the failure of the great Chartist petition
of 1848 and his own symbolic rebirth does he finally submit to the
influence of Christian Socialism. These ideals are preached by his
beloved Eleanor in a series of anticlimactic concluding chapters
which insist that freedom, equality and brotherhood will be achieved
not by democratic agitation but through exemplary Christian patience
and suffering, 'by the cross, and not the sword'.

While patriotic novelists such as Harrison Ainsworth (1805–82)
tried unsuccessfully to revive the tradition of Scott, the historical
novel as an arena for political debate is evident in the work of the
prolific and versatile Edward Bulwer-Lytton (1803–73). In *The Last
Days of Pompeii* (1834), for example – a novel marred by pedantic
research and contrived dialogue – Bulwer-Lytton concentrated on
individuals crushed in moments of historic change and a period that
suggests parallels with the troubled England of the Reform Bill.

Bulwer-Lytton also developed many other genres of fiction. *Paul Clifford* (1850), for example, is a 'novel with a purpose' in which the author campaigned against 'a vicious prison-discipline, and a sanguinary penal code'. His resurrection of the eighteenth-century 'Newgate novel' was to influence the Dickens of *Oliver Twist* (1838), while occult fantasies such as *Zanoni* (1842), ghost stories such as 'The Haunted and the Haunters' (1859) and works of science fiction furthered Bulwer-Lytton's popularity. So did *The Caxtons* (1849), a gentle saga of domestic family life, and one of a trilogy of pleasantly reassuring works which include *My Novel* (1853) and *What Will He Do with It?* (1858). Compromise and good humour are the essence of these works.

Two contemporary exponents of comic fiction were Charles Lever (1806–72) and R.S. Surtees (1805–64). Lever's works were principally concerned with Ireland and the Irish, and range from picaresque military adventure through to *Lord Kilgobbin* (1872), a more sombre reflection on the life of the Irish aristocracy. The picaresque was also to be favoured by Surtees in *Jorrocks's Jaunts and Jollities* (1838), his sporting sketches of a rumbustious 'Fox 'unting' grocer whose Sancho-Panza-like servant Pigg is introduced in *Handley Cross* (1843).

With such novels as these, the enormous range of Victorian prose fiction had begun to be explored. Social and political theory, protest, and historical and domestic works had all been essayed, but it is with the comic possibilities opened up by social reportage that we come to the early career of one of the supreme figures of nineteenth-century English literature: Charles Dickens (1812–70).

3

Dickens began his career as a freelance journalist, reporting legal and parliamentary affairs with an accuracy that was to win him a high reputation. An increasingly informed and passionate response to Victorian social conditions sustained the great achievements of his maturity, while the exuberance apparent in his early pieces led to the writing of anecdotal sketches, character studies and tales. Derived in part from the essays of Leigh Hunt and the young Dickens's extensive reading in the novels and journalism of the eighteenth century, these very successful essays were issued in volume form and under Dickens's pseudonym as *Sketches by Boz* (1836).

The publishers Chapman and Hall were aware of this early work, and when the failing artist Robert Seymour approached them with some sporting illustrations of cockneys in the countryside, they asked the newly contracted Boz for linking passages of narrative prose. Confident now of his imaginative power, Dickens insisted that the illustrations serve the narrative rather than the other way around. The publishers agreed, and at the close of March 1836 they began the monthly serial publication of one of the great comic works in the language, *Pickwick Papers*. As the novel developed along its haphazard route and the plump and prosperous hero acquired his worldly wise servant Sam Weller – a figure who shows Dickens's remarkable powers of characterization through speech – so this genial comedy of middle-class life slowly became a publishing phenomenon. The eighteenth-century picaresque novel had been given fresh life, and the newly married author of twenty-four eventually found his work circulated in print runs of 40,000 a month.

The commercial success of this experiment in serial publication was to have an immense influence on subsequent Victorian fiction. Authors and publishers were now often to issue their works in parts before republication as a 'three-decker' or later as a single volume. The demands and conventions of issuing a novel in what was often as many as twenty monthly parts of three or four chapters, with a concluding double issue, challenged authors to organize their themes, plots and character development within a regular framework of climaxes. In addition, writers learned how to bind their material together through parallelism and imagery. The enormous length of such publications encouraged the depiction of a comprehensive social range, while the relatively low cost of serial publication – a shilling an issue compared to the guinea and a half charged for a bound novel – greatly enlarged the market.

In *Pickwick Papers* itself, many of the technical possibilities offered by serial form are still unexplored. However, with Jingle as the none-too-serious villain of the work and the humorously contrived misunderstanding whereby the innocent Pickwick is mistakenly supposed to have offered marriage to his landlady Mrs Bardell, the work develops via such hilarious scenes as Bob Sawyer's bachelor party (later one of Dickens's favourite recital episodes) towards the high comedy of the trial of *Bardell* v. *Pickwick*. Pickwick's refusal to pay damages and his consequent stay in the debtors' prison gave Dickens the chance to confront boyish innocence and the charitable high spirits of Dingley Dell with a suggestion of the claustrophobic horror that characterizes the world of his maturity. Against this he then set the hero's magnanimity – the essential Pickwickian benevolence – by which Pickwick himself contrives to relieve the wretchedness of his fellow prisoners. The rich man who intervenes to alleviate suffering was to remain a standard figure in Dickens's fiction.

With *Pickwick* gaining ever-greater popularity, Dickens began a work whose characters were to obsess his imagination and whose incidents began to probe the painful worlds of abused childhood and official incompetence in a manner that reveals the great social critic. The sentiment and high melodrama of *Oliver Twist* (1838) derive from the popularity of the Newgate novel, while the somewhat clumsily handled conventions of the wronged woman, the dispossessed heir and the death-bed secret explore the social horrors of Victorian England with considerable power.

Oliver in the Malthusian hell of the workhouse is an image of eternal innocence caught in Victorian corruption, in particular the evils of the 1834 Poor Laws and the blighted imagination and sheer ineptitude of Bumble the beadle. The institutionalized physical hunger of the workhouse is at one with the emotional starvation, and both lead to legendary pathos: 'The gruel disappeared; the boys whispered each other, and winked at Oliver; while his next neighbours nudged him. Child as he was, he was desperate with hunger, and reckless with misery. He rose from the table; and advancing to the master, basin and spoon in hand, said: somewhat alarmed at his own temerity: "Please, Sir, I want some more."' Here is an emblem of a heartless, system-dominated world that tries to crush the individual and stands perpetually indicted for failing to protect the innocent and the weak. Dickens's loathing of the mechanical inhumanity of systems places him firmly in the line of the great Victorian sages.

Where supposedly respectable adults have abused their trust the Devil steps in, here as Fagin the red-bearded master of the underworld frying sausages with a toasting fork and ironically encouraging the cockney resilience of the Artful Dodger and his school of thieves in the Victorian values of hard work, family loyalty and useful education. If official charity is heartless, the criminal world at first appears warm. The irony is scathing, but it leads to the nightmare of the Devil trying to reclaim his own, of Nancy menaced by Fagin and Sikes, and Dickens's portrayal of the wicked pursued by justice after the brutal murder of Nancy herself.

Perhaps no moment in Dickens more surely raises melodrama to high art than this last – the strands of Nancy's hair crackling in the fire as Sikes burns his murderous club echo for ever in the mind – and it is the sheer imaginative force of Dickens's underworld that remains with the reader long after the machinery that leads to Oliver's security in the middle-class world of Mr Brownlow has been forgotten. A simplistic faith in acceptable Victorian values pales when confronted by the anarchic forces that underlay them and suggests that the artist and the moralist were not yet at one.

Such problems of focus are also evident in *Nicholas Nickleby* (1839) and *The Old Curiosity Shop* (1841), where they partly derive from both works being novels of the road. However, where the first is comic and resilient, the second is often sentimental to a maudlin degree.

In his previous novels, Dickens's heroes had been a portly old gentleman and a child. In *Nicholas Nickleby*, he took what he described as 'a young man of impetuous temper and of little or no experience' and placed him in a plot that is too often dependent on eavesdropping and coincidence. It is also uncomfortably suspended between the stage villainy of Uncle Ralph and the sickly benevolence of the Cheeryble brothers. Such effects suggest the world of Victorian melodrama, and Dickens's love of the theatre is evident throughout. Popular culture, indeed, was one of the mainstays of his art.

If the stage villainy of Ralph, the pathos of the mentally defective Smike and the often rather priggish virtue of the hero strain credibility, what gives the novel its continuing fascination is Dickens's portrayal of a cast of grotesques acting out their roles with conscious hypocrisy like Ralph or the superabundant dottiness of Mrs Nickleby. The success and limitations of such a proceeding can be seen in the book's most famous character: Mr Squeers, the sadistic and rapacious principal of a nightmare school for the unwanted sons of the gentry.

Evil is here tempered by broad comedy. Indignation Squeers certainly rouses but also laughter, and in the end it is sufficient that he is flogged by Nicholas who then absconds with his chief victim, Smike.

In contrast to Squeers are the Crummleses, that marvellous theatrical family who become ever more vivid as their plays become ever more absurd. Mr Crummles's memory of falling in love with his consort as she stood 'on the butt-end of a spear surrounded with blazing fireworks' has a bizarre yet heart-warming innocence, a richly imaginative psychological verisimilitude. Such invention suggests that uniquely Dickensian gallery of snobs, fools and minor villains, obsessives who are often the life of his work. Among such figures here are Mrs Nickleby herself whose mental flutterings rise to the greatness of Mistress Quickly as she hears of the death of Smike:

'I am sure,' said Mrs Nickleby, wiping her eyes, and sobbing bitterly, 'I have lost the best, the most zealous, and most attentive creature that has ever been a companion to me in my life – putting you, my dear Nicholas, and Kate, and your poor papa, and that well-behaved nurse who ran away with the linen and the twelve small forks, out of the question of course.'

In *The Old Curiosity Shop*, a novel developed out of a story in Dickens's unsuccessful periodical *Master Humphrey's Clock* (1840), the death of Little Nell is a transfiguration of innocence in a corrupt world, the world of London and the industrial cities of the Midlands, of darkness, vain hope and the evil Quilp.

In a work built on contrasts of light and dark, Quilp is the deformed embodiment of evil, the Rumpelstiltskin in the fairy-tale elements of the plot. As a grotesque, he is a masterly creation. 'He ate hard eggs, shell and all, devoured gigantic prawns with the heads and tails on . . . and in short performed so many horrifying and uncommon feats that the women were nearly frightened out of their wits, and began to doubt if he were really a human creature.' And therein lies the problem. Compelling as he is and revolting as the sexual and financial plots he hatches are, Quilp is unable fully to embody Dickens's loathing for 'the mountain heap of misery' in the novel. He is a figure of fear rather than a means of analysis. He belongs to fairy-tale, and the lurid hellishness of his death is too obviously his creator's revenge on horrors not yet fully understood.

By contrast, the plangently sentimental death of Little Nell, exhausted after forced wanderings with her grandfather, is too obviously an attempt by Dickens to come to terms with his own very personal feelings about the deaths of girls whose lives were too good for the world. Nell and her grandfather's flight from the city to the supposed innocence of the countryside is essentially a pursuit of sentiment and a place 'where sin and sorrow never came . . . a tranquil place of rest, where nothing evil entered'. Only here, Dickens seems to suggest, silent under a moonlit tomb, can innocence finally be left in peace with God. Meanwhile, the world goes on in the life of the stalwart Kit (one of Dickens's most delightful heroes) while the dead and the houses in which they lived pass away 'like a tale that is told'.

One of the most alarming horrors faced by Little Nell was violent industrial unrest in the Midlands. With *Barnaby Rudge* (1841), Dickens's historical novel on the Gordon Riots of 1780, the mob surges to the centre of attention. While the Scott of *The Heart of Midlothian* was an important influence here, the range of Dickens's social analysis had now been deepened by his contact with Carlyle, and in *Barnaby Rudge* itself a number of important elements from Carlyle's thought are clearly present. In the opening chapters, for example, we are shown the sins of the fathers that are to be visited on the sons. Sir John Chester – 'soft-spoken, delicately made, precise and elegant' – personifies Carlyle and Dickens's loathing of the eighteenth-century 'Dandiacal Body', of feckless patrician government and of the paternal irresponsibility by which Chester himself casts off his son Edward while also causing the bestial Hugh, his 'natural' or illegitimate child, to join in the destruction of the Maypole inn and the traditional values suggested by the nearby great house. Hugh is the personification of the corrupt old order, 'that black tree of which I am the ripened fruit'. In this, he forms the perfect complement to the simple-minded Barnaby Rudge, the 'natural' or idiot son of a murderous servant. Together, Hugh and Barnaby suggest the brutality and idiocy which will lead a rebellion in society against the values their parents have betrayed.

The forces of the Terror as presented by Carlyle made a deep impression on Dickens, and the wanton destructiveness of the mob roars through his novel with a power that is as ruthlessly conceived as his master's. The mob gives frightening expression to contemporary fears of a Chartist uprising, and its mindless fury is exactly caught when Dickens describes the sacking of Lord Mansfield's house. To ravage the work of the father of the common law is to bring about a society where all coherence has gone. In the end, the heroes of the novel – Varden, Joe, Edward Chester – are obliged to align themselves with the older forces whose weakness they all too painfully know. For Dickens, society must redeem itself through traditional resources, however corrupt these may have become.

Between the completion of *Barnaby Rudge* and starting on *Martin Chuzzlewit* (1844), Dickens made the journey described in his *American Notes* (1842), much of which had in fact been toned down from the private letters on which his book was based. In *Martin Chuzzlewit* – and partly as a response to criticisms levelled at *American Notes* – Dickens painted an even harsher picture of the United States. It becomes a morass where the 'cash nexus' had reached such appalling dimensions that 'men were weighed by their dollars, measures gauged by their dollars; life was auctioned, appraised, put up, and knocked down for its dollars'. Dickens's powerful symbol of this self-destructive greed is the putrid swamp which his hero is tricked into investing in and which goes by the name of Eden.

The American scenes in *Martin Chuzzlewit*, excellent though their satire is, are nonetheless too loosely connected to a novel which is itself messily constructed. Martin is sent to the States (partly, it has been suggested, to boost the book's poor sales) after falling in love with his grandfather's ward and becoming a victim of the machinations of that ogre of hypocrisy, Mr Pecksniff. And it is with figures like Pecksniff and Sarah Gamp that Dickens's genius for moral caricature is seen at its most splendidly developed. The energy with which these figures have been created takes over the book, while their actions and speech lead in the case of Pecksniff especially to a portrait of hypocritical duplicity and self-seeking that was without parallel in Dickens's work so far.

Pecksniff is financially ruined by the trickster Montague Tigg, a character who again took Dickens's imagination into areas that had never been so powerfully explored, a world not just of financial chicanery, but of claustrophobic criminal psychology, nightmare and murder. The death of Tigg at the hands of Jonas Chuzzlewit points forward to *Edwin Drood* (1870) and the horrors of Dostoevsky's *Crime and Punishment* (1866). If the focus of *Martin Chuzzlewit* as a whole is rather too diffuse, it is nonetheless one of the most richly inventive of all Dickens's works and suggests powers that his mature genius was to harness to triumphant effect.

Part of this discipline was provided by Dickens's deepening awareness of social problems, and throughout his career he was to turn to journalism as a means of publicizing abuses and venting his anger. For a brief period he was editor of the *Daily News*, but the most telling of his journalistic pieces from this period are the 'Letters on Social Questions' (1846–50), published in his friend and biographer John Forster's *Examiner*. In these articles (so superior in their passion to the contemporary *Pictures from Italy* (1846) and their laboured travelogues) Dickens railed against capital punishment, ragged schools, 'Ignorance and Crime', the vile exploitation to be found on paupers' farms and the wretchedness of a legal system where 'A Truly British Judge' could linger over the possibilities of flogging, transporting or imprisoning a ten-year-old child who had stolen 5s 3d.

In *A Christmas Carol* (1843), the first and finest of the *Christmas Books* Dickens issued up to 1848, the heartless forces of Malthus, the Utilitarians and the market-place are presented by means of a fairy-tale that has become a permanent part of the mythology of modern man. Scrooge – 'hard and sharp as a flint, from which no steel had ever struck out a generous fire; secret, and self-contained, and solitary as an oyster' – is the eternal type of the miser. His solipsistic existence is at once a psychological deformity and a satire on the hard-faced Victorian business man bound to his work, dutifully contributing a pittance to the workhouse, yet ultimately indifferent to the means that serve to 'decrease the surplus population'.

The ghost of Christmas Present shows Scrooge the reverse of this state. The domestic virtues of Bob Cratchit his wretched ·clerk – values which, in *The Cricket on the Hearth* (1845), Dickens was to dwell on to a maudlin degree – reveal a Christian benevolence that allows the Cratchits to toast Scrooge's health amid the poverty he has inflicted on them. When the ghost of Christmas Future shows Scrooge the scenes after his own death, the miser is finally converted into that essential Dickensian figure, the wealthy but benevolent man who, far from seeing money as his chief business, can say with the ghost of Jacob Marley: 'Mankind was my business. The common welfare was my business; charity, mercy, forbearance, and benevolence, were all my business. The dealings of my trade were but a drop of water in the comprehensive ocean of my business.'

Dicken's next work again conveys the conversion of a hard and life-denying business man, but where *A Christmas Carol* is a moral fable, *Dombey and Son* (1848) is the first work of Dickens's maturity and a novel of exceptional range and subtle suggestiveness. In offering a panoramic view of a society in the throes of change, Dickens here emerges as one of the supreme figures of nineteenth-century fiction, the first great English novelist to describe the discontents of urban industrial life. His genius at last stands fully revealed.

So great an advance required a major extension of technique. What in Dickens's earlier works often appears improvised or even careless is here focused through telling juxtapositions of character and a play of imagery that at once probes the personal and social influences at work in the late 1840s and relates these to a view of the ultimately mysterious forces of life, a view that is truly poetic in its subtle comprehensiveness.

At the centre of the novel stands Dombey himself, the representative of the great business house of Dombey and Son. And it is the implications of a 'house' as both a commercial enterprise and a home for living souls that lie near the heart of the work. In a world of pride and money-consciousness however the first meaning brutally crushes the second:

The earth was made for Dombey and Son to trade in, and the sun and moon were made to give them light. Rivers and seas were formed to float their ships; rainbows gave them promise of fair weather; winds blew for or against their enterprises; stars and planets circled in their orbits, to preserve inviolate a system of which they were the centre.

Dombey is stiff and cold with commercial pride, a man whose blinkered, utilitarian vision reduces all around him to the chilling soullessness of the cash nexus, a brutal, masculine and ultimately self-defeating rigidity. The birth of his son, little Paul Dombey, is seen by him not as the coming into the world of a human being but as the arrival of a commodity that will extend the life-denying existence of the firm. Paul's coldly funereal christening at which Dombey's glance seems to freeze even the water in the font is a brilliantly ironic rendering of a heartlessness that turns all to ice.

But the boy's birth has been accompanied by his mother's death, and with this comes a source of imagery opposed to that associated with Dombey. We are shown the warm salt tears of his daughter Florence, the novel's heroine and the apparently redundant female embodiment of sentiment and love. And with Florence's tears are associated the great, ever-moving expanses of the sea. Throughout the novel, the ocean suggests death, eternity and the natural rhythms of life – mysterious, profound, but ultimately spiritual and free. It is to such forces as these that the dying Mrs Dombey surrenders when, with Florence in her tearful embrace, and 'clinging fast to that slight spar within her arms, the mother drifted out upon the dark and unknown sea that rolls round all the world'. The dying Paul is also identified with the waves. Later, the sea cruelly separates Florence from her father's clerk Walter Gay when Dombey and Son has become merely Dombey and Daughter. Nautical images also sustain the warm but threatened world of Captain Cuttle and his kin.

One threat posed to these old and often decaying forces of life is that of modern industrial progress, here symbolized by the railway. Dickens's handling of this theme shows the power of his imagination whereby social forces can be portrayed almost as characters. The railway invades lives, is praised or reacted against, but changes all about it irrecoverably. People like the inhabitants of Staggs Gardens see an old-fashioned life transformed into a new world of threat and promise. As the tracks are laid, so such characters are forced to recognize how 'the yet unfinished and unopened Railroad was in progress; and from the very core of all this dire disorder, trailed smoothly away, upon its mighty course of civilization and improvement'.

But if the railway is a power for new life in the novel it is also a force for death. After he has been left a widower, Dombey marries into a hollow and heartless aristocracy (the ancient nobility and the *nouveaux riches* are lethally described) only to have his new wife deceive him with his villainous employee Carker. But Carker himself is eventually crushed beneath the iron forces of progress. In addition, Florence deserts her father and Dombey's business fails. His house is reduced to a hollow shell for thoughts of suicide and despair.

The ending of *Dombey and Son* is not pessimistic however. The man who froze his daughter with a stare is humanized and redeemed.

Florence returns amid rain and tears in a scene of the greatest Dickensian melodrama. Nor are Walter and Florence herself finally parted. The sea brings the boy home while turning to good his uncle's investments. Walter's path to success is now assured and is tempered by our knowledge of his humanity. Hearts do change. An improvement in the sometime leaders of society can be wrought. As the ageing Dombey sheds tears of love over his family, so a mechanistic world is redeemed by natural feeling.

David Copperfield (1850) was Dickens's own favourite among his novels and has remained so with generations of his readers. The reasons for such popularity are not far to seek. In this work, Dickens drew on the traumas of his own childhood and the unhappiness of his youth to create a fictional autobiography in which the psychological forces of personal experience are revealed through a series of the most vivid characters and incidents, thereby suggesting a richly human passage to maturity.

The hero's boyhood is deprived of strong parents (David's father is dead, his mother is flighty and empty-headed) and it is populated by good fairies and ogres: Peggotty, the loving, rough-handed opposite to David's mother, and the sadistic Murdstone and his repellent sister by whom David is humiliated on his return from his idyllic stay in Yarmouth. It is Murdstone who also sends the boy first to a cruel school and then to the horrors of the blacking factory. Here Dickens the novelist touches the anguished centre of Dickens the man. His own parents, confined to the debtors' prison, had obliged him to similar degradation, and it left a permanent scar on his emotions. As Dickens wrote to Forster:

The deep remembrance of the sense I had of being utterly neglected and hopeless; of the shame I felt in my position; of the misery it was to my young heart to believe that, day by day, what I had learned and delighted in, and raised my fancy and my emulation up by, was passing away from me, never to be brought back any more; cannot be written. My whole nature was so penetrated with the grief and humiliation of such considerations, that even now, famous and caressed and happy, I often forget in my dreams that I have a dear wife and children; even that I am a man; and wander desolately back to that time in my life.

In the novel, only the Micawbers, feckless and irresponsible as they are, can bring laughter into this hell. Mr Micawber – comically orotund, hopelessly optimistic that 'something will turn up' – is an image of Dickens's father and one of the most memorable of the author's inventions. That he is later used to work the downfall of Uriah Heep, whose hypocritical fawning makes him an equally effective character, suggests the novel's intricate patterning of good and evil, of thwarted childhood innocence and fallen idols, themes personified in the lubricious Steerforth and his seduction of Little Em'ly. Similarly, David's first wife Dora, a psychologically telling simulacrum of his mother, proves to be an illusory angel. It is only when David has married Agnes Wickfield, dispatched many of the figures of his childhood to Australia and then established himself as a successful novelist that this archetypal Victorian hero finally feels able to count his blessings.

During the composition of *David Copperfield*, Dickens launched his weekly periodical *Household Words* (1850–59). 'Conducted', as the rubric expressed it, by Dickens himself, this twopenny magazine was to reach a circulation of 40,000. Dickens's own contributions, some of which were later issued as *Reprinted Pieces* (1858), reveal the passionate social commentator. In 'A Nightly Scene in London' (January 1856), for example, we see him shake a ragged bundle by the workhouse door. 'The rags began to be slowly stirred within, as little by little a head was unshrouded.' Asked if she has eaten, the woman twice denies it. But proof leads to helpless compassion. 'She bared her neck, and I covered it up again.'

Such was the Victorian England of Malthus and the disciples of *laissez-faire*, the butts of Dickens's profound moral indignation. 'I utterly renounce and abominate them in their insanity,' he wrote, 'and I address people with respect for the spirit of the New Testament, who do mind such things, and who think them infamous in our streets.' These streets were now those of the richest capital in the Western world, of an England mounting to the high plateau of mid-Victorian prosperity, and celebrating its confidence in the Great Exhibition of 1851. Against the vulgarity of the Crystal Palace however, Dickens now juxtaposed the nightmare of *Bleak House* (1853). The most famous novelist of Victorian England became one of its greatest critics. Dickens's engagement with his age was complete.

Bleak House is a labyrinthine indictment of contemporary conditions and a work in which Dickens's range of techniques was wrought to its highest pitch and then augmented with a new daring. Brooding over the whole is the Court of Chancery and the case of Jarndyce and Jarndyce, Dickens's fog-bound, life-denying symbol of what John Jarndyce himself calls 'trickery, evasion, procrastination, spoilation, botheration . . . false pretences of all sorts'. The Court of Chancery and the case of Jarndyce and Jarndyce itself which eventually swallows the disputants' moneys are Dickens's images of an England debilitated by 'the system' and a hideously perverse society.

This last ranges from the magisterial pomposity of Sir Walter Dedlock to little Jo the crossing-sweeper, ignorant, abused, neglected, yet central to the whole vast and hideous machinery of the Victorian England that crushes him. As in his life, so in his death from smallpox, Jo is a figure who links the highest to the lowest. He is the most pathetic of many victims of political mismanagement and complacency, of filth, the slums and the absurdity of philanthropists who ignore the wretched sitting on their own doorsteps. In *Bleak House*, these forces collide as Victorian society gropes its way through a fog of corruption, greed and terrible spiritual deadness.

Dickens's imagery of corruption is one of his supreme techniques for exposing the society about him while binding together a novel whose social range – the awareness of a whole society – is an imaginative achievement of the highest order. Yet within the complex entanglements of *Bleak House*, and worked out with an assured narrative mastery, are other devices which, for original readers of the monthly parts, provided a degree of suspense comparable to the detective fiction Dickens here helped to inaugurate. These techniques also offered a diversity of comment and a range of incidents that were without precedent. The interconnectedness of this huge work is a phenomenal achievement, and repeated readings bear out Forster's claim that 'nothing is introduced at random, everything tends to the catastrophe, the various lines of the plot converge and fit to its centre'.

The narrative of Esther Summerson is one of these devices. Virginal, self-deprecating and sensitive, Esther is Dickens's largely passive voice of human decency and a figure who develops from a maudlin dependence on John Jarndyce, through a recognition of her love for the worthy Alan Woodcourt and the ravages of smallpox (no figure is immune to the contamination of society), and on to the nightmare revelation that she is the illegitimate daughter of Lady Dedlock. Finally, she achieves domestic happiness.

Esther observes nearly all the characters in the novel and provides a moral register against which to measure them. She is involved, for example, with many of the victims of Chancery: Ada Clare and the weak Richard Carstone who inevitably deteriorates as he is drawn into its workings; Gridley, another figure destroyed by the system; and the marvellous figure of Miss Flite, half-crazed yet full of humanity and suggesting in her confused way that the day of judgement in Jarndyce and Jarndyce will be at one with the Day of Doom itself. Miss Flite's cracked mind prompts thoughts of the fall of the mighty and the coming of divine vengeance. We might laugh at her obsessions, but she also suggests that in this corrupt land the day of the Apocalypse may well be nigh.

Such an awareness of doom is also suggested through other grotesque yet sinister figures in the subplot, above all 'Chancellor' Krook, the villainous rag-and-bone dealer with his 'liking for rust and must and cobwebs' and his sadistic sense of power and greed. The masterpiece of symbolic narrative that is Krook's death by 'Spontaneous Combustion' suggests the inevitable end of an entire way of life. 'Chancellor' Krook is incinerated by a force 'inborn, inbred, engendered in the corrupt humours of the vicious body itself'. An incident so amazing that only a novelist of genius could have risked it provides a grotesque summation of all the evils in Victorian society.

Dickens's comic genius flays the social parasites in the novel with merciless inventiveness, while Esther's appalled response deepens his criticism of such figures as Mr Skimpole, the irresponsible and mercenary aesthete, and Turveydrop, the dandy and exploiter of his wife. Other grotesques include Chadband, the nauseating voice of evangelical Anglicanism; Mrs Pardiggle, the High Church philanthropist 'pouncing upon the poor, and applying benevolence to them like a strait-jacket'; and Mrs Jellyby, reducing her home to slovenly chaos and ignoring the likes of Jo as she pursues plans for 'cultivating coffee and educating the natives of Borrioboola-Gha on the left bank of the Niger'.

Yet the comic grotesque is only one aspect of the rottenness in *Bleak House*. Nearer Chancery and the rapacious centre of a corrupt society move figures of sinister and sterile energies. There are the Smallweeds, that 'horny-skinned, two-legged, money-getting species of spider'. There is 'Conversation' Kenge who, as he praises the law, gently moves 'his right hand as if it were a silver trowel, with which to spread the cement of his words on the structure of the system and consolidate it for a thousand ages'. There is Vholes the solicitor glimpsed as he 'takes off his close black gloves as if he were skinning his hands', and, above all, there is Tulkinghorn. Lone, sadistic, secret, 'mechanically faithful without attachment', dead to all feelings save his own perverse relish of power, Tulkinghorn stalks through Chancery, the slums and the houses of the great, closing in on Lady Dedlock in order to blackmail her over her long-dead affair with Jo's friend the drug-addict Nemo and his knowledge of Esther, the child of Lady Dedlock's liaison. Tulkinghorn's murder is one of the novel's greatest moments and ironically deprives the lawyer of his victory over his prey.

In these terrible areas, the voice of the third-person narrator carries the weight of Dickens's indignation by the exhilarated variety of its language. This range is one of the supreme achievements of nineteenth-century fiction. Here is the voice that can create the image of a fog-bound Chancery and connect it to the inertness and horror of the Dedlocks' home at Chesney Wold. It is the voice of invocation and apostrophe that winds about Nemo in his pauper's grave, the voice that conjures up the slum of Tom-All-Alone's. The narrator's is a voice that explores every variety of hell and hypocrisy in Victorian England and, as a result, it is finally the voice of righteous indignation. Nowhere does Dickens more effectively combine pathos with prophetic denunciation than as Woodcourt watches over the dying Jo:

'Jo, can you say what I say?'

'I'll say anythink as you say, sir, fur I knows it's good.'

'OUR FATHER.'

'Our Father! – yes that's weery good, sir.'

'WHICH ART IN HEAVEN.'

'Art in Heaven – is the light a-comin', sir?'

'It is close at hand.

'HALLOWED BE THY NAME!'

'Hallowed be – thy—'

The light is come upon the dark benighted way. Dead! Dead, your majesty. Dead, my lords and gentlemen. Dead, Right Reverends and Wrong Reverends of every order. Dead, men and women, born with Heavenly compassion in your hearts. And dying thus around us every day.

As Dickens here speaks out in his own person and addresses the whole community of his readers, so, in a manner of the greatest importance to nineteenth-century fiction, we hear the novelist himself rousing what he can assume to be the best, fundamental and shared values of his audience. His art is an appeal to the experience of stable and universal moral truths. However bizarre his characters, however contrived his events and however far the world he criticizes has veered from these assumptions, Dickens believes he can share with his readers an essentially New Testament morality, a core of timeless values against which to denounce the aberrations of the present.

In *Hard Times* (1854), Dickens's voice of denunciation is levelled at the irresponsible excesses of industrial *laissez-faire* and the blighting force of utilitarianism. Coketown, Dickens's image of the industrial cities of the North, is an unnatural hell sweltering in machine oil, a place where nature has been ousted by industry and 'the whir of shafts and wheels'. Such an environment is the hideous outcome of a hideous philosophy, the utilitarianism caricatured (much to Mill's annoyance) in Dickens's portrayal of Gradgrind and his school:

Now, what I want is, Facts. Teach these boys and girls nothing but Facts. Facts alone are wanted in life. Plant nothing else, and root out everything else. You can only form the minds of reasoning animals upon Facts: nothing else will ever be of service to them. This is the principle on which I bring up my own children, and this is the principle upon which I bring up these children. Stick to Facts, sir!

This is a philosophy that brings its terrible revenges. The life of Gradgrind's daughter is blighted, while his son finds relief in compulsive gambling. When Tom Gradgrind is eventually tracked down by Bitzer, a product of Gradgrind's school, a callous system rebounds on its patron's head. Bitzer brings a villain to justice but also serves his own ends. He will be promoted to Tom's job. Gradgrind himself is horrified at this, but he is the victim of the very rules he has promulgated. '"I beg your pardon for interrupting, sir," returned Bitzer; "but I am sure you know that the whole social system is a question of self-interest."'

The paranoid logic of this belief is personified in Josiah Bounderby the self-made industrialist, a man wholly devoid of compassion and yet, by a telling paradox, driven partly by the forces of imagination he himself would deny. So obsessive is his ideal of the self-made man that he invents for himself a destitute childhood, an imaginary gutter from which he has risen by a triumph of commercial drive. In his delusion, Bounderby believes that he has genuinely brought about the greatest happiness of the greatest number. For him, the pollution and industry of Coketown are not a nightmare but a dream come true. Smoke becomes 'the healthiest thing in the world', while the grinding toil of the factory is 'the pleasantest of work there is, and it's the lightest work there is, and it's the best paid work there is'. With a bizarre flight of fantasy, Bounderby even claims that Turkey carpets on the factory floors might be a final refinement of felicity, but this is an expense he will not be put to. Inflated with self-satisfied delusion, Bounderby is Dickens's horrific image of the triumph of modern industrial man and *laissez-faire* gone mad.

Dickens's portrayal of his working-class characters is less successful, and points to the limits of his social criticism. Massively indignant though his response to contemporary suffering was, his anger was essentially what Walter Bagehot (1826–77), the miscellaneous gentleman journalist and mildly progressive authority on *The English Constitution* (1867), was to call 'sentimental radicalism'.

The crushing effect of the mechanical and unimaginative is sharply delineated in *Hard Times*, yet in the character of Stephen Blackpool, Dickens fails to give a wholly adequate account of the industrial proletariat. Blackpool is too easily the martyr, a victim of the plot as much as of the system. His refusal to join a trade union leads to him being ostracized by his fellow workers and paradoxically to his being sacked. Dickens's portrayal of the union movement itself as a hectoring and aggressive centre of self-interest is crude and suggests the author's failure adequately to come to terms with the forces of the industrial world about him. In the end, what stands against heartless exploitation is not the genuine efforts of the workers and a real engagement with society but a retreat into the innocent glitter of the circus world of Mr Sleary and his kind. 'There was a remarkable gentleness and childishness about these people,' Dickens wrote, 'a special inaptitude for any kind of sharp practice and an untiring readiness to help and pity one another, deserving often of as much respect, and always of as much generous construction, as the everyday virtues of any class of people in the world.' But this is mere sentimentality, and its obverse was the profound pessimism embodied in *Little Dorrit* (1857).

Little Dorrit is an intricate maze of real and metaphorical prisons and of characters trapped in the worlds of self-seeking aristocratic patronage, bungling bureaucracy, criminal financial schemes, rigid class loyalties, wretched families and corrupting self-deceit. It is Dickens's darkest work. 'I have no present political faith or hope – not a grain,' Dickens had written to a friend in 1855. His disillusion with public life is conveyed in *Little Dorrit* through one of his most telling social symbols: the Circumlocution Office. Here, under the pompous sway of the Barnacle and Stiltstalking families, nepotism and incompetence thrive, while the England that this corrupt civil service is supposed to administer is paralysed by institutional inertia and jobbery. 'The Circumlocution Office went on mechanically, every day, keeping this wonderful, all-sufficient wheel of statesmanship, How not to do it, in motion . . . The Circumlocution Office was down upon any ill-advised public servant who was going to do it, with a minute, and a memorandum, and a letter of instructions, that extinguished him.'

Where the Circumlocution Office is an image of corruption in high and public places and of a system that emasculates those who come into contact with it, Bleeding Heart Yard is a prison for the unfortunate, a poverty trap of soul-destroying squalor. Here live families like the Plornishes whose father has eventually to be consigned to the workhouse. This prison of the spirit has its governor in Casby 'the Last of the Patriarchs', the useless and exploitative landlord who in his turn is the victim of his agent who eventually exposes him for the sham he is.

It is part of Dickens's purpose in the novel to show that Casby is a bad father, a man who has played his part in separating the novel's middle-aged and depressive hero Arthur Clennam from his first love.

Dickens's most telling image of parental irresponsibility and the effects of imprisonment however is William Dorrit, the 'Father of the Marshalsea'. Twenty-three years in the debtors' prison turn the feckless Dorrit into a foolish and often heartless victim of self-delusion. Just as society outside the prison is conceived as a series of gaols and cells, of lying and hypocritical characters trapped in the confinement of their fantasies, so the Marshalsea sets up its own absurd and debilitating illusions. As Mr Dorrit languishes his life away, 'a disposition began to be observed in him, to exaggerate the number of years he had been there; it was generally understood that you must deduct a few from his account; he was vain, the fleeting generations of debtors said'.

Among these drunken and shabby inmates, Dorrit himself acquires a spurious social status and with it an ever-deepening moral blindness. This is suggested when he suddenly inherits the money that frees him, throws a party for the prisoners and leaves the Marshalsea in a triumphal procession but without Little Dorrit herself who has fainted and been forgotten. Shades of the prison house never leave the family however. The proudly *nouveaux riches* Dorrits roam Europe, constantly meeting people whose empty lives 'greatly resembled a superior sort of Marshalsea'. Finally, in Dorrit's pathetic speech to his horrified dinner guests in Rome, the senile recidivist is transported back in imagination to the gaol he has never really left.

The world of high society is likewise a gaol and place of corruption. Mrs Merdle the financier's wife believes society has 'made its mind up on the subject, and there is nothing more to be said'. Her caged parrot hideously mimics such attitudes, and together mistress and bird suggest a claustrophobic and foolish world that is a sham beneath. Mr Merdle the financier, as mysterious in his origins as in his activities, admired and courted by society, proves to be a villain whose suicide removes from the world 'the greatest Forger and the greatest Thief that ever cheated the gallows'. This was nonetheless the man whom bishops courted and politicians praised.

But just as society is seen in terms of fraud and the prisons in which it would place its erring members, so the dour religion of Mrs Clennam is a monstrous hypocrisy which masks criminal actions, emasculates the man she pretends is her son and reduces the woman herself to a neurotic cripple imprisoned in a crumbling house. The worst excesses of Victorian piety are here revealed as a festering gaol of the spirit. In such a world, heroes and heroines can be no glittering figures. Amy Dorrit, living by the New Testament, forgiving, meek and loving, and Arthur Clennam, blighted yet eventually finding love and a home, suggest by their marriage the only positives Dickens could now offer. After a ceremony solemnized in the shadow of the Marshalsea, they go down the church steps together and to 'a modest life of usefulness and happiness . . . and as they passed along in sunshine and in shade, the noisy and the eager, and the arrogant and the froward and the vain, fretted, and chafed, and made their usual uproar'. The couple find an autumnal happiness in a world of stifling corruption and psychological constraint. The romantic triumphalism that concludes *David Copperfield* is here chastened to a brave and modest ordinariness which marks the deepening of Dickens's mature thought.

The psychological effects of long imprisonment are one of the more telling areas in a novel that is otherwise a historical melodrama written to launch Dickens's magazine *All the Year Round* (1859–95). *A Tale of Two Cities* (1859) clearly shows the influence of Dickens's reading of *The French Revolution* and Carlyle's analysis of a decadent aristocracy. Dickens's use of the identical figures of Charles Darnay and Sidney Carton is deft rather than analytical however. Much of the tension and historical detail are well handled, while Carton's last speech is perhaps the best-known passage in all of Dickens's work – a highly professional tear-jerker. It is in the figure of Dr Manette however, imprisoned for nearly eighteen years and just holding on to his sanity through the exercise of his shoemaking craft, that the novel's most telling power resides.

Great Expectations (1861) is an altogether finer work. Here Dickens turned from corruption in society to the corruption of the individual. The novel is much concerned with the nature of true gentility and discusses this theme through the voice of an autobiographical narrator. Pip's chastened reflections after the collapse of his hopes reveal his youthful aspirations to status to have been a hollow and heartless sham. Such a procedure allowed Dickens to ally shrewd and sensitive moral awareness to a plot in which mystery and suspense are expertly controlled. *Great Expectations* also reveals the mature dramatic mastery that allowed its author to create some of his greatest set-piece scenes.

None of these is more powerful than the boy Pip's first encounter with the convict Magwitch. The superbly sensationalistic effects are nonetheless subtly related to the book's main themes. The innocent and frightened charity that provides food and a file for the starving prisoner, for example, is finely contrasted to the disdain with which the adult Pip observes Magwitch's gross manners on his illicit return from transportation. We see not only how the child has matured to a snob, but how the snob is a product of his ignorance of his true nature and circumstances. Pip's growing charity and Christian forgiveness however show a reawakening of moral virtue. In addition, the dawning realization that it is the criminal Magwitch who is both the true source of his wealth and the father of his beloved Estella unites the narrative to the theme of growing self-awareness.

Pip slowly realizes that his aspirations to gentility have been founded on money rather than goodness of heart. But that money itself proves illusory. As the worldly wealth of an illegally returned convict it is forfeit to the Crown. In the midst of growing self-awareness, Pip is suddenly left penniless. He has been trained for nothing useful and is also deeply in debt after a feckless life spent dancing attendance on Estella. The discovery that this superbly characterized embodiment of frigid sexual allure – the product of the jilted Miss Havisham's desire for revenge on men – is also Magwitch's child reduces all Pip's expectations to dust.

At the nadir of his fortunes he is saved by the resources of true gentility. First, Herbert Pocket, the natural gentleman, offers his friend a job. Pip must now earn his keep. He must also recognize who his true benefactors are. The orphan boy, who, led into moral delusion by Magwitch's money, thought he was Miss Havisham's heir and wilfully adopted her values, finally discovers that his real mainstay is neither a criminal nor an old and embittered woman but Joe the blacksmith who first took him in as a child. Big-hearted, honestly simple, well adapted to his world and his work, it is Joe who nurses Pip in his sickness and Joe who wins Biddy, the country girl Pip in his pride had shunned.

Self-awareness and the knowledge that human goodness is true gentility are bought by Pip at the cost of painful isolation and suffering, a process that Dickens, swayed by his friend Bulwer-Lytton, brought to an end in the revised close to the novel by hinting that

Pip would eventually marry Estella. Many readers however may prefer his first thoughts and the original anticlimax of Pip's last meeting with the chastened woman who has wrecked his emotional life and who, in truth, he can never marry.

Dickens's concern with the moral damage inflicted by the obsessive pursuit of wealth and social position is again central to his last completed novel. In *Our Mutual Friend* (1865), the blighting effect of money on individuals and their society and environment is luridly symbolized by the mounds of 'dust' – the accumulated piles of human waste – that are at once the sources of wealth and of corruption in the work. At the centre of the immensely intricate plot, and suggesting the forces of death and power Dickens associated with money, are the will of Old Harmon and the wealth he has built up from 'coal-dust, vegetable-dust, bone-dust, crockery-dust, rough dust and sifted dust – all manner of Dust'. In life a miser gaoling the spirits of those around him, in death Harmon still asserts his power. His servants the Boffins inherit his wealth, while his son, required by the terms of his father's will to marry Bella Wilfer, is obliged to watch the seeming corruption of both the Boffins and his future bride as they appear to sink into the depths of mercenary corruption.

Around the Boffins gather the forces of society in a world where money is all and the vulgarity of the *nouveaux riches* is triumphant. 'Have no antecedents, no established character, no cultivation, no ideas, no manners; have shares.' Such a society becomes a chorus of bigotry and banality. We are shown the Veneerings whose name aptly suggests the brittle and gaudy surface glued over the rotten wood beneath, and Podsnap that incarnation of the worst excesses of Victorian jingoism and prudery who waves aside any topic whose impropriety might raise a blush on his repellent daughter's cheek. A bored, languid and trivial aristocracy swells these ranks. As Boffin's money buys him position, so we see 'all manner of crawling, creeping, fluttering and buzzing creatures, attracted by the gold dust of the Golden Dustman'. Dickens offers a compelling picture of the gaudy and complacent society of the new rich in alliance with an emasculated nobility. These voices are his most powerful satire of a money-obsessed world and of a Victorian England whose leaders are portrayed as gilded scavengers on a waste tip.

Around and beneath these stifling figures, choking in the shadows of the dust mounds or drawn to the polluted waters of the Thames, move other figures variously caught in speculation and fraud. The Lammels, victims of the mutual deceit by which each wrongly believed the other to be rich, batten on society to exploit it. Dickens's presentation of this couple, his mixing of narrative with symbol, reveals depths of psychological and technical resource which are again reflected in his presentation of extreme states of violent and barely repressed emotion. Indeed, the most successful parts of the novel are much concerned with sterile lives and dark forces. The grotesquely gilded London of high society, of lowering dust heaps and emotional death, is also the London of the night river, murder and attempted murder.

Of the two rivals for Lizzie Hexam the boatman's child, Bradley Headstone is Dickens's portrait of emotional and social dislocation and of suppressed passion. Eugene Wrayburn, his victim, is initially presented as his perfect complement: blasé, privileged and spiteful. His love for a girl wholly outside his class and his symbolic rebirth after Headstone has nearly drowned him in the Thames suggest Dickens's concern with the regeneration of society through the education of the heart. Nonetheless, it is Headstone himself we most vividly recall as, in defeat, he sinks to the floor 'and grovelled there, with the palms of his hands tight-clasping his hot temples, in unutterable misery, and unrelieved by a single tear'. Such melodrama points forward to Dickens's last and uncompleted novel, *Edwin Drood* (1870) with its atmosphere of murder, drug addiction and confused identity.

4

Dickens both learned from and inspired his contemporaries, and the melodramatic atmosphere of *Edwin Drood* suggests the influence of his friendship with the first and greatest of the Victorian 'sensation' novelists, Wilkie Collins (1824–89). In the works of Collins himself and such writers as Charles Reade (1814–84), the influence of serial publication, along with a craving for excitement amid calm, mid-century prosperity, contributed to the development of convoluted plots and thrilling effects. These were then allied to a concern with such social issues as prison abuse, enforced restraint in lunatic asylums, bigamy and criminal womanhood.

In *The Woman in White* (1860), Collins explored such themes through an originally contrived mixture of testamentary evidence, diaries, letters and sensational events. Walter Hartright's first encounter with the heroine, for example – the ghostly woman in white who accosts him on a lonely Hampstead high road – opposes the ordinary to the melodramatic with startling effect, an effect deepened by Collins's powers of characterization. The fat, chain-smoking Count Fosco is a memorable 'Napoleon of crime', while the plain, intelligent and forceful Marian Halcombe effectively subverts many stereotypes of the Victorian woman in fiction. Even more sensationally, in *Lady Audley's Secret* (1862) by Mary Braddon (1837–1915), the heroine turns to murder and, after a powerful denunciation of women's social and sexual frustration, feigns madness and dies in exile.

The emergence of an organized police force led to the inevitable portrayal of the detective in fiction. Dickens had offered the first such figure in *Bleak House*, but it is with Sergeant Cuff in Collins's *The Moonstone* (1868) that we have what T.S. Eliot described as 'the first, longest and best of English detective novels'. The work vividly combines the surface respectability of the Victorian great house with drugs, suicide and the sinister menace of Hindu thuggees.

Collins's interest in the supernatural suggests the Victorian development of the ghost story, a genre explored by Dickens in *The Haunted Man* (1848). It is with Sheridan Le Fanu (1814–73) however that we find the first Victorian writer whose finest work is all in a supernatural or occult mode. *The House by the Churchyard* (1863) contains excellent ghostly incidents, while *Uncle Silas* (1864) shows the physical world dissolving horribly into supernatural fear, a haunting that is a truly psychological terror.

5

Dickens's interest in the 'condition-of-England question' brought him into contact with other novelists concerned with social problems. 'I do honestly know that there is no living English writer whose aid I would desire to enlist in preference to the authoress of *Mary Barton*,' he wrote in his role as the editor of *Household Words*. *Mary Barton* (1848), the first published novel of Mrs Elizabeth Gaskell (1810–65), draws on her experience of life in the great cotton-spinning town of Manchester, then the most advanced city of the nineteenth-century industrial world. Presenting a finely observed view of the working people, and observing their lives with deep but far from sentimental passion, the work was an important contribution to the 'condition-of-England question' and to what Gaskell herself called 'the struggle on the part of the work people to obtain what they esteem their rights'.

Gaskell shows both how evil and eventually how tragic this lack of communication between the classes is. Only at the end when John Barton has murdered Harry Carson, and factory owner and employee are brought together for a last time, are they obliged to confront their mutual humanity and recognize that they are 'brothers in the deep suffering of the heart'. The humanitarianism that ran so deeply in Mrs Gaskell's Unitarian world of Manchester's Cross Street Chapel is here pitted against the wrongs of the industrial world. Once again, it is suggested that necessary social change must spring from a change of heart.

In *Ruth* (1853), Mrs Gaskell took as her heroine a serving girl forced into the anguish of unmarried motherhood and yet rising above conventional condemnation to become a figure of genuine moral strength and independence. At the close of the work, Ruth gives of herself so generously that she can nurse the man who fathered her child while rejecting him as a partner. As Ruth herself dies of typhus, so she underlines what was then seen as Mrs Gaskell's controversial conviction that the 'fallen woman' may yet achieve moral grandeur.

North and South (1855) returns to the theme of industrial conflict and juxtaposes the traditional values of Mrs Gaskell's heroine Margaret Hale to the uncaring exploitation of the northern industrial world personified in the factory owner John Thornton. The scenes of urban squalor and unrest are again powerfully presented, but Gaskell's principal interest is less in working-class consciousness than in the moral and emotional growth of her leading figures. Margaret, for example, comes to appreciate the values of an alien culture, while

Thornton comes to recognize the need for an altogether more humane approach to his work-force. Carlyle's belief that the cash nexus is not the sole relationship of man to man is here explored through excellent characterization, thereby allowing Gaskell to wed moral purpose to the techniques of fiction. The success with which she portrays the social implications of Thornton's pride and Margaret's prejudice places her in the tradition that evolved from Jane Austen, and Gaskell's other works show further aspects of this side of her craft.

Cranford (1853), for example, although a collection of incidents rather than a true novel, portrays life in a small town with both shrewdness and charm. In this very female world – the vaunted independence of Gaskell's provincial amazons is slyly but gently handled – propriety is all. The incidents that ruffle this demure surface (the embarrassments of Miss Matty in particular) are handled with smiling humanity, and *Cranford* breathes a warm and innocent pleasure that is wholly delightful.

Sylvia's Lovers (1863), Mrs Gaskell's only historical novel, is one of her less successful works, but the unfinished *Wives and Daughters* (1865) is a deeply satisfying study of character viewed through a mature and unobtrusive mastery of technique. Beautifully observed in its physical details and subtle in its presentation of its central characters, *Wives and Daughters* is a fragment of life illuminated by richly experienced understanding and an intelligence that has no need to reach out to explicit moral statement. The work shows the full development of Gaskell's art and places her far above the category of the merely interesting minor novelist.

6

Elizabeth Gaskell was also the author of one of the most esteemed Victorian biographies, *The Life of Charlotte Brontë* (1857). Her portrayal of her friend is an account (much revised after threats of libel prosecution) of a strong-minded and selfless woman's fortitude in the face of psychological extremism and remorseless personal tragedy. Above all, it is a portrait of a major author and her background in a family whose contribution to English literature is of incalculable richness. Enshrined in national legend, the Brontës remain the great radicals of nineteenth-century fiction.

Mrs Gaskell powerfully evoked the isolation and proximity to death that marked the Brontës' life in the remote Yorkshire village of Haworth. At the parsonage itself, intense introversion was enforced by a depressive father and a strict aunt, thereby obliging children of the highest intelligence to develop without ready contact with the outside world. As Charlotte herself wrote: 'we were wholly dependent on ourselves and each other, on books and study, for the enjoyments and occupations of life. The highest stimulus, as well as the liveliest pleasure we had known from childhood upwards, lay in attempts at literary composition.'

Among these early attempts were epic sagas in verse and prose. From the characters given to some toy soldiers, Charlotte (1816–55) and her brother Branwell (1817–48) created the imaginary world of Angria, Emily (1818–48) and Anne (1820–49) the realm of Gondal. Extremes of passion fed by the children's reading of Shakespeare and the Bible, Bunyan, Byron and Scott, created worlds of elemental intensity. For Emily, such worlds offered a vocabulary for imaginative experiences of mystic intensity. For Anne and above all for Charlotte, realization of a more mundane existence helped shape a fiction in which the passionate individual is obliged to face the constraints of her daily life.

Charlotte's first novel *The Professor*, published posthumously in 1857, draws on aspects of her experience as a teacher. *Jane Eyre* (1847) also draws on its author's work as a governess but transcends the merely local to offer a challenging account of the demands made on the world by a strong and passionate woman obliged to challenge conventional social and spiritual constraints. Moral freedom, sexual desire and Charlotte Brontë's intuition of the forces of the unconscious are felt as imperatives throughout *Jane Eyre*, while imagery and symbolism shape the novel's development with compelling resource.

Just as *Jane Eyre* draws on the romantic tradition of Byron, Scott and the Gothic to challenge ideas of realism – Scott's 'art of copying from nature as she really exists in the common walks of life' – so the novel also develops a deeply held and radical Christian belief. In particular, conventional Christian morality and the place it assigned to women are here felt to crush the spirit. In what we may see as a Victorian reworking of *Pilgrim's Progress*, we come to realize that Jane's development is the growth to maturity of a strong-minded Christian gentlewoman living under the sway of Providence. A too easy assumption of conventional beliefs and social roles is thus challenged by a mind at once devout but enquiring. Fiction creates imagined worlds which have the power to disturb and criticize the normal and the given. *Jane Eyre* assumes one of the great purposes of art as it challenges the limits of the culture in which it was created.

The child is mother to the woman, and Jane's defiance of her repulsive aunt shows both her early awareness of the freedom she needs for her emotional health as well as, in the horrors of the red room, the fear and isolation suffered by those obliged to rebel. Her subsequent incarceration in the hypocritical and evangelical world of Mr Brocklehurst, the 'black marble clergyman', creates another prison of the spirit. While the Christian stoicism of Helen Burns and the nourishing, cultivated influence of Miss Temple suggest the defences some women could develop in a world of patriarchal dominance, Jane herself is obliged to go beyond these. She longs to 'surmount the blue peaks'. Nonetheless, as merely a poor female in a world of men and money, her escape can only be into the apparently restricting role of governess. She goes to Thornfield and there meets Rochester.

The passion of Jane and Rochester is Charlotte Brontë's mightiest achievement. It is above all her assertion of the importance of sexual passion in a woman's quest for experience. This recognition is powerfully supported by a natural imagery which is also symbolic of supernatural moral agency. The mighty tree by which the lovers plight their troth is struck by lightning and split in two while remaining joined at the roots. The naturalness of the lovers' passion is thereby suggested but so too are the mysteries and moral prohibitions which prevent its immediate fulfilment. For Jane, Rochester's house is at once a new Eden and Bluebeard's castle. It is a place of hope but also a place of terror where Bertha Mason, Rochester's first wife, lives as a restrained lunatic. Thornfield, as its name implies, is truly a place of tribulation.

But it is also a focus for the operation of Providence, for a recognition of the laws of God and man and for the testing of moral fortitude. Jane's bigamous wedding is prevented by the last-minute arrival of Mason and his revelation of Rochester's secret marriage. Crime is avoided, but in the terrible aftermath of disappointment we are shown both the anguish Rochester himself has suffered in his dark night of emotional deprivation and Jane's assertion of morality over passion. She quits Thornfield and the man she loves for she knows not what future in the valley of humiliation.

The twenty-eighth chapter of *Jane Eyre* presents the heroine's lowest point of isolation. Whitecross is a desert of solitude, and yet, as its name suggests, a place of Christian hope as well. Even in her loneliness, Jane is not wholly abandoned. Nature, grace and charity surround the suffering Christian. The heavens above her and the heath around reveal the glory of God, while a distant light providentially beckons Jane to a world of charity – to Diana, Mary and their brother St John Rivers.

St John Rivers is one of Charlotte Brontë's most daring creations, her portrait of an extreme puritanical Christianity which for all its moral fortitude is shown to be contrary to the heroine's true nature. St John Rivers's belief is hard and despotic. It is bound to the worship of a vindictive God and, for Jane herself, is ultimately a denial of life. Eventually, she comes to feel the influence of St John Rivers as an 'iron shroud'. This is a chilling image of emotional death and of a religious vocation to which, for all her deep belief, Jane herself is not called. Rather, it is the voice of nature and of Rochester that summons her to her true vocation in the marvellous moment when Jane hears her beloved call out through the night 'in pain and woe, wildly, eerily, urgently'. This is the cry of an all-mastering human love, of a maimed and repentant Rochester open to affection and an equality of joy. In one of the most moving moments in nineteenth-century fiction, the narrator finally declares: 'Reader, I married him.' The Christian gentlewoman has found her role in the natural world, while St John Rivers toils on alone towards a more arduous vision of the celestial city.

Charlotte Brontë's next novel, *Shirley* (1849), explores with great clarity the roles forced on Victorian women in a patriarchal society. 'Their good woman is a queer thing, half doll, half angel; their bad woman almost always a fiend,' the heroine declares. Though the plot is principally concerned with a re-creation of Yorkshire at the start of the century and the troubles of the mill owner Robert Moore, the greatest interest of the book now lies in its portrayal of Caroline Helstone and the eponymous heroine. Through these figures, Charlotte Brontë develops feminist views that are at once pessimistic and defiant. Caroline, for example, speaks out ardently on behalf of the depressed state of the nineteenth-century spinster, urging the belief that 'single women should have more to do – better chances of interesting and profitable occupation than they possess now'.

Many single women in reduced circumstances were nonetheless condemned to the role of governess, a humiliation portrayed with devastating accuracy in Anne Brontë's *Agnes Grey* (1847). It is in *Villette* (1853) however that Charlotte provides the most radical analysis of the lot of the socially dislocated woman. Lucy Snowe, estranged in Brussels (the 'Villette' of the novel), finds her 'innate capacity for expanse' constricted by an alien world. Madame Beck's school – an over-regulated hell of surveillance and espionage – depersonalizes the heroine until she is in danger of becoming merely an object among a mass of things. Such an alien world takes on a hallucinatory power, and Lucy wandering in drugged confusion through the streets of the town provides Charlotte Brontë with the most extreme of several opportunities for portraying the mind at the end of its tether.

In such a world, Lucy is obliged to define herself and discover her identity as a woman. As in *Jane Eyre*, Providence is central to this process. Lucy comes to understand that in her suffering there is an element of God's will. Her love for Paul Emanuel (a vibrantly emotional affair which centres on the clash of independence and submission) eventually allows Lucy to glimpse the possibility of future married happiness. The ambiguous conclusion of the novel however leaves the reader in doubt as to whether this will come to pass.

For many contemporaries, Charlotte Brontë's radical probing of a woman's needs and struggle for independence were profoundly shocking. Even her vocation as a writer was considered by some as an affront in an age that was increasingly trying to limit such women as continued to write to romance, domestic issues and narrowed horizons. 'Literature cannot be the business of a woman's life,' Southey wrote in reply to Charlotte Brontë's enquiry, 'and it ought not to be. The more she is engaged in her proper duties, the less leisure she will have for it, even as an accomplishment and a recreation.' In a world of such poisonous pomposity, the Brontës themselves initially felt obliged to issue their work under male pseudonyms: Charlotte as Currer Bell, and Anne and Emily as Acton and Ellis Bell. The deceit involved in this was discussed by Charlotte when she wrote about the sisters' 'vague impression that authoresses are liable to be looked on with prejudice'.

This fear was justified in the case of Anne Brontë's second novel, *The Tenant of Wildfell Hall* (1848). A number of readers saw through her pseudonym and were either shocked or enthralled by the novel's radical subject matter and the brutal scenes of alcoholism which drive Helen Huntingdon to leave her dissolute husband and, in defiance of law and convention, take her son with her when she adopts a new life and identity at Wildfell Hall itself. Though marred by its narrative method, the novel is a frank and clear-sighted account of its subject, while Anne's defence of her work is as startling as the book itself. 'All novels are or should be, written for both men and women to read,' she declared in her Preface, 'and I am at a loss to conceive how a man should permit himself to write anything that would be really disgraceful to a woman or why a woman should be censured for writing anything that would be proper and becoming for a man.'

Despite such powerful assertions, and the passionate and radical intelligence with which both Charlotte and Anne defied the conventional social restrictions and realist norms of much nineteenth-century fiction, it is Emily Brontë who remains the greatest of the sisters. Her only novel, *Wuthering Heights* (1847), races with a uniquely poetic and amoral force. Of all the Brontë children, Emily has the chief claim to poetic stature.

The sisters' only published volume of verse, the *Poems* of Currer, Acton and Ellis Bell (1846), received favourable reviews but sold pitifully. Modern editorial work has shown that much of Emily's output is connected with the Gondal epic and is couched in the form of dramatic monologues. These express a knowledge of love and defeat and a response to the natural world that rises to mystic intensity. 'High waving heather' throbs with the splendour of the Yorkshire moors incandescent with 'midnight and moonlight and bright shining stars'. In one of her best-known poems, 'No coward soul is mine', spiritual love rises to a triumphant assertion of the divine. In other lyrics, intimations of holiness are glimpsed through the natural world.

The poetry of *Wuthering Heights* is instinct in every line of these lyrics, while the extremes of grief and the enduring, terrifying anguish of a love so strong that it touches on death thrill through the moorland world powerfully evoked in the following stanza:

> Cold in the earth, and fifteen wild Decembers
> From these brown hills have melted into spring –
> Faithful indeed is the spirit that remembers
> After such years of change and suffering.

We are close here to the agony of Heathcliff after he has opened Cathy's grave and tells Ellen Dean how 'she has disturbed me, night and day, through eighteen years – incessantly – remorselessly – till yesternight – and yesternight, I was tranquil'.

Desire, dream, death and the awe-inspiring amorality of passion surge through *Wuthering Heights*. The novel was, wrote Charlotte Brontë, 'hewn in a wild workshop, with simple tools, out of homely materials. The statuary found a granite block on a solitary moor: gazing thereon, he saw how from the crag might be elicited the head, savage, swart, sinister; a form moulded with at least one element of grandeur – power.' This is vividly expressed and accurately reflects a memory of the novel, yet it is not altogether just to the experience of reading it, to the distances and subtle ambiguities through which Emily Brontë filtered her archetypal narrative. The Byronic excess and black majesty of Heathcliff's passion are actually recounted by the foppish Lockwood who has learned about them from the honest but unsophisticated Ellen Dean. She, in turn, has been obliged to reconstruct events from her own observation and the confessions of characters who move on a plane altogether different to hers. Such effects reinforce the ambiguity by which the central characters themselves move in worlds at once natural and supernatural, physical and diabolic.

Heathcliff's possibly diabolic origins are frequently suggested, while the childhood love that grows between him and Cathy is nurtured by the elemental and amoral moors. It is a natural growth. When Cathy, won to the artificial sophistication of the Lintons, denies it, she denies and eventually destroys her own nature.

Heathcliff knows that the elemental takes a hideous revenge on those who violate it. Cathy, too, has understood this. Her dying agony lies in her realization that she is bound body and soul to Heathcliff, to the moors and to earthly passion. 'Nelly, I *am* Heathcliff – he's always, always in my mind – not as a pleasure, any more than I am always a pleasure to myself – but as my own being.' In her last moments, Cathy achieves a wild vindictiveness and ruthless intensity, while Heathcliff howls 'not like a man, but like a savage beast getting goaded to death'.

Cathy's denial of their passion leads Heathcliff to the self-destructive extremes of revenge. He tries to work the misery of all around him. Nonetheless, in the end, he is defeated and loses even the relish of revenge itself. The love of the younger generation is stronger than his hate. Such a belief in the self-destructive nature of evil is a conventional Christian consolation, yet as Lockwood makes his pious parting at the graves of Heathcliff and Cathy, we might wonder how reliable his feelings are. After the revelation of such passion, can we really trust this mild-mannered man? *Wuthering Heights* provides no ready answers to the issues of elemental passion it so thrillingly portrays. Rather, its radical originality of subject and technique make it the most remarkable and in some respects the most unsettling of all the major works of Victorian fiction.

7

When Charlotte Brontë dedicated *Jane Eyre* to William Makepeace Thackeray (1811–63), she praised her fellow novelist for 'the Greek fire of his sarcasm'. The combination of such satire with scenes of sentiment in Thackeray's fiction suggests the intellectual and formal debts discussed in his major work of literary criticism, *The English Humorists of the Eighteenth Century* (1853).

Thackeray's earlier work, much of it published in *Fraser's Magazine* and, after 1841, in *Punch*, includes both travel sketches and grotesque stories. In *The Memoirs of Barry Lyndon* (1856), Thackeray attempted a rogue's tale in the manner of Fielding's *Jonathan Wild*. In *Catherine* (1839–40), he exposed what he saw as the moral dangers of the

Newgate novel as practised by Bulwer-Lytton, Ainsworth and Dickens, while in 'Novels by Eminent Hands' (1847), he extended his literary satire to other writers of popular adventure fiction. *The Yellowplush Papers* (collectively published 1856) present a servant's view of fashionable life, but it is *The Book of Snobs* (1848) that most clearly looks forward to *Vanity Fair*.

Vanity Fair (1848) is Thackeray's most assured success, a re-creation of England on the eve of Waterloo in which a 'set of people living without God in the world' are exposed to mercenary obsessions in a life of vicarious social survival. The title of the novel and, in part at least, its tone of moral indignation derive from Bunyan's *Pilgrim's Progress*. Here 'Vanity Fair' is the place where honours, preferments and titles are sold, and where there is nothing to be seen but 'juggling, cheats, games, plays, fools, apes, knaves and rogues'. In such a world as this, Thackeray's Becky Sharp is obliged to make her way from the precarious position of governess to the equally uncertain role of society lady. She does so with a degree of resource and ruthlessness that wins our ambiguous admiration. The career of this Napoleonic upstart (Thackeray's imagery as well as his illustrations to his novel frequently enforce the parallel) also exposes the hypocrisy and sheer brutishness of the upper ranks of English society.

Here is a world where money and social position are all, and where Becky and Rawdon Crawley learn 'How to Live Well on Nothing a Year'. Becky's amoral energy constantly exposes the corruption about her. Miss Pinkerton's Academy, which she symbolically dismisses for its second-hand learning by throwing her gift of Johnson's dictionary out of her carriage, is one minor though memorable example of this. Becky's awareness of her physical attractiveness and mental superiority reveals the world of sinecure hunting, boorishness and sheer stupidity that characterizes the aristocracy and the upper middle classes. These are worlds in which many are made to suffer. Rawdon Crawley himself is horribly punished for his marriage to Becky. The decline of the older Osborne and Sedley is as ruthless as that of Sir Pitt Crawley. Such portraits constitute a hideous picture of the moral and emotional depravity underlying the lives of the great.

Yet even the virtuous are not without their faults. Amelia Sedley, conceived by Thackeray as Becky's opposite, suffers over George

Osborne's emotional vacillation and, after the memorable pathos of his death, from increasing poverty. She morbidly reveres his memory, and it is only Becky's tart intelligence which can finally rouse her from the foolish worship of a 'padded booby' to accepting Dobbin, Thackeray's portrait of an English gentleman proper to the point of dullness. Becky's own adventures however have by now reduced her to a picaresque existence of adultery and crime. Finally she establishes herself as an apparently respectable English lady on the strength of Joss Sedley's life insurance, a prize almost certainly gained at the cost of his murder. The power of *Vanity Fair* lies partly in Thackeray the disillusioned gentleman's profound disgust at the betrayal of conventional ethical values. His often over-obtrusive commentaries take on a tone of disillusioned resignation. 'Ah! Vanitas, Vanitatem! which of us is happy in this world? Which of us has his desire? or having it, is satisfied?'

Thackeray's subsequent novels were never to attain quite the level of achievement reached in *Vanity Fair*. *Pendennis* (1850) contains many scenes skilfully re-created from the author's own life (his experiences as a hack journalist are finely used), and shows a young man's development from boyish worldliness, through increasing cynicism, to final marriage to the virtuous Laura Bell. The Preface contains a well-known complaint about the restrictions placed on the contemporary novelist by Victorian prudery in sexual matters, but Major Pendennis, an excellent portrait of a Regency buck, helps in part to alleviate this problem. The episodic construction of the work and the somewhat clumsy handling of a complex inheritance issue serve nonetheless to justify Henry James's criticism of many Victorian novels as 'loose, baggy monsters'.

The hero of *Henry Esmond* (1852) is also in some degree a self-portrait, though the historical setting of the work allowed Thackeray to develop his admiration of Addison as an epitome of eighteenth-century rectitude. This he does to the point where his own style becomes pastiche. The historical re-creation is somewhat flat, and the novel ends with the disillusioned hero marrying his faithful beloved and emigrating to America. Such a situation provides the setting for Thackeray's next novel, *The Virginians* (1859), a collection of episodes and pen portraits of the lives of Henry's grandsons. In *The Newcomes* (1855), Thackeray offered a rambling and often sentimental vision of

Victorian society, of villains excessively villainous, of the moral dangers and suffering imposed on young women by the marriage market and, in the last moments of the fond and foolish Colonel Newcome, a death scene of genuinely touching pathos. Sentiment and nostalgia abound, but their obverse is not necessarily cynicism. Thackeray considered himself to be a satirical moralist and in his best work such tensions give his writing its power.

8

For Anthony Trollope (1815–82), the novel was a 'picture of common life enlivened by humour and sustained by pathos'. His energetic mother had tried to salvage the family fortune with her pen (the fate of many Victorian women writers) but Trollope himself was condemned to drudgery in the General Post Office. This was an existence he partly described in the life of Charlie Tudor, the redeemed 'hobbledehoy' in *The Three Clerks* (1857). A severe illness was followed by some seventeen years working for the Post Office in Ireland, experiences on which Trollope was to base his early and commercially unsuccessful novel *The Kellys and the O'Kellys* (1848). By 1851 however, Trollope had returned to the west of England, and in Salisbury, 'one mid-summer evening round the purlieus of the Cathedral', he conceived the idea of *The Warden* (1855), the first of the Barsetshire novels that were finally to establish his fame.

The Warden is a satire of clerical abuse and its ruthless exposure in the newspapers, but in the character of the gentle Mr Harding integrity and sympathy are embodied as Trollope's true values. This compassion for unspectacular characters, along with Trollope's conservative and somewhat sentimental reverence for older proprieties, helped shape his wide-ranging awareness of the tensions within his society. In *Barchester Towers* (1857), he captured the ethos of life in a cathedral close with a shrewd awareness of competition in spiritual places and the machinations of unscrupulous evangelicals such as Obediah Slope and Mrs Proudie.

Doctor Thorne (1858), the work in which, as Henry James declared, Trollope 'settled down steadily to the English girl', is a novel of fine moral discrimination in which integrity is balanced against the financial pressures of the marriage market. *The Small House at Allington* (1864) uses the device of the unwise engagement to show how the career of the ambitious Adolphus Crosbie is blighted after jilting the weakly conventional Lily Dale for the aristocratic Lady Alexandrina de Courcy, while the 'hobbledehoy' Johnny Eames flourishes even though he does not win Lily's hand. Such disappointment is again discussed in *The Last Chronicle of Barset* (1867), but the real centre of the work is the pain inflicted on the rebarbative Josiah Crawley as he is falsely arraigned for theft. This is one of Trollope's finest studies, and we see both the pain caused to his worthy daughter along with the painful manipulations of Mrs Proudie who, since some readers declared in Trollope's hearing she had become a bore, he now decided to kill off.

'Since her time others have grown equally dear to me, – Lady Glencora and her husband, for instance.' As the Pallisers and later the Duke and Duchess of Omnium, these figures move through Trollope's series of 'parliamentary' novels in which he skilfully suggests some of the larger social and political shifts of his time. The series was begun with *Can You Forgive Her?* (1865), a novel which contains a powerful confrontation between the major figures as Glencora begs to be allowed to break her arranged marriage with Palliser because of her love for a worthless man. 'If you cannot love me, it is a great misfortune to us both. But we need not therefore be disgraced.' Palliser's words suggest the starchy moral rectitude, the resolve in the face of political and family disillusion, that will give him his dignity in both *The Prime Minister* (1876) and *The Duke's Children* (1888).

In *Phineas Finn* (1869) and *Phineas Redux* (1874), Trollope offered a portrait of a political figure obliged to operate on the outside of the world in which Palliser moves. Both works question moral probity in political society. In the first, political success is compromised partly by the hero's failure to secure a rich wife, while in the second and darker work, faded beauty, madness and murder blight Phineas's hopes of preferment. Disillusioned with British justice, Phineas eventually marries his wealthy saviour, retires from Parliament and ends an unfulfilled man.

In *The Eustace Diamonds* (1873), a novel loosely connected with the Palliser series, Trollope essayed a portrait of the criminal woman in a manner reminiscent of Wilkie Collins and the 'sensation' novel, a theme he had skilfully touched on in *Orley Farm* (1862). Here, for much of the work, we are genuinely sympathetic towards the misdirected maternal love of the guilty heroine. The novel has considerable power, but among Trollope's forty-seven works of fiction, his most powerful indictment of Victorian society is *The Way We Live Now* (1875).

This is the longest of Trollope's novels and his most powerful exposure of corruption and the commercial England which Bagehot in *Lombard Street* (1873) had called 'the greatest monied country in the world'. For Bagehot, the English commercial system was a vast enterprise relying entirely on trust. For Trollope, it was an enticement to corruption and the collapse of old values and decencies. Melmotte, the merchant prince of no clear origins and distinctly Napoleonic lack of scruple, 'rises above honesty as a general rises above humanity when he sacrifices an army to conquer a nation'. In a glittering six weeks of lies, Trollope's shady financier tricks City, church and state with his phoney schemes for railway projects. Working on their gullibility, Melmotte rises to the position where he entertains the Emperor of China (Trollope's satire on the absurd excesses of the worship of social status), is selected by the voters of Westminster and is then to be ushered into the House of Commons.

Melmotte's fall is as spectacular as his rise, and round it Trollope lavishes his satire on the cash nexus and the idle aristocracy. Trollope's deeply conservative outrage contains disturbing elements of xenophobia and anti-Semitism, but his savage indignation nonetheless attains a comprehensive fury. We are shown how new money corrupts every element of traditional society. As Trollope wrote in his posthumously published *Autobiography* (1883): 'I went beyond the iniquities of the great speculator who robs everybody, and made an onslaught also on other vices – on the intrigues of girls who want to get married, on the luxury of young men who prefer to stay single, and on the puffing propensities of authors who desire to cheat the public into buying their volumes.' In this comprehensive range, Trollope's novel forms a major attack on the complacency of Victorian values.

9

Trollope was much reviled for his productivity, especially after his *Autobiography* told of his writing novels by the clock and then advised the would-be author that his efforts should be to him 'as is his common work to the common labourer'. Such productivity was typically Victorian nonetheless, and it occurred against the background of a rapidly rising population, an ever-increasing literacy rate and the metamorphosis of publishing into a modern, multi-million-pound industry.

By about 1840, and in a population of nearly 27 million, literacy rates appear to have reached 66 per cent for men while perhaps half the women in the country could also read. These percentages were to improve dramatically over the next hundred years, and the 1870 Education Act especially was to help create a vast new population of the reading poor. Print had become the unchallenged medium of mass communication.

Both writers and readers could also draw on the resources of an ever-increasing vocabulary. Though eighteenth-century purists had objected to foreign borrowings, the expansion of the empire had brought a great wealth of new words. American Indian terms and words from the Caribbean entered the language along with a multitude of Indian importations and phrases used by Dutch and Portuguese traders in southern Africa. The growth of science was to become a rich source of new words, and terms from medicine and physics (many of them derived from Greek originals) rapidly became familiar.

While grammarians in the later eighteenth century had tried to impose prescriptive rules, codify the language, point out what were believed to be errors and settle disputed matters of usage (the correct choice of *shall* and *will*, for example), the great Victorian philologists concerned themselves with spelling and lexicography. Their monument is *The Oxford English Dictionary*. In 1857, members of the Philological Society resolved to collect words not found in earlier dictionaries, and the following year proclaimed their intention of initiating a new dictionary of their own. This would record every word found in English after *c.* 1100 and exhibit its history and development through a generous use of quotations. Hundreds of volunteers offered to read historical works in the search for ancient forms, and one by-product of this effort was the founding of the Early English Text Society. After the premature death of Herbert Coleridge, editorship of the *Dictionary* passed to Frederick Furnivall and then to James Murray. Although he did not live to see the completion of the great task, the scholarly foundations on which Murray established the enterprise meant that by 1928 – seventy years after the original resolution had been made – work on the first version of the *Dictionary* was complete, supplements being issued from 1933 onwards.

Victorian England also saw a huge expansion of the publishing trade and the development of new methods of printing, marketing and distribution. The success of *Pickwick Papers*, for example, obliged Chapman and Hall to investigate the latest printing techniques for their publication of multiple editions of the work, to advertise and to begin using the new railways for distribution. The 'yellow backs' issued for railway travellers by the Victorian business man W.H. Smith (1825–91) were to help form a commercial empire that exists to this day, while others pioneered cheap reprints, George Routledge's Railway Library (founded 1848) eventually running to some 1,000 volumes and including among its authors both Disraeli and Bulwer-Lytton.

Another force that was to exert a profound influence on Victorian publishing and reading habits was the growth of the circulating library. The great expansion of these is associated with Charles Mudie who, by 1875, was the proprietor of some 125 branches. The scale of Mudie's purchases is the measure of his power. He would regularly buy upwards of 2,500 copies of a new novel (he subscribed 3,000 copies of Disraeli's *Lothair*), while in total he may have purchased as many as 180,000 volumes a year. Since Mudie could charge his borrowers three times over for a three-decker novel, the influence the circulating libraries had on literary form was of the greatest importance. This is nowhere more powerfully illustrated than by the fact that, faced with increased competition, especially after the 1850 Public Libraries Act, Mudie was obliged to join with his rival W.H. Smith and insist on single-volume novels. In 1894, the year in which these men issued their request, 184 three-decker works were published. The following season saw a mere 52. Market forces had clearly triumphed and helped clear the way of 'loose, baggy monsters'. Authors could now concentrate on discovering the possibilities opened up by the modern one-volume novel.

In a market where for a long time there was no satisfactory means of maintaining retail prices (the Bookselling Regulations of 1829 had proved almost impossible to enforce) fierce competition among book-sellers led to a severe narrowing of retail outlets. Further efforts at regulation were made in 1848, but by the 1880s matters had reached a crisis. At the opening of the next decade, Macmillans seized the initiative and set up the Publishers' Association, and by 1900 had negotiated the Net Book Agreement whereby publishers would offer booksellers a discount on their purchases provided they agreed to sell their wares at the fixed and agreed price. The Net Book Agreement was to remain the foundation of British publishing.

Other changes in the law during the nineteenth century suggest the growing status and security of the author. In 1842, for example, and helped by Wordsworth's lobbying for change, the period of copyright was extended to forty-two years or seven years after the author's death, whichever proved the longer. Authors such as Mrs Henry Wood (1814–87) whose melodramatic *East Lynne* (1861) sold upwards of 400,000 copies in thirty years, benefited enormously from this legislation, and such sales meant that major authors could demand high prices and often end their careers as wealthy people. Carlyle, for example, though never a rich man, sold the rights to an edition of 5,000 volumes of the first two parts of *Frederick the Great* for £2,800. Dickens cleared £10,000 on *Dombey and Son*.

Such sums inevitably encouraged a greater professionalism, and the end of the century saw the rise of such literary agents as A.P. Watt (*c.* 1875) and Curtis Brown (from 1899), men whose firms negotiated on behalf of their authors and who, against considerable initial hostility from the publishers, began to press for writers to be paid on a royalty basis from which the agents themselves then earned their 10 per cent. In addition, Walter Besant (1836–1901), a minor novelist but a campaigner of immense talent, gave a huge boost to the profession of letters in Britain by founding the Society of Authors (1883) and its journal *The Author*. Both institutions continue to this day to campaign tirelessly and effectively for their members.

These developments mark the dawning of the modern age of

publishing, and not the least brilliant of Besant's successes was to secure Alfred, Lord Tennyson (1809–92) as the first President of the Society of Authors. As Laureate, a peer and a poet whose works sold in editions of 40,000 and more, Tennyson represented the pinnacle of respectability a Victorian author might hope to attain.

10

Tennyson had written verse since his boyhood, and his juvenilia reveal his wide reading in the Greek and Latin classics as well as in the English tradition from the Elizabethans onwards. His contributions to *Poems by Two Brothers* (1827) were much influenced by Byron and by Burke's notions of the sublime, but in the poorly received *Poems, Chiefly Lyrical* (1830) we begin to hear Tennyson's true voice and glimpse the range of his intellectual concerns.

What is immediately striking about Tennyson's early works is their metrical variety and aural refinement. These are often combined with melancholia and a powerful ability to express mood through landscape. 'A Spirit haunts the year's last hours', for example, suggests both the effects of the strained circumstances of Tennyson's life at the rectory at Somersby and a young man's vivid sense of a psychological inertia that is at once oppressive yet alluring:

> The air is damp, and hushed, and close,
> As a sick man's room when he taketh repose
> An hour before death;
> My very heart faints and my whole soul grieves
> At the moist rich smell of the rotting leaves,
> And the breath
> Of the fading edges of box beneath,
> And the year's last rose.
> Heavily hangs the broad sunflower
> Over its grave i'the earth so chilly;
> Heavily hangs the hollyhock,
> Heavily hangs the tiger-lily.

In 'Mariana', this hushed sense of decay and solitude is combined with a remarkably suggestive visual imagination and allusions to Shakespeare and Ovid. Mariana is also the first of a type that was of great importance to the early Tennyson: the sensitive and often female figure caught in the lassitude of solipsistic retreat. But if such a life has its dangers, so too does exposure to the world. 'The Kraken' wakes from his 'ancient, dreamless, uninvaded sleep' only to die.

As undergraduate works, such poems are exceptional, but the intellectual influence of Cambridge, and of earnest debate among 'the Apostles' of Trinity College especially, can be seen in 'Supposed Confessions of a Second-Rate Sensitive Mind Not in Unity with Itself'. Here Tennyson broaches a subject as central to his own life as it was to those of many eminent Victorians: the belief that 'it is man's privilege to doubt' and the spiritual pain consequent upon the loss of simple religious faith. In both his questioning and his search for that degree of moral certainty on which to base his art, Tennyson is a paradigm of a major aspect of Victorian literary endeavour.

In *Poems* (1833), Tennyson further developed his concern about social engagement and retreat from the world. A number of these works, which are among the poet's most familiar, were revised in the light of hostile criticism however and were later republished in the first volume of *Poems* (1842). It is in these versions that the verses are now most generally read.

The withdrawn female as a focus for Tennyson's meditation on the private and public worlds is used in both 'The Palace of Art' and the more powerful 'The Lady of Shalott'. Both works are concerned with the dangers of what Shelley had called 'the Poet's self-centred seclusion', but where the first hints at optimism, the Lady of Shalott, 'half sick of shadows' and of recording the reflections of a life merely glimpsed in her mirror, eventually goes out into the real world to perish. The work's strongly Keatsian appreciation of sensuous beauty vividly dramatizes the artist's dilemma in being caught between oppressive solipsism and a dangerous engagement with reality. The need to struggle and commit oneself to the world of action is the implied ethos underlying 'The Lotos-Eaters', one of the most verbally sophisticated of Tennyson's early poems. Based on an episode from the *Odyssey*, the work favourably contrasts the vigour of the heroic leader to the lassitude of his companions as they give way to drugged self-indulgence:

All things have rest, and ripen toward the grave
In silence; ripen, fall and cease:
Give us long rest or death, dark death or dreamful ease.

The *Poems* of 1833 had been seen through the press by the charismatic figure of Arthur Hallam, a member of the Apostles of whom Tennyson was to write: 'he was as near perfection as a mortal man could be'. In October 1833 however Hallam suddenly died. Tennyson, always prone to melancholy and self-doubt, and still uncertain of his religious convictions, entered a long period of painful spiritual reflection. In 'Tithonus', written at this time but not published until 1860, he used a figure from Greek myth to explore the idea that immortality could be a curse and that, contrary to the heroic acceptance of struggle suggested in 'The Lotos-Eaters', death may, in fact, be a blessing – the natural and even desirable end of life.

In 'The Two Voices', Tennyson expressed his determination to resist the suicidal impulses that plagued his grief, while other poems show him developing his 'passion of the past' and for seeing how old modes and genres could be remade into vehicles for contemporary awareness. The idylls of Theocritus offered him the opportunity to mix topical political and scientific interests with a conversational form in 'Audley Court' and then to blend these with comedy and the grotesque in 'Walking to the Mail'. The most extended of such experiments however, and a work that points forward to Tennyson's later concerns, is the 'Morte d'Arthur'. This Tennyson inserted into a conversational poem entitled 'The Epic'.

The opening sections of 'The Epic' are set during Christmas and so allow Tennyson to elaborate the problems of reviving ancient literary and religious forms in a period much concerned with evolution and the knowledge that 'nature brings not back the Mastodon'. In other words, he questions the place of past culture in a world of progress, a world which, in the view of the parson, has seen 'the general decay of faith'. A discussion of poetry and religious belief is thus prepared for, while in the 'Morte d'Arthur' itself, Tennyson merges these themes with his abiding grief at the death of Arthur Hallam. In presenting the final moments of the once and future king, Tennyson probed the decline of political, religious and intellectual orthodoxy, thereby drawing a parallel between ancient legend and modern conditions. The chapel to which Arthur's body is brought is merely a ruin: 'a broken chancel with a broken cross'. Political and moral instability combines with an awareness of religious decay and the painful loss of 'the true old days'. In a world of constant evolution, new values must one day be found by new men:

> The old order changeth, yielding place to new,
> And God fulfils himself in many ways,
> Lest one good custom should corrupt the world.

Tennyson's concern with the Victorians' faith in progress and moral evolution is again the subject of one of his early dramatic monologues, 'Locksley Hall'. The speaker here is a bitter and rejected lover whose invective against a crude, money-obsessed world, and against a woman who has rejected him for a better financial prospect, combines reminiscences of Juvenal and Donne. The situation in the poem was partly suggested by a translation of an Arabic work, but if the culture of the East contributed to the making of the poem, its ethos rejects anything other than Western values of scientific progress. 'Better fifty years of Europe than a cycle of Cathay.' Though the emotional state of the lover might make us question the validity of what he says (a technique Tennyson was to use far more subtly in *Maud*) the poem itself has a superficial optimism that expressed many aspects of the Victorian ideal.

Two finer dramatic monologues from *Poems* (1842) are 'St Simeon Stylites', a work derived from the history of early Christianity, and 'Ulysses', a poem drawing on both Dante and Homer. Where Simeon emerges as a filthy and psychologically warped personality whose life has been wasted in spiritual pride, Ulysses suggests heroic resolution. The poem subtly combines the zeal of Tennyson's ageing hero for fresh quests and adventures with the suggestion that the 'newer world' he longs for is in fact a last spiritual home.

'Ulysses' also expresses Tennyson's belief in gradual political progress, settled government and freedom broadening down 'from precedent to precedent'. In large part, this was an anti-radical stance, but in *The Princess* (1847) Tennyson brought his belief in slow evolutionary improvement to one of the most controversial subjects available to him: feminism and the position of women in Victorian England. Tennyson's treatment of this theme is both visionary and comic. His story of the invasion of the princess's university by young men *en travestie*, their overthrow and the heroine's growing love for the wounded and passive prince suggests the comic world of *Love's Labour's Lost*. Tennyson's essential theme however was that time will eventually abolish male supremacy. The freedom of women is a natural process of evolution which will allow them to develop their separate and distinct natures independent of dominating male influence. In the end, both sexes will grow more alike. 'Come down, O maid, from yonder height' – one of the exquisite lyrics that mark the points of crisis in *The Princess* – suggests that the princess herself, a woman who has put off enforced childish dependence in a patriarchal society, must eventually return to the natural world of human love, marriage and procreation. United in equality, modern men and women will be able to overcome the barbarous customs of the past and together scale 'the shining steps of nature'.

In Memoriam A.H.H. (1850) again ends with marriage as an image of progressive human fulfilment. Written over nearly seventeen years, the volume is a collection of lyrics on loss, spiritual isolation and the dawning of a new and intuitive sense of Christian consolation. Petrarch and Shakespeare contributed to individual poems, while the *Vita Nuova* and the *Divine Comedy* of Dante were influential on Tennyson's shaping his collection into a progress from despair at the death of Arthur Hallam to some measure of Christian consolation and an acceptance of transience. He is seeking a public voice through the gradual quietening of private doubt.

Time and mortality occupy the greater number of lyrics nonetheless. Throughout the work, the constant, painful stirring of memory and the agony of loss cause the poet to see himself as a widow, a neglected wife or a hopelessly infatuated girl. Grief seems an endless repetition of dreams, tears and emotional paralysis. It is in this picture of a mind grappling with the great Victorian problems of science and faith that the true strength of the poem lies, the quatrains of Tennyson's verses being most resonant not when conveying a mystical theology of evolution but when depicting a wilderness of human grief amid the horrors of the Victorian world:

> Dark house, by which once more I stand
> Here in the long unlovely street,

Doors, where my heart was used to beat
So quickly, waiting for a hand,

A hand that can be clasped no more –
Behold me, for I cannot sleep,
And like a guilty thing I creep
At earliest morning to the door.

He is not here; but far away
The noise of life begins again,
And ghastly through the drizzling rain
On the bald streets breaks the blank day.

A simple and poignant gesture of affection – a love that has behind it all the conscious weight of the Petrarchan tradition – has been swallowed up in death. Tennyson the lover, made furtive by the very force of his delicacy, is unable emotionally to accept the finality of death. Feeling pathetically imagines an unrecapturable life, while around the poet, trespassing on fantasy, the ghastliness of Victorian urban squalor asserts its philistine roar – the oppressive materialism that eventually only faith can redeem.

In 1850, and after the public success of *In Memoriam*, Tennyson was appointed Poet Laureate, the successor to Wordsworth. Two years later, and as a tribute to another great Englishman, Tennyson composed his 'Ode on the Death of the Duke of Wellington', praising the victor of Waterloo for his selfless ideal of duty.

With *Maud* (1855), an altogether more complex poem, Tennyson chose as his central figure an unstable young man tormented by the death of his father after a business failure. He is also racked by love and 'at war with myself and a wretched race'. In his state of heightened morbidity, and in a series of diverse lyrics through which we darkly learn the development of the plot, the speaker becomes the critic of his society. We are shown a world where 'only the ledger lives' and where the horrors of poverty described by Carlyle are rampant. Opposed to these are a heartless and wealth-obsessed upper class, the England of the 'dandy-despot' and the life-denying 'stony British stare'. Though the narrator at first tries to bury his discontent in stoic withdrawal, he comes to see that 'nature is one with rapine, a harm no preacher can heal'. This appalling background of exploitation, indifference and natural violence, of a money-obsessed and apparently godless Victorian world, drives the speaker to distraction.

To such sufferings are then added the torments of love. The narrator falls for the daughter of the man who ruined his father and is obliged to endure the anguish of passion:

> There has fallen a splendid tear
>   From the passion-flower at the gate.
> She is coming, my dove, my dear;
>   She is coming, my life, my fate;
> The red rose cries, 'She is near, she is near;'
>   And the white rose weeps, 'She is late;'
> The larkspur listens, 'I hear, I hear;'
>   And the lily whispers, 'I wait.'

In his maddened state, the narrator becomes Tennyson's 'little Hamlet'. The highly disjointed and episodic nature of the work is appropriate to the speaker's state of mind and develops the techniques of the so-called 'Spasmodics', poets like Alexander Smith (1830–67), author of *A Life-Drama* (1853), and Sydney Dobell (1824–74) whose unfinished *Balder* (1854) is a protracted and preposterous verse drama in which a depressed wife goes mad and raves until her poet husband smothers her to death. In *Maud* – a work of incomparably greater sophistication – Tennyson's speaker, having accepted the madness of love, causes his beloved's death after killing her brother in a duel. He himself then goes insane with remorse.

Amid this psychological and social violence flowers 'the blood-red blossom of war'. Colour symbolism plays an important part in binding the diverse elements of *Maud* together. White becomes the colour of negation and 'passionless peace', while red is the colour of blood, love and what, in *In Memoriam*, Tennyson had described as 'nature red in tooth and claw'. Finally, red is the colour of Mars and the Crimean War. The madman, trapped in the atrocities of Victorian society, comes to see the battlefield as the panacea for both his own miseries and the nation's ills. 'Love of a peace that was full of wrongs and shames' will now be swept aside as the banner of battle is unrolled and lets the world see 'the glory of manhood stand on his ancient height'. What the world in fact saw was grotesque mismanagement and the futile heroism of 'The Charge of the Light Brigade'

(1854). As Tennyson, adapting the words of a *Times* editorial declared: 'someone had blundered'.

In *The Idylls of the King*, published in parts between 1859 and 1885, Tennyson's purpose was to show 'the dream of man coming into practical life and ruined by one sin'. This sin, uncondemned by Malory, was the sexual incontinence of Guinevere that brings the ideal of Camelot to its tragic end. 'I tried in my *Idylls*', Tennyson wrote, 'to teach men the need of the ideal.' The public poet had found his public voice and what a contemporary critic was to call 'a sound view of human life and the condition of man in the world'. Tennyson can now speak with the authority conferred by what are taken to be the dominant ethical beliefs of his day. National saga and morality are thus merged.

The ten idylls are framed by the 'Coming' and 'Passing' of Arthur, while the image of the wheel of Fortune helps give Tennyson an organizing principle for the whole. The wheel's revolutions become identified with the wheels of change and the cycles of time. The first three idylls – 'Gareth and Lynette', 'The Marriage of Geraint' and 'Geraint and Enid' – show the rise of the wheel of Fortune. Nonetheless, as the poet's son Hallam wrote: 'the sin of Lancelot and Guinevere begins to breed'. The next three idylls – 'Balin and Balan', 'Merlin and Vivien' and 'Lancelot and Elaine' – heighten the poet's concern with the excesses of sexuality. Merlin is seduced by a woman who denies all that is good or ideal, while 'Lancelot and Elaine' is a rapidly told tale of unrequited love and of the Fair Maid of Astolat brought low by the best impulses of her nature.

To such sexual dangers are added spiritual ones, and in 'The Holy Grail', which Tennyson regarded as one of his finest achievements, he discussed the perils of extreme religious idealism and its potentially antisocial effects. Arthur himself disapproves of the quest, and of all the knights who seek the Grail only Galahad gains full beatific vision. This is achieved at the cost of never returning to the community of the Round Table itself. Probing the forces of social disintegration, Tennyson here reveals, in his son's words, how 'faith declines, religion in many turns from practical goodness to the quest after the supernatural and marvellous and selfish religious excitement'. The wheel, in other words, is turning.

'Pelias and Ettarre' shows the world of Camelot relapsing further into the sexual obsession whose catastrophic results, less tragically conceived than in Malory, are finally seen in 'The Last Tournament' and 'Guinevere'. In 'Guinevere' itself, Tennyson's parallels between medieval legend and Victorian England are particularly clear since this description of marital separation was published two years after the divorce courts were founded. Indeed, much of the underlying pessimism of the work reflects Tennyson's own disgust with what he saw as the contemporary spiritual and moral decline caused by passionate sexuality and intellectual individualism. Against these, Tennyson the Laureate set his own belief in the values of traditional morality and an imperialist ethic. The contemporary embodiments of the Arthurian ideal become Queen Victoria, 'loyal to the royal in thyself', and Prince Albert whom Tennyson chose to·describe as 'scarce other than my king's ideal knight'. The British Empire now had its poet, and Tennyson's patriotism was to be expressed in other historical narratives such as 'The Revenge' (1878) and 'The Defence of Lucknow' (1879).

While Tennyson's plays have little literary interest, his later monologues are of more value. Those like 'Northern Farmer, Old Style' (1870) and its companion piece in the 'New Style' are written in the dialect of his native Lincolnshire and are shrewd, humorous and unsentimental. 'Luvv? what's luvv? thou can luvv thy lass an' 'er munny too,' declares the New Style Victorian farmer. The 'Idylls of the Hearth' again deal with social abuses. 'Sea Dreams' (1860) combines Tennyson's strong dislike of a Christianity centred on a vengeful God with criticisms of an obsession with money rather than the heart. 'Aylmer's Field' and 'Enoch Arden' (1864) develop such themes. The first, a poem influenced by Crabbe, condemns pride in social status and asserts that true virtue is a matter of charity rather than birth. In the words of 'Lady Clara Vere de Vere': 'kind hearts are more than coronets'. The poem shows the ravages wrought by family pride. Nonetheless, the rector in the work preaches forgiveness rather than resentment at aristocratic excess and so asserts an essentially conservative and Christian ethic. In 'Enoch Arden', Tennyson dealt with the problems of unintentional bigamy (a fashionable theme among novelists), doing so with sentimentality but also some psychological acuteness.

Two of Tennyson's late tragic monologues were taken from

real-life incidents and show the force of the satire and anger he could still direct at social abuse. 'Rizpah' and 'Despair' both condemn a cruel, Calvinist religious attitude, 'a God of eternal rage'. The first also speaks out against social injustice and a barbarous penal system. The second work reveals the spiritual perils of both a dour religion and agnosticism.

Towards the end of a life deeply troubled by the loss of religious certainty, Tennyson himself still felt the pains of doubt. 'Vastness' (1889) ends on a brief note of consolation, but the most powerful sections of the work offer a frightening picture of the dead 'swallow'd in Vastness, lost in Silence, drown'd in the deeps of a meaningless Past'. In 'The Ancient Sage' (1885), a melancholy young sceptic is told by his mentor of those mystical glimpses of another world Tennyson had shown sustaining the narrator of *In Memoriam*. Such faith and hope were perilously won nonetheless, and in 'Locksley Hall Sixty Years After' (1886), anti-democratic and wholly disillusioned with the ideal of progress, the narrator can still ask:

> Is it well that while we range with Science, glorying in the Time,
> City children soak and blacken soul and sense in city slime?

Where the earlier poem was a paean to progress, its companion is a lament for what progress has actually wrought.

Myth still served Tennyson as a means of exploring moral issues. In 'Lucretius' (1868), he voiced his lifelong mistrust of sex, adding to this an indictment of the irrational threat he saw posed by 'civic tumult'. In 'Demeter and Persephone' (1889), Tennyson outlined an evolutionary view of religion, while in both 'The Voyage of Maeldune' (1880) and 'The Death of Oenone' (1892) he emphasized the importance of forgiveness. It is in Tennyson's late and brief lyric 'Crossing the Bar' however, a work that Tennyson himself always wished to be placed at the conclusion to editions of his work, that his most moving acceptance of religious hope is found:

> though from out our bourne of Time and Place
> The flood may bear me far,
> I hope to see my Pilot face to face
> When I have crost the bar.

After a lifetime of questioning, Tennyson here places his faith in God with a surrender that is itself like a quiet and tranquil death.

I I

Where Tennyson aspired to be the spokesman of his age, the finest work of Robert Browning (1812–89) reveals him as the ventriloquist of Victorian moral dilemma, the poet whose psychological subtlety and reach of intellect dramatized the conflicts of his period through a diverse range of characters. Browning thereby offered his readers 'truth broken into prismatic hues'.

The ideal medium for such an approach was the dramatic monologue, and after the failure of *Pauline* (1833) – an autobiographical poem of religious doubt much influenced by Shelley – Browning began *Paracelsus* (1835). In this work he gave more objective form to an intellect wrestling with the multiplicity of experience. Paracelsus is a Faust-like figure aspiring to universal knowledge who learns that such a pursuit, when severed from human love, leads only to despair. Despite his disillusion with mankind however, Paracelsus eventually sees the ultimate perfection of the human race lying in man's inherent 'tendency to God'. The theories of the early Victorian evolutionists supply a measure of moral affirmation. *Paracelsus* was also important in Browning's career for establishing the use of dramatic form and the degree of intellectual force he could bring to this. Nonetheless, the latter is almost wholly lost in *Sordello* (1840), a historical work on the poet's role in society which long established Browning as a poet of impenetrable obscurity.

Browning was now to embark on a sterile decade of writing for the theatre, but his true voice emerged with *Pippa Passes* (1841), the first of a series of pamphlets he issued under the collective title *Bells and Pomegranates*. In this work, the song of Pippa the child factory worker echoes innocently through Asolo as she celebrates her one day's annual holiday:

> God's in his heaven –
> All's right with the world.

Such optimism works a profound but ambiguous change on the inhabitants of the small town. In her simplicity, Pippa envies what she imagines to be the romantic love of Ottima and Sebald, but her song actually rouses the murderous couple to remorse and death.

Similarly, under the influence of Pippa's song, the newly wedded Jules is obliged to reconsider the duplicity that has led him to a false marriage. Luigi's faltering patriotism is also rekindled by the song, but unknown to Pippa, Luigi himself sets out on an anarchist's mission closely observed by the Austrian police. Finally, the Monsignor learns that Pippa is the true inheritor of the wealth he is expecting. The power of her song nonetheless appears to conquer his resolve to have her raped and sold into prostitution. Pippa's innocence has indeed wrought change in Asolo, but it is unclear whether this is wholly for good or whether Pippa herself is an agent of God or merely of chance. Issues of innocence, guilt, punishment and mortality are thus raised only to be left ambiguously unresolved.

It is 'My Last Duchess' (1842) that marks Browning's first complete success with the dramatic monologue. The manipulative duke, stiff with family pride, unconsciously exposes his mercenary nature as he bids his listener enjoy his art collection:

> That's my last Duchess painted on the wall,
> Looking as if she were alive. I call
> That piece a wonder, now: Fra Pandolf's hands
> Worked busily a day, and there she stands.
> Will't please you sit and look at her?

As we overhear the scene, so we perceive how art can freeze the warmth and beauty of life into a merely inert if marvellous object. The speaker's lovely young wife has died (perhaps at her husband's hands) only to achieve immortality in her frescoed portrait. The bronze statue of Neptune taming a seahorse may indeed reveal the skill of the Renaissance sculptor, but it nonetheless symbolizes a highly questionable mastery over the forces of nature. We are shown here a world where power and objects are more important than people and love. The satire on Victorian materialism is allusive and deft.

Browning's Nonconformist suspicion of Roman Catholic and High Church practices was first voiced in the figure of the spiteful monk who recites the 'Soliloquy of the Spanish Cloister' (1842). It is in 'The Bishop Orders his Tomb at St Praxed's Church' (1845) however that Browning more subtly questions what Ruskin, the advocate of a medieval purity, was to call Renaissance 'worldliness, insincerity, pride, hypocrisy, ignorance of itself, love of art, of luxury, and of good Latin'. Browning's monologue is spoken by a sensual, grasping churchman whose religion is little more than an obsession for a religious art that trumpets worldly success. The bishop confuses the spiritual and secular, piety with paganism, and the poem is finally as humorous as it is satiric.

An altogether more serious approach to religious problems is evident in Browning's finest collection of poems, *Men and Women* (1855), much of which was written during his Italian exile with Elizabeth Barrett Browning. Four works in particular examine central Victorian questions of faith and doubt.

In the first part of 'Christmas-Eve and Easter-Day' (1850) Browning's typical Victorian, the man from Manchester, experiences various modes of the modern Christian life: the shrewdly observed vulgarity of a Zion chapel, Roman Catholic worship choked by 'the frankincense's fuming' and the airless rationalism of the German Higher Criticism. At the close of the first section, and with a somewhat jingoistic lack of subtlety, Browning's speaker opts for English Nonconformity. The second part of the work however raises further problems as a new spokesman, a man of scientific convictions, longs for objective proof of the Bible's words and then recounts a visionary trance in which the Incarnation made evident to him God's love for man. Two different and irreconcilable impulses are here forced together:

> But Easter-Day breaks! But
> Christ rises! Mercy every way
> Is infinite, – and who can say?

Though Browning himself maintained his Christian faith, 'Cleon' and 'An Epistle Containing the Strange Medical Experience of Karshish' suggest the range of doubt that Browning and all Victorians were exposed to. Both works are skilful historical re-creations and again use antiquity to probe the present. Both poems also draw on the techniques of the Higher Criticism whereby documentary evidence from the past was used to examine the personality of the writer in terms of his particular historical situation. Browning's poems provide two such imagined documents and personalities.

In 'Cleon', Browning took a highly educated Greek of the early first century, a man who, like many Victorian Englishmen, believed that his own culture expressed the highest reach of human progress. Such a combination of pride and xenophobia nonetheless leaves a hollowness in the heart, a fear of death and a longing for 'some future state revealed to us by Zeus'. Divine reassurance is felt as an aching need, but the sophisticated Greek ends his letter by describing St Paul as a 'mere barbarian Jew', a man wholly inferior to himself in culture. Such a character's ideas can only be an affront to the glory of Greece. In the second poem, Karshish is an Arab medical student, a representative of the scientific mind. His training however has left him wholly unprepared for the half-admiring and half-sceptical sense of wonder roused in him by the story of Lazarus. On the one hand this appears merely as a 'case of mania', on the other it might be a profound intimation of the love of God, a miracle. Karshish in his doubting wonder is, like many a Victorian, a man caught in the dilemmas of faith.

'Bishop Blougram's Apology' is both the longest and the most sophisticated of the poems on religious questions in *Men and Women*. The work is full of references to contemporary intellectual life, and it is partly this re-creation of the timbre of modernity and the patterns of contemporary speech that makes the poem so fine an achievement. Browning also brings all his intellectual and psychological finesse to bear on his bishop, a seemingly hypocritical man holding on to old dogma for largely materialistic reasons – reasons which he nonetheless defends with such subtlety that he wholly confuses the free-thinking but less wily Gigadibs.

Gigadibs despises the bishop with a naïve if honest earnestness that is no match for the prelate's brilliant casuistry. While Gigadibs himself, with superbly observed discomfort, plays with the spoons and ranges olive stones round the edge of his plate, the bishop, with the skill of a great prosecuting counsel, anticipates and then answers all the young man's questions, placing worldly comfort and ideas of an afterlife against Gigadibs's threadbare liberalism. This last the bishop exposes as a philosophy in which, with all supernatural sanctions removed, all things become possible. This is an intolerable state for man, yet we must surely be equally suspicious of the plump, self-satisfied bishop's murmuring: 'Come, come, it's best believing, if we can.'

In 'Andrea del Sarto' and 'Fra Lippo Lippi', Browning returned to the world of Renaissance art to unsettle modern assumptions. In the first poem, mere technical excellence in painting leads to lifeless creations as sterile as the painter's own marriage. The bourgeois, the domestic and the safe – those cardinal values of Victorian respectability – are shown to be inimical to true art. The painter's wife, waiting for her lover, pulses with a truer passion. In 'Fra Lippo Lippi', such sexual experience is contrasted to a life spent painting soulful saints. Lippi's monologue gives a powerful picture of the psychological pressures on an artist saved from childhood poverty by a church whose asceticism is nonetheless too often a form of hypocrisy. Lippi is an artist who has sold out to comfort, and who is guilty and resentful about this. He tries to suggest that a dangerous sensuality is the real basis of an art that can give glory to God. In both his life and his painting however, Lippi remains caught in an uneasy compromise between the sacred and the profane – the Victorian dilemma of prudery and licence.

It is a measure of Browning's greatness that the volume which contains these works also prints one of the most troubling and mysterious of Victorian poems, 'Childe Roland to the Dark Tower Came'. Browning himself claimed that the work was inspired by a dream and that he was not wholly sure what it meant. Its combination of horror and hysteria however, and its sense of endless and repetitive search, is both disturbing and suggestive of a terrible spiritual nihilism.

In strong contrast are 'Meeting at Midnight' and 'Parting at Morning', a pair of verses which, in their blend of romantic situation and physical suggestiveness, are among the finest evocations of the erotic in Victorian poetry:

I

The grey sea and the long black land;
And the yellow half-moon large and low;
And the startled little waves that leap
In fiery ringlets from their sleep,
As I gain the cove with pushing prow,
And quench its speed i' the slushy sand.

II

Then a mile of warm sea-scented beach;
Three fields to cross till a farm appears;

A tap on the pane, the quick sharp scratch
And blue spurt of a lighted match,
And a voice less loud, thro' its joys and fears,
Than the two hearts beating each to each!

Other lyrics such as 'A Lovers' Quarrel' present passion painfully re-created in memory. The intensity and evanescence of the deep feeling experienced in a mature relationship are suggested by 'Two in the Campagna', while 'Love among the Ruins' is an affirmation of the passion felt by each generation of men and women as this is viewed amid the cycles of European history. The most powerful of these poems however is 'Love in a Life'. In this remarkable lyric, Browning captures with great subtlety the mind's awareness of the multifariousness of the physical world, the sheer crush of things. With the speed almost of thought itself we see how the poet's imagination transforms the objects in an old Italian palace into a phantasmagoria of his own restless emotion.

Where *Men and Women* was written in the married joy of Italian exile, *Dramatis Personae* (1864) was composed in London where Browning had returned a widower. The love lyrics in this collection are studies in disillusion and missed opportunity, while two of the finer philosophical pieces are darker than anything Browning had so far composed. In *Mr Sludge, 'The Medium'*, over-long as it is, Browning portrayed a spiritual impostor playing to the weaknesses of the middle-class audience whose property he has become. Sludge suggests his 'inventions' have the same validity as the inspiration of a great poet. This is a purely cynical view of the role of the artist in society, but even more shocking for a Victorian audience is Sludge's claim that the revelations of the supernatural he apparently provides offer proofs of another world, proofs that lay 'the atheist sprawling on his back'. We are to think that revealed religion is comparable to hocus-pocus.

Just how controversial Browning was being in these works can be gauged by Bagehot's response to 'Caliban upon Setebos'. Verminous and theologically troubled, the very image of the ignoble savage, Caliban lies in his cave picking fleas off his body and meditating on the nature of the deity. For Bagehot, Caliban was 'a nasty creature – a gross animal, uncontrolled and unelevated by any feeling of religion or duty'. He apparently denies the Victorian poet's assumed responsibility to ennoble and inspire. The irony lies in the fact that Caliban is actually shown evolving an image of God in his own likeness. In this he may be compared both to the natural theologians and to the Higher Critics who saw Christ as no more than such a man-made myth – 'as I: so He'. And 'He', for Caliban, is the vengeful God of Calvinism ordering some to damnation on a whim just as Caliban himself considers throwing stones at every twenty-first crab that happens to crawl by his den.

Much of Browning's later work shows a diminishing of his powers and an excessive verbal imagination, but poems such as *Prince Hohenstiel-Schwangau* (1872) effectively satirize political events, while the over-long *Red Cotton Night-Cap Country* (1873) remains an interesting black comedy about religious despair and the need felt by a sane but foolish and suffering man to 'put faith to proof, be cured or killed at once!' The Epilogue to *Asolando: Fancies and Facts* (1889), though Browning recognized its confidence might sound boastful, has a defiant optimism which some find merely philistine.

To this general decline in Browning's later work there is one magnificent exception. In its reconstruction of a particularly brutal seventeenth-century Roman murder, *The Ring and the Book* (1868–9) is Browning's triumphant vindication of the dramatic monologue as a means for capturing the 'facet-flash' of the world's variety. The work shows his genius for reanimating the past, for exploring religious and moral dilemmas and above all for conveying a sense that truth lies at a level deeper than the play of individual intellects – minds whose various lights can only partly illuminate and in part distort the facts.

Browning tells us what these facts are at the start. Amid the detritus of the Florentine flea-market, the poet has found a collection of old legal records. These recount how at the close of the seventeenth century, Count Guido Franceschini, along with four peasants, murdered his wife Pompilia (herself the bastard daughter of a prostitute deceitfully reared by a merchant couple) when she had fled to Rome with her priest and there given birth to a child. The count was tried for the murder, found guilty and, after an unsuccessful appeal to the pope, executed along with his fellow conspirators. These facts are the 'Book' of the poem's title. The 'Ring' is the golden artefact wrought by the poet's imagination working on recorded incidents and bringing them to life through dramatic monologues.

The first three monologues present the public's view of the events reflected through the 'plague of squint'. Excuses for the count are voiced by One Half-Rome who fears for the loyalty of his own wife. Other Half-Rome sentimentally exonerates Pompilia. Tertium Quid then comments on the case with would-be wit in an attempt to advance his social prestige. The facts are already being moulded afresh by the various energies of various minds, but it is when the protagonists of the drama themselves speak that Browning's art reveals its full inventiveness.

Count Franceschini at first masks his evil nature under a rational and strategically cunning defence of traditional values. His murder of the base-born woman who married him only to run off with a priest is presented as the worthy act of an old aristocrat, an act which will see 'manners reformed, old habits back once more'. Murder thus becomes a means to morality. It is the monologue of the priest Caponsacchi however that is the more moving, a revelation of the complex spiritual life of an aristocrat genuinely devoted to the church, sickened by institutional corruption and reanimated in his belief by an intense but chaste devotion to a woman whose beauty was like a revelation of grace – a revelation it is his Christian duty to protect. Pompilia's monologue, sentimental though it now appears, is an example of the suffering female innocent popular with Victorian writers as different as Dickens and Thackeray.

After sentiment comes satire in the portraits of the two lawyers who hope that the whole world will eventually become 'one lawsuit', not for the sake of justice but in order to fill their purses. The monologue of the pope, by contrast, achieves genuine moral grandeur as he struggles with the evidence and then with his own doubts about erring human judgement and the need to curb the spread of individualism. These dilemmas were given a particular edge for the original audience by fears over recent discussions of papal infallibility and the growth of Newmanite Catholicism.

One of the finest achievements of *The Ring and the Book* is the count's second monologue in which he appears to present himself as a primal, almost Nietzschean superman – a figure beyond conventional moral judgement. Such an image collapses nonetheless, and the

Venetian visitor's account of his execution (satirizing the Roman Catholic rites Browning so abhorred) gives a final suggestion of the human meanness of the man. The facts have been stated, justice done and moral order reaffirmed, but in the interplay of differing and highly individualized points of view – in his re-creation of human society driven to interpret the world through its own conflicting energies – *The Ring and the Book* is Browning's supreme expression of his art and its attempt to capture the multifariousness of existence.

12

The love affair of Robert and Elizabeth Barrett Browning (1806–61) was portrayed by the latter in her *Sonnets from the Portuguese*. These were first published in the *Poems* of 1850, a volume which caused one reviewer to nominate the widely popular Barrett Browning for the laureateship. Since then her stock has fallen.

The *Sonnets* themselves draw on a broad classical education, but the doubts and triumphs of a forbidden passion have the force of genuine feeling and show the victory of love over emotional death. This experience is often conveyed in original and powerful imagery, as in Sonnet 24. Here, free at last from the suffocating inertia of Victorian propriety, Barrett Browning suggests that the cruel knife of worldly criticism now lies shut in the enfolding warmth of love's hand. Mutual passion has triumphed over social constraint, and a woman has asserted her personal freedom in love.

Mrs Browning used the sonnet form again in *Casa Guidi Windows* (1851), a somewhat too effusive response to the struggle of Italian patriotism, but in her verse novel *Aurora Leigh* (1857) she created a work which recent criticism has resurrected as a central document of Victorian feminism, a woman writer's powerful claim to establish her independent identity through her work. *Aurora Leigh* discusses issues of gender, class and the relation of art to politics. To achieve this it drew on a range of contemporary or near-contemporary works, remoulding them into an independent and 'unscrupulously epic' poem – a woman's invasion of what had hitherto been regarded as an exclusively male preserve. Mme de Staël's *Corinne* (1807) provided the basic situation of the female artist torn between the sensuous and passionate world represented by Italian culture and a life-denying English Puritanism. Barrett Browning's satire on the aunt with whom her heroine passes her later childhood is a particularly effective image of the suppression of women in Victorian society:

> She stood straight and calm,
> Her somewhat narrow forehead braided tight
> As if for taming accidental thoughts
> From possible pulses; her brown hair pricked with grey
> By frigid use of life (she was not old,
> Although my father's elder by a year),
> A nose drawn sharply, yet in delicate lines;
> A close mild mouth, a little soured about
> The ends, through speaking unrequited loves
> Or peradventure niggardly half-truths;
> Eyes of no colour . . .

As her heroine develops, the poet explores a woman's struggle to establish her identity as an·independent and passionate being whose radical energies drive her to a successful career in literature. In this she is contrasted to the masculine, mechanical and logic-bound idealism of Romney Leigh, the Christian Socialist. Worlds suggested by the Brontës and *Alton Locke* are here contrasted, while Mrs Gaskell's *Ruth* contributed to the portrait of the working-class Marian Erle. Romney's rejection by Marian, her subsequent rape and her absorption into the independent, feminist world of the heroine explore gender roles and class warfare in a male-dominated society. At the close, when Romney's social experiments have brought him personal disaster, his acceptance by Aurora herself creates a relationship in which the mutuality of the sexes allows Aurora to become the voice of a social criticism in which the roles of women and art can be asserted. Poetry and a moderate feminism are seen as effective answers to social problems, thereby making Barrett Browning's own text the truest response to the society it criticizes.

A wholly different approach to relations between the sexes can be found in the reactionary mysticism of *The Angel in the House* (1854–63) by Coventry Patmore (1823–96). Here the man is 'unconditionally lord', a figure who, as Patmore later suggested, 'interprets woman to herself as God interprets his own nature to man'. Patmore was to declare that 'nuptial love bears the clearest marks of being nothing other than the rehearsal of a communion of a higher nature' – an idea he was to elaborate in his Roman Catholic-inspired *The Unknown Eros* (1877). The narratives that make up *The Angel in the House* however are altogether fresher and shrewder than such beliefs might suggest. Patmore was capable of the psychologically telling epigram, of a sense of the interplay of man and wife and of a joy and passion that the cavalier grace of his style redeems from the merely mawkish.

Patmore wrote that 'the death of nuptial joy is sloth', but *Modern Love* (1862) by George Meredith (1828–1909) charts with an altogether more terrible accuracy the break-up of a marriage through mutual incompatibility:

> Lovers beneath the singing sky of May,
> They wandered once; clear as the dew on flowers:
> But they fed not on the advancing hours:
> Their hearts held cravings for the buried day.
> Then each applied to each that fatal knife,
> Deep questioning, which probes to endless dole.
> Ah, what a dusty answer gets the soul
> When hot for certainties in this our life!

Derived in part from his disastrous marriage to Thomas Love Peacock's widowed daughter, the fifty sixteen-line sonnets portray the mutual deceits and recriminations of two powerful characters trapped like 'falcons in a snare'. The marriage ends with the woman's suicide, and the sequence as a whole represents a passionate and disturbingly honest criticism of the mutual damage inflicted by a society where marriage was a sacred ideal and divorce a disgrace.

Other aspects of modern love were discussed in the work of Arthur Hugh Clough (1819–61). His journal records his late adolescent struggles between physical desire and sexual shame as well as the opposing forces of 'muscular' Christianity, Tractarianism and doubts raised by the Higher Criticism. Ten undergraduate poems collectively entitled 'Blank Misgivings of a Creature Moving About in Worlds Not Realized' suggest a deep-seated psychological inertia. Clough was eventually to renounce his Oxford fellowship after difficulties with the Thirty-Nine Articles proved insurmountable and, during the ensuing period of release, he wrote the first of his long hexametrical poems, *The Bothie of Tober-na-Vuolich* (1848). The work proposes a revision of normal male and middle-class ideas of marriage through a form of social miscegenation. The hero, having wisely earned a first-class degree and then questioned whether social divisions are the work of Providence, marries a farmer's daughter and goes to New Zealand in order to find satisfaction working the land.

Some of the poems Clough contributed to *Ambarvalia* (1849) further explore the problems of sexual choice or, as in 'Natura Naturans', the relation of desire to procreation. 'The Questioning Spirit' suggests the constant mood of doubt that is so much more truly representative of Clough's verse than either the better-known idealism of 'Say not the struggle naught availeth' or the tart cynicism of 'The Latest Decalogue' with its list of Victorian hypocrisies.

And it is the endless self-analysis of the doubting mind that underlies Clough's greatest poem, the *Amours de Voyage* (written 1849, published 1858). Here, the letters sent from the Continent by the vacillating and intellectual Claude to his more stalwart friend in England are a unique and subtle extension of the Victorian poetic monologue. The accentual hexameters, although originally inspired by an interest in Homeric translation (a concern Clough was to pursue intermittently throughout his short life), reveal not so much an academic antiquarianism as a fastidious intellectual scrupulousness:

> I do not like being moved: for the will is excited: and action
> Is a most dangerous thing; I tremble for something factitious,
> Some malpractice of the heart and illegitimate process;
> We are so prone to these things with our terrible notions of duty.

The fall of the short-lived Roman republic after the French siege reveals Claude's political vacillation, while his pursuit of an ultimately rather ordinary English girl – a passion that is a combination of reticence and desire stirred by the workings of a mind arguing itself into love – creates a psychological truthfulness foreshadowing the subtlety of Henry James. Such an intellect eventually finds truth to be made in its own image: 'flexible, changeable, vague, and multiform, and doubtful'. As a result, even the stabilities of religious consolation seem at once simplistic and fantastic. Their cultural authority however could not easily be brushed aside, and Clough is a fine poet of Victorian religious doubt.

'My God, my God, that I were back with Thee!' The cry of Clough's fallen Adam echoes in many of his works, whether 'pent up in crowded pews' on a Sunday or in the scenes of Clough's tragicomic *Dipsychus* (published 1865). Here, the alternation of a morbid religious sense with colloquial satire creates a highly subversive work which Clough forbade his girl-friend to read. The blank agony of the Victorian loss of faith could rouse a devastating spiritual homesickness, and the allusions to St Paul amid the hopeless materialism of 'Easter Day. Naples 1849' deepen despair by referring to words that no longer have the power to save:

> Eat, drink, and play, and think that this is bliss!
>> There is no Heaven but this!
>> There is no Hell; –
> Save Earth, which serves the purpose doubly well,
>> Seeing its visits still
> With equallest apportionments of ill
> Both good and bad alike, and brings to one same dust
>> The unjust and the just
>> With Christ, who is not risen.

Its very hopelessness makes this one of the great Victorian religious poems, even if its almost blasphemous power to shock has today been somewhat blunted.

13

Clough's early death was mourned in the pastoral elegy 'Thyrsis' by Matthew Arnold (1822–88), a work composed at the end of a brief and intermittent poetic career that had begun with *The Strayed Reveller, and Other Poems* (1849). These works reveal a struggle between the epicurean and the stoic that surprised Arnold's contemporaries by its force. 'The Strayed Reveller' himself, drunk on Circe's wine, is finally seen as a lesser figure than the poem's strenuous

Ulysses. 'The New Sirens' sing of a romantic passion that leads only to spiritual sloth. In the end, the true props of the confused modern soul are not enchantresses but philosophers and poets: Epictetus, Homer and Sophocles, the wide Greek vision which 'saw life steadily, and saw it whole'.

Such a view from the Acropolis was more sustaining than that from the Victorian city or, Arnold suggests, from Windermere and the Lakes. Wordsworth's mystical intuitions in 'Tintern Abbey' are countered in 'Resignation' by a world where intimations of immortality give way to 'the soiled glory and the trailing wing'. In the 'Memorial Verses' written after Wordsworth's death in 1850, 'the freshness of the early world' is found to be staled by the adult's 'time-ridden consciousness'. The surfaces of modern life are hopelessly agitated, while the submarine depths of 'The Forsaken Merman' try Margaret's soul with too great a solitude. She remains a restless figure torn between the love of society and the call of the spirit. A woman named 'Marguerite' is also the subject of a sequence of eight poems Arnold entitled 'Switzerland'. Here, he reveals an inescapable isolation and a stoic acceptance that for two at least among the world's 'mortal millions' love was a pre-ordained impossibility:

> A God, a God their severance ruled!
> And bade betwixt their shores to be
> The unplumbed, salt, estranging sea.

Again, it was the Greeks who, Arnold believed, could provide the most telling equivalents for his spiritual state, and *Empedocles on Etna* (1852) is the century's finest attempt to measure Victorian despair in a Grecian light. Although nominally a drama, *Empedocles on Etna* is essentially a series of dramatic monologues in which, as the ageing hero examines his 'dwindling faculty of joy', so he moves up the side of the volcano into whose crater he will eventually throw himself rather than endure a compromise with a world of lost emotions. While Empedocles' extreme and destructive responses are reminiscent of Byron's *Manfred*, the most attractive figure in the work is the young Callicles, still fresh in his enjoyment of life. As a poet, Callicles is able to uphold the Greek ideal of literature in which extremes are counterbalanced with the taut grace of a perfectly tuned string:

> The day in his hotness,
> The strife with the palm;
> The night in her silence,
> The stars in their calm.

But classic poise was perhaps only for a classic world. In 'Future', Victorian society brings the cities that cluster darkly along the river of time and an existence ravaged by industrialism. This is a life without culture, without community and ultimately without God. Even the receding tide heard in 'Dover Beach' becomes an emblem of the 'Melancholy, long, withdrawing Roar' of faith, and at the close a modern man and woman are left clasped in each other's arms as they stare at

> a darkling plain
> Swept with confused alarms of struggle and flight
> Where ignorant armies clash by night.

Frequent anthologizing has barely staled the terror of these lines and their evocation of a godless Victorian waste land and so of a central Victorian moral dilemma.

In the Preface to his *Poems* of 1853, Arnold advanced a concept of poetry which would appeal to 'the great primary human affections, to those elementary feelings which subsist permanently in the race and which are independent of time'. In 'Sohrab and Rustum', Arnold attempted to give Homeric grandeur to a tragic plot, but it is partly the personal application of a poem about a son's death at the hands of his father that gives the work its undoubted force. *Merope* (1858), by contrast, is no more than an academic exercise in ancient tragic modes. Arnold's greatest poem in his 1853 volume however is an altogether more passionate engagement with modes of escape from Victorian spiritual despair.

The Scholar Gipsy, imagined in an Oxfordshire landscape re-created with Keatsian sensuousness, depicts a seventeenth-century free spirit, a timeless representative of 'glad perennial youth'. Introspective, dedicated, natural, he is the image of the unstrained well-being that Victorian society could only contaminate:

> O born in days when wits were fresh and clear,
> And life ran gaily as the sparkling Thames;

Before this strange disease of modern life,
With its sick hurry, its divided aims,
 Its heads o'ertax'd, its palsied hearts, was rife –
 Fly hence, our contact fear!
Still fly, plunge deeper in the bowering wood!
 Averse, as Dido did with gesture stern
 From her false friend's approach in Hades turn,
Wave us away, and keep thy solitude!

But, in the end, this is the solitude of escapism. The closing allusion to Virgil's Dido suggests that life cannot be spent in self-indulgent reverie, and for modern man commitment must take the place of nostalgia and yearning after will-o'-the-wisps. Arnold realized that other engagements with his society must be sought. 'I am glad you like the Gipsy Scholar,' he wrote to Clough, 'but what does it *do* for you? Homer *animates* – Shakespeare *animates* ... the Gipsy Scholar at best awakens a pleasing melancholy. This is not what we want.'

What the age did want, Arnold believed, was something to quicken and ennoble its responses, and if his own poetry could not provide this then criticism might point the way. Arnold's essays and lectures brought a broad and humane critical intelligence to bear on the discussion of literature, social questions and issues of religious belief. Against pedantry and the narrowly provincial, against dogmatism, self-interest and 'the elaborate machine-work of ... the logicians', he opposed the calm and comprehensive poise of mind which he identified with culture:

The great men of culture are those who have had a passion for diffusing, for making prevail, for carrying from one end of society to the other, the best knowledge, the best ideas of their time; who have laboured to divest knowledge of all that was harsh, uncouth, difficult, abstract, professional, exclusive; to humanize it, to make it efficient outside the clique of the cultivated and the learned, yet still remaining the best knowledge and thought of the time, and true source, therefore, of sweetness and light.

This passage from *Culture and Anarchy* (1869) is central to Arnold's entire enterprise. Olympian but not aloof, it suggests how a humane intelligence longs to communicate to a troubled society the restorative poise by which it has established its own integrity. To do this meant seeing beyond the narrowly partisan, the capricious and the eccentric. It meant above all 'a *critical* effort: the endeavour, in all branches of knowledge – theology, philosophy, history, art, science – to see the object as in itself it really is'. The call is for a Grecian light, and 'On the Modern Element in Literature', the inaugural lecture Arnold delivered after his appointment to the Oxford Professorship of Poetry in 1857, proclaims that 'Greek Literature, and, above all, Greek poetry', provide the necessary illumination for a humane survey of the present, culminating epoch of the world.

But even Oxford could nurture a *trahison des clercs*. Modern versions of the Greek poets are attacked in 'On Translating Homer' (1861) for their pedantry and failure to understand that 'the critic of poetry should have the finest tact, the richest moderation, the most free, flexible, and elastic spirit imaginable'. Arnold was to show in *Essays in Criticism* (1865) that a failure to preserve such standards is a national danger. Not only does it encourage absurd exercises in biblical literalism, but it suggests the narrowness of 'general culture' itself. A country like Arnold's much admired France is saved from such ignorant enthusiasm, he suggests, by 'The Literary Influence of Academies', not by the promulgation of rules but by the public recognition of high and comprehensive standards.

'The Future of Criticism at the Present Time' argues for the supreme importance of rising above the materialistic, the utilitarian, the John Bullish 'practical view of things'. Arnold here suggests that a free play of mind is only to be achieved by the intellect 'steadily refusing to lend itself to any of those ulterior, political, practical considerations about ideas, which plenty of people will be sure to attach to them, which in this country at any rate are certain to be attached to them ... but which criticism really has nothing to do with'. The poised, open intelligence and, above all, 'the disinterested desire to learn and propagate the best that is known and thought in the world' are the only means of preserving a humanity that joys in the mainstream of European thought. The opposite is the deafening din of 'a confused, loud-talking, clap-trappy country like this'. Victorian values were never more mercilessly exposed.

In *Culture and Anarchy*, Arnold also discussed the broader social and political issues such beliefs entailed. 'The difficulty for democracy', he had written in 1861, 'is how to find and keep high ideals.' The role of the state moves closer to the centre of his thought, as do those enemies of civilization he memorably denounced as the 'Barbarians', or the entrenched and ill-educated aristocracy, the 'Populace', and that particular object of his contempt, the 'Philistines', or the narrow, *nouveaux riches* and often Nonconformist members of the Victorian middle classes.

It was the 'bad civilization' of the latter group which Arnold saw as especially pernicious. He believed that a rigid ethic of work and commercial *laissez-faire* left such people aesthetically impoverished amid material wealth. In addition, a narrow biblical literalism cut them off from the true spirit of the Gospels and the broader traditions of the Anglican Church. Low in their cultural aspirations, provincial in their bigotry, Arnold alleged that such people could contribute little of value to 'the nation in its collective and corporate character'. Arnold christened this rigid outlook 'Hebraism' and then contrasted it to his ideal of 'Hellenism', or what, following Swift, he called 'sweetness and light'. With the emotive pithiness that often distinguishes his style, he declared: 'the governing ideal of Hellenism is *spontaneity of consciousness*; that of Hebraism, *strictness of conscience*'. Ideally, these two forces, the biblical and the pagan, should operate in harmony. What Arnold saw as the triumph of Hebraism however made him concentrate on his favoured world of the Greek ideal in order to suggest to the Victorian public his belief in a balanced culture, the 'harmonious expansion of *all* the powers which make for the beauty and worth of human nature'.

In the political sphere, Arnold advocated an ideal of 'firm State-power'. In 'Equality', published in *Mixed Essays* (1879), he saw inequalities of class and property as a threat to both strong government and civilization itself since they tended to 'materializing our upper class, vulgarizing our middle class, and brutalizing our lower class'. It was against such 'anarchy' that Arnold evolved his concept of the state as a humane force which would unify the people in an elevated ideal body 'which is not manifold, and vulgar, and unstable, and contemptuous and ever varying, but one, and noble, and secure, and peaceful, and the same for all mankind'.

At the end of his career, Arnold turned back to his literary interests and a renewed concern with religion. In 'The Study of Poetry', a work republished at the start of *Essays in Criticism: Second Series*

(1888), he described poetry in a famous phrase as 'a criticism of life', an attempt to see things as they truly are. These later works nonetheless show Arnold moving towards a concept of culture more clearly coloured by religious aspiration than before, since literature (and poetry in particular) is now seen to make moral truth uniquely telling. Hence in part Arnold's preference for lines which suggest a stoic acceptance of suffering. Such lines are the 'touchstones' which he suggested the reader should house in his memory 'for detecting the presence or absence of high poetic quality, and also the degree of this quality, in all other poetry which we place beside them'.

It was in the Bible that Arnold believed the mass of ordinary people could find the poetry of 'joyful and bounding emotion' which would enliven their morality. For Arnold himself, religion was nothing other than 'morality touched by emotion', a vague but ennobling sense of transcendent values 'whether we find it in Sophocles or in Isaiah'. This is notoriously imprecise, but when Arnold turned to analyse the Prophets as he might have done the classical poets – in other words, when he looked at the Bible as a literary text – he inevitably roused the anger of those who believed the Testaments to be divinely inspired.

Works such as *St Paul and Protestantism* (1870), *Literature and Dogma* (1873) and *God and the Bible* (1875) show Arnold developing these concerns. A narrow, literalistic dependence on the sacred text (whether that of the scholar or the bigot) is tellingly criticized here when Arnold declares that the language of Scripture is fluid rather than fixed, literary rather than legalistic, and so requires an experience of life, a flexibility of spirit and the wide culture of the true critic if it is to be fully appreciated. That form of narrow Puritanism which builds a vengeful doctrine on a poetic insight is skilfully analysed, while the value Arnold himself set on the Anglican Church as a broad, historical growth and 'a beneficent social and civilizing agent' suggests his lifelong concern that Victorian society should be joined in one truly organic community based on the highest values of culture, sweetness and light. Such was the enormous authority granted to the Victorian man of letters from Carlyle onwards – the prestige attributed to literary culture itself – that the sage could assume something of the influence once reserved for the priest. His consciousness, searching for moral truth, is admitted as central to an age of diverse and often conflicting values.

14

The effort to create a fully humane life in an age of religious doubt is also central to the work of George Eliot (1819–80). In a famous conversation on God, immortality and duty, she told the writer Frederick Myers how she considered the first inconceivable, the second unbelievable and the third peremptory and absolute. Her path towards so magisterial a response was marked by the influence of some of the central figures of European thought, and such philosophic gravity was in turn to transform the writing of the English novel. With George Eliot, works of fiction become vehicles in which a human response of the greatest subtlety and warmth is at one with the novelist's ability to make ideas 'incarnate'. Imaginative prose gains a new power, a new range of moral grandeur.

Such mastery required a long apprenticeship, and the development of the sternly evangelical Mary Ann Evans into the novelist George Eliot shows a mind being gradually 'liberated from the wretched giant's bed of dogmas on which it has been racked and stretched'. In particular, the religious beliefs among which George Eliot had been reared were shaken by her early reading in sceptical and determinist thinkers, and by her completion of a version of Strauss's *Das Leben Jesu* (1846). After the death of her father, and when John Chapman took over the *Westminster Review* in 1851, George Eliot became his editorial assistant and was introduced to liberal and free-thinking circles in London. These included Mill and Harriet Martineau; Herbert Spencer (1820–1903), the philosopher of social evolution; Thomas Huxley (1825–95), the defender of Darwin; and the man with whom George Eliot herself was to form the extra-marital relationship that sustained her most creative years, G.H. Lewes (1817–78).

During this period of personal change and fulfilment, Eliot was to further her involvement with German literature and criticism. In 1854, there appeared her translation of Ludwig Feuerbach's *Essence of Christianity*, a work in which the author argued that God is an imaginative projection of man's deepest instincts about his own nature, and that the true divinity of humankind is best revealed not in religious observances but in loving relationships. 'Man and woman are the complement of each other, and thus united they first present the species, the perfect man.' At this time too, Lewes's work on a biography of Goethe also led Eliot to a new appreciation of *Wilhelm Meister's Apprenticeship*, and so of an art which, she wrote, 'brings us into the presence of living, generous humanity – mixed and erring, and self-deluding'. Goethe, she continued, 'quietly follows the stream of fact and life; and waits patiently for the moral processes of nature as we all do for her material processes'. This was a response deepened by Eliot's personal sympathy with the value of tradition, an approach which was reinforced by her study of the German sociologist W.H. von Reihl, who proposed a view of men and women as beings formed by the deeply rooted local society they and their predecessors have created.

Such ideas were to help shape George Eliot's fiction, but both her own writing and that of Goethe were strongly influenced by Spinoza's *Ethics* (1677), a work which Eliot herself translated but never published. Here, Spinoza not only showed the social importance of religious belief but outlined a subtly philosophical psychology in which a determinist view of man is moderated by a concern with the degree of his mastery over his emotions, a partial control which gives him moral dignity. This becomes a central issue in Eliot's fiction.

So, too, does the role of the woman writer. Eliot's essays in the *Westminster Review* at this period outline not only her resentment at women's legal and educational disadvantages but also her belief in the 'special qualities' of feminine experience itself, qualities based on sexual differences which involve women in wholly different areas to men. In 'Silly Novels by Lady Novelists', Eliot argued that these feminine qualities of imaginative and loving sympathy must be preserved from the degrading clichés peddled by popular writers of fiction with their boudoir fantasies and fairy-tale endings. Compassion, acute observation and realism are for Eliot the hallmarks of true women's fiction – the female writer's claim to the high moral ground – and the three stories that make up *Scenes from Clerical Life* (1858) were designed as experiments in this mode.

In her first story, 'The Sad Fortunes of the Reverend Amos Barton', the lower-middle-class provincial background is beautifully observed not only in its physical characteristics but as a world at once traditional and subject to modern forces of improvement. Amos Barton himself however is far from an idealized figure, being 'palpably and unmistakably commonplace'. The death from over-work of his wife Milly rouses compassion in both parishioners and readers alike, and so kindles that 'religion of humanity' which is central to Eliot's writing. 'Depend upon it,' she wrote, 'you would gain unspeakably if you would learn with me to see of the poetry and the pathos, the tragedy and the comedy, lying in the experience of a human soul, that looks out through dull grey eyes, and that speaks in a voice of quite ordinary tones.'

The climax of 'Amos Barton' has something of the melodrama seen again in 'Mr Gilfil's Love-Story'. In 'Janet's Repentance' how-ever, Eliot portrays a heroine at once noble and loving but tempera-mentally flawed, vulnerable in a world of male dominance, yet finding through sacrifice and a community of suffering the 'quiet submissive sorrow, patience and gratitude' by which, the author suggests, women may alter the world. Human pity, the woman writer's 'power of sympathy', reaches down into the depths of such feeling to show a love 'not calculable by algebra, not deducible by logic, but mysterious, effectual, mighty as a hidden process by which the tiny seed is quickened and bursts forth into full stem and broad leaf, and glowing tasselled flower'.

It is such a force that is personified in Dinah Morris, the Methodist preacher in George Eliot's first full-length novel, *Adam Bede* (1859). This work again aims at faithful pictures of 'a monotonous homely existence', the realism George Eliot so marvellously conveys through descriptions such as that of Bede's carpenter's shop where a rough grey shepherd dog lies bedded down on the shavings and occasionally wrinkles his brows as he stares at his master. Description, speech and the outward appearance of the characters all create a vividly realized environment. Nonetheless, in the story of the seduction of Adam's beloved Hettie Sorrel by the young squire Arthur Donnithorne and the agony of Hettie herself when, abandoned, she leaves her illegiti-mate child to die, George Eliot shows how the world she describes may be distorted and made tragic by the fantasies and partial aware-ness of those who inhabit it.

Adam has to learn that moral values cannot be simply measured with a carpenter's rule. Arthur, entranced by Hettie, has to learn that in sexual attraction there is an unconscious power so forceful that it is 'as if his horse had wheeled round from a leap, and dared to dispute his mastery'. As a man with no very strong control over his emotions, Arthur is also obliged to realize that the rousing of such powerful and unconsidered emotion weaves men against their will into an all-involving pattern of cause and effect where 'consequences are unpitying'.

It is Hettie who is the chief victim of these consequences, but she is also the dupe of her own weakness: her fantasy that the taboos of class may be broken with ease and that the world will readily shape itself to her wishes. Such naïvety is shown as blameworthy in so far as it debars her from responsible moral choice, but when the real world cruelly impinges on her she can only wander in the agonizing winter nightmare of unmarried motherhood in which she abandons her baby. Finally, in the condemned cell and in the presence of that Comtian 'priestess of Humanity' Dinah, she can finally come to terms with her plight. 'Dinah, do you think God will take away that crying and that place in the wood, now I have told everything?' The deep, female sympathy of Dinah brings the realization of truth even as it rouses sympathy. But just as Hettie's last-minute reprieve from the gallows is merely melodramatic, so Dinah's marriage to Adam Bede is a somewhat contrived image of the union Feuerbach had seen as the perfection of human life.

The web of duties and local love that makes up character while constraining its higher flights is most movingly explored in *The Mill on the Floss* (1860). Of all George Eliot's heroines, Maggie Tulliver is her most autobiographical and the one in whom the influences of childhood are most subtly traced. Maggie's love for her brother Tom and the intensity of the early passions that bind her to her world are presented with such acuteness that we feel them to be her true moral centre as she grows to maturity. Numerous incidents go to make up this impression, and each is presented with great subtlety:

He threw a line for her and put the rod into her hand. Maggie thought it probable that the small fish would come to her hook, and the large ones to Tom's. But she had forgotten all about the fish, and was looking dreamily at the glassy water, when Tom said, in a loud whisper, 'Look, look, Maggie!' and came running to prevent her from snatching her line away.

Maggie was frightened lest she was doing something wrong, as usual, but presently Tom drew out her line and brought a large tench bouncing on the grass.

But the growing Maggie is also a creature of more wayward passions and dreams. She is a seemingly ordinary girl yearning for beauty, love and knowledge. In this she becomes one of her creator's tragic heroines who tries to rise above 'the mental level of the generation before them, to which they have been nevertheless tied by the strongest fibres of their hearts'. Maggie's aspirations to culture and romantic love constantly conflict with the reality of her life. Most painfully of all, they conflict with the rigid moral certainties of Tom, especially after Mr Tulliver's ruin, and with the responsibilities that are then thrust on the boy.

Though Maggie attempts to subdue her emotions, her aspiration to the cultured world of Philip Wakem is cruelly stifled by Tom, while her affection for the somewhat lifeless Stephen Guest threatens to sever her from her roots. The townsfolk of St Oggs see this liaison as reducing Maggie to a fallen woman, while she herself realizes that surrendering to impulses regardless of others is contrary to her whole being. Her childhood summons her: 'I must go back to it, and cling to it, else I shall feel as if there were nothing firm beneath my feet.' But Maggie's return leads to chaos and death as, in the hurried symbolic narrative of the third volume, brother and sister, drowning in the great flood of the mill-race, are at last united and redeemed by reawakened love.

After the somewhat diffuse structure of The Mill on the Floss, the moral fable of Silas Marner (1861) appears an altogether more disciplined account of community, love and the discovery of self. Much influenced by Wordsworth's narrative poetry, the work focuses many of George Eliot's principal concerns. Marner himself, having been unjustly expelled from his narrow religious community, becomes exiled from all men in solipsistic miserliness. After the theft of his money however, he begins to learn the 'religion of humanity' when the golden locks of an abandoned child replace his affection for his stolen wealth. 'There was love between the man and the child, and love between the child and the world.'

Godfrey Cass, the squire's son who is both little Eppie's legal father and the thief of Marner's gold, is Eliot's figure of moral weakness trapped and eventually defeated by the circumstances he has created. In the regeneration of Marner however, and in the loyalty of Eppie to her 'real' father, George Eliot suggests the power of love and community. This she presents in Old Testament terms. Although today no angels lead men from the city of destruction, she declares 'a hand is put into theirs, which leads them forth gently towards a calm and bright land, so that they look no more backwards; and the hand may be a little child's'.

George Eliot's earlier works are set in the immediate past, but with *Romola* (1863) she attempted a historical novel centred around the fifteenth-century Florence of Savonarola and exploring the philosophy of Comte. Critics from Henry James onwards have disliked the work for smelling of the lamp. *Felix Holt, the Radical* (1866), Eliot's social problem novel, is again only a partial success. Written at the time of the Second Reform Bill, it re-creates the England of 1832 in order to argue that the true welfare of the working classes lay in moral improvement rather than access to political power. The eponymous hero is the mouthpiece for such radical conservatism, but the novel fails to 'incarnate' his ideas in a fully convincing way, and the true greatness of the work lies elsewhere. George Eliot's portrait of the indomitable Mrs Transome, harried by the secret of her son's illegitimate birth and by this radical dandy's failure to touch the humanity beating within her, remains a fine account of a woman gnawed by unassuageable bitterness.

The greatness of George Eliot's reputation remains founded on one of the supreme works of English fiction. *Middlemarch* (1872) is the novel in which the writer's compassion and range of analysis are blended with an artistic control of the greatest subtlety and scale. Henry James described *Middlemarch* as 'an organized, moulded, balanced composition, gratifying the reader with a sense of design and construction'. He was to declare that George Eliot's artistic intelligence marked the beginning of a new era in English fiction, an era in which the novel could be accorded the highest dignity as 'the expression of an artistic faith, the result of choice and comparison'.

The quest of the ardent Dorothea Brooke for her true vocation and her squandering of youthful idealism on the dry-as-dust scholar Casaubon are portrayed with a magnificent interplay of compassion and irony. The author's detailed sympathy and the comments of the townsfolk of Middlemarch itself give further verisimilitude to Eliot's depiction of exceptional individuals caught in an ordinary world. We watch the tragedy of Dorothea's disillusion, seeing it as the result both of her naïve and even arrogant assumption of being a St Theresa called 'to lead a grand life here – now – in England', and of the equally reckless innocence that believes 'the really delightful marriage must be that where your husband was a sort of father, and could teach you even Hebrew, if you wished it'. This denial of sexuality in a longing for submission leads to the desperate entrapment of Dorothea's marriage to Casaubon.

But Casaubon also has his tragic aspects. Ladislaw tells Dorothea that her husband's life work, the 'Key to All Mythologies', merely opens the door to hopelessly dated modes of scholarship. Dorothea's tactless insistence that he complete the work nonetheless shows the heroine in a new light. 'Dorothea was not only his wife,' Eliot comments, 'she was a personification of that shallow world which surrounds the ill-appreciated or desponding author.' In such ways, we come to see the characters with ever-greater objectivity, while, in her disillusion, Dorothea herself begins to gain the imaginative sympathy and poise that lay at the heart of Eliot's reading of Spinoza. The famous conclusion to the twenty-first chapter of the novel describes this process:

We are all of us born in moral stupidity, taking the world as an udder to feed our supreme selves: Dorothea had early begun to emerge from that stupidity, yet it had been easier for her to imagine how she would devote herself to Mr Casaubon, and become wise and strong in his strength and wisdom, than to conceive with that directness which is no longer reflection but feeling – an idea wrought back to the directness of sense, like the solidity of objects – that he had an equivalent centre of self, whence the lights and shadows must always fall with a certain difference.

The novelist speaks out in her own voice, but the appeal is less to an established belief than to what, through the precision of her analysis, she has to convince us is a shared experience. Dorothea has moved from that immature state which naïvely sees the world as a reflection of her own desire to an awareness that she and hence others are autonomous moral beings. By recognizing the separateness of others, she can develop the mature awareness of relationship that lies at the heart of the novel.

A second fate deepens our appreciation of Dorothea's plight. Lydgate, seduced by the spots of commonness in his own nature, marries the lethally trivial Rosamund Vincey, falls into debt and loses the fine and high idealism which spurred him to scientific research. He is brought down by the very society he hopes to serve: by Rosamund, by himself and by the choric voices of Middlemarch society. The name of the town suggests the level of its inhabitants' aspirations. Such representative townsfolk as Mrs Cadwallader are as ready to pass their partial verdicts on Dorothea's marriage and Lydgate's aspirations as they are on efforts to secure the passage of the 1832 Reform Bill. When Mr Brooke's absurd speech at the hustings has been parodied into derision, Ladislaw remarks: 'it seems as if the paltry fellows were always to turn the scale'. Similarly, Mrs Dollop of the Tankard Inn spreads the rumour that Lydgate's medical efforts are directed solely by a wish to 'let people die in the Hospital, if not to poison them, for the sake of cutting them up without saying by your leave'.

The most subtle and tragic effect of this chorus of local comment comes when Lydgate appears compromised by the unmasking of the odious banker Bulstrode. At a public meeting called on health matters, Bulstrode is obliged to give an account of his affairs. 'A crisis of feeling almost too violent for his delicate frame to support' ensues. Lydgate is torn between his duty as a doctor and the effect that showing sympathy will have on his reputation. He rises to help the tottering man, but what might have been merely a simple act of compassion associates him with the corrupt banker in the eyes of the townsfolk. Lydgate's reputation is destroyed and he is compelled to squander his life with a woman he cannot respect and in a demeaningly fashionable medical practice. The aspirations of the erstwhile scientist produce nothing more than a tract on gout.

But pessimism is absorbed in a broader view. What George Eliot calls 'the stealthy convergence of human lots' leads to Dorothea gaining ever-greater moral stature. Her sympathy for Lydgate is a 'saving influence', and not on the doctor alone. A widow now but debarred by the terms of her husband's will from marrying the somewhat weakly characterized free-spirit Ladislaw, Dorothea wrongly believes Rosamund is having an affair with the young man. Her pain is intense and, in the dawn light, her thoughts turn to Lydgate, Rosamund and Ladislaw himself. 'What should I do – how should I act now, this very day if I could clutch my own pain, and compel it to silence, and think of these three!' Her mind begins to find a greater moral dignity through an imaginative and altruistic effort of the will. Other people, seen objectively, demand her help and thereby connect her to the real world in all its sullied ordinariness and potential glory. 'Far off in the bending sky was the pearly light; and she felt the largeness of the world and the manifold wakings of men to labour and endurance. She was part of that involuntary, palpitating life and could neither look out on it from her luxurious shelter as a mere spectator, nor hide her eyes in selfish complaining.'

Dorothea goes to see Rosamund on Lydgate's behalf. The great eighty-first chapter of *Middlemarch* presents the heroine's moral triumph and liberation. Rosamund, by a 'reflex' of Dorothea's moral strength, is able to disabuse her about Ladislaw and so prepare for the scene in which the couple declare their love. The meeting of the two women is one of the supreme moments of Victorian fiction and was recognized as such by contemporaries. Frederick Myers offered a reaction that encapsulates the response of many subsequent readers. In a world where God and the hereafter no longer provide man's spiritual goals, he told George Eliot, human contact is the only means of self-realization. Dorothea's night of struggle and visit to Rosamund, though only a fiction, reveal the best the contemporary spirit can offer. 'The interest of such conceptions', he continued, 'is more than artistic; they are landmarks in the history of the race, showing the height to which, at successive periods, man's ideal of his own life has risen.'

We are no longer in the world of St Theresa, Dorothea's earlier heroine, but in that of a Victorian gentlewoman quietly charged with moral grandeur. From this basis, happily married to Ladislaw, himself now 'an ardent public man', Dorothea works her modest goodness on society. Neither saint nor martyr, 'the effect of her being on those around her was incalculably diffusive: for the growing good of the world is partly dependent on unhistoric acts; and that things are not so ill with you and me as they might have been is half owing to the number who lived faithfully a hidden life, and rest in unvisited tombs'.

George Eliot's last novel *Daniel Deronda* (1876) has both a contemporary and a European setting. In the character of Deronda himself, in his slowly dawning awareness of his Jewish ancestry and his growing commitment to Zionism, George Eliot attempted to widen her English readers' cultural vision. Community is again of central importance. The community between Christianity and Judaism is suggested through Deronda's upbringing in a gentile house, while his Zionist vision emphasizes the community of races.

If the Jewish characters in the novel are not always wholly convincing, in the figure of Gwendolen Harleth, obliged by financial necessity to marry the sadistic Grandcourt, George Eliot created one of her finest studies of a female mind. In particular, the effects of a spoiled childhood have ill prepared Gwendolen for the adult world. Her relationship with Deronda is a subtle blend of love and renunciation and is skilfully contrasted to the egotism of Grandcourt. However, when Grandcourt drowns there is no marriage between Gwendolen and Deronda, who leaves with his Jewish bride on a Zionist pilgrimage. Novelistic convention is replaced by an altogether deeper knowledge of separateness and community.

15

Eliot's contemporaries were also pursuing intellectual experiment in the novel, a fact which suggests the growing divide between those readers content with the conventional and the run-of-the-mill and those few interested in literary developments, in particular the analysis of characters' mental and moral lives. Such developments suggest that ever-increasing diversity, the stress on individual sensibility and experiment, that is one of the hallmarks of later nineteenth-century fiction.

'Brainstuff is not lean stuff,' wrote George Meredith (1828–1909), 'the brainstuff of fiction is conscious internal history, and to suppose it dull is the profoundest of errors.' After the oriental fantasy *The Shaving of Shagpat* (1856), Meredith turned to a fiction in which optimism based partly on the Darwinian-inspired belief that man must be responsible for developing his consciousness in co-operation with nature is tempered by a recognition of the egoism that alienates and divides him from his world and his kind. As Meredith suggested in his lecture *On the Idea of Comedy and the Uses of the Comic Spirit* (1877), it is the 'volleys of silvery laughter' hurled by Comedy herself at the bigoted, the pretentious and the self-deceived that are life's principal means of maintaining healthy psychological balance.

Meredith's comic irony is often grim nonetheless, and nowhere more so than in *The Ordeal of Richard Feverel* (1859) where the attempts of the hero's father to rule his son's sexual life offer a picture of an egotism that causes suffering, tragedy and death. The novel is also important for showing how Meredith used the resources of the poet to suggest personal crises. Extended metaphor was particularly valuable, and one of the great set-piece passages in the work shows the hero's reaction to the news that the wife from whom he has separated has borne his child. Climbing through a magnificent German landscape, Richard's initial indifference gives way to warmth, to love and eventually to that deep natural joy once experienced with his wife in their youth and now revived by the vista of 'a plain clothed with ripe corn under a spacious morning sky'. Such exaltation is in sharp contrast to the book's portrayal of sex without love which so offended contemporary readers.

Both *Evan Harrington* (1861) and *The Adventures of Harry Richmond* (1871) are conceived in a more high-spirited vein reminiscent of Peacock. They also reveal Meredith's ability to create female characters whose strengths subdue the egotism of men. Feminism and the theme of the estranged married woman are developed in *Diana of the Crossways* (1885) and in Meredith's last novels, but it is Clara Middleton in *The Egoist* (1879) who helps create Meredith's most successful work. Constructed from scenes and dialogues that resemble drama, the novel offers a portrait of quintessential egoism in Sir Willoughby Patterne. For all his faults – a preference for the set-piece scene over careful construction, grandiloquence, obscurity and intrusive theorizing – Meredith is a figure of great importance in the development of the English novel. Though he lamented that 'my name is celebrated, but nobody reads my books', writers such as Hardy, James, Woolf, Joyce, Lawrence and Forster were all to benefit from his courage to experiment for a small readership, to present a cosmic view of human life and to develop analysis through imagery.

One writer to whom Meredith gave practical encouragement was George Gissing (1857–1903), recommending to Chapman and Hall that they publish his second novel, *The Unclassed* (1884). Like *Workers in the Dawn* (1880), this novel is an attempt to offer a vision of life in the slums – of what Gissing himself called 'untouched social strata' – and to let the appalling facts speak for themselves as he exposes the blight inflicted on the poorest at the hub of empire.

George Moore (1852–1933) was to attempt a similar realism in *A Mummer's Wife* (1885) and his horrifying description of a lying-in hospital in *Esther Waters* (1894). In this he was much influenced by the French Naturalists and by Zola, a translation of whose *La Terre* was prosecuted in England for obscenity. Gissing however asserted the novelist's right to order the external world in the light of his own impressions and ideas. *Demos* (1886) satirizes working-class aspirations and the socialists' attempts at improvement, while in *The Nether World* (1889) – a work written after the sordid death of his alcoholic wife – Mad Jack is told by an angel that 'this life you are now leading is that of the damned; this place to which you are confined is Hell!'

The influence of the artistically more self-conscious French novel was viewed with great suspicion by literary conservatives – Tennyson referred bitterly to 'maiden fancies wallowing in the troughs of Zolaism' – but it is an important aspect of the English avant-garde in the later nineteenth century and their attempt to create a fiction which had, in Henry James's words, 'a consciousness of itself behind it'. The influence of Flaubert, Zola and Maupassant allowed writers to deal with issues unavailable to those who saw themselves as spokesmen of an older moral consensus. Here, indeed, was one vitally important way beyond what we can now see as Victorian prudery.

Gissing's *Born in Exile* (1892) deals with the unconscious motivation of Godwin Peak, a man of great ability who tries to overcome the barriers of class through hypocrisy and deceit, but perhaps the finest of Gissing's novels is *New Grub Street* (1891). Here Gissing offers his most telling analyses of marriage, thwarted artistic creation and the human spirit crushed by a competitive world in which only those who sell out appear to survive. Edward Reardon, the well-educated novelist without money, sees the breakdown of his marriage and his literary hopes. His friend Biffen, the avant-garde realist, toils at a would-be essay in the style of Flaubert called 'Mr Bailey, Grocer' and dies. 'Success has nothing whatsoever to do with moral deserts', and the odious Whelpdale makes a living from the lowest reaches of journalism. His greatest success is to convert the magazine *Chat* into *Chit-Chat* and there print articles no more than two inches in length and broken into at least four paragraphs. In the real world, *Tit-Bits* had been started a decade earlier.

Gissing's is a world of alienation, a world without God. The novel of religious doubt remained an important genre, and while J.H. Shorthouse's *John Inglesant* (1880) could view the choice between Rome and Canterbury as 'a conflict within a man's own nature – nay, a conflict between the noblest parts of man's nature arranged against each other', J.A. Froude's notorious *The Nemesis of Faith* (1849) had earlier presented the agony of Markham Sutherland as doubts lead him to resign his Anglican living and die in despair after he has been saved from suicide by a Roman Catholic priest. *Robert Elsmere* (1888) by the distinguished novelist Mrs Humphry Ward (1851–1920), by contrast, develops from muscular Christianity, through the Higher Criticism and the resigning of a living, to the hero's involvement in East End charity work and 'the London of democracy, of the nineteenth century, and of the future'.

The narrow spiritual ugliness of much Victorian religious dissent is described in the semi-autobiographical novels of 'Mark Rutherford', the pseudonym of William Hale White (1831–1913). *The Autobiography of Mark Rutherford* (1881) is a quiet study of spiritual problems in a depressing environment, of dishonest conversion, the effect of reading Wordsworth and escape to London where the author endures an unhappy love affair. *Mark Rutherford's Deliverance* (1885) is a sad account of mediocrity accepted and of a passive response to dispiriting circumstances finally relieved by death.

16

For many Victorian children and, no doubt, their parents, escape and succour lay in the realms of fantasy and nonsense, though even here the best works preserve the disturbing undertones of a song recorded by Gerard Manley Hopkins in his Journal:

> Violante
> In the pantry
> Gnawing at a mutton bone,

How she gnawed it
How she clawed it
When she felt herself alone.

A similar note is found in 'Up the airy mountain', the best-known poem of William Allingham (1824–89), while isolation and fear underlie much of the anarchic comedy in *A Book of Nonsense* (1846), *Nonsense Songs* (1871) and *Laughable Lyrics* (1877) by Edward Lear (1812–88). Though Lear himself was not the inventor of the limerick (its origins are to be found in the 1820s), verses containing such figures as the Old Man of Cape Horn who wished he had never been born have led to the limerick being closely identified with Lear. Such verses also suggest how, in more sophisticated narrative works such as 'The Owl and the Pussy-Cat' and the haunting, visionary 'Jumblies', Lear could combine melancholy with exquisite inventiveness and a refined ear. 'The Courtship of the Yonghy-Bonghy-Bo' and 'The Dong with the Luminous Nose' develop Lear's fundamental pathos, the sense of hopelessness and futility seen again in such works as 'Incidents in the Life of my Uncle Arly' from the posthumous *Nonsense Songs and Stories* (1895).

With Lewis Carroll – the pen-name of the Oxford mathematician Charles Lutwidge Dodgson (1832–98) – the sense of unease created by much Victorian nonsense writing comes from pushing rationality to its limits and leaving the mind surprised by its tenuous hold on the worlds created by words and ideas:

> He thought he saw an Argument
>   That proved he was the Pope:
> He looked again, and found it was
>   A Bar of Mottled Soap.
> 'A fact so dread', he faintly said,
>   'Extinguishes all hope!'

These Gardener's songs are perhaps the best things in Carroll's late work *Sylvie and Bruno* (1899), but Carroll had been writing nonsense lyrics as early as 1855 when he copied 'Jabberwocky' into an album. The marvellous linguistic inventiveness of this piece derives partly from Carroll's attempt to parody Old English poetry, and many of its coinages have passed into everyday usage. They recur in Carroll's finest narrative poem, *The Hunting of the Snark* (1876), a parody of the quest poem developed by Carroll after the work's last line had risen spontaneously in his mind. He always claimed that the poem had no meaning beyond itself, but it remains a haunting evocation of wasted effort and the fallacies of hope.

Carroll's gift for parody is revealed again in his version of Isaac Watts's 'How doth the little busy bee' in *Alice's Adventures in Wonderland* (1865). Begun originally to entertain the young Alice Liddell, daughter of the lexicographer and Dean of Christ Church, a finely illustrated version of a four-chapter story called *Alice's Adventures Underground* was first given to the little girl. This was subsequently expanded into the text most commonly read today. Carroll's additions included such scenes as the Mad Hatter's Tea Party, while the work as a whole contains not only the most exhilarating and challenging series of puns and word games, but a very perceptive response to the child's place in the adult world, a place where he or she is sometimes dwarfed, sometimes capable of shrewd insight into the fallacies of older people. *Through the Looking-Glass* (1872) is nonetheless the finer achievement. The tighter structure provided by the chess references, and even more by the inversion of the familiar world caused by seeing it through a mirror, offers the most unsettling insights and makes for subtle combinations of comic nonsense, cruelty and pathos. Such effects can be seen in the destruction of Humpty Dumpty and also as the Walrus and the Carpenter eat their way through the all-too-trusting oysters.

Carroll's fictions are largely free of the didactic purposes behind much Victorian writing for children. Some of these works nonetheless display a fine gift for fantasy. For example, the belief of Charles Kingsley (1819–75) that the moral squalor of the poor was at one with their physical conditions is among the many ideas suggested in *The Water Babies* (1863), the finest of his writings for children. A humanitarian approach to animals and, in particular, horses underlies Anna Sewell's (1820–78) *Black Beauty* (1877), but the greatest creator of the animal world for the children of the late nineteenth century was Beatrix Potter (1866–1943). A small masterpiece like *Peter Rabbit* (1902) shows with what power and poetry she could combine the delicate observation of the naturalist with both the charm and the fear inherent in true fantasy writing. Later, this combination was to be achieved in a new way in *The Wind in the Willows* (1908) by Kenneth Grahame (1859–1932).

Novels by George MacDonald (1824–1905) such as *The Princess and the Curdie* (1877) and, with its finer mixture of fairy-tale and poetic apprehension, *At the Back of the North Wind* (1868–9) discuss moral and social problems with surprising force, as does *The Princess and the Goblin* (1870–71), a work of great psychological interest. The most memorable play for children from before the Great War is *Peter Pan* (1904) by J.M. Barrie (1860–1937), a work whose charm must, for an adult audience, lie in an imagined pre-Freudian innocence.

We may conclude here with two works of moral instruction and fantasy by two altogether more significant writers. Thackeray's *The Rose and the Ring* (1855), designed 'for Great and Small Children', mixes satire and parody with a warning against complacency as the fairy tells the new-born heroine: 'the best thing I can wish her is a *little misfortune*'. Finally, *The King of the Golden River* (1851) by John Ruskin (1819–1900) combines the influences of Dickens and Grimm with Ruskin's love of mountain scenery in order to instruct his future bride in the ethics of selflessness and the belief later expressed in Ruskin's dictum: 'there is no wealth but life'.

17

The King of the Golden River gives fairy-tale expression to ideas Ruskin developed in those mature writings that make him one of the great Victorian sages. Ruskin was brought up in a wealthy evangelical home by parents who, as the autobiographical series of visions and interpretations contained in *Praeterita* (1885–9) makes clear, were devoted to nurturing their son's aesthetic genius. After a carefully protected childhood and youth, Ruskin emerged as the apologist of the great English artist Turner.

The first volume of *Modern Painters* (1843) defended Turner's work against the complaints of contemporary critics by arguing 'that Turner *is* like nature, and paints more of nature than any man that ever lived'. In order to prove this, Ruskin developed his remarkable gift for word-painting, a skill he was later to disparage. *Modern*

Painters describes the effects of nature and art with the greatest sensitivity to detail, a faculty nurtured in Ruskin by his own experiences as a draughtsman. He records in *Praeterita* how sketching a branch of ivy near his home and later drawing a tree in the forest at Fontainebleau convinced him of the artificiality of mere rules, teaching him instead that the beauty of the woods revealed 'the same laws which guided the clouds, divided the light, and balanced the wave'. Such an awareness of unity prepared Ruskin to appreciate Turner's profound knowledge of a similar intuition. In addition, the natural descriptions in *Modern Painters* encouraged Ruskin's audience to view the world with fresh eyes and, thus prepared, to contrast the allegedly mannered representations of nature achieved by the old masters with those attained by Turner himself. Having been taught to see, they would now be taught to interpret.

For Ruskin, Turner's loving and accurate response to nature constituted his 'Truth'. In the second volume of *Modern Painters* (1846), such truth is allied to an evangelical concept of beauty as typifying the attributes of God. The appreciation of the natural world becomes an act of moral and religious awareness which leads to the realization that 'All great art is the expression of man's delight in God's work, not in *his own*.'

The five volumes of *Modern Painters* were not completed until 1860, and during this period Ruskin embarked on two major books which reveal his powerful appreciation of how art is related to the social context in which it is created. In *The Seven Lamps of Architecture* (1849), Ruskin urged that truth and beauty must stem from honest construction and from that love of nature by which a Gothic arch is seen to be at one with 'the termination of every leaf that shakes in summer wind'. The medieval world becomes a criterion of excellence, and Ruskin juxtaposes its aesthetic qualities to the tawdry opulence of much Victorian decoration and the horrors of the new suburban houses which he characterized as 'gloomy rows of formalized minuteness, alike without difference and without fellowship, as solitary as similar'. A contrary ideal of community and the joy of the workman as he creates within that community became increasingly important to Ruskin's thought, and in *The Stones of Venice* (1851–3), aesthetic, historical, social and moral analysis combines with remarkable imaginative force.

Written for an audience proud of the achievements of the Great Exhibition, Ruskin's work is an investigation of the fall of a great mercantile power as its religious beliefs declined from the values expressed in Gothic architecture to those allegedly enshrined in Renaissance building. The organic and spiritual give way to the rational and mercenary, while in the book itself social polemic, travelogue and jeremiad combine with some of the finest examples of Ruskin's skill as a word-painter.

A number of the great descriptive passages in *The Stones of Venice* show Ruskin achieving what he admired in Turner: the creation of accurate descriptions of landscape and the man-made world which transcend the merely topographical and so allow the reader to be a sharer in the artist's own 'strong feelings and quick thoughts'. Ruskin's description of Torcello, for example, coloured like sackcloth and barely emerging from the stagnant waters to support a ruined church, conveys with extraordinary vivacity his belief that such desolation is a punishment for sin – for commercial pride severed from the roots of faith.

An analogy to the possible fate of Victorian England is made explicit in the central and polemical section of the work: 'The Nature of Gothic'. Where the regularity of Renaissance architectural forms or, Ruskin suggests, the mechanical repetitiousness of mass production kills the spirit, the Gothic gives life. The natural and unconfined abundance of Gothic architecture reflects the joy of men in their work, while industrialism and the division of labour are modes of bodily and spiritual slavery:

We have much studied and much perfected, of late, the great civilized invention of the division of labour; only we give it a false name. It is not, truly speaking, the labour that is divided; but the men: – Divided into mere segments of men – broken into small fragments and crumbs of life; so that all the little piece of intelligence that is left in a man is not enough to make a pin, or a nail, but exhausts itself in making the point of a pin or the head of a nail. Now it is a good and desirable thing, truly, to make many pins in a day; but if we could only see with what crystal sand their points were polished, – sand of the human soul, much to be magnified before it can be discerned for what it is – we should think there might be some loss in it also.

This is the cry of the heart against *The Wealth of Nations*. Societies built on such values may fall as Venice has fallen, and for the art critic and moralist, a nation's decline is to be read in its artefacts.

This passionate concern with social well-being is continued in the later volumes of *Modern Painters* where it is also suggested that the spirit of the modern artist, deprived of firm religious consolation, is 'forced to seek in history, and in external nature, the satisfaction it cannot find in ordinary life'. Artists dramatize these mental states by projecting them on to nature, and such romantic distortions Ruskin calls the 'Pathetic Fallacy'.

Ruskin himself had been bred in a biblical tradition which habitually saw events in the Old Testament prefiguring those in the New and which regarded both as shadowing forth a multiplicity of spiritual truths. Such methods of interpretation had allowed him to write his lastingly valuable account of Tintoretto's San Rocco *Annunciation* in the second volume of *Modern Painters*. After his abandonment of Christianity however, such techniques were developed in the light of German studies of myth. This can be seen in Ruskin's powerful analysis of Turner's *The Garden of the Hesperides*, a work that allowed him to continue probing the spiritual dilemma of modern man.

Ruskin attempts to show how Turner's canvas offers a symbolic account of the state of the nation. Ruskin believed that, whether consciously or not, Turner's imagination had reached to the archetypal core of the Greek myth and restated it in terms of contemporary society. The dragon guarding the golden fruit suggests a country that has abandoned innocence for greed, industrialism and 'a paradise of smoke'. Turner's picture thus symbolizes Ruskin's belief – expressed in 'Traffic' in *The Crown of Wild Olive* (1866) – that the English middle classes had given their belief and energies to the 'great Goddess of "Getting-on"'. Such social criticism now became his principal concern. 'Government and co-operation are in all things and eternally the laws of life. Anarchy and competition, eternally, and in all things, the laws of death,' he wrote.

Many of Ruskin's central ideas on politics, economics and society were developed in the lectures he now gave in the industrial towns of the Midlands and the North – the very centres of the forces to which he was opposed. *The Political Economy of Art* (1857), reissued as *A Joy for Ever* in 1880, suggests how aesthetics were still his starting-point, while a phrase from these texts suggests the basis of his entire social thinking: 'the beauty which is indeed a joy for ever, must be a joy for all'. Community lies at the heart of Ruskin's belief, and, against the doctrines of *laissez-faire*, he argues that a 'paternal government' should intervene in all aspects of the economy to promote social cohesion.

Though a number of these works of criticism – *Munera Pulveris* (1862–3), for example, or the second part of *Sesame and Lilies* (1865) with its condescending attitude to the position of women – are very far from promoting enlightened attitudes, there is much in this work that remains permanently interesting and powerful. The analysis of 'Lycidas' in the first half of *Sesame and Lilies*, for example, shows Ruskin's etymological analysis at its best and most orderly, even as *The Queen of the Air* (1869) and *Fors Clavigera* (1871–84) show them at their most chaotic. In *Time and Tide* (1867), Ruskin admits that his analysis has 'now branched, and worse than branched, reticulated, in so many directions, that I hardly know which shoot of it to trace, or which knot to lay hold of first'. Utopias and moral espionage, profound comments on the use of natural resources and state education, the virtues of manual work, myth and quixotic digressions on the social abuses wrought by garlic jostle here with intimate revelations of the author's private life. Such a torrent of matter and impertinency suggests what was in fact the case – the energies of a brilliant mind constantly threatened by insanity. One of these works of social criticism nonetheless remains of enduring value, clear and powerfully argued: *Unto This Last* (1862). Here is Ruskin's central statement of his social beliefs.

The essays that make up *Unto This Last* were originally issued in the *Cornhill Magazine*, but proved so tendentious that they eventually had to be issued in volume form. Ruskin had already suggested in *The Political Economy of Art* that the true use of wealth consisted in tackling poverty and unemployment rather than leaving these ills to *laissez-faire*. Now he proceeded to attack the philosophy that gave rise to such notions in the first place. He was determined to show that the self-interest and unfettered accumulation of wealth proposed by classical economists since the time of Adam Smith (and exemplified chiefly for Ruskin by Mill's *Principles of Political Economy*) had neither a scientific nor a moral basis.

To achieve this, the great word-painter became a master of

impassioned exposition and the satirical grotesque. Writing of the much vaunted 'science' of getting rich, Ruskin declared: 'Observe, I neither impugn nor doubt the conclusion of the science if its terms are accepted. I am simply uninterested in them, as I should be in a science of gymnastics which assumed that men had no skeletons.' In other words, classical economists have forgotten the human with the result that their rationalism has become the merest folly.

Arguing in the mode of a biblical prophet, as a paternalist and 'a violent Tory of the old school', Ruskin now attempted to substitute for the myth of 'economic man' the Christian ethics expounded by the parable of the workers in the vineyard. Economic relations are to be based not on the pursuit of individual advantage but on justice since, in the end, the needs of all members of society are the same. 'Production does not consist in things laboriously made,' Ruskin declared, 'but in things serviceably consumable; and the question for the nation is not how much labour it employs, but how much life it produces. For as consumption is the end and aim of production, so life is the end and aim of consumption.' Instead of a few growing rich on industrial exploitation, the true purpose of creating wealth is 'the production of as many as possible full-breathed, bright-eyed, and happy-hearted human creatures'.

Inspired by such a vision, Ruskin came to realize that gross inequalities of wealth are a comprehensive denial of opportunity. 'The rich not only refuse food to the poor; they refuse wisdom; they refuse virtue; they refuse salvation.' They thus deny the less fortunate the very benefits offered by the Christian faith the rich themselves profess. Such a realization led Ruskin mercilessly to expose the emotional dishonesties of those who attempted to hide behind the 'invisible hand' of classical economics. To men who argued that raising the standards of the poor would merely lead them to idleness and drink, he retorted:

Suppose it were your own son of whom you spoke, declaring to me that you dare not take him into your firm, nor even give him just labourer's wages, because if you did he would die of drunkenness, and leave half a score of children to the parish. 'Who gave your son these dispositions?' – I should enquire. 'Has he them by inheritance or by education?'

Ruskin believed that an enhanced concept of the state was essential to achieving the social cohesion for which he longed. *Unto This Last* therefore advocates state education and state care for the elderly and the poor, as well as recommending the founding of state-subsidized factories to employ those out of work and encourage excellence in standards of production. His social programme – radical and quixotic – was of profound influence on thinkers as diverse as Tolstoy, Gandhi, William Morris and the first elected members of the Parliamentary Labour Party. In the end, the Victorian sage points forward to the modern Welfare State.

18

Ruskin's concern with the accurate representation of nature in art made him the natural ally of a group of radical young painters who, in 1848, briefly set themselves up as the 'Pre-Raphaelite Brotherhood'. Their name suggests their interest in the Gothic, while their short-lived magazine *The Germ* (1850) contains some of the poems of the group's most powerful personality, Dante Gabriel Rossetti (1828–82).

Just as in painting Rossetti and his friends looked back beyond Raphael to the Italian and Flemish primitives, so in poetry Rossetti himself looked back beyond Petrarch to his own thirteenth-century namesake, issuing in translation *The Early Italian Poets* (1861) and revising this in 1874 as *Dante and his Circle*. Rossetti's own early works were not published in volume form until the *Poems* of 1870, a collection expanded in 1881, the year in which he also issued his *Ballads and Sonnets*. Rossetti had, nonetheless, been writing poetry since the 1850s when he began early versions of 'The Blessed Damozel'. This work suggests a number of characteristic features. Dante's Beatrice has here been metamorphosed into a woman longing to be reunited with her earthly lover. Eroticism and the religiose, sensuously realized detail of a vaguely medieval, Keatsian variety and anguish suffused with languorous ardour all become the keynotes:

> And still she bowed herself and stooped
>   Out of the circling charm;
> Until her bosom must have made

> The bar she leaned on warm,
> And the lilies lay as if asleep
> Along her bended arm.

The warmed bar carries a sexual charge which suggests elements in Rossetti's work some were to find disturbingly frank.

Rossetti's other early work ranges over the lyrical, the dramatic, the erotic macabre and pieces of social commentary such as 'Jenny', a monologue set in a prostitute's bedroom. 'Even so' suggests Rossetti's sometime love for his wife Elizabeth Siddal, in whose coffin he buried his early manuscripts after her probable suicide, being later obliged to exhume them for publication. The most important of Rossetti's muses however was the woman he was to represent as the incarnation of Pre-Raphaelite beauty: Jane Morris, the wife of his most ardent disciple. Their affair is recorded in what eventually became a series of 101 sonnets entitled *The House of Life*.

Though the 1881 version of the sequence is organized with an intricacy that suggests the 'fundamental brainwork' Rossetti considered essential to good poetry, the cycle remains at best a series of effective moments interspersed with much that is marred by Rossetti's characteristic faults of turgid and self-conscious literariness. 'Nuptial Sleep' – a sonnet of post-coital lassitude suppressed by Rossetti after Robert Buchanan's prurient attack in 'The Fleshly School of Poetry' (1871) – is a greater achievement however. The haunted guilt of the four 'Willowood' sonnets constitutes a powerful re-creation of remorse and death, but Rossetti's finest evocation of this state is 'The Woodspurge', a lyric whose delicacy of image and plain but dramatic expression achieve a forcefulness that is genuinely affecting.

'I want to imitate Gabriel as much as possible,' declared William Morris (1834–96) in the first flush of his enthusiasm for one of the several masters who were to guide him towards his final role as a great Victorian sage. Morris had gone up to Oxford believing he was called to the High Church ministry, but the writings of Carlyle and Ruskin convinced him that his vocation lay elsewhere. The influence of Ruskin was to be particularly profound, and at the close of a prodigiously diverse and energetic career, when Morris printed an edition of Ruskin's 'The Nature of Gothic', he declared it to be 'one of the very few necessary and inevitable utterances of the century'.

This is the voice of the committed social reformer, and Morris's life and writing (along with his multifarious work as a designer) can be seen as an ever-broadening attempt to juxtapose Utopian visions to squalid contemporary reality. He was both a dreamer and a critic.

The early work Morris published in the short-lived *Oxford and Cambridge Magazine* (1855) suggests his imaginative response to the natural world and to a variety of medieval interests ranging from Gothic art to Scandinavian myth, themes that were to sustain him throughout his life. While many of these early pieces are in prose, the verses gathered in *The Defence of Guenevere and Other Poems* (1858) show Morris treating subjects from Froissart and Malory with considerable originality. In the title piece of the collection, the queen challenges the knights to dare to condemn her for what we know is her adultery. The poem's tormented power and syntax are finely achieved, as is the stark brutality of 'Sir Peter Harpendon's End' and 'The Haystack in the Floods'. '*Beata mea Domina*', perhaps the best-known poem in the volume, shows Morris transforming his future wife's silent beauty into a torturing image from romance.

Though *The Defence of Guenevere* was well received among the discerning and remains a highly original contribution to Victorian Gothic, public criticisms were harsh. When Morris re-emerged as a poet with *The Life and Death of Jason* (1867), it was as a very different writer, a man embroidering a narrative of elegiac disillusion with pretty vignettes in a distinctively Pre-Raphaelite mode. Such self-conscious escapism from the personal unhappiness inflicted by his wife's affair with Rossetti and his own deepening revulsion at the sordid commercialism of the age again underlies the work that was to make Morris famous among his contemporaries, the twenty-four verse narratives collected in *The Earthly Paradise* (1868–70). Here escapism is openly avowed:

> Dreamer of dreams, born out of my due time,
> Why should I strive to set the crooked straight?
> Let it suffice me that my murmuring rhyme
> Beats with light wings against the ivory gate,
> Telling a tale not too importunate
> To those who in the sleepy region stay,
> Lulled by the singer of an empty day.

'Why should I strive to set the crooked straight?' Morris's line suggests his hopelessness in the face of the problems raised by late Victorian industrial society and his recourse to the anodyne effects of a poetry that swings between the pursuit of beauty and the discovery of pain. Despite its excessive and often flaccid prolixity, such poetry was to have considerable influence, and Henry James was not alone when he declared of *The Earthly Paradise*: 'to the jaded intellects of the present moment, distracted with the strife of creeds and the conflict of theories, it opens a glimpse into a world where they will be called upon neither to choose, to criticize, nor to believe, but simply to feel, to look and to listen'. In a world of increasingly stressful complexity, the avant-garde poet is no longer the spokesman of an agreed moral and ethical vision. What he asserts and satisfies is a common ideal of escape from a noisome existence. Art is becoming an end in itself, a radical development others were soon to take much further.

By the late 1870s however, the protean range of Morris's activities was obliging Morris himself to test such views ever more critically. His work as a designer concerned to counter the gimcrack qualities of much Victorian mass production, the lectures in which he sought to define a satisfactory relationship between man and his labour and, increasingly, Morris's involvement in political activities were all convincing him that literary escapism was not a sufficient response to his age. Morris's growing radicalism in these years was a reaction to profound shifts in Victorian society and to divisions that were becoming increasingly evident in the last quarter of the nineteenth century. These, in their turn, were to challenge writers into analysing a complex of evolving problems and to develop solutions for representing them. Literary developments were thus being compounded with social and political changes whose pace, scale and diversity many were to find threatening and to which none were immune.

What writers were facing in fact was those profound uncertainties that mark the origins of the modern world. By the 1870s, the broadly liberal concerns which had brought the country immense material wealth and prestige – the high and sunny plateau of mid-century prosperity – were under threat from both external circumstances and developing internal strains. By creating an industrial nation dependent on world trade, men like the entrepreneurial heroes of Samuel Smiles's *Self-Help* (1859) had made the nation vulnerable to economic changes largely beyond their control. Both Germany and the United States were becoming major competitors and, more and more, increasing numbers of the working population were the victims of recession, slumps and unemployment. The problems of mass socialization were becoming frighteningly evident, and Disraeli, now Prime Minister, began to lay the foundations of a Conservative policy designed to contain these.

Traditional Conservative support was enhanced by disaffected Liberals and many of those working men to whom Disraeli had given the vote in 1867. Disraeli himself now began an active campaign of social reform in housing, public health, factory regulation, trade unionism and education. Such a revision of *laissez-faire* attitudes marked the beginning of the thorough overhaul of state machinery characteristic of the decades from 1870, a process which in turn was to lead to an inevitable and massive growth in centralized power. The modern bureaucratic state was coming into existence.

An England of cities and the masses was being created at home, while events abroad were to focus national consciousness in new and troubling ways. The popular poetry of the music hall expresses this with raucous certainty. When Disraeli appeared ready to join the Turks against Russia in a dubious alliance designed to maintain trade routes with India, a new song added a new word to the English language:

> We don't want to fight,
> But by jingo, if we do,
> We've got the ships, we've got the men,
> We've got the money too!

Nationalism on such a scale gave the mass of the people one easy form of popular identity, and its potency was to be enhanced by the ever more hectic scramble for empire and the markets opened up by the colonies. This growing sense of imperial pride was crowned, quite literally, when Disraeli made Victoria Empress of India in 1876. The way had thus been prepared for those quintessential manifestations of Victorian imperialism – the Golden Jubilee of 1887 and the Diamond Jubilee ten years later. England was coming to see its duty as being to pick up 'the white man's burden'.

Morris himself was appalled not only by such attitudes as these but by the squalor, social injustice and threats to the well-being of the countryside wrought by industrialism. Above all, he was deeply concerned about the spiritual damage inflicted on men themselves by 'mere unmitigated slavish toil' in factories turning out vulgar and shoddy goods. In a series of powerful lectures, he developed Ruskin's principles and argued for the necessity of 'an art which is to be made by the people and for the people, as a happiness to the maker and user'. He came to believe that a profound change in society must be wrought in order to bring this about. Mistrusting both the growth of trade unions and the activity that was to lead to the founding of the Parliamentary Labour Party, Morris became an early convert to what remains one of the greatest indictments of the Victorian industrial world, Marx's *Das Kapital* (1867).

The extremism that underlay the opulent surface of late Victorian England could hardly be clearer, and it was epitomized by Morris himself in his lecture 'Art and Socialism' (1884) when he declared: 'these, I say, are the days of combat, when there is no external peace possible to an honest man'. The Victorian sage had mounted the barricades, and the evils inherent in Victorian values might be redeemed, it appeared, by class warfare and revolution.

Morris campaigned tirelessly for Marxist principles. His newspaper *The Commonweal* (1885) played a major part in this, publishing not only *A Dream of John Ball* (1886–7) – a Marxist analysis of the Peasants' Revolt – but the greatest of Morris's prose works, *News from Nowhere* (1890). Offered as a Utopian vision of English life after the socialist revolution, *News from Nowhere* portrays a society where the state has been abolished and men and women live in equality. Work has taken on the delight of art, and competitive individualism has ceased. Common ownership means that there can be no crime against property and therefore no need for prisons. Sexual relationships are free, while women have achieved liberation by being no longer regarded as chattels to be exchanged in the marriage market. The result is an 'epoch of rest' and a life of small concerns and decent living in harmony with nature and the past. In this, *News from Nowhere* is far superior to Morris's other romances – *The Story of the Glittering Plain* (1891), for example, or *The Well at the World's End* (1896) – with their mannered prose and fantastic, allegorical quests.

Where Morris developed in these strenuous years from the influence of Rossetti and the Pre-Raphaelites to revolutionary socialism, Rossetti's sister revealed an equally passionate attachment to the extremes of High Anglicanism, a force whose social and artistic influence was of considerable importance. Christina Rossetti (1830–94) indeed is one of the most interesting Victorian woman poets, and the traumas of her secret emotional life broke forth in a verse at once subtle and seemingly spontaneous. Lyrics such as 'When I am dead, my dearest' and the excellent sonnet 'Remember' imagine the effects of her death on her lover with great psychological finesse. 'From the Antique' and 'Cobwebs' express a terrible nihilism, but Christina Rossetti was also capable of using Pre-Raphaelite imagery to express the rapture she shows in 'A Birthday'.

Her masterpiece is *Goblin Market* (1862). Written with a freedom of metre that recalls Skelton, the poem suggests allegory without ever quite giving up a clear reading. Laura and Lizzie's encounters with the goblins hint at temptation, surrender, a repressed eroticism expressing itself in symbolic form and being punished for its indulgence. Laura's restoration through Lizzie's actions defeats the Christian suggestions raised without ever quite denying them, while the insistent sensuality of the work is in powerfully ambivalent contrast to the poem's nursery ending.

Christina Rossetti's purely religious poems spring from a profound and absolute devotion coupled to a powerful awareness of personal sin. 'A Better Resurrection' re-creates with great force the idea of dying into Christ to be reborn, a commitment made again at the close of 'In the bleak mid-winter', a work whose taut simplicity of form and powerful feeling makes it one of the very greatest of English hymns.

19

It is in the work of Gerard Manley Hopkins (1844–89) that Victorian religious poetry finds its most magnificent expression. Hopkins was educated in an Oxford alive with the controversies raised by Newman and Ruskin, and he was profoundly influenced by both. Just as Ruskin, when drawing the Norwood ivy and the Fontainebleau ash, had come to perceive an underlying organic unity in nature, so Hopkins (himself a more than competent draughtsman) developed the keenest perceptions of those outer qualities which declare an object's inner and distinctive nature. His Journals, vivid with an etymologist's love of language, attempt to record these qualities of what Hopkins himself called 'inscape'. In his mature poetry, the traditions of English prosody were recast in the effort to capture the divine particularities of the natural world.

Hopkins's sympathy for the individual uniqueness of things – their special energies or 'instress' – was given a philosophic basis after his discovery of the work of the medieval philosopher Duns Scotus, and Hopkins himself came to see individual loveliness or *haecitas* as an aspect of God. 'I do not think I have ever seen anything more beautiful than the bluebell I have just been looking at,' he wrote. 'I know the beauty of our Lord by it.'

Such an overwhelming sense of Christian devotion was stirred by the writings of Newman. The *Apologia* was published in the year Hopkins went up to Oxford, and in 1866, after intense self-examination and a painful rift with his family, he was received by Newman into the Roman Church. Then, after graduation, Hopkins began his decade of training for the Jesuit priesthood. Duty and submission to authority became the prelude to donning 'The Habit of Perfection'. As Hopkins wrote to his friend the minor religious poet R.W. Dixon (1833–1900): 'What I had written I burnt before I became a Jesuit and resolved to write no more, as not belonging to my profession, unless it were by the wish of my superiors; so for seven years I wrote nothing but two or three little presentation pieces which occasion called for.'

So complete a surrender to external discipline suggests another of the forms of extremism that were gaining ground in the later decades of the nineteenth century and which are evident in the history of the Roman Church itself. In 1864, for example, the papacy issued its *Syllabus of Errors* which codified the pronouncements of Pius IX against the forces of secularism, liberalism and freedom of conscience. The work concluded that the Pope could never reconcile himself to the progress of modern civilization. Six years later, the concept of papal infallibility was made dogma. This assertion of papal power was to cause widespread opposition, Germany in particular passing punitive laws against Roman Catholics. As Hopkins continued in his letter to Dixon: 'when in the middle of '75 the Deutschland was wrecked in the mouth of the Thames and five Franciscan nuns, exiled from Germany by the Falk laws, were drowned I was affected by the account and happening to say so to my rector he said that he wished someone would write a poem on the subject. On this hint I set to work.' Hopkins's long silence was broken by the revolutionary torrent of verse he called 'The Wreck of the *Deutschland*':

> Loathed for a love men knew in them,
> Banned by the land of their birth,
> Rhine refused them, Thames would ruin them;
> Surf, snow, river and earth
> Gnashed: but thou art above, thou Orion of light;
> Thy unchancelling poising palms were weighing the worth,
> Thou martyr-master: in thy sight
> Storm flakes were scroll-leaved flowers, lily showers – sweet heaven was
> astrew in them.

The agony of the nuns trapped in their thirty-hour torment of death is watched by God the hunter – luminous, all-powerful and ultimately benevolent – as He presides over a heroic martyrdom. God is present in all He has made. He is the inscape of even the 'endragoned' elements as He works salvation out of terror. What in human eyes are the death-dealing snow and waves becomes, in the eyes of eternity, the flowers of paradise. The faithful, driven to exile and death in the world, have an immortal home. In the end they may even become the means of intercession whereby the Roman faith will be returned to an England from which it has been exiled. 'Let him easter in us, be a dayspring to the dimness of us.'

To achieve so vivid a re-creation of God's presence amid the hurtling destructiveness of nature, Hopkins brought a radical and critical intellect to play on the conventions of prosody. Among the most obvious features of this are a concern with alliteration and assonance and a syntax that challenges accepted notions of rhythm. All these concerns are directed to the ear. Poetry, Hopkins wrote, is *'a figure of spoken sound'*, and his own work challenges us to discover the aural resources of English afresh.

The possibilities inherent in spoken language – its emphases, vigour and occasional colloquialism – are an important element in this. Rhythm is also fundamental to Hopkins's pursuit of 'the current language heightened'. Hopkins himself considered accent (or what he often called 'stress') to be a principal factor here. His concept of 'sprung rhythm' is thus dependent on the fall of the emphases in a line and disregards regularity in the use of unaccented syllables. In the end, the final arbiter is the sensitive ear. As Hopkins wrote in a note to 'The Wreck of the *Deutschland*': 'which syllables . . . are strong and which light is better told by the ear than by any instruction that could be in a short space given'.

This was a type of poetry very few of Hopkins's contemporaries were prepared to accept. The Jesuit journal *The Month* reluctantly refused the '*Deutschland*', just as they were also to turn down Hopkins's elegiac 'The Loss of the Euridice'. His rector at Stonyhurst considered 'May Magnificat' to be below the college's standards, and Hopkins's only artistic support now came from his correspondence with Dixon and the future Poet Laureate Robert Bridges (1844–1930). The latter, whose own best works have a compassionate, melancholy charm, carefully garnered his friend's poems in an album which he first published in 1918. The most innovative poet of the century was thus obliged to work almost in secret and alone. His pursuit of extreme aesthetic concentration however, his intellectual and emotional complexity, his daring intensity and the rich texture of verbal association by which Hopkins challenged and extended conventional forms were all to appeal to the founders of modern literature. If Hopkins is the most radical of the Victorians, he is, by adoption and influence, one of the first of the moderns.

Hopkins completed *The Wreck of the Deutschland* while training at St Beuno's, and the beauty of the surrounding Welsh countryside inspired a number of sonnets in which he developed his techniques while discussing the place of the Christian amid the glory of the natural world. 'Spring' and 'Pied Beauty' re-create the inscape of an innocent beauty which, in its highly particularized loveliness of flowers, thrushes' eggs and 'rose-motes in all stipple upon trout that swim', is an offering of praise to their Maker. 'In the Valley of the Elwy' however suggests that even amid so much beauty man remains a fallen being, while 'God's Grandeur' tells how, in his original sin, man has polluted the innocent landscape around him:

The world is charged with the grandeur of God.
　It will flame out, like shining shook from foil;
　It gathers to a greatness, like the ooze of oil
Crushed. Why do men then now not reck his rod?
Generations have trod, have trod, have trod;
　And all is seared with trade; bleared, smeared with toil
　And wears man's smudge and shares man's smell: the soil
Is bare now, nor can foot feel, being shod.

The conclusion of the work is not pessimistic however. What was then believed to be nature's infinite power of self-renewal is finally equated with the might of the Holy Ghost as it broods in life-restoring love over the universe.

But if the beauty of the world is a manifestation of God, its very allure may be a snare that prevents mankind from acknowledging the true Creator. In 'The Starlight Night', for example, the 'piece-bright paling' of the stars can act as a barrier between man's soul and its Redeemer. 'Hurraring in the Harvest' presents another rapturous but potentially deceptive evocation of the natural world. Here, the instress of a rich, autumnal landscape is re-created in lines of breathtaking and beautiful audacity:

Summer ends now; now, barbarous in beauty, the stooks rise
　Around; up above, what wind-walks! what lovely behaviour
　Of silk-sack clouds! has wilder, wilful-wavier
Meal-drift moulded ever and melted across skies?

In response, the ecstatic soul beats its wings and attempts to fly to its Maker. But the sonnet is not a pantheistic hymn. Man may only truly commune with God through the sacraments, and the soul's rapture is finally a frustrated flight reminding man of both the beauty of the world and his own fallen place within it.

An image of frustrated flight is again central to what is perhaps the finest of these sonnets. 'The Windhover' is a work in which Hopkins's technical resources are seen at their most experimental. The soaring rhythm and alliteration of the opening lines exactly convey the ecstasy of the princely falcon's riding 'the rolling level underneath him steady air'. We feel how a heart in spiritual retreat could indeed be stirred by 'the achieve of, the mastery of the thing!' The natural world is momentarily exultant. However (and although precise explication of this work is tendentious) the sudden reversal of the bird's flight suggests both the human spirit brought down from proud aspiration and Christ's descent to suffering in the mortal world. Once again, nature encourages man to joy in God's universe while revealing to him that salvation can only be found through the recognition of sin and by toiling in a fallen world.

Hopkins's concern with how man is destroying that world is expressed in both 'Duns Scotus' Oxford' and 'Binsey Poplars'. In the last poem, the felling of the trees is a revelation of man's appalling capacity to wreck the sources of his happiness. 'After-comers cannot guess the beauty been.' Again, time's ruin of human loveliness means that men and women must give their deepest faith to the beauty of God's grace rather than to worldly things, an idea suggested by 'To What Serves Mortal Beauty' and the marvellous virtuosity of 'The Leaden Echo and the Golden Echo'. The most moving of these meditations on mutability however is 'Spring and Fall' with its poignant examination of mortality.

Such poems suggest an elated response to human beauty, and the magnificence of the muscular body in action is re-created in the densely knotted syntax of 'Harry Ploughman', a work which is perhaps the best introduction to that handful of poems concerned with Hopkins's ministry to the working classes. In 'The Bugler's First Communion', the physical beauty of young men is embodied in a uniformed soldier 'breathing bloom of a chastity in mansex fine'. The poet's evident excitement rekindles his priestly vocation, and the offering of the Eucharist becomes both a union in God and a portent of paradise. In 'Felix Randal', by contrast, the decay of physical strength and the tenderness that grows between a dying Christian and his confessor become the basis of a meditation on man's inevitable passage from physical splendour to decay, from glory in this world to salvation in the next.

Under such certainties there lay what emerges in 'Tom's Garland' as Hopkins's rigidly hierarchical and anti-liberal political views – the extremism characteristic of much thought in this period. In a letter explicating what remains an exceptionally difficult poem, Hopkins wrote that working-class life 'if it wants one advantage, glory or public fame, makes up for it by another, ease of mind, absence of care'. This is naïve to the point of being callous, and when Hopkins turns to the evils of unemployment he can only see its victims as 'outcasts' from his feudal commonwealth.

At the close of his brief life, Hopkins was harrowed by intense personal struggles, with 'fits of sadness' which, he told Bridges, 'resemble madness'. He was grappling with despair, and to lose was to sin against the Holy Ghost. It was from this struggle however that Hopkins wrested some of the greatest sonnets in the language:

> O the mind, mind has mountains; cliffs of fall
> Frightful, sheer, no-man-fathomed. Hold them cheap
> May who ne'er hung there. Nor does long our small
> Durance deal with that steep or deep. Here! creep,
> Wretch, under what comfort serves in a whirlwind: all
> Life death does end and each day dies with sleep.

Night, purgatory, exhaustion and the alienated stranger longing for patience in torment provide images of awe-inspiring intensity. One reads these poems with chastened gratitude for their author's heroism. 'No worst, there is none.' The power of these sonnets shows how Hopkins had earned the right to say this, and his exploration of the dark night of the soul gives poignant authenticity to his dying words: 'I am so happy.'

20

While some writers in the troubled later years of the nineteenth century clung to communism or Roman Catholicism, others pursued sensation in decadence and aesthetics. Algernon Charles Swinburne (1837–1909) was early associated with Morris and the Pre-Raphaelites, but a range of other influences – among them Shelley, Baudelaire and de Sade – led him to write poems in which a remarkable metrical dexterity (when not carried away by its own inventiveness) was embroidered with images of hedonism and morbid satiety. These traits can be seen in *Atalanta in Calydon* (1865), a work modelled on Greek tragedy. Here, 'the holy spirit of man' is pitted against the 'supreme evil God', while the famous first chorus attempts a Dionysiac fury at once hypnotic but largely meaningless:

When the hounds of spring are on winter's traces,
    The mother of months in meadow or plain
Fills the shadows and windy places
    With lisp of leaves and ripple of rain;
And the brown bright nightingale amorous
    Is half assuaged for Itylus,
For the Thracian ships and the foreign faces,
    The tongueless vigil and all the pain.

From here it was a short step to *Poems and Ballads* (1866) where the 'Hymn to Proserpine' suggests the lassitude of a defeated paganism, an elegant, world-weary blasphemy which, in the sado-masochistic 'Dolores', beatifies the mistress as 'Our Lady of Pain'. Vampires, lesbians and hermaphrodites make up much of the rest of the dramatis personae.

As a critic, Swinburne wrote perceptively on Baudelaire and Blake, two poets with whom his complex personality could identify. While the voluminous writings of his later years contain much that is merely turgid, some still show the power of 'The Triumph of Time' and the haunting 'Itylus' from his 1866 volume. Among such works is 'A Forsaken Garden', a poem in which Swinburne's metrical virtuosity and deep response to the sea are combined with a convincing atheistic vision of a world doomed to destruction, a place where meaning can only be found in the brief sensation of love.

The pursuit of an albeit highly refined sensation tempered by the awareness of mortality is again a major focus in the work of Walter Pater (1839–94). Pater's writings mark a significant and influential development away from the man of letters as the spokesman of an agreed, explicit morality, developing instead a concept of the artist as a man who can foster 'a quickened, multiplying consciousness'. Inspiration and aesthetic empathy replace moral earnestness in a world where all other values appear tendentious.

Realizing the importance of William Morris to this process, Pater celebrated *The Earthly Paradise* for offering a poetry of evanescent mood in accord with its age. Such poetry is at once a balm and a revelation: 'for art comes to you proffering frankly to give nothing but the highest quality to your moments as they pass, and simply for the moment's sake'. To be able to appreciate such experiences, 'to burn always with this hard, gemlike flame, to maintain this ecstasy is success in life'. When Pater printed a revised version of this statement in the Conclusion to the first edition of *Studies in the History of the Renaissance* (1873), he gave the generation of the 1890s the central doctrine of the Aesthetic Movement. The English version of 'art for art's sake' had been born.

The essays that make up Pater's volume suggest both the importance of the past as a source of inspiration and the belief that the great value of the Renaissance itself lay in its 'care for physical beauty, the worship of the body, the breaking down of those limits which the religious systems of the Middle Ages imposed on the heart and the imagination'. This last was a profoundly influential if misleading idea. For Pater however it led both to the pure aestheticism of his essay on Giorgione, with its elegant variations on the theme that '*All art constantly aspires towards the condition of music*', and to his essay on Leonardo (or the Leonardoesque) with its famous description of the *Mona Lisa*. This exquisitely mannered passage (reprinted as *vers libre* by the admiring Yeats in his 1936 edition of the *Oxford Book of Modern Verse*) is important as Pater's symbol of the contemporary mind living amid the myriad, evanescent details of history:

She is older than the rocks among which she sits; like the vampire, she has been dead many times, and learned the secrets of the grave; and has been a diver in deep seas, and keeps their fallen day about her; and trafficked for strange webs with Eastern merchants: and, as Leda, was the mother of Helen of Troy, and, as Saint Anne, the mother of Mary; and all this has been to her but as the sound of lyres and flutes, and lives only in the delicacy with which it has moulded the changing lineaments, and tinged the eyelids and the hands. The fancy of a perpetual life, sweeping together ten thousand experiences, is an old one; and modern philosophy has conceived the idea of humanity as wrought upon by, and summing up in itself, all modes of thought and life. Certainly Lady Lisa might stand as the embodiment of the old fancy, the symbol of the modern idea.

Time and ideas fall as lightly on consciousness as music or sunlight, and in his Conclusion, Pater rejects any 'theory or idea or system which requires of us the sacrifice of any part of this experience'. Such sceptical and hedonistic relativism (especially, perhaps, the mild tinge of the homoerotic with which Pater originally endowed it) was considered subversive. The second edition of *Studies in the History of the Renaissance* suppressed the passage, while to the modified version offered in the third edition Pater added: 'I have dealt more fully in *Marius the Epicurean* with the thoughts suggested by it.'

Marius the Epicurean (1885), a slow and euphuistic novel on the life of a young second-century Roman, reveals Pater advancing a little beyond the refined hedonism of his earlier work. The reality of evil is now recognized and accepted, even if an answer to it is still seen in purely aesthetic terms. Though Marius himself is influenced by traditional beliefs, by a range of classical philosophies and finally by a delightful community of early Christians, his deepest loyalty remains to his stern Epicureanism. At the close of the work he has a vision of Christianity as 'a perfect beauty, in a perfect world'. He finds the courage to die in the place of his friend and is buried after receiving the last rites. There is no suggestion he has been truly converted however. 'His Sensations and Ideas', in the words of the subtitle, remain the ultimate source of his morality.

Marius the Epicurean and *Studies in the History of the Renaissance* were widely influential. James Joyce and W.B. Yeats were indebted to both. To the critic Arthur Symons (1865–1945), the latter work in particular sometimes seemed 'the most beautiful book of prose in our literature', while Oscar Wilde (1854–1900) called it 'that book which has had such a strange influence over my life'.

And it was into his life that Wilde poured his genius. His talent, he declared, he reserved for his books. By making himself the personification of artifice and by his ultimately tragic belief that the world can be controlled by wit, Wilde became a central symbol of the English *fin de siècle*:

'*Fin de siècle*,' murmured Lord Henry.

'*Fin du globe*,' answered his hostess.

'I wish it were *fin du globe*,' said Dorian with a sigh. 'Life is a great disappointment.'

The Picture of Dorian Gray (1891), Wilde's only novel, builds on popular psychological melodrama and the pursuit of hedonism cultivated by the hero of J.K. Huysman's quintessential decadent text *A Rebours* (1884). Though its puritanical sense of retribution is its own, both Wilde's artifice and his borrowings suggest the talent revealed in

'The Decay of Lying'. Published along with 'The Critic as Artist' in *Intentions* (1891), the aphoristic brilliance of these works shows a dependence on such figures as Pater, Morris and Arnold. Short stories like 'The Happy Prince' and 'The House of Pomegranates' (1888) suggest Wilde's awareness of the perils underlying the artistic life, while his drama *Salomé* (1893) – a work which was to inspire both Aubrey Beardsley, illustrator of the *Yellow Book* (1894) and Richard Strauss – is a central work of decadence to which the Lord Chamberlain refused a licence.

The series of Wilde's comedies, *A Woman of No Importance* (1893) and *An Ideal Husband* (1895), culminates in one of the classics of the English stage, *The Importance of Being Earnest* (1895). Even the title of the work is a marvellous riposte to the ethos personified by Carlyle, and shows that for Wilde the time for levity and insincerity had returned. Wit here creates a world self-sufficiently supercilious in which artifice constructs its own reality. 'The telling of beautiful untrue things, is the proper aim of Art.'

But this was a brilliance fluttering over the abyss. Challenged to bring an action for libel against the father of his lover Lord Alfred Douglas, Wilde embarked on the most foolhardy of aesthetic enterprises – the attempt to prove that wit is more powerful than the law. Two years of imprisonment produced the mannered *De Profundis* (1897) and *The Ballad of Reading Gaol* (1898), a work in which bleakness and refined, tender ferocity create a powerful picture of human isolation. As Arthur Symons wrote: 'In this poem, where a style formed on other lines seems startled at finding itself used for such purposes, we see a great spectacular intellect, to which, at last, pity and terror have come in their own person, and no longer as puppets in a play.' Three years later, dying in self-imposed French exile, Wilde was received into the Roman Church.

A number of other figures, some of them associated with the Rhymers' Club, also pursued aesthetic and decadent experience, often exploring these though a poetry of fastidious lyric artifice. Such verse was in part influenced by the Elizabethans, while in 'The Decadent Movement in Literature' (1893) Arthur Symons related the group's characteristic over-refinement and 'spiritual and moral perversity' to the decadence of late classical literature. This last is an influence seen in the work of Ernest Dowson (1867–1900):

I cried for madder music and for stronger wine,
But when the feast is finished and the lamps expire,
Then falls thy shadow, Cynara! the night is thine;
And I am desolate and sick of an old passion,
   Yea hungry for the lips of my desire:
I have been faithful to thee, Cynara! in my fashion.

It was with *The Symbolist Movement in Modern Literature* (1899) that Symons developed his analysis of another influence on these poets – the new poetry evolved in France by Rimbaud, Verlaine, Laforgue and Mallarmé. The very considerable work of these men sought to expose subjective states of mind through what Rimbaud himself called a 'disordering of all the senses'. This it did partly by means of an imagery that was believed to give immediate and intuitive access to the deeper levels of the mind. Both W.B. Yeats (the dedicatee of Symons's volume) and T.S. Eliot were to be greatly influenced by Symons's analysis which thus points forward to major poetic developments in the twentieth century.

The city, glimpsed either through a detached impressionism or with the grim futility of James Thomson's 'City of Dreadful Night' (1874) and John Davidson's 'Thirty Bob a Week' (one of the first poems to discuss underground trains and the suburban life these made possible), was also a common theme in the work of these poets. So too was their frequent recourse to religious experience. For some, like the alcoholic Lionel Johnson (1867–1902), conversion to the Roman Church was largely a matter of stirring up controversy and seeking a *nouveau frisson*. Perhaps the best-remembered Roman Catholic poet of what Yeats called the 'tragic generation' however was Francis Thompson (1859–1907) whose often over-inflated *Hound of Heaven* (1893) embodies a sense of religious experience that is less purely aesthetic than that of many of his contemporaries.

An altogether more considerable figure ironically deprecated his place among these men of the *fin de siècle*. A.E. Housman (1859–1936) wrote to Symons that 'to include me in an anthology of the Nineties would be just as technically correct, and just as essentially inappropriate, as to include Lot in a book on Sodomites'. Housman nonetheless shares with the figures of this decade their concern with lyric artistry, while his own work draws on Heine and the classics as well as the songs of Shakespeare, the Border Ballads and Burns. In his lecture *The Name and Nature of Poetry* (1932), Housman placed the emotional appeal of poetry above intellectual analysis, while mood, tone and temperament are the chief vehicles of his own work from *A Shropshire Lad* (1896) through to *Last Poems* (1922) and the posthumous *More Poems* (1936).

Such moods swing between a poignant love of the English countryside and an awareness of the pathos of a short life of embittered frustration spent in a world where inexorable moral laws no longer have their foundations in conventional belief. The 'brute and blackguard' who made the world has condemned all to pain. Such sufferings are from eternity 'and will not cease'. They afflict equally the ancient Roman centurion and the modern 'lad' as he purses his lips at the failure of love or is visited by moments of inspiration. These last, at once luminous and anguishing, give rise to such lyrics as 'Into my heart an air that kills', works that are an important part of a native English tradition of pastoral that survived into the twentieth century.

21

In the work of Thomas Hardy (1840–1928), such anxieties as Housman expresses are greatly developed to become one origin for what Hardy himself called 'the ache of modernism'. Hardy is among the leading novelists of the late Victorian era and one of the greatest poets of the early twentieth century. He wrote poetry throughout his career, but his first published work was in prose.

After the rejection of *The Poor Man and the Lady* in 1868, George Meredith suggested Hardy write a work in the sensationalist mode of Wilkie Collins. The result was *Desperate Remedies* (1871), a densely plotted novel of coincidence and intrigue, much concerned with class conflict, that some were to censure on moral grounds. Others had praised the rural scenes in Hardy's earliest work however, and on this hint he wrote *Under the Greenwood Tree* (1872). Here his amused but delicate sympathy with country people and his intimate knowledge of their ways of life create a gentle comedy of love and pastoral incident as Hardy shows the activities of the Mellstock choir and how Fancy Day eventually chooses the humble Dick Dewy as her husband.

In *A Pair of Blue Eyes* (1873), Hardy returned to the ironically constructed novel of youthful love and class difference. The plot, in which the young architect Stephen Fitzmaurice Smith, commissioned to restore a church tower, falls in love with the vicar's daughter, owes something to the circumstances of Hardy's own first marriage to Emma Gifford. In the novel however, the hero's nerve fails him as the couple plan to elope. Elfride is pursued by the cold and literary Knight, Stephen's erstwhile patron, but when Knight learns of her earlier affair with Stephen he rejects her. At the conclusion of the work, both men travel down to Cornwall on the same train only to discover that Elfride's corpse has accompanied them in the baggage van.

Such 'Satires of Circumstance' point to fundamental concerns in Hardy's fiction. The situation is grotesque, while it also suggests a preoccupation with how passion and aspiration are constantly thwarted by the indifferent Immanent Will. As a young man, Hardy had lost his faith amid the doubts unleashed by Darwin, and the scene in *A Pair of Blue Eyes* where Knight clings desperately to the side of a cliff while a fossilized trilobite stares blindly across at him gives early expression to Hardy's view of man living in an uncaring universe that stretches back over aeons of time and in which man himself is no specially favoured creation.

That Hardy often chose to suggest such ideas through the grotesque is a further important aspect of his technique. In his *Life* (1928–30) – a work published under his second wife's name but now believed to be largely autobiographical – Hardy wrote: 'Art is a changing of the actual proportions and order of things, so as to bring out more forcibly than might otherwise be done that feature in them which appeals most strongly to the idiosyncrasy of the artist.' This ability to shape action to personal philosophic purpose is frequently juxtaposed in the novels to Hardy's deeply poetic gifts of realistic observation. Such a contrast helps account for the power of works like *Far from the Madding Crowd* (1874).

It is in this novel that Wessex first becomes Hardy's great imaginative domain. His account of the loves of Bathsheba Everdene – her relationships with the dashing Sergeant Troy, with the luckless Bold-wood and finally with Gabriel Oak – is distinctly sensational in its plotting, and Hardy achieves such fine effects in this mode as the moment when lamplight suddenly reveals to Bathsheba the presence of Troy himself. The grotesque and the pathetic merge in the scene where water from a gargoyle washes away the flowers the repentant Troy has placed on Fanny Robin's grave. It is the integration of such action with the seasons however that gives the novel its satisfying resonance. The ageless cycles of the life of the land and the relation of human passion to the turning year are excellently achieved. Hardy's Wessex – his evocation of the life and landscapes of the West Country and of Dorset in particular – place his characters against a universal setting. Generations appear to have brought man into some unity with such a world, and no passage in the novel more clearly shows Hardy's deep response to this than the twenty-second chapter, describing the place occupied in the lives of these people by the great barn.

In *Far from the Madding Crowd*, the natural world is fruitful, restorative and ultimately benevolent. In *The Return of the Native* (1878), Hardy's remarkable ability to fuse the local with the cosmic shows aspects of nature that are altogether more narrowing and malign. Egdon Heath is timeless and indifferent nature itself, enduring rather than picturesque, chastening rather than kind. It crushes or subdues to its own wisdom those who live there, and for Hardy, the heath is nature itself as modern man must see her. Those like Clym Yeobright who are disillusioned by 'the defects of the natural laws' come to love the heath precisely for its reflection of their own disenchantment. In this they are late Victorians wracked in a world where 'old-fashioned revelling in the general situation grows less and less possible'. They are thus representative modern men:

In Clym Yeobright's face could be dimly seen the typical countenance of the future. Should there be a classic period to art hereafter, its Pheidias may produce such faces. The view of life as a thing to be put up with, replacing that zest for existence which was so intense in early civilizations, must ultimately enter so thoroughly into the constitution of the advanced races that its facial expression will become accepted as a new artistic departure. People already feel that a man who lives without disturbing a curve of feature anywhere upon himself, is too far removed from modern perceptiveness to be a modern type.

Science and agnosticism reveal an inimical world where man must either endure or, as with Michael Henchard in *The Mayor of Casterbridge* (1886), become the victim of his own character as its energies weave his fate.

Michael Henchard, Hardy's 'Man of Character', is his creator's most heroic figure. Henchard is at once both agent and victim in a plot where remorseless tragic coincidence provides far more than sensationalism. *The Mayor of Casterbridge* offers one of Hardy's most elaborate examples of his changing the natural order and proportion of events to show how, in an indifferent universe, man is trapped by his character, his past and the far-from-benevolent march of progress. This last eventually replaces Henchard with the thin and bloodless Farfrae, the accountant and man of the machine. But if the plot has an almost Sophoclean inevitability, *The Mayor of Casterbridge* achieves at its climax especially something of the grandeur and pathos of *King Lear*. Henchard's death inspires both pity and awe. Farfrae and Elizabeth-Jane arrive too late, and Abel Whittle's account of the hero's death and the reading of his will are moments unbearably poised between rustic simplicity and an annihilating, universal despair.

The Woodlanders (1887) returns to Hardy's themes of frustrated love and class division in a rustic setting, offering in the figures of Grace Melbury, Giles Winterborne and Marty South a tragedy of frustrated affection. We feel that we know what the proper and natural outcome of events should be, but Hardy's intensely realized descriptions of the woods themselves – descriptions darkened by a more-than-Darwinian pessimism – suggest the inherently cruel and frustrating operations of the natural world. The woods are a place of conflict and decay, of rotting and twisted forms. 'Here, as everywhere, the Unfulfilled Intention, which makes life what it is, was as obvious as it could be among the depraved crowds of a city slum. The leaf was deformed, the curve was crippled, the taper was interrupted; the lichen ate the vigour of the stalk, and the ivy slowly strangled to death the promising sapling.' Nature is a continuous thwarting, and yet, in such a world, pathos approaching the sublime is achieved in scenes such as that where Marty South mourns at Winterborne's grave.

For the most part, Hardy's lesser novels have, like his short stories, a displeasing air of contrivance and strained effect. *The Hand of Ethelberta* (1876) is an experiment in the alien world of polite comedy, while *A Laodicean* (1881) is frankly dull. *Two on a Tower* (1882) aims to set 'infinitesimal lives against the stupendous background of the stellar universe' but fails to unite local anguish to cosmic awareness in the manner of Hardy's greater works. *The Trumpet-Major* (1880) is rather more successful in relating Hardy's familiar world to a re-creation of the Napoleonic period, but the grotesque situation in *The Well-Beloved* (serialized 1892) suggests the relish of irony for its own sake that is seen again in Hardy's four volumes of short stories.

Hardy's two last novels tower above these lesser works, *Tess of the D'Urbervilles* (1891) in particular being one of the supreme achievements of English fiction. The tragic passions of an obscure country girl perfectly integrate Hardy's abiding concern with love thwarted by an implacable universe and the ruthless dislocations wrought by class. The landscapes of Wessex, evoked with great poetic power, relate the particular to the universal with consummate mastery, while the narrative also allows Hardy to engage with contemporary issues of religion and morality.

The day of Tess's wedding to Angel Clare shows how perfectly these themes are fused with high drama. Tess and Angel have courted each other through a long summer of heady pastoral luxuriousness. Nature pulses through them and all the world. But the wedding itself takes place in the dismal greyness of New Year's Day and, on their first evening as man and wife, each confesses to an earlier affair as the fire glows with a 'Last Judgement luridness'. Tess, in particular, tells her husband of her seduction by the feckless Alec D'Urberville, a supposed aristocratic relative whose child she bore. Though nature does not condemn her for what has happened, memories of a vindictive Christian morality have troubled Tess with thoughts of the child's eternal damnation, and in a little ceremony of her own devising she christened the baby Sorrow before burying it in a scene of the utmost pathos.

It is the restorative power of nature that brought Angel and a revived Tess together. Though Angel has discarded most of the

Christian beliefs in which he has been reared (his progress to agnosti-cism was that of many intelligent young Victorians) he is horrified to discover that his wife is not, in his opinion, a 'pure' woman. His love freezes under the withering spectre of conventional morality and he departs for Brazil. With Angel gone, Tess endures the purgatory of winter farm work until her family is all but ruined by the death of her foolish father. In order to support them, Tess, flawed by her 'reckless acquiescence in chance', returns to the worldly and rootless D'Urberville. Her love however is still for Angel: 'She tried to pray to God, but it was her husband who really had her supplication. Her idolatry of this man was such as she herself almost feared it to be ill-omened.' That fear is justified.

Angel returns in chastened humanity, and Tess herself, hysterically grieving, murders D'Urberville and rushes to give herself to the one man she loves. The great closing scene at Stonehenge – Hardy's symbol of an ancient and malevolent natural world of human sacrifice – is one of his supreme achievements. As the policemen take Tess away to trial and execution, so we see how, in this brutal and implacable world, '"Justice" was done, and the President of the Immortals, in Aeschylean phrase, had ended his sport with Tess.'

Hardy's last novel, *Jude the Obscure* (1895), deals with what he called the 'deadly war waged between the flesh and spirit' and with the tragedy of unfulfilled aims. The work's remarkable discussions of the perils of sexuality and religious belief place it on the frontiers of the modern world, a world Hardy glimpses with profound pessim-ism. For example, after Jude's first son has murdered the other child-ren and then committed suicide (a scene so grotesque and poignant as to strain the limits of Hardy's art) the author has his hero reflect about the child's character:

The doctor says there are such boys springing up amongst us – boys of a sort unknown in the last generation – the outcome of new views of life. They seem to see all its terrors before they are old enough to have any staying power to resist them. He says it is the beginning of the coming universal wish not to live.

Such pessimism derives from a world where all aspiration is thwarted. Jude Fawley himself is caught between the sensuous and degrading Arabella, who smothers his yearning for knowledge, faith and the spirit, and Sue Bridehead, a woman of intellectual inclinations reduced to neurasthenia by contradictory impulses of freedom and guilt in matters of sexual and religious commitment.

Irony underlies the agony of both Jude and Sue. For all his efforts to educate himself, Jude never rises above being a stonemason. Apparently freed from his first wife Arabella, his relationship with Sue is constantly thwarted and the couple only achieve sexual union after Arabella reappears. Unable to face the constraints of marriage – 'a sordid contract, based on material convenience' – the newly divorced Sue and Jude are harried by the social pressures placed on their relationship. The death of the children drives Sue herself (Hardy's remarkable portrait of a woman caught in the birth pangs of the modern world) to an abject surrender to a vindictive Christian faith and a loveless remarriage to her first husband. Jude is tricked into remarrying Arabella. Only at their last meeting does Sue reveal the true depths of her passion, but by this time Jude himself is mortally ill.

The frankness with which Hardy discussed his themes – the emotional crippling inflicted by an illusory but socially powerful religious faith and, above all, the difficulties faced by sexual morality when conventional props have been removed – outraged many of his contemporaries. Hardy was to write no more novels and turned instead to the publication of his poetry. *The Dynasts* (1904–8) is Hardy's 'epic-drama of the war with Napoleon, in three parts, nineteen acts, and one hundred and thirty scenes'. This vast work shows the workings of history from a cosmic perspective. A chorus of Phantom Intelligences observe the operation of the Immanent Will, while what we may loosely call the stage directions sometimes offer the powerful sweep of a vast panorama in which Hardy's characters appear like labouring ants.

Hardy's purely philosophical lyrics are perhaps the least satisfying part of his large output, while a number of his anecdotal 'Satires of Circumstance' reveal the faults also seen in his short stories. Works influenced by ballad forms – 'The Tramp Woman's Tragedy' in particular – are more successful however. Hardy's often criticized diction and rhythm frequently show him using dialect or archaic forms, a practice in which he was influenced by the self-taught Dorset poet and polymath William Barnes (1801–86), author of

Poems of Rural Life in the Dorset Dialect (1844). Hardy's best work nonetheless shows his ability to handle complex verse forms with an appearance of freshness and ease. It is when these characteristics are under the control of his own chastened speaking voice that he achieves the absolute emotional integrity which helps make him one of the greatest poets of the twentieth century.

This is nowhere clearer than in those lyrics gathered in *Poems of 1912–13* where Hardy relives in bereavement and remembered joy his earliest days with his first wife. The ironies of love in the novels – the loss of desire for those we have and the kindling of passion for those we may no longer possess – are here a personal tragedy at once wholly understood and inescapable:

> Yes: I have re-entered your olden haunts at last;
> > Through the years, through the dead scenes I have tracked you;
> What have you now found to say of our past –
> > Scanned across the dark space wherein I have lacked you?
> Summer gave us sweets, but autumn wrought division?
> > Things were not lastly as firstly well
> > > With us twain, you tell?
> But all's closed now, despite Time's derision.

The strength and delicacy of subtle evocation, the undemonstrative ironies of deep emotion and – elsewhere in the poem – the exact observation of a natural world more enduring than man's are at once the essential Hardy and a vision of modern humanity itself. Though Yeats, Eliot and, later, Auden were to work their immense influence on twentieth-century literature, the importance of Hardy can be seen as continuously active. In 1966, Philip Larkin declared how he 'would not wish Hardy's *Collected Poems* a single page shorter', and regarded it as 'many times over the best body of poetic work this century so far has to show'.

22

Larkin's generous tribute nonetheless obliges us to remember that for all his contemporary influence Hardy's roots and his work as a novelist especially lie deep in the late Victorian period – the period that saw the phenomenal expansion of British imperialism. Several late-nineteenth-century writers were drawn to the imperialist ethos while also developing techniques of moral instruction and sensation fiction. This is clear in a number of works originally intended for younger readers. Such stories include *Tom Brown's Schooldays* (1857) by Thomas Hughes (1822–96). This is a portrait of life at Rugby and of the reformed public-school movement led by Thomas Arnold (1795–1842), the influential father of the poet. The novel itself is a down-to-earth celebration of the supple-thewed and clean-thinking Christian English boy and of 'the great army of Browns who are scattered over the whole empire on which the sun never sets'. The work may be compared to the dire warnings contained in *Eric, or Little by Little* (1858) by Frederick Farrar (1831–1903), a melodramatic account of a boy's decline into smoking, drinking, thieving and further discreetly suggested public-school vices.

Other writers for boys include Frederick Marryat (1792–1845) whose delightful if over-plotted narratives offer harmless and amusing adventure, usually of a nautical kind, as well as R.M. Ballantyne (1825–94), author of *The Coral Island* (1858), and G.A. Henty (1832–1902). Both these last developed the 'manly' and often vigorously imperialistic hero, while other novelists took aristocratic young men through a series of spectacular adventures and morally uplifting deaths. It is Charles Kingsley's *Hereward, the Last of the English* (or *Hereward the Wake*; 1866) which most clearly shows this 'muscular' school's concern with the hero as a representative of the crude but allegedly revitalizing forces of English nationalism. In Kingsley's novel, such primitive strength is duped and overcome, but he suggests that it must never be wholly abandoned if the Victorian Englishman is to preserve his racial purity.

The adventure and sensationalistic effects required of detective fiction were perfected by Sir Arthur Conan Doyle (1859–1930) in the figure of Sherlock Holmes who made his first appearance in *A Study in Scarlet* (1887). Though Conan Doyle himself lamented that Holmes distracted him from better things – Conan Doyle wrote profusely in the fields of historical fiction – his attempt to bring strict logic to the detective story ensured that Holmes remained his best-loved creation. Another writer to make his name and fortune out of escapist romance was Sir Henry Rider Haggard (1856–1925). *King Solomon's Mines* (1885), drawing on its author's African experiences, was one of the most popular adventure stories of its day, as was the yet more dramatic and psychologically suggestive *She* (1887).

The exotic settings and high sensationalism to be found in Haggard's work are all but equalled by some of the real-life adventures recounted in Victorian travel writing. Sir Richard Burton's *Personal Narrative of a Pilgrimage to El-Medinah and Mecca* (1855–6), for example, offers the adventures of this extraordinary linguist as, variously disguised as a Persian prince and an Afghan doctor, he made his way to a city prohibited to non-Muslims. The popularity of travel in such areas had been initiated by Alexander Kinglake's *Eothen* (1844), while the field of African exploration was to offer similar excitements.

In his *First Footsteps in East Africa* (1856), Burton describes how he and his rival John Hanning Speke (1827–64) – author of *Journal of the Discovery of the Source of the Nile* (1863) – escaped attack only after Speke himself had been wounded eleven times and Burton had been speared through both his cheeks. In such ways could the reader on the Clapham omnibus vicariously participate in the expansion of empire. To such imperialist motives for exploration however could be added the evangelical Christianity seen in *Missionary Travels and Researches in South Africa* (1857) by David Livingstone (1813–73), a work enlivened by the author's love of both the people and the landscape.

George Borrow (1803–81) posed as a missionary distributing Bibles in order to write *The Bible in Spain* (1843), a work which, like many other of his travel volumes, shows Borrow's profound interest in languages and his gift for describing vivid incident and picturesque personalities. Charles Doughty's *Travels in Arabia Deserta* (1888), written to show 'my dislike of the Victorian English', is one of the most remarkable of contemporary travel books, not only for its author's reckless bravery but for the mannered and often beautiful archaism of its style.

Wholly different are the travel books of Robert Louis Stevenson (1850–94). In *An Inland Voyage* (1878) and *Travels with a Donkey* (1879), Stevenson often took relatively small incidents on which to bring to bear his humour, introspection and determined agnostic views. There is certainly excitement in these books, but also more sophisticated pleasures mediated through a high degree of verbal mastery and the credo of the true traveller: 'For my part, I travel not to go anywhere, but to go. I travel for travel's sake.'

Stevenson was also to emerge as one of the great Victorian masters of adventure and sensation fiction. In contrast to the 'intense illusion of reality' Henry James had advocated in 'The Art of Fiction' (1884), Stevenson argued in 'A Humble Remonstrance' (1884) for a literature of action, suspense and primal feeling that transcends the mundane. Though he could swing somewhat ambiguously between the costume drama he labelled 'Tushery' and a contempt for the sort of public that relished this kind of writing, Stevenson's best work reveals a profound and often poetic grip on those characters and situations which stir the energies of the unconscious mind.

Treasure Island (1883), for example, wonderfully re-creates a boy's world of wish-fulfilment and, in the figure of Long John Silver – vital, attractive and amoral – offers a first suggestion of Stevenson's interest in the ambiguously grotesque. While *Kidnapped* (1886) and to some extent its sequel *Catriona* (1893) show Stevenson bringing to his Highland subjects something of the manner of Scott, the troubling allure of evil is powerfully evoked in *The Master of Ballantrae* (1889). *Weir of Hermiston* remains a suggestive fragment, but the full force of Stevenson's power is to be seen in *Dr Jekyll and Mr Hyde* (1886). The use of three narrators shows Stevenson's command of the techniques of sensation fiction, but the abiding force of the novel lies in its powerful investigation of the fact that the public and shadow selves of a man are both parts of a single personality.

Stevenson's vivid romances of action were greatly admired by the young Rudyard Kipling (1865–1936) who, newly arrived from India, was swept to immediate success with *Plain Tales from the Hills* (1888). Kipling was at once at odds with the 'long-haired things' he found in the drawing rooms of the Aesthetes, and nothing perhaps more surely suggests the range of extremes to be found in late Victorian literature than this confrontation. On the one hand is Marius the Epicurean, on the other Files-on-Parade.

Kipling nonetheless remains a most difficult writer to focus on. His reputation as the unofficial laureate of empire, 'the Jelly-Bellied Flag-Flapper' of his own *Stalky & Co.* (1899), has obscured the range and subtlety of his achievement, notably in the short story. There is no question that Kipling could be jingoistic, absolutist and philistine. His public-school and barrack-room bruisers have the hair-raising stand-ards revealed in 'His Private Honour', a story in which fist fights and anti-Semitism are all part of subduing raw recruits to what nonetheless remain high military ideals of personal honour and community. Such young men's submission to Kipling's concept of 'the Law' becomes increasingly important, and as readers of *The Jungle Books* (1894, 1895) and the *Just So Stories* (1902) were told: 'the head and the hoof of the Law and the haunch and the hump is – Obey!'

'At the End of the Passage' shows how Kipling was sympathetically aware of the boredom and repetitiousness of much Anglo-Indian life, while 'Without Benefit of Clergy' and 'Love-o'-Women' also suggest he knew its tragedies. The latter story is particularly well told, using contrasts and framing devices with great skill to achieve a fine effect of pathos as the death of a syphilitic gentleman ranker is recalled in strongly characterized demotic speech. Such sophistication is allied to high adventure in 'The Man Who Would Be King', perhaps the finest of Kipling's stories of this type.

The pain in Kipling's early autobiographical novel *The Light that Failed* (1890) is at once intense but somewhat naïvely handled. From about 1892 however Kipling's work develops a number of his recog-nizable themes. 'The Bridge Builders' from *The Day's Work* (1898) shows his fascination with machines and technology (a subject of otherwise near-universal loathing among Victorian writers) along with his sympathy for the white men who work it. Findlayson and Hitchcock are the dutiful, unglamorous servants of empire Kipling so admired. Nonetheless, when Findlayson is wounded and, drugged with opium, is stranded on an island in the Ganges, he has a vision of the Hindu gods which shows the power of Kipling's mythopoeic imagination. The story also suggests the subtle symbolism by which the bridge spans both the Indian and European worlds, while offering a vision of daily toil seen in the eye of eternity.

Many of these themes are brought together in Kipling's finest work for children, *Kim* (1901). Free from the ritualistic public-school beastliness of *Stalky & Co.*, *Kim* is its author's marvellously rendered vision of a unity between Indian and European culture, the imperial ideal and a boy's world of adventure and passage to maturity.

But *Kim* is a fantasy, and Kipling believed his imperial dream was threatened from many quarters: from 'flannelled fools' obsessed with sport as much as by the cultivated minority of progressive intellectuals demanding Irish Home Rule and votes for women. What was for Kipling the profoundly pessimistic belief that British power would pass away like the Roman empire is embodied in *Puck of Pook's Hill* (1906). Kipling had already felt the severe wound dealt to imperial honour by Britain's defeat in the Boer War, while, at the very apogee of empire – Queen Victoria's Diamond Jubilee of 1897 – he warned his enormous public of the dangers of hubris:

> If, drunk with sight of power, we loose
> Wild tongues that have not Thee in awe,
> Such boastings as the Gentiles use,
> Or lesser breeds without the Law –
> Lord God of Hosts, be with us yet,
> Lest we forget – lest we forget!

Kipling's poetry, if it only rarely achieves the trembling and sugges-tive power of 'The Way through the Woods' or 'Cities and Thrones and Powers', draws very effectively on the hymn, the ballad and the music-hall song to create works in which the language really used by ordinary people combines with a quite exceptional gift for phrase-making. Kipling's eulogies of 'The Blood' and 'The Pride of Race' are self-evidently repellent, but 'For All We Have and Are' gives voice to a grave and noble patriotism, while 'The Absent-Minded Beggar' was remarkably effective in raising funds for the dependants of those fighting the Boers. Kipling's poetry could indeed touch the nerve of empire with exceptional finesse (this is why he was so powerful as its critic) and it is often his poems about the imperial army that show him at his best. Verses like 'Gentlemen-Rankers' or 'Danny Deever' powerfully combine technical resource with an understanding of the emotions of ordinary men.

And it was in these last that Kipling placed his deepest trust. Looking about him in 1897, he firmly believed that 'we're about the only power with a glimmer of civilization in us'. He had been watching the review of the Channel Fleet, as had the future Kaiser. Kipling's knowledge of the ordinary man however led him to comment: 'the big smash is coming one of these days, sure enough, but I think we shall pull through not without credit. It will be the common people – the 3rd class carriages – that'll save us.'

In this perceptive comment, the late-nineteenth-century concern with class, nation and race – those often crudely comforting tokens of identity and purpose – leads less to jingoism than to an awareness of the dangers lurking in the heart of the international situation. Kipling is the single most important writer to engage on the side of the hugely influential complex of idealism, nationalism and colonialism that characterizes the late-nineteenth-century English view of the country's role. That he had a remarkable insight into the forces that threatened this is a partial measure of his greatness, and it points to the subtle and often tragic short stories he wrote in response to the First World War – but these properly belong to twentieth-century literature.

Among the lesser but highly versatile conservative writers active before the First World War, two in particular deserve mention: G.K. Chesterton (1874–1936) and Hilaire Belloc (1870–1953). Christened by Shaw 'the Chesterbelloc', both were Roman Catholic apologists concerned to promote a vision of a medieval social order inimical to both socialism and capitalism. Though Chesterton's *The Victorian Age in Literature* (1913) reveals him as an interesting critic of Dickens, Chesterton regarded himself principally as a journalist. His entertaining style of paradox owes something to the writers of the *fin de siècle* and contrasts effectively with his moral seriousness. *The Man Who Was Thursday* (1909) shows him pitting the dream world against reality, while the Father Brown stories show Chesterton's ingenuity as well as bringing his religious awareness to the detective genre. Belloc however remains the more combative of the two. An excellent writer of light verse tinged with the macabre, he also argued vehemently for a Latin and Roman Catholic culture to place against what, in *The Servile State* (1912), he saw as the tendencies of modern collectivism.

Some writers such as Max Beerbohm (1872–1956) in *Zuleika Dobson* (1911) maintained the satiric edge of the Aesthetic Movement or, like H.H. Munro (1870–1916) – the short-story writer 'Saki' - used epigram to heighten a sadistic inventiveness. Others meanwhile, some of whom Virginia Woolf was tartly to christen 'the thick dull middle class of letters', continued to pursue realism in the novel. Among such figures are Arnold Bennett (1867–1931), John Galsworthy (1867–1933) and the writer who was to carry both the style and financial success of these men into the twentieth century, W. Somerset Maugham (1874–1965).

Bennett's most lasting novels portray the commercially minded success and the resigned and pessimistic stoicism he considered characteristic of his native Potteries. *Anna of the Five Towns* (1902) paints the area with particular vividness and density of physical detail, but Bennett's human understanding is perhaps best shown in *The Old Wives' Tale* (1908). Here he portrays passing time, stifled spontaneity, the narrowed and miserly spirit preserving itself in a hard and practical world yet eventually managing some final affirmation.

The Man of Property (1906), the first novel in John Galsworthy's perennially popular series *The Forsyte Saga*, is a powerful attack on Victorian and Edwardian materialism – the narrowness that allows Soames Forsyte to see both his house and his enigmatic wife Irene as property. Galsworthy had an intimate knowledge of the people he professed to despise but, as D.H. Lawrence wrote in a coruscating essay, he 'had not quite enough of the superb courage of his satire. He faltered and gave in to the Forsytes.'

The most powerful satirical response to the deadening effects of Victorian smugness is to be found in the work of Samuel Butler (1835–1902). *Erewhon* (1872) is a picaresque Utopian satire in which the inhabitants of the ideal land do not themselves escape censure. A complex topsy-turveydom creates continuous moral ambiguity. Healthy, handsome, caring for their environment and deriding the machine in superstitious fear that it will take over their lives, the Erewhonians hospitalize criminals, punish the sick and are not above a stultifying reverence for shibboleths. If 'they smell a rat about the precincts of a cherished institution, they will always stop their noses to it if they can'. Hence their worship of Ygrun or Mrs Grundy, a figure Butler opposes to his own ideal of the gentleman as the one 'potent humanizing influence' who can set the mind free.

Butler was deeply influenced by the sceptical debates of the 1870s, and in his non-fiction works questioned Christian orthodoxies, Darwinian evolution and Homeric scholarship. It is with his posthumously published *The Way of All Flesh* (1903) however that Butler presented his most violent attack on Victorian values. The protest of a man injured by the constraints of his inheritance, the work also attempts to find a way beyond these. Scenes such as that where the clergyman Theodore Pontifex beats his stammering son till he screams and then summons the family servants for evening prayers allow us to see why writers of the succeeding generation such as George Bernard Shaw could hail Butler as the greatest writer of his time and see his work as full of 'fresh, free, and future piercing suggestions'.

If Butler's work helped liberate many of the younger generation from the shackles of Victorian prejudice, H.G. Wells (1866–1946) preached to a vast popular audience on the potential of science and the baleful results of a fossilized English class system. In his first 'scientific romance', *The Time Machine* (1895), these concerns are combined in a carefully crafted novel in which evolution has led to an illiterate proletariat menacing the descendants of the nineteenth-century middle classes. While the first group suggests the ignorant urban crowds of late Victorian England, the second portrays its feckless intelligentsia. Science fiction thus offers a baleful picture of evolution while satirizing the contemporary world.

The Invisible Man (1897) again shows how Wells's finely developed scientific imagination blended easily with the fantastic, while both *Kipps* (1905) and *The History of Mr Polly* (1910) suggest how Wells could create comic characters with a depth of sympathy and pathos that approaches Dickens. *Tono-Bungay* (1909) reveals that he could also approach Dickens's social range and insight into financial and personal corruption. Nonetheless, Wells's pessimism, his belief that human history is 'a race between education and catastrophe', underlies not only his warning on the perils of dehumanized science in *The Island of Dr Moreau* (1896) but his attack on what he called 'the false securities and fatuous self-satisfaction' of his times in *The War of the Worlds* (1898). Here, the invasion of the Martians provides a terrible warning of the dangers of advanced technology and the perils that underlay man's (and particularly imperial Victorian man's) easy assumption of superiority. Wells thus portrays the crises that seethed below the mass industrialized society of late Victorian England with considerable power, and his work can be seen as a terrible prophecy addressed to a people moving yearly towards the unprecedented horrors of the First World War.

For Wells, the novel was little more than a medium for his message. Such an approach was vigorously attacked by Henry James (1843–1916) whose absolute devotion to the 'sacred office' of the novelist was an attempt to broaden the reader's experience through a fiction of scrupulous moral and psychological awareness. This was achieved in works that are triumphs of self-conscious technique.

So demanding a purpose required a wholesale revision of the practice of the past, a critical engagement with the achievements of Dickens and his generation and their alleged belief 'that a novel is a novel, as a pudding is a pudding, and that our only business with it could be to swallow it'. It was such an approach, James believed, that had led to the 'loose, baggy monsters' of the middle years of the century. He criticized *Our Mutual Friend* for these faults and decried Trollope for admitting in *The Eustace Diamonds* 'that the events he narrates have not really happened, and that he can give his narrative any turn the reader may like best'. To kill off Mrs Proudie because of the whispers of the clubmen, for example, was an artistic crime only possible when the novel had 'no air of having a theory, a conviction, a consciousness of itself behind it'.

The truly artistic and self-conscious novel – and James's works are nothing if not this – must be various, full and held together not by the clear controlling voice of the narrator but by an organic unity rising naturally from its parts. In 'The Art of Fiction', such beliefs led James to take on the mantle of Coleridge. 'A novel is a living thing, all one and continuous, like any other organism, and in proportion as it lives will it be found, that in each of the parts there is something of each of the other parts.'

It would be wrong however to see this concern with fiction as a highly crafted and self-sufficient entity purely as an aesthetic pursuit. James's art is profoundly concerned with morality. For him, the greatness of the novel lies partly in its power to awake such a consciousness in the reader through what, in his Preface to 'The Lesson of the Master', James was to call the 'high and helpful public and, as it were, civic use of the imagination'. The processes of fiction themselves thus become a matter of what Matthew Arnold termed 'high seriousness', and James's was an imagination partly nourished on Arnoldian principles. An American expatriate of the widest culture, well versed in the main European languages and their literatures, he believed that literature itself was an index to an era's well-being and that its creator should be a detached yet penetrating observer of life, one whose craft might even 'forward the cause of civilization'.

James's Notebooks, those fascinating quarries of genius, portray a writer for whom social life was above all the source for the refining experiments of fiction. Dinner-party anecdotes become the origins of moral drama. In addition, James's position as the cultivated American observer, 'the visiting mind', gave him his international subject: the relation of Americans and an America 'young with its own juvenility' to Europeans and a Europe 'vast and various and dense'. Such a meeting of opposites became, by extension, James's theme of ingenuous youth entangled in the meshes of an older civilization.

Among James's early works, *Roderick Hudson* (1875) portrays the conflict of an American artist opening himself to Europe and wavering between a wealthy American fiancée of high moral tone and Christina Light, a woman of refined aesthetic sensibilities who has been reared in a corruptly sophisticated Europe. In *The American* (1877), for all its melodramatic effects, James portrays how the wealthy and significantly named Christopher Newman is betrayed by Europeans 'pretending to represent the highest possible civilization' but who are in fact hidebound by their place in a ruthlessly authoritarian social order. *The Europeans* (1879), James's first assured success, is a delightful comedy, not without its darker moments, in which a European brother and sister confront Puritan America and so allow James to pit old social codes against more democratic values.

The danger presented to innocent American girls by their own headstrong naïvety provides the pathos in James's beautiful short story 'Daisy Miller'. Related from the point of view of her American admirer – a device that allows James to explore the situation with a subtly oblique awareness – the tale shows the plight of American ingenuousness in Europe as Daisy risks reputation, ostracism and life itself in the pursuit of her youthful ideal of personal freedom.

In *The Portrait of a Lady* (1881), James's theme of the young American heroine trapped in the snares of the international situation received its most subtle and extensive handling so far. James's portrayal of 'a certain young woman affronting her destiny' is one of his finest achievements – indeed, one of the finest novels in the English language. *The Portrait of a Lady* is at once a large and subtle tissue of psychological action and moral responsiveness. It is also a work of ruthless dramatic clarity. 'The idea of the whole thing', James wrote in his Notebooks, 'is that the poor girl, who has dreamed of freedom and nobleness, who has done, as she believes, a generous, natural, clear-sighted thing, finds herself in reality ground in the very treadmill of the conventional.' The situation is at once tragic and delicate, and the supreme achievement of the work is to focus its whole burden of hope and disillusion in the consciousness of the heroine herself. James's discussion of what he was seeking to achieve in *The Portrait of a Lady* conveys all the obsessive excitement of a writer working at the limits of his art. 'Place the centre of the subject in the young woman's own consciousness, I said to myself, and you get as interesting and as beautiful a difficulty as you could wish.'

James's heroine Isabel Archer draws, as do some of his later heroines, on his love for his cousin Minny Temple, 'radiant and rare, extinguished in her first youth'. Isabel herself comes to England, having already rejected the millionaire Caspar Goodwood. Here, at the ancient house of the expatriate Touchetts, she is approached by a second suitor, Lord Warburton, the great English gentleman with his 'air of a happy temperament fertilized by a high civilization'. For James, such social tone could be an outward, visible sign of the personal integrity nurtured by an ancient élite. Isabel declines his proposal nonetheless. 'She couldn't marry Lord Warburton; the idea failed to support any enlightened prejudice in favour of the free exploration of life that she had hitherto entertained.' At once noble and naïve, Isabel longs for the romantic freedom to give herself to some great cause. In this, we may see her as a younger cousin of Dorothea Brooke.

The consumptive Ralph Touchett is moved by such idealism and persuades his father to leave Isabel the family fortune. Isabel falls victim to the meretricious Osmond, collector of *objets de vertu*, and Mme Merle, Osmond's erstwhile mistress who has borne him his daughter Pansy. Freedom is thus snared and idealism squandered on the sterile. The gradual revelation of the truth – of Osmond's emasculated dilettantism and Mme Merle's cunning vulgarity – is handled with an exquisite sense that only moral worth can be the true source of human value. When Isabel, trapped in her Roman palace, reflects on her situation, narrative, symbol and heightened consciousness combine as she recognizes that her daily anguish springs from the choice she has made and from her husband's commonplace evil:

It was the house of darkness, the house of dumbness, the house of suffocation. Osmond's beautiful mind gave it neither light nor air; Osmond's beautiful mind indeed seemed to peep down from a small high window and mock at her. Of course it had not been physical suffering; for physical suffering there might have been a remedy. She could come and go; she had her liberty; her husband was perfectly polite. He took himself so seriously; it was something appalling. Under all his culture, all his cleverness, his amenity, under his good-nature, his facility, his knowledge of life, his egoism lay hidden like a serpent in a bank of flowers.

Situation, moral awareness, narrative and character are perfectly fused. Nothing is obtrusive yet all is made clear. The passage perfectly illustrates James's contention in 'The Art of Fiction' that he could not imagine in a great novel

a passage of description that is not in its intention narrative, a passage of dialogue that is not in its intention descriptive, a touch of truth of any sort that does not partake of the nature of incident, or an incident that derives its interest from any other source of the success of a work of art – that of being illustrative.

As a result, our awareness is deepened by the processes of fiction themselves.

And for Isabel, there is no escaping her prison. Though she returns to England to nurse the dying Ralph and there receives another proposal from Goodwood, the life of the heroine – the Lady – admits no compromise with second chances. Isabel has an absolute respect for 'all the traditionary decencies and sanctities of marriage'. Her implacable moral sense identifies self with the conventions that the novel takes as the register of a high civilization. She returns to Rome and to Osmond. As a young woman she had hoped 'she should have the pleasure of being as heroic as the occasion demanded'. She now finds that the cost of such heroism is life itself.

James was to return to the American scene for *Washington Square*

(1881), his portrait of a plain woman's brutally disillusioned hopes of love and marriage, and for his sharply satirical *The Bostonians* (1886). Both works are perhaps best seen in the context of the American novel, though the reception of the last, like that of James's inferior *The Princess Casamassima* (1886), caused his reputation to plummet. In these works he had tried the novel of social commentary and realism – feminist causes in *The Bostonians*, the opposition of anarchist ideals to traditional values in *The Princess Casamassima* – and lost much of his audience.

Just as disturbingly, he had tried to gain public recognition through the drama and had been mortified by the reception of *Guy Domville* (1895). 'All the forces of civilization in the house', he wrote to his brother after the first night, 'waged a battle of the most gallant, prolonged and sustained applause with the hoots and jeers and catcalls of the roughs, whose *roars* (like those of a cage of beasts at some infernal "zoo") were only exacerbated (as it were!) by the conflict.' James had been seeking a mass popularity his art could not sustain. On the one hand were the 'gallant' and civilized few, on the other the vulgar mass, loud, ill mannered, gross by the very weight of their numbers and involved in the strident late-nineteenth-century world of mass opinion, mass entertainment, jingoism and economic uncertainty. In what relation to such an audience could a writer like James stand?

If, like Ray Limbert in 'The Next Time', he strained after vulgarity, then his true talent would out and show him a world where 'even twaddle cunningly calculated was far above people's heads'. The democratization of sensibility was seemingly impossible. For Hyacinth Robinson, the hero of *The Princess Casamassima*, it had meant cutting up the old masters 'so that everyone might have a little piece', and from such a solution even the would-be anarchist had turned away. For James himself, the answer lay in an ever more arduous devotion to the subtleties of his craft, the pursuit of those quiveringly sensitive discernments that are, as Hyacinth Robinson knows, among 'the splendid accumulations of the happier few'. Great art becomes of necessity élitist, and the artist himself the consciousness of that élite. 'Art', James was to insist to H.G. Wells, '*makes* life.'

The integrity of the artist and the threats to his preserving 'the tradition of a high aesthetic temper' became central to a large group of James's novellas and short stories. In 'The Death of the Lion', the great author succumbs, through a mixture of weakness and excessive delicacy, to the world of the sycophantic philistines who worship him without reading his books. By contrast, the narrator of this beautifully constructed and often sharply humorous story leaves the world of fashionable journalism and, under the influence of the master, writes a serious critical essay on him. 'The Figure in the Carpet' concentrates on the enigmatic and ultimately unknowable sources of a refined and esoteric fiction, while 'The Coxon Fund' and 'The Lesson of the Master' concentrate on the dangers money poses to artistic integrity. In the first story, financial independence results in artistic silence. In the second, the need to keep a wife and family means a reduction in literary quality. Nonetheless, the literary lion portrayed here quickly remarries after the death of his first wife and ceases to write, thereby contradicting the advice given to his acolyte to dedicate himself 'to intellectual not to personal passion'.

The greatest of these works is 'The Aspern Papers'. Based on an anecdote about a cache of Byron's letters, the novella is partly about the would-be biographer's invasion of the private life from which great art springs. It is also partly about the temptations offered by the market price of the invaluable papers guarded by two old women. Their various obsessions make both sides rapacious and ultimately defeated by mutual misunderstanding. From their collision in the marvellously evoked Gothic of James's Venetian palace, there emerge only death, loneliness and frustration. The papers themselves are burned. A similar fate is visited on the treasures gathered in *The Spoils of Poynton* (1897). Here we see how James's experiments in the drama and the short story had encouraged him to explore what he called 'the sacred mystery of structure' and so develop his exceptional control over narrative. His fiction now offers the indirect presentation of climaxes through the reactions of his characters and, above all, the dramatization of the often partial consciousness of his narrators.

After the opening chapter of *The Spoils of Poynton*, for example, James's point of view is focused on Fleda Vetch. With her capacity for refined discernment, Fleda becomes the centre of a plot to wrest a fabulous collection of antiques from the vulgar grasp of the woman engaged to their owner's son. Though Fleda herself falls in love with this young man, her scrupulousness in personal relations is greater even than her aesthetic discrimination. She renounces him and he, in his turn, is obliged to marry the vulgarian he now despises and who eventually leaves Poynton itself in the hands of careless servants who let it burn to the ground. Possession, discrimination and the multiple meanings of 'spoils' create a work whose moral focus is at once ironic and poignant.

The subtlety with which James could now use the figure of the dubiously reliable narrator is given virtuoso display in his ghost story 'The Turn of the Screw' (1898). Here, the governess's account of events at Bly suggests both a genuine haunting and a frustrated young girl's self-deception. The current of illicit and suppressed sexuality that runs through the story – in the governess herself, in the affair between the ghostly Quint and Miss Jessel and in the effects these have on the questionable innocence of the children – greatly increases the tension. The terror lies in the constantly shifting uncertainties, the art in creating the impossibility of assured interpretation.

In *What Maisie Knew* (1897), the consciousness of a growing child is used to refract an experience of a life in which Maisie herself is the victim of hollow and worldly adults as they move through exquisitely paired and balanced adulteries. The process of coming to 'know' – of maturing consciousness itself – is both James's subject and his method of evaluating his characters. The effect is a quite exceptional subtlety of register as Maisie progresses from innocence to the state where, near the close of the work, 'she looked at the pink sky with a placid foreboding that soon she should have learnt All'. The passing of childhood is suggested through an extraordinarily refined art working on a situation which, as James wrote in his New York Preface to his works (1907–9), was 'dignified by the most delightful difficulty'.

It was during the composition of *What Maisie Knew* that James began dictating his works to a stenographer, a fact which perhaps partly accounts for the richly eddying air of improvisation – the constant parenthetical play of suggestion and qualification – that is a characteristic of his mature style and the three great novels that crown his career.

The Ambassadors (1903), James's reflection on the unlived life, was his own favourite among his novels. It is a work whose power and pathos are focused in the consciousness of the provincial American Strether as he is exposed, too late, to the refined enjoyments of

Parisian civilization. Sent to redeem young Chad Newsome from a supposed world of vice, Strether discovers the life he has missed and can now no longer have. The technical mastery and human depth by which James shows a consciousness at once limited in its understanding yet slowly unfolding towards the poignant awareness of its own deprivations is achieved with absolute assurance. Indeed, the scene at the garden party where Strether observes in partial ignorance yet growing self-awareness the European ideal of high and graceful refinement (the figures on the lawn, we feel, like those on some oriental screen, go about their daily lives in the all-involving radiance of a great civilization) is one of the high points of James's art. The crossing of the older man's path with the young – the gradual broadening of Strether's awareness, and Chad's exercise of the heartless privileges of youth – is achieved not merely with the greatest technical subtlety but finally with the sadness and strength of profoundly considered experience.

In *The Golden Bowl* (1904), James's 'international subject', his concern with materialism and moral values, with deception and evil, and his use of symbolism and the refined consciousness are developed to a degree that is often oppressive, and it is perhaps in *The Wings of the Dove* (1902) that the greatness of his late period can be most readily seen.

The dramatic power and range of *The Wings of the Dove* reveal the style of the late James as the most subtle medium for focusing the consciousness of his narrators. In the opening sections especially, it weaves its way around the physical world and then, with a richness of metaphor that equals Dickens or Donne, raises the physical world to an image of the moral values that underlie it. Kate Croy's Aunt Maud, for example, is at once a great society lady and an embodiment of the forces working in the imperial heyday of Edwardian England.

Monstrously glossy in her dress, Aunt Maud becomes metamorphosed in Kate's mind into Britannia – 'Britannia of the Market Place', the mythical embodiment of the fabulous wealth of a trading empire. But Aunt Maud is not a figure to be lightly dismissed with an amusing analogy. 'There was a whole side of Britannia, the side of her florid philistinism, her plumes and her train, her fantastic furniture and heaving bosom, the false gods of her taste and the false notes of her talk, the sole contemplation of which would be dangerously misleading.' Britannia is passionate as well as practical, aggressive, defensive and wise. Above all, armed with 'a reticule for her prejudices as deep as that other pocket, the pocket full of coins stamped in her image', she is the focus of power and materialism. For Kate and her equally impoverished fiancé Merton Densher, she represents 'the general attestation of morality and money, a good conscience and a big balance'. It is this relationship between materialism and the spirit that the novel will explore.

The work having opened with various attempts at financial deviousness, there now comes into the lovers' world Milly Theale, the American princess of fabulous wealth, eager for life but smitten with a mortal disease. Ardent, innocent and poetic, Milly is inveigled into the revolting plan whereby Densher will marry her for her money and, after her death, share it with Kate. As Milly's rare and precious spirit becomes enmeshed in materialism, so she is the Psalmist's dove trapped in a world of duplicitous friends. This terrible interplay of innocence and corruption is raised by James to a work of the most profound moral subtlety.

To achieve this, the melodramatic grounding of the plot is constantly subverted by James's refusal to dramatize the majority of its 'great' moments, in particular those where Milly comes to understand the trap laid for her by her beloved Densher. We do not know what she says in her final letter to him. We do not see her die. Motives and events are, as James declared, 'subject to varieties of interpretation'. For example, the dying Milly apparently forgives Densher his duplicity and certainly leaves him her wealth. The result is a curse on his life that has a tragic intensity. Obsessed with Milly's memory and stricken with guilt, Densher's violation of another person's sanctity seems to mean the collapse of his own relationship with Kate. A guilty horror falls on a man who appears to be forced into a life forever tortured by his consciousness of the love he has defiled. The golden feathers of Milly the dove brood over the world as the conspirators work their own torment. 'We shall never be again as we were!' Kate and Densher's powerfully dramatized last dialogue allows for no neat narrative conclusion. Instead, it concentrates our awareness of moral dilemma by adding 'the sharp taste of uncertainty to a quickened sense of life'. By thus straining all his resources of construction and the presentation of consciousness, James has here created a novel that stands on the borders of the modern world.

24

Joseph Conrad (1857–1924) called Henry James 'the historian of fine consciences', and his admiration reflects both his own interest in the mind facing moral dilemma and the sophisticated technical devices he too elaborated to explore this.

Conrad was born Jozef Teodor Konrad Korzeniowski, and his early life was spent first in his native Poland and then in sharing his literary father's Russian exile. Although nurturing the ambition to be a writer, Conrad was deeply attracted to the sea, and by the time he was seventeen was sailing the Mediterranean where he appears to have been involved in a number of escapades including gun-running. Exile, the sea, adventure, violence and espionage contributed much to the plots of his novels, but although he was to become one of the masters of English fiction Conrad did not speak the language itself until he was twenty-three. That he was to explore its resources to the limit is an indication of his overmastering commitment to trial and heroic endeavour.

From his youth, Conrad read widely in the Russian, French and English classics, but he did not begin writing seriously until he was thirty-two. His first novel, *Almayer's Folly* (1895), was not published until he was thirty-eight. Like its successor, *An Outcast of the Islands* (1896), the work is concerned with the moral decay of Europeans amid Far Eastern landscapes where primeval energies constantly threaten to engulf and choke their lives. The style is adjectival and slow, the sense of character less strong than the vivid realization of the threats posed by the natural world and the relapse into barbarism.

It is with *The Nigger of the 'Narcissus'* (1898) that Conrad's genius revealed its qualities. This short novel is, first of all, a magnificent re-creation of heroic adventure and of life aboard ship in the great days of sail. The long battle with the storm, the picture of the ship itself 'shaken like a rattle in a madman's hand' and the effort to right it in its battle with the elements are among the finest achievements of

English writing in this manner. But Conrad was concerned with more than evocation. In *Some Reminiscences* (1912) he wrote: 'Those who read me know my conviction that the world, the temporal world, rests on a few very simple ideas: so simple that they must be as old as the hills. It rests, notably, among others, on the idea of Fidelity.' It is what happens when this virtue is under threat, when circumstances conspire to untie conventional bonds and expose man to the insidious forces of evil lurking both within him and without, that Conrad is principally concerned.

In *The Nigger of the 'Narcissus'*, the sea tests to the limits man's role as both an individual and a member of a society, a crew. The ship is a man-made embodiment of what for Conrad should be the ideal values that hold human society together: discipline, hierarchy, authority. It is these that are pitted against both the destructive forces of nature and the more insidious human weaknesses that undermine society from within. The dying Negro James Wait appears to put a curse on the ship, and the sympathy he evokes is inextricably bound up with egoism, the sense of self that works against the habitual and necessary submission to community. 'He was demoralizing. Through him we were becoming highly humanized, tender, complex, excessively decadent: we understood the subtlety of his fear, sympathized with all his repulsions, shrinkings, evasions, delusions – as though we had been over-civilized and rotten, and without any knowledge of the meaning of life.' Liberal individualism – the progressive and optimistic values of the nineteenth century – threatens chaos. Only the heroic and aptly named Singleton maintains an absolute fidelity to his task as he steers the ship through. Nonetheless, at the close of the work, when Singleton has been paid off, Conrad is careful to emphasize the man's ordinariness, the unremarkable quality of the figure who embodies fundamental values.

Singleton is one of 'the everlasting children of the mysterious sea', and a number of the novellas and short stories Conrad wrote throughout his career are concerned with exploring the moral nature of man through just such characters. They range from the most doggedly ordinary, through youths exhilarated by their first command, to man's mysterious encounter with his sinister shadow self. In 'Typhoon' (1902), for example, a ship is once more in the grip of a furious storm which the crew fight while the coolies below threaten mutiny. Only Captain MacWhirr – taciturn, unromantic, but strong in 'the loneliness of command' – can impose his authority on the men and so bring the *Nan-Shan* safely through the fury of nature. Conrad's double vision shows us the captain as both unprepossessing and heroic, the man whose limited imagination poses no threat to the personal integrity that allows him to impose his will.

'Youth' (1899) introduces Marlow, the figure whom Conrad was to use in many of his works to recount adventures and suggest the complex issues of morality and perception these raise. Here, the older Marlow tells a group of mature men bound by 'the strong bond of the sea' about the euphoric moment in his early life when, after a storm, his lifeboat arrived in a Far Eastern port. Youth's romantic illusions of power and an existence untouched by time – feelings at once poignant, genuine and absurd – are contrasted to the older Marlow's deeper wisdom, the experience of life he shares with his listeners.

The crises by which men pass beyond youthful confidence to maturity are explored in some of Conrad's finest works. In *The Shadow Line* (1917), the narrator tells of his first command and the rite of passage by which, through ordeal, he comes to a measure of adult self-awareness. The narrator knows that by being the captain of his ship 'I stood, like a king in his country, in a class by myself.' A black cloud of doubt and insecurity hangs over him nonetheless. The trial imposed by responsibility and the sea becomes an investigation of the secret recesses of weakness – the imprecise but potent sense of evil and nihilism which both surrounds a man and is within him. 'I always suspected', the narrator declares, 'that I might be no good.'

In *The Shadow Line*, this sense of psychological and moral threat is personified by the spectre of the previous captain who had sold the ship's supply of quinine and replaced it with worthless powder. The ship becomes becalmed, the men fall ill, and only the narrator and Ransome, the mortally ill cook, can bring her to port. However, the captain's horror at physical distress is compounded by a more subtle personal dread. He feels an affinity with his predecessor's wrongdoing. 'That man had been in all essentials but his age just another man as myself. Yet the end of his life was a complete act of treason, the betrayal of a tradition which seemed to me as imperative as any guide on earth could be.' The threat to 'Fidelity' is everywhere present and is here met by straining the limits of human endurance. In so doing, the captain passes the shadow line between youth and maturity. It is Ransome however, dying and undemonstratively heroic, who places such experience in its true context: 'I saw under the worth and comeliness of the man the humble reality of things,' the narrator declares. True greatness is quotidian, ordinary, human.

The meeting with the shadow self is also presented in 'The Secret Sharer' (1909), but Conrad's most profound and comprehensive treatment of man's encounter with evil is to be found in the novella that remains his most assured artistic success, *Heart of Darkness* (1902). Here, Marlow's river journey into the forests of the Belgian Congo to find the trader Kurtz is enveloped with a many-layered significance. A penumbra of moral awareness is cast by a story that is at once a display of technical mastery and a poetic response to the notion of the quest.

Conrad had himself made a similar journey and been profoundly disillusioned by what he saw of Belgian colonialism, describing it in an essay as 'the vilest scramble for loot that ever disfigured the history of human conscience'. In his novella, the European traders are compared to burglars breaking into a safe. The pointless firing of the man-of-war and, above all, the treatment of the Negro slaves in the chain gang strongly underline Conrad's revulsion at contemporary standards. Throughout, such incidents are related to a timeless sense of evil. 'Going up that river was like going back to beginnings,' Marlow declares. The frenzied sounds of the natives faintly revive in him distant, primeval memories, and his journey towards Kurtz becomes a journey of increasing spiritual self-discovery. Finally, it becomes an encounter with moral and spiritual nihilism – the shadow self. Kurtz has 'stepped over the edge' into a darkness that defies adequate description and all but occludes humanity. Only in the moment of his death does he glimpse the scale of his enormity:

It was as though a veil had been rent. I saw on that ivory face the expression of sombre pride, of ruthless power, of craven terror – of an intense and hopeless despair. Did he live his life again in every detail of desire, temptation, and surrender during that supreme moment of complete knowledge? He cried in a whisper at some strange image, at some vision – he cried out twice, a cry that was no more than a breath –

'The horror! The horror!'
I blew out the candle and left the cabin.

Kurtz's desperately whispered phrase is at once an affirmation of moral values and an expression of incommunicable despair. The evil at the heart of darkness remains mysterious and terrifying – something glimpsed and intuitively guessed at rather than something to be explained. It is also all-pervasive. As Marlow finishes his story, the narrator raises his head and looks out across the Thames. 'The offing was barred by a black bank of clouds, and the tranquil waterway leading to the uttermost ends of the earth flowed sombre under an overcast sky – seemed to lead into the heart of an immense darkness.' Evil is both timeless and omnipresent. In *Heart of Darkness*, Conrad sees imperialism as its contemporary manifestation, but by connecting London and all men to the primordial and savage, he also reveals his sense of the precariousness of modern civilization and the depth of his metaphysical despair.

Lord Jim (1900) was begun as a short story but grew under Conrad's hand until his discussion of lost honour and broken fidelity became a full-length novel in which the author's sophisticated manipulation of point of view allows his audience both to sympathize with Jim and to see his fundamental unworthiness, his essential human contradictions. As Marlow himself says of his story: 'I put it down here for you as though I had been an eyewitness. My information was fragmentary, but I've fitted the pieces together, and there is enough of them to make an intelligible picture.' The result of this technique is a subtle enrichment of moral awareness.

Jim is the victim of his own delusive dream of heroism. For him the sea means glamour and romance, and the divide between his vision and reality is a gulf of tormenting guilt. As a boy Jim besmirched his ideal when he failed to jump overboard to save a drowning colleague. As a young man he again corrodes his ideal when he leaps from the *Patna* and so abandons a ship he wrongly believes to be sinking. For him, this moment of profound dishonour, of broken fidelity, 'was as if I had jumped into a well – into an everlasting deep hole'. Baffled and guilty in his moral isolation, harried by his vivid imagination with the shame of his cowardice, Jim willingly submits to the guilty verdict passed at the official inquiry.

'The real significance of crime', Marlow comments, 'is in its being a breach of faith with the community of mankind, and from that point of view he was no mean traitor.' Conrad's abiding themes of fidelity and moral chaos are here combined in a figure whose appearance is that of the upright young public-school Englishman. His inner reality however is the existential uncertainty of a figure cut loose by weakness from his moral bearings. Jim must drift.

Marlow's reluctance to play the omniscient narrator and so provide a clear, consecutive view of his relationship with Jim is an aspect of the literary technique Conrad was evolving with Ford Madox Ford (1873–1939). In order to suggest the complexity of experience as it is actually received, Conrad has Marlow stress to his listeners his own sense of baffled awe as Jim's story unfolds. We see the hero through clouds, obliquely and with a constant quickening of moral awareness rather than through simple assertions of guilt and shame.

Jim the moral exile drifts ever further from Western man until, in a remote district of the Far East, he eventually becomes the loved and trusted moral centre of a primitive community – 'Tuan' Jim, Lord Jim. But weakness is inexpiable. The arrival in Patusan of the corrupt Brown is the arrival of nemesis in the form of the tempter, the shadow self. As the two men confront each other, 'there ran through the rough talk a vein of subtle reference to their common blood, an assumption of common experience; a sickening suggestion of common guilt, a secret knowledge that was like a bond of their minds and of their hearts'. In pursuit of his code of honour, Jim spares Brown, sacrifices himself and so breaks his promise to his mistress and his people. Refracted through the subtlety of Conrad's narrative technique, our glimpses of Jim allow us to see him as idealist, sinner and finally, in Marlow's words, 'one of us'.

Conrad's concern with his characters' ideal conception of themselves, with the corruption of those ideals and with the advanced techniques by which such matters may be explored is seen at its finest in *Nostromo* (1904), Conrad's most intricately structured work. The imagined South American state of Costaguana, hemmed in by mountains and the sea, becomes his focus for a deeply pessimistic and disillusioned view of modern man in his political and moral dimensions.

The importance of Costaguana itself lies in its silver mine, and, as

Conrad wrote, 'silver is the pivot of the moral and material events, affecting the lives of everybody in the tale'. Since these characters represent the various forces operating in the modern world, the insidious corruption wrought by the silver becomes the means by which Conrad can offer his analysis of contemporary *malaise*.

Financed by the absentee American business man Holroyd, the mine itself has been inherited by the Englishman Charles Gould. The greed and instability of earlier Costaguanian governments have broken Gould's father, and the silver is already regarded as a curse. Gould himself however, the doctrinaire liberal capitalist, is determined to salvage the mine and his family name by asserting his faith in 'material interests'. Only through these, he believes – through the efficient making of wealth – will the moral and social benefits of law and order come to the benighted state.

This conventional nineteenth-century ideal hardens into an obsession which eventually separates Gould from the finer human sympathies of his wife. It also blinds him to the true nature of material progress. Mrs Gould – the most sympathetic of Conrad's female characters – pays the personal price of Gould's obsession in her lovelessness and loneliness. The embittered Dr Monygham meanwhile realizes the awful social cost of Gould's materialism. Though prosperity does indeed eventually come to the state, Monygham knows that wealth without morality is another form of tyranny:

There is no peace and no rest in the development of material interests. They have their law, and their justice. But it is founded on expediency, and is inhuman; it is without rectitude, without the continuity and the force that can be found only in a moral principle. Mrs Gould, the time approaches when all that the Gould concession stands for shall weigh as heavily on the people as the barbarism, cruelty, and misrule of a few years back.

It is this threat of barbarism and cruelty that triggers the central action. Gould has backed a regime which he hopes will bring better order to the state, but this regime is overthrown in a military coup. As much silver as possible must now be removed from the town, and the 'incorruptible' Nostromo, the reliable man of all work, is required to achieve this.

The subtle construction of *Nostromo* – Conrad's continuous shuttling back and forth across the movements of time – keeps this central episode as the focus of attention while allowing a great range of political implications to play over it. Similarly, Conrad's pairing and contrasting of characters allow him to deepen his moral commentary. Such structural richness is at one with the novel's analytical sophistication, and any attempt at a brief overview must necessarily distort Conrad's purposes.

Nonetheless, in the great scene where the silver itself is taken to the island, we can begin to see something of Conrad's achievement. Here we are presented with Nostromo, with Martin Decoud and with the luckless Hirsch. Decoud, the anti-idealist who has yet been won to some measure of affirmation by his surprised discovery of love, believes he can see into the true nature of Nostromo. For him, Nostromo is a man whose vanity and desire for personal prestige have apparently made him incorruptible. Nostromo's is 'that finest form of egotism which can take on the aspect of every virtue'. Left alone on the island however, and overpowered by his own scepticism, 'the deep unbroken solitude of waiting without faith', Decoud weights himself down with some of the silver ingots and commits suicide.

The apparently invincible Nostromo has meanwhile returned to the mainland and helped so to transform the military situation that the province can secede from Costaguana and enter on a period of prosperity. Nostromo feels slighted nonetheless and eventually enriches himself from the treasure it is generally believed has been lost at sea. Corrupted by the silver like nearly all who come in contact with it, Nostromo is eventually shot in a love intrigue, his integrity entirely compromised. Mrs Gould prevents the dying man from telling her where the silver lies, but if she preserves her refusal to submit to material interests, we are shown how the moral values of the state itself are being progressively undermined by its new wealth. Against a facile belief in progress stands Monygham's bitter wisdom. The political revolutions that have racked Conrad's world underline the abiding spiritual emptiness of the modern condition and raise disturbing doubts about the viability of all human values.

The political pessimism of *Nostromo* is so developed in *The Secret Agent* (1907) as to create a world of madness and despair set against a background of moral squalor. The novel's situation was suggested by an anarchist attempt to blow up Greenwich Observatory, an incident which Conrad described as 'a blood-stained inanity of so fatuous a kind that it was impossible to fathom its origin by any reasonable or even unreasonable process of thought'.

In *The Secret Agent*, this shiver of revulsion animates the gruesome account of how Mr Verloc, pornography seller and spy, when told by his paymasters to create an incident that will frame the anarchists that haunt his shop, uses his wife's weak-minded brother to deliver a bomb that prematurely explodes. When the crime has been detected, Winnie Verloc murders her unresisting husband with the knife used to cut the meat he is eating. She is then abused by one of his erstwhile anarchist associates and drowns herself. Anarchism itself thereby becomes the expression of a world in which action is destructive and social values are intensely precarious. The heart of darkness is a desperate and corrosive pit of loneliness and negativity, the seat of a violence at once fatuous and terrible. Part farce and part tragedy, Conrad's analysis of betrayal and lovelessness is a terrible insight into nihilistic violence, a masterpiece of sustained irony.

Political anarchy is also the theme of *Under Western Eyes* (1911), though here it is triggered by Conrad's hatred of Russia. He had discussed the dangers of both Russian and German imperialism in 'Autocracy and War' (1905) and was convinced that both powers had crushed 'all that is faithful in human nature'. His Preface to *Under Western Eyes* makes the political dangers of extinguishing such fidelity clear. Here, outlining the political theme of his work, Conrad declared that 'the ferocity and imbecility of an autocratic rule rejecting all legality and in fact basing itself upon complete moral anarchism provokes the no less imbecile and atrocious answer of a purely Utopian revolutionism encompassing destruction by the first means to hand'.

Chance (1913), a rather unlikely story of modern chivalry, brought Conrad the popular acclaim that had so far eluded him, while *Victory* (1915) was his last assured artistic success. Axel Heyst, protected in his disillusion by a philosophy of non-attachment, saves an English-woman from humiliation but fails to achieve a harmonious relation-ship with her. Only after she has given her life for him and Heyst is dying by his own hand does he realize the spiritual damage inflicted on him by his philosophy. 'Woe to the man whose heart has not learned while young to hope, to love – and to put his trust in life!'

Fidelity remains the ideal, but it is the sophisticated and often guilt-ridden analysis of its collapse – the apprehension of the heart of darkness – that makes Conrad one of the first masters of the modern novel.

25

The great achievements of Victorian fiction and poetry were not remotely approached by the drama until the closing decades of the nineteenth century. The theatre itself suffered from generally low esteem, and farce, melodrama and burlesque provided the staple fare. This was the age of the Crummleses, of Nicholas Nickleby hurriedly adapting French plays, of *Black-Eyed Susan* (1829) and *Maria Marten, or The Murder in the Red Barn*.

Melodramas like *The Shaughraun* (1875) by Dion Boucicault (1820–90) have some genuine tenderness in their scenes of everyday Irish life, and Boucicault himself was to influence future Irish dramatists, if only by serving as a model against which to react. T.W. Robertson (1829–71) in plays such as *Caste* (1867) attempted to deal with social issues in dialogue trimmed of the rant and excess that characterized much of the work favoured by Victorian actor-managers. Robertson had a genuine comic gift, while the threat his new style of drama appeared to pose to the old school of actors is sensitively portrayed in *Trelawny of the 'Wells'* (1898) by Arthur Wing Pinero (1855–1934). Nonetheless, in Pinero's *The Second Mrs Tanqueray* (1893), the victory of conventional social pieties over the author's exploration of a woman's past suggests the mortmain of respectability from which the drama still had to free itself.

Though poetry was considered appropriate to high drama, few serious verse plays of the Victorian era are to any degree memorable, and it is to the librettos written by W.S. Gilbert (1836–1911) for the Savoy Operas that we must turn for the most effective use of dramatic verse in this period. Gilbert had first shown how his talent for complex verse forms could be allied to social satire in the *Bab Ballads* (1869). This combination is revealed again in such 'patter songs' from the operas as 'I've got a little list' in *The Mikado* (1885).

The satire and parody in *HMS Pinafore* (1878) and *The Pirates of Penzance* (1880) are often surprisingly sharp, while the portrait of Bunthorne in *Patience* (1881) is a lasting comment on Wilde and the Aesthetic Movement.

Though Wilde's *The Importance of Being Earnest* remains one of the great works of the English comic stage, Victorian drama had to find sources more nourishing than the native tradition if it was to reform itself and thrive. These were in large part provided by the Norwegian dramatist Henrik Ibsen (1828–1906). In such plays as *Pillars of Society* (1877), *A Doll's House* (1879), *Ghosts* (1881) and *An Enemy of the People* (1882), Ibsen developed a naturalistic drama of private anxiety and social comment that discussed such issues as marriage and the position of women with a power that was felt to be deeply threatening. *Ghosts*, for example, which uses hereditary syphilis as a metaphor for the blighting power of a corrupt past, was regarded by many as a loathsome sore, an open drain.

Ibsen's work was championed in England by the critic and translator William Archer (1856–1924) whose articles in the *London Figaro* were to attract the attention of George Bernard Shaw (1856–1950), then a reviewer, unsuccessful novelist and ardent Fabian socialist. The two men became friends. In 1891, Shaw published his highly partisan study *The Quintessence of Ibsenism*, while the following year saw the production of the play Shaw had at first collaborated on with Archer, *Widowers' Houses*. This was staged by the Independent Theatre, which the previous year had mounted Ibsen's *Ghosts*.

In the Preface to *Plays Pleasant and Unpleasant* (1898), his first published collection of his dramas, Shaw warned his readers that his attacks were 'directed against themselves, not against my stage figures'. The English theatre was at last becoming a place for a critical engagement with English society. *Widowers' Houses* somewhat clumsily suggests Shaw's indignation at the hypocritical lives of slum landlords, but with Vivie, the newly liberated heroine of *Mrs Warren's Profession* (1894), Shaw portrayed a type to whom he was often and effectively to give his more radical sentiments. Here, Vivie asserts a woman's right to earn her own income, and reveals herself as the sort of person who would later read Shaw's *The Intelligent Woman's Guide to Socialism and Capitalism* (1928).

The young girl from Newnham is nonetheless horrified when she learns that her mother earns her money by running a chain of brothels. Not having had Vivie's opportunities, Mrs Warren has had to survive in a world where 'the only way for a woman to provide for herself decently is for her to be good to some man that can afford to be good to her'. As a whore and later a madam, Mrs Warren has capitalized on the mores of a society that makes women financially dependent, and she has done so with all the thrift and efficiency admired in the Victorian business man. If Mrs Warren herself is at once amusing, corrupt and horrific – Shaw himself called the play 'a cold-bloodedly appalling one' – she is nonetheless an effective device for exposing the hypocrisy in conventional nineteenth-century ideas of sexual relationships.

'My method is to take the utmost trouble to find the right thing to say,' Shaw declared, 'and then to say it with the utmost levity.' Many of his comedies from this period reveal how his witty and vivacious dialogue, given to characters of brilliant conversational ability, can indeed support a drama of ideas and so 'chasten morals with ridicule'. His exchanges are far more lively, his craftsmanship more adept, than those revealed by those who followed his lead such as J.M. Barrie in *The Admirable Crichton* (1902).

A number of dangers threaten to cloud an audience's pleasure nonetheless. The first of these is the fact that some of Shaw's butts of ridicule have simply passed into history. Shaw is engaging with problems and satirizing attitudes that are no longer central to our experience. Nor does his language, for all its brilliance, necessarily succeed in reaching more enduring aspects of life. He is only intermittently as felicitous as Congreve, while his tendency to the argumentative results in a too laborious didacticism. Though these faults were to become more dominant, they are not entirely avoided in the earlier work.

In *Arms and the Man* (1894), Shaw attacked the military triumphalism that lay behind much contemporary melodrama and patriotic feeling. Shaw's Bluntschli, though he seems to be involved in the most romantic situations, is no swaggering hero but a practical, unromantic Swiss biding his time as a mercenary until he inherits his father's hotels. Eventually he converts others to the view that the glorification of war is, like romantic love, no more than a hollow sham.

Continuing his high-spirited attack on Victorian prejudice, Shaw offered in *Candida* (1894) a carefully constructed domestic drama in which he contrasted the selfish demands made on the heroine by her Christian Socialist husband to those made by the young poet Marchbanks. In conventional domestic comedies, the wife finally chose her husband in preference to her would-be lover, having discovered he was the stronger man. Here, Candida chooses the weaker man – her limited and distinctly prosaic spouse. While *You Never Can Tell* (1897) is often highly proficient as comedy, its presentation of the sex war rapidly palls, and Shaw's second play of that year, *The Devil's Disciple*, is an altogether more interesting work. In this play directed against the contemporary theatre's 'deification of Love' – a sentiment the dramatist found absurd – Shaw inverts the conventions of melodrama. The anti-romantic Dick Dudgeon endures personal sacrifice, court martial, the threat of execution and a last-minute reprieve, not for love but out of a cold-blooded regard for his own moral dignity.

In *Caesar and Cleopatra* (1898), the contrast Shaw makes between the ageing Roman man of destiny and Cleopatra, the alluringly spoiled and even spiteful young queen, amusingly sets worldly values against Shaw's portrayal of a figure who was to be increasingly important to him – the superman with his high and dispassionate moral intelligence. After the ironic presentation of revenge and justice in *Captain Brassbound's Conversion* (1900), this figure comes to prominence in one of Shaw's most important plays, *Man and Superman* (1903).

If *Man and Superman* shows Shaw's comedy of ideas at its most brilliant, it also suggests his defects. The first act is enlivened by Jack Tanner the socialist intellectual's virtuoso speeches on woman as the embodiment of the Life Force or Creative Evolution. The virtuoso didacticism here is masterfully undercut by Tanner's own inability to see clearly what is going on around him. First, his ward Ann Whitefield is destined to snare Tanner himself rather than the poetic Octavius. In addition, when Tanner launches on a vigorous defence of Octavius's sister's apparently illegitimate pregnancy, he is floored as he discovers she is in fact secretly married. This is the comedy of ideas at its most effective.

The second act, which introduces that 'very momentous social phenomenon' 'Enry Straker, the educated working-class mechanic, concludes with Tanner in full flight from his ward in his expensive motor car. In most productions this is followed by the fourth act. Here, finally cornered, Tanner admits that he is indeed the victim of the Life Force embodied in Ann and falls in with her ruse to marry him. Shaw's original third act however greatly extends his drama of ideas. It offers a dream dialogue in hell where Tanner (now metamorphosed into Don Juan) tries to reject 'the seven deadly virtues' of contemporary life for a vision in which the philosophic mind of the superman can guide the Life Force directly in its task of bringing forth human perfection.

For all its moments of theatrical brilliance, *Major Barbara* (1905) is a less coherent drama of ideas. After a deftly amusing first act, the visit of Undershaft the weapons manufacturer to his daughter's Salvation Army post skilfully proves that charity is ultimately dependent on the capitalists who create poverty in the first place. Undershaft's offer of £5,000 is gratefully accepted by the Army, and Barbara's realization that even salvation has its price shatters her faith. When the leading characters then visit the model armaments factory in the third act, Undershaft himself (propelled, as he seems to admit, by the Life Force) progresses from a vehement support of capitalist enterprise, through a powerful attack on the 'crime' of poverty, to something that appears close to revolutionary ardour. Barbara seems similarly to grasp at the idea of the Life Force and to find renewed energy in preaching for the good of Undershaft's employees. Quite what she will preach to them however is unclear.

After *Major Barbara*, Shaw was to write a number of minor comedies. Then, in 1913, came the first performance of *Pygmalion*. This play, in which the cold and scholarly Professor Higgins buys Eliza Dolittle the flower-seller from her cockney father and proceeds to educate her as a lady, is a superb satire on the English class system and on language and accent as its most insidious manifestations. *Pygmalion* is also a delicate and effective exposure of the wrongs done by treating people merely as items of convenience. 'You have no idea', Higgins tells his mother, 'how frightfully interesting it is to take a human being and change her into a quite different human being by creating a new speech for her. It's filling up the deepest gulf that separates class from class and soul from soul.'

Higgins's experiment proceeds through some marvellous comic

scenes, that where the half-formed Eliza attends a ladies' tea-party being particularly effective. Nonetheless, beneath this brilliant surface stirs Eliza's realization that aside from a few little social proprieties 'the difference between a lady and a flower girl is not how she behaves, but how she's treated'. Eliza has learned true gentility from Higgins's friend Pickering. Higgins himself however continues to treat her badly – this Pygmalion does not fall romantically in love with his Galatea – while a conventional happy ending is replaced by what Shaw regarded as an altogether more likely conclusion. Eliza marries the asinine Freddy Eynsford Hill with whom she eventually sets up a flower shop.

Pygmalion makes clever use of myth for comic purposes, and is a play which draws on a human situation deeply understood yet brilliantly adapted to satiric attack. *Heartbreak House* by contrast, probably begun in the year before the outbreak of the First World War but not performed until 1921, is 'a fantasia in the Russian manner on English themes'. The obvious debt is to Chekhov, and the work attempts to portray the state of a nation on the brink of disaster. Heartbreak House itself is inhabited by the great and the good of Shaw's Edwardian England: 'charming people, most advanced, unprejudiced, frank, human, unconventional, democratic, and everything that is delightful to thoughtful people'. Utter catastrophe faces them nonetheless.

Under the brilliant surface, the same boredom and 'the same utter futility' mark the lives of these English country-house dwellers as they do those of the characters in *The Cherry Orchard*. Farce and despair go hand in hand, and a profound, nihilistic pessimism emerges. 'I tell you, one of two things must happen. Either out of that darkness some new creation will supplant us as we supplanted the animals, or the heavens will fall in themselves and destroy us.' The elderly Captain Shotover sits and drinks rum and spins plans for universal death while the young people pursue disillusioned and cynical affairs. England is a drifting ship of state while, at the close, Shotover himself retreats into dreams as the heroine waits exultantly for the falling of the bombs.

Heartbreak House is a vision of the end of a society. An era that had begun with Carlyle's warnings about the dangers of the machine and the mechanized mind was now plunged into the horrors of scientific mass destruction. The First World War is the true and catastrophic end of the nineteenth century, its terrible climax. As Henry James wrote on the eve of hostilities: 'to have to take it now for what the treacherous years were all the while really making for and meaning is too tragic for any words'.

Aspects of Twentieth-Century Literature

___

I

Early in the spring of 1915 Henry James gave an interview to the *New York Times Magazine*. 'The war has used up words,' he told the reporter despondently, 'they have weakened, they have deteriorated like motor-car tyres.' Old beliefs, James acknowledged, were perishing in the unprecedented horrors of mass destruction, and with them died the language in which they could be expressed. If literature were to survive at all – if it were to be remotely adequate to the appalling violence and uncertainty of the new age – then writers would have to re-create it out of a profoundly critical engagement with what they had inherited. Nowhere is this process clearer than in poetry.

For many who marched to the trenches in 1914, the best modern verse was collected in the anthologies of *Georgian Poetry* issued from 1912 under the guidance first of the cultivated amateur Edward Marsh (1872–1953) and then of J.C. Squire (1884–1958). Here could be found the work of such figures as John Masefield (1878–1967) and W.H. Davies (1871–1940), the finely honed, melancholy lyrics of the rural poet Edward Thomas (1878–1917) and the celebrated poem by Rupert Brooke (1887–1915) which Marsh persuaded him to publish as 'The Old Vicarage, Grantchester'. Influenced by both Housman and Hardy, this was widely popular verse, deriving its inspiration from the native countryside, which cultivated a lyricism that found its most able exponent in Walter de la Mare (1873–1956), and which was supported by poetic dreams of 'an English heaven' enshrined for many in Brooke's 'The Soldier'. Here was a poetry of unrecapturable innocence. It remained to be seen what was left when its flowers had been squashed in the Flanders mud.

In *Undertones of War* (1928), the Georgian poet Edmund Blunden (1896–1974) juxtaposed the traditional language of English Arcadian dream to contemporary horror – nature and art to mechanized death.

As Blunden described how 'deep red poppies, blue and white corn-flowers, and darnel thronged the way to destruction', so the rape of a landscape at once actual and literary becomes the ruin of the spirit, the progress towards experience of 'a harmless young shepherd in a soldier's coat'. This enforced brutalizing of the pastoral tradition, along with the mild homoerotic quality of much of the best First World War poetry, is seen again in the work of Ivor Gurney (1890–1937). A poem such as 'To his Love', for example, poignantly contrasts Arcadian innocence to the mute body of a friend – the 'thing I must somehow forget'.

References to myth, to Malory and the New Testament were used by David Jones (1895–1974) in *In Parenthesis* (1937) to relate the First World War to an explanatory tradition of timeless evil. The most effective use of literary allusion in such work however is to be found in the verse of Isaac Rosenberg (1890–1918). In poems such as 'Returning, we hear the larks' or 'Break of Day in the Trenches', the traditions of lyric from the Elizabethans to Shelley give a terrible and clear-eyed pathos to the horrors recounted in Rosenberg's 'Dead Man's Dump'.

'The pity of war, the pity war distilled' makes Wilfred Owen (1893–1918) the most widely regarded of these poets. In a language of bitter assonance and alliteration, Owen offers a nightmare landscape of mud and rain, gas, bullets and boredom. He reveals the trenches in which the blinded limp 'blood-shod' through a world 'where death becomes absurd and life absurder'. This is the world of 'Exposure', 'Futility' and 'Mental Cases'. Though 'the monstrous anger of the guns' is briefly stilled in the hell that forms the background to 'Strange Meeting', in the end Owen recognized that the language of shared humanity now belongs only to those who know the horrors inflicted by scientific warfare and crassly sentimental patriotism. In such a world, new forces of destruction require a new poetry to excoriate deceitful traditions:

> If you could hear, at every jolt, the blood
> Come gargling from the froth-corrupted lungs,
> Obscene as cancer, bitter as the cud
> Of vile, incurable sores on innocent tongues, –
> My friend, you would not tell with such high zest

> To children ardent for some desperate glory,
> The old Lie: Dulce et decorum est
> Pro patria mori.

Dulce et decorum est . . .: *it is sweet and becoming to die for one's homeland*

The ancestral voice of patriotism has been devalued and must be replaced by a new and bitterly accurate verse.

The intolerable division between conventional attitudes and the realities of war gave rise to the satirical works gathered in *The Old Huntsman* (1917) and *Counter-Attack and Other Poems* (1918) by Siegfried Sassoon (1886–1967). In the three volumes of his *Memoirs of George Sherston* (1928–36), Sassoon also suggested something of the mental distress that led him to write 'A Soldier's Declaration' in the hope of being court-martialled. In a world without meaning, self-destruction becomes a desperate gesture of revolt.

Sassoon was saved from what he later came to regard as the futility of such a proceeding by Robert Graves (1895–1985) who described the incident in *Goodbye to All That* (1929). This comedy of humours – the work of one of the war's survivors – refuses to dignify horror as tragedy, preferring instead to present the ultimately indescribable in terms of farce, caricature and sheer grotesque invention. 'The memoirs of a man who went through some of the worst experiences of trench warfare', Graves declared, 'are not truthful if they do not contain a high proportion of falsities.' Like other poets of the First World War, Graves discovered that when old criteria of truth have been destroyed – when the world lies in ruins about him – the modern writer must seek to create his own reality through his work.

This sense of coherence and truth lost in universal breakdown, along with the belief that the techniques of the writer offer the only means of structuring the random motions of consciousness, is again fundamental to the tetralogy of novels by Ford Madox Ford (1873–1939) collectively entitled *Parade's End* (1924–8). Ford was a friend of Henry James and a mentor to Conrad with whom he collaborated on two works of fiction. He thus has his place among the great experimenters of the decades either side of 1900. *The Good Soldier* (1915), a novel of upper-middle-class adultery, shows the dexterity with which Ford could manipulate point of view and suggest shifting consciousness. The novel is marred however by an airless perfectionism and an unlikely central situation. These shortcomings persist in the greater work, but *Parade's End* is a moving and important attempt to portray the collapse of the high but obsolete beliefs embodied in Ford's hero Christopher Tietjens.

Tietjens begins the work as a representative of received patrician values but ends it purely as an item in the consciousness of others. He thus moves from the pre-war society of the superb opening scene – a world where Tietjens's class and sex are masters in an empire as comfortable to them and as prestigious as a first-class railway carriage – to find himself eventually in a culture that has spun with terrifying completeness off the old, accustomed tracks. Amid the psychological horrors of trench warfare and sexual combat – the nightmare of embattled France and the insane cruelty of his wife – Tietjens has been endlessly humiliated and seen his inheritance of values destroyed.

The literature of chronicle has here given way to the recording of consciousness. The aristocracy has bowed to the meritocracy. The great house has been superseded by the bureaucratic nation state and chivalry has surrendered to the claims of the New Woman. Imperial Britannia, Ford realized, would no longer be able to usher in an era of peace to the strains of 'Land of Hope and Glory'. As Tietjens himself declares, after 1918 'there will be no more Hope, no more Glory, no more parades for you and me any more. Not for the country ... not for the world I dare say.' With the ending of the war, old Europe and its dynasties had collapsed: the Habsburgs crushed by the Treaty of Versailles, the Romanovs shot after the looting of their Russian palaces. The English and their empire, ceding influence to the Americans, were uncertain of their role and, Ford declared, 'fitted neither for victory nor defeat'. This, at its broadest, is the birth of the modern Western world.

2

'It was at home the world was lost,' wrote D.H. Lawrence (1885–1930) of the war. 'At home stayed all the jackals, middle-aged male and female jackals. And they bit us all. And blood-poisoning and mortification set in.' Lawrence's attack is sharp, but it is directed here at what he saw as symptoms of an altogether more pervasive *malaise* – the profound problems engendered in European civilization since the 1870s.

In particular, enormous rises in population had led to the unprecedented difficulties of mass socialization. Many people, intellectuals especially, felt threatened by a world where the bourgeois values of the market-place had replaced old, aristocratic hierarchies and where nineteenth-century ideals of progress seemed to be little more than a capitulation to herd values. The positivism that underlay both the expansion of science and the triumph of the machine appeared increasingly inert and materialistic, and this in its turn engendered responses based on irrationalism – on the unconscious, the vitalistic and the intuitive.

Philosophers such as Friedrich Nietzsche (1844–1900) had suggested that reason was powerless when divorced from passion and that in a world where God is dead man must exercise his will to power, assert his instincts and free himself for a life of creative activity. Lawrence himself was profoundly aware of these tensions and was convinced that the problems of the English in particular (the nationalism is typical of the period) lay in their resolute denial of the body and the life of the senses. In the exploration of these, Lawrence was to work a profound change in the nature and form of both poetry and the novel. It is this that helps make him one of the undisputed masters of twentieth-century literature.

Lawrence's early fiction suggests a number of these themes. Annable, the gamekeeper in *The White Peacock* (1910) for example, is 'a man of one idea; – that all civilization was the painted fungus of rottenness. He hated any sign of culture,' Lawrence continued. 'When he thought, he reflected on the decay of mankind – the decline of the human race into folly and weakness and rottenness. "Be a good animal, trust to your animal instinct," was his motto.'

Here is a first expression of a fundamental Lawrentian idea: the belief that modern men and women are ruinously trapped between nature and civilization. When the female embodiment of the latter triumphs, the man is destroyed. Annable himself sees the sophisticated and dominant woman – the embodiment of culture as opposed to nature – as being 'all vanity and screech and defilement'. As Lawrence wrote in his next novel, *The Trespasser* (1912): 'these deep, interesting women don't want *us*; they want the flowers of the spirit they can gather from us. We, as natural men, are more or less degrading to them and to their love of us; therefore they destroy the natural man in us – that is, us altogether.' In *The Trespasser*, Lawrence's Siegmund experiences an adulterous if hysterically repressed affair and then, returning to his cold wife, commits his second 'trespass' by killing himself.

Such melodrama is transcended in the greatest of Lawrence's early works – the autobiographical masterpiece *Sons and Lovers* (1913). The novel is set in Lawrence's familiar North-country mining community, a working-class environment he describes with great poetic precision. In addition, Lawrence's feeling for forces of life operating more deeply and powerfully than on the mere carapace of personality is rendered in a way at once lyrical and elemental. The hero's mother Mrs Morel, for instance, locked in the terrible battle between her own aspirations and her miner husband's earthy and ultimately extinguished 'sensuous flame of life', has far more than a purely social existence. Raising her head from the heavily scented lilies, we are shown her as a figure borne on tides at once unconscious and dangerous:

Mrs Morel leaned on the garden gate, looking out, and she lost herself awhile. She did not know what she thought. Except for a slight feeling of sickness, and her consciousness in the child, herself melted out like scent into the shiny, pale air. After a time the child, too, melted with her in the mixing-pot of moonlight, and she rested with the hills and lilies and houses, all swum together in a kind of swoon.

The identification of the mother with her son – the Oedipal situation which, largely independent of Freud, Lawrence was here exploring – is responsible for Paul Morel's dislocation from the world of his father and his inability to form satisfactory relationships with women. Miriam, for example, is both a rival and in some respects a simulacrum of Mrs Morel herself. When the older woman analyses her own jealousy, it is in words that are a comment on the threatening nature of both characters: 'She wants to absorb him. She wants to draw him out and absorb him till there's nothing left of him, even for himself. He will never be a man on his own feet –

she will suck him up.' It is such emotional sapping that the novel explores.

Paul becomes a moderately successful part-time painter. He temporarily abandons Miriam for the initially less troubling sexuality of the married Clara, but is finally obliged to recognize in his mother's presence that she herself will triumph over his feelings for all other women while she is alive. Mrs Morel, however, has the cancer which Lawrence was to suggest in a letter was an unconscious response to the emotional damage she has inflicted on her son.

After Paul has helped contrive his mother's euthanasia, he urges Clara to mend her marriage but finds sex with Miriam distressingly involved in 'the sense of failure and death'. With that quickening awareness of the multiplicity of truth Lawrence saw as one of the great potentials of fiction, Paul seems to blame this failure on Miriam even while his creator suggests that the horror Miriam herself feels stems from Paul's own inherent weakness. There is no apparent salve for these psychic wounds however, nor does Lawrence create easy sympathy in the reader for his increasingly complex and sometimes antipathetic hero. The uncertain ending of the novel nonetheless is suggestive rather than defeatist. It is alive with possibility. Turning from Miriam, Paul finally walks 'towards the city's gold phosphorescence', towards light and life. The concluding promise is thus of possible renewal.

The circumstances which led to the liberation Lawrence himself found in his relationship with Frieda von Richthofen-Weekley, the sometime wife of his tutor at Nottingham University, are charted in both the second part of *Mr Noon* (published complete 1984) and the wonderful volume of verse he entitled *Look! We Have Come Through!* (1917). Lawrence's 'Argument' in the latter work is frankly suggestive of his poetry's autobiographical content and contains a sentence full of implications for his mature fiction. 'The conflict of love and hate goes on between the man and the woman,' he wrote, 'and between the two and the world around them, till it reaches some sort of conclusion, they transcend into some sort of blessedness.' Conflict, transcendence and the hope of spiritual fulfilment become central Lawrentian themes. So too, expressed in a free verse of seemingly effortless control, does a sensuous joy unmatched in any English poet since Donne:

> She spreads the bath-cloth underneath the window
> And the sunbeams catch her
> Glistening white on the shoulders,
> While down her side the mellow
> Golden shadow glows as
> She stoops to the sponge, and her swung breasts
> Sway like full-blown yellow
> Gloire de Dijon roses.

By the summer of 1912 however, Lawrence was already cursing 'the snivelling, dribbling, dithering palsied pulseless lot that make up England today'. By the autumn of the following year he was in Italy writing a novel with the projected title of 'The Sisters', but in the middle of 1914, when he returned to England to marry Frieda, the couple found themselves trapped by the Great War. Its duration was to be a period of intense pain and humiliation for Lawrence, an agony later recounted in the 'Nightmare' chapter of *Kangaroo*. Nonetheless, out of this time were to emerge those revised versions of 'The Sisters' which constitute two of the supreme English novels of the twentieth century: *The Rainbow* (1915) and *Women in Love* (1920).

Lawrence was now convinced that the spiritual *malaise* which had led to the destructiveness of war derived from the English people's misunderstanding of the physical life. As a result, he believed that 'only through a readjustment between men and women, and a making free and healthy of this sex, will she get out of her present atrophy'. In both *The Rainbow* and *Women in Love*, Lawrence explored his radical doctrine that the spiritual is revealed by the sensuous, portraying it through an evocation of the successive marriages of the Brangwen family.

So original a purpose required a wholly new formulation of fiction itself, a concentration less on the externals of plot and character than on 'some unnamed and nameless flame behind them all'. In his 'Study of Thomas Hardy' (written 1914) and 'The Crown' (1915), Lawrence developed his ideas of continuously developing consciousness, of life flowering like the poppy rather than limiting itself to the static, the personal and the egocentric. 'When I assert an identity in the temporal flux,' he wrote, 'I become like a cabbage that folds over itself in its effort to contain the flux in static individuation.'

At the same time, in a letter to Edward Garnett, Lawrence

described his attempts as a novelist to get beyond 'the old stable *ego* of character' and so develop fictional means of realizing his concept of forces of life deeper and more potent than personality and social appearance. 'Again, I say, I don't look for the development of the novel to follow the lines of certain characters: the characters fall into the form of some other rhythmic form, as when one draws a fiddle-bow across a fine tray delicately sanded, the sand takes lines unknown.' Only in such ways, Lawrence believed, could he trace the developing relations between men and women at a fundamental level, expose his fears about society and then probe the possibilities of new ideals. The result of this revolutionary approach was a prosecution for indecency and the public vilification of its author.

Today, we can see the opening chapter of *The Rainbow* as one of the supreme achievements of Lawrence's prose. It is a passage in which he suggests the irrecoverable community between the ancient Brangwens and their land, a harmony at once potent, teeming and spiritual. Nonetheless, dissension is already clear in the longings of the women as they 'looked out from the heated, blind intercourse of farm-life, to the spoken world beyond'. The women desire more than the natural universe can offer and, in their ascendancy, begin to dominate their men. Sexual conflict has become established. Industrialism then adds social pressures to emotional ones, its encroaching rhythms having already become 'a narcotic to the brain' for Tom Brangwen and his generation. Tom's future wife Lydia, a woman of Polish origins, brings yet a further element of estrangement into his relations with the world. The couple's moments of mutual incompatibility are powerfully described, but out of such conflict emerge expressions of intense, reinvigorating intimacy.

Tom's relation to Lydia's daughter by her previous marriage is deepened in the marvellous scene that takes place during the birth of his own child. We here see Anna emerging as self-contained, dominating and rejoicing in the maternal – the combination of characteristics Lawrence had explored in Mrs Morel. Above all, Anna suppresses her sense of the numinous and the mystical, feeling these as a menace to her awareness of self – the stable, socially aspiring ego. As a result, although she at first finds Will Brangwen's sensual attraction at once stirring but a threat, his failure to lead her to where 'the sunshine blazed on an outside world' ruins their relationship.

Lawrence nonetheless describes their moments of aroused awareness with the intense prose-poetry he lavished on the great harvesting scene. Here, the plenitude, the eddying prose rhythms and the suggestions of simultaneous sharing and separation portray a relationship in which transcendence will be powerfully if spasmodically known. However, in the end, Anna rejects transcendent spiritual awareness. 'She would forfeit it all for the outside things.' Will, loathing the surface world because of the radiance he has glimpsed, swings between furious desire and moody lassitude until finally subdued by 'Anna Victrix' – the maternal, the worldly and the limited.

Ursula Brangwen, born of the triumphant mother and her father's 'black torment of unfulfillment', is one of Lawrence's supreme creations, the figure who must realize both self and oneness with the infinite, both the world and the spirit. An important stage in this self-realization is Ursula's affair with Anton Skrebensky. At its most intense, Ursula feels her sexuality pulsing with universal vitality, and in a passage of typically Lawrentian rhythm and imagery, he describes how 'she had the potent, dark stream in her own blood, she had the glimmering core of fecundity, she had her mate, her complement, her sharer in fruition'. Nonetheless, the dominance Ursula eventually achieves over a man she comes to realize is spiritually enfeebled destroys their relationship. 'She knew him all round, not on any side did he lead into the unknown.' For Ursula, the ego alone is inadequate compared to 'the unexplained, the undiscovered'. Her freedom to experiment physically is suggested by her all-female relationships, while the novel itself concludes with Ursula's belief that the commonplace industrial world must be transformed by the numinous – the gift of revelation and the new self symbolized by the rainbow.

The Ursula of *Women in Love* is an altogether more inward figure, a woman whose still budding life awaits the experience offered by Rupert Birkin, Lawrence's partial self-portrait and a character whose fluctuating irritability and aspiration voice many of his creator's sometimes unresolved concerns. For example, Birkin expresses Lawrence's intense belief in the natural wisdom of blood and flesh, 'the great dark knowledge you can't have in your head'. As a result, Birkin is deeply opposed to the mechanistic and life-suppressing social structure he sees as deriving from the denial of intuitive awareness. The novel itself draws much of its denunciatory energy from Lawrence's similar dismay at contemporary conditions.

'The stiffened, exhausted, inflexible loins of our era are too dry to give us forth in labour,' Lawrence wrote, 'the tree is withered, we are pent in, fastened, and now have turned round, some to the source of darkness, some to the source of light, and gone mad, purely given up in frenzy.' England is falling apart, a decay manifested in 'the ghastliness and mechanical, obsolete, hideous stupidity of war'. Against such social decay and the bankruptcy of old ideals, Birkin feels obliged to rear a personal, psycho-sexual concept of salvation: 'the old ideals are dead as nails – nothing there', he declares. 'It seems to me there remains only this perfect union with a woman – sort of ultimate marriage.'

Such a relationship cannot be achieved with a woman like Hermione Roddice – frigid, possessive, domineering and lacking spontaneity. Birkin rounds on Hermione in Ursula's presence, claiming that perhaps if he cracked her skull 'one might get a spontaneous, passionate woman out of you'. However, it is Hermione herself who eventually attacks Birkin at a house party and, after he has partly warded off her blow, he walks out into the countryside to renew his contact with the natural world by rolling naked in the flowers. In a way characteristic of the mature Lawrence, observation and symbolic narrative merge.

In contrast to Hermione, Ursula can respond to Birkin's 'wonderful, desirable life-rapidity' – she also realizes he can be the stiffest of prigs – but in the end she feels she is 'held to him by some bond, some deep principle. This at once irritated and saved her.' Lawrence shows that such a bond is not 'the mingling of love' in any conventionally romantic sense, though Ursula for a while confuses her feelings with this. Rather, she is involved in a relationship at once challenging and abrasive which may, nonetheless, finally attain Birkin's ideal of human balance and an independence in which 'The man is pure man, the woman pure woman, they are perfectly polarized. But there is no longer any of the horrible merging, mingling and self-abnegation of love. There is only the pure duality of polarization, each one free from any contamination of the other. In each, the individual is primal, sex is subordinate, but perfectly polarized.' Yet even this 'star-equilibrium' cannot provide complete psychological wholeness.

Birkin is exercised by 'the problem of love and eternal conjunction between two men'. This theme introduces a third major character in the book, Gerald Crich.

Gerald is a physically magnificent embodiment of aristocratic English manliness, a figure at once compelling yet thwarted by the efficient view of life with which he has revolutionized his mines and subdued his workers to a perverse satisfaction in the mechanical. Gerald's is thus a life of the will – of a man who can subdue his Arab horse to face an oncoming train, and who believes that the England he deeply cares for 'is artificially held *together* by the social mechanism', by work that is as mechanical as the society it creates. Such a defiance of the organic is seen in the novel as a form of the spiritual death which encircles Gerald himself in 'pale gold, arctic light' – the snow amid which he will eventually die.

Between Gerald and Birkin there is nonetheless 'a strange, perilous intimacy which was either hate or love, or both'. Birkin seeks to explore this, to enjoy the physical contact described in 'Gladiatorial', and to urge a blood-brotherhood which will be 'an impersonal union that leaves one free'. Gerald however retreats in fear and is lethally attracted to Ursula's sister Gudrun. 'They were of the same kind, he and she, a sort of diabolic freemasonry subsisted between them.' Theirs is a kinship of dominance and ultimately of death. Gudrun has already been exhilarated by Gerald's treatment of his horse at the railway crossing, but it is the chapter entitled 'Rabbit' that most cruelly suggests their self-debasing and unnatural compact. The couple's association of sex with death and of love with dominance is also vividly revealed when Gerald, panicked by the spiritual void left in him after his father's death, comes to Gudrun's room:

He had come for vindication. She let him hold her in his arms, clasp her close against him. He found in her an infinite relief. Into her he poured all his pent-up darkness and corrosive death, and he was whole again ... And she, subject, received him as a vessel filled with his bitter potion of death. She had no power at this crisis to resist. The terrible frictional violence of death filled her, and she received it in an ecstasy of subjection, in throes of acute, violent sensation.

Instead of star-equilibrium and freedom, there is spiritual eclipse and emotional death, that laceration of false sentiment and dominance seen again in the passage of mutual humiliation the couple endure in the *Gasthaus*. While Gudrun, mocking, malicious and destructive, pursues 'the very stuff of the underworld of life' with the reptilian denial of the true artist embodied in Loerke, a murderous Gerald wanders off into the snow to die 'fulfilled in the destructive frost mystery'. Only Birkin has offered him love, but Gerald has made the great refusal, and Birkin is finally left to tell a disbelieving Ursula how 'I wanted eternal union with a man too: another kind of love.'

Neither the Arnold-Bennett-like realism of *The Lost Girl* (1920) nor *Aaron's Rod* (1922) achieves the psychological and technical brilliance of *The Rainbow* and *Women in Love*. In these earlier novels, Lawrence had shown a sufficient control of his art for his work effectively to 'contain the essential criticism on the morality to which it adheres'. It avoided, that is, the dogmatic expression of those near-Fascist tendencies Bertrand Russell (1872–1970) detected in Lawrence's wartime letters and non-fictional works.

Aaron's Rod however, with its revolt against debilitated post-war society and the smothering woman, its affirmations of male separateness and its urging of 'a real committal of the life-issue of inferior beings to the responsibility of a superior being', is an ugly statement of doctrines Lawrence was also pursuing in *Psychoanalysis and the Unconscious* (1921) and *Fantasia of the Unconscious* (1922). Merging arcane notions of cosmology and physiology, and passionately asserting both individual uniqueness and a rejection of 'idealism', Lawrence here urges separateness of gender and ridding the race of 'mental consciousness' – all those consequences of conventional romantic sentiment he described as 'beastly benevolence, and foul good-will, and stinking charity, and poisonous ideals'. Such highly questionable notions are found again in *Sea and Sardinia* (1921), but much of the sheer lyrical beauty of this book – its assurance of a knowledge that is not acquired through the desiccating abstractions of science – makes it an admirable introduction to 'the delicate magic of life' evoked again in Lawrence's magnificent collection of poems: *Birds, Beasts and Flowers* (1923).

Among Lawrence's short stories, it is in 'The Captain's Doll' that his narrative symbolism is seen at its most effective. The little mannequin of Captain Hepburn made by the Countess Hannele is 'a perfect portrait of an officer of a Scottish regiment'. As the story develops however so it also becomes an image of that false and conventional sentimentality – the woman's making a man into a doll – which Lawrence saw as a denial of the depths of being and separateness on which a true relationship must be founded.

These ideas were given further development in the novels *Kangaroo* (1923) and *The Plumed Serpent* (1926). The first, written in a mere six weeks, evokes with impressive power the 'saurian torpor' of the Australian landscape in which Lawrence was briefly staying. It also registers, with a deal of anti-colonial snobbery, an antipodean world of mateship in which 'the women seem almost effaced'. Male dominance is again a major theme. Somers, involved with the right-wing Diggers, is Lawrence's tetchy self-portrait. He is a man who seeks to go beyond the social ideals of the ambiguously evoked Jewish lawyer Kangaroo and so find a new religion of 'lordship' in the worship of the dark God of 'the phallic self'. This is a faith which will, apparently, replace the outworn and emasculated Judaeo-Christian tradition. As Somers portentously declares: 'it is time for the Son of Man to depart, and leave us dark, in front of the unspoken God: who is just beyond the dark threshold of the lower self, my lower self'.

Such an exaltation of 'the lower self' becomes Lawrence's major subject in *The Plumed Serpent*. Set in the landscape beautifully described in his *Mornings in Mexico* (1927), the work takes Kate Leslie as its critic of an emasculated, post-war civilization in search of 'the slow, great change to something else'. In this case, the change takes the ridiculous and often repulsive form of the reincarnation of the Aztec pantheon dominated by Quetzalcoatl and here embodied in Ramon Carrasco and the suitably subdued Don Cipriano. Kate, as the avatar of the goddess Malintzi, marries Cipriano – her 'young and clean' Huitzilopochtli – amid costumed scenes of human sacrifice, sacred fire and what even Kate herself is occasionally obliged to admit is 'high-flown bunk'. She also watches Ramon's Roman Catholic wife destroyed amid this factitious exploration of the archaic mind. Her own experience of sexual wisdom finally consists in the willing suppression of female orgasm – Lawrence's old bogy of 'the seething, frictional, ecstatic Aphrodite'.

This is a doctrine modified in Lawrence's last and most notorious novel. *Lady Chatterley's Lover* (1928) returns to the north of England and to themes familiar from Lawrence's earlier work: the spiritual blight inflicted by the modern industrial world and the necessity of countering this through the natural wisdom of the body. It is this last that Lady Chatterley herself is perforce denied by a husband crippled in the war. His emasculation symbolizes what Lawrence himself called 'the paralysis, the deeper emotional or passional paralysis, of most men of his sort and class today'.

Constance Chatterley must be resurrected to a new life by the sexual tenderness possible only after initiation by the gamekeeper Mellors into 'phallic reality'. This alone, in Lawrence's telling play of imagery, can 'burn out the false shames and smelt out the heaviest ore of the body into purity'. Only the phallus, he suggests, can penetrate to 'the last and deepest recesses of organic shame'. For Connie, anal intercourse is a mystic rite which leads to freedom from inhibition, to an awe of the male and to the possibility of psycho-sexual rebirth. The novel itself, at first privately issued, only became generally available after the historic trial in 1959–60 which established artistic merit as a defence against alleged obscenity. Paradoxically, this was a judicial decision which heralded the sexual mores of the 1960s, and so a culture which Lawrence himself would almost certainly have found antipathetic.

For Lawrence's philosophy is not in the limited sense permissive. It does not allow anything but insists on the All. It is numinous with that chaste, apocalyptic vision, the knowledge of a mystic communion with the cosmic, anticipated by the heroines of 'St Mawr' and 'The Woman Who Rode Away'. It is a view beautifully suggested in both the ancient mysteries evoked in *Etruscan Places* (1932) and those late poems which celebrate the discovery that

> There is no god
> apart from the poppies and the flying fish,
> men singing songs, and women brushing their hair in the sun.

In 'The Man Who Died', Christ himself, resurrected into the fullness of redeemed physical life and making love to a woman 'who can lure my risen body, yet leave me my aloneness', becomes the true Lawrentian ideal. Life, fully understood, is freedom and the divine, the here and now hymned in *Last Poems* (1932) and experienced, finally, as *Apocalypse* (1931):

We ought to dance with rapture that we should be alive and in the flesh, and part of the living, incarnate cosmos. I am part of the sun as my eye is part of me. That I am part of the earth my feet know perfectly, and my blood is part of the sea. My soul knows that I am part of the human race, my soul is an organic part of the great human soul, as my spirit is part of my nation. In my own very self, I am part of my family. There is nothing of me that is alone and absolute except my mind, and we shall find that the mind has no existence by itself, it is only the glitter of the sun on the surface of the waters.

Lawrence's vision is ultimately a religious one: his awe in his belief that redemption is of the body and that eternity is here and now.

3

Wide reading in ancient mystery religions and modern spiritualist writers underlay *Apocalypse*, but Lawrence's fundamental purpose was not an academic one. 'What does the Apocalypse matter,' he wrote, 'unless in so far as it gives one imaginative release into another vital world?' The arcane and mysteriously potent life of the past leads beyond modern sterility, helping at once to expose and redeem contemporary existence.

Such a discovery is again fundamental to the work of W.B. Yeats (1865–1939), and his heroic attempt to find private, aesthetic and political coherence through the manipulation of myth and symbol in a world which, no longer sustained by conventional faith, appears otherwise meanly materialistic and incoherent. Yeats's poetry thereby becomes a response – a personal, idiosyncratic, yet profoundly sugges-tive response – to one of the greatest of modern issues: the problem of finding spiritual value in a world without God. The long develop-ment of Yeats's complex art is dedicated to such an end, and this helps in part to account for his exalted position in the history of modern poetry.

As Yeats wrote in *The Trembling of the Veil* (1922), after he had lost his Christian faith as a young man he 'made a new religion, almost an infallible Church of poetic tradition, of a fardel of stories, and of personages, and of emotions, inseparable from their first expression, passed on from generation to generation by poets and painters with some help from philosophers and theologians'. Such imaginary worlds were 'created out of the deepest instinct of man, to be his measure and his norm', and for Yeats they were most readily to hand in the stories he eventually published as *Fairy and Folk Tales of the Irish Peasantry* (1888). Such roots lay deep in his own childhood, while to the young man there also opened up 'all things Pre-Raphaelite'.

Yeats's first sustained success, *The Wanderings of Oisin* (1889), draws on Celtic narrative sources to create a poem reminiscent of Keats, Tennyson, Morris and Swinburne. As Yeats's Irish hero relates to a despairing St Patrick his adventures with the magical Nimah on three illusory island paradises, so he passes through what, at the end of his career, Yeats himself was to call 'vain gaiety, vain battle, vain repose'. Though the poem for the most part is repetitious, its concern with arcane mystery and with the opposition between Christian and pagan and between what, following Browning, Yeats was later to call 'objective' eras of obedience and periods of hierarchical, beauty-loving aristocracy are all themes of enduring importance to his mature poetry.

So too was Yeats's work as a playwright. *The Countess Cathleen* (1892), slight and occasionally reminiscent of Jacobean drama though it is, tells of a lady who, during a famine, sold her soul to the Devil to feed her people. The work is intimately connected with Maude Gonne, achingly beautiful and ardently nationalist, who was to absorb Yeats's emotions throughout his life. In the lyrics first published with the play and then reprinted in his *Collected Works* as *The Rose*, Maude Gonne is the embodiment of beauty and the inspiration of verses written to celebrate the Irish spirit.

The Rose also illustrates Yeats's widening researches into the occult. This last was pursued by him with considerable learning and was to admit some artistically invaluable developments. In the context of an age when Madame Blavatsky and the Theosophists were listened to by many and the occult was an interest among even the finest minds, Yeats's researches may seem less eccentric than at first appears. They were above all his means of apprehending the mystical, and 'the mystical life', he was to declare, 'is the centre of all that I do and all that I think and all that I write'.

In an increasingly materialistic age, these 'stylistic arrangements of experience' as Yeats chose to call them could provide classifications, polarities, structures and, above all, the imagery that a poet's intuition could translate into imaginative gold. The esoteric learning of the Rosicrucians, the pangs of misprized love, the folk magic of *The Celtic Twilight* (1893) and Ireland herself (sometimes sentimentalized as in 'The Lake Isle of Innisfree') now became central factors in his work. To these sources however were also added the influences of modern French poetry mediated through Arthur Symons's *The Symbolist Movement in Modern Literature*. The result was Yeats's volume *The Wind among the Reeds* (1899).

The poet of *The Wind among the Reeds* was still as much the follower of the Pre-Raphaelites as of Mallarmé however, as the exquisite 'He Wishes for the Cloths of Heaven' reveals:

> Had I the heavens' embroidered cloths,
> Enwrought with golden and silver light,
> The blue and the dim and the dark cloths
> Of night and light and the half-light,
> I would spread the cloths under your feet:
> But I, being poor, have only my dreams;
> I have spread my dreams under your feet;
> Tread softly because you tread on my dreams.

To move beyond this, purely beautiful though it is, required the pressure of greater and more varied forces. Among these was a deepening involvement with poetic drama. From the first decade of the twentieth century, Yeats was intimately connected with the work of the Abbey Theatre and the Irish theatrical renaissance. 'Players and painted stage took all my love.'

Yeats once declared that his interest in drama sprang from the wish 'to hear Greek tragedy spoken with a Dublin accent'. More modestly, in his Nobel Prize acceptance speech, he said he wanted to bring 'the imagination and speech of the country, all that poetical tradition descended from the Middle Ages, to the people of the town'. Nationalism, poetry and the idiom of the people were giving birth to an Irish dramatic movement focused on the Abbey Theatre. Here Yeats worked with those people who were to enter deeply into his personal mythology: the dramatist John Synge, the aristocratic patroness Lady Gregory of Coole Park and Maude Gonne who played the leading role in Yeats's play *Cathleen ni Houlihan* (acted 1902).

Like so much of the work of the Abbey Theatre, this drama is a political piece. Written in dialect and representing Ireland herself as an old woman who stirs the 'thoughts that men had felt, hopes they had died for', Yeats was to ask at the end of his career whether the play had sent out 'certain men the English shot' in the Easter Rising of 1916. Others of Yeats's early plays include *The Unicorn from the Stars* (acted 1907), a work which engages with the anarchy that shrilly enveloped Maude Gonne's brand of nationalism, while *On the Baile's Strand* (acted 1904) develops Yeats's mythological concerns and his interest in such character types as the poet, overlord, blind man and fool.

Yeats was to experiment widely with dramatic forms: with ideas taken from Japanese Noh plays, with esoteric symbolism – both of which contributed to *Purgatory* (1938) – and with the strange, haunting combination of seance, realism and prose seen in *The Words on the Window-Pane* (acted 1930). It is in the work of his fellow dramatist J.M. Synge (1871–1909) however that dramatic prose reaches a true poetic force and an exceptional exaltation of Celtic consciousness. This can be seen in *The Playboy of the Western World* (1907), a work that caused a riot on its first production. It is also to be found in *Riders to the Sea* (1904) where the dialect of the Aran Islanders reaches tragic intensity. Synge's unfinished *Deirdre of the Sorrows* (1910) uses legendary material, but it is a measure of the diversity of the Irish dramatic revival that Sean O'Casey (1884–1964) could write of urban life in plays like *Juno and the Paycock* (1925) and *The Plough and the Stars* (1926).

The volume of poems Yeats issued in 1904 as *In the Seven Woods* indicates many of the directions his art was now taking. Like his earlier publications, *In the Seven Woods* is usually read in the form he prepared for the 1908 edition of his *Collected Works*. This constant process of revision eventually offers Yeats's *oeuvre* as a considered sequence, a conscious working of personal emotion into an evolving but solid structure. Art is seen as an ordering beyond the reach of the random and chaotic, an artifice that both communicates its own considered values while allowing for a summing up before moving on to fresh developments. Integration – 'blood, imagination, intellect, running together' – becomes the ideal.

The title poem of *In the Seven Woods* refers to Lady Gregory's

Coole Park and hints at the life of patrician ceremoniousness that later poems would celebrate as a stay against the vulgar contemporary world. Yet even in this aristocratic paradise there is anxiety. Maude Gonne is turning grey, while the poet's veneration remains painfully that of a man in thrall to an archetype of female beauty. Love hovers on the edge of myth and knows 'The Folly of Being Comforted'. Lyrics of anguished disillusion follow, and they work with the new idiomatic directness that was to be praised by Lady Gregory's son-in-law, the American poet Ezra Pound. Such apparent ease was only achieved however by the hardest labour:

> A line will take us hours maybe;
> Yet if it does not seem a moment's thought,
> Our stitching and unstitching has been nought.

Art is both inspiration and conscious effort, and in the end it has a permanence denied to those who make it. The old Ovidian faith that his art outlives the artist moves to the centre of Yeats's vision in such poems as 'The Players Ask for a Blessing on the Psalteries and on Themselves'.

Such themes are greatly developed in four succeeding collections: *The Green Helmet* (1910), *Responsibilities* (1914), *The Wild Swans at Coole* (1919) and *Michael Robartes and the Dancer* (1921). This last volume in particular contains a work that draws several of Yeats's most potent motifs together and places them amid a moving and magnificent celebration of that life of friendship and high, deep-rooted civilization which Yeats associated with Coole Park. This poem, 'A Prayer for my Daughter', remains one of the supreme creations of twentieth-century poetry.

The work is set in Yeats's tower at Ballylee, the ancient stone-built home that was soon to become one of his most powerful symbols of ancestral value, an expression of a life lived among things 'the great and passionate have used'. Outside however the night storm screams of a new historical era soon to emerge from 'the murderous innocence of the sea'. Stone securities and untameable nature surround both the poet and his child. He prays for her, and such fatherly love, tender amid the changing cosmos, provides the poem's ground bass of elemental human feeling.

As Yeats imagines the coming of his daughter's womanly loveliness, so his thoughts are a prayer that she may have the kindly and intimate beauty of blessed ordinariness. In contrast, he fears the destruction inseparable, it seems, from the queens and goddesses of romance. Maude Gonne, evolving in Yeats's imagination as Helen of Troy or 'A Woman Homer Sung', is seen here as the anti-type of all that fatherly feeling could wish. By contrast, calm like that of his friend Olivia Shakespear is shown as the ideal of feminine courtesy. Such values are profoundly natural, and Yeats conveys this intuition through his image of a secluded tree burgeoning skywards from the earth and bright with birdsong. In such passages, the poem creates the sense of blessedness its speaker longs for, a unity with the world suggested through symbolism.

Hatred, by contrast – 'intellectual hatred' especially – destroys. It robs both the tree of its birds and the poet of his song. Maude Gonne once again enters the poem as both the Helen of Yeats's heart and the shrill politician shouting her 'opinionated mind' on the Dublin street corners. From the 'radical innocence' of Yeats's daughter, by contrast, there will hopefully flow a true abundance, the richness of the horn of plenty, the perpetual greenness of the laurel which is the poet's tree. In the end, love and a marriage founded on decorous convention fully and truly unite man and woman with the world. The concluding stanza of the poem is a vision of matchless dignity:

> And may her bridegroom bring her to a house
> Where all's accustomed, ceremonious;
> For arrogance and hatred are the wares
> Peddled in the thoroughfares.
> How but in custom and in ceremony
> Are innocence and beauty born?
> Ceremony's a name for the rich horn,
> And custom for the spreading laurel tree.

One has to go back to Spenser for such a celebration of marriage, to Jonson for such a praise of the ideal of nobility and to Coleridge for such deep, paternal love.

But for Yeats, outside the patrician, traditionalist circle of ceremony and innocence, there snarled the vulgar tumult of the street: the audience that booed Synge's *Playboy of the Western World* and which now threatened the very existence of Coole itself. To Yeats, the courtier in ancestral houses, the life-denying, catchpenny tradesmen of 'September 1913' show how 'romantic Ireland's dead and gone'. The modern crowd cannot nourish the roots of art, and 'To a Wealthy Man Who Promised a Second Subscription to the Dublin Municipal Gallery if It Were Proved the People Wanted Pictures' takes the Renaissance court of Urbino as its timeless model of true patronage. For Yeats, art is the flowering of an élite munificence, the expression of a culture that has no place in a bourgeois democracy. Rather, art finds its natural home amid the 'passion and precision' of the landed aristocrat or, by contrast, in the freedom of the beggar, the hermit and the fool. For the rest – even for the poet George Russell or 'A.E.' (1867–1935), author of a rudely inaccurate autobiography – the works of Yeats and his friends are less than nothing, 'a post the passing dogs defile'.

Against such philistinism stand the world of Coole, the members of the Rhymers' Club invoked in 'The Grey Rock' and, above all, Yeats's own devotion to the 'priceless things' that are his art. This last is the subject of some of his finest work from this period. 'The Scholars', for example, is a satire written out of a romantic poet's contempt for the dry-as-dust pedantry that extends its mortmain over passion. 'The Fascination of What's Difficult' displays a deep personal insight into the deadening effect that comes after too prolonged an immersion in an intractable art – in this case the drama – and the consequent longing to let Pegasus freely wing the air. The finest meditation on the poet and Yeats's abiding theme of his ageing self are to be found however in *The Wild Swans at Coole*.

The title poem, pellucid yet mysterious, holds within it Yeats's themes of the aristocratic life, passion and ageing, death and the orders of art and change, viewing these through an intuition that suggests without ever making explicit a fundamental relationship between the earth-bound and the sky mirrored in the water below.

Of the many deaths and losses in the volume, that of Robert Gregory in the First World War most profoundly affects Coole. The patrician ideal of high and heroic liberty, at once vigorous and refined, obliges Yeats to mourn him as 'our Sidney and our perfect man'. 'In Memory of Major Robert Gregory' and 'An Irish Airman Foresees his Death' are age's tribute to youth and the aristocratic hero celebrated by Yeats from his earliest work. The ageing poet of 'Men

Improve with the Years' however sees himself as no more than 'a weather-worn, marble Triton', his lust fed by fantasy and finding in the fact that the heart grows old one of his greatest themes. Maude Gonne, too, is the subject of his praise while also being the victim of time. The seven poems 'Upon a Dying Lady' deepen this pathos.

Juxtaposed to defeat however is a new, mystical sense of life struggling to find an identity. In particular, the poems in *The Wild Swans at Coole* begin to include material from *A Vision* (1925–37), Yeats's records of the automatic writing practised by his new wife Georgie Hyde-Lees. As with his earlier experiments in the occult, Yeats was to refine this turgid and sometimes embarrassing farrago into a 'lunar parable' which in turn prompted some of the greatest and richest poetry of the century.

The mystical elements in *A Vision* centre around astrology, celestial mechanics and Yeats's concepts of the Great Wheel, the Gyres and the Mask. Some account of their working is essential. The spokes of the Great Wheel, for example, are the twenty-eight 'phases of the moon' in Yeats's poem of that title. Ranging from the dark to the full of the moon, they represent all the types of the human personality. Those on the sun side are 'primary' or 'objective' men – scientists, business men, scholars, saints, and so on – while those more interestingly placed on the opposite side are 'subjective' or 'antithetical' people who must complete their natures by putting on the mask of their complementary type, an idea discussed in 'Ego Dominus Tuus' and 'Per Amica Silentia Lunae'. Yeats, who saw himself along with Dante and Shelley as the daimonic man of lunar phase seventeen, is drawn to intensity, to passionate simplification and to the transformation of desire into art. He imagines his ideal audience as the patrician, self-contained Irish fly-fisher, and

> Before I am old
> I shall have written him one
> Poem maybe as cold
> And passionate as the dawn.

The Gyres are to be imagined as two perfectly intersecting cones, the tip of the primary, objective and solar gyre touching the base of the antithetical, subjective and lunar one. Between these lie all the possible degrees of the combination of opposites that make up Yeats's essentially dynamic view of both the individual personality and the history of races. Yeats's is thus a theory of both self and society, and what, once we have set aside its naïve determinism, is remarkable about his system is the sophisticated relationship it encouraged with his own personality and his times. We now watch a great poet engage with both his nation and his self. Amid world war and 'Easter 1916' – the bitter Irish struggle to establish independence – Yeats sees how 'a terrible beauty is born'. In 'The Second Coming', the primary gyre of the self-effacing Christian era is at its turning-point and Antichrist now ushers in a new age:

> Turning and turning in the widening gyre
> The falcon cannot hear the falconer;
> Things fall apart; the centre cannot hold;
> Mere anarchy is loosed upon the world,
> The blood-dimmed tide is loosed, and everywhere
> The ceremony of innocence is drowned;
> The best lack all conviction, while the worst
> Are full of passionate intensity.

Such is the all-too-painfully recognizable modern era and the background to Yeats's next volume, *The Tower* (1928).

'*The Tower* astonishes me by its bitterness,' Yeats wrote. The volume must also astonish by the force of its heroic engagement with the destructive violence of modern civilization, by its passionate picture of an Ireland in the throes of civil war and by its images of an ageing man distracted by the torments of his heart and seeking desperately for symbols of self and artistic purpose.

'Sailing to Byzantium', the first poem in the volume, establishes these themes with tremendous force. Old age, recognizing its hopeless inability to be any longer part of a natural world at once fecund yet dying – a world which the poet's very separation allows him to capture in the phrases of a matchless art – seeks out a new and permanent life of the imagination. Byzantium and the impersonal art of a great and strong civilization lure him with a vision of 'the artifice of eternity'. The poet must now try to be integrated with something at once exotic and courtly, something beyond the reach of time. The tattered man must fashion the golden bird.

The real world, nonetheless, threatens such ordering with its intrusive chaos, and 'Meditation in Time of Civil War' presents 'a lamentation over lost peace and lost hope'. We are shown first the collapse of patrician gracefulness and then, in the second section, Yeats's tower itself, the symbolic and moral centre of a mind desperately searching for symbols with which to express a sense of worth in an era bent on self-destruction. One of the finest of these symbols is the Japanese sword given to Yeats by Junzo Sato. To be placed among the things 'the great and passionate have used', the 'changeless sword' is an ancient emblem of moral purpose. It suggests at once the razor edge of human endeavour and the perfect, timeless work created by 'an aching heart' amid a great ancestral culture. The force with which Yeats reveals his own emotional desperation, the pained honesty of the opening lines of 'The Tower' itself for example, makes such longings far more than mere aesthetic escape:

> What shall I do with this absurdity –
> O heart, O troubled heart – this caricature,
> Decrepit age that has been tied to me
> As to a dog's tail?

The chaos of the heart is a bitter complement to political chaos in a world enduring the ravages of change.

'My Descendants' acknowledges that Yeats's tower itself might remain in the mind at least as some witness of value amid historic change, and though the civil war may swagger right up 'The Road at my Door', perhaps the starlings and the honey bees building in the tower's stone crevices give some cause for hope. Nonetheless, a phantasmagoria of destruction, the contemporary chaos wrought as the turning gyres usher in historic change, leave us with a poet who can only turn back to his occult studies in the hope of finding some sense of purpose amid modern chaos and 'the innumerable clanging wings that have put out the moon'.

In such a world, art becomes increasingly unable to express the life on which it draws and, in 'Nineteen Hundred and Nineteen', Yeats suggest that all high traditions have gone. Drunken soldiers commit atrocities. Man the philosopher wakes to find that he and his fellows 'are but weasels fighting in a hole'. Art is no more permanent than a dancer's evanescent image. For the poet, there is only 'the half-written page' in a world where mockers and the depraved work the black magic of catastrophe. The poem is one of the great, terrible glimpses into the chaos that lies at the heart of the century. The age of Christ indeed gives way to that of the slouching 'rough beast', just as that time itself was preceded by the heroic age, the glory and destructiveness of the Homeric era whose birth is described in that supreme modern sonnet 'Leda and the Swan'.

Love and age, the poet's personal experience of passion and time, re-emerge as central themes in *The Tower* and of one of its greatest poems, 'Among School Children'. Here, at the centre of Yeats's volume, and with that universality of response which is one of the indications of his genius, the uncommunicating, broken images of 'Nineteen Hundred and Nineteen' and the personal anguish of 'The Tower' itself are superseded by radiant symbols of unity of being, of life glimpsed as a potent and flourishing whole. Beyond the educationalists' world of neat and pretty categorizations and the poet's reflections on youth and age, there comes to Yeats an image of self-delighting work, physical pleasure, radiance and joy:

> Labour is blossoming or dancing where
> The body is not bruised to pleasure soul,
> Nor beauty born out of its own despair,
> Nor blear-eyed wisdom out of midnight oil.
> O chestnut tree, great-rooted blossomer,
> Are you the leaf, the blossom or the bole?
> O body swayed to music, O brightening glance,
> How can we know the dancer from the dance?

This is an image powerfully contrasted to the partial visions of the earlier stanzas, yet it is an intimation – something aspired to – rather than an absolute assertion of knowledge. There is no assurance of its attainment, and the deep, subtle pathos the poem casts over the children lies, as Yeats wrote in a note, in 'the thought that life will waste them, perhaps that no possible life can fulfil their own dreams or even their teacher's hope'.

Finally, 'All Souls' Night' draws on *A Vision* to conclude the volume with an incantation to a spectral gathering and those modes of thought which, wound as intricately as mummy cloths, envelop the mind in eternity, allowing it to know both the howling of the damned and the dance of the blessed. A volume that began with lapidary images of art, descended to sufferings both private and public, stared into chaos and then elaborated an image of longed-for unity of being, ends with mortality as it hovers on the edge of time.

The Winding Stair (1933) also opens with ghosts – the remembered spectral beauty of Eve Gore-Booth and Con Markiewicz. Their loveliness has been destroyed, Yeats suggests, by time and the debasing popular politics again excoriated in 'The Seven Sages'. Yeats implies that both these forces attacking beauty are man-made ravages of the spirit. 'Man has created death.' At the conclusion of the opening lyric, Yeats sees himself as the arsonist of materialism burning up the bodily world in order that the spirit may be exalted. Such purgatorial fire is a repeated image in the volume and suggests the antinomies of body and soul – the opposing forces of the gyres between which, in these works especially, mankind seems destined to suffer.

The Winding Stair is not however a volume of unmitigated defeat. Indeed, it marks Yeats's progress towards an acceptance of the fullness of life that is to be the hallmark of his final volumes. 'A Dialogue of Self and Soul', for example, reversing an ancient preference for the ascetic, suggests the gradual triumph of the body's gyre over the soul. In particular, the second part of the poem celebrates in language at once astringent and colloquial the poet's acceptance of his reincarnation into the humiliations and distress of human existence. 'I am content to live it all again.' In the end, the taking up of such a burden is, for the poet, the true joy and blessedness of his vocation, his revelling in life's antinomies.

Nowhere is the crisis wrought by the antithetical gyres of body and soul explored with a richer or more subtle rhetoric than in 'Byzantium'. The ancient city, emptying in preparation for its nocturnal metamorphosis, becomes, as the sound of the great gong dies away, a phantasmagoria. The curve of a dome, silent and weightless in the moonlight, disparages everything except its own authority. Then, as 'the fury and the mire of human veins' evaporate, superhuman forms, barely embodied by the syntax that describes them, lead the newly arrived soul to the dance of abundance and purgation, the 'agony of a flame that cannot singe a sleeve'. The soul is completed, disembodied. Yet, by a paradox that goes to the heart of Yeats's volume, process is as vital as perfection. If fire is the ultimate, it is fed with the bodies borne by the euphoric energies of the dolphins as they plunge into the waters of materialism between life and the after-life:

> Astraddle on the dolphins' mire and blood,
> Spirit after spirit! The smithies break the flood,
> The golden smithies of the Emperor!
> Marbles of the dancing floor
> Break bitter furies of complexity,
> Those images that yet
> Fresh images beget,
> That dolphin-torn, that gong-tormented sea.

It is this vigour of man exultant between corrupt body and purged soul with which Yeats concludes the poem – the image at once heart-rending and mysterious of 'that dolphin-torn, that gong-tormented sea'. Though admitting the ascendancy of the soul, the last line of the poem suggests the ecstasy of bounding between water and fire, the body and spiritual perfection.

A more boisterous acceptance of the earthly life underlies the early lyrics in the section entitled 'Words for Music Perhaps'. Jack and Crazy Jane assert phallic intimacy against hypocritical denial, an earth-bound passion that is of both the body and the soul. 'Fair and foul are near of kin.' Love and 'the place of excrement' are one. It is 'A Woman Young and Old' however that remains the most beautiful of Yeats's lyric investigations of passion – perhaps the finest song cycle on a woman's love in English literature. The largeness of such a claim is justified by the pellucid and seemingly effortless imagery which describes a girl's awakening emotions. Her boy's hair, 'cold as the March wind in his eyes', causes the girl to put on the mask of coquetry and seek to satisfy 'the craving in my bones'. Thus freed by passion, the couple 'stare astonished at the sea', the mysterious potency of the physical world. Their love-making is both guilty and a pleasure, connecting them wholly each to each and, in the exquisite 'Chosen', to the forces of the cosmos as the boy circles his beloved like the sun. Sun and earth, light and dark, man and woman, merge in reminiscences of Shakespeare and Donne as the lovers meet and then part. But the body is finally defeated. Death is their passion's inevitable end and is presented as a universal and terrible wrong – a private tragedy and a cosmic outrage. Only the poet, uttering words from Sophocles' *Antigone*, is equal to the extremity of it all.

'The Gyres' which opens Yeats's *New Poems* of 1938 presents an impassioned, general picture of decline in a world where 'irrational streams of blood are staining earth'. Amid cultural and moral collapse however the poet now mourns neither for past graciousness nor for present vulgarity. Rather, in the confident belief that the turning gyres will one day restore his 'unfashionable' values, he rejoices in his knowledge that there is 'in the creative joy . . . an energy so noble, so powerful, that we laugh aloud and mock, in the terror or the sweetness of our exultation, at death and oblivion'.

Such for Yeats was 'tragic joy', and his magnificent 'Lapis Lazuli' takes this idea further. Yeats here suggests that, in a world of modern problems, the 'hysterical women' of the opening stanza foolishly reject the 'gay' arts of painting, sculpture, music and poetry for lesser and merely political solutions to human woe. They are unaware that the tragic hero, like the sculptor and the musician of the concluding stanzas, holds within his intensities an absolute acceptance that 'all things fall and are built again'. As a result, such women fail to realize that artists alone can take on the burden of the world and in tragic joy sing amid despair. The true artist's is a wisdom at once vibrant and philosophical against which, in a world ruled by the phases of the moon, politics is merely the art of the makeshift.

For Yeats, 'beautiful lofty things' included friendship as well as art, and 'The Municipal Gallery Revisited' places this generous idea against the political and artistic background of the Ireland Yeats and his contemporaries were trying to create, a culture at once patrician and peasant-like in its authentic simplicity and freedom from the modern bourgeois world. Among the portraits in the gallery is that of Maude Gonne, celebrated again in 'A Bronze Head' from Yeats's posthumous *Last Poems* (1939). This work brings the poet's meditations on her ageing to a climax. The wrinkled bust, lifeless in all but its terrible, penetrating eyes, suggests both private madness and divine possession – both psychological and spiritual trance. Winds of terrible emptiness seem to play over this shrivelled vision of a once beautiful woman, and the mysteries of her true identity – the relation between youthful beauty and horrific age, the gentle woman and the wild, soul-shattered activist – preoccupy the poet as his beloved becomes the embodiment of both private anguish and divine anger in a world wrecked by futile vulgarity.

Yeats believed that it is the passion of the artist which brings fully human meaning to the ideal forms underlying art. 'Only passion sees God,' Yeats wrote, and 'The Statues' again uses sculpture to meditate on how it is the artist who creates those evolving concepts of the ideal which embody and inspire a civilization: Greek beauty, Asiatic indolence, the heroic Celtic Cuchulain whose statue stands outside the Dublin Post Office where the Easter Rising began. It is not by their armies but by their embodiments of spiritual insight that nations rise or fall. Indeed, cut adrift 'upon this flitting modern tide', man can only be redeemed by artists creating images with which all may identify and so find heroic resolve.

But if men are to aspire Godwards, the immortals must in turn incline to man. 'News for the Delphic Oracle' offers a comic picture of 'the golden codgers' or the gods themselves satiated in the Islands of the Blest. At such a time, the gyre of the spiritual must give way to the mortal. The choir of celestial love must retune its note to the 'intolerable music' of Pan's orgiastic revelry and that copulation in the foam which gives birth to the heroic life and so to man extended to the ultimate of tragic joy.

Two major works at the opening and close of *Last Poems* define the poles of Yeats's late achievement. 'Under Ben Bulben' contains both his epitaph and his ideas of spiritual, artistic, national and personal fulfilment. These are in large part conveyed by the symbolic horsemen of the opening, people assured of the truth of immortality and rejoicing in 'completeness of their passions won'. Such figures derive from the Irish folk ballads told to Yeats by a servant in his childhood. They are also, as Yeats wrote elsewhere, 'that horde that will sweep down the mountains as the harbingers of a new phase of history'. It is one of their number whom Yeats addresses at the close of the poem, bidding him ride past his grave and on into the future.

The true Irish spirit it is here suggested must be tense and even violent in order to accomplish its destiny of going, as Yeats declared in his Nobel acceptance speech, 'below all that is individual, modern and restless, seeking foundations for an Ireland that can only come into existence in a Europe that is still but a dream'. To assist its birth, the great image-makers – the poets, artists and sculptors – must, especially in this corrupt age, abhor the modish and the shapeless. Confident in the assertion of such traditional values, Yeats himself can now rest among his ancestors and bid the horseman of the future '*pass by!*' In a way typical of much European social and political thought before the Second World War, the poem offers the ideal of the national destiny of a truly organic society — a race at once patrician, soil-conscious and visionary. Such values are held to be a talisman against the onslaughts of the modern world and an attack on its confused, debilitating herd values, the aimless anonymity of the mass and the market-place.

If beneath this reactionary nationalism there is a troubling suggestion of Yeats's commitment to eugenics outlined in *Under the Boiler* (1939), 'The Circus Animals' Desertion', true to the polarities of Yeats's art, suggests that his poetry has its foundations not only in political ideals but in the striving human spirit, the artist's need to find some relation between the sublimities of his craft and the common mess of personal feeling. In old age, and aware of 'being but a broken man', Yeats reviews his career. Acknowledging now that the myths he reanimated, 'masterful' though they seem, were fashioned as an escape from private anguish, he is forced finally to confront the squalor and incoherence that gave rise to his art in the first place. The imagination's images recede and, too frail now to aspire after them, the ageing poet is left with the ordinary human world from which all longing comes:

> A mound of refuse or the sweepings of a street,
> Old kettles, old bottles, and a broken can,
> Old iron, old bones, old rags, that raving slut
> Who keeps the till. Now that my ladder's gone
> I must lie down where all the ladders start
> In the foul rag-and-bone shop of the heart.

Yeats seems resigned to imaginative and physical decay, to death. The contrasts in the poem however, indeed the whole progress of this final volume from the epitaph at its opening to its longing for life and ardour in the concluding lines of 'Politics', refuse a wholly quiescent acceptance. Yeats remains to the end the poet of moral polarities, moving between vision and mundane reality like his great compatriot James Joyce (1882–1941).

4

In January 1900, Joyce gave a talk to the Literary and Historical Society of University College, Dublin. He lamented the passing of chivalry and romance, commented on the dullness of contemporary life and then added a crucial manifesto: 'I think out of the dreary sameness of existence, a measure of dramatic life may be drawn. Even the most commonplace, the deadest among the living, may play a part in a great drama.' From most seventeen-year-olds, such a statement might have seemed merely pretentious. For Joyce, it was a first declaration of an artistic aim which, in its developing, profound range and originality, was to make Joyce himself one of the heroic figures of the early twentieth century – the literary peer of Picasso, Schoenberg and Einstein.

The thirty-six lyrics gathered in *Chamber Music* (1907) give barely an indication of this promise. Borrowing from both the Elizabethans and the Symbolists, they tell of young love's failure, and offset literary reminiscence with mild irony. 'This suggestion of relativity', as the autobiographical narrator of Joyce's unfinished *Stephen Hero* (published 1944) declares, 'mingling itself with so immune a passion is a modern note.'

More truly modern are the series of prose 'Epiphanies' written at the same time but only issued posthumously. Here, drawing on the French realist and symbolist schools, Joyce attempted to invoke those moments which, once again, the narrator of *Stephen Hero* most aptly defines: 'by an epiphany he meant a sudden spiritual manifestation, whether in the vulgarity of speech or of gesture or in a memorable phrase of the mind itself. He believed it was for the man of letters to record these epiphanies with extreme care, seeing that they themselves are the most delicate and evanescent of moments.' The search for contemporary techniques in which to render such illuminations through the combining of realism, symbol and spiritual revelation is profoundly indicative of Joyce's maturing purpose. So too is his critical engagement with a sterile society.

This is seen again in his first completed prose work, the collection of short stories eventually issued in 1914 as *Dubliners*. Joyce himself provides the best description of his purpose here in a letter to his publisher:

My intention was to write a chapter of the moral history of my country and I chose Dublin for the scene because the city seemed to me the centre of paralysis. I have tried to present it to the indifferent public under four of its aspects: childhood, adolescence, maturity and public life. The stories are arranged in this order. I have written it for the most part in a style of scrupulous meanness.

The paralysis at the heart of the national waste land is the condition of the Irish themselves. Joyce sees their lives and aspirations as constantly thwarted by an oppressive and far from virtuous Roman Catholic Church as well as by the sycophancy and pocket-lining of small-time politicians in a country enduring oppressive English rule. He shows the squalor of the drink-sodden urban lower middle classes and, most subtly of all, the mountain of the dead who seem never to let the living go.

This constellation of ideas was crucial to Joyce's own endeavour to free himself for a life of artistic creation. Though his encyclopaedic intelligence was to relish scholasticism and the immense resources of the Roman Catholic tradition (Newman was a favourite modern stylist) Joyce personally rejected the priesthood as a way of life. He also decried the church's broader influence in Ireland which he saw as stunting what he believed was an already oppressively provincial society. He further condemned contemporary Irish nationalism, whether this was the aesthetic cult of the Celtic Twilight, the chauvinism of the Abbey Theatre when it decided to mount only Irish plays and so prohibit productions of his greatly admired Ibsen, or the oscillation of extreme violence and apathy he saw as characteristic of the political scene after the fall of Parnell – a figure who was to take on a Christ-like status in Joyce's eyes.

Childhood discovers death and paralysis in 'The Sisters' when a little boy hears of Father Flynn's demise from what might well be tertiary syphilis. The moral, spiritual and physical collapse of the church is both grotesque and sinister, as is two other little boys' meeting with an ineffective pervert in 'An Encounter'. The subject of 'Eveline', hesitating on the quayside and so perhaps fortunately not joining her lover in what he alleges is a plan to emigrate to South America, is yet again caught in the general Dublin paralysis.

'Ivy League in the Committee Room' is an excellently contrived satire on the state of contemporary Irish politics. Here we are shown time-servers going about their chilly little duplicities, while it is the absent and the departed figures who are more truly present than those we actually see or hear. In the end, the ghost of Parnell has more life than the living. But if the world of Irish politics is inert, its spiritual existence is grotesque. The sheer comedy of this is explored in 'Grace', originally the concluding story of the volume. Here, the adventures of a commercial traveller, as he is shown drunkenly falling in a public lavatory, recovering and then going to a business men's religious retreat, parodies the three stages of the Christian afterlife amid a welter of theological confusion. This combination of religious reference and modern banality is an important indication of developments to come.

The final version of *Dubliners* however does not close on this comic note but with one altogether more subtle and moving. 'The Dead' is Joyce's first assured masterpiece and one of the greatest short stories in the language. While his inspiration in *Dubliners* generally owes something to Chekhov, the personal development of a style of 'scrupulous meanness' emerges with particular power in 'The Dead'. It is both apt for its subject and immensely subtle in its variety of register. Scrupulous meanness becomes moral accuracy, the omniscient distance from their subjects cultivated by Ibsen and Flaubert. This virtue was later to be discussed by Joyce's hero Stephen Dedalus when he described the writer as one who 'remains within or behind or beyond or above his handiwork, invisible, refined out of existence, indifferent, paring his fingernails'.

It is such objectivity that allows Joyce in 'The Dead' to offer wholly without sentimentality Gabriel Conroy's discovery that his wife's affection truly belongs to a dead boy who once courted her. The young man's ghost now draws out the life of Conroy's own soul. The dead do indeed inflict their paralysis on the living, and Conroy's epiphany – his realization of truth – is expressed through one of the supreme passages of English symbolist prose:

A few light taps upon the pane made him turn to the window. It had begun to snow again. He watched sleepily the flakes, silver and dark, falling obliquely against the lamplight. The time had come for him to set out on his journey westward. Yes, the newspapers were right: snow was general all over Ireland. It was falling on every part of the dark central plain, on the treeless hills, falling softly upon the Bog of Allen and, farther westward, softly falling into the dark mutinous Shannon waves. It was falling, too, on every part of the lonely churchyard on the hill where Michael Furey lay buried. It lay thickly drifted on the crooked crosses and headstones, on the spears of the little gate, on the barren thorns. His soul swooned slowly as he heard the snow falling faintly through the universe and faintly falling, like the descent of their last end, upon all the living and the dead.

Realized with intense physical immediacy, the snow is at once a benediction and a valediction — a quiet smothering of the land and soul of Ireland in a gentle yet deathly paralysis.

The artist himself must refuse such living death in order that he may 'forge in the smithy of my soul the uncreated conscience of my race'. This is the theme that underlies the fragmentary *Stephen Hero* and its metamorphosis into *A Portrait of the Artist as a Young Man* (1916). The title of the completed work is particularly apt, for it was part of Joyce's maturing genius so to present his autobiographical material that he both establishes his Olympian sense of vocation while showing the growth to maturity of a young man rich in the pain and confused conceit of youth. This he achieves in part by a variety of language that obliges us to recognize how all-pervasively linguistic the writer's experience of the world is. From the radical use of baby-talk at the start to the cadences of Newman and Pater at the close, Joyce's symbolically named Stephen Dedalus is caught in a labyrinth of languages, and only the realization that, as an artist, he may at last be able to create his own speech frees him from the oppressive maze of other people's words.

Experience is scrupulously registered in terms of Stephen's evolving consciousness, and one of the first languages that impinges on this is the deadly stridency of politics as his father and aunt Dante quarrel over the Christmas dinner. To words is then added the untransformed beastliness of the physical world: bed-wetting, the brutality of a football game and the unjust, excruciating punishment meted out at school by the prefect of studies. The artist, Ibsen taught, will always be persecuted by a world he must transform. Stephen challenges the ignominy of the punishment inflicted on him, and in a boys' world the heroics of boys' stories provide the literary language for exploring this.

Soon however Stephen goes through another linguistic development. 'Words which he did not understand he said over and over to himself till he had learnt them all by heart; and through these he had glimpses of the real world about him.' Adolescence plays exuberantly with its growing sense of potency, finding in the language of romantic fiction and schoolboy gossip images of sex. But neither the language of a school play nor that of a prize-winning essay is sufficient to contain Stephen's burgeoning desire for experience, and he precociously and promiscuously begins to visit the brothel quarter.

The tremendous sermon on hell that follows is an appalling revelation of the church's power to bring into action the rhetoric of the spiritual bully. Through its rites it also claims to transform the physical into the metaphysical and so offers a tempting but false vocation to Stephen the 'priest of the eternal imagination'. On the verge of a Christian calling, Stephen narrowly escapes apostasy by feeling the pressure of real life about him. 'The faint sour stink of rotten cabbages came towards him from the kitchen gardens on the rising ground above the river. He smiled to think that it was this disorder, the misrule and confusion of his father's house and the stagnation of vegetable life, that was to win the day in his soul.'

The artist needs an aesthetic however, and Joyce has the undergraduate Stephen elaborately spin one out of Aquinas and Ruskin. But Stephen's aims are most truly brought together in his moment of epiphany on the beach. Here his untrammelled soul takes flight as a glimpse of an unknown girl seems to hold sky and earth together in a moment of perfect synthesis. He is at last enabled to utter the language of his own poetry: 'a day of dappled sea-borne clouds'. Stephen's discovery of the power of his own language (that it is, in fact, deeply dependent on Pater is part of Joyce's fathomless subtlety) gives him an elated sense of vocation. Soon, he will be able to assert the full force of his authenticity:

I will not serve that in which I no longer believe, whether it call itself my home, my fatherland, or my church: and I will try to express myself in some mode of life or art as freely as I can and as wholly as I can, using for my defence the only arms I allow myself to use – silence, exile, and cunning.

In this defiant independence, the young man becomes the young artist, a Daedalus freely flying above the labyrinth of social constraint and other people's words. He is transcendent, exiled and visionary amid the 'dreary sameness of existence' from which, nonetheless, he must pluck the matter to transform into art.

But for Stephen art is still poetry, and the Stephen who reappears in *Ulysses*, first published after immense and long-continued difficulty in 1922, is the uncertain poet now returned to Ireland from France. He continues to be harassed by the social and political constraints his inheritance forces on him and, above all, by the pervasive sense of guilt inflicted on his conscience as a lapsed Roman Catholic who has refused to make a confession of faith at the bedside of his dying mother.

Intensely and even obsessively intellectual, embittered and confused, Stephen will, during the course of Joyce's fictional re-creation of 16 June 1904, explore a range of the experiences open to the impoverished young Dublin intellectual. He will pass from involved speculation to physical debauch and, in the process, encounter the novel's central character, Leopold Bloom. Stephen will be taken to Bloom's home but eventually leave the older man's orbit while Bloom himself moves ever closer to the sleeping, dreaming body of his unfaithful wife to end the novel curled in foetal slumber beside the reveries of this image of the all-accepting earth.

Bloom is thus the Ulysses indicated by the work's title. He is the traveller home from his day's and lifetime's wandering the Dublin world. His wife Molly is Penelope, while Stephen suggests Telemachus, the son seeking the father. Between the morning and night of a single day, and in the eighteen sections of the work, the adventures of Stephen and Bloom will recapitulate the tripartite action of the *Odyssey* itself: the Telemachia or the search of the son, the wanderings of Odysseus and finally the Nostos or homecoming.

But *Ulysses* is notoriously more complex than this simplified account suggests. Some way into writing it, Joyce developed his purpose and revised his earlier chapters in the light of his ambitious aim to create 'a kind of encyclopaedia'. This suggests that contained within *Ulysses* is a series of allusions and techniques altogether more complex than the parallels manipulated between Homeric epic and the contemporary world. A convincing case has been made out for scriptural references which relate Stephen and Bloom to the narrative of the New Testament and, in the Nostos especially, to the Passion and the three regions of the Christian afterlife. Since Joyce declared *Ulysses* was the epic of two suffering and often alienated races – the Jews and the Roman Catholic Irish – such parallels are appropriate.

In addition, each section of the novel also contains its characteristic part of the body, colour and ruling art or 'technic'. Further, leitmotivs or repeated verbal clusters help, in the manner of the repeated musical phrases in Wagnerian opera, to weld each section into the work's totality. Joyce's encyclopaedic interests also spread out into the minutely described topography of Dublin, to the intricacies of Irish history and to the disastrous effects of nationalistic violence. Finally, he shows an intense interest in all physical and mental activities, from evacuation, masturbation and menstruation to the mind's conscious endeavours at philosophy and literary criticism and its constant, unconscious play of memory and desire.

In terms of the novel's literary techniques, Joyce's radical experimentation ranges from the so-called 'stream of consciousness' or the internal monologues through which he establishes the inner being of Stephen and Bloom in eight of the nine opening sections, to his fantastic engagements with rhetoric, sentimental romance, historical stylistics, fugue, counterpoint and expressionist drama. Faced with such all-inclusive variety, the reader of *Ulysses* is tempted to murmur with Stephen himself as he stares bewildered at the sea: 'signatures of all things I am here to read'.

In the novel itself, as the reader who has advanced some way with it will know, the sea is, in the Homeric analogy, Proteus, the ever-changing god. Proteus' symbol is the tide of the natural world, while philology is the chapter's 'technic'. The 'signatures' refer to the evidences of the divine that God (according to Jacob Boehme) has implanted in his works so that the spiritual eye may read the signs of their Creator's purpose. As in the world, we may say, so in the book. We are here to interpret a cosmos, a myth and a physical existence.

And it is the real world that is so magnificently present in the Telemachia. By the time Stephen has begun his walk on Sandymount beach (11.00 a.m. on 16 June 1904 to be precise), Joyce has already presented aspects of both his day-to-day existence in the Martello tower and his grinding work as a schoolmaster, doing so with vivacious and subtle all-inclusiveness. Here indeed is Joyce's matchless ability to make the reader aware of a life-giving sense of the ordinary as it blossoms in individual minds, minds borne along on currents and preoccupations which are at once their own, their nation's and experiences which, the literary allusions suggest, are to be faced over and over again in all the cycles of human history.

Here, specifically, we see Stephen the broke and guilty young man, the Irishman wanting to escape the influences of nationalism and the church, and the Telemachus who is searching for a true father. By extension, he is also the Jesus-artist figure thwarted by the English devil Harris and the incomplete, cynical Mulligan. Only when Stephen has met Bloom his spiritual Father will he be able truly to become the Son and so allow the Holy Ghost of literary inspiration to be manifested. Neither the gold nor the inaccurate racial bigotry of Mr Deasy the garrulous headmaster (the Nestor of the Homeric analogy) must distract him. For the moment, however, Stephen can only stare at the flux of the waves, a frustrated mind ill at ease in an uncomprehending natural world.

While Stephen is walking on the beach, Leopold Bloom is attending Paddy Dignam's funeral. In terms of the Homeric parallel, the scene represents the hero's visit to the underworld. What is so powerfully engaging about the episode however is its exceptional evocation of Bloom's idiosyncratic and minute-to-minute selfhood, the density and quick associations of his mental and physical life. Amid the jocularity, anger and unthinking anti-Semitism of the other mourners, and in response to their careless discussion of suicide especially (Bloom's own father killed himself), Bloom remains placid, looking for the good, exposing the pompous through his comic humanity.

His response to the priest and the funeral service, for example, reduces what in his eyes seems a superstitious and mechanical ceremony to the absurd. 'Said he was going to paradise or is in paradise. Says that over everybody. Tiresome kind of a job. But he has to say something.' The Roman Catholic Church is, as ever, woven through this scene along with the constant pressure of Irish politics. Bloom's responses to these last are not the cant and lies of the group and the crowd. They come out of his own battered and rather commonplace self, a self that is nonetheless so intimately shown and sympathetic that Bloom does indeed become the modern hero – the hero as Everyman in his unique selfhood and constant eddying life. A world without God and an afterlife has no meaning beyond itself, but this is not in Bloom's case a cause for sentimental pessimism. A Bloom, a flower, a Jew lightly rooted in Irish soil, commonplace and doomed to fade, he quietly asserts the albeit troubled worth of sheer living. A Ulysses navigating the tides of existence, here, in the midst of death, he is in life.

And his life is one we know with a wonder-working richness and intimacy, a completeness which the opacities and discretions of normal existence, the incommunicable quick privacies of other beings, almost invariably deny. Riding the stream of his consciousness, we have watched Bloom as he prepares breakfast for the wife who is at once Calypso the ensnaring enchantress and, later, Penelope the faithful: Molly Bloom, professional singer, slattern and object of consummated desire to Blaizes Boylan. Infidelity is also the subject of Joyce's play *Exiles* (1918), and in *Ulysses* we are again in the realm of the body and a cuckolded, early-middle-aged man, patient amid the disappointments of his frowsty household, mature in his acceptance, a Ulysses metamorphosed into the wandering Jew.

After food comes defecation, and after wiping his bottom on *Tit-Bits* comes the ten-o'clock warmth and gentle lotus-eating of Sir John Rogerson's Quay and the letter from Martha Clifford with its coy, onanistic fantasies. Bloom is a fetishist, the physical side of his marriage having ended after the death of his son. This exploration of his fantasy life marks the historic entry of the Freudian unconscious into literature. The mind is borne on currents both familiar and perverse, and dreams of abasement and flagellation, of society ladies digging their spurs into Bloom's flesh 'up to the rowel', are as real to him as the Dublin streets themselves. Bloom's thoughts of his body in the bath bring us to the presiding organ of this section and fuse fantasy with the physical.

After the funeral and the body in its little sadnesses, shame-joys and defeats, comes work and one of Joyce's great technical innovations. Bloom has a small job in advertising − one of the lowest forms of literature if we discount the writing of mildly titillating romances to which Bloom also aspires − and this takes him to the offices of various newspapers. Here Stephen will also be found. The highest and the lowest in literature briefly coincide in the cave of Aeolus, the wind god of the hacks.

The special 'technic' of this section is rhetoric, the framing of public speech. The passage is itself constructed around the six parts of a classical oration and takes examples of oratory in both the high and low styles as its subject matter. Joyce here plays with the linguistic theory underlying the giving of speeches and proves through a fantastication of wind imagery that all rhetoric is hot air. The whole passage, in the words of the sports writer, is 'Clamn dever' (the spoonerism must play its part in this anthology of linguistic abuse) but if some find its ingenuity irksome, it is also important to see the passage as the very foundations of humanism blowing themselves to bursting point before a new and truly modern literature can be written.

After the heroically disgusting episode with the Laestrygonian cannibals (lunch, in fact), Bloom, aware that his wife's adultery is soon to occur, goes on business to the National Library where Stephen is holding forth on literature with an argument about the biographical basis of Shakespeare's art and, in particular, the importance of the relation of father to son. The whole is a sustained passage of dense allusion brilliantly suggesting a mind of the highest order still not in sympathy with itself and expressing the very need for a father that is the subject of the discourse. Before the son and the father of the novel meet in the phantasmagoric hell that is the 'Circe' episode however, Joyce offers more.

Three of these sections – the 'Wandering Rocks', 'Sirens' and 'Cyclops' – present a vast panorama of Dublin itself. In the first we see its citizens navigating between the twin dangers of the church and the state, while the 'Sirens' episode sophisticates Joyce's technique of mingling the myriad voices of the novel into what is the literary equivalent of a musical fugue. It is 'Cyclops' however which offers one of Joyce's most powerful treatments of the theme of voices, here the oppressive voice of Irish nationalism and insular hatred satirized in the figure of Homer's one-eyed giant. Polyphemus has here been metamorphosed into 'the citizen' who mouths an oafish triumphalism that is at once deflated by the welter of Joyce's Rabelaisian literary techniques and Bloom's own modest affirmation of 'Love . . . I mean the opposite of hatred.'

Where the styles of 'Cyclops' are those of a debased politics, those of 'Nausicaa' parody a debased literature. 'Far away in the west the sun was setting and the last glow of all too fleeting day lingered lovingly on sea and strand.' Joyce's name for this threadbare style of popular literature was 'tumescence'. The eye is the organ of the chapter, and Gerty MacDowell's underwear becomes the object of Bloom's fetishistic fantasies, fantasies which eventually cause him to masturbate in a darkness lit up by a firework display. In his unfertilizing, post-orgasmic sadness, Bloom prepares us for a greater expense of spirit in a greater waste of shame as well as for the profound themes of birth, resurrection and Stephen the artist's progress towards that recognition of the Father whereby the Trinity is completed and the Holy Spirit of true art may hover redeemingly over the world and its words.

In Homer, the slaughter of the Oxen of the Sun is an act of blasphemy. In *Ulysses*, these beasts are symbols of fertility, of the creative principle in life and literature. Stephen himself is the 'bullock-befriending bard', but now he has joined his drunken medical school friends at the maternity hospital prior to an expedition to the brothel quarter. On the one hand is birth, on the other non-procreative sex. There is also Bloom, father of father-figures, who has come to the hospital out of sheer kindness to witness the birth of a friend's child. The processes of literary and physical gestation are suggested by Joyce's artful (for some merely factitious) evocation of events through a re-creation of the history of the English language. Female Latin here mingles with muscular Old English, and from this union springs all literature from Malory to Carlyle. As is the growing language, so is the evolving foetus. Stephen however, drunk and sexually eager, opts for sterility among the whores. He turns against creativity, but the ever-protective Bloom follows him to the brothel quarter and into Joyce's great experimental drama of sex and the unconscious – 'Nighttown', where the enchantress Circe turns men into swine.

Just as in Freudian interpretation dreams have a manifest and a latent content, a surface narrative and a deeper personal application, so also Bloom's hallucinations – his fetishes and flagellations, his encounters with figures of the day and of the more distant past – are offered here through a series of grotesque incidents which incorporate both the profoundest layers of his being as well as the motifs he has been involved with during the recent hours. 'Nighttown' is a creation of extraordinary virtuosity. On the purely psychological level, it is further enriched by Krafft-Ebing's belief that sado-masochism such as Bloom's is the source of all deviation. Bloom's fantasies conform to many of the standard types of mental disease then recognized from anxiety to the schizophrenia apparent in his imagined change of sex.

But if this episode is the greatest of literary explorations of the unconscious – a supreme twentieth-century glimpse into the chaos of the irrational – Stephen's fantasies are a black mass, a vision of the end of the world, a dance of death during which his mother rises terribly from her coffin 'in leper grey with a wreath of faded orange blossoms and a torn bridal veil, her face worn and noseless, green with grave mould'. But the dead and the Roman Catholic Church must both be cast off. The true artist is bound, like Wagner's Siegfried, to forge 'Nothung' or the sword 'Needful' and free himself from the constraints of time and place:

STEPHEN: *Ah non, par exemple!* The intellectual imagination! With me all or not at all. *Non serviam!*

FLORRY: Give him some cold water. Wait. (*She rushes out.*)

THE MOTHER: (*Wrings her hands slowly, moaning desperately*) O Sacred Heart of Jesus, have mercy on him! Save him from hell, O divine Sacred Heart!

STEPHEN: No! No! No! Break my spirit all of you if you can! I'll bring you all to heel!

THE MOTHER: (*In the agony of her death rattle*) Have mercy on Stephen, Lord, for my sake! Inexpressible was my anguish when expiring with love, grief and agony on Mount Calvary.

STEPHEN: *Nothung!*

(*He lifts his ashplant high with both hands and smashes the chandelier. Time's livid final flame leaps and, in the following darkness, ruin of all space, shattered glass and toppling masonry.*)

THE GASJET: Pwfungg!

The Irish situation, the nightmare of history from which Stephen has been trying to escape, must finally be discarded. While the forces of family and church have been overcome by Stephen's heroic '*non serviam*', Irish nationalism works its repulsive end in the lurid death of the Croppy Boy. For the artist however, there remains the mental struggle to clean consciousness of its staining inheritance. As Stephen tells Bloom as he taps his brow: 'but in here it is I must kill the priest and the king'. Father and son, Irishman and Jew, mind and body, have finally met. In taking on the role of the artist, Stephen is both a fully human man and Christ the son.

As such, crucifixion awaits him. Privates Carr and Compton, the forces of English imperialism, are, in this book of voices, the lowest levels of speech and the basest reaches of humanity. The Roman soldiers on Calvary mock their redeemer: 'PRIVATE CARR: (*With ferocious articulation*) I'll do him in, so help me fucking Christ! I'll wring the bastard fucker's bleeding blasted fucking windpipe!' Christ is recrucified as Stephen is knocked to the ground. Only Bloom can take the fainting young man away in that moment at once moving and sentimental when Stephen becomes both Bloom's spiritual son and his own Rudy, the dead child of his loins.

After the Crucifixion come the rest of Good Friday, the stages of the Passion liturgy leading to Easter Sunday, Christ's descent into hell and the Resurrection – inferno, purgatory and paradise. After the escape from Circe comes the Nostos or homecoming. Such, in part at least, is the schematic background as Bloom takes the barely conscious Stephen across Dublin to his home in Eccles Street. Both men are tired, and in the cabman's shelter where they rest, their minds wander the inferno of cliché. Voices, words and literature are threadbare. This is the writer's hell, properly terrifying and one of Joyce's most threatening achievements.

'Ithaca', the penultimate section of the novel, is a catechism, a reduction of the world through question and answer to its essential physical attributes. As Joyce's 'ugly duckling', this was a passage he came to prefer above even the 'Circe' episode. The experienced reader of the book might agree while being unable to account for the fact that it also verges on the inexpressibly moving. Stephen and Bloom, sipping their cocoa and desultorily talking, become planets briefly circling each other. The 'technic' of the chapter is, appropriately, astronomy. Perhaps it is this scrupulous objectivity, Bloom's knowledge after Stephen's departure of both 'the cold of interstellar space' and his own place within this – the world of ugly but domestic and cosy furnishings and of slightly shameful things hidden in drawers – that is so affecting. Here is a purgatory where the feverishness of the commonplace is absolved and where there is hope because of human contact achieved, rebirth suggested and, above it all, 'the heaventree of stars hung with humid nightblue fruit'.

Stephen has found a measure of redemption through contact with the ordinary. The meeting of Father and Son creates the Holy Spirit of art. Bloom meanwhile, earth-bound man, must find his particular salvation, his own redemption, in the all-accepting and life-affirming processes that are the earth itself – Molly Bloom in her dream of consciousness knowing herself as both a sexual being and a mystic rose:

I was a Flower of the mountain yes when I put the rose in my hair like the Andalusian girls used or shall I wear a red yes and how he kissed me under the Moorish wall and I thought well as well him as another and then I asked him with my eyes to ask him again yes and then he asked me would I yes to say yes my mountain flower and first I put my arms around him yes and drew him down to me so he could feel my breasts all perfume yes and his heart was going like mad and yes I said yes I will Yes.

Faced with such plenitude, the heart knows it can be whole.

But Molly Bloom, flower of earth and rose of the only heaven we can know, was not Joyce's final creation. Bloomsday yields to night, and the epic of the night is *Finnegans Wake* (1939). *Finnegans Wake* nonetheless defies ready description and all too often baffles analysis. It is a book into which the literature of the world has been poured along with its words, its myths and its music. The cycles of history and the turnings of the dreaming mind weave a language of pun, of allusion and ultimately of high poetry for a consciousness absorbed in universal sleep. And it is with Joyce the encyclopaedist in exile, dreaming of Dublin and its rivers while time flows into eternity, that we must leave him – 'beside the rivering waters of, hitherandthithering waters of. Night!'

5

The older generation of English writers who published during the First World War and its aftermath point to the enormous disparities of tradition and innovation in the period. The year that saw the first edition of *Ulysses* also saw Housman's *Last Poems* (1922) and Hardy's *Late Lyrics and Earlier*. Hardy's *Winter Words*, that volume which so movingly witnesses to the continuities between Victorian disillusion and the modern world, did not appear until 1928. In drama, 1922 also saw the first production in New York of Shaw's 'metabiological Pentateuch', *Back to Methuselah*. These five plays are a laborious examination of Shaw's views on Creative Evolution and the Life Force, and are in the strongest contrast to his greatest work, *Saint Joan*, published the following year.

Though sufficiently effective as a historical pageant, *Saint Joan* is a deeply felt, highly entertaining and ultimately tragic analysis of the Life Force conceived not as an arid abstraction but as a truly vital principle. Interpreted by Joan herself as the voice of God, her spiritual intimations give this simple country girl the combination of innocence and moral grandeur by which she can at first overcome the rebuffs of a ridiculously prejudiced male world and then lead France to victories over the English. Shaw thereby develops two favourite themes: women's ability to see through the self-deceit of men and the unmasking of the more ludicrous excesses of English nationalism.

These last are memorably embodied in Warwick, but Warwick's dialogue with the Bishop of Beauvais points forward to the cruel and self-defeating machinations whereby men and their institutions invariably conspire against the Life Force and whoever embodies it. The destruction of Joan at the hands of the politicians and the Inquisitor is thus the withering of her destroyers too. Joan's personal tragedy is deepened by the fact that it represents men's inveterate attempts to poison and seal off 'the fountain of inspiration which is constantly flowing in the universe'. Shaw himself was never to equal the combination of comedy, deep feeling and intellectual coherence achieved in *Saint Joan* however, and his later political fantasies are works of declining power.

Among the older writers of fiction, Kipling dealt with the war in short stories that are often of exceptional formal and emotional subtlety. 'A Madonna of the Trenches' is one such, and if the conclusion of 'The Gardener' is slightly too contrived and sentimental, it nonetheless suggests the masterpiece contained in *A Diversity of Creatures* (1917). This story, 'Mary Postgate', offers an extraordinary insight into the heart barbarized by loneliness, by the male chauvinism of the pre-war upper middle classes and by the actions of both English and Germans in the war itself. As the heroine burns her dead and callous beloved's effects, so she ignores the crashed and dying German airman who has just bombed near her village. The insoluble moral dilemma and the flowering of Miss Postgate in her triumph of hate are Kipling's expression of the moral damage inflicted on ordinary people by the cruelties of sex, class, war and racial hatred.

Writers influenced by French realism continued their analyses of man in his material world: Galsworthy in the later volumes of *The Forsyte Saga*, Bennett in *Riceyman Steps* (1923), Somerset Maugham in *Of Human Bondage* (1915). H.G. Wells, still immensely prolific and influential, wrote an increasingly didactic and pessimistic fiction as well as such non-fictional work as *The Outline of History* (1919–20). Spurning the 'drum and trumpet' narratives devalued by the war, Wells here offers, in beautifully lucid form, his heroic myth of man's struggle to achievement and return to the dark.

Wells was, like Samuel Butler, a writer concerned to expose the cruel sham of Victorian and Edwardian class-consciousness, and this crusade, strengthened by the older English and modern continental traditions, is central to the novelist who remains the most eloquent spokesman of the late-nineteenth-century liberal humanist ideal, E.M. Forster (1879–1970).

His first novel, *Where Angels Fear to Tread* (1905), juxtaposes a class-bound England to the liberation of personal feeling, the unfreezing of icy propriety, offered by Forster's far-from-sentimental image of Italy and the spontaneous Mediterranean soul. *A Room with a View* (1908) develops this motif. Italy again provides the stimulus to a depiction of human nature triumphing over narrow culture and the limitations imposed by class. Forster's technique here is firmly within older traditions of social comedy and Victorian fiction which allowed him both the melodrama by which he hints at the fundamental insecurities and violence of the world and to comment directly on his characters' moral standing. This he does from the point of view of a man wholly and delicately committed to the values he believed he had found in the Cambridge of his youth – 'not an aristocracy of power based upon rank and influence, but an aristocracy of the sensitive, the considerate and the plucky'. Such people, he continued, 'represent the true human condition, the one permanent victory of our queer race over cruelty and chaos'.

In *The Longest Journey* (1907), these values are expressed (sometimes in curiously lush prose) as a means of measuring the progressive spiritual paralysis of Rickie Elliott as he attempts to pass for conventional in a world he cannot be true to. The strong if repressed current of homosexuality that runs through the work was made explicit in Forster's posthumous *Maurice* (written 1913–14, published 1971), a disappointing novel that fails to give its central subject a real and abiding relation to life within society. Maurice and his working-class boy-friend retreat to the 'greenwood' and an existence strongly influenced by the philosophy of Edward Carpenter (1844–1929), the pioneer sexologist and minor man of letters whom Forster praised 'for his courage and candour about sex, particularly about homosexuality; for his hatred of snobbery while snobbery was still fashionable; for his support of Labour before Labour wore dress-clothes; and for his cult of simplicity'.

In *Howards End* (1910), Forster essayed a 'condition-of-England' novel, but achieved a work whose generous sentiments are marred by too artificial a structure and too limited an experience of the social range Forster tries to present. 'Only connect', the work's well-known motto, reflects an attempt at an Arnoldian ideal of seeing life steady and whole. The individual must connect body and soul, poetry and prose, the much criticized business world of the Wilcoxes with the personal relationships and culture embodied in the Schlegels – an ethos prone nonetheless to the dangers of smugness and preciosity.

After the publication of *Howards End*, Forster issued his short stories as *The Celestial Omnibus* (1914) and *The Eternal Moment* (1928), while his volume of essays entitled *Pharos and Pharillon* appeared in 1923. Later essays were issued as *Abinger Harvest* (1936) and the admirable *Two Cheers for Democracy* (1951), while Forster's most influential work of literary criticism was the highly readable *Aspects of the Novel* (1927). Later short stories, some with homosexual themes, were posthumously published as *The Life to Come and Other Stories* (1972). Nonetheless, with one very considerable exception, Forster's career as a novelist was over, brought to an end, he suggested, by the obligation to write about marriage.

The last, culminating work in Forster's career in fiction was *A Passage to India* (1924), his study of imperialism. By focusing on a historical situation, Forster could here go beyond the intricate social comedy and marriage themes of his earlier work. He could also concentrate on his preoccupations with class, division and the search for wholeness in the light of politics and race. *A Passage to India* can be read as a carefully observed account of power relations. It is also a novel in which symbolism offers a poetic and subtle commentary on the action. These qualities are clear in the novel's best-known episode.

Mrs Moore, Fielding and Adela Quested – Forster's morally sensitive English people – go with the Indian Dr Aziz on a visit to the Marabar caves. Their journey begins in confusion. Trains are missed and the promised sunrise proves a disappointment. India is a bafflement, a muddle embodying Forster's conviction that the rational surface of life sheers rapidly away into chaos. In the caves themselves, Mrs Moore and Adela are separated, and the older woman's moral being is profoundly moved by hearing the cave's famous echo: '"Pathos, piety, courage – they exist, but are identical, and so is filth. Everything exists, nothing has value." If one had spoken vileness in that place, or quoted lofty poetry, the comment would have been the same – "ou-boum".'

The mind is baffled by its failure to grasp the wholeness it seeks – the effort to 'only connect' aspiration with physical reality – and in its confusion, its muddle, it recognizes something alien in the universe itself. This power will always keep the spirit partial and confused, individuals separated.

The hostility of things and events, individuals and races, is given narrative expression in the events following Adela's being left alone in the caves with Dr Aziz. We are told of a mysterious incident that occurs there – almost certainly a fantasy of rape – and watch the progress towards Aziz's trial and its inconclusive ending when the charges against him are dropped. In this, the main action of the novel, Forster skilfully explores the self-awareness of both Adela and Fielding as they are caught in racial antagonism. Fielding's relation to the bigots at the club (Forster's final image of partial-hearted English public schoolboys) and to the Indians he seeks to address as equals is particularly finely achieved. Nonetheless, though Aziz is not found guilty and, after the trial, genuine friendship between him and Fielding seems possible, harmony between races and individuals is prevented even by the stones on the road both men are riding – by the muddle of India all about them. 'Only connect' becomes a motto for the highest humanist endeavour and for an aspiration doomed to incompleteness.

Forster's liberal humanism, his disparagement of the narrowed heart and contempt for the values of imperialism, drew him into the orbit of the remarkable Bloomsbury group. Their revolt against the immediate past can be seen in *Eminent Victorians* (1918) by Lytton Strachey (1880–1932). Here, in a series of shrewd and erudite biographical essays, Strachey cut through the cant of hagiography to reveal his subjects in an altogether more human perspective. General Gordon, the hero of Khartoum, is shown as a religious obsessive in the mould of his enemy the mad Mahdi. Florence Nightingale, 'the lady with the lamp', is viewed as a power-hungry autocrat using others and driving them to exhaustion and death. Newman and Manning engage in ruthless worldly battles for eminence in the Roman Church. Such astringency is lost in the latter parts of *Queen Victoria* (1921) and the strained heroics of *Elizabeth and Essex* (1928), but Strachey's literary criticism (his appreciation of Racine especially) shows his recognition of art as a centre of the truly humane life.

This fundamental Bloomsbury doctrine inspired the pioneering critical work of Roger Fry (1866–1934) and Clive Bell (1881–1962) in the field of modern French painting especially. As the latter wrote in his *Civilization* (1928): 'works of art being direct means to aesthetic ecstasy are a direct means to good'. This is a belief derived in large measure from the *Principia Ethica* (1903) of G.E. Moore (1873–1958) whose criticism of the idealist philosophy developed by F.H. Bradley (1846–1924) among others led Moore to suggest that, far from seeking truth in the abstract, people should discover good in beauty and personal relationships. Individual perception and freedom from conventional morals, from received wisdom and from sexual stereotyping became the means of throwing off earnest Victorianism. As the great Bloomsbury economist John Maynard Keynes (1883–1946) wrote in 'My Early Beliefs' (published 1949): 'social action as an end in itself and not merely as a lugubrious duty had dropped out of our Ideal, and, not only social action, but the life of action generally, power, politics, success, wealth, ambition'.

For the luminous intelligence of Keynes himself, this 'struggle of escape from habitual modes of thought and expression' led to his writing *The Economic Consequences of the Peace* (1919), a quietlv magisterial polemic on the folly of levying excessive reparations on a defeated Germany and a work enlivened with excellent pen portraits of leading political figures. This was followed in 1936 by *The General Theory of Employment, Interest and Money*, a modification of capitalist theory towards the humane and deliberate management of national economies. In the period of the Great Depression, the work was to have world-wide importance in suggesting alternatives to the extremes of Bolshevism and Fascism. Meanwhile, as Keynes wrote of the minute and comfortably funded world of 1920s Bloomsbury: 'nothing mattered except states of mind, our own and other people's of course, but chiefly our own'.

It is such a philosophy that lies behind one of the best-known manifestos of the group's most prominent writer, Virginia Woolf (1882–1941)·

Examine for a moment an ordinary mind on an ordinary day. The mind receives a myriad impressions – trivial, fantastic, evanescent, or engraved with the sharpness of steel. From all sides they come, an incessant shower of innumerable atoms; and as they fall, as they shape themselves into the life of Monday or Tuesday, the accent falls differently from of old . . . Life is not a series of gig-lamps symmetrically arranged; life is a luminous halo, a semi-transparent envelope surrounding us from the beginning of consciousness to the end. Is not the task of the novelist to convey this varying, this unknown and uncircumscribed spirit, whatever aberration or complexity it may display, with as little mixture of the alien and external as possible?

The alien and the external are the techniques of what Virginia Woolf called the 'Edwardian' novelists: Wells, Galsworthy and Bennett. Both here in 'Modern Fiction' (1919) and in 'Mr Bennett and Mrs Brown' (1924), she assailed what she saw as these writers' materialism, their contrived plots and emphasis on externals. Bennett himself had asserted that characterization is the basis of fiction and opined that the characters in *Jacob's Room* (1922), Woolf's first experimental novel, 'do not vitally survive in the mind'.

Woolf's reply asserted that such a concern with received conventions of fiction was now redundant, for, 'in or about December 1910' – the date of Roger Fry's seminal exhibition of modern French art – 'human nature changed'. The precise date is a debating point skilfully made, but it suggests Woolf's recognition that in post-war England old social hierarchies had broken down and that literature must rediscover itself in a new and altogether more fluid world. As a result, the realist novel must be superseded by one in which objective reality is replaced by the impressions of subjective consciousness. The writer's principal concern is with states of mind. The knitting of a stocking or a ride on a bus becomes an experience altogether more dramatic and humanly revealing than a contrived chain of events.

Defining her role among the moderns – the 'Georgians' as Woolf confusingly called them – meant defining her role as both a writer and a woman. This agonized process of confronting 'the tyranny of sex' was to lead to repeated nervous breakdowns and eventual suicide. The essays gathered in the two volumes of *The Common Reader* (1925, 1932) reveal Woolf's deep engagement with the women writers of the past, while *A Room of One's Own* (1929) gives painful expression to what she saw as the female writer's essential predicament. 'It needs little skill in psychology to be sure that a highly gifted girl who has tried to use her gift for poetry would have been so thwarted and hindered by other people, so tortured and pulled apart by her own contrary instincts, that she must have lost her own health and sanity to a certainty.'

To be a woman writer was, for Woolf, to threaten both personal well-being and, in the resulting agony, the artistic integrity of the work she may produce. Even in the greatest women's fiction of the past – in the novels of Charlotte Brontë, for example – 'we constantly feel an acidity which is the result of oppression, a buried suffering smouldering beneath her passion'. The male principle becomes a mode of artistic death, and the woman writer must isolate herself from its threats. She must have independent means and a room of her own into which she can withdraw from psychic conflict and cultivate the androgynous mind – 'that curious sexual quality which comes only when sex is unconscious of itself'. The Bloomsbury emphasis on private mental states, bisexuality and social disengagement here leads to intense isolation. A room of one's own can be a womb, but it can also be an ivory tower, a prison and a grave. Its dangers and promise are inherent in all Virginia Woolf's work.

Mrs Dalloway (1925), her first major novel, clearly reveals Woolf's allegiance to her modern contemporaries. The work presents its heroine's consciousness during a day of her fashionable London life, a day during which her mind moves in its own internal time and space and amid the often threatening awareness of drift and death. This last invades even her party that evening when Mrs Dalloway is told of the death of Septimus Smith, a neurasthenic victim of the war with whom throughout her own mental states have been compared. Woolf suggested that these two consciousnesses were in some respects identical, and the fact that Septimus is created from Woolf's own experiences of mental asylums suggests that the book draws on conflicts between the roles of the Bloomsbury hostess and the victim of insanity.

Mrs Dalloway is marred by the rather obvious devices Woolf used to give her work structure. For all her enthusiasm for recording the atoms of experience as they fall on the mind, she knew, as Lily Briscoe in *To the Lighthouse* (1927) suggests, that a true work of art must be both very delicate and extremely strong. 'Beautiful and bright it should be on the surface, feathery and evanescent, one colour melting into another like the colours on a butterfly's wing; but beneath the fabric must be clamped together with bolts of iron.' Virginia Woolf is at one with the great modern masters of fiction in seeking to forge these bolts anew.

Woolf realized that in freeing the reader 'from the perpetual demand of the novelist that we shall feel with his characters', modern writers such as Proust and Henry James had sought 'an equivalent for the processes of the mind'. She also appreciated that the dexterity of their solutions called on the pleasurable use of previously unexercised responses in the reader while drawing attention to novels themselves as created artefacts. Such processes, along with the mind's attempt to interpret and structure the flux experience, are both the subject and the substance of *To the Lighthouse*.

The first part of the novel ingeniously plays with ambiguities of time as Mrs Ramsay's consciousness is presented to us through the flow of her memories. This mingling and even confusing of past and present is an effective evocation of mental life and is made the more moving by Mrs Ramsay's awareness of chronological time, of the hours hastening her towards death. Hers is thus the central consciousness of the book: of the first part which describes an evening of her life, and of the last part in which, after her death and the decade described in the baroque prose of 'Time Passes', those who have known her come to appreciate her focal place in their lives. Mrs Ramsay is thus enabled to become a centre of Woolf's major themes, the contrary forces of male and female especially. The one, embodied in Mr Ramsay, a figure based on Sir Leslie Stephen (1832–1904), Woolf's father and the editor of the *Dictionary of National Biography* (founded 1882), is rational and aggressive. The female principle by contrast is nurturing, intuitive and ultimately transcendent.

To the Lighthouse was followed by *Orlando* (1928), Woolf's fantasia on her love affair with Vita Sackville-West (1892–1962), but it is in *The Waves* (1931) that she developed to its fullest extent her concern with dematerializing the world into almost pure consciousness. The inner lives of her characters as they change over time are presented against the rising and setting of the sun over the sea. All becomes flux. Nonetheless, by excluding so much of the normal world while developing a strained style of prose-poetry, the novel too often appears preciously hermetic. *The Years* (1937) makes some attempt to right this balance, while the posthumous *Between the Acts* (1941) sets an amateur pageant of England's history against the menace of war. And it is the Second World War as a supreme expression of male destructiveness that Woolf attacked in her hectoring and unpopular *Three Guineas* (1938). Here she urged that women should found an 'Outsiders' Society' wholly detached from masculine enormity.

Other women writers were also concerned to portray a refined and distinctively female awareness. Although the term 'stream of consciousness' is rightly and invariably applied to the work of Virginia Woolf, it was first borrowed in 1918 from the American philosopher William James (1842–1910) to describe the novels of Dorothy Richardson (1872–1957). These were eventually to make up the twelve-volume sequence *Pilgrimage* (1915–38). Richardson defined her work as an attempt to 'produce a feminine equivalent of the current masculine realism'. She was reacting in particular to the writing of her erstwhile lover H.G. Wells, and Virginia Woolf praised her as an ally who had engaged with the nature of language itself to create a style that could reflect a genuinely female awareness.

It was the distinguished if neglected May Sinclair (1863–1946) who first labelled Richardson's stream of consciousness technique. Her own *Life and Death of Harriet Frean* (1922) is a sharply experimental analysis of waste and destructive relationships, and has something of the ironic observation seen again in the short stories of Katherine Mansfield (1888–1923). The best of these offer the finely crafted insights into female self-betrayal and destruction exemplified in such works as 'Miss Brill'. Like Sinclair, Mansfield was aware of the work of Freud, and the early novels of Rebecca West (1892–1983) such as *The Judge* (1922) again reveal the influence of Freudian theory. It is however in her awareness that the destructive male 'does not belong to the same race as woman' that West most fully suggests her feminist sympathies and portrays a world of often hideous recrimination.

The brittle glamour of the period between the end of the First World War and the Great Depression is exemplified by Noël Coward (1899–1973) both in plays of the technical deftness and sheer comedy of *Private Lives* (1930) as well as in the lyrics whose wit and verve make Coward one of the great masters of English light verse, just as P.G. Wodehouse (1881–1975) is the master of the English light novel. That the highest camp is also tinged with an aura of threat is suggested by the novels of Ronald Firbank (1886–1926). The eponymous hero in *Concerning the Eccentricities of Cardinal Pirelli* (1926), for example, dies of a heart attack while pursuing a choirboy round his cathedral dressed only in his mitre. Norman Douglas (1868–1952) in conversational novels such as *South Wind* (1917) also threw off inhibition, while another *jeu d'esprit* of the period is David Garnett's essay in the surreal, *Lady into Fox* (1922). The surreal is also found in the early poetry of Edith Sitwell (1887–1964) such as her sequence *Façade* (1922).

Wit and high-spirited satire again characterize such early novels of Aldous Huxley (1894–1963) as *Crome Yellow* (1920) and *Antic Hay* (1923), but *Those Barren Leaves* (1925) reveals the darker side of the 1920s. The novel as a morality is seen in such works of T.F. Powys (1875–1953) as *Mr Weston's Good Wine* (1927), while satire on what he regarded as the shiftless, the spurious and the artistically confused is to be found in *Tarr* (1918) by Percy Wyndham Lewis (1882–1957). Though of a far lesser talent than they, Lewis was the ally of Ezra Pound and T.S. Eliot – 'the Men of 1914' as he called them – and thus of writers who stared appalled into what they saw as the cultural chaos of the post-war modern world.

6

As an expatriate American deeply versed in the European literary tradition, Ezra Pound (1885–1972) was well placed to expose what he saw as contemporary European cultural decline. This he believed had reached its nadir in the First World War, in the nightmare vision of mass slaughter and 'laughter out of dead bellies'. The condensed, highly allusive sections of his *Hugh Selwyn Mauberley* (1920) portray this 'botched civilization' which has left its heirs mere fragments of greatness: 'two gross of broken statues' and 'a few thousand battered books'.

Pound believed that his ambition to resuscitate poetry, to remake tradition anew, could not be fulfilled in an age dominated by tabloid headlines, the demand for instant, gimcrack vulgarities and 'tawdry cheapness'. High civilization, he considered, now stood battered and empty amid modern mass society. The poet, alienated from such standards, moves in a world and is obliged to write a verse where quotations from the rich culture of the past are shockingly juxtaposed to a society that wants neither truly potent sensuality nor 'the saint's vision'. Both flesh and the spirit have been denied amid modern rootlessness and the disparagement of those life-giving traditions Pound referred to as 'Beauty'.

Pound suggested that the emasculation of the pre-war generations was partly responsible for this deplorable state of affairs. *Hugh Selwyn Mauberley* shows us the Pre-Raphaelites' 'vacant gaze' and what Pound regarded as the shoddy sensationalism of the Rhymers' Club. In the contemporary world, successful literary enterprise is measured by the pursuit of wealth, and Mr Nixon (probably a portrait of Arnold Bennett) advises the young man to give up poetry since 'there's nothing in it'. Art for art's sake, the second half of the poem suggests, is also a process of emasculation and a retreat from life.

In addition, the great ladies who should inspire and support civilization now pursue squalid affairs or mere petty dilettantism. They are no longer the apt focus of the ideal, and the 'Envoi' to *Hugh Selwyn Mauberley*, which is one of Pound's finest achievements, exactly suggests this sense of crisis and betrayal. Written in a manner designed to recall the aristocratic grace of Waller and a high civilization, it suggests the current impossibility of reviving the very conditions it evokes. The 'Envoi' is thus intended as a last poem in the tradition of 'Beauty'. Western civilization has now run its course, Pound suggested, and the radical experimentation of his own poetry – its violent juxtapositions, range and frustration – expresses the dilemma of modern cultural emptiness. As T.S. Eliot wrote of *Hugh Selwyn Mauberley*: 'it is compact of the experience of a certain man in a certain place at a certain time; and it is also a document of an epoch; it is genuine tragedy and comedy; and it is, in the best sense of Arnold's worn phrase, a "criticism of life"'.

Pound himself had first met T.S. Eliot (1888–1965) when the younger man came to England in 1914 to work on the philosophy of F.H. Bradley. Pound was greatly impressed by Eliot's independent efforts to engage with the literary problems he himself was facing, and he arranged for the publication of Eliot's *Prufrock* (1917). Behind this and Eliot's other important early work lies an attempt to explore the possibilities for a truly contemporary poetry. Here was experimentation based on the widest range of cultural reference, on great critical acumen and on imaginative powers at once formidable and subtle.

Eliot's early education in French, German, history and the classics was broadened at Harvard by studies of ancient art, philosophy and religion. It was at Harvard too that he first studied Dante and Eastern mysticism, read Arthur Symons's *The Symbolist Movement in Modern Literature* and encountered in Irving Babbit (1865–1933) a man who, embodying 'the aristocratic aloofness of the ancient humanist', was deeply to influence the reactionary cast of Eliot's thought.

This last was deepened during a period of study in France in 1911 when Eliot was first attracted to L'Action Française, a right-wing group led by Charles Maurras (1868–1952). This body, guided by a man Eliot regarded as a major literary critic, advanced royalist and hierarchical ideas in a period when, as we have seen, liberal individualism seemed under threat and the new complexities of mass society were finding expression in the simplifications of nationalism, racism and anti-Semitism. For Eliot, Maurras's traditionalist beliefs and religious sympathies freed the mind from a vague humanism and encouraged a vigorously critical attitude to both literature and society. Maurras is thus an important figure in Eliot's development towards Christian orthodoxy, and Eliot himself was later to refer to him as 'a kind of Virgil who led us to the doors of the temple'.

Eliot's involvement with so wide a range of influences, his panoramic eclecticism, is an example of what Henry James had asserted as the American's right to 'pick and choose and assimilate and in short (aesthetically etc.) claim our property where we find it'. For Eliot, this was both a process of establishing his cultural traditions and one of engaging with an increasingly desperate view of modern man's place in a secular, fragmented and ultimately sterile society – a society that had lost contact with the spiritual abundance of the past.

Among the work of the French Symbolists, Eliot had first been attracted to Laforgue's figure of the sad, fastidious dandy, the figure who in such works of Eliot's own as 'Humoresque', 'Spleen' and 'Conversation Galante' waits in his patent leather boots 'on the doorstep of the Absolute' – a man both elegant and diffident in the face of spiritual intensities. 'Hysteria' and several of Eliot's poems in French suggest a deep psycho-sexual unease amounting to terror, but it is in the 'Preludes' and more especially 'Rhapsody on a Windy Night' that Eliot's narrator is presented as the anxiously sensitive young man, his acute and well-stocked mind revolving unconnected fragments of memory as he wanders the hell of the modern city.

Influenced by the French philosopher Henri Bergson (1859–1941) – a figure also of central significance to Proust – the mind of Eliot's narrator reaches down into the depths of consciousness to convince him that his life in time is a continuum, a 'duration' to be perceived aesthetically rather than through rational analysis. The young narrator experiences his memories as images, symbols of consciousness which create similar emotions in the reader in the manner advocated by the French Symbolist poets. The world such images convey is one of deep unease however, of crabs in primeval pools and a pointless, debilitating daily world of materialism:

> The bed is open; the tooth-brush hangs on the wall,
> Put your shoes at the door, sleep, prepare for life.

It is these areas of response that Eliot greatly developed in 'Portrait of a Lady' and 'The Love Song of J. Alfred Prufrock'. Both are portrayals of a Boston like Henry James's, a society 'quite uncivilized', as Eliot was to call it, 'but refined beyond the point of civilization'. In 'Portrait of a Lady', Eliot evoked a world of half-lived lives, of tea and subordinate clauses, while in the greater poem an American cousin of Laforgue's dandy, trapped in a society where he has measured out his life with coffee spoons, can neither face his own intuitions of life's deeper purposes nor, in the words of the American moralist Ralph Waldo Emerson (1803–1882), 'affront and reprimand the smooth mediocrity and squalid contentment of the times'.

As the epigraph from Dante suggests, Prufrock is a man afflicted by a spiritual sloth so all-pervasive that he no longer recognizes his moral responsibility for his lack of action. The sharp confrontation of Dante's *Inferno* with the early twentieth century emphasizes contemporary moral hollowness and draws a literary comparison between worlds of spiritual authority and decline in a manner fundamental to Eliot's technique. That this confrontation finds its diminished echo in Prufrock's own contrasts between daringly anti-romantic descriptions of the hell of the modern city, the natural forces of the sea and the silken claustrophobia of the salons gives added pathos to this image of the modern anti-hero trapped in the hell of his own mediocrity.

Prufrock and Other Observations (1917) thus offers a confrontation between an emasculated civilization of high material comfort and its half-acknowledged discontents. In the quatrain verses from *Poems* (1920), this sense of opposition is altogether more extreme. A force gathering to itself the widest range of anecdote and illustration is here counterpointed to the cold and barely containing contrivance of the form. 'Burbank with a Baedeker: Bleistein with a Cigar' presents this opposition at its most troubling. The poem is set in Venice: the Venice of Renaissance art, of Ruskin and Henry James, but also the Venice of Othello ruined by sexual torment and of the Jew Shylock. For Eliot, the city has now become a seat of ultimate degradation. This is wrought, we are asked to believe, by an alliance of degrading feminine sexuality and the rootless degeneration of Jewish financiers. To illustrate this, the action shows a raddled princess slumming in small hotels. She first corrupts the cultured if morally uncertain Burbank, a figure imagined here as both a Prufrock and an Antony left to decline as his Cleopatra's lust stretches out to the world of the Jews. This last is personified by Bleistein himself – 'Chicago Semite Viennese' – and Sir Ferdinand Klein with his 'money in furs'.

For Eliot, pained by what he saw as ruinous cultural decline, the crudest stereotypes of anti-feminism and anti-Semitism – of sex as the destroyer and the 'wandering Jew' as the virus of cultural death – are here fused. That such repellent attitudes were commonplace in the 1920s is suggested by the fact that Sir Alfred Mond – a founder of ICI, Minister of Health and the token 'rich Jew' in Eliot's 'A Cooking Egg' – was regularly attacked in the House of Commons with cries of 'Silence in the ghetto!' Eliot's own anti-Semitism was publicly expressed as late as *After Strange Gods* (1934), a deeply unhappy work he later suppressed. Anti-Semitism and disgust at female sexuality again characterize the second half of 'Whispers of Immortality', a poem whose opening stanzas nonetheless convey with profound originality the influence of Eliot's reading of the Jacobean dramatists and the 'metaphysical' poets. The seventeenth century's obsession with the body of love as the food of worms has here been genuinely rediscovered and re-created.

The spiritual confidence of its Anglican Church however still eluded Eliot. Both 'The Hippopotamus' and 'Mr Eliot's Sunday Morning Service' suggest a painful awareness of the problems raised by the Word becoming incarnate in the hated flesh, and of spiritual truth maintained by an institution here derided as both worldly and obscurantist. Eliot's emotional extremism is also maintained. Origen, the early church father who castrated himself for the greater love of God, is here contrasted to Sweeney, Eliot's gross embodiment of the merely physical, *l'homme moyen sensuel*. In 'Sweeney Erect' and 'Sweeney among the Nightingales', this figure rakes through a sordid bed-sit world of one-night stands, a world that is godless, meaningless and violent. In the 'Fragment of an Agon' from the unfinished *Sweeney Agonistes* (1926–7), amid the jazz and hysteria, Sweeney himself expounds his philosophy:

> Birth, and copulation, and death.
> That's all the facts when you come to brass tacks:
> Birth, and copulation, and death.
> I've been born, and once is enough.

Finally, in *Poem*, the ageing central figure in 'Gerontion', his life unrelieved by spiritual vision and trapped in the deceits of time, revolves 'thoughts of a dry brain in a dry season'.

Parts of Gerontion's soliloquy are cast in a language reminiscent of the seventeenth-century playwright Tourneur, and Eliot wrote in an essay how it was 'from these minor dramatists that I had learned my lessons'. Eliot viewed his criticism as a by-product of his poetic activity, and the essays gathered in *The Sacred Wood* (1920) and those published separately or in his magazine *The Criterion* (1922–39) aim at a definition of poetry as an activity justified in its own right rather than one dependent on other modes of thought or faith. As Eliot wrote in an early number of *The Criterion*: 'to maintain the autonomy, and the disinterestedness, of every human activity, and to perceive it in relation to every other, require a considerable discipline'. This strenuous endeavour – along with the novel insistence on close reading and analysis in 'The Function of Criticism' and the definition of poetic activity contained in 'Tradition and the Individual Talent' – not only clarified the basis of Eliot's own aesthetic but helped lay the foundations of modern academic criticism.

Eliot believed that criticism should be 'the common pursuit of true judgement', and his work aimed to free literature from critics who saw it wholly in terms of its historical context or merely as the individual writer's self-expression. Eliot constantly insisted on the 'impersonality' of the poet and the 'autotelic' or self-sufficient nature of his art. Great poetry, Eliot suggested, does not express the unique concerns of the private self, for 'the progress of an artist is a continual self-sacrifice, a continual extinction of personality'. Nor is it the poet's purpose to express purely philosophical ideas, though he will often voice the feelings raised by these. Finally, it is not the job of poetry itself to be a substitute for religion. By contrast, and in a famous if polemically extreme image, Eliot saw the true poet as a catalyst working on the given elements of his culture and the traditions contained within that culture. His mind fuses elements of these into a new compound without itself leaving a trace in the result. Thus the poet neither expresses his personality in his work nor merely voices the commonplaces of his time. If he has succeeded in realizing Eliot's ideal, he has nonetheless made something new and permanently valuable – true poetry.

Eliot illustrated this idea through a discussion of Dante and Shakespeare. Both wrote '*equally* great poetry' but neither was an original thinker. Though Dante could draw on the high philosophic culture of Thomas Aquinas and the thirteenth-century Roman Catholic Church while Shakespeare (it is suggested) was dependent on the poorer civilization that nurtured a taste for Seneca, 'the essential is that each expresses, in perfect language, some permanent human impulse'. The catalytic poet has thus realized his essential function and his work stands (or Eliot at this stage wished it to stand) independent of philosophy or religion while nonetheless providing a sense of absolute value. Only much later, in 1935 and after his conversion to Anglicanism, would Eliot come to see the church as the true arbiter of poetry's moral worth and declare: 'the "greatness" of literature cannot be determined solely by literary standards; though we must remember that whether it is literature or not can be determined only by literary standards'.

The direction of Eliot's early thought thus led to the need to escape from ideas of the 'reflective' poet and the manner of Victorian writers such as Tennyson and Browning, men who for Eliot could feel and think but 'do not feel their thought as immediately as the odour of a rose'. For Eliot himself, such poets as these stood on the near side of a 'disassociation of sensibility'. On the far bank stood the poets of the seventeenth century. These men 'possessed a mechanism of sensibility that could devour any kind of experience'. Their work can be 'simple, artificial, difficult, or fantastic', while Donne especially provided Eliot with a model of the integrated poetic mind. 'A thought to Donne', he wrote, 'was an experience; it modified his sensibility.' Here was an image of the true poet's proper functioning, and it is this tradition of psychological and artistic well-being Eliot wished to re-establish. He sought to be of such poets' company without being anachronistic. In other words, he had to engage creatively with tradition. 'We need an eye that can see the past in its place with its definite differences from the present, yet so lively that it shall be as present to us as the present. This is the creative eye.'

For the creative artist, the past is not static, an object for antiquarian specialists. It is a living body that is both dynamic and organic. It lives under the true writer's creative gaze. As a result, the true poet not only is shaped by his perceptions of his inheritance but can change others' perceptions of that inheritance. Discussing such matters in 'Tradition and the Individual Talent', Eliot declared: 'No poet, no artist of any art, has his complete meaning alone. His significance, his appreciation is the appreciation of his relation to the dead poets and artists. You cannot value him alone; you must set him, for contrast and comparison, among the dead.' And in this company, the 'really new' poet and his work will lead to a reordering of the old hierarchy because of the novel light he sheds on received tradition.

Eliot was profoundly aware however that the creation of the really new in the twentieth century faced the formidable problems created by the twentieth century itself. 'Our civilization comprehends great variety and complexity,' he wrote, 'and this variety and complexity, playing upon a refined sensibility, must produce various and complex results. The poet must become more and more comprehensive, more allusive, more indirect, in order to force, to dislocate if necessary, language into his meaning.' This passage aptly defines the technique of *The Waste Land* (1922). The extreme tensions in the *Poems* of 1920 (as well as those in Eliot's marriage) are here at breaking point. In the modern world the poem presents, tradition has become merely a cracked mirror reflecting fragments of sterile existence.

Eliot's technique for weaving together the strained voices and diverse cultural allusions in *The Waste Land*, its agonized confrontation of modern despair with ancient spiritual plenitude, was influenced by both Pound and James Joyce. Writing of *Ulysses*, which appeared in the same year as *The Waste Land*, Eliot suggested that by juxtaposing contemporary Dublin to the world of Homeric narrative Joyce had found 'a way of controlling, of ordering, of giving a shape and a significance to the immense panorama of futility and anarchy which is contemporary history'. The writer was now free of the tyranny of a plot and could rely instead on his informed readers' knowledge of myth to provide the sense of structure. Eliot himself defined this process as 'manipulating a continuous parallel between contemporaneity and antiquity'. In *The Waste Land*, this technique is taken to its extreme.

The great range of myth on which Eliot drew refers to the hopes men and women once had that the sterile Waste Land could indeed be made to blossom again. Fundamental here were two contemporary works of anthropology: Sir James Frazer's *The Golden Bough* (1890–1915) and Jessie L. Weston's *From Ritual to Romance* (1920). The first of these is one of the most influential works of late-nineteenth-century scholarship.

From his study of the ancient fertility cults of Adonis, Attis and

Osiris especially, Frazer deduced that there were strong parallels between the pagan rites surrounding a fertility god who died and rose again to redeem the winter waste land of his worshippers and the Christian mystery of the Resurrection. Christianity, in other words, was not a divine revelation but merely one of several similar cults that had become politically dominant. Summing up this argument, Frazer declared that the coincidences of Christian and pagan ritual could not be an accident. 'They mark the compromise that the Church in the hour of its triumph was compelled to make with its vanquished yet still dangerous rivals.'

According to Jessie L. Weston, these rivals lived on to become the knights who sought the Holy Grail, the chalice of divine truth guarded by a wounded Fisher King whose country was again a waste land to be redeemed. Esoteric fertility ritual was thus metamorphosed into medieval romance, while the symbols of the original cult could still be found on Tarot cards. These, Weston believed, had once been used by the Phoenicians to predict the rise and fall of the waters that brought fertility to the waste land. Now, in Eliot's poem, the cards are used for nothing of the kind. Madame Sosostris, the famous clairvoyante, snivels over her 'wicked pack of cards' and tells her visitor to 'fear death by drowning', the very death from which some of Frazer's fertility gods rose to redeem the waste land. There is no redemption in the modern world however. The land is parched, Phlebas the Phoenician merely sinks in the tranquil sea, while his corrupt inheritors importune homosexual favours. The chapel of the Grail is empty, and contemporary man, devoid of the positive resources of myth, gropes round a land apparently irredeemably wasted.

A second structural device in the poem is the figure of Tiresias. The blind seer is a suffering, ambiguous, timeless figure who has lived in the bodies of both genders, has untangled the doom of Oedipus in the waste land of sexually polluted Thebes and now, as the central character in Eliot's poem, is the figure whose consciousness is the substance of the whole work. In particular, Tiresias is aware of the hopeless failure of sexuality in the modern world: the neurosis and the aborted children in 'A Game of Chess', the joyless fornication of the typist and the small house-agent's clerk in 'The Fire Sermon':

> She turns and looks a moment in the glass,
> Hardly aware of her departed lover;
> Her brain allows one half-formed thought to pass:
> 'Well now that's done: and I'm glad it's over.'

The reflection in the tawdry room, the anonymity and the mental vacuousness and utter banality of the woman's words are at once an indictment and the searing engagement of a truly modern poetry with the world in which it is created. Sexuality is impotent without spiritual vision, and, as 'The Fire Sermon' comes to its climax, so Eliot juxtaposes the Eastern and Western philosophies of the Buddha and St Augustine and their teaching on the suffering caused by desire.

It is a measure of the enormous range of *The Waste Land* that in these central sections of the work ideas of the great religious teachers mingle with jazz rhythms and pub talk as well as a poetry expressing terrible psychological exhaustion. As the neurotic woman bares her soul in her boudoir, so Eliot combines the world of Freud with the rootlessness, the *anomie*, detected by such contemporary sociologists as Emile Durkheim (1858–1917) and Max Weber (1864–1920). Both men considered that some revitalization of man's need for myth and religion was an overriding necessity if modern society were to preserve itself from collapse, but the masses in Eliot's poem – the crowd that flows over London Bridge, for example – have no such hope. 'I had not thought that death had undone so many,' says the narrator in the words of Dante surveying the countless hordes of the morally neutral in hell. London itself becomes an equivalent of the *Inferno*, as well as the 'place of unreality' imagined by Bertrand Russell at the outbreak of the First World War and which, according to his autobiography, he spoke about to Eliot 'who put it into *The Waste Land*'.

Hopelessness, violence and spiritual and material destruction reached a climax in the war, but the period after hostilities ceased appeared profoundly threatening too. Marxism in Russia, along with political and economic instability in the rest of Europe, seemed to accord with the pessimism of Oswald Spengler's *The Decline of the West* (1918–22), a work which offers a vision of the cycles of history passing away like the falling cities in 'What the Thunder Said'. For Spengler, sustained violence had become the norm, and that Eliot himself thought in terms of anarchy taking over is confirmed by

Stephen Spender whom he told of his fears of internecine warfare and people killing each other on the streets. Nonetheless, the thunder in the last section, which Eliot associated with the philosophy of the East, will eventually bring redeeming rain. Meanwhile, in the agonized period of waiting, the narrator can only revolve his memories of brief, unconnected moments of illumination, and ponder the significance of the disparate patchwork of quotations garnered from the lost greatness of his culture. 'These fragments I have shored against my ruins.'

That *The Waste Land* organizes such a range of material so powerfully, that it conveys with dramatic immediacy the plight of the highly cultured mind amid the wreckage and despair of twentieth-century life, is in part due to the editorial work of Ezra Pound. The publication of the drafts of *The Waste Land* allows us to see how decisive an effect this had. What previously was loose and anecdotal, what suggested the purely private confusions of Eliot himself, was skilfully removed. Because of this, *The Waste Land* itself now stands as a more agonizing statement of the reality of a world without God.

Eliot's work however is a continual spiritual progress, and in *The Hollow Men* (1925) he suggested that to deny God was to commit a form of spiritual suicide and so live in a world that is bleakly and terribly placed in a 'valley of dying stars'. Spiritual terror blows through this poem. It is bleak with the despair of those too inured to their own deaths to have the strength to hope for life in eternity. If God does exist, it is at an infinite, exhausting remove, and words offered to the Word fail to cross the divide. Instead they fade, dying with the dying in a world that merely peters out. There is no final apocalypse, only a tired whimper. *The Hollow Men* thus portrays the hell of those who have abandoned hope. It is a vision of life in the Dantesque darkness of despair from which Eliot himself was slowly to emerge, becoming as he did so the greatest Christian poet of the twentieth century writing in English, a man whose work suggests that eventually he glimpsed beatitude.

In 1927, Eliot became a British citizen and was received into the Anglican Church, activities which he saw as complementing each other. The poetry that ensued however shows no sense of crude spiritual triumphalism. It is puzzled, pained even, offering a profound and mysterious sense of birth, rebirth and the death of the old material self. The narrator of 'The Journey of the Magi', for example, expresses an old man's bewilderment as he awaits his end in a state hovering between two incompatible worlds: the world of his life in time and a barely perceived eternity. Intuitions of the latter render the former inert and meaningless, despite the exquisite precision with which it is expressed and the feeling that the Christian symbols hidden within it have not yet acquired a full meaning. Similarly, in 'A Song for Simeon' – like 'Mariana', one of the most beautiful of the Ariel Poems – the narrator knows that his glimpse of his Redeemer marks the hour of his death.

It is in *Ash Wednesday* (1930) that this sense of moving between two worlds, of groping tentatively towards spiritual light, is most subtly rendered. The language of the poet becomes prayer – words seeking a relationship with the Word. Consciousness is now the spiritual self divested of the material world of history and imploring the intercession of the Lady after the body has been cast aside. The Word has not yet been heard however, nor has the certainty of a mystical perception of truth been achieved. Rather, in a poem profoundly influenced by the *Purgatorio*, we may see the narrator as purged and penitent, living in the hope that the light of paradise may one day be glimpsed and that words and the Word will eventually be one.

This sense of the soul divesting itself of the love of created things did not mean that Eliot ceased his creative and critical engagement with literature. The unfortunate *After Strange Gods* dates from this period, while a central issue in *The Use of Poetry and the Use of Criticism* (1933) is the degree to which the reader can appreciate poetry written out of beliefs one cannot actually share – a matter of great importance to a devoutly Christian writer. Eliot was also to broaden his range into the literature of the eighteenth and nineteenth centuries, but the inspirational quality of his earlier writing – the excited relation of practice to theory – is here replaced by the sense of a man of the widest and deepest culture considering matters with an almost judicial impartiality. In fact, Eliot's finest prose from the 1930s is concerned less with literature than with the place of faith and the church in a deeply troubled world.

The harrowing divisions and uncertainties of the 1930s offer an essential background to Eliot's concern. He was writing in an England facing the social and economic trauma of financial depression and a European-wide polarization of political views into the twin evils of Communism and Fascism. As early as 1924, Eliot the right-wing traditionalist described what he heard as the true note amid the turmoil of British political life. 'The note is not "the great middle class liberalism" or the great lower-middle class socialism; it is of authority not democracy, of dogmatism not tolerance, of the extremity and never of the mean.' Eliot here rejected Communism for its unrelieved materialism, the worship of the golden calf. Such ideas as Fascism could boast, he claimed, he found 'in a more digestible form in the works of Maurras'. To Eliot however all forms of secularism seemed ultimately doomed to disaster, and it appeared that only the church – militant, continuously influential and unmuddied by liberalism – could offer a satisfactory view of mankind striving to build a better world, the City of God.

Thoughts after Lambeth (1931) sounds this theme. It is in *The Idea of a Christian Society* (1939) however, written after what Eliot saw as the country's moral failure over the Munich settlement, that he described his vision of a society founded on the traditional morality stemming from received spiritual truths. The High Anglican Church represented by such revered figures as Lancelot Andrewes became Eliot's refuge. Such a church offered him 'a society in which the natural end of men – virtue and well being in community – is acknowledged for all, and the supernatural end – beatitude – for those who have the eyes to see it'. The church, as the choruses of *The Rock* (first performed 1934) suggest, provides the only viable foundation for society. *Murder in the Cathedral* (1935), Eliot's great verse play of the following year, shows the church in action.

The play presents ideas of ritual slaughter within a Christian context. The Women of Canterbury, like the pagan mourners of Adonis, live in a winter world reduced to 'brown sharp points of death in a waste of water and mud'. The analogy to the landscapes of *The Waste Land* is marked. However, while in the earlier poem redemption was barely glimpsed, here the women are drawn into an action where the timelessness of God intersects with the historical world of man. The death of Thomas à Becket becomes, through the paradoxes of Christian theology, the means whereby they can have life more abundantly.

A martyrdom, as Thomas explains in his Christmas sermon, is that state of annihilation wherein the sufferer's will is completely identified with God. For Thomas, to realize this state is to realize his vocation. In the dialogues with the Four Tempters, he throws off the lures of pleasure, worldly power (even the power to work material good in the world) and finally the last and greatest temptation: 'to do the right deed for the wrong reason'. Thomas will not choose martyrdom, rather God will choose him as a martyr. In his death, and as the pure instrument of divine will, Thomas becomes the means by which the resonant poetry of the Women of Canterbury's chorus is turned from lamentation to prayer, from horror at the waste land to the hope of redemption within the church.

The discovery of religious vocation is also the central subject of Eliot's succeeding verse dramas: *The Family Reunion* (1939), *The Cocktail Party* (1950), *The Confidential Clerk* (1954) and *The Elder Statesman* (1958). Their Christian basis means they show Eliot's preoccupation with the temporal and the eternal, with contrition, expiation and sacrifice. Technically, they reveal the influence of both the English dramatists of the seventeenth century and the Greek tragedians. The degree of their success is disputable, but it was an omitted passage from *Murder in the Cathedral* that underlay *Burnt Norton* (1935), the first of Eliot's *Four Quartets*. Here, his magisterial and deeply felt discussion of religious and poetic vocation, of words and the Word, and his concern with the intersection of the timeless with time are worked into the crowning achievement of his career.

All of the *Four Quartets* – *Burnt Norton*, *East Coker* (1940), *The Dry Salvages* (1941) and *Little Gidding* (1942) – are constructed from five sections whose themes are repeated with variations in each. The conscious analogy is to the late works of Beethoven, and like those sublime achievements, they move in a world of the highest intellectual meditation while being suffused with a knowledge of suffering and a perception of joy which touch on the furthest reaches of the spirit.

Eliot's fusion of the religious and the poetic in these works aspires to the ideal he was later to express in *Notes towards the Definition of Culture* (1948). 'To judge a work of art by artistic or religious standards, to judge a religion by religious or by artistic standards should come in the end to the same thing: though it is an end at which no individual can arrive.' In attempting this fusion of religion and poetry however, the *Four Quartets* make wide use of what Eliot in 'The Three Voices of Poetry' (1952) was to call the first of the poet's voices: 'the voice of the poet talking to himself'. He is alone with spiritual concerns and draws strength from a profound humility as he explores the significance and waits for the actual moment of the intersection of the timeless with time, the mystic insight that will confirm his view that truth is ultimately a spiritual experience and that his words and the Word can be one.

The opening section of *Burnt Norton* is a remarkable fusion of the philosophic mind, the spiritual impulse and the poetic imagination. These three combine to offer a uniquely satisfying impression of the consciousness that underlies the whole work: the image of the spirit moving in a world of time and illuminated by those moments out of time which let it know that eternity is its true goal. In *East Coker*, Mary Stuart's motto 'In my beginning is my end' prefaces Eliot's vision of natural time which is also a vision of history working itself out in an English landscape described with a visionary power which is one of Eliot's most distinctive mature achievements. In *The Dry Salvages*, which looks back to the Massachusetts of Eliot's childhood, the river and the sea become his images of the physical world of time.

In the second sections of the *Four Quartets*, high lyric artifice is followed by meditations on the world of time, on God as 'the still point of the turning world', on humility and the confusion inherent in the natural world. Deprivation, the conscious unburdening of the soul and pilgrimage made amid darkness are the characteristics of the third sections, while each of the fourth sections is an exquisite lyric of increasing Christian emphasis. These lyrics develop from the beautiful apprehension of time and the natural world in *Burnt Norton*, through Good Friday meditation and the prayer to the Virgin in *The Dry Salvages*.

In *Little Gidding*, the supreme masterpiece among these works, the fourth section is a pentecostal vision of divinity descending on the world and its words, a revelation of the power of tongues:

> The dove descending breaks the air
> With flame of incandescent terror
> Of which the tongues declare
> The one discharge from sin and error.

Little Gidding subsumes the other Quartets and offers one of the supreme expressions of the spiritual life in English literature. Written in the darkest period of the Second World War, the work draws on the bleakness and desolation of a culture apparently facing annihilation by evil, working this into a vision of redemption gloriously sustained by Christian symbolism and the force of a poetic inspiration which indeed suggests the 'continual extinction of personality' dominant in Eliot's work since the essay on 'Tradition and the Individual Talent'. The High Church community at Little Gidding was, we should recall, deeply influential on George Herbert among other seventeenth-century poets, and is the place of prayer and of tradition seen by Eliot in a season of tremulous delicacy. In the poem, it becomes the place for 'the intersection of timeless moment', of spiritual revelation. Little Gidding is both in time and rich in experience out of time.

In the second section of the work, the physical world and the record of civilization are imagined as having been purged away. For the believer, there is no final truth within time. Nor can human experience fully answer human needs. The passage which concludes this section, written in the metre of Dante and alluding to figures as diverse as Valéry, Blake and Yeats, is perhaps Eliot's supreme achievement. The life lived within literature and the literature of renunciation here fuse in the encounter with 'the familiar compound ghost'.

The long night's watch is over, the 'dark dove' of the Nazi bomber planes has passed by, 'interminable night' gives way to dawn. In the *Purgatorio* that is wartime London and all human history, Eliot and the ghost meet like Dantesque figures moving in a universe where meaning is divine rather than human, and the human spirit itself longs to be immersed in the refining fire. The modern poet – in an image that had preoccupied Eliot since the time of *The Waste Land* – must be at one with Dante's Provençal lyricist Arnaut Daniel rejoicing in the purgatorial flames and so working out his redemption. He must detach himself from the worldly and purify the true longing that can only be expressed in prayer. Then at last the pentecostal dove can descend, the word be at one with the Word, private vision be accorded spiritual certainty. This is the moment of illumination, timeless but ephemeral, when poet and prayerful believer are united, and

> all shall be well and
> All manner of thing shall be well.

It is a moment both of exaltation and of humility, an intimation of beatitude.

7

The immense influence of Eliot's criticism is closely connected with the rise of academic English studies, particularly at Cambridge University where an honours school of English was founded in 1917. Free of the philological bias of the older Oxford school, Cambridge had, in I.A. Richards (1893–1979), an innovator at once enthusiastic and rigorous. Richards's earlier studies had been in philosophy. He had been influenced especially by G.E. Moore, and he brought to the study of poetry both a linguistic exactitude and a moral concern with the value of literature in a world where the absolutes of God and the soul no longer seemed to have philosophic credence. Literature as the storehouse of values now supplies 'the best data for deciding what experiences are more valuable than others'. Though the moral and intellectual foundations of the greater part of earlier English literature are no more than 'pseudo-statements', nonetheless, when freed from belief, such statements remain 'the main instruments by which we order our attitudes to one another and to the world'. They are fragments to shore against moral ruin, and it is important that they be accurately read. As in Eliot's earlier essays, so in Richards's *Principles of Literary Criticism* (1924), he recoiled from the lack of method evident in so much contemporary literary study, while in *Practical Criticism* (1929) he both documented such looseness and began to provide a vocabulary for aiding more accurate description.

This new rigour was widely influential and can be allied to the close reading practised by Robert Graves and Laura Riding (b. 1901) in *A Survey of Modernist Poetry* (1927). Here, a reading of Shakespeare's sonnet 'The expense of spirit in a waste of shame' revealed the multiplicity of interwoven meanings the work contained, a richness that was itself a criterion of value. Inspired by this approach and encouraged by Richards, the poet and critic William Empson (1906–84) began work on *Seven Types of Ambiguity* (1930), a work whose insight into the layers of possible interpretation in a poem has been of incalculable influence in the universities. Such approaches were popularized for schools in the work of the poet James Reeves (1909–78) who also collaborated with Denys Thompson on various works, but it is Thompson's collaboration with F.R. Leavis (1895–1978) in *Culture and Environment* (1933) that introduces the most influential of the Cambridge critics.

Culture and Environment was intended to promote in schools Leavis's concern with what he believed were the values of the organic societies of the countryside. These values – nostalgic, conservative and almost certainly mythical – were, he thought, being lost amid the vulgarity of modern mass society with its jazz, journalism and junk novels. Leavis's own writing thus attempted to consolidate the work of Eliot, Richards and Empson by basing itself on a strongly urged moral concern with the state of the nation's culture. In this, Leavis was the heir of Arnold and the Victorians, and his critical writing was an honest and serious, if often bitterly contentious, effort to preserve literary study – 'concrete judgements and particular analyses' – as the humane centre of a modern education. *New Bearings in English Poetry* (1932) reveals Leavis's debts to the Cambridge school while making explicit his social concerns. His comment on *The Waste Land* – that very complex reaction to a disintegrating culture – focuses both these interests within the typical Leavisite tone:

that the public for it is limited is one of the symptoms of the state of culture that produced the poem. Works expressing the finest consciousness of the age in which the word 'highbrow' had become current, are almost inevitably such as to appeal only to a tiny minority. It is still more serious that this minority should be more and more cut off from the world around it – should, indeed, be aware of a hostile and overwhelming environment.

The modern university as the open élite of the intelligent and culturally aware, as the centre for the maintenance of true sensibility in an age of cultural decadence, was central to Leavis's thought. The magazine *Scrutiny* (1932–53) which he edited with his wife Q.D.

Leavis (1906–81) served as a forum of immense prestige, while the recipients of Leavis's charismatic teaching were to carry his influence into the newer universities. *Revaluation* (1936) extended the range of Leavis's criticism beyond the modern works he had previously analysed and opened up discussions at once critically fresh and acrimonious on Shakespeare, Milton and others. Many major critics and important critical works emerged from these decades, and English literature was now beginning to attract some of the finest academic minds of the time, a new professional breed often bitterly opposed to Bloomsbury, to the young socialist writers of the 1930s and to the Oxford tradition represented by the polymath C.S. Lewis (1898–1963).

Lewis and the critics of the 'Anglo-Oxford' school – Lewis himself, Charles Williams (1886–1945) and J.R.R. Tolkien (1892–1973) – were all concerned in different ways with literature as a humane source of spiritual nourishment in the modern world. C.S. Lewis's *The Allegory of Love* (1936) and his magisterial contribution to the *Oxford History of English Literature* both indicate the medieval and Renaissance bias of his Olympian scholarship. Similarly, his moralistic and Christian writings suggest the group's concern for traditional spiritual values. Tolkien's *The Lord of the Rings* (1954–5) is the finest among their attempts to find value in myth and romance rather than in more conventional modern prose.

This was an ambience that was to attract the mature Eliot whose increasing differences from Leavis (most clearly seen in their disagreement about Milton) led Leavis himself to find critical guidance in the work of D.H. Lawrence. The beliefs that underlay this development are most clearly expressed in a passage from Lawrence's *Studies in Classic American Literature* (1924). 'The novel', wrote Lawrence, 'is the perfect medium for revealing to us the changing rainbow of our living relationships. The novel can help us to live, as nothing else can: no didactic Scripture, anyhow.' The result was Leavis's *The Great Tradition* (1948) which established a new hierarchy for the English novel. 'Jane Austen, George Eliot, Henry James, Conrad, and D.H. Lawrence: the great tradition is there.' What this tradition embodied was the values Lawrence himself – later the subject of Leavis's *D.H. Lawrence, Novelist* (1955) – held as most precious in literature. Justifying a selection which omits Fielding, Thackeray, Joyce and Dickens (the latter an omission eventually made up) Leavis declared: 'their essential claim to greatness is that they are all distinguished by a vital capacity for experience, a kind of reverent openness before life, and a marked moral intensity'.

It was this moral intensity that characterized Leavis's later pronouncements against popular culture and what the Cambridge novelist L.H. Myers (1881–1944) called 'the deep-seated spiritual vulgarity' of the age. In her *Fiction and the Reading Public* (1932), Q.D. Leavis had traced this cultural decline to the commercial exploitation of growing literacy rates during the nineteenth century. Exacerbated by the modern demands of mass culture, the disastrous result of the worship of the best-seller was, she suggested, national decline engendered by books whose effect was to 'work on and solidify herd prejudice and to debase the emotional currency by touching grossly on fine issues'.

8

Such pessimism is in a long tradition. It is analogous to the cultural despair of the *Dunciad* and to Wordsworth's fulminations against 'frantic novels, sickly and stupid German Tragedies and deluges of idle and extravagant stories in verse'. For the Leavises and their disciples, the popularity of contemporary best-selling novelists offered 'convincing proof of the incapacity of the twentieth century to manage its emotional life for itself'. Such portentous gloom is not entirely supported by the facts.

During the 1930s, the number of new titles published each year fell consistently, and a strong back-list was a financial necessity for the publishers' survival. Cheap reprints have a long history, and the fact that in the twentieth century they could be edited to a relatively high standard is suggested by the founding of the Everyman Library in 1904 and the purchase by Oxford University Press of the World's Classics series in 1906. Both lists survive today, and the original success of the former was such that production had to be moved to the new garden city of Letchworth in order that conditions of supply could meet the great demand. The move is only one illustration of the desire for high-quality literature in modern mass society.

Middlebrow tastes were catered for by the Book Society and the Readers' Union, founded in 1929 and 1937 respectively, the first selecting its titles under the guidance of J.B. Priestley and the once popular Hugh Walpole (1884–1941). Far more immediately influential however was the Left Book Club founded by Victor Gollancz (1893–1967) in 1935 to counter the rise of Fascism by providing 'the indispensable basic *knowledge* without which a really effective United Front of all men and women cannot be built'. The club soon had a membership of 50,000 many of whom met in active discussion groups amid the harrowing social conditions of the time described in the club's most famous title, George Orwell's *The Road to Wigan Pier* (1937). If the relation of the Left Book Club to the Labour Party was distinctly uneasy, there can be little question of the contribution it made to the Labour victory of 1945 and the founding of the modern Welfare State.

By far the most significant event in modern British publishing however was the paperback revolution engineered from 1935 by Allen Lane (1902–70) at Penguin Books. That Lane was an innovator of genius is suggested by his being, while still at the Bodley Head, the first English publisher to risk issuing *Ulysses*. It was in his realization of the full potential of the paperbound volumes already familiar on the Continent however that Lane's abiding importance lies.

Paperbound books had occasionally appeared in seventeenth-century England where the Stationers' Company immediately regarded them with suspicion. Tauchnitz had long issued such volumes in Germany, and it was in challenging the somewhat dated appearance of these with his Albatross series, issued in Germany from 1932, that John Holroyd-Reece invented the format of the modern, mass-market paperback. This Lane took over while simultaneously revolutionizing the traditions of book marketing. Lane believed that cheap, attractive reprints of quality books could be sold not just in bookshops but in the retail chains where ordinary people did their daily shopping. The first ten Penguin paperbacks issued on 30 July 1935 were retailed by Woolworth's among other places at sixpence each. The venture was a tremendous risk. To maintain such low prices involved printing 20,000 copies of each title and selling most of them immediately. That Lane succeeded in clearing a million volumes in six months is an enormous tribute to his trust in the intelligence and interests of ordinary English men and women.

The titles Lane chose to launch with reflect this. While including such quintessentially English genres as the detective story with Agatha Christie's *The Mysterious Affair at Styles* (1920), Lane also issued André Maurois's life of Shelley and Ernest Hemingway's *A Farewell to Arms* (1929). Classic English works soon followed, and in April 1937 Lane issued six Penguin Shakespeare plays. Mass society and high literary culture now coincided, with the public able to buy '*Hamlet* for the price of ten Gold Flake'.

9

But for many in the 1930s cigarettes were a luxury beyond easy reach. In *English Journey* (1933), the popular playwright, novelist and broadcaster J.B. Priestley (1894–1984) described the moral and physical desolation wrought by unemployment in such northern towns as Jarrow. 'There is no escape anywhere in Jarrow from its prevailing misery,' Priestley wrote, 'for it is an entirely working-class town.' This background of the Depression, of social injustice and the divisions of class, was also to shape the attitudes of a rising generation of poets, the young W.H. Auden (1907–73) especially.

Auden's was a great talent that never revealed its full promise in a major and sustained work. His verse is often brilliant and troubling, but it rarely maintains its highest qualities. Indeed, it is frequently marred by a facility that degenerates into phrase-making and a merely irksome smartness. Characteristic lines – 'Watching the traffic of magnificent cloud' or 'Prohibit sharply the rehearsed response' – eventually reveal a manufactured, inert quality. It is as a lyric poet that Auden is at his best, as in the exquisite tenderness of 'Lay your sleeping head, my love' from *Look, Stranger!* (1936). Nonetheless, even in some of his lyric work there is a tendency to over-elliptical syntax and the muddled thought seen in 'Our hunting fathers'.

Such faults are also present in Auden's dramas of the 1930s where he shows his interest in the psychology of Freud and his followers. In *The Orators* (1932), fear and stifling inertia are the enemy in a society obsessed with intrigue. *The Dance of Death* (1933) is structured round Marxist propaganda. The verse in *The Dog beneath the Skin* (1935) and *The Ascent of F6* (1936) – works on which Auden collaborated with Christopher Isherwood – again tends towards the ponderous, though the feeling of a world headed irrecoverably for war is strong.

As Auden later declared of *Letters from Iceland* (1937), a volume on which he collaborated with Louis MacNeice (1907–63): 'though writing in a "holiday" spirit, its authors were all the time conscious of a threatening horizon to their picnic – world-wide unemployment, Hitler growing every day more powerful and a world-war more inevitable'. Works from this volume such as 'Letter to Lord Byron' express horror at economic collapse and proclaim that, in the suffering north of England, the idea of progress is 'not a white lie, it's a whacking big 'un'.

The pathos of poverty and working-class hopelessness which Auden helped to make subjects for modern poetry are seen again in 'An Elementary School Classroom in a Slum' by Stephen Spender (b. 1909) and Louis MacNeice's 'Birmingham'. A hatred of the sterile materialism of the south of England was also exposed by John Betjeman (1906–84) in his early and satiric 'Come friendly bombs and fall on Slough', as well as in the work of Cecil Day-Lewis (1904–72). Day-Lewis himself and MacNeice especially were to move beyond this to write a mature poetry which, while often in a traditional pastoral vein, has a craftsmanship and emotional subtlety too often ignored by critics in search of more obvious novelty. Betjeman was in turn to become the most widely read of modern English poets, his apparently safe and sometimes cloyingly cute persona belied by sharp, urbane satire and the unselfpitying pathos that characterizes the best passages in his autobiographical *Summoned by Bells* (1960).

Auden's sense of cultural decay and death-wish, his loathing of injustice, also profoundly influenced the generation associated with the *Left Review* (1934), with John Lehmann's *New Writing* (1936) and with Michael Roberts's two anthologies *New Signatures* (1932) and *New Country* (1933). Charles Madge (b. 1912) expressed a typical response when he wrote of Auden's work: 'I read, shuddered, and knew.'

The opposition of Fascist and left-wing forces in the Spanish Civil War (1936–9) became the testing ground for the political beliefs of writers and intellectuals of the time. While some like Ezra Pound and

Roy Campbell (1901–57) sided with Franco, many more agreed with Cecil Day-Lewis when he wrote: 'as a writer and as a member of the Communist party I am bound to help in the fight against fascism, which means certain destruction or living death for humanity'. In his 'Autumn Journal' (1936), MacNeice saw Spain as 'ripe as an egg for revolt and ruin', while in 'Spain, 1937', Auden spoke for those young idealists like John Cornford (1915–36) and Rex Warner (b. 1905) who believed that only the far Left could bring social justice to both Spain and Britain. Auden's poem, with its repeated insistence on 'today the struggle', captures the often tragic courage of such idealism. Describing those who actually made the journey to Spain, he wrote:

> They clung like burrs to the long expresses that lurch
> Through the unjust lands, through the night, through
>   the alpine tunnel:
>   They floated over the oceans;
> They walked the passes. All presented their lives.

The appeal of Communist ideas for many intellectuals in the 1930s has been analysed in the essays by various hands in Stephen Spender's *The God that Failed* (1950). Such figures, Spender suggests, often from public-school and professional backgrounds, were sickened and made guilty by the distress around them, the distress revealed by the old Etonian George Orwell (pseudonym of Eric Blair, 1903–50) in *Down and Out in Paris and London* (1933) and *The Road to Wigan Pier*. As a result, such young men often 'combined a belief in the inexorable Marxist development of history with mystical confidence in the workers'. A vision of justice was thus sustained by the false but alluring certainties of a dogma and a faith. The faith, nonetheless, was blind. John Lehmann (b. 1907), looking back on the period in *The Whispering Gallery* (1951), realized what he had not seen or had not been shown in Moscow: 'the total absence of political freedom, the fatal lack of open critical check in bureaucratic one-party government, the concealed poisoning of truth and corruption of values'.

Orwell's *Homage to Catalonia* (1938) suggests that disillusion with Marxism had set in by 1937, especially after revelations of Stalin's duplicity in the Spanish Civil War. This was soon followed by the terrible speed of approaching war. Just what was entailed in 'the frock-coated diplomat's social aplomb' described in Auden's 'Song for the New Year' (1937) was revealed eight months later when Chamberlain returned from Munich having tried to appease Hitler.

Auden himself, much to the anger of many, now sailed for New York. There, in 'September 1, 1939', seated in one of the 'dives' off Fifty-Second Street, he brooded fearfully on the 'low dishonest decade' as it expired. The later Auden, the Christian-Existentialist of *New Year Letter* (1941) and *The Age of Anxiety* (1948), of *Nones* (1951) and *The Shield of Achilles* (1959), is also the American Auden. In 1939, it was left to George Orwell in *Coming Up for Air* to imagine how, when the bombs fell on England, there would be 'plenty of broken crockery, and little houses ripped open like packing-cases, and the guts of the chartered accountant's clerk plastered over the piano that he's been buying on the never-never'.

Orwell's first novel, *Burmese Days* (1934), suggests his propagandist approach to fiction and is a misanthropic exposure of the moral blight inflicted by imperialism. This is a theme dealt with again in such essays as 'Shooting an Elephant' where Orwell's appearance of a rigorously objective style is in effective contrast to his very real anger. *Keep the Aspidistra Flying* (1936) portrays a life ruined amid modern urban poverty, and Orwell was eventually to declare: 'every line of serious work that I have written since 1936 has been written, directly or indirectly, *against* totalitarianism and *for* democratic socialism, as I understand it'. To Orwell, the period offered no alternative. Returning disillusioned from Spain to England, Orwell joined the Independent Labour Party, an extreme left-wing ideological group espousing pacifist principles. The outbreak of the Second World War however was to make Orwell realize 'that I was patriotic at heart', and his war work involved him – as it did many other writers – in broadcasting.

By 1945, when British public opinion was still strongly pro-Russian as a result of that nation's heroic effort in the war, Orwell eventually managed to publish *Animal Farm*. This exposure of Stalinist totalitarianism was to make Orwell's international reputation. Couched in the form of a beast fable, the work provided a short and lucid exposure of Orwell's fundamental conviction that revolutions encourage tyranny and that those who try to bring about equality eventually ensure that 'some are more equal than others'. Mankind, Orwell suggests, is not in the least capable of continuous moral improvement, and at the close of the work humans and pigs are indistinguishable.

In *Nineteen Eighty-Four* (1949), such defeatism works the annihilation of the individual in the totalitarian state. Winston Smith, the anti-hero, is at first in secret revolt against the tyranny of 'Ingsoc', Big Brother and the corruption of 'doublethink' and 'Newspeak' – dangers analysed again in Orwell's essay 'Politics and the English Language'. The novel nonetheless portrays the gradual and terrible alienation of the self from freedom as Smith, arrested by the Thought Police, eventually succumbs to the inquisitor's arguments on the nature of absolute state power and ends up worshipping the very force that has destroyed him. The prison scenes in *Nineteen Eighty-Four* owe something to Arthur Koestler's exposure of Communism in *Darkness at Noon* (trans. 1940), while in *Brave New World* (1932), Aldous Huxley portrayed a third dystopia and a minimal, tragic affirmation of human freedom amid the tyranny of scientific bureaucracy.

The early novels of Christopher Isherwood (1904–86) also deal with the effects of totalitarianism, in particular the warping of life and thought as Hitler came to power in the Weimar Republic. *Mr Norris Changes Trains* (1935) evokes the underlying violence of a country racked by unemployment, while Mr Norris himself, the sleazy, bewigged author of a pornographic novel, suggests the shifty corruption of moral values and the abasement of language accompanying the degradation of a nation. In *Goodbye to Berlin* (1939), a corrupt society preparing for war and the extermination camps is portrayed, while *Prater Violet* (1946) contains visions of the catastrophic horror of a nation corrupted by 'a cult based upon the most complex system of dogmas concerning the real nature of the Fuehrer, the utterances of *Mein Kampf*, the ten thousand Bolshevist heresies, and the sacrament of Blood and Soil; and upon elaborate rituals of mystic union with the Homeland, involving human sacrifice and the baptism of steel'.

Isherwood's first two novels – *All the Conspirators* (1928) and *The Memorial* (1932) – present the emotional paralysis, the sense of personal and social neurosis, evident in Auden's work of the period. The conspirators in the first work are a mother and her son who allow the youth's hypochondria to shield him from life's issues and keep him dependent on his possessive parent. The novel is constructed through a highly effective cinematographic technique of juxtaposition and flashback, as is *The Memorial*, a picture of a generation blighted in the aftermath of the First World War. The characters' hollow lives are here recorded with the moral impartiality suggested by Isherwood's well-known manifesto: 'I am a camera with its shutter open, quite passive, recording, not thinking.'

Isherwood's characters in these two novels expose themselves through their dialogue, a technique brought to remarkable sophistication in the novels of Ivy Compton-Burnett (1892–1969). Such dialogues are here less a matter of individual nuance however than of defence and aggression in an upper-middle-class world of deep-seated and shocking emotional instability. The late-nineteenth-century family is viewed by a writer who understands violence in the manner of the generation that matured during the First World War and who were to live through the years of neurosis leading to the Second World War. The dialogues in *Men and Wives* (1931), for example, filter a chilling narrative of failed suicide, emotional blackmail, murder, thwarted freedom and thwarted love. 'Dear, dear, the minute world of the family!' declares a character in *Parents and Children* (1941), 'all the emotions of mankind seem to find a place in it.' The result is emotional claustrophobia, the contrast of melodrama and dry irony, which often produces the tension of a barely suppressed scream.

The emotional suffocation of women in love is powerfully suggested by Rosamund Lehmann (b. 1901) in *Dusty Answer* (1927) and *The Echoing Grove* (1953). In such novels as *The Death of the Heart* (1938) by Elizabeth Bowen (1899–1973), emotional paralysis is registered through a sensibility and moral awareness greatly influenced by Henry James and a feeling for social comedy that clearly reflects Jane Austen. The young Portia, for example, progressively reveals the inert emotional life of the Quaynes, and the confrontation of the innocent with the experienced leads through paradox to tragedy.

The paralysis and underlying sense of fear characteristic of much fiction of the 1930s are powerfully rendered in *Party Going* by Henry Green (pseudonym of Henry Vincent Yorke, 1905–73), a novel published in the month that the Second World War broke out. Green had previously shown his technical ingenuity in *Blindness* (1926) – a remarkable evocation of the experience of a boy facing the loss of his sight, begun while Green was still at Eton – and also in *Living* (1929), a work that treats factory life in a humane and moving manner free of the overt political concerns characteristic of most of Green's contemporaries.

Party Going offers an equally emphatic neutrality in its presentation of a collection of upper-middle-class characters trapped by fog in the luxurious hotel of a crowded railway station and so unable to embark on a trip to France arranged by their benefactor. What Green characterized in his prose style as 'a gathering web of insinuation' here becomes his subject: a class-divided and fog-bound England waiting in a state of suspended animation and obscure threat. 'What targets, what targets for a bomb,' declares one character in the waiting crowd. The symbolism is deepened, and the sense of menace increased, by the repeated motif of the pigeon that falls dead at the feet of one of the characters who then takes it to the ladies' lavatory where she washes it and wraps it in brown paper. No moral is drawn, but the tone of fecklessness and imminent disaster is very strong.

These qualities are found again in such early novels by Anthony Powell (b. 1905) as *Afternoon Men* (1931) with its combination of fascination and patrician disdain for a slovenly and gossiping bohemian world endlessly involved in alcohol, sex and the disappointments of mechanistic hedonism. Beyond the frantic trivia lie 'vistas of triteness', and in *Venusburg* (1932) these stretch out to eastern Europe. Here, political and social insecurity and the sense of a decayed and unsustaining culture and of personal enslavement to dreary sexual passion are conveyed with laconic pathos as Lushington and his mistress wander in a decaying rococo palace.

The sense of frantic futility in Powell's early work becomes a form of tragic farce in the early novels of Evelyn Waugh (1903–66). The misadventures of Paul Pennyfeather in *Decline and Fall* (1928) set the form of these pre-war novels, while *Vile Bodies* (1930) captures the world of the Bright Young Things and the desperate hedonism of the decade:

'Oh, Nina, *what a lot of parties.*'
(. . . Masked parties, Savage parties, Victorian parties, Greek parties, Wild

West parties, Russian parties, Circus parties, parties where one had to dress as somebody else, almost naked parties in St John's Wood, parties in flats and studios and houses and ships and hotels and night clubs, in windmills and swimming baths, tea parties at school where one ate muffins and meringues and tinned crab, parties at Oxford where one drank brown sherry and smoked Turkish cigarettes, dull dances in London and comic dances in Scotland and disgusting dances in Paris – all that succession and repetition of massed humanity . . . Those vile bodies . . .)

The futile is here rendered through the comic, but it was largely the extensive travels that Waugh undertook after his divorce and conversion to Roman Catholicism in 1930 that broadened his approach and enabled him to juxtapose the heartlessness of Mayfair to the savagery of the primitive. The playboy figure of Basil Seal in *Black Mischief* (1932), Waugh's representative of a decaying Europe, is seen by an African emperor, for example, 'as the personification of all that glittering, intangible Western culture to which he aspired'. The tone of heartless farce is also maintained. 'You're a grand girl, Prudence, and I'd like to eat you,' Basil murmurs. Later, at a tribal feast, he unwittingly does just that.

The finest of these pre-war novels is *A Handful of Dust* (1934). The allusion to *The Waste Land* in the title suggests the greater seriousness of approach. Waugh's Tony Last is his image of the upright English gentleman, worthy but slightly absurd, who is destroyed by his own illusions of chivalric honour and the trivial selfishness of his wife. The moment when their son is killed while Brenda is having her fortune read from the soles of her feet exactly suggests the brittle and tragic world of the novel, moods heightened by the elegance and economy of Waugh's style and construction.

In *A Handful of Dust*, Tony Last is criticized for his anachronistic delight in the Gothic values symbolized by his home. In *Brideshead Revisited* (1945), the stately home that is the seat of the great Roman Catholic family of the Marchmains is Waugh's symbol of the traditional and hierarchical values that are so pronounced a feature of his later work. When Lord Marchmain finally returns to Brideshead, these values so move him that he dies in the faith he earlier renounced. Indeed, Waugh declared that the subject of his novel was 'the operation of divine grace on a group of diverse but closely connected characters'. It is partly her father's death that recalls his daughter Julia to ideals of devotion and duty, thereby preventing her marriage to the hero Charles Ryder. Similarly, Julia's brother, the alcoholic and homosexual Sebastian Flyte, ends up being cared for by a group of Christian brothers in North Africa.

Another Roman Catholic writer whose works involve what he called 'the appalling strangeness of the mercy of God' was Graham Greene (1904–91). Greene's novels of the early 1930s rehearse the great themes of the period – strikes, international finance, the Spanish Civil War, religion and Marxism – and do so in Greene's typical manner. Here is a world in which seediness is the background for the isolation of spiritual struggle and very often for the operation of political tyranny as well. Greene's novels frequently use such popular genres as the spy story and the political thriller to portray a vision influenced by Conrad and by newsreels, the cinema and Greene's belief that the sinner is at the very heart of Christianity. Many of these elements are clear in his first major novel, *Brighton Rock* (1938), a thriller and murder story set in a gangland where the seventeen-year-old Pinkie chooses evil and damnation amid the squalid world that has brutalized him: '"... it's the only thing that fits. These atheists, they don't know nothing. Of course there's Hell, Flames and damnation," he said with his eyes on the dark shifting water and the lighting and the lamps going out above the black struts of the Palace Pier, "torments."'

Such spiritual drama is particularly well achieved in *The Power and the Glory* (1940), Greene's study of the struggle between Marxism and Christianity. The 'whisky priest' is the one surviving representative of the church in a remote Mexican state whose secular values are represented by the police lieutenant. Both are men of dedication, and the policeman himself is an excellently conceived and humane foil to the more flamboyant priest – a drunken coward and fornicator – who yet rises to the stature of a martyr. The confrontation between the spiritual and the material is conceived with the greatest drama and humanity, an intelligence and moral passion that make this perhaps Greene's finest novel.

The operation of grace in sexual passion is dealt with in both *The Heart of the Matter* (1948) and *The End of the Affair* (1951). In the former, the hero is eventually driven to suicide, partly to prevent the suffering of his wife and mistress. According to strict Roman Catholic orthodoxy, he therefore dies in a state of mortal sin and so must be consigned to the hell so luridly described by Pinkie. But what does divine justice amount to if God so condemns an essentially good man? In the end, men and women cannot know. God cannot be limited by their understanding, nor can His love be measured by human horizons. As the priest says to Scobie's widow: 'Don't imagine that you – or I – know a thing about God's mercy.' Such mysterious and ruthless working of grace again underlies *The End of the Affair*. This moving novel, set in wartime London, appears to be a study of obsessive sexual jealousy yet, in the end, the hero Maurice Bendrix is forced to realize that he has lost his mistress not to her husband or another man but to God.

The narrator of *The End of the Affair* is himself a novelist, and it is the creative imagination which is a central subject in the work of Joyce Cary (1888–1957). 'We are the children of creation,' one of his characters declares, 'and we cannot escape our fate, which is to live in creating and re-creating.' Cary himself came late to fiction after a career spent variously in the fine arts and the imperial civil service. Among Cary's African novels, *Mister Johnson* (1939) portrays his characteristic theme of individual imagination in conflict with authority, doing so with a comedy that turns to tragedy as his expansive black hero dies as a result of the justice of the white man he so admires. *Charley is My Darling* (1940) stems from the experience of wartime evacuees in the countryside, but it is in the first of his trilogies that Cary's full powers are seen.

These novels – *Herself Surprised* (1941), *To Be a Pilgrim* (1942) and *The Horse's Mouth* (1944) – take three representative lives to portray English society between the close of the nineteenth century and the outbreak of the Second World War. In the first, Sara Monday describes her life with Thomas Wilcher and the artist Gully Jimson, the heroes of the second and third volumes. Cary wrote of her that Sara had 'the elementary morals of a primitive woman, of nature herself'. She surveys her career from prison where she has been sent for fraud, but in the unfolding of her life Cary creates a superb evocation of the earth mother and the eternal feminine. Thomas Wilcher in *To Be a Pilgrim* is an equally fine rendering of a wholly different type: the repressed, ageing and puritanical male whom Sara can only pity but through whom Cary created a remarkable portrait of English Nonconformity and the life of achievement in which Wilcher himself has failed. Finally, Gully Jimson is the artistic genius, an embattled and visionary Blake and one of the great comic characters in Cary's fiction. Sadly, this zest is not maintained in Cary's second trilogy where his philosophical concerns outweigh his interest in fiction.

One of the greatest novels of this era is *Under the Volcano* (1947) by Malcolm Lowry (1909–57). The work describes the last hours in the life of the alcoholic British Consul Geoffrey Firmin as he flees the call of love in the Mexican town of Quauhnahuac. It is the Day of the Dead 1938, and in this remote location and amid a grim celebration, Lowry creates his vision of the modern world as hell. If Joyce and Conrad stand behind him, Lowry's technical ability and visionary depth are magnificently his own and perfectly fused. Firmin's alcoholism, for example, is a symptom of his damnation, of his being separated from those who love him and who, for all his passion, he cannot respond to. He is seen as alienated modern man in flight from bar to bar as the two great volcanoes lour over the town and proclaim the entrance to the underworld. In Europe, meanwhile, the Spanish Civil War is coming to its dreadful end and Hitler is rising to power. If the novel offers its glimpses of paradise, it is thoroughly acquainted with hell – the hell of politics, the hell of loneliness, the hell of love. Its central figure, focused with the strongest moral clarity, ends his life at the hands of Fascist thugs, his corpse thrown into the ravine between the volcanoes.

The poets who began to establish their reputations in the early 1940s were also seeking modes of visionary expression. As Cyril Connolly (1903–74), author of *Enemies of Promise* (1938) and editor of the influential magazine *Horizon* (founded 1940), declared: 'the flight of Auden and Isherwood to a land richer in incident and opportunity is also a symptom of the failure of social realism as an aesthetic doctrine'. Dylan Thomas (1914–53) again opined at Auden's 'sanitary science', and his own work suggests the awareness of the senses, the deep and even mystical love of landscape, as well as the determined regionalism of these younger poets. Both 'Fern Hill' and 'Poem in October' evoke the landscapes of Wales with a visionary intensity and in a language at once dense with imagery and loaded with the weight of Thomas's own bardic voice. Indeed, the poems are almost inseparable from Thomas's reading of them, as are parts of the poetic prose of his radio play *Under Milk Wood* (1954). *Portrait of the Artist as a Young Dog* (1940) suggests this aspect of the performer in Thomas, but his early and tragic death from alcohol poisoning suggests something of the enormous tension that was involved in his trying to preserve a vision at once innocent and rapturous.

Both Vernon Watkins (b. 1906) and R.S. Thomas (b. 1913) have written with passion and humour about the landscapes and people of Wales, while Thomas's poetry especially has been deepened and made more personal by his restless Christianity and his dialogue with 'an untenanted cross'. Humble prayer for redemption in a visionary landscape is a characteristic of some of Thomas's finest work.

The shrewd poetic intelligence of John Heath-Stubbs (b. 1918) castigated the worst excesses of this neo-romantic school, and his own work is altogether more astringent. Nonetheless the neo-romanticism espoused by Dylan Thomas is also to be found in the work of George Barker (b. 1913) and David Gascoyne (b. 1916) whose 'Ecce Homo' again suggests, in its praise of a 'Christ of Revolution and of Poetry', the deep longing for spiritual affirmation that underlies the work of many of the poets of this period. 'The Horses' by Edwin Muir (1887–1959), for example, offers a suggestive myth about the redemption of the natural world after the death of our industrialized, mechanistic civilization. A visionary attitude to the natural world is again characteristic of the poetry of Andrew Young (1885–1971). In the tense, spare language of Kathleen Raine (b. 1908), nature mysticism combines with a deeply felt sexual passion to create poems of considerable stature. Again, *The Anathemata* (1952) by David Jones (1895–1974), offers in its immense complexity an attempt at visionary history.

A number of poets were to make their reputations in exile. Wartime Cairo, for example, was home to Lawrence Durrell (1912–91), Bernard Spencer (b. 1909) and Terence Tiller (b. 1916) whose well-crafted poems, vivid with Mediterranean light, appeared in the magazine *Personal Landscape*, much of which was anthologized in volume form in 1945. The greatest of these poets living abroad however was Robert Graves.

Graves wrote some of the finest love poetry of the twentieth century. In 1929, after the publication of *Goodbye to All That*, he moved to Majorca with Laura Riding with whom he had collaborated on the immensely influential *Survey of Modernist Poetry*. Here he began to support himself by writing novels in the genre he invented – the imaginary historical autobiography. *I, Claudius* and *Claudius the God*, both published in 1934, coolly and amusingly show the Gravesian theme of a man struggling for sanity in a mad world, while *Wife to Mr Milton* (1943) is a skilful example of stylistic pastiche and literary criticism. Graves's classical interests were revealed by his many translations, while *The Greek Myths* (1955) suggests a fundamental concern fully embodied in *The White Goddess* (1948).

The basis of this work, and of Graves's art generally, was outlined in a letter to a friend in 1946. 'Poetry has always supplied my religious needs,' he wrote. 'This may seem a stupid statement but I am realizing, have been realizing for the last three years, that real poetry . . . is an epitome of the ancestral religion of Europe which made the Minoans what they were, and which was submerged by the Arian invaders about 2000 BC and finally stamped out by the Christians.' Pagan, mythical, the centre of a cult of erotic love, the White Goddess is the muse who has her embodiment in the woman whom she 'may make her instrument for a month, a year, seven years or even more'.

For Graves, the writing of poetry was thus a central spiritual exercise, an engagement with an experience at once physical and numinous. Many of the lyrics gathered in *Poems 1938–45* reveal the power of the art generated by such beliefs. These poems include 'To Juan in the Winter Solstice', a deeply satisfying example of Graves's mythopoeic imagination, 'Through Nightmare' and one of his greatest love poems, 'Mid-Winter Waking'. This last shows Graves at his best and most typical. The poem is ordered with a rigorous craftsmanship, while the terseness of the greater part of the diction is effectively juxtaposed to a subtlety of rhythm, to coinages and a vocabulary altogether richer and more evocative of the emotion that underlies the work. The poem is a celebration of human love both exquisitely tender and direct. As, in 'this mid-winter', the poet wakes, so

> I found her hand in mine laid closely
> Who shall watch out the Spring with me.
> We stared in silence all around us
> But found no winter anywhere to see.

Such love is a waking to art and vocation. New life buds in midwinter, and 'I knew myself once more a poet.'

Graves published his earliest work during the First World War and was a contemporary of Owen and Rosenberg. The poets of the Second World War – Alun Lewis (1915–44), Keith Douglas (1920–44) and Sidney Keyes (1922–43) – wrote less of the battlefield than of the circumstances surrounding hostilities: parting in Lewis's 'Goodbye', decadent civilian life in Douglas's 'Cairo Jag' or the hopeless fate of victims in 'Europe's Prisoners'. The talent that was destroyed by the tragically early deaths of these men is best seen in Douglas's 'Simplify me when I'm dead', a poem of the deepest pathos and intellectual sensitivity.

For many during the war however the commanding voice was that of Winston Churchill (1874–1965). Churchill's entertaining autobiography *My Early Life* was published in 1930, while as a historian his style has something in common with Macaulay. Churchill's rhetoric and theatricality have been much disparaged. Nonetheless, in the darkest years of the war, when the people of Britain had nothing to rely on save their courage and their language, Churchill's speeches, delivered on the BBC, wrought both to the highest pitch and so helped inspire the eventually victorious struggle against evil.

IO

But with the coming of victory Churchill's imperial tone seemed an anachronism, and in the election of 1945 he was swept aside by the democracy he had fought to preserve. No passage more movingly expresses the profound change the war wrought to the old order than the exchange between Guy Crouchback and a Jewish refugee in Evelyn Waugh's *Sword of Honour* trilogy (1952–61, 1965):

'Is there any place that is free from evil? It is too simple to say that only the Nazis wanted war. These Communists wanted it too. It was the only way in which they could come to power. Many of my people wanted it, to be revenged on the Germans, to hasten the creation of the national state. It seems to me there was a will to war, a death wish, everywhere. Even good men thought their private honour would be satisfied by war. They could assert their manhood by killing and being killed. They would accept hardships in recompense for having been selfish and lazy. Danger justified privilege. I knew Italians – not very many perhaps – who felt this. Were there none in England?'

'God forgive me,' said Guy. 'I was one of them.'

It is into the world built out of the wreckage of this realization that many of us were born and in which all of us live. The literature produced in the decades after the war is one of the means by which our culture defines itself. Here, more than anywhere, commentary must recognize that it is personal and provisional. Conscious of the risk of being merely bland and bibliographic, what follows is simply an attempt to suggest some of the main lines of development to about 1970 and indicate those works that appear to me particularly valuable.

For all its harsh shrewdness and moments of humour, Waugh's *Sword of Honour* trilogy is marred by its author's snobbery, with the result that Guy Crouchback, the officer and gentleman displaced in the modern world, is a lesser creation than Augustine Penry-Herbert, the hero of *The Human Predicament* (1961–73) by Richard Hughes (1900–76). This series is unfinished, but *The Fox in the Attic* (1961) and *The Wooden Shepherdess* (1973) are among the greatest achievements of post-war British fiction.

Hughes's first novel, *A High Wind in Jamaica* (1929), is a remarkable and original analysis of the mind on the borders of adolescence. His next work, *In Hazard* (1938), challenges Conrad on his own ground and suggests the working of self-discovery and virtue as a ship encounters an unexpected hurricane. It is *The Human Predicament* however that shows the immense range and subtlety of Hughes's imagination and a mind that had the reach of both the great novelist and the great historian. Through what we are shown of the life of Augustine Penry-Herbert, we come to see the forces at work in a world headed for the catastrophe of war. Penry-Herbert himself is the last heir of the British great-house tradition, but the most remarkable scenes are those set in a Germany declining into Fascism. Old and weakening order and the new, barbarous forces of chaos are superbly juxtaposed, while the sheer power of Hughes's imagination is suggested by his being able to weave into his account of imaginary characters a portrait of a Hitler sufficiently spiritually minimal to attract Goering and the degenerates of the Nazi Party. To achieve this without appearing factitious is a major attainment, yet quite as subtle is Hughes's later presentation of old British culture confronting new American forces – a relationship of fundamental importance to twentieth-century experience.

Olivia Manning's (1908–80) *The Balkan Trilogy* (1960–65) and *The Levant Trilogy* (1977–80) suggest the rootless internationalism forced by the war on Britons adrift in a world they no longer automatically control. The depiction of the relationship between Harriet and Guy Pringle is finely rendered through the consciousness of Harriet herself, while Guy, the working-class intellectual, suggests both the values of British culture in a world of unreason as well as the admirable humanitarianism of the new men who would help build the Britain of the Welfare State.

Lewis Eliot, the hero of the *Strangers and Brothers* (1940–70) sequence by C.P. Snow (1905–80), charts the rise in this new world of a self-made man. The novels are an account of public and private struggles in those closed communities of national influence that Snow himself was to call 'the corridors of power'. The sequence lacks the sense of a permanently quickening spirit however, and the more important *roman-fleuve* of the post-war era is Anthony Powell's *A Dance to the Music of Time* (1951–75).

This work also partly concerns itself with the rise of the meritocracy, but where Lewis Eliot is a central consciousness in Snow's work, Powell's Nicholas Jenkins, a minor literary man, is essentially a reflector of his society, its anecdotalist in the manner of Powell's favourite John Aubrey. Private consciousness is less the issue here than the revelation of character in set-piece scenes ranging from bohemia to the world of the upper middle classes. These areas are populated by a myriad of figures whose complex inner compulsions are often at odds with their clipped, laconic conversations. The background of political and cultural developments is skilfully suggested, nowhere more acerbically than in the career of the absurd Kenneth Widmerpool, a philistine exploiting the trends of his time. And it is the passage of time that is Powell's chief concern. A passage on a painting by Poussin in *A Question of Upbringing* (1951) is beautifully evocative of this idea and of the methods of the sequence itself:

The image of Time brought thoughts of mortality: of human beings, facing outwards like the Seasons, moving hand in hand in intricate measure: stepping slowly, methodically, sometimes a trifle awkwardly, in revolutions that take recognizable shape: or breaking into seemingly meaningless gyrations, while partners disappear only to reappear again, once more giving pattern to the spectacle: unable to control the melody, unable, perhaps, to control the steps of the dance.

Lawrence Durrell's *The Alexandria Quartet* (1957–60) offers a view of life – especially the erotic life – in a feistily polyglot city, doing so in highly wrought prose. The work's philosophic ambitions are somewhat pretentious however and Durrell's style is highly and even wearisomely ornate. Other novels on international themes dealt shrewdly with Britain's retreat from her imperial role. Her relation to India, for example, is evoked in J.G. Farrell's (1935–79) *The Siege of Krishnapur* (1970), an account of the Mutiny of 1857 that is as densely wrought as a Victorian novel while offering a modern assessment of imperialism. *The Raj Quartet* (1966–75) by Paul Scott (1920–78) is an account of the personal and racial tensions on the subcontinent in the era of independence, and is touchingly complemented by *Staying On* (1977).

One of the most interesting analyses of imperial decline is *The Malayan Trilogy* (1972) by Anthony Burgess (b. 1917). This is a pessimistic vision of Britain's role, not just of the decline into irrelevance of old ideals of colonial service, but of England herself as a land culturally emasculated. Burgess's vision has been deeply influenced by his Roman Catholic upbringing, and novels like *Earthly Powers* (1980) – rich with erudition, wit and puns – suggest that the forces of evil and destruction are more likely to triumph than those of good.

Burgess is one of the most prolific novelists of his generation and also one of the most consistently experimental. He has a polymath's range and a deeply informed knowledge of the great masters of his craft. His critical works on Joyce and Lawrence are admirable, alive with the novelist's need to relate to his predecessors. His own works of fiction are the products of an imagination that refuses to be confined by the conventional and the formulaic.

Language itself is one of Burgess's abiding preoccupations. *Nothing Like the Sun* (1964) experiments with Elizabethan pastiche, while language and futuristic social criticism combine in what has become his most notorious work, *A Clockwork Orange* (1962). Burgess himself disparages the emphasis placed on this work, particularly after its filming. Nonetheless, the account of the hoodlum Alex and his 'droogs' or mates in a society riven by depravity, along with the morally complex irony whereby the 'cured' Alex is merely a vegetable compared to his former self oscillating between high art and criminal bestiality, creates a deeply disturbing work. Two further novels suggest Burgess's extraordinary range. *The Wanting Seed* (1962) is a nightmare vision of the hideous measures taken to control an overpopulated world and of the political manipulation of the heroic myths of the First World War. *MF* (1971), by contrast, is an intricate and highly inventive attempt to engage with the structuralist theory fashionable in the 1960s and 1970s, and is a work that does not shrink from poking fun at anthropological solemnities.

Fantasy as a means of social satire and moral investigation was particularly influential in the early post-war era. Wyndham Lewis had published *The Childermass* in 1928. Here he exposed the hollowness of modern so-called civilized values, and the Dantesque elements in the work were developed in *Monstre Gai* and *Malign Fiesta*. Published as a trilogy under the title *The Human Age* (1955), the novels suggest a parallel between materialism and a modern *Inferno* where the threat of the atomic bomb forever lurks. Among other trilogies, Tolkien's *The Lord of the Rings* and its mythopoeic concern with good and evil has already been mentioned, while *Gormenghast* (1946–59) by Mervyn Peake (1911–68) can be read in part as an allegory of a hidebound, bureaucratic post-war society. Finally, after such novels of rural life as *Wolf Solent* (1929) and *Weymouth Sands* (1934), John Cowper Powys (1872–1963) developed his concern for the forces of nature and the spirit in the mythological and apocalyptic tones of *A Glastonbury Romance* (1932).

The post-war novels of Graham Greene are works by one of the few British novelists of his era to have a truly international reputation. These works show Greene not only as a Roman Catholic writer but as a considerable political novelist, a writer with an extraordinary sensitivity to areas of international conflict. This is clear from *The Quiet American* (1955) with its sophisticated structure, skilfully contrived elements of mystery and depiction of the political evil worked in Saigon. 'Sooner or later, one has to take sides.' Nonetheless, affirmation in Greene's world is only achieved with difficulty. In *The Comedians* (1966), for example, those who give their name to the title are those who opt out of moral responsibility in the Haiti of Papa Doc. For a long while the narrator is included among them, but even he is eventually shown to have at least some knowledge of higher values amid his sordid existence.

Where Greene was a figure of international repute, many English writers chose to stay within the traditions that derive from Jane Austen and Henry James. Here, social comedy, moral sensitivity and irony are addressed through works where refined craftsmanship is often contrasted to the violence and cruelty lurking in everyday life.

The finest of these figures to come to prominence after the war was L.P. Hartley (1895–1972) whose *Eustace and Hilda* trilogy (1944–7) is a carefully observed account of the relationship between a sensitive young man and his more passionate sister, mutual victims locked in destruction and a tragedy constructed with delicacy and ruthless clarity of purpose. These qualities are seen again in *The Hireling* (1957) and *The Go-Between* (1950), this last being a finely wrought account of the blighting of a life at the very moment when it is beginning to unfold.

Among women novelists writing in the tradition influenced by Elizabeth Bowen was Elizabeth Taylor (1912–75) whose maturity of insight and gift for pathos can be seen in such novels as *A Wreath of Roses* (1950) and *Mrs Palfrey at the Claremont* (1972). Barbara Pym (1913–80) was an altogether more precious observer of provincial and Anglican life among the middle classes, while two further figures must also be mentioned. Pamela Hansford Johnson (1912–81) has rendered the intricacies of English life with a sure awareness of the moral duties underlying individual complexity. Rose Macaulay's (1881–1958) *The Towers of Trebizond* (1956) is written in a manner that tries to avoid the stereotypes of gender and so suggest the universality of emotions.

One of the principal modern writers who has felt herself 'obliged to repudiate the shackled woman of the past' is Doris Lessing (b. 1919). The early volumes of her sequence *Children of Violence* (1952–69) are set in Rhodesia before independence, and her heroine Martha Quest – a British woman locked in the unresolved conflicts of race, class and gender – is Lessing's focus for an analysis of the range of pained experience that finds expression in *The Golden Notebook* (1962). The narrative entitled 'Free Woman' in this work suggests Lessing's concern with 'what is known as free lives, that is, lives like men'. Lessing suggests that such freedom may lead to dependence and breakdown in a world where stable relationships fail, where men are deficient in the capacity to love, and 'feminine sensibility' is seen in a Marxist light 'since the emotions are a function and a product of society'. The struggle of the female intellectual in the worlds of imperialism and Marxist politics and the spheres of sex and the imagination eventually leads to a searing sense of hopelessness. *The Golden Notebook* is a frighteningly pained work. Lessing's later novels use science fiction as a basis for a cosmic exploration of her themes.

The first novel by Iris Murdoch (b. 1919) was *Under the Net*, published in 1954. Its picaresque form was abandoned in later work, but the philosophic preoccupation with getting 'under the net' of theory and language to apprehend the 'unutterably particular' – a concern which in part accounts for the saturation of Murdoch's work with descriptive detail – is juxtaposed in her later books to her use of an elusive yet often richly suggestive symbolism. This in its turn helps to suggest both the similarities and the differences, the areas of individual growth and conflict, in her characters' developing personalities. The beautiful object that provides the title for *The Bell* (1958), for example, bears the Latin inscription 'I am the voice of love'. Its discovery and subsequent lifting from the bed of a lake at a religious community is a focus for the self-realization of both Michael Meade, a homosexual torn between romantic and religious passion, and Dora, the would-be artist. The religious community itself disintegrates, but the bell's motto underlies the Abbess's declaration that 'all our failures are failures in love'.

The highly stylized construction of *A Severed Head* (1961) is a further typical feature of the Murdoch novel, and again shows the author trying to suggest a reality beyond the tyranny of easy generalization. At its best, in novels such as *The Black Prince* (1971), these concerns are vividly explored, but there is also a tendency in some of Murdoch's work – *The Nice and the Good* (1968), for instance, or *A Fairly Honourable Defeat* (1970) – to drift into philosophic essay.

Contrivance as a deliberate fiction 'out of which a kind of truth emerges' is a characteristic of the work of Muriel Spark (b. 1918) At its best, particularly in such early novellas as *Memento Mori* (1959) with its artful yet chilling final revelation of the reality of death, this contrast is highly effective. An awareness of powerful forces working under appearance – frustration leading to Fascism in *The Prime of Miss Jean Brodie* (1961), for example, or the operation of evil and grace in *The Girls of Slender Means* (1963) – points to another feature of Spark's work: the reality of eruptive violence seen most clearly in *The Driver's Seat* (1970).

Angus Wilson (1913–91) was to turn in his later works towards the self-conscious manipulation of fictional devices, but his earlier novels – written after two brilliant collections of short stories, *The Wrong Set* (1949) and *Such Darling Dodos* (1950) – are an ambitious attempt both to re-create a Victorian richness and to convey a sense of the evil underlying contemporary society. This last is a force that the liberal values of Bernard Sands, the married but homosexual hero of *Hemlock and After* (1952), cannot effectively combat. In *Anglo-Saxon Attitudes* (1956), Wilson again examined the traditions of English liberalism, relating his hero's processes of reflection and self-discovery to the broader framework of historic change. The novel is distinguished by its fine re-creation of social milieux, by its idiomatic dialogue and by Wilson's awareness of how people hide behind social roles. These are aspects of Wilson's art ambitiously pursued in *The Middle Age of Mrs Eliot* (1958).

In *The Old Men at the Zoo* (1961), Wilson turned to futuristic fable to suggest man's dependence on the world of nature in a Britain that is now a minor post-colonial power whose society has become a meritocratic dystopia – a self-destructive horror of bureaucracy and materialism. The critical and imaginative force of Wilson's vision here makes this one of his most important novels, though the depths of misery and rootlessness he detected in post-war England are again movingly portrayed in *Late Call* (1964).

Wilson's was a vision of the *malaise* of the England of his time. The novels of William Golding (b. 1911), especially those of his earlier period, offer a troubling insight into mankind's inherent sinfulness, that innate capacity for evil which appears to render ideas of human perfectibility a sentimental sham. Such works as *The Spire* (1964), in which man's aspirations towards God are shown as having been reared amid dreadful suffering, exploitation and pride, are a powerful indictment of complacency and facile optimism. *The Spire* also suggests the mythopoeic cast of Golding's imagination. Indeed, he is one of the greatest inventors of moral allegory since Bunyan and shares with the earlier writer the artist's knowledge that such narratives must be firmly rooted in the world of physical reality. Golding's response to the natural world can be shiveringly intense. *The Inheritors* (1965), for instance, is a vividly realized evocation of the life of Neanderthal man and the Fall.

These qualities of moral, imaginative and technical resource are seen fully matured in Golding's first work, *Lord of the Flies* (1954). Here, the gung-ho Victorian optimism of R.M. Ballantyne's *The Coral Island* (1857) is replaced by a vision of shipwrecked boys relapsing into barbarism and destroying civilized social order in their worship of the Devil – Beelzebub, the lord of the flies. The self's realization of its natural tendency to evil is conveyed in *Pincher Martin* (1956) with the technical ingenuity that is yet more highly wrought in *Darkness Visible* (1979). This novel, produced after long silence, also suggests the possibility of redemption, while Golding's latest work – the trilogy *Rites of Passage* (1980), *Close Quarters* (1987) and *Fire Down Below* (1989) – seems to suggest the possibility of man's maturing towards an acceptance of his moral responsibility in an evil world.

Lessing, Spark, Wilson and Golding emerged as novelists in the 1950s, a decade also associated with the defiant provincialism of the Angry Young Men and a literature suggesting an allegiance to lower-middle- and working-class life. This is seen at its most affecting in Alan Sillitoe's (b. 1928) *The Loneliness of the Long Distance Runner* (1959). Much of this writing has dated nonetheless. It lacks the intellectual weight and sensitivity of one of the most important works of the time, Richard Hoggart's (b. 1918) *The Uses of Literacy* (1957) with its careful analysis of the threatened status of working-class culture in post-war affluent society.

The university-educated hero of John Wain's (b. 1925) *Hurry On*

Down (1954) eventually compromises with a society whose hypocrisy he reviles, while Joe Lampton in John Braine's (b. 1922) *Room at the Top* (1957) suggests something of the new affluence, a theme investigated again in Alan Sillitoe's *Saturday Night and Sunday Morning* (1958). *Lucky Jim* (1954) by Kingsley Amis (b. 1922) is an altogether finer work, a satire on life in one of the newer universities and a narrative of the misadventures of a young lecturer unable to prevent himself from exposing the academic racket he would nonetheless be part of. Amis has subsequently widened and deepened his satiric range, and if he sometimes seems mechanically bitter, he can also inveigh against trivial standards with considerable force and elicit from his characters a genuine sense of pathos.

Look Back in Anger (1956) by John Osborne (b. 1929) gave the Angry Young Men their group name and helped revolutionize the expectations of a theatre-going public who for a long time had been fed either on the safe, well-made plays of J.B. Priestley and Terence Rattigan (1911–77) or on the experiments in dramatic verse made by T.S. Eliot and Christopher Fry (b. 1907). Then, in 1955, Samuel Beckett's *Waiting for Godot* came to London, followed the next year by the work of Ionesco and Bertolt Brecht's Berliner Ensemble. In this year too there emerged the hugely influential English Stage Company at the Royal Court Theatre, their season opening with Angus Wilson's *The Mulberry Tree*, Arthur Miller's (b. 1915) *The Crucible* (1953), and Osborne's *Look Back in Anger*.

Though the conclusion of this last work now seems weakly structured, its bitter analysis of the decline of the hopes nurtured in 1945 and, above all, its realistic presentation of the brutalized lives of the young, educated, but poor, was both original and challenging. Stimulated by the policies of the Royal Court and the critic Kenneth Tynan (1927–80) especially, a number of plays directed against middle-class conventions rapidly followed. These included the powerful combination of tenderness and bitterness in Shelagh Delaney's (b. 1939) *A Taste of Honey* (1958), John Arden's (b. 1930) *Live Like Pigs* (1958), Arnold Wesker's (b. 1932) *Roots* (1959) and, most politically challenging of all, Brendan Behan's (1923–64) *The Hostage* (1958). Here indeed was a powerful literary engagement with contemporary British society, while, with Samuel Beckett (1906–89), drama in the English language at last seemed part of the European mainstream.

Beckett had been an amanuensis to James Joyce, but where Joyce's vision is all-encompassing and accepting, Beckett's prose fiction works through great intellectual subtlety to affirm a radically minimal image of man. The hero of *Murphy* (1938), tied in his rocking-chair, inhabits an uncertain, ambiguous world which in *Watt* (1944) is yet more terribly a world of the writer's contrivance. In *Molloy* (1951), such contrivance is of great formal and stylistic beauty – Beckett wrote a genuine prose-poetry – but the events described are both humiliating and pointless. In *Malone Dies* (1952), the elderly man amusing himself by inventing narratives seems almost to converge with the creature of his imagination. It is *The Unnameable* (1960) who is the most terrible of these twilight figures however. Playing his 'wordy-gurdy', he recognizes he has spent his life churning out 'a ponderous chronicle of moribunds in their courses, moving, clashing, writhing or fallen in shortlived swoons'. The armless and legless man kept in a bell-jar by the proprietress of a restaurant is one of the most wretched of these figures.

It was with his drama and with *Waiting for Godot* (1954) especially that Beckett gave the best-known expression to his pessimistic philosophy of 'Nothing to be done.' The opening line of the play sets its theme with the result that the action is continuous inaction: suffering, fear, uncertainty and long waiting. The full effect (which is extremely difficult to achieve in production) is of comedy and tragedy fused in a dialogue of evocative yet beautifully economic power – a language spoken in defiance of circumambient silence. In *Endgame* (1958), Beckett's familiar themes and situations reveal what he called 'the power of the text to claw', but it is *Krapp's Last Tape* (1959) that most movingly reveals the life of an old man trapped in memory and nearly impotent, the problems of his early middle age still unresolved. Nonetheless, it is Winnie in *Happy Days* (1960) who remains perhaps Beckett's greatest theatrical invention. Persistent and brave in a futile world, her very ordinariness seems to take on an appearance of the heroic.

The influence of Beckett, and also to some degree of Ionesco, can be felt in the work of Harold Pinter (b. 1930). In plays such as *The Birthday Party*, first performed in 1958, *The Dumb Waiter* and *The Caretaker* (both published 1960), Pinter established his characteristic blend of minimal realism constantly threatened by failures of communication and the troubled sense of personal identity in a world menaced by violence. In *The Caretaker*, speech at once suggests the banal hopes and fantasies of Aston, Mick and Davies while imprisoning them in an obsessive language that seems to come from some other and more superficial parts of their minds than their deep and ultimately inarticulate privacies. In such a world as this, fantasy carries the constant threat of sliding from the absurd into madness. Such experiences are suggested in *A Night Out* (1961) and the hallucinatory radio play *Landscape* (1968), while *No Man's Land* (1975) derives comedy, suffering and horror from a language that is again an entrapment.

This undertow of violence is also seen in plays as various in date and subject as Anne Jellicoe's (b. 1927) *The Sport of my Mad Mother* (1958, revised 1964), John Whiting's (1917–63) *The Devils* (1961) and Peter Terson's (b. 1932) depiction of football hooliganism in *Zigger-Zagger* (1964). In Joe Orton's (1933–67) *Entertaining Mr Sloane* (1964) and *Loot* (1965), violence and farce create an effect in which the self-consciously theatrical borders on hysteria. David Rudkin's (b. 1936) *Afore Night Come* (1962) chillingly evokes ritual murder.

Plays on historical themes could also offer a perspective on modern concerns. The heroes of Robert Bolt's (b. 1924) *A Man for All Seasons* (1960) and John Osborne's (b. 1929) *Luther* (1961), for example, suggest the pursuit of integrity in worlds of political and spiritual corruption. Peter Shaffer's (b. 1926) *The Royal Hunt of the Sun* (1965) depicts the ruinous greed of Western colonialism. Joan Littlewood and the Stratford (East) ensemble's *Oh What a Lovely War!* (1963) offered a depiction of the First World War deeply influenced by the work of Brecht. Previously, John Arden's *Sergeant Musgrave's Dance* (1959) had shown the bewilderment of historical characters trapped in a world meant partly to reflect contemporary struggles of labour and capitalism.

One of the most important figures to emerge out of the Writers' Group at the Royal Court is Edward Bond (b. 1934). The stoning of a baby in Bond's *Saved* (1965) is a moment that focuses more sharply than any other the emphasis on violence in the plays of this period. It caused the inevitable uproar which led eventually to the abolition of stage censorship under the office of the Lord Chamberlain in 1968. In Bond's work, such violence is not meant as gratuitous. It is an essential part of his awareness of oppression, of class brutalization and human suffering. These are seen again in *Narrow Road to the Deep North* (1968) and *Lear* (1972). In *Bingo* (1971), Bond's political message is of the overriding necessity for changing the human consciousness that can accept such a world of violence and cruelty.

Some of the senior poetic figures whose stature only emerged after the Second World War had written important work during the 1930s. Much of this suggests a major intellectual and emotional commitment both to the past and to the broadest traditions of European culture. Austin Clarke (1896–1974), for example, was influenced by the Irish poetic tradition and by myth. Christopher Murray Grieve (1892–1978), writing as Hugh McDiarmid, was a disciple of Pound's whose own *Cantos* (1925–69) with their moments of undoubted greatness and frequent profuse pretentiousness were appearing at this time. From the publication of *Sangschaw* (1925) onwards however, McDiarmid also attempted to revitalize the traditions of Scottish verse and make these international. His political affiliations are suggested by his *Second Hymn to Lenin*, while 'O Wha's Been Here afore Me Lass' shows the power of his lyric achievement.

David Jones (1895–1974) in *The Tribune's Visitation* (1969) continued his exploration of the continuities of the Christian past and present. The widely eclectic verse in *The Spoils*, written by Basil Bunting (1900–85) in 1951, only became generally available in 1965. Like McDiarmid, Bunting's work was deeply influenced by Pound, while *Briggflats* (1966) mingles cobby Northumberland landscapes and dialect to create an individual music which was to have more influence in the United States than in his homeland.

Bunting's faults of a too contrived vocabulary are sometimes matched by the prolixity of the man who, at his best, remains the most moving of these poets, George Barker (b. 1913). *Lament and Triumph* and *Eros and Dogma* appeared in 1940 and 1944 respectively, but it is in *The True Confessions of George Barker* (1965) that he is seen at his best: sonorous yet muscular, his emotional honesty deepened by elegiac meditation. Stevie Smith (1902–71), the true eccentric of this older generation, produced a volume of work unique in its combination of doggerel and ironic subtlety. Traumatic events and perceptions are here regarded almost in the light of whimsy, a juxtaposition that at its best is persistently disturbing.

Both Geoffrey Grigson (1905–85) and Roy Fuller (b. 1912) asserted the importance of what Fuller called 'brain power allied at least to a dogged alertness and integrity'. It is the poets in the so-called 'Movement' however who most creatively pursued what Donald Davie (b. 1922) in the 1967 Postscript to his influential *Purity of Diction in English Verse* (1952) was to call 'an originally passionate rejection, by one generation of British poets, of all the values of Bohemia'. Davie's work promoted the ideals of an eighteenth-century decorum, and though he himself was to become more than what he called 'a pasticheur of late Augustan styles', his astringency is one element in the work of the poets published by Robert Conquest (b. 1917) in the poetry magazine *Listen* and later in *New Lines 2* (1967). These figures include Kingsley Amis, John Wain, D.J. Enright (b. 1920), Davie himself and Elizabeth Jennings (b. 1926) whose *Collected Poems* (1967) reveal her as a poet of the clear, cool gravity and compassion seen in 'Sequence in Hospital'. The outstanding member of this group however was Philip Larkin (1922–85).

After *The North Ship* (1945, revised 1966), Larkin's volumes *The Less Deceived* (1955), *The Whitsun Weddings* (1964) and *High Windows* (1974) reveal him as the poet of isolated observation resigned to the failure of love, the inevitability of loneliness and death, yet recognizing too the need for transcendence however frail its foundations might be. Such qualities are seen in the title poem from *The Whitsun Weddings*. Here, the ancient metaphor of life as a journey has been subsumed in a train ride, much of it through the banal urban world of disfigured advertising hoardings and false paradises seen again in 'Sunny Prestatyn'. The frail lives and hopes of the wedding couples who come on board the train heighten the pathos even as they distance the poet from the world he watches, the only passenger to know that the common terminus is death. 'Mr Bleaney' and 'The Old Fools' are perhaps Larkin's most troubled depictions of this essentially modern loneliness and defeat, while 'Ambulances' is his most assured poem on the inevitability of death.

The longing for transcendence glimpsed from the time of 'Church Going' finds its most subtle fulfilment in 'An Arundel Tomb', a poem of exceptional technical accomplishment, verbal originality and emotional strength. And it is such strength that supports the pathos which is perhaps the greatest quality in Larkin's work. It is this last which enabled him to achieve the combination of plenitude and transience seen, for example, in the last verse of 'The Trees'. The pain of life and growth and the certainty of death are all acknowledged here, but so too, in the sheer energy of the poetry itself, is something beyond these:

> Yet still the unresting castles thresh
> In fullgrown thickness every May.
> Last year is dead, they seem to say,
> Begin afresh, afresh, afresh.

Thom Gunn (b. 1929) is another figure early associated with the Movement who has continued to develop his own distinct vision. This has matured from the defiant juxtaposition of angst and machismo in his early collections *Fighting Terms* (1954) and *The Sense of Movement* (1959). 'In Santa Maria del Popolo' shows a subtlety some have compared to Donne, and both *My Sad Captains* (1961) and *Touch* (1967) admit gentleness in a world where ferociousness and lust prowl within the confines 'built by an exercised intelligence'. 'Misanthropos' from this collection is a powerful expression of the twentieth century's terror of nuclear war. The poems in *Moly* (1971) nonetheless suggest a tentative approach to some means of affirmation, while both *Jack Straw's Castle* (1976) and *The Passages of Joy* (1982) reveal a continuing range of experimentation. Some of this, such as the formally over-loose 'Autobiography', was influenced by American Beat poetry, and is less successful than poems where Gunn's technique is more disciplined.

In the work of Geoffrey Hill (b. 1932), a mannerly, intense precision – a sensibility at once patrician yet contemporary – negotiates the abyss: the political evil, the violence and banality, the ravaged continuities of a broken and erstwhile Christian society. This is a poetry of the highest difficulty – Coleridge and Eliot are among Hill's English peers in this regard. The early poems in *For the Unfallen* (1959) show a young man's attempt to create his own distinctive use of the resources of history, language and imagery. The volume also conveys the sense of a great talent discovering the sources of its power.

Occasionally, as in 'Three Baroque Meditations' from *King Log* (1968), the drive for rhetorical complexity takes over truer perception and the result is questionable. *King Log* nonetheless contains two sequences of the finest quality. The first of these, 'The Songbook of Sebastian Arrurruz', comprises poems about defeated love which move with a quick and often terrible sense of desolation hardly borne, of the imagination driven to images by the vivifying reality of pain. It is such subtlety of response that also underlies 'Funeral Music', the second sequence in the volume.

Like much of Hill's finest work, 'Funeral Music' is a meditation on history. Through the poems he explores what it means to try to be a twentieth-century figure of full and authentic imagination, a poet aware of the claims both of the spirit and of the past in a land saturated with tradition. The Wars of the Roses become in these works a way of connecting with the timeless recrudescence of human violence, with the needs of the soul and 'with an England crouched beastwise beneath it all'. The result, as Hill himself has described it, is 'a grim florid music broken by grunts and shrieks'.

The prose-poems that make up *Mercian Hymns* (1971) are an attempt to broaden this imaginative, philosophical and essentially a-chronological view of history. They are at once archaeology and autobiography, works where high culture shoulders the demotic, creating an authentic, modern polyphony in 'coiled entrenched England'. Fine as these works are however, it is *Tenebrae* (1976) that shows Hill at his full and remarkable stature. The sequence called 'The Pentecost Castle' is as sparse and sophisticated as the great, anonymous masterpieces of the European ballad tradition, while the sonnet sequence 'Lachrimae' and 'An Apology for the Revival of Christian Architecture in England' are pieces in an opposite mode.

The poems in *Tenebrae* are fundamentally religious, imbued with a troubled longing for transcendence and suggestions of spiritual reality. They are also rooted in a profound and subtle response to a country that is at once both its past and its landscape:

> Platonic England, house of solitudes,
> rests in its laurels and its injured stone,
> replete with complex fortunes that are gone,
> beset by dynasties of moods and clouds.

There is nothing here of the besetting vice of sentimental ruralism. Hill's England of the ring-dove and the Holy Spirit, its history glimpsed between 'goldgrimy shafts and pillars of the sun', is also an England politically uncertain, threatened by the insidious banality of urban sprawl and, more terribly, by that alliance of man with nature which makes the menace of nuclear holocaust an ever-present reality, a permanent feature of the physical and mental landscape. It is such qualities of considered, broad response, and of a fully contemporary verbal and emotional refinement, that make *Tenebrae* one of the greatest achievements of post-war British poetry – the work of an élite but focal voice.

From his first collection *Death of a Naturalist* (1966), Seamus Heaney (b. 1939) has shown an awareness of the violence and threat underlying a natural, soil-conscious world. This might rise from the remembered sensitivity of a small boy's longing to explore birds' nests in a river bank but holding back 'because he once felt the cold prick of a dead robin's claw' or, as in 'Limbo' from *Wintering Out* (1972), the response of a poet born an Ulster Catholic to the fate of the soul of a murdered country child glittering where even Christ cannot fish for its redemption.

Such violence, inevitably and painfully, touches on the political, and many of the poems in *North* (1975) and *Field Work* (1979) are the response – sincere, unstrident, horrified – to political catastrophe. In 'Exposure', Heaney refers to this as 'my responsible *tristia*', and a poem such as 'The Toome Road' displays this state with a subtlety of courage by which poetry becomes the means of asserting an essential humanity amid sectarianism. In the eponymous verses from *Station Island* (1984), these themes of moving in the natural, religious and political worlds are treated with Dantesque power as the poet affirms his vocation. And it is this that is precious above all. The range of Heaney's work, the emotional integrity of his tested, unhardened humanity, affirms poetry as a matter of fundamental importance in preserving a full and modern humanity.

Hill and Heaney are the leading poets of their generation. Of the 'Group' poets once gathered around Philip Hobsbaum (b. 1932) and later Edward Lucie-Smith (b. 1935), Peter Porter (b. 1929) appears the most variously talented. Porter is a poet of wide cultural reference, a satirist influenced by Latin poetry and the Elizabethans as well as being the tender elegiac poet of 'An Exequy'. Other Group poets include George Macbeth (b. 1932), whose *Poems from Oby* (1982) especially are finely achieved meditations on love; Alan Brownjohn (b. 1931) and Edwin Brock (b. 1927), who are poets of sharp social comment; while Peter Redgrove (b. 1932) is a poet of vital energies and occasionally of the grotesque.

The vital qualities of the natural world are often associated with the work of Ted Hughes (b. 1930) whose poems on animals in *The Hawk in the Rain* (1957) and *Lupercal* (1960) evoke the wordless energies of nature – its pride, violence and death – in a language of harsh rhythms and sharp, consonantal attack. In poems such as 'Hawk Roosting', 'Thrushes' and 'The Thought Fox', this juxtaposition of animal life to human consciousness leads to a subtle and interesting poetry. In later works however, the volume *Crow* (1970) particularly, Hughes's development has been towards a self-conscious brutalism. This, along with suggestions of myth and shamanistic inspiration, do not save these poems from the charge of inverted sentimentality nor, in the case of *Gaudete* (1977), from very dubious success. *Season Songs* (1976) and *Remains of Elmet* (1979) contain work of superior quality however as do the vivid 'diary' poems in the first sequence of *Moortown* (1979).

The work of Hughes's ex-wife Sylvia Plath (1932–63) is altogether more tragic in its revelation of a first-rate poetic intelligence eventually driven to self-destruction. Poems such as 'Candles' have exceptional tension and tenderness, the qualities of a vital and original sensibility seen again in 'Among the Narcissi' or the evocation of motherhood in 'Morning Song'. Nor, at its strongest, was Plath's a mind moving in purely personal circles. A poem such as 'The Thin People' approaches one of the central and terrible dilemmas of post-war experience – the exercise of the imagination in a world that made Dachau and Hiroshima realities. 'The Thin People' is a profound and terrible response to the Nazi extermination camps and the fact that their obscene images must permanently affect our perception.

Nonetheless, the forces within Plath herself which allowed her to identify with the victims of the Holocaust were symptomatic of a terrible personal desolation. 'All day I feel its soft, feathery turnings, its malignity.' The terror and pity here are the more awful for the growing knowledge of impotence before the forces of self-destruction. The lacerations of 'Daddy' speak finally of an ineluctable private extremism, just as 'Fever 103' is the most terrible self-portrait of psychosis. Poems such as 'Elm' and 'Lady Lazarus' however, fraught with the appalling urge to dehumanize and destroy the self, suggest a surrender which is ultimately tragic.

Plath herself was an expatriate American, and this fact suggests the international perspective that gives the work of the post-war world much of its breadth and scope. One thinks of Beckett and Lessing, while remembering that the contribution of writers from the Commonwealth is exceptional. Indeed, it is perhaps in the work of authors as various as Patrick White (1912–90), Derek Walcott (b. 1930), V.S. Naipaul (b. 1932) and others that a future historian will trace the major developments in late-twentieth-century literature written in English.

This must be a matter for conjecture, and the same is true of the attempt to assess the relative merits of the youngest contemporary writers. What is clear nonetheless is that much of the most interesting modern literature is inseparable from the wealth of history lying behind it. This book began with the Old English poet or *scop* singing the lives of his ancestors. I would like to conclude with some lines by Seamus Heaney as he seeks inspiration by returning to these first creators:

> to the scop's
> twang, the iron
> flash of consonants
> cleaving the line.

It is in such ways as this – in the constant, critical quest for a fully humane language of self-definition – that writer and reader combine in the unending task of creating the history of English literature.

Bibliographical Essay

This bibliography does not attempt to be comprehensive but merely to provide some directions for further critical reading. All the books listed have detailed bibliographies. Since most of the major works of English literature are available in reliable modern editions, I have listed only some of those I consider outstanding. Unless otherwise stated, the place of publication is London.

Histories of English literature and general critical surveys

There are several multi-volume histories of English literature. The fifteen volumes of the *Oxford History of English Literature* have been published over a long period. Some show their age; others, like *Poetry and Prose in the Sixteenth Century*, by C.S. Lewis, 1964, are classics. The eight volumes of the *New Pelican Guide to English Literature*, edited by Boris Ford, show the influence of Leavis. Many of the essays are excellent, and the *Guide* contains useful biographical material. The *Sphere History of English Literature*, its ten volumes edited by various hands, contains some of the highest-quality introductory essays. To these should be added the *Macmillan History of English Literature*, a number of volumes of which are individually listed in the relevant sections below, and the Longman Literature in English series, edited in forty-six volumes by David Carroll and Michael Wheeler. The volumes on the intellectual and cultural context in the latter series are particularly to be welcomed.

Useful series on individual works and authors include Macmillan's Casebook series and Penguin Critical Studies. Studies in English Literature, edited by Davis Daiches for Edward Arnold, is also useful. The Past Masters series, edited by Keith Thomas for Oxford University Press, is outstanding on the earlier European and British figures;

as is Fontana's Modern Masters series, edited by Frank Kermode, for more recent figures.

Two important books on general subjects are: *A History of the English Language*, by A.C. Baugh and Thomas Cable, revised edn 1978; and *A History of British Publishing*, by John Feather, 1988. Students will also find David Daiches's *Critical Approaches to Literature*, 2nd edn 1981, an admirable introductory survey to the history of criticism.

Old English literature

Introductory works on Old English literature include C.L. Wren, *A Study of Old English Literature*, 1967; and Michael Alexander, *Old English Literature* in the *Macmillan History of English Literature*, 1983. Michael Alexander has usefully translated *Beowulf* and the greater part of the corpus of Old English poetry for Penguin Books. Translations of Old English prose may be found in *Anglo-Saxon Prose*, translated and edited by Michael Swanton, 1975; and *Alfred the Great*, translated and edited by Simon Keyes and Michael Lapidge, Penguin Books, 1983. Those wishing to know more about Old English itself are commended to the two classic volumes by Henry Sweet: his *Anglo-Saxon Primer*, revised, edited by Norman Davis, Oxford, 1952; and *Anglo-Saxon Reader in Prose and Verse*, revised, edited by Dorothy Whitelock, Oxford, 1967.

Medieval English literature

Important general books on the Middle Ages include: *The Making of the Middle Ages*, by R.W. Southern, 1953, a work both scholarly and approachable; and, for the end of the period, *The Waning of the Middle Ages*, by J. Huizinga, 1924, reprint, Penguin Books, 1965, a vivid and beautiful re-creation of an era. Two books by C.S. Lewis remain important: *The Allegory of Love*, Oxford, 1936, though some of its theses are disputable, is a classic work; *The Discarded Image*, Cambridge, 1964, is fundamental on pre-scientific views of man and the cosmos.

R.M. Wilson's *Early Middle English*, 3rd edn 1968, is a valuable introduction and is to be supplemented by *Early Middle English Verse and Prose*, edited by J.A.W. Bennett and G.V. Smithers, revised 2nd edn, with a glossary by Norman Davis, Oxford, 1974. Much Early Middle English and Middle English verse and prose has been translated for Penguin Books by Neville Coghill, Brian Stone and others.

General studies of medieval English literature include: *English Gothic Literature*, by Derick Brewer, in the *Macmillan History of English Literature*, 1983; and J.A. Burrow, *Medieval Writers and their Work*, Oxford, 1982, a particularly valuable account of the social and intellectual contexts of creativity. Useful books on general topics include: H.J. Chaytor, *From Script to Print*, revised edn, Cambridge, 1967; John Stevens, *Medieval Romance*, 1973; and A.C. Spearing, *Medieval Dream-Poetry*, Cambridge, 1976.

F.N. Robinson (ed.), *The Works of Geoffrey Chaucer*, 2nd edn, Oxford, 1966, is essential, but may usefully be supplemented by Barry Windeatt (ed.), *The Book of Troilus*, 1990. Of the innumerable general books on Chaucer, Derick Brewer's *Introduction to Chaucer*, 1984, is particularly to be recommended for its directness and suggestiveness.

For lyric poetry and other medieval genres, see J. Spiers (ed.), *Medieval English Poetry: The Non-Chaucerian Tradition*, revised edn, 1962. For the Gawain poet, A.C. Spearing's *The Gawain-Poet: A Critical Study*, Cambridge, 1970, is extremely approachable. Standard editions include *Sir Gawain and the Green Knight*, edited by J.R.R. Tolkien and E.V. Gordon, 2nd edn, revised by N. Davis, Oxford, 1967; and *Pearl*, edited by E.V. Gordon, Oxford, 1953. Langland should be approached through *The Vision of Piers Ploughman: A Complete Edition of the B-Text*, edited with a fine Introduction by A.V.C. Schmidt, revised edn 1984. Useful commentaries include E. Salter's *Piers Ploughman: An Introduction*, Oxford, 1962. Medieval drama should be approached through W. Tydeman, *The Theatre in the Middle Ages*, Cambridge, 1978; and R. Woolf, *The English Mystery Plays*, 1972. *English Mystery Plays*, edited for Penguin Books by P. Happé, 1975, is a useful introductory text as, for the same publishers, is his *Four Morality Plays*, 1979. There is a useful essay on 'Late Medieval Prose' by N.F. Blake in the Sphere volume on *The Middle Ages*, edited by W.F. Bolton, 1970. A particularly varied and valuable anthology is *The Oxford Book of Late Medieval Verse and Prose*, edited by Douglas Grey, Oxford, 1985.

Humanism and reform

Peter Burke's *The Renaissance*, 1987, is a brief but brilliant introduction to the European setting and to later historians' interpretations. It also contains excellent bibliographical material. The introductory lectures published as *Background to the English Renaissance*, edited by J.B. Trapp, 1974, though difficult to obtain, comprise essays by historians of the first eminence. *Reformation Thought: An Introduction*, by Alister E. MacGrath, 1988, is an indispensable brief account of its subject.

General studies of the English literature of the period include C.S. Lewis's classic *English Literature in the Sixteenth Century (Excluding Drama)*, Oxford, 1964; and Julia Briggs, *This Stage-Play World: English Literature and its Background, 1580–1625*, Oxford, 1983. For the transition from medieval to early Renaissance literature, H.A. Mason's *Humanism and Poetry in the Early Tudor Period*, 1959, is particularly recommended.

Geoffrey Shepherd's edition of *An Apology for Poetry*, Manchester, revised edn 1973, is a magnificent introduction to Renaissance rhetoric and other topics – a bridge into the Renaissance literary mind. Rhetoric is also well discussed and its classical background briefly and lucidly sketched in *Rhetoric*, by Peter Dixon, 1971, in The Critical Idiom series.

For Sidney, Spenser, Shakespeare and the sonneteers, J.W. Lever's *The Elizabethan Love Sonnet*, revised edn 1965, remains indispensable. *The Faerie Queene*, edited by A.C. Hamilton, 1980, in the Annotated English Poets series, is invaluable, each book being clearly introduced and the dense web of allusions and linguistic intricacies lucidly glossed. Graham Hough's *A Preface to 'The Faerie Queene'*, 1962, is invaluable on the European background, while Anthea Heale's *'The Faerie Queene': A Reader's Guide*, Cambridge, 1987, is a lucid and admirable introduction to a field that all too rapidly runs to the arcane. The epyllion is well discussed by Elizabeth Story Donno in *Elizabethan Minor Epics*, 1963.

'Sixteenth and Seventeenth Century Prose' by John Carey in the second volume of the *Sphere History of English Literature*, edited by Christopher Ricks, revised edn 1986, is an essay of almost book length and the point from which everyone will take their bearings.

Shakespeare and the drama: 1500–1642

The most useful and accessible general survey is *English Drama to 1700*, volume 3 of the *Sphere History of English Literature*, edited by Christopher Ricks, 1971. Each chapter contains well-chosen and manageable bibliographies in a field saturated with critical studies.

Pre-Shakespearian drama is well served by D.M. Bevington's *From 'Mankind' to Marlowe*, Cambridge, Mass., 1968. *English Tragedy before Shakespeare*, by Wolfgang Clemen, 1961, offers comprehensive treatment. J.B. Steane's *Marlowe: A Critical Study*, Cambridge, 1964, is useful.

The classic survey of general matters is the six volumes by M.C. Bradbrook collectively entitled *A History of Elizabethan Drama*, Cambridge, 1980 edn. A particularly useful single-volume work on the companies, players, playhouses, staging and audiences is Andrew Gurr's *The English Stage, 1574–1642*, 2nd edn, Cambridge, 1980.

Perhaps the best starting-point for building up a general picture of Shakespeare is *The Cambridge Companion to Shakespeare Studies*, edited by Stanley Wells, Cambridge, 1986. This is a collection of essays by leading experts that is broad, reliable and comprehensive while also containing manageable bibliographies. Wells and Gary Taylor have edited *William Shakespeare: The Complete Works*, Oxford, 1986. This is one of the great triumphs of modern textual scholarship. Minor editions are legion, though those by Penguin Books are particularly to be recommended for the quality of their introductions and – a not inconsiderable factor – their clear design and typography.

The field of Shakespeare studies is daunting in the extreme. A partial list of general books would include, on the comedies: C.L. Barber, *Shakespeare's Festive Comedy*, revised edn, New York, 1973; Kenneth Muir, *Shakespeare's Comic Sequence*, Liverpool, 1979; A. Righter, *Shakespeare and the Idea of the Play*, 1962; L.G. Salingar, *Shakespeare and the Traditions of Comedy*, Cambridge, 1974; and

E.M.W. Tillyard, *Shakespeare's Early Comedies*, 1965. On the history plays: M.M. Reese, *The Cease of Majesty*, 1961; and chapters 1–3 of A.P. Rossiter's *Angel with Horns*, 1961. On the Roman plays, two useful books are: M. Charney, *Shakespeare's Roman Plays: The Function of Imagery in Drama*, Cambridge, Mass., 1961; and R. Miola, *Shakespeare's Rome*, 1983. The classic though now disputed work on the tragedies is A.C. Bradley, *Shakespearian Tragedy*, 1904. See also: J.F. Danby, *Shakespeare's Doctrine of Nature*, 1949; G.W. Knight, *The Wheel of Fire*, revised edn 1949, and *The Imperial Theme*, revised edn 1951; M. Mack Jnr, *Killing the King: Three Studies in Shakespeare's Tragic Structure*, New Haven, 1973; and R. Nevo, *Tragic Form in Shakespeare*, Princeton, 1972. On the late plays: G.W. Knight, *The Crown of Life*, 1947; and E.M.W. Tillyard, *Shakespeare's Last Plays*, 1938. The most recent approaches to Shakespeare are discussed by Cedric Watts in the volume of the *Sphere History* listed above.

For the study of individual plays, I would recommend the student to the Casebook and Penguin Critical Studies series.

Ben Jonson: Dramatist, by Anne Barton, Cambridge, 1984, is excellent. The masque and, indeed, the whole conspectus of Jacobean and Caroline court culture are given excellent analysis in *The Golden Age Restor'd: The Culture of the Stuart Court, 1603–42*, by Graham Parry, Manchester, 1981. Later tragedy is well surveyed in I. Ribner, *Jacobean Tragedy: The Quest for Moral Order*, revised edn 1965. On Middleton, particularly to be recommended is Margot Heinemann, *Puritanism and Theatre: Thomas Middleton and Opposition Drama under the Stuarts*, Cambridge, 1980, a valuable clarification of the period.

From Donne to Dryden

The Seventeenth Century: The Intellectual and Cultural Context of English Literature, 1603–1700, by Graham Parry, 1989, in the Longman Literature in English series, is an admirable survey of its field – broad, stimulating and richly informed. Douglas Bush's volume *English Literature in the Early Seventeenth Century*, revised edn 1962, is one of the great works in the *Oxford History*, at once magisterial but approachable.

Among general works on the earlier lyric poets, A. Alvarez, *The*

School of Donne, 1961, and J. Bennett, *Five Metaphysical Poets*, revised edn, Cambridge, 1964, are particularly to be recommended. An important but very advanced book is Rosamund Tuve's *Elizabethan and Metaphysical Imagery*, Chicago, 1947. Two books on Donne can be particularly recommended: J.B. Leishman, *The Monarch of Wit*, 5th edn 1962; and John Carey's *John Donne: Life, Mind and Art*, 1981. Jonson is sympathetically analysed in Parry, *The Seventeenth Century*, see above. For Herbert, Vaughan and Traherne, see especially Louis Martz, *The Poetry of Meditation*, revised edn 1962. Marvell has been particularly well served by R.L. Colie, *My Echoing Song*, Princeton, 1970, and J.M. Wallace, *Destiny his Choice: The Loyalism of Andrew Marvell*, Cambridge, 1968. Readers should also note William Empson, *Some Versions of Pastoral*, 1935.

Every student of Milton will be indebted to Alastair Fowler's edition of *Paradise Lost* and John Carey's edition of Milton's *Complete Shorter Poems*, issued separately in the Annotated English Poets series in 1971. The glosses are particularly well crafted and informative. Modern classics of Milton criticism include: William Empson, *Milton's God*, 2nd edn 1965, a book calculated to stir controversy; Helen Gardner, *A Reading of 'Paradise Lost'*, Oxford, 1965; C.S. Lewis, *A Preface to 'Paradise Lost'*, 1942; and Christopher Ricks's vigorously combative *Milton's Grand Style*, Oxford, 1963.

For utilitarian prose in Bacon, Ralegh and Hobbes, see Christopher Hill's masterly *The Intellectual Origins of the English Revolution*, 1965. Joan Bennet's *Sir Thomas Browne*, Cambridge, 1962, remains useful; as do George Williamson, *The Senecan Amble*, 1951, and K.G. Hamilton, *The Two Harmonies: Poetry and Prose in the Restoration*, Princeton, 1948.

Restoration satire is well covered in Rachel Tricket's *The Honest Muse*, Oxford, 1967. A particularly fine edition of Rochester's poems is David M. Veith, New Haven, 1968. For Dryden, see T.S. Eliot, *Homage to John Dryden*, 1924; and Earl Miner, *Dryden's Poetry*, Bloomington, 1967. Dryden as a satirist is discussed in Ian Jack's *Augustan Satire 1660–1750*, revised edn, Oxford, 1966; while for Dryden as a critic, see Daiches's *Critical Approaches*, above. For the heroic play, see D. Hughes, *Dryden's Heroic Plays*, Lincoln, Nebr., 1981. Restoration comedy is discussed in T.H. Fujimura, *The Restoration Comedy of Wit*, Princeton, 1952.

Science, satire and sentiment

The European background to the Enlightenment is charted comprehensively but most readably in P. Gay, *The Enlightenment*, 2 vols, New York, 1967–70. N. Hampson, *The Enlightenment*, Penguin Books, 1968, is elegant and broadly based; while Paul Hazard's *European Thought in the Eighteenth Century*, Penguin Books, 1965, is detailed but stimulating. Basil Willey's *The Eighteenth Century Background*, 1940, remains valuable; Paul Fussell's *The Rhetorical World of Augustan Humanism: Ethics and Imagery from Swift to Burke*, Oxford, 1965, is a major work by a great scholar; while by far the best recent general survey is James Sambrooke's *The Eighteenth Century: The Intellectual and Cultural Context of English Literature, 1700–1789*, 1986, in the Longman Literature in English series.

Locke, Shaftesbury and Addison are discussed with breadth and grace in Basil Willey's *The English Moralists*, 1964. Defoe is discussed in *The Rise of the Novel*, by Ian Watt, 1957, a now classic work of criticism. Addison and Steele are discussed in Janet Todd, *Sensibility: An Introduction*, 1986.

Swift is the subject of an excellent critical biography: *Jonathan Swift: A Hypocrite Revers'd*, by David Noakes, Oxford, 1985. Among other works are: D. Donoghue, *Jonathan Swift: A Critical Introduction*, Cambridge, 1969; Irwin Ehrenpreis, *The Personality of Swift*, 1958; C.J. Rawson, *Focus: Swift*, 1971; and Clive Probyn (ed.), *The Art of Jonathan Swift*, 1978.

There is a useful edition of Thomson's *Seasons* and *The Castle of Indolence*, edited by James Sambrooke, revised edn, Oxford, 1987. See also James Sutherland, *A Preface to Eighteenth Century Poetry*, Oxford, 1948. *The New Oxford Book of Eighteenth Century Verse*, chosen and edited by Roger Lonsdale, Oxford, 1984, is a wide-ranging and important challenge to the familiar canon and a delightful field in which to browse.

For the poetry of Pope there is the great ten-volume *Twickenham Edition* with invaluable introductions and the most extensive notes and glosses. It is these in particular that make James Sutherland's edition of the *Dunciad*, 3rd edn 1963, essential for a serious study of the poem. Ian Jack's *Augustan Satire*, see above, is still a useful starting-point, as is Pat Rogers's *An Introduction to Pope*, 1975. Rogers's *Hacks and Dunces: Pope, Swift and Grub Street*, 1972, is both fascinating and informative.

For Fielding and Richardson, see Ian Watt, *The Rise of the Novel*, above, and also Terry Eagleton, *The Rape of Clarissa*, Oxford, 1982. Christopher Ricks's introduction to his Penguin edition of *Tristram Shandy*, 1970, offers an excellent vantage-point. For contemporary women writers, see Dale Spender, *Mothers of the Novel: Ten Good Women Writers before Jane Austen*, 1986.

For Hume and Burke, see Willey, *The English Moralists*, above. Later eighteenth-century poetry is discussed in *From Sensibility to Romanticism*, edited by F.W. Hilles and H. Bloom, New York, 1965; and also in Patricia Spacks, *The Poetry of Vision: Five Eighteenth Century Poets: Thomson, Collins, Gray, Smart, Cowper*, Cambridge, Mass., 1966. There is an excellent edition of the poetry of Gray, Collins and Goldsmith by Roger Lonsdale in the Annotated English Poets series, 1969. David Daiches's *Robert Burns*, revised edn 1966, is sensitive and illuminating. A stimulating essay on Crabbe is E.M. Forster's 'George Crabbe and Peter Grimes' in *Two Cheers for Democracy*, 1951.

There is a compendious and useful selection in *Samuel Johnson*, edited by Donald Greene, Oxford, 1984. Boswell's *Life* remains indispensable, along with Walter Jackson Bate, *The Achievement of Samuel Johnson*, New York, 1955, and his biography of 1977. Johnson's importance as a critic is clearly analysed in Daiches's *Critical Approaches to Literature*, see above. John Burns's study of Gibbon, 1985, in the Past Masters series is admirable, as is D.D. Raphael's of Adam Smith, 1985, in the same series. There is a useful essay by C.W. Parkin on 'Burke and the Conservative Tradition' in *Political Ideas*, edited by David Thomson, reprint, Penguin Books, 1969. Burke is also the subject of a Past Masters study by C.B. Macpherson, 1980.

Revolutions, reaction and reform

Raymond Williams's *Culture and Society: 1780–1850*, 1959, is a classic study of this period, as is the massive yet fascinatingly detailed Elie

Halévy, *A History of the English People in the Nineteenth Century*, reprint, with an Introduction by Asa Briggs, 1987. D. Thomson, *England in the Nineteenth Century*, Penguin Books, 1950, is a brief and masterly synthesis. Basil Willey's *The Eighteenth Century Background*, 1940, remains useful. By far the most stimulating recent account of the literature of this period and its relation to social and political developments is Marilyn Butler's *Romantics, Rebels and Reactionaries: English Literature and its Background, 1760–1830*, Oxford, 1981.

The period is also rich in major biographies: Richard Holmes's *Shelley: The Pursuit*, 1974, is admirable, as is his work on Coleridge, 1989 and 1990. There is also an excellent life of Keats by Robert Gittings, 1968; and a one-volume abridgement by the author of Leslie Marchand's three-volume *Byron*, 1957.

For Burke, see above. For Godwin and Mary Wollstonecraft, see the Introduction to *Enquiry Concerning Political Justice*, edited by F.E.T. Priestley, Penguin Books, 1976; and M.B. Kramnick (ed.), *A Vindication of the Rights of Woman*, Penguin Books, 1975. J.R. Watson's *English Poetry of the Romantic Period, 1789–1830*, 1985, in the Longman Literature in English series, is a sound and useful introduction.

A very usefully glossed edition of Blake is that by W.H. Stevenson in the Annotated English Poets series, 1971. Important studies of Blake include: H. Bloom, *Blake's Apocalypse*, 1963; and S.F. Damon's indispensable *A Blake Dictionary*, 1973. Northrop Frye's *Fearful Symmetry*, 1947, remains a classic work.

F.W. Bateson's *Wordsworth: A Reinterpretation*, revised edn 1956, is questionable on the William–Dorothy relationship. J.F. Danby's *The Simple Wordsworth*, 1960, is a moving book that re-creates the original impact of Wordsworth. M. Jacobus's *Tradition and Experiment in Wordsworth's Lyrical Ballads (1798)*, 1976, is penetrating on their historical context. D.B. Pirie, *William Wordsworth: The Poetry of Grandeur and Tenderness*, 1982, is fresh. J. Wordsworth's *William Wordsworth: The Borders of Vision*, 1983, is the product of a keen textual knowledge. M.H. Abrams's *Natural Supernaturalism*, New York, 1971, is particularly good on Wordsworth.

Coleridge, the towering intellect among these poets, is the subject of an excellent Past Masters study by his biographer Richard Holmes, 1989. J.B. Beer's *Coleridge's Poetic Intelligence*, 1977, is excellent.

Coleridge's reading and the vexed question of plagiarism are discussed in G. Lowes Dickinson, *The Road to Xanadu*, 2nd edn 1930; and N. Fruman, *Damaged Archangel*, 1972. The first of these is a classic work.

The great study of the Gothic element in Romantic poetry and prose is M. Praz, *The Romantic Agony*, translated by A. Davidson, revised edn 1951.

Two very stimulating books on Jane Austen are: M. Butler, *Jane Austen and the War of Ideas*, 1975; and B. Hardy, *A Reading of Jane Austen*, 1975. The early novels of Scott and his poetry are well discussed in Ian Jack's volume of the *Oxford History*, 1990 edn.

Byron's *Letters*, edited in twelve volumes by Leslie Marchand, 1973–82, are a source of continuous delight and entertainment. Studies of his poetry veer widely between praising everything and lacking the essential gift of humour. The most reliable remains A. Rutherford, *Byron: A Critical Study*, Edinburgh, 1961.

One of the best introductions to Shelley is T. Webb, *Shelley: A Voice Not Understood*, Manchester, 1977. Other useful works include: K.N. Cameron, *Shelley: The Golden Years*, 1974; and R. Cronin, *Shelley's Poetic Thought*, 1981.

A particularly fine introduction to Keats is *John Keats*, by Douglas Bush, 1966; to this should be added W. Walsk, *Introduction to Keats*, 1981. Two very interesting books on more recondite areas are: Ian Jack, *Keats and the Mirror of Art*, Oxford, 1967; and Christopher Ricks, *Keats and Embarrassment*, Oxford, 1974.

John Clare's works have not yet received a definitive edition, though an Oxford edition by E. Robinson and D. Powell is in progress. The most sympathetic introduction is *The Poetry of John Clare: A Critical Introduction*, by M. Storey, 1974.

The writers of critical prose and their relationship to the major poets are well discussed in Butler, *Romantics, Rebels and Reactionaries*, see above.

Victorian values

The following all provide essential background reading to this diverse and immense period: Raymond Williams's *Culture and Society: 1780–1850*, 1959; Halévy, *A History of the English People in the Nineteenth*

Century, see above; and D. Thomson, *England in the Nineteenth Century,* Penguin Books, 1950. In addition, W.E. Houghton, *The Victorian Frame of Mind, 1830–1870,* New Haven, 1957 is a fundamental study of the intellectual context. J. Holloway, *The Victorian Sage: Studies in Argument,* 1953, is useful on Carlyle, Disraeli, George Eliot, Newman, Arnold and Hardy.

The earlier Victorian sages are all subjects of excellent studies in the Past Masters series: Carlyle, by A. le Quesne, 1982; Newman, by Owen Chadwick, 1983; Mill, by William Thomas, 1985; and Darwin, by Jonathan Howard, 1982.

The Longman Companion to Victorian Fiction, by John Sutherland, 1988, is an indispensable reference book and a constant source of delight. The relevant volumes of both the Pelican *Guide* and the *Sphere History* offer excellent introductory essays on the main figures, while a useful overview is provided by both Walter Allen, *The English Novel,* 1991 edn; and R. Williams, *The English Novel: From Dickens to Lawrence,* 1970. The early period is particularly well covered in K. Tillotson, *English Novels of the Eighteen-Forties,* Oxford, 1954.

Among studies of particular themes and genres, the following are especially recommended: E. Showalter, *A Literature of their Own: British Women Novelists from Brontë to Lessing,* Princeton, 1977, is a major feminist study which will surely establish its place as a classic; rather more eccentric though stimulating is *The Madwoman in the Attic: The Woman Writer and the Nineteenth-Century Literary Imagination,* by S.M. Gilbert and S. Gubar, 1979. Other useful studies are: *The Newgate Novel, 1830–47,* by K. Hollingsworth, Detroit, 1963; *The Silver Fork School,* by M.W. Rosa, reprint, Port Washington, NY, 1964; *The English Historical Novel: Walter Scott to Virginia Woolf,* by A. Fleishman, 1971; and *The Realist Novel in England: A Study in Development,* by I. Williams, 1974. *The Maniac in the Cellar: Sensation Novels of the 1860s,* by W. Hughes, Princeton, 1980, is interesting on an important genre.

A useful overview of Dickens is offered by K.J. Fielding, *Charles Dickens: A Critical Introduction,* revised edn 1966. J. Carey, *The Violent Effigy,* 1973, and J. Lucas, *The Melancholy Man,* revised edn 1980, offer more idiosyncratic though stimulating accounts. Also useful are: Humphrey House, *The Dickens World,* Oxford, 1941; and

F.R. Leavis and Q.D. Leavis, *Dickens the Novelist*, 1970. Individual novels are best approached through the Penguin Critical Studies and Casebook series.

Mrs Gaskell can be approached through *Mrs Gaskell, Novelist and Biographer*, by John Chapple, Manchester, 1965. In addition to the feminist studies mentioned above, the Brontës are interestingly discussed in I.S. Ewbank, *Their Proper Sphere: A Study of the Brontë Sisters as Early-Victorian Female Novelists*, 1966. 'The Structure of *Wuthering Heights*', an important early essay by C.P. Sanger, 1926, is reprinted in A. Everitt (ed.), *Wuthering Heights: An Anthology of Criticism*, 1967.

J. Carey, *Thackeray: Prodigal Genius*, 1977, presents a modern critical overview that gives prominence to the earlier work; while Thackeray as a moralist is particularly well discussed in *The Exposure of Luxury: Radical Themes in Thackeray*, by Barbara Hardy, 1972. Useful studies of Trollope include: A.O.J. Cockshut, *Anthony Trollope: A Critical Study*, 1955; and P.D. Edwards, *Anthony Trollope, his Art and Scope*, 1977.

Christopher Ricks's *New Oxford Book of Victorian Verse*, 1990, offers a useful and important revision of the canon and by far the best starting-point for study. Among general studies of Victorian poetry, the essays in the *Sphere History* are excellent, while the relevant volume in the *Oxford History*, by Paul Turner, 1990 edn, contains studies that are brisk, informative and approachable. E.D.H. Johnson, *The Alien Vision of Victorian Poetry*, Princeton, 1952, is a seminal work. On the later period, John Heath-Stubbs, *The Darkling Plain: A Study of the Later Fortunes of Romanticism in English Poetry from Darley to W.B. Yeats*, 1950, is excellent.

Christopher Ricks's edition of Tennyson, 1989, in the Longman Annotated English Poets, is a remakable achievement; his *Tennyson: A Biographical and Critical Study*, 1972, is useful, as is Paul Turner's *Tennyson*, 1976. Two useful books on Browning are: I. Jack, *Browning's Major Poetry*, 1973; and P. Drew, *The Poetry of Robert Browning: A Critical Introduction*, 1970. For Elizabeth Barrett Browning, *Aurora Leigh* has been edited with an excellent Introduction by Cora Kaplan, 1978. Among general studies are A. Hayter, *Mrs Browning: A Poet's Work and its Setting*, 1962. An interesting historical and social perspective on Coventry Patmore is offered in *The Worm in the Bud* by

Ronald Pearsall, 1983. Among studies of Clough are *Too Quick Despairer: The Life and Work of A.H. Clough*, 1969. Arnold is the subject of an excellent Past Masters study by Stefan Collini, 1988, a work which discusses the criticism with particular insight.

Classic works on George Eliot include G.S. Haight's *George Eliot: A Biography*, Oxford, 1968; F.R. Leavis's discussion in *The Great Tradition: George Eliot, Henry James, Joseph Conrad*, 1948; and Barbara Hardy's *The Novels of George Eliot: A Study in Form*, 1959.

G. Beer, *George Meredith: A Change of Masks. A Study of the Novels*, 1970, is sensible; while A. Poole, *Gissing in Context*, 1975, is excellent.

For children's literature, see J.S. Bratton, *The Impact of Victorian Children's Fiction*, 1981.

Ruskin is well discussed by Turner in the *Oxford History*, above, and is also the subject of a Past Masters study by George P. Landow, 1985. Among introductions to the Pre-Raphaelites, Gay Daley's *Pre-Raphaelites in Love*, New York, 1989, is important for its feminist perspective, an approach seen again in Kathleen Jones, *Learning Not to Be First: The Life of Christina Rossetti*, Moreton-in-Marsh, Glos., 1991. The range of William Morris's career is discussed in Stephen Coote, *William Morris: A Life*, 1990. Hopkins is well introduced in G. Storey, *A Preface to Hopkins*, 1981. For Swinburne, see Praz, *The Romantic Agony*, above. The importance of Pater is particularly well emphasized in Peter Faulkener, *Modernism*, 1977, in The Critical Idiom series. Wilde may be approached through Richard Ellmann's *Life*, 1987, a major modern literary biography. There is a finely introduced collection of Housman's poetry edited by Christopher Ricks, Penguin Books, 1989.

Among important studies of Thomas Hardy that relate him to the work of other novelists is J. King's *Tragedy in the Victorian Novel: Theory and Practice in the Novels of George Eliot, Thomas Hardy and Henry James*, Cambridge, 1978. A useful general study is I. Gregor, *The Great Web: The Form of Hardy's Major Fiction*, 1974. Among modern studies of the verse are D. Taylor, *Hardy's Poetry*, 1981.

Stevenson and the Art of Fiction, by David Daiches, New York, 1951, is sensible and acute; while Kipling's *Something of Myself*, reprint, Penguin Books, 1971, is sympathetic. Eliot's selection of Kipling's poems is important. For Butler, see T.L. Jeffers, *Samuel Butler Revalued*, 1981.

Useful discussions of Henry James may be found in Leavis, *The Great Tradition*, see above, and F.O. Matthiessen, *Henry James: The Major Phase*, 1946; while a useful introduction is S.G. Putt, *A Reader's Guide to Henry James*, 1966. James's own Prefaces are an essential introduction to his aesthetic.

For Conrad, see: J. Berthoud, *Joseph Conrad: The Major Phase*, 1978; C.B. Cox, *Joseph Conrad: The Modern Imagination*, 1974; and F.R. Karl, *A Reader's Guide to Joseph Conrad*, 1960.

For Victorian drama, see M.R. Booth, *The Revels History of English Drama*, volume 6, 1975. One of the best critical introductions to Shaw is R. Williams's *Drama from Ibsen to Brecht*, 1968.

Aspects of twentieth-century literature

A useful account of the prodigious changes in the modern era can be found in David Thomson, *England in the Twentieth Century (1914–79)*, 2nd edn, with additional material by Geoffrey Warner, Penguin Books, 1981. The European – and, to some extent, the American – background is ably presented in Michael D. Biddis, *The Age of the Masses: Ideas and Society in Europe since 1870*, Penguin Books, 1977. A brief but extremely lucid account of the major literary changes is provided by Peter Faulkener, *Modernism*, see above. There are surprisingly few one-volume general surveys. The most readily available – in addition to the relevant volumes in the *Pelican Guide* and the *Sphere History* – is W.W. Robson, *Modern English Literature*, Oxford, 1970.

The impact of the First World War on literature is charted in Paul Fussell's *The Great War and Modern Memory*, Oxford, 1975, a work of exceptional range and brilliance.

In addition to F.R. Leavis's *D.H. Lawrence, Novelist*, 1955, a more balanced discussion may be found in Graham Hough's *The Dark Sun: A Study of D.H. Lawrence*, 1956. There is also good criticism of Lawrence in L. Lerner's *The Truth Tellers*, 1967. A. Niven, *D.H. Lawrence: The Novels*, Cambridge, 1978, surveys the field, though perhaps overvalues the later works.

The edition of Yeats's poems edited by Daniel Albright for the Everyman series, 1990, is a volume every student will wish to have. Among major studies are T.R. Henn, *The Lonely Tower*, revised edn

1965. A.N. Jeffares, *A Commentary on the Collected Poems of W.B. Yeats*, 1968, remains useful, as does J. Unterecker's *A Reader's Guide to W.B. Yeats*, 1959. Richard Ellmann's *Yeats: The Man and the Masks*, 1948, is admirable.

Ellmann's *James Joyce*, 1959, and *The Consciousness of James Joyce*, 1977, are both excellent. Joyce criticism rapidly runs to the dry and arcane, and Anthony Burgess's *Here Comes Everybody: An Introduction to James Joyce for the Ordinary Reader*, revised edn 1982, is admirably fresh, enthusiastic and informed. Also useful is M. Hodgart, *James Joyce: A Student's Guide*, 1978.

The most sympathetic and informed account of E.M. Forster is to be found in G. Gaveliero's *A Reading of E.M. Forster*, 1979. Woolf and many of her contemporaries are well discussed in Douglas Hewitt, *English Fiction of the Early Modern Period*, 1988, in the Longman Literature in English series. The two volumes of Quentin Bell's biography of Woolf, published together in 1982, are admirable. The novels are very intelligently discussed in H. Lee's *The Novels of Virginia Woolf*, 1977; while J.K. Johnstone, *The Bloomsbury Group*, 1954, is one of innumerable accounts of this perennially fascinating movement.

The best general account of Eliot's work and development (and, to some extent, his life) is to be found in Stephen Spender's Modern Masters volume, revised edn 1977. A more detailed account of *The Waste Land* may be found in my volume on the poem in the Penguin Critical Studies series, 1988. Helen Gardener's *The Composition of the 'Four Quartets'*, 1978, is excellent. Also useful is G. Williamson, *A Reader's Guide to T.S. Eliot*, revised edn 1967.

Essential background and intelligent analysis are offered by Valentine Cunningham's *British Writers of the Thirties*, 1988; but see also Samuel Hynes, *The Auden Generation: Literature and Politics in England in the 1930s*, 1976; and Ronald Carter, *Thirties Poets: 'The Auden Group'*, 1984. A useful, brief and well-constructed introduction to the period is Norman Page, *The Thirties in Britain*, 1990.

By far the best introductory essays to the contemporary period are to be found in the *Pelican Guide* volume entitled *The Present*, 1983. While every reader will want to question some of the emphases in this collection, the introductory material by Krishan Kumar and John Holloway performs its immensely difficult task comprehensively and exactly and forms an ideal starting-point for further discovery.

Index